D1493292

EAST SUSSEX COUNTY COUNCIL
WITHDRAWN
19 APR 2023
3

01488864 - ITEM

LOST VICTORIES

The Author, 1944

LOST VICTORIES

BY

FIELD-MARSHAL

ERICH VON MANSTEIN

Edited and translated by

ANTHONY G. POWELL

Foreword by

CAPTAIN B. H. LIDDELL HART

Introduction to this Edition by

MARTIN BLUMENSON

EAST SUSSEX

V.	W	INV. No.	454605
CLASS No,		940·5482	U
BOOK No.		694979	731

COUNTY LIBRARY

First published as "Verlorene Siege"
© 1955 by Athenaum-Verlag, Bonn
English translation © 1958 by Methuen & Co. Ltd.
Copyright © 1982 edition by Bernard & Graefe Verlag, Munich

1982 edition published in Great Britain by
Arms and Armour Press,
Lionel Leventhal Limited,
2–6 Hampstead High Street,
London NW3   IQQ

ISBN 0-85368-555-X

Printed in the United States of America

DEM ANDENKEN UNSERES
GEFALLENEN SOHNES GERO V. MANSTEIN
UND ALLER FÜR DEUTSCHLAND
GEFALLENEN KAMARADEN

CONTENTS

ILLUSTRATIONS

MAPS

PLATES

The Author, 1944   *frontispiece*

facing page 272

With members of the German minority in Siebenbürgen,
    accompanied by his son, Gero, and Lt. Specht
At H.Q. 50 Division in the Crimea
With Col.-Gen. Dumitrescu
Southern coastline in the Crimea
Maxim Gorki I
Sevastopol on fire
Russian Battery at entrance to Severnaya Bay
Crimean meeting with Marshal Antonescu
With Baron v. Richthofen at Kerch, May 1942
Caravan conference before Leningrad
Conference with Gen. Kempf and Gen. Busse, during 'Citadel'
H.Q. at Vinnitsa

KEY TO SYMBOLS
USED IN MAPS

XXXXX
Army Group*

XXXX
Army

XXX
Corps

*Flagstaff indicates Headquarters' location

XX
Division

X
Brigade
(or Regimental Combat Team)

━━XXXXX━━
Army Group Boundary

━━XXXX━━
Army Boundary

TACTICAL SYMBOLS FROM DIVISION DOWNWARDS ALSO
INCLUDE ARM OF SERVICE—

Infantry

Cavalry

Armoured

Mountain

Airborne

Air force unit

Enemy formations

INTRODUCTION
by Martin Blumenson

E VERYTHING in war is simple, Clausewitz said; but the
simplest thing, he added, is incredibly difficult.

Consider the basic relationship between politics and war.
Clausewitz made the equation crystal clear, even simplistic, in his
classic dictum that war is an extension of politics by different
means. In other words, political ends govern the exertions of war.
Or, the military are the means by which to gain political goals. The
political leaders establish the objectives, the military men seek to
attain them.

Nothing could be simpler or more obvious. This is the essential
definition of war: organized violence in quest of political advantages. Otherwise, conflict and killing are meaningless and
immoral.

Clausewitz expressed this very plainly in his monumental study
of the nature of war. But beyond some general observations and
several specific illustrations, he could not systematically examine
the other side of the coin, the politics to which war is attached, for
he lacked a complementary treatise on the nature of international
politics.

If the primacy of the political over the military is beyond question, the application of the relationship in the real world poses
problems of terrible complexity. Political wishes and the military
methods to realize them, political motives and the military pro-
cedures to support them, are seldom clear-cut and in balance at
any given moment. They are anything but easy to synchronize.
Furthermore, where is the fine and sometimes invisible line
between the political and military spheres?

The case of Adolf Hitler is instructive. Apart from the fatal flaws
that finally crushed him, he was for a time a political genius.

Whether he followed a blueprint or extemporized, he gained striking political triumphs. Without resorting to force, he remilitarized the Rhineland, annexed Austria, and conquered Czechoslovakia. He thereby expanded the territory and the power of Germany. Even when he used military means in Poland to obtain his political desires, he demonstrated the close connection between politics and war.

Unfortunately for him, his invasion of Poland precipitated World War II. From then on, his direction of the war became increasingly military and less political. Toward the close, the fighting he exhorted degenerated into senseless destruction for the sake merely of continuing the struggle, and that was hardly a proper political objective.

Erich von Manstein, whether deliberately or unconsciously, has illuminated the steady decline of Hitler's outlook and the constant deterioration of Germany's war effort. As Hitler assumed more and more the military functions and concerned himself with military decisions, no one exercised the political role. And without that, the bloodshed and the sacrifice were without reason.

That is what Field Marshal von Manstein suggests in his title, *Lost Victories*. By the summer of 1940, after defeating France, Hitler's Germany was master of western Europe. What next? Manstein plaintively asks. Hitler had no long-range plans, and as a result could neither conclude peace with Britain nor invade the island.

By the following summer, having overrun Denmark and Norway, Germany and Hitler stood victorious. Only Britain breathed defiance, and that was of little significance at the moment.

What next?

Germany's power had never been higher when in June 1941, heady with success, Hitler miscalculated both his resources and the immensity of his task and struck into the Soviet Union. Unable to determine which political and economic targets to pursue, he diluted and fragmented his endeavors. In the end he lost all, for himself and for Germany.

The tragedy for all thoughtful, knowledgeable, and sensitive German soldiers like Manstein was the dilemma of trying faithfully to serve their country while disapproving the Fuehrer's aims and methods. True to their tradition of blind obedience, most of them, again like Manstein, kept their gaze unwaveringly on the military role they were expected to play even as they deplored the growing vacuum of direction at the political top.

In a magisterial, even noble account of the war from the German perspective, Manstein has written a personal narrative of his place in the unfolding events. In the process, he has explained, in a manner comprehensible to laymen, the battles in Poland, France, and Russia. Because professional officers must understand the political dimension that is off limits to them, he has offered a panoramic view of the strategic opportunities that beckoned and were missed.

Brilliantly dissecting Hitler's policies and methods of command, he has graphically detailed the growing disenchantment among the officer corps with Hitler's leadership, including Manstein's own dramatic personal clashes, face to face, with the Fuehrer; "*I* am a gentleman," he told Hitler pointedly. And finally he has related what to him was the heartbreaking story of bright prospects turning to ruin.

Dismissed by Hitler in March 1944, Manstein sat out the rest of the war at home, watching, no doubt with dismay, the unnecessary prolongation of a conflict that had already been decided. Afterward he was charged and tried in Britain for war crimes in Russia; convicted and sentenced to eighteen years of imprisonment, he was released from confinement four years later.

Although he served an evil and brutal regime, he was patriotically motivated to fight for his country. He maintained the highest personal standards of comportment and character according to the soldiers' code and became the officer most widely respected and admired by his colleagues.

Through his book, he says, he hoped to give insight into "how the main personalities thought and reacted to events." He has succeeded in his intention and achieved much more. His is the best book of memoirs on the German side and it is indispensable for understanding the conditions and circumstances of Hitler's war.

December 1981

FOREWORD

by Captain B. H. Liddell Hart

THE general verdict among the German generals I interrogated in 1945 was that Field-Marshal von Manstein had proved the ablest commander in their Army, and the man they had most desired to become its Commander-in-Chief. It is very clear that he had a superb sense of operational possibilities and an equal mastery in the conduct of operations, together with a greater grasp of the potentialities of mechanised forces than any of the other commanders who had not been trained in the tank arm. In sum, he had military genius.

In the earlier stages of the war he exerted a great influence behind the scenes as a staff officer. Later he became an outstanding commander, and played a key part from 1941 to 1944 in the titanic struggle on the Russian front. His detailed account of the campaigns, pungent comments, and very significant revelations combine to make his book one of the most important and illuminating contributions to the history of World War II.

An extraordinary aspect of Erich von Manstein's career is that he is best known, outside Germany at any rate, in connexion with operations that took place when he was a relatively junior general, and in which he took no part. For his fame primarily arose from his influence on the design – or, rather, on the recasting – of the plan for the German offensive of 1940 which broke through the Western Front, and led to the fall of France, with all its far-reaching results. The new plan, for making the decisive thrust through the hilly and wooded Ardennes – the line of least expectation – has come to be called the 'Manstein Plan'. That is tribute to what he did in evolving it and striving to win acceptance for it in place of the old plan, for a more direct attack through Belgium – which would in all probability have resulted in a repulse.

At that time Manstein was Chief of Staff to Rundstedt's Army Group, and when his arguments for changing the plan became irritating to his superiors he was honourably pushed out of the way by promotion to command a reserve corps, of infantry, just before the new plan was adopted under Hitler's pressure – after hearing Manstein's arguments. The book provides much fresh information on the course of this operational controversy and the evolution of the plan that led to victory.

In the crucial opening stage of the offensive, which cut off the Allies' left wing and trapped it on the Channel coast, Manstein's corps merely had a follow-on part. But in the second and final stage it played a bigger role. Under his dynamic leadership, his infantry pushed on so fast on foot that they raced the armoured corps in the drive southward across the Somme and the Seine to the Loire.

After the collapse of France, Hitler hoped that Britain would make peace, but when disappointed he began, belatedly and half-heartedly, to make preparations for a cross-Channel invasion. Manstein was entrusted with the task of leading the initial landing with his corps, which was moved to the Boulogne–Calais area for the purpose. His book has some striking comments on the problem, on the strategic alternatives, and on Hitler's turn away to deal with Russia.

For the invasion of Russia in 1941 Manstein was given his heart's desire – the command of an armoured corps, the 56th. With it he made one of the quickest and deepest thrusts of the opening stage, from East Prussia to the Dvina, nearly 200 miles, within four days. Promoted to command the Eleventh Army in the south, he forced an entry into the Crimean peninsula by breaking through the fortified Perekop Isthmus, and in the summer of 1942 further proved his mastery of siege-warfare technique by capturing the famous fortress of Sevastopol, the key centre of the Crimea – being Russia's main naval base on the Black Sea.

He was then sent north again to command the intended attack on Leningrad, but called away by an emergency summons to conduct the efforts to relieve Paulus's Sixth Army, trapped that winter at Stalingrad, after the failure of the main German offensive of 1942. The effort failed because Hitler, forbidding any withdrawal, refused to agree to Manstein's insistence that Paulus should be told to break out westward and meet the relieving forces. The long chapter on 'The Tragedy of Stalingrad' is full of striking revelations, and the more illuminating because of the penetrating analysis of 'Hitler as Supreme Commander' in the preceding chapter.

Following Paulus's surrender, a widespread collapse developed on the Germans' southern front under pressure of advancing Russian armies, but Manstein saved the situation by a brilliant flank counter-stroke which recaptured Kharkov and rolled back the Russians in confusion. That counterstroke was the most brilliant operational per-formance of Manstein's career, and one of the most masterly in the whole course of military history. His detailed account of the operation is likely to be studied, for its instructional value, so long as military studies continue.

Then in the Germans' last great offensive of the war in the East, 'Operation Citadel', launched in July 1943 against the Kursk salient, Manstein's Southern Army Group formed the right pincer. It achieved a considerable measure of success, but the effect was nullified by the failure of the left pincer, provided by the Central Army Group. Moreover, at this crucial moment the Anglo-American landing in Sicily led Hitler to direct several divisions to the Italian theatre. Having checked the German offensive, the Russians now launched their own on a larger scale along a wider front, and with growing strength.

From that time onwards the Germans were thrown on the defensive, strategically, and with the turn of the tide Manstein was henceforth called on to meet, repeatedly, what has always been judged the hardest task of generalship – that of conducting a fighting withdrawal in face of much superior forces.

He showed great skill, against heavy odds, in checking successive Russian thrusts and imposing delays on the westward advance of the Russian armies. His concept of the strategic defensive gave strong emphasis to offensive action in fulfilling it, and he constantly looked for opportunities of delivering a riposte, while often ably exploiting those which arose. But when he urged that a longer step back should be made – a *strategic* withdrawal – in order to develop the full recoil-spring effect of a counter-offensive against an overstretched enemy advance, Hitler would not heed his arguments.

Hitler's unwillingness to sanction any withdrawal forfeited each successive chance of stabilizing the front, and repeatedly clashed with Manstein's sense of strategy. Unlike many of his fellows, Manstein maintained the old Prussian tradition of speaking frankly, and expressed his criticism forcibly both to Hitler in private and at conferences, in a way that staggered others who were present. That Hitler bore it so long is remarkable evidence of the profound respect he had for Manstein's ability, and a contrast with his attitude to most of his generals, and to the General Staff as a body. But the cumulative effect became in the end more than Hitler could stand – and all the more because the course of events continued to confirm Manstein's warnings. So in March 1944 Hitler reached the limit of his endurance, and put Manstein on the shelf, although with far more politeness than he normally showed in making changes of command.

That ended the active career of the Allies' most formidable military opponent – a man who combined modern ideas of mobility with a classical sense of manœuvre, a mastery of technical detail and great driving power.

January 1958

AUTHOR'S PREFACE

THIS BOOK is the personal narrative of a *soldier*, in which I have deliberately refrained from discussing political problems or matters with no direct bearing on events in the military field. In the same connexion it is perhaps worth recalling a statement of Captain B. H. Liddell Hart's:

'The German generals of this war were the best-finished product of their profession—anywhere. They could have been better if their outlook had been wider and their understanding deeper. *But if they had become philosophers they would have ceased to be soldiers.*'

I have made every effort not to view things in a retrospective light, but to present my experiences, ideas and decisions as they appeared to me at the time. In other words, I write not as a historical investigator, but as one who played an active part in what I have to relate. But even though I have tried to give an objective account of all that happened, of the people involved and of the decisions they took, my opinion, as that of a participant, is bound to be subjective. I still hope, nevertheless, that the account I give will be of some use to historians, for even they cannot get the truth from files and documents alone. The essential thing to know is how the main personalities thought and reacted to events, and the answer to this will seldom be found – certainly not in a complete form – in files or war diaries.

In describing how the plan for Germany's 1940 offensive in the west came about, I have departed from Colonel-General v. Seeckt's precept that General Staff officers should be nameless. I feel I am at liberty to do this now that – through no action of my own – the subject has so long been open to general discussion. It was actually my former Commander-in-Chief, Field-Marshal v. Rundstedt, and our Chief of Operations, General Blumentritt, who told Liddell Hart the story of the plan. (At that time I had not had the pleasure of meeting him.)

In this account of military problems and events I have occasionally included items of a personal nature in the belief that there must be a place for the human element even in war. The reason for the absence of such personal reminiscences from the later chapters of the book is that worry and the burden of my responsibilities overshadowed everything else during that period.

My activities in World War II have led me to deal with events largely from the viewpoint of leadership at a higher level. I hope, nonetheless, to have made it consistently clear that the *decisive factor* throughout was the self-sacrifice, valour and devotion to duty of the German *fighting soldier*, combined with the ability of *commanders* at all levels and their readiness to assume responsibility. These were the qualities which won us our victories. These alone enabled us to face the overwhelming superiority of our opponents.

By this book I should at the same time like to express gratitude to my Commander-in-Chief in the initial phase of the war, Field-Marshal v. Rundstedt, for the trust he always placed in me; to the commanders and soldiers of all ranks who served under my command; and to the men who served at my various headquarters, in particular my chiefs-of-staff and General Staff officers, who constantly supported and advised me.

Finally I must also thank those who have assisted me in preparing these memoirs: my former Chief-of-Staff, General Busse, and our staff officers v. Blumröder, Eismann and Annus; Herr Gerhard Günther, who encouraged me to commit my memoirs to paper; Herr Fred Hildenbrandt, who gave me valuable assistance in composing them; and Herr Dipl.-Ing. Materne, who showed great understanding in his work on the sketch-maps.

VON MANSTEIN

Part I
THE CAMPAIGN IN POLAND

I

BEFORE THE STORM

I WATCHED POLITICAL developments after the Austrian *anschluss* from a point far from the centre of military affairs.

At the beginning of February 1938, after I had risen to the second most senior post on the German Army Staff – that of *Oberquartiermeister I* – the deputy to the Chief-of-Staff, my career as a General Staff officer had abruptly ended. When Colonel-General Baron v. Fritsch was eliminated as Commander-in-Chief of the Army through a diabolical party intrigue, a number of his closest collaborators, myself included, had been removed from the Army High Command (O.K.H.) along with him. Since then, as commander of 18 Division, I had naturally ceased to be informed of matters falling within the High Command's jurisdiction.

Indeed, since the beginning of April 1938 I had been able to devote myself entirely to my job as a divisional commander. It was a particularly satisfying task – even more satisfying in those years than at any other time – but it also called for every ounce of one's energy, since the expansion of the army was still far from complete. The continual formation of new units entailed a constant reorganization of those already in existence, while the speed of rearmament, and especially the attendant growth of both the officer and non-commissioned officer corps, meant that the most exacting demands were made on commanders at all levels if we were to fulfil our aim of creating intrinsically stable and highly trained troops who would guarantee the security of the Reich. To succeed in this work was more gratifying still, especially in my own case, now that, after several years in Berlin, I once again had the pleasure of being in direct touch with combat units. It is with immense gratitude, therefore, that I remember that last year and a half of peace, and, in particular, the Silesians of whom 18 Division was largely composed. Silesia had produced good soldiers from time immemorial, so the military education and training of the new units was a rewarding task.

It is true that the brief interlude of the 'floral war' – the occupation of the Sudetenland – had found me in the post of Chief-of-Staff of the army commanded by Colonel-General Ritter v. Leeb. As such I had learnt of the conflict that had broken out between the Chief-of-Staff of the Army, General Beck, and Hitler over the Czech question and which, to my intense regret, had ended with the resignation of the Chief-of-Staff I so revered. This resignation, however, snapped the thread which had kept me in touch with O.K.H.

And so it was not until summer 1939 that I learnt of Operation 'Order White', the first offensive deployment against Poland to be prepared on Hitler's orders. No such thing had existed before the spring of 1939. On the contrary, all military preparations on our eastern frontier had been based on defence.

In the above operation order I was earmarked as Chief-of-Staff of Southern Army Group, the Commander-in-Chief of which was to be Colonel-General v. Rundstedt, then already living in retirement. It was planned that this Army Group should deploy in Silesia, eastern Moravia, and partly in Slovakia, in accordance with the detailed arrangements which we were now to work out.

As the Army Group Headquarters did not exist in peacetime and would be set up only in the event of general mobilization, a small working party was formed to deal with the new operation order. It assembled on 12th August 1939 in the Silesian training area of Neu-hammer. It was to work under the direction of Colonel Blumentritt, a General Staff officer who was destined to become the Army Group's chief of operations (Ia) on mobilization. This was an unusual stroke of luck as far as I was concerned, for my relationship with that exception-ally able man was one of the closest confidence. The bond had been forged while we were both serving at the headquarters of v. Leeb's army during the Sudeten crisis, and I considered it extremely valuable to have a colleague on whom I could rely in times like these. As often as not, the things that attract us to another person are quite trivial, and what always delighted me about Blumentritt was his fanatical attach-ment to the telephone. The speed at which he worked was in any case incredibly high, but whenever he had a receiver in his hand he could deal with whole avalanches of queries, always with the same imperturbable good humour.

In mid-August the future commander of Southern Army Group, Colonel-General v. Rundstedt, arrived at Neuhammer. Every one of us knew him. As an exponent of grand tactics he was brilliant – a talented soldier who grasped the essentials of any problem in an instant. Indeed, he would concern himself with nothing else, being supremely indifferent to minor detail. He was a gentleman of the old school – a type, I fear, which is now dying out, but which once added a delightful variant to life. The General had a charm about him to which even Hitler succumbed. The latter seemed to have taken a genuine liking to him, and, surprisingly enough, there was even a glimmer of this left after he had twice dismissed him. What probably attracted Hitler was the indefinable impression the general gave of a man from a past which he did not understand and to the atmosphere of which he never had access.

As a matter of interest, when our working party assembled at Neuhammer, my own 18 Division was also in the training area for the annual regimental and divisional exercises.

That everyone among us, disquieted by the number of emergencies through which the Fatherland had passed since 1933, wondered where all this would lead, I need hardly say. Our thoughts and private conversations at this time were centred on the signs of the gathering storm on the horizon around us. We realized that Hitler was fanatically resolved to dispose of the very last of the territorial problems Germany had inherited through the Treaty of Versailles. We knew that he had begun negotiations with Poland as far back as autumn 1938 to clear up the whole Polish–German frontier question, though what progress, if any, these negotiations had made we were not told. At the same time we were aware of the British guarantee to Poland. And I can safely say that not one of us in the army was so arrogant, thoughtless or shortsighted as not to recognize the deadly seriousness of the warning that guarantee implied. This factor alone – though it was not the only one – convinced our party in Neuhammer that there would in the end be no war. Even if the deployment plan on which we were now engaged went into operation, that still need not, in our opinion, mean war. We had watched Germany's precarious course along the razor's edge to date with close attention and were increasingly amazed at Hitler's incredible luck in attaining – hitherto without recourse to arms – all his overt and covert political aims. The man seemed to have an almost infallible instinct. Success had followed success in a never-ending progression – if one may initially refer to the glittering train of events that ultimately led to our downfall as successes. All those things had been achieved without war. Why, we asked ourselves, should it be different this time? Look at Czechoslovakia. Though Hitler had drawn up a menacing array of troops against her in 1938, there had still been no war. Yet the old adage about taking the pitcher to the well once too often still echoed in our ears, for the position was now a much trickier one and the game Hitler seemed intent on playing had a more dangerous look about it. There was the British guarantee to contend with this time. But then we recalled Hitler's assertion that he would never be so mad as to unleash a war on two fronts, as the German leaders of 1914 had done. That at least implied that he was a man of reason, even if he had no human feelings left. Raising that coarse voice of his, he had explicitly assured his military advisers that he was not idiot enough to bungle his way into a world war for the sake of Danzig or the Polish Corridor.

THE GENERAL STAFF AND THE POLISH QUESTION

Poland was bound to be a source of great bitterness to us after she had used the dictated peace of Versailles to annex German territories to which neither historical justice nor the right of self-determination gave her any claim. For us soldiers she had been a constant cause of distress in the years of Germany's weakness. Every time we looked at the map we were reminded of our precarious situation. That irrational demarcation of the frontier! That mutilation of our Fatherland! That corridor whose severance of East Prussia from the Reich gave us every reason to fear for that lovely province! For all that, however, the army had never dreamt of fighting an aggressive war against Poland to end this state of affairs by force. Apart from anything else, such forbearance had a perfectly simple military reason: any attack on Poland would have plunged the Reich into a war on two or more fronts, and with this it could never have coped. In the period of weakness imposed on us at Versailles we had always had the *cauchemar des coalitions* – a nightmare that disturbed us all the more whenever we thought of the aspirations for German territory still harboured with such ill-concealed longing by wide circles of the Polish people. Yet although we had no wish to fight an aggressive war, we could hardly hope, even taking the most unprejudiced view of the Polish mentality, to sit down peacefully at the same table as the Poles to revise those senseless frontiers. Neither did it seem beyond the bounds of possibility that Poland might herself take the initiative one day and set out to solve the frontier question by force. We had gained some experience in this respect since 1918, and in Germany's years of weakness it had been just as well to be prepared for such a thing. Once Marshal Pilsudski's voice was silent and certain nationalist circles had gained a decisive influence in Poland, an incursion into East Prussia or Upper Silesia was just as feasible as the Polish raid on Vilna before it. For that contingency, though, our military deliberations had found a political answer. If Poland were proved to be the aggressor and we succeeded in warding off the attack, the Reich might well have an opportunity to get the unhappy frontier question revised on the political rebound.

At all events, there was no exaggerated wishful thinking on the subject on the part of any army leaders. Although General v. Rabenau, in the book *Seeckt, Aus Meinem Leben*, quotes the Colonel-General as saying that 'Poland's existence is intolerable and incompatible with Germany's essential needs: she must disappear through her own internal weakness and through Russia ... with help from ourselves', this was in fact an attitude already overtaken by developments in the political and military fields. We had a pretty fair idea of the growing military power of the Soviet Union; and France, the land under whose spell one so easily fell, still faced us with the same hostility as ever. She would always seek allies in Germany's rear. But if the Polish State were to disappear, the mighty Soviet Union could become a far more dangerous ally of France than a buffer State like Poland was at present. Any elimination of the buffer formed by Poland (and Lithuania) between Germany and the Soviet Union could lead only too easily to differences between the two big Powers. While it might be a matter of mutual interest to carry out frontier revisions *vis-à-vis* Poland, the complete removal of that State would hardly be to Germany's advantage in view of the entirely changed situation that now prevailed.

So whether we liked her or not, it was preferable to keep Poland between us and the Soviet Union. Aggrieved though we were as soldiers by the senseless and explosive frontier demarcation in the east,

Poland was still less dangerous as a neighbour than the Soviet Union. Like all other Germans, of course, we hoped a revision of the frontier would come about sometime and return the predominantly German-populated areas to the Reich in accordance with the natural right of their inhabitants. At the same time it was most undesirable from the military point of view that the size of our Polish population should increase. As for the German demand for a union of East Prussia with the Reich, it could well have been harmonized with Poland's desire for a seaport of her own. This, and none other, was the trend of thought on the Polish problem favoured by the majority of German soldiers in the days of the Reichswehr – let us say from the end of the nineteen-twenties onwards – whenever the question of armed conflict cropped up.

Then the wheel of fate turned once again. Adolf Hitler appeared on the stage. Everything changed, including the basis of our relationship with Poland. The Reich concluded a non-aggression pact and treaty of friendship with our eastern neighbour. We were freed from the nightmare of a possible Polish attack. At the same time relations between Germany and the Soviet Union cooled off, our new ruler having only too clearly voiced his hatred of the Bolshevik system in public speeches. Poland was bound to feel less constrained politically in consequence of this new situation, but that was no longer a danger as far as we were concerned. German rearmament and Hitler's series of successes in the field of foreign policy made it improbable that she would use her new freedom of action against the Reich. And when she proved only too ready to take a hand in the partitioning of Czechoslovakia it seemed not unlikely that we could talk business about the frontier question.

Until spring 1939, then, the High Command of the German Army never had any plan for offensive deployment against Poland on its files. Before that all our military measures in the east had been purely defensive in character.

WAR OR BLUFF?

Was it to be the real thing this time – in autumn 1939? Did Hitler really want war, or would he, as with Czechoslovakia in 1938, bring the very limit of pressure to bear – militarily and otherwise – to settle the Danzig and Corridor questions?

War or bluff? That was the question exercising the mind of everyone without any real insight into political developments, primarily into Hitler's own intentions. And who, for that matter, was vouchsafed any insight whatever into those intentions?

At all events, it was entirely conceivable that the military measures taken in August 1939 – despite Operation 'Order White' – were directed towards increasing political pressure on Poland. Since the summer, on orders from Hitler, work had been proceeding at feverish speed on an *Ostwall* – an eastern equivalent of the Siegfried Line. Whole divisions, the 18th among them, were moved to the Polish frontier in constant rotation to work on this fortification for several weeks at a stretch. What was the point of all this effort if Hitler were going to attack Poland? Even if, contrary to all his assurances, he were contemplating a war on two fronts, the *Ostwall* would still have been quite out of place, since the only proper action for Germany in such circumstances would be to attack and overwhelm Poland first while remaining on the defensive in the west. The reverse solution – offensive action in the west and defensive measures in the east – was quite out of the question with the present ratio of forces, especially as neither plans nor preparations for an offensive in the west had been made. So if the construction of an *Ostwall* were to have any rhyme or reason in the present situation, it could surely only be to exert pressure on Poland by placing large troop concentrations on her frontier. Even the deployment of infantry divisions on the east bank of the Oder in the last ten days of August and the movement of the armoured and motorized divisions into assembly areas initially west of the river need not really have been preparations for an attack: they could just as well have been a form of political pressure.

Be that as it may, the peacetime training programme went on just as usual for the time being. On 13th and 14th August I had my last divisional exercise at Neuhammer, winding up with a march-past at which Colonel-General v. Rundstedt took the salute. On 15th August there was a big artillery shoot in co-operation with the Luftwaffe. It was marked by a tragic accident. An entire dive-bomber squadron, obviously wrongly informed about cloud altitude, failed to pull out of a dive in time and tore straight into a wood. There was one more regimental scheme the next day, and then the divisional units went back to their normal garrisons – though they were to leave for the Silesian frontier again only a few days later.

On 19th August v. Rundstedt and I received instructions to attend a conference at the Obersalzberg on the 21st. On 20th August we drove from Liegnitz to my brother-in-law's estate near Linz and spent the night there, reaching Berchtesgaden the following morning. All the army group and army commanders and their Chiefs-of-Staff were reporting to Hitler, as well as the appropriate navy and Luftwaffe leaders.

The conference – or rather Hitler's address, as he was not going to let the occasion turn into an open discussion after his experience at a conference with the Chiefs-of-Staff the previous year, before the Czech crisis – took place in the big reception-chamber of the Berghof that looked out towards Salzburg. Shortly before Hitler appeared Göring came in. He was an extraordinary sight. Up till now I had assumed that we were here for a serious purpose, but Göring appeared to have taken it for a masked ball. He was dressed in a soft-collared white shirt, worn under a green jerkin adorned with big buttons of yellow leather. In addition he wore grey shorts and long grey silk stockings that displayed his impressive calves to considerable effect. This dainty hosiery was offset by a pair of massive laced boots. To cap it all, his paunch was girded by a sword-belt of red leather richly inlaid with gold, at which dangled an ornamental dagger in an ample sheath of the same material.

I could not resist whispering to my neighbour, General v. Salmuth: 'I suppose the Fat Boy's here as a strong-arm man?'

Hitler's speech on this occasion was the subject of various prosecution 'documents' at the Nuremberg trial. One of these asserted that he had indulged in the vilest of language and that Göring, delighted at the prospect of war, had jumped on the table and yelled '*Sieg Heil!*' All this is quite untrue. It is equally untrue that Hitler said anything about 'his only fear being a last-minute offer of mediation from some pig-dog or other'. While the tone of his speech was certainly that of a man whose mind was firmly made up, he was far too good a psychologist to think he could impress a gathering of this kind with tirades or bad language.

The substance of the speech has been correctly reported in Greiner's book *Die Oberste Wehrmachtführung 1939–43*. This report is based on a verbal summary given to the author by Colonel Warlimont for inclusion in his war diary and on shorthand notes taken by Admiral

Canaris. A certain amount of information on the speech may also be gathered from Colonel-General Halder's diary – although here too, as in the case of the statements made by Warlimont and Canaris, I feel a number of things may have been included which were actually heard from Hitler on other occasions.

The impression left on those of us generals who did not belong to the top circle of military leaders was approximately this:

Hitler was absolutely determined to bring the German–Polish question to a head this time, even at the price of war. If, however, the Poles were to give in to German pressure, now approaching its climax in the deployment – albeit still camouflaged – of the German armies, a peaceful solution still did not seem excluded, and Hitler was convinced that when it came to the point the Western Powers would once again not resort to arms. He was at special pains to develop the latter thesis, his main arguments being: the backwardness of British and French armaments, particularly with regard to air strength and anti-aircraft defence; the virtual inability of the Western Powers to render Poland any effective help except by an assault on the Siegfried Line – a step which neither power was likely to risk in view of the great sacrifice of blood it would entail; the international situation, particularly the tension in the Mediterranean, which considerably reduced Britain's freedom of movement; the internal situation in France; and last but not least the personalities of the responsible statesmen. Neither Chamberlain nor Daladier, Hitler contended, would take upon themselves the decision to go to war.

Logical and conclusive though his appreciation of the Western Powers' position appeared to be in many respects, I still do not think Hitler's audience was entirely convinced by his exposition. The British guarantee was certainly the only real obstacle to his designs, but it was nevertheless a pretty weighty one!

What Hitler had to say about an eventual war with Poland could not, in my opinion, be interpreted as a policy of annihilation, which was the sense given to it by the Nuremberg prosecution. When Hitler called for the swift and ruthless destruction of the Polish Army, this was, in military parlance, merely the aim that must be the basis of any big offensive operation. At all events, nothing he had said could give us any hint of how he was to treat the Poles later on.

The biggest surprise, and also the deepest impression, was caused, quite naturally, by the announcement of the impending pact with the Soviet Union. On our way to Berchtesgaden we had already read newspaper reports of the conclusion of an economic agreement, and that in itself was quite a sensation. Now we were told that Foreign Minister v. Ribbentrop, who was present at the conference and took leave of Hitler in our presence, was flying to Moscow to sign a non-aggression pact with Stalin. By this move, Hitler declared, he was depriving the Western Powers of their trump card, for even a blockade of Germany would be ineffectual from now on. Hitler hinted that in order to facilitate the pact he had already made considerable concessions to the Soviet Union in the Baltic and in respect of Poland's eastern frontiers, but his remarks gave no reason for inferring that there would be a complete partition of Poland. Indeed, he is now known to have still been considering leaving a Polish rump state in existence even after the campaign had started.

As a result of Hitler's address neither v. Rundstedt nor I – and presumably none of the other generals either – concluded that war was now inevitable. Two factors in particular persuaded us that – as at Munich – there would be an eleventh-hour settlement.

The first was that the pact with the Soviet Union now rendered Poland's position hopeless from the start. If Britain, virtually deprived of the weapon of blockade, were compelled to take the bloody course of attacking in the west in order to aid Poland, it seemed likely enough that, under pressure from the French, she would advise Warsaw to give in. Similarly it must henceforth be clear to Poland that the British guarantee was now practically inoperative. If it came to a war with Germany, moreover, she must expect the Russians to take action in her rear with a view to accomplishing their old demands on her eastern territory. What else could Warsaw do in this situation but give way?

A further consideration was the conference we had just attended. What was its purpose? Hitherto, on the military side, the intention to attack Poland had been camouflaged in every possible way. The presence of divisions in the eastern areas had been explained by the construction of an eastern rampart; and to conceal the purpose of the troop movements to East Prussia, an enormous Tannenberg celebration had been arranged. Preparations for big motorized troop manœuvres had been going on until the very last moment. There had been no official mobilization. Though these measures could not possibly escape the notice of the Poles and were obviously intended as political pressure, they had still been enveloped in the greatest secrecy and accompanied by every form of deception. Yet now, at the very height of the crisis, Hitler had summoned every one of his senior commanders to the Obersalzberg – an action that could not possibly be concealed. To us this seemed to be the climax of a policy of deliberate bluff. In other words, was Hitler not after all working for a settlement, despite his bellicose utterances? Was not this very conference meant to apply the final squeeze?

Such were the thoughts of Colonel-General v. Rundstedt and myself as we left Berchtesgaden. While he travelled on ahead to our Neisse headquarters, I stopped on in Liegnitz for a further day with my family. This alone was a measure of my inner disbelief in the likelihood of an imminent outbreak of war.

At noon on 24th August Colonel-General v. Rundstedt assumed command of the Army Group. On 25th August, at 3.25 in the afternoon, we received the following cypher message from the High Command of the army:

'Operation Plan White: D-Day = 26.8: H-Hour = 0430.'

So the decision to go to war – the decision we had not wanted to believe possible – had apparently been taken.

I was at dinner with Colonel-General v. Rundstedt in our quarters at the Monastery of the Holy Cross in Neisse when the following order from the High Command came through by telephone:

'Do *not* – repeat *not* – commence hostilities. Halt all troop movements. Mobilization to continue. Deployment for Plans White and West to proceed as scheduled.'

Every soldier can judge what an eleventh-hour counter-order of this kind implied. Within the space of a few hours three armies moving straight for the frontier across a zone extending from Lower Silesia to the eastern part of Slovakia had to be brought to a halt – not forgetting that all headquarters staffs up to at least divisional level were also on the march and that there was still a security ban on wireless traffic. Despite all the difficulties, we managed to notify everybody in good time – a first-rate piece of work by the operations and signals staffs. Nevertheless, one motorized regiment in eastern Slovakia could only be stopped after an officer in a Fieseler Storch aircraft had landed at the head of the column in the darkness.

We were not told Hitler's reasons for what seemed to be an eleventh-hour reversal of his decision to fight. All we heard was that the negotiations were continuing.

It will be appreciated that we as soldiers were considerably shaken by leadership of this kind. The decision to go to war is, after all, the gravest that a head of state ever has to take.

How could any man reach such a decision and then cancel it again in the space of a few hours – least of all when that cancellation placed him, in the military sense, at a severe disadvantage? As I pointed out above when describing the Obersalzberg conference, everything in the military sphere was aimed at taking the enemy by surprise. There was no public announcement of the mobilization, the first call-up being scheduled for 26th August – the day of the invasion that had this very moment been stopped. This meant that we were to march into Poland with nothing more than our sum total of armoured and motorized formations, plus a limited number of infantry divisions that were already in the frontier areas or in the process of being made 'immediately operational'. There could be no question now of catching the enemy unawares. For even though the movement of troops into their final concentration areas behind the frontier was being carried out by night, it could certainly not elude the enemy's attention, particularly as the motorized units in assembly areas west of the Oder had to form up in daylight in order to cross the river. Consequently, if there really were to be war, the other alternative must now come into effect – invasion with all our mobilized forces. The element of surprise was lost in any case.

As the original decision to start hostilities could not be regarded as an act of ill-considered frivolity on Hitler's part, we could only deduce that the whole thing was simply a continuation of diplomatic tactics to bring ever-increasing pressure to bear on the Poles. So when, at 1700 hours on 31st August, we received a fresh order

$$D = 1.9: H = 0445,$$

Colonel-General v. Rundstedt and I were sceptical, particularly as no mention was made of the negotiations having failed. Within our own Army Group, at any rate, we were all set this time, in view of what had occurred on 25th August, to cope with another last-minute stoppage of the operation. The General and I stayed up till midnight in anticipation of the countermand we thought might still come through.

Only when midnight had passed and the last possibility of halting the operation had gone could there be no further doubt left: from now on the weapons would speak.

2

THE STRATEGIC POSITION

THE FOLLOWING factors were decisive in determining the strategic position in the Polish campaign:

First, the *superiority* of the German forces – provided that the German leadership were prepared to accept a considerable risk in the west in order to commit the bulk of its strength against Poland.

Secondly, the *geographical situation*, which enabled the Germans to take the Polish Army in a pincer movement from East Prussia on one flank and Silesia and Slovakia on the other.

Thirdly, the latent *threat* present in Poland's rear from the outset in the form of the Soviet Union.

GERMAN ORDER OF BATTLE AND PLAN OF OPERATIONS

The German planners accepted the above-mentioned risk in the west to the full.

O.K.H. launched its attack against Poland with forty-two divisions of regular troops (including one newly formed armoured division, 10 Panzer) and one new infantry division formed from fortress troops in the Oder–Warta basin (the 50th). They consisted of twenty-four infantry divisions, three mountain divisions, six armoured divisions, four light divisions, four motorized infantry divisions and one cavalry brigade. Then came sixteen new divisions not formed until after the general mobilization and destined for use between the second and fourth waves. These could not initially be regarded as first-rate troops. Also assigned for the Polish campaign were the SS division *Leibstandarte Adolf Hitler* and one or two reinforced SS regiments.

For the west this left only eleven regular divisions, some fortress troops amounting to about a division in strength (later to be formed into 72 Infantry Division), and thirty-five newly constituted divisions of second- to fourth-line troops. No armoured or motorized troops were available. There was thus a total of forty-six divisions, of which only three-quarters were conditionally fit to go into action.

22 Infantry Division, which had been trained and equipped as an airborne division, was retained at the disposal of O.K.H. in the interior of the Reich.

The bulk of our *air forces* were likewise committed against Poland in the form of two air fleets, a third, weaker one being kept in the west.

The risks which the German leadership ran by distributing its forces in this way were undoubtedly very great indeed. Because of the un-expected brevity of the Polish campaign (a development due in part to the loser's own mistakes) and, above all, as a result of the complete inaction of Poland's Western allies at the time of her defeat, these risks have hardly ever been properly appreciated.

It should be realized that at that particular juncture the German command had to reckon with a French Army some ninety divisions strong. In autumn 1939 (according to v. Tippelskirch) France actually raised 108 divisions in the space of three weeks! These consisted of fifty-seven infantry, five cavalry, one armoured and forty-five reservist or 'territorial' divisions, supported by strong army troops of tanks and artillery.[1] The last category had the advantage of being made up of fully trained reservists, whereas the new German formations consisted to a great extent of raw recruits or reservists from the First World War.

There can be no doubt, then, that the French Army far outnumbered Germany's forces in the west from the very first day.

The British contribution of land forces, on the other hand, was quite insignificant. It amounted to a mere four divisions, and even these did not arrive until the first half of October.

The basis of the German plan of operations against Poland was to make maximum use of the way the frontier ran in order to envelop the enemy from the start. Thus the German armies deployed in two widely divided flank groups which left the central sector (the Oder–Warta basin) almost wide open.

Northern Army Group (Commander Colonel-General v. Bock, Chief-of-Staff General v. Salmuth) comprised two armies embracing a

---

[1] It should be noted, however, that part of these forces remained in North Africa and on the Alpine frontier in the initial stages. *Author.*

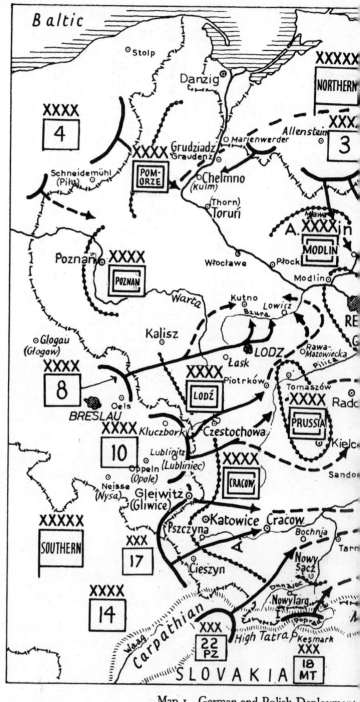

Map 1. German and Polish Deployment,

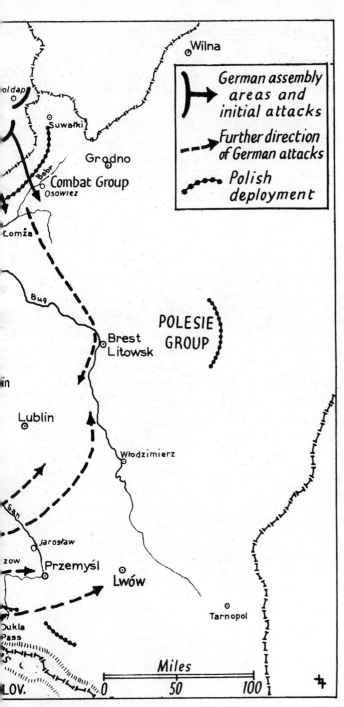

Wilna

oldap

Suwałki

Grodno

Bobr
Combat Group
Osowiez

Łomża

Bug

Brest
Litowsk

POLESIE
GROUP

Lublin

Włodzimierz

San

Jarosław

zow
Przemyśl

Lwów

Tarnopol

Dukla
Pass

LOV.

	German assembly areas and initial attacks
	Further direction of German attacks
	Polish deployment

Miles

0   50   100

nd Execution of German Offensive.

total of five infantry and one armoured corps. Under command of these were nine regular infantry divisions (including the newly formed 50 Infantry Division, which consisted of fortress troops and was not up to strength), eight infantry divisions established on mobilization, two armoured divisions (plus the newly formed tank task force 'Kemp'), two motorized infantry divisions and one cavalry brigade – in all twenty-one divisions. Supplementing these in East Prussia were the fortress troops of Königsberg and Lotze; in Pomerania, the Netze Brigade.

Of this Army Group, Third Army (General v. Küchler) deployed in East Prussia and Fourth Army (Colonel-General v. Kluge) in East Pomerania.

The task of the Army Group was to thrust through the Polish Corridor, to throw the mass of its forces on the east of the Vistula towards the south-east or south, and then, after forcing the Narew line, to take any Polish defence of the Vistula from the rear.

Southern Army Group (Commander Colonel-General v. Rundstedt, Chief-of-Staff General v. Manstein) was considerably stronger. It consisted of three armies – Fourteenth (Colonel-General List), Tenth (Colonel-General v. Reichenau) and Eighth (Colonel-General Blaskowitz). In all, the Army Group had eight infantry and four armoured corps, totalling fifteen regular infantry divisions, three mountain divisions, eight newly drafted divisions and the bulk of the mechanized formations – four armoured, four light and two motorized infantry divisions. This made a total of thirty-six divisions.

The Army Group deployed Fourteenth Army in the Upper Silesian industrial region, eastern Moravia and western Slovakia, Tenth Army in Upper Silesia around and to the south of Kreuzberg, and Eighth Army in central Silesia eastward of Oels. Its task was to defeat the enemy in the large bend of the Vistula and in Galicia, to dash for Warsaw with strong motorized forces, taking the Vistula crossings as fast as possible on a broad front, and then, in conjunction with Northern Army Group, to destroy the remainder of the Polish Army.

POLISH ORDER OF BATTLE AND PLAN OF OPERATIONS

Peacetime Poland had thirty infantry divisions, eleven cavalry brigades, one mountain brigade and two motorized (armoured) brigades. In addition to these there were a few Frontier Corps regiments, a large number of Home Defence (O.N.) battalions and naval troops stationed in the Gdynia–Hel area.

In other words, her aggregate strength was pretty considerable. Her weapons, however, dated mainly from World War I, and her air force, of some 1,000 aircraft, was also not up to modern standards.

Germany had expected Poland to double the number of her divisions in the event of war, though it seemed doubtful whether the requisite arms were available. According to v. Tippelkirch in his *History of the Second World War*, Poland drafted only enough regiments for ten reserve divisions prior to the outbreak of hostilities, and even then she apparently had no time to embody all of them in their scheduled divisions. Nevertheless, German Intelligence did identify a number of reserve divisions in the course of the campaign.

The Polish High Command disposed its forces as follows:

Deployed along the *East Prussian frontier*, in *front* of the Bobr-Narew–Vistula line, were:

(i) a *combat group* of two divisions and two cavalry brigades between Suwałki and Łomza, and

(ii) the Modlin Army of four divisions and two cavalry brigades on both sides of Mława.

In the *Corridor* was the *Pomorʒe Army* of five divisions and one cavalry brigade.

Facing the *German frontier from the Warta to the Slovakian frontier* were three armies:

(i) the *Poʒnań Army*, with a strength of four divisions and two cavalry brigades, in the western part of Poznań Province;

(ii) the *Łódʒ Army* (four divisions and two cavalry brigades) around Wieluń; and

(iii) the *Cracow Army* (six divisions, one cavalry and one motorized brigade) between Częstochowa and Nowy Targ. Behind the two last-named armies was the *Prussia Army* (six divisions and one cavalry brigade) in the area Tomaszow–Kielce.

Finally, the deep flank along the *Carpathian frontier* was to be covered by a *Carpathian Army* – composed mainly of reserve units and O.N. battalions – in echeloned formation.

A reserve group (General Piskor's Army), consisting of three divisions and one motorized brigade, remained on the Vistula in the area Modlin–Warsaw–Lublin. In the course of the campaign, moreover, an independent *Polesie Group* was formed east of the Bug, presumably for protection against Russia.

In the event, the Polish deployment was still in progress when the German invasion started, and for this reason it was probably never properly completed in the form described above.

SOME REFLECTIONS ON THE POLISH DEPLOYMENT

It is difficult to decide the strategic aim of the Polish deployment, unless it was based on a wish to 'cover everything' and surrender nothing voluntarily. It was a policy that usually leads to the defeat of the weaker party. Hitler was to have a similar experience only a few years later – without ever learning his lesson from it.

Now, the difficulty of Poland's strategic position was really quite obvious, consisting as it did in the inferiority of the Polish forces and the fact that the line of the frontier enabled Germany to attack from two – later even from three – sides at once. So when the Polish High Command still could not resist trying to 'hold on to everything', this only went to show how difficult it is to reconcile psychological and political inhibitions with hard military fact.

Apart from Marshal Pilsudski and one or two sober-minded politicians, probably no one in Poland ever quite realized in what a dangerous situation the country had landed itself by enforcing its unjustified territorial demands on the neighbouring States of Russia and Germany. Yet this same Poland numbered only 35 million inhabitants, of whom a mere 22 million were of Polish nationality, the rest belonging to the German, Ukrainian, White Russian and Jewish minorities, all of which had been oppressed to one degree or another.

Besides, in their reliance on their French allies, people in Poland had undoubtedly spent far too long in the years of Germany's (and the Soviet Union's) military weakness dreaming of a chance for aggression against the Reich. Some had dreamt of raids on isolated East Prussia or – thanks to the propaganda of the Polish Insurgents' League – on German Upper Silesia; others had even considered a march on Berlin, either by the shortest route through Poznań and Frankfurt or by first conquering Upper Silesia and then advancing on the capital west of the Oder.

Admittedly such dreams had been frustrated by Germany's fortification of East Prussia and the Oder–Warta basin and later by her rearmament. But it is unlikely that Poland's politicians and soldiers, banking on a simultaneous French offensive in the west, ever put such aggressive ideas right out of their minds. Defensive though the above dispositions may well have been in the first instance, it is reasonable to infer that they were meant to leave the door open for offensive action at a later date, as soon as the first French assistance had made itself felt.

For the rest, the Polish General Staff did not possess its own tradition of generalship shaped by long experience. On the one hand the Polish temperament was more disposed towards attack than defence. It is fair to assume that the mind of the Polish soldier was still coloured, at least subconsciously, by romantic notions from bygone days. I am reminded here of a portrait I once saw of Marshal Rydz-Smigły painted against a background of charging Polish cavalry squadrons. On the other hand the newly founded Polish Army was French-taught. This, in view of the fact that French military thought since 1918 had been based on experience of static warfare, could hardly have imbued the Poles with a sense of operational speed and mobility.

It is conceivable, then, that except for a desire not to abandon anything to the enemy, the Polish deployment plan had no clear-cut operational objective whatever and amounted merely to a compromise between the aggressive ambitions of yesteryear and the necessity of preparing for defence against a superior opponent. At the same time the Poles made the mistake of assuming that the Germans would carry out an offensive on the French pattern and that this would soon degenerate into positional warfare. Of some interest in this connexion is a confidential report which we received just before the outbreak of war on the subject of Poland's allegedly *offensive* intentions. It emanated from a source – hitherto regarded as completely reliable – in the immediate circle of either the Polish President or Marshal Rydz-Smigły, and contended that the Polish deployment would be offensive in character and include the concentration of strong forces in the province of Poznań. Most remarkable of all was the allegation that this plan of campaign had actually been proposed, if not demanded, by the British! In the circumstances we found the whole thing rather improbable. Yet it was to emerge later that the Poles actually did assemble relatively strong forces in Poznań Province, notwithstanding the fact that from their own point of view this was the least likely direction from which to expect a German attack. The Poznań Army was to meet its fate in the battle on the River Bzura.

In point of fact there had been no lack of sensible suggestions on the Polish side. As Colonel Hermann Schneider reported in the *Militär-wissenschaftliche Rundschau* in 1942, General Weygand had suggested putting the defence behind the line of the rivers Niemen, Bobr, Narew, Vistula and San. Operationally this was the only proper recommendation to make, since it eliminated the possibility of encirclement by the Germans and would also, by virtue of the river obstacles, have considerably strengthened the defence *vis-à-vis* the German tank formations. What was more, this line was only about 375 miles long, in contrast to the 1,125-mile arc described by the Polish frontier from Suwałki to the Carpathian passes. Acceptance of this suggestion would, of course, have necessitated abandoning the whole of western Poland, which embraced the country's most precious industrial and agricultural areas, and it is hardly likely that any Polish Government would have survived such a step. What also had to be borne in mind was the fact that a withdrawal as extensive as this at the very start of hostilities was hardly likely to increase French aggressiveness in the west, and it was an open question whether surrendering the whole of western Poland to the Germans would not encourage the Russians, for their part, to take immediate steps to secure their share of the spoils in the east.

Consequently, Colonel Schneider tells us, another solution was put forward by General Kutrzeba, Director of the Polish Military Academy, in a memorandum he submitted to Marshal Rydz-Smigły at the beginning of 1938. He insisted that there could be no question of giving up 'Poland's vital strategic zone', which embraced both the industrial regions of Łódz and Upper Silesia and the valuable agricultural areas of Poznań, Kutno and Kielce. Accordingly he proposed a deployment plan which, while dropping any attempt to hold the Corridor or Poznań Province, substantially resembled the one ultimately implemented in 1939. To buttress the Polish defences, a far-reaching system of fortifications was to be built south of the East Prussian frontier, in a wide arc from Grudziadz to Poznań, and along the Silesian frontier from Ostrowo, through Częstochowa to Cieszyn. At the same time, General Kutrzeba pointed out, attention should be paid to preparing 'sally-ports' for later attacks against both East and West Prussia and Silesia. That to build such far-flung fortifications in adequate strength would have exceeded Polish potentialities was only too clear. Nevertheless, General Kutrzeba had recognized Poland's military inferiority *vis-à-vis* the Reich. His appraisal of French support was equally clear-sighted, since he took it for granted that, even if France rendered the maximum military assistance, Poland would be thrown on her own resources for the first six or eight weeks. He therefore envisaged a 'strategic defence' along the western periphery of the above-mentioned 'vital zone', in the interior of which reserves were to assemble for the decisive operations later on.

As I have said, the deployment carried out by the Polish Army in 1939 was very similar to that recommended by the General. The latter, however, had envisaged making the main effort in the area Toruń-Bydgoszcz–Gniezno, whereas in 1939 there tended to be two focal points—one in the area around East Prussia and the other opposite Silesia.

The Polish deployment of 1939, aimed as it was at covering everything, including the forward province of Poznań, was bound to bring defeat, in view of the Germans' superiority and their ability to outflank. How, then, should Poland have operated to avoid such a defeat?

The first question to settle was whether the 'vital strategic zone' referred to by General Kutrzeba was to be lost *by itself* or – as a result of a German envelopment from East Prussia, Silesia and Slovakia – together with the *Polish Army*. It was the same sort of question as I kept asking Hitler in the years 1943–4 every time he called on me to hold the Donetz Basin, the Dnieper and other areas of Russia.

To my mind, the answer to Poland's problem was perfectly clear. As far as her High Command was concerned, everything must hinge on the Polish Army's ability to hold out at all costs until an offensive by the Western Powers compelled the Germans to withdraw the mass of their forces from the Polish theatre. Even though the loss of the industrial areas would appear on the face of it to render Poland incapable of fighting a war of any length, the army's continued existence as a combat force would still have held out the prospect of winning them back. Whatever happened, the Polish Army must not allow itself to be encircled to the west or on both sides of the Vistula.

The whole crux of Poland's problem was *to play for time*. Obviously no *decisive* defence could be contemplated anywhere forward of the Bobr–Narew–Vistula line, although it might be possible on the southern flank to move this front up as far as the Dunajec with a view to holding on to the central Polish industrial area between the Vistula and the San.

The most important thing of all would have been to eliminate any possibility of encirclement by the Germans from East Prussia and western Slovakia. A means of doing so in the north was offered by the line of the Bobr–Narew and the Vistula down as far as the fortress of Modlin or Wysograd. This, at any rate, formed a strong natural obstacle, and additional support was afforded by the former Russian fortifications, obsolete though they were. A further point was that if any German armour at all appeared from East Prussia, it was unlikely to be in great strength.

The problem in the south was to obviate an outflanking manœuvre deep in Poland's rear by defending the Carpathian passes. Both tasks could undoubtedly have been fulfilled with limited forces. To deploy the Polish forces forward of the Bobr–Narew line was just as big a blunder as pushing strong forces out into the Corridor and the bulge of Poznań Province.

Once the necessary guarantees had been created against such deep outflanking in the north and south, it would have been possible to fight a delaying action in the west of Poland, always bearing in mind that the main German thrust was to be expected from Silesia. One reason for this was that the rail and road network in that part of the world allowed a quicker concentration of powerful forces than could be effected in Pomerania or, for that matter, in East Prussia; the other was that a drive on Warsaw via Poznań, being purely frontal, would have been operationally the least effective, and was therefore improbable.

The Polish assembly of forces should not have taken place in the vicinity of the frontier, as happened in 1939, but far enough back for the defenders to identify the main direction of the German thrusts. This would have meant managing with a bare minimum of forces in the Corridor and the Poznań area in order to oppose the main thrust from Silesia in the greatest possible strength and, above all, to keep an adequate strategic reserve in hand. Had Poland concentrated on improving the former German fortifications on the Vistula between Toruń and Grudziadz, instead of so long indulging in dreams of aggression, she could at least have delayed the link-up of the German forces advancing from Pomerania and East Prussia; similarly, by properly fortifying Poznań, she could have curtailed the Germans' freedom of movement in that province.

One further point is that the idea of utilizing the inner defence line to deal counterblows in the north or south of western Poland, according to the way the situation developed, would hardly have worked out in practice. There was insufficient space available for operations of this sort, and the Polish railway network would not have stood the strain. Besides, the possibility had to be borne in mind that big troop movements would very soon have been hampered by the Germans' air forces and tank formations. Consequently there was nothing for it but to plan the really decisive defence as far back as the Bobr–Narew–Vistula–San (or –Dunajec) line, and merely to fight for time anywhere forward of this – always remembering that one had to place the main effort opposite Silesia from the very start and simultaneously ensure due protection on the northern and southern flanks.

No one can argue that any of these measures would have saved Poland from ultimate defeat if – as proved to be the case – she were abandoned to her fate by the West. Nevertheless, they would have saved the Poles being so easily overrun in their frontier areas, as a result of which the Polish High Command was unable either to fight a set battle in the Vistula bend or to withdraw its forces behind the great line of rivers and take up a prepared defence.

From the very first day Poland could only fight for time. All she could do was to hold out against German attacks – ultimately behind the river line – until an Allied offensive in the west compelled the Germans to pull back. It should therefore have been incumbent on the Polish military leaders to tell their Government quite bluntly that they could not go to war against the Reich without a binding guarantee from the Western Powers that the moment hostilities broke out they would launch an offensive in the west with all the resources at their disposal.

No Government could have disregarded such a warning in view of the decisive influence wielded at the time by the Polish Commander-in-Chief, Marshal Rydz-Smigly. The Government ought to have come to terms on the Danzig and Corridor question while there was still time, if only to postpone a war with Germany.

In 1940 our troops in France captured a letter, dated 10th September

1939, from General Gamelin to the Polish military attaché in Paris. It was obviously a reply to an inquiry from the Poles as to when they could expect any effective military assistance. The comments made by Gamelin for onward transmission to Marshal Rydz-Smigły were as follows:

'More than half our regular divisions in the north-east are in action. Since we crossed the frontier the Germans have been resisting energetically, despite which we have made some headway. However, we are tied down in a static war with an enemy well prepared for defence, and I have not yet all the necessary artillery. . . . There has been aerial warfare from the outset in conjunction with the operations on the ground, and we are conscious of having a considerable part of the Luftwaffe opposite us.

'I have thus fulfilled in advance my promise to start the offensive with my main forces a fortnight after the first day of the French mobilisation. It was impossible for me to do more.'

It follows from this that Poland did in fact have a guarantee from the French in her possession. The only question is whether the Polish High Command should have been satisfied with one which did not commit the French to 'start the offensive' till a whole fortnight had elapsed. In any case, events have since shown that the above promise was meant to imply anything but swift and effective aid to Poland.

Poland's defeat was the inevitable outcome of the Warsaw Government's illusions about the action its allies would take, as well as of its over-estimation of the Polish Army's ability to offer lengthy resistance.

3

THE OPERATIONS OF SOUTHERN ARMY GROUP

WHEN OUR troops crossed the Polish frontier at daybreak on 1st September 1939, we of the Army Group Staff were naturally at our posts in the Monastery of the Holy Cross at Neisse. This was a training establishment for Catholic missionaries situated outside the town and offered an ideal wartime setting for a senior headquarters staff by virtue of its size and seclusion and the unembellished state of its classrooms and cells. To a certain extent the Spartan existence of its normal inmates, from whom we had taken over part of the building, reflected itself in our own standard of living, for though our camp commandant came from the famous *Löwenbräu* in Munich, he showed little inclination to pamper us. As a matter of course we drew ordinary rations like any other troops, and the midday stews we got from the field kitchen certainly gave us no cause for complaint. On the other hand, I really cannot believe that the evening menu need have been limited day after day to army bread and hard preserved sausage, which our older gentlemen had considerable difficulty in masticating. Fortunately the monks helped out with occasional lettuces or vegetables from their kitchen garden. On a number of evenings the Army Group commander and his senior staff were joined by the Abbot, who retailed fascinating accounts of the self-sacrificing work of the missionaries in distant parts of the globe. This was a welcome distraction, however brief, from the burning problems which the immediate future presented.

September 1st put an end to these talks, however. Henceforth the battle claimed every moment of our time. The fact that we were in our offices so early that morning was due less to any practical necessity than to the feeling that we had to be in readiness from the very moment our troops made contact with the enemy. For it was certain that many hours would pass before we heard any vital news from the armies under our command. These were the hours familiar to anyone who has worked on a higher formation staff – the phase in which events have already begun to take their course and one can only await developments.

The soldier at the front knows the tremendous tension that mounts before an attack, as the platoon commander's watch ticks steadily on to the moment of release when the assault can go in. From then on, however, the front-line fighter is completely taken up with the battle around him and quite oblivious of anything else. The difference with a formation staff – and the higher one goes the more this applies – is that the moment of attack marks the beginning of a period of waiting that is charged with suspense and anxiety. Subordinate formations quite rightly dislike getting inquiries about the progress of a battle, which they are liable to interpret as a sign of nervousness. Consequently it is better just to sit and wait. A point worth noting in this respect is that the saying about bad news travelling fast seldom applies in the military sphere. Whenever things are going well, news usually finds its way back quickly enough. If, on the other hand, the attack gets stuck, a blanket of silence descends on the front, either because communications have been cut or because those concerned prefer to hang on till they have something more encouraging to report.

And so the tension breaks only when the first reports come in, whether these be good or bad. Pending their arrival we, too, could only sit and wait. Would the troops on whom we had expended so much labour and effort, but whose training had been carried out far too quickly, come up to expectation? In particular, would the big armoured formations, the organization and use of which constituted something completely new, justify the hopes of their creator, General Guderian, and ourselves? Would the German headquarters staffs, in particular our own Army Group, be able to master the opening situation and go on to win a complete victory that would destroy the enemy while he was still west of the Vistula and remove any danger of a war on two fronts? Such were the questions running through our minds in those hours of tension and uncertainty.

It was envisaged in O.K.H.'s plan for a large-scale outflanking operation against the Polish Army from East Prussia and Silesia that *Northern Army Group*, having once established a link between East Prussia and Pomerania by expelling the Polish forces from the Corridor, would be able to get straight behind the Vistula in order to attack the main enemy forces in the large bend of the river from the rear.

The task that must devolve on *Southern Army Group*, on the other hand, was to try to engage the enemy as far forward as the Vistula and to frustrate any attempt he might make to withdraw behind the line of the Vistula and San. This meant that Tenth Army's tank formations, with its infantry divisions following as closely as possible behind, must make a concerted effort to over-run the enemy troop assemblies that would probably be taking place near the frontier, and that the tanks should if possible reach the Vistula crossings from Demblin to Warsaw ahead of the enemy. It also presupposed that Fourteenth Army, which was to advance through Galicia, would reach and cross the San with the greatest possible speed. In the event of the enemy's intending to place his decisive resistance as far back as the San and Vistula, this army could immediately unhinge the river defences from the south and join up – deep in the enemy's rear – with the eastern wing of Northern Army Group as it approached from the north. Fourteenth Army was bound to be assisted here by the fact that its right wing, by extending so far eastward into Slovakia, constituted an immediate threat to the deep flank of the enemy forces concentrating in the Cracow area, and thereby made it impossible to effect any protracted defence of Galicia.

Such was the course of action on which Southern Army Group based its operations in Poland. It strove throughout to engage and destroy the main body of the enemy forward of the Vistula, but at the same time remained ready to anticipate any attempt he might make to avoid accepting the decisive battle until he was behind the San–Vistula line.

Instead of giving a day-to-day account of the operations, useful though a detailed survey of this 'lightning' campaign would undoubtedly be, I would rather confine myself to a broad outline of its essential phases. These, partly in chronological sequence and partly simultaneous, were as follows:

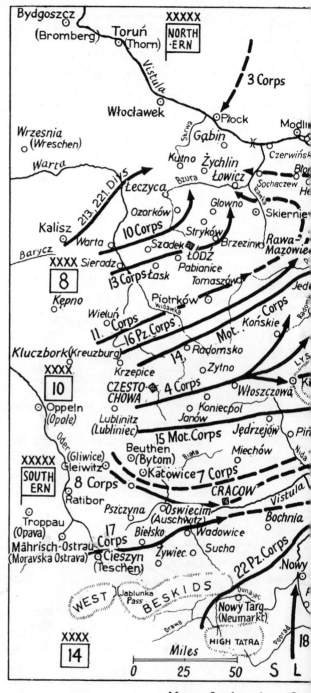

Map 2. Southern Army Gro▪

erations in Polish Campaign.

The heavy frontier battles fought by *Fourteenth Army* in *Galicia* and the latter's subsequent pursuit of the beaten enemy to Lwòw and over the San.

Tenth Army's breakthrough to the Vistula and the *Battle of the Radom Pocket*.

The *Battle of the Bzura*, which was conducted direct from H.Q. Southern Army Group and led to the destruction of the strongest enemy grouping by Eighth and Tenth Armies.

The *attack on Warsaw* and the *final battles* which resulted from the frequent changes in the agreements entered into by Germany's political leaders with the Soviets, who were by now marching into Eastern Poland. The latter crossed the Polish frontier on 17th September 1939.

FOURTEENTH ARMY'S ASSAULT MARCH THROUGH GALICIA

The first object of Fourteenth Army was to encircle the strong enemy forces believed to be in the area of Cracow. This encirclement was already inherent in the army's extensive deployment from Silesia through the region of Moravska Ostrava (Mährish-Ostrau) to the Carpathians.

While 8 Corps (General Busch – 8 and 28 Infantry and 5 Panzer Divisions) was to break through the strong Polish frontier fortifications in eastern Upper Silesia and then advance on Cracow along the north of the Vistula, 17 Corps (General Kienitz – 7 and 44 Infantry Divisions) moved on Cracow to the south of the Vistula from Moravia.

The task of directly outflanking the enemy forces thought to be around Cracow fell to two further army corps:

22 Panzer Corps (General v. Kleist – 2 Panzer and 4 Light Divisions), which was to drive on Cracow from the south out of the Orava Valley in the western Carpathians, and 18 (Mountain) Corps (General Beyer – 2 and 3 Mountain Divisions), which was to break out of the Poprad Valley east of the High Tatra with the aim of advancing through Nowy Sącz (Neu-Sandez) on Bochnia (west of Tarnow) and taking the enemy at Cracow in the rear.

Still further east the Slovakian forces later released by O.K.H. had to attack through the Dukla Pass, so well known from World War I days. 1 Mountain Division, a seasoned Bavarian formation, and two reserve divisions were allocated to this enveloping wing later on.

Though Fourteenth Army's initial battles – in particular those

fought by 8 Silesian Corps for the Polish frontier fortifications –
proved hard going, the issue in these frontier regions was virtually decided already from the operational point of view by the outflanking
movement from the Carpathians. Admittedly the proposed encirclement of the enemy grouping around Cracow did not come off in the
literal sense, as the enemy recognized the danger threatening him and
duly evacuated western Galicia. But the bulk of his forces were still
smashed in these first battles and the chase that followed, in the course
of which 22 Panzer Corps succeeded in overhauling its quarry. They
took the army's right wing, the Mountain Corps and 17 Corps, as far
as Lwòw and the fortress of Przemyśl, both of which were captured.
The left wing, consisting of the Panzer Corps, 8 Corps and 7 Corps
allocated to the army by the Army Group, was able to cross the San
above its junction with the Vistula, and though our opponents fought
back bravely in the subsequent battles, which were in part extremely
heavy, further enemy forces – some of them coming from Warsaw or
Northern Army Group's front – were wiped out. In due course we
joined hands with the left wing of Northern Army Group.

By 15th September, Lwòw and Przemyśl having fallen, the pursuit
was virtually over, even if the destruction of the remaining Polish
units in this area and east of the San was to call for further fighting.

THE BREAKTHROUGH OF TENTH ARMY AND THE BATTLE OF THE RADOM POCKET

While the object of Fourteenth Army's operations – apart from annihilating the forces deployed in western Galicia – was to pursue and
catch a retreating enemy, and thereby prevent him at all costs from
making a fresh stand behind the Vistula, the task of the two armies
attacking from Silesia was to make him accept a decisive battle *forward*
of the river. The crucial role of thrusting through to the Vistula devolved on the stronger Tenth Army, with its powerful complement of
armour, while the weaker Eighth Army was to cover the northern
flank of the operation against the enemy forces believed to be in the
Kalisz–Łòdz area and Poznań Province.

Tenth Army attacked from Upper Silesia – the left wing from around
Kreuzburg – with fours corps up. Reading from right to left, these
were 15 Motorized Corps (General Hoth – 2 and 3 Light Divisions), 4
Corps (General v. Schwedler – 4 and 46 Infantry Divisions), 16

Panzer Corps (General Hoepner – 1 and 4 Panzer Divisions, 14 and 31 Infantry Divisions) and 11 Corps (General Leeb – 18 and 19 Divisions). 14 Motorized Corps (General v. Wietersheim – 13 and 29 Motorized and 1 Light Divisions) followed up.

Following behind the army as an Army Group reserve were 7 Corps (General v. Schobert – 27 and 68 Infantry Divisions) and 62 Infantry Division.

Eighth Army, composed of 13 Corps (General v. Weichs – 10 and 17 Infantry Divisions and the motorized Leibstandarte) and 10 Corps (General Ulex – 24 and 30 Divisions), had to advance in deeply echeloned formation in the direction of Łòdz. This army, too, was followed by two divisions (213 and 221) of the Army Group reserve.

Immediately after the German armies had crossed the frontier at dawn on 1st September 1939, violent fighting started, in the course of which the enemy was thrown back. For the next few days our big problem was whether he would still seek to join the decisive battle forward of the Vistula or whether his object in the present fighting was to gain time in which to get his forces back behind the river. Initially, at all events, there were signs of strong enemy groupings forming in the mountainous country of Łysa Gora around Kielce, at Radom and around Łòdz.

What decided the battles of these first few weeks, however, were probably two factors which had appeared for the very first time in this campaign.

One was the tearing open of the enemy's front by tank formations which penetrated deep into his rear areas and with which, incidentally, our infantry divisions were hard pressed to keep up.

The other was the almost complete elimination of the enemy's air force and the crippling of his staff communications and transport network by the effective attacks of our Luftwaffe. For these reasons no centralized control of operations was ever really achieved by the Poles.

By reason of the situation on the enemy side, Army Group H.Q. found it necessary to set Tenth Army two objectives. One group on the right (14 Motorized Corps and 4 Corps), followed through by 7 Corps (which was not moved over to Fourteenth Army until later on), had to attack and defeat the enemy grouping still assembling around Radom. Another group on the left, consisting of 16 Panzer Corps, 14 Motorized Corps and 11 Corps, was to cut off the enemy's line of retreat from the Łòdz area to Warsaw while Eighth Army attacked from the west.

In pursuit of these orders, Tenth Army succeeded in engaging the Radom grouping in the wooded mountains of Łysa Gora while the mobile 15 Motorized Corps moved in between it and the Vistula crossings of Opatow and Demblin and the 14 Motorized Corps, operating from the army's left-hand group in the north, also barred the way to Warsaw. By 9th September the first 'pocket' of the war had closed round an enemy army. Though the fighting in the Kielce–Radom region went on till 12th September as a result of the enemy's efforts to burst out of the ring enclosing him, his fate was already sealed. By the end of the battle 60,000 prisoners and 130 guns were in our hands and the enemy had forfeited seven divisions. Even if he had succeeded in getting back across the Vistula, this would not have helped him, for on the day the Battle of Radom ended Fourteenth Army already had its 1 Mountain Division at the gates of Łwòw, and the army's left wing, through having crossed the lower San, was in a position to unhinge any enemy defence of the Vistula.

Meanwhile 16 Panzer Corps, which belonged to the left-hand group of Tenth Army, had fought its way to the Vistula crossing of Gora Kalwaria, south of Warsaw, and one armoured division had penetrated into the south-west suburbs. These forces were actually too weak to capture a city fortified as Warsaw was, and the armoured division had to be pulled out again. The fact remained, however, that the enemy's western approach to the capital was now blocked.

THE BATTLE OF THE BZURA

While fighting was still going on in the Radom area, even if signs of victory there were already apparent, our attention was drawn to the northern wing of the Army Group as a result of an enemy initiative.

During the first nine days of the campaign everything had run so smoothly and so completely according to plan that one was tempted to believe that little could happen now to interrupt or cause any real change in the scheduled course of operations. Nonetheless I still had a vague feeling that something was brewing on the northern flank of the Army Group. We knew, after all, that the enemy had assembled strong forces in Poznań Province which had not yet come to light. For this reason, on 8th and 9th September I had repeatedly pointed out to the

Chief-of-Staff of Eighth Army that he must pay special heed to reconnaissance on his northern flank. Discussions between ourselves and O.K.H. regarding the location of these Poznań forces had produced a teleprinter message from O.K.H. on 9th September to the effect that the enemy was moving them off to the east with all the transport he could muster, and that a threat to Eighth Army's deep flank need no longer be feared. Nevertheless we reckoned that there must be some ten enemy divisions south of the Vistula between Łòdz and Warsaw.

It will be recalled that the Army Group had intended to use Tenth Army to block the route back to Warsaw of an enemy grouping of five or six divisions thought to be around Łòdz, while Eighth Army had also been directed to attack this force from the west. Eighth Army's original task – the provision of deeply echeloned protection to the entire Army Group operation on its northern flank – naturally still held good.

It would appear, nevertheless, that H.Q. Eighth Army paid rather more attention to the afore-mentioned task than to developments in the north, for early on 10th September it reported a surprise attack from that quarter against its 30 Division, launched by considerably stronger enemy forces. The situation threatened to become critical, as attempts by the army to restore it by counter-attacks failed one after the other. However, the army still reckoned on halting the enemy – who was undoubtedly present in strength and presumably composed in the main of forces drawn back from Poznań Province – and for this purpose wheeled both its corps round to form a defensive front facing north. All the same it asked to be quickly reinforced by one panzer corps in order to prevent any southward enemy breakthrough to Łòdz, which had been occupied without resistance on 9th September.

Army Group H.Q., however, was by no means disposed to see the situation of Eighth Army restored by a reinforcement of its front. Even if a local crisis – and possibly a serious one at that – were to arise here, it would have not the least bearing on the operations as a whole. On the contrary, it actually offered us the chance of winning a big victory, since strong enemy forces had now been committed to a battle west of the Vistula, and this, if the right actions were taken on our own side, would end in their destruction.

Instead of acceding to Eighth Army's request for the additional support of a panzer corps, therefore, Army Group H.Q. started making preparations for the enemy's encirclement. The two divisions following Eighth Army as an Army Group reserve were anyway still approaching from the west, and these could be presented against the western flank of the enemy now attacking Eighth Army from the north. For the same purpose a light division was ordered over from the battle now drawing to a close around Radom. What the Army Group desired above all was to compel the enemy to fight a battle with reversed front. To this end it directed Tenth Army to turn round 16 Panzer Corps, now at the southern perimeter of Warsaw, and 11 Corps, which was following the latter, in order to intervene in Eighth Army's battle from the east. The latter's own task was to hold off the enemy as long as he kept up his assault, but once this perceptibly slackened off, to go over to the attack.

As a result of impressions gathered by Colonel-General v. Rundstedt and myself on visits to H.Q. Eighth Army at this time (during one of which Hitler was also present), Army Group decided to assume direct control of the operation. The attack by the two corps of Tenth Army intervening from the south and south-east was to be directed by Colonel-General v. Reichenau himself, while H.Q. Eighth Army was left in charge of the fighting of its two corps facing north and the envelopment of the enemy from the west. Finally, at the request of our Army Group, 3 Corps, which had crossed the Vistula from the north in the enemy's rear as part of Northern Army Group, was brought in to close the ring. When it became apparent in the course of the battle that large elements of the enemy were striving to escape along the Vistula to the fortress of Modlin, Army Group even pulled up 15 Motorized Corps from the Radom region to block this last escape route.

After heavy fighting in which the enemy had tried to break out first to the south, then to the south-east and ultimately to the east, his resistance finally collapsed on 18th September. By 20th September Tenth Army had reported the capture of 80,000 prisoners and booty amounting to 320 guns, 130 aircraft and 40 tanks. Eighth Army reported 90,000 prisoners and as yet uncalculated amounts of captured equipment. Nine enemy infantry divisions, three cavalry brigades and elements of ten further divisions had been involved in this defeat – in point of fact many more formations than we had supposed.

The *Battle of the Bzura* was the biggest self-contained action of the

Polish campaign and constituted its climax, even if not its decisive engagement.

The latter, operationally speaking, lay in the far-flung envelopment of the entire Polish forces by Northern Army Group in the north and Fourteenth Army in the south. Whether this one large-scale counter-move arose from a hope on the part of the Polish Command that it could still change its fortune in the Vistula Bend, or whether it was merely directed towards clearing the way to Warsaw for the enemy forces south of the Vistula, it could have no further influence on the fate of the Polish Army.

Even if the Battle of the Bzura did not measure up in actual results to the big battles of encirclement fought in Russia later on, it was still the largest of its kind to date. It was not one which could be planned from the outset through penetration of the enemy front by powerful tank formations, but arose from counter-moves made on the German side when the enemy's own actions unexpectedly gave us our big opportunity.

THE CAPTURE OF WARSAW

After the Battle of the Bzura and a series of actions in the wooded country south of Modlin against enemy elements trying to escape from the fortress towards Warsaw, our Army Group was given the task of taking the capital. Even now certain of its formations were being moved off to the west, where the French and British, much to our surprise, had looked idly on as their Polish ally was being annihilated.

We had already reported to O.K.H. that the preparations for the assault on Warsaw could not be complete before 25th September, our main motive being a wish to avail ourselves of the whole of the army artillery, including that of Fourteenth Army.

However, after the Soviet intervention on 17th September and the establishment of the Vistula as a demarcation line, Hitler was in a great hurry to take the city, and ordered that it must be in our hands by the last day of the month. While it is not abnormal, I suppose, for politicians to expect the generals to win a victory, it was undoubtedly a new departure for them to go as far as fixing the actual date.

Apart from this, Army Group was disposed to conduct the attack in a manner which would keep casualties down to a bare minimum. The only reason why the city had to be attacked at all was that the enemy had taken steps to defend it with an entire army and that the Polish Commander-in-Chief had announced that it would be held to the last.

The Army Group was well aware that in the circumstances nothing could be expected of a surprise attack on the city. On no account, however, did it wish to become involved in a battle inside Warsaw, whatever reasons might be given for doing so. This would inevitably have caused extraordinarily high losses both to the attacking troops and the civil population.

Eighth Army, which had been charged with the capture of the city, was accordingly ordered to confine its attack to investing the fortress area with a tight, unbroken ring of troops roughly coinciding with the line of the circular railway. The city would then be compelled to surrender by a combination of artillery bombardments and air raids or, if these did not produce results, by a food and water shortage. I might mention here that Army Group H.Q. had successfully opposed an earlier wish of Hitler's to have the city bombed by the Luftwaffe, our argument then being that no air raid at that particular juncture would have had a direct bearing on, or in any way benefited, military operations. In the present instance, however, these same reasons served to justify bombardment.

On 25th September fire was opened on the outer forts and strongpoints, as well as on important supply centres. At the same time the localized attacks to reach the predetermined siege line began. On 26th September we dropped leaflets warning that the city was about to be shelled and calling on its occupants to surrender. As the Polish troops continued to offer a stubborn resistance, the actual bombardment was begun on the evening of the same day.

At noon on 27th September Colonel-General v. Rundstedt and I learnt during a visit to my old 18 Division, which had just taken two forts, that the enemy had offered to capitulate. The shelling was immediately stopped.

The capitulation was signed next day by the Polish army commander and Colonel-General Blaskowitz, commander of the German Eighth Army. It provided for immediate succour to the civil population and enemy wounded and in every way upheld the military honour of an enemy defeated after a gallant struggle. It was agreed that the officers should retain their swords and that the non-commissioned officers and men should go into captivity for only as long as it took to dispose of the necessary formalities.

According to the Polish plenipotentiary, 120,000 officers and men capitulated in Warsaw.

When signing the instrument of capitulation, the Polish general said: 'A wheel always turns'. He was to prove right in the end, though hardly – as far as the subsequent fate of his fatherland was concerned – in the sense his words had been meant to convey.

THE FINAL BATTLES EAST OF THE SAN AND VISTULA

Although the bulk of the enemy forces committed forward of the Vistula had been eliminated in the Battle of the Bzura and the fall of Warsaw, numerous other engagements, some of them quite heavy, were still being fought in Fourteenth Army's area in eastern Galicia and on the far side of the lower San against individual groups of the enemy who had so far escaped destruction. In the meantime Tenth Army had also got a corps across the Vistula at Demblin to advance on Lublin. In the midst of this fighting we suddenly received orders from the Supreme Command to hand over Lwòw – which had just capitulated to the troops of Fourteenth Army – to the Soviets and to retire along the whole Army Group front behind the demarcation line arranged by Ribbentrop in Moscow. This ran from the Uzok Pass to Przemyśl and then along the San and Vistula to the north of Warsaw. Thus the battles fought on the far side of those two rivers had been wasted effort as far as the units of Southern Army Group were concerned, and had only benefited the Soviets!

To get back across the San we had to disengage from an enemy grouping whose strength we still estimated at two or three divisions and one or two cavalry brigades. These forces now showed tremendous courage – though at the same time a complete misunderstanding of the overall situation – in going over to the attack themselves in an attempt to prevent our 7 and 8 Corps from reaching the river. Here again heavy fighting ensued purely in consequence of the political haggling still going on between the German and Soviet Governments. The extent of this was best shown by the fact that on 1st October a further alteration was made to the demarcation line. This time our orders were to re-occupy Lublin Province. 14 Motorized Corps therefore crossed the Vistula again and received the capitulation of the last enemy grouping still in action as it withdrew towards the river before the advancing Soviets.

The Polish campaign was over. In the course of it Southern Army Group had taken 523,236 prisoners and captured 1,401 field-pieces, 7,600 machine-guns, 274 aircraft, 96 fighting vehicles and an incalculable quantity of other equipment. The enemy's losses in blood were undoubtedly very high indeed, for he had fought with great gallantry and had shown a grim determination to hold out in even the most hopeless situations.

Our own Army Group's losses were as follows:

Officers: 505 dead; 759 wounded; 42 missing. N.C.O.s and other ranks: 6,049 dead; 19,719 wounded; 4,022 missing.

On 5th October Hitler held a victory parade in Warsaw of all the divisions stationed in and around the city, taking the salute at a march-past on the big avenue leading from the Belvedere to the Castle. Unfortunately the occasion ended on a discordant note which only too clearly revealed his attitude towards the leaders of the army.

It had been arranged that before flying back to Germany Hitler should meet the commanders and commanding officers of the troops that had taken part in the parade, and for this purpose a table had been laid in a hangar where they were to be served with plates of soup from a field kitchen. When he came into the hangar and caught sight of the white cloths and autumn flowers on the table, however, Hitler turned on his heel and joined the troops at a field kitchen outside. Having swallowed a few spoonfuls of soup and chatted to the men around him, he made straight for his waiting aircraft. It was a patent attempt to demonstrate his 'attachment to the popular masses'. Yet I very much doubt whether he really won the approval of those gallant grenadiers of ours by such behaviour. They would, I am sure, have fully appreciated the gesture if, after the victories they had won, the Head of State had honoured the troops as a whole by a visit to their commanders. His treatment of the latter was a snub which, happening when it did, inevitably set one thinking.

Before long the Polish campaign was being described as the *blitz-krieg* – the 'lightning war'. Indeed, as far as its speed of execution and the outcome were concerned, it did constitute something almost unique until the German offensive in the west produced a similar development on an even bigger scale.

In order to assess it fairly, however, one must bear in mind what was said in a previous chapter about Poland's prospects in this war.

In point of fact the Germans were *bound* to win this campaign by virtue of their superiority and their infinitely more favourable starting conditions, provided that two stipulations were fulfilled.

One was that the German command accepted a very high degree of risk in the west in order to have the necessary superiority in the east.

The other was that the Western Powers did not in any way exploit this risk to render timely aid to the Poles.

There cannot be any doubt that things might have turned out very differently had the Western Powers taken the offensive in the west at the earliest possible moment. This would, of course, have presupposed the existence of a Polish command with a rather greater sense of reality – a command which, instead of scattering all its resources from the outset in an effort to cling on to what could not be held, would have concentrated its forces at the crucial points and fought systematically for the time needed to confront the Germans with the dilemma of a real war on two fronts. The bravery with which the Polish troops fought right up to the end would have been an adequate guarantee of their ability to hold on until the Allies reached the Rhine and forced the German command seriously to consider calling off the campaign in Poland.

And so in this case too – as Count Schlieffen had once put it – the weaker party made their own contribution to the victory of their adversaries. On the other hand, it must also be recognized that the speed and completeness of our success in Poland were ultimately due – apart from our operational advantage at the start and the numerical superiority we had achieved by accepting a big risk in the west – to the better leadership and higher quality of the German fighting troops.

A vital factor in the speed of our success was the unorthodox use of big, self-sufficient tank formations supported by a far superior air force. But what had been really decisive, next to the steadfast courage and devotion of the German soldier, was the *spirit* pervading the German staffs and fighting troops. While the material achievement of rearmament had certainly been largely due to Hitler's own efforts, material superiority alone would by no means have guaranteed so swift and conclusive a victory.

The most important thing of all was that our little Reichswehr, once rather looked down upon by many people, had revived Germany's great tradition of training and leadership after carrying it through the aftermath of the 1918 defeat. The new German Wehrmacht, as the child of that Reichswehr, had found – and was probably alone in doing so – how to prevent warfare from degenerating into a static war or – as General Fuller expressed it in connexion with the final stage of World War I – into 'ironmongery'. In the German Wehrmacht it had been found possible, with the help of the new means of warfare, to reacquire the true art of leadership in mobile operations. Individual leadership was fostered on a scale unrivalled in any other army, right down to the most junior N.C.O. or infantryman, and in this lay the secret of our success. The new Wehrmacht had passed its first test with flying colours. So far, even the army staff had been able to act without interference from outside. So far, the military commanders had retained full authority of command. So far, the troops had had a purely military battle to fight, and for that reason it had still been possible to fight chivalrously.

On 15th October Colonel Heusinger of the O.K.H. Operations Branch came to see us with the welcome news that our headquarters was also to be moved to the Western Front at the end of the month. Our place was to be taken by H.Q. Eighth Army under Colonel-General Blaskowitz. Shortly afterwards I myself was instructed to present myself at O.K.H. in Zossen on 21st October for the purpose of receiving our operation orders for the west.

I left Łòdz on the 18th to pay a brief visit to my family and brother-in-law, who was lying severely wounded in a Breslau hospital.

Then there was a new task to be faced.

Part II

THE CAMPAIGN IN THE WEST

INTRODUCTORY NOTE

'Now is the winter of our discontent
Made glorious summer. . . .'

(Richard III)

APPY TO have escaped the thankless task of having to act as the occupying Power in Poland, our headquarters arrived on the Western Front on 24th October 1939 to take command of the newly formed Army Group A. The armies under command (Twelfth and Sixteenth) had their forward divisions in position along the frontiers of southern Belgium and Luxembourg and their rear units strung out as far back as the right bank of the Rhine. It had been decided that Army Group H.Q. would be located in Coblenz.

We duly moved into the Hotel Riesen-Fürstenhof beside the Rhine – a place which in my early days at the cadet school in the nearby market town of Engers I had regarded as the very peak of elegance and culinary refinement. But now wartime restrictions had left their mark even on this famous establishment. Our offices were situated in a once-charming old building near the *Deutsches Eck* which until the outbreak of war had accommodated the Coblenz Division. The lovely Rococo rooms of yesteryear were now bare and gloomy. Not far from this building, in a small square lined with ancient trees, stood an obelisk of considerable interest. It bore a bombastic inscription, having been erected by the French commandant of Coblenz in 1812 to mark the crossing of the Rhine by Napoleon's Grand Army on its march to Russia. Below the original inscription another had been engraved. Its approximate purport was: 'Noted and approved', and it bore the signature of the Russian General who had become commandant of Coblenz in 1814.

What a pity Hitler never saw this!

At my suggestion our command staff had received the valuable addition of a second, older General Staff officer for the operations branch. He was the then Lieutenant-Colonel v. Tresckow, who put an end to his life in July 1944 as one of the main forces behind the conspiracy against Hitler. Tresckow had already worked under me in peacetime in the First Department [1] of the General Staff of the army. He was a most talented officer and an ardent patriot. With his quick brain, his many accomplishments and his cosmopolitan and gentlemanly ways, he had a special charm of his own, and his elegant, aristocratic appearance was fully complemented by his beautiful and equally intelligent wife, a daughter of the former War Minister and Chief of the General Staff, v. Falkenhayn. In those days there could hardly have been a more charming couple in Berlin army circles than the Tresckows.

Tresckow and I were linked by an intimate bond of sympathy that was closely akin to friendship and dated from the time we had worked together in the Operations Branch. Here in Coblenz, too, he was to render me valuable assistance in our struggle for the adoption of our own Army Group's plan for the offensive in the west. When I later became commanding general of a panzer corps and then an army commander, I asked in each case to have Tresckow as my Chief-of-Staff. However, my request was turned down on the rather original grounds that I 'did not need so clever a man'. When he was finally offered to me in the spring of 1943 to be chief of my Army Group staff, I could not give him precedence over my Chief of Operations, General Busse, who was of the same age and had proved his mettle in the many battles we had fought together. My only reason for mentioning this is that a gentleman close to Tresckow has given currency to a story that I refused to have the latter because he was not a reliable National Socialist. Anyone who knows me will be aware that I did not select my staff on that basis.

If those months in Coblenz were to become the 'winter of our discontent', this arose from the strange suspense of the 1939–40 Shadow War or 'drôle de guerre', as the French called it. It would have been easier to bear had we been able to pin our attentions from the outset on systematically preparing the troops under our command for an offensive in the coming spring. Unfortunately Hitler was known to want an offensive late that same autumn and when this proved impossible, at least during the winter. Every time his 'weather boffins', the Luftwaffe meteorologists, predicted a period of fine weather, he issued the

---

[1] Order of Battle and Operations. *Tr.*

code-word which was the signal for the troops to start moving into their final assembly areas. On each occasion the meteorologists had to climb down again, either because heavy downpours of rain had made a hopeless mess of the ground or because a sharp frost and falls of snow had raised doubts as to the advisability of using tanks and aircraft. The result was a process of vacillation between warning orders and counter-mands – a most frustrating state of affairs for troops and commanders alike. During this period Hitler's mistrust of military reports which did not suit his own wishes revealed itself most strikingly. After Army Group H.Q. had once again stated that continuous rainfall made it temporarily impossible to form up for the offensive, he sent his military assistant, Schmundt, to us with orders to examine the state of the ground himself. Tresckow was the ideal man to deal with this. He spent an entire day dragging his erstwhile regimental comrade along well-nigh impassable roads, across sodden ploughland and marshy meadows and up and down slippery hillsides, so that by the time they got back to our headquarters in the evening, Schmundt was in a state of complete exhaustion. From that day on Hitler dispensed with such wholly improper methods of verifying our weather reports.

The person who had most to suffer as a result of this absurd chopping and changing and the consequent wastage of effort was, of course, our Army Group commander, Colonel-General v. Rundstedt, with whom patience had never been a strong point. Very soon our headquarters was swamped with the flood of paper which regularly descends on fighting units and formation headquarters during the quieter phases of war. Thanks to a very proper unwritten law in the German Army that the general commanding a formation be kept free of all minor detail, however, v. Rundstedt was hardly affected and was able to take a long walk every morning on the Rheinpromenade. Since I, too, had to take some sort of exercise, I often used to meet him. Even in that freezing winter, when the Rhine was already covered with ice, Rundstedt still wore only a thin raincoat. When I protested that he would catch his death of cold, he merely retorted that he had never possessed a greatcoat in his life and was certainly not going to buy one at his age! And neither did he, for even after all these years the old gentleman still bore the imprint of his spartan training in the Cadet Corps. Another habit of v. Rundstedt's served to remind me of my own days as a cadet. On returning to his desk to await the verbal reports which he daily received from myself and other members of the staff, he would fill in the time by reading a detective thriller. Like many other prominent people, he found a welcome distraction in such literature, but since he was rather shy about this taste of his, he regularly read the novel in an open drawer which could be quickly closed whenever anyone came in to see him. It was the very same thing we had done as cadets whenever an instructor came into our quarters during a private-study period!

However, our discontent that winter was due in only small measure to Hitler's vacillations and their prejudicial effect on the troops – who were in time liable to doubt the good sense of orders which were repeatedly being cancelled – to say nothing of the fact that the inter-formation training schedules, which had a particular relevance in the case of the newly formed divisions, were seriously upset.

The real cause of our discontent – or, to put it more exactly, our uneasiness – was twofold.

In the first place it arose from a development which I can only describe as the eclipse of O.K.H. I personally found this development particularly distressing, having fought right up to the winter of 1937–8, as *Oberquartiermeister I* of the General Staff and assistant to Fritsch and Beck, to ensure that in the event of war O.K.H. would be given its proper position within the framework of overall war policy.

Secondly, Army Group H.Q. sought in vain throughout the winter to get O.K.H. to accept an operations plan which – in our own opinion, at all events – seemed to offer the only guarantee of a decisive victory in the west. This was not adopted as the basis of the offensive until Hitler had finally intervened – and only then after O.K.H., undoubtedly as the result of our badgering, had removed me from my post as Chief-of-Staff of the Army Group.

These two facts – the 'demotion' of O.K.H. and the struggle over the operations plan – largely form the background to the western campaign to which this part of the book is devoted. Its later course is already known in such detail that there is no need for me to go through it all again. All I intend to tell of it is what I saw as a corps commander.

Nonetheless, the 'winter of our discontent' was still followed by a 'glorious summer'!

4

THE ECLIPSE OF O.K.H.

THE ELIMINATION of O.K.H., or the General Staff of the Army, as the authority responsible for war policy on land is generally assumed to have been effective from the time when Hitler dismissed Field-Marshal v. Brauchitsch and took over the leadership of the army in addition to that of the Wehrmacht as a whole. In actual fact, however, the General Staff was eliminated for all practical purposes – even if this was not yet formally the case – in the weeks immediately following the Polish campaign.

After my visit to Zossen on 21st October 1939 to receive 'Operation Order Yellow' on behalf of Army Group A, as Southern Army Group was henceforth to be designated, I noted in my diary: 'Musical accompaniment by Halder, Stülpnagel and Greifenberg extremely depressing.' At that time General v. Stülpnagel, as *Oberquartiermeister I*, was the right-hand man of Halder, the Chief of the Army Staff, while Colonel Greifenberg headed the O.K.H. Operations Branch.

It was perfectly evident from the remarks of these three gentlemen that O.K.H. had issued a war plan forced on it by Hitler. They, as well as the Commander-in-Chief himself, obviously took a thoroughly negative view of the idea of an offensive in the west and did not consider it the proper way to bring the war to a close. From what they had to say it could also be gathered that they did not think the German Army would be in a position to enforce a decisive dénouement in the west. This impression was corroborated both by the Operations Order, which will be analysed in due course, and by the various visits to be paid to Army Group H.Q. by the Commander-in-Chief and his Chief-of-Staff.

Now it was quite clear that opinions might differ – particularly during the period of the late autumn and winter of 1939 – as to the expediency and prospects of a German offensive in the west. What horrified me was my realization of the extent to which O.K.H.'s status had declined within the scope of the Supreme Command. And this just after it had conducted one of the most brilliant campaigns in German history!

Once before, admittedly, Hitler had disregarded the views of O.K.H. That had been during the Sudeten crisis. But on that occasion something entirely different had been at stake – not a matter of military leadership but one of *political* decision. Hitler's dispute with O.K.H. – primarily with Beck as Chief of the General Staff – had arisen not over the handling of an army operation but over the question of whether action against Czechoslovakia would lead to intervention by the Western Powers, and thereby to a war on two fronts which the German Army could not have the capacity to fight. The appraisal of *this* problem, however, had ultimately been a matter for the *political* leadership, in whose power it had lain to obviate by political measures any trend towards a war on two fronts. So although the Commander-in-Chief had taken on a grave military responsibility by bowing to the primacy of politics on that occasion, he had still in no way renounced the prerogative of military leadership in his own exclusive sphere.

At the time of the Polish crisis no such divergence of views between Hitler and O.K.H. had reached our ears. Indeed, I am inclined to think that after Hitler's political assessment of the Western Powers had proved correct in the case of Czechoslovakia, O.K.H. hoped that the same would apply in autumn 1939. In any case I believe that throughout those final crucial days of August O.K.H. assumed right up to the last – just as we did at Southern Army Group – that the whole business would again end in a political settlement similar to that reached at Munich. At all events, if one disregards the wishes he expressed regarding the deployment in East Prussia – to which O.K.H. agreed – Hitler cannot be said to have interfered in the conduct of operations in Poland.

Now, however, the position was quite different. It is true, of course, that the question of how the war should be continued after the defeat of Poland was a matter of *overall war policy* which ultimately had to be decided by Hitler as the Head of State and Commander-in-Chief of the Wehrmacht. However, if the solution were to be a land offensive in the west, this must depend entirely on *how*, *when* and *whether* the army would be able to tackle the task. In these three respects the primacy of the army leadership was inalienable.

Yet in all three Hitler confronted the High Command of the army with a *fait accompli* when on 27th September – without prior consultation of the Commander-in-Chief of the Army – he informed the Commanders-in-Chief of all three services of his decision to take the offensive in the west that same autumn and, in so doing, to violate the neutrality of Holland, Belgium and Luxembourg. The decision presently found expression in an O.K.W. directive of 9th October 1939.

I was bound to infer from the remarks made by the three above-named officers when I took over 'Operation Order Yellow' that O.K.H. had resigned itself to this *capitis diminutio*. It had issued a directive for an offensive of which it steadfastly disapproved and in whose success – in the decisive sense, at least – it had no confidence. In view of the relative strengths on the Western Front, one had to admit that such doubts were not unjustified.

I could only deduce, therefore, that O.K.H. had in this case renounced any claim to be the authority responsible for land warfare and had resigned itself to acting as a purely technical, executive organ. The very thing had now come to pass which Colonel-General Beck and I had once sought to prevent by our recommendations for a rational distribution of responsibility at the summit in time of war. What we had called for was one single authority which would alone be responsible for advising the Head of State on questions of military policy and have joint control of army operations and the overall conduct of the war. For at least as long as it took to decide the issue on the Continent, either the Commander-in-Chief of the Army was to have command of the Wehrmacht as a whole or a Reich Chief-of-Staff responsible for running the Wehrmacht should simultaneously make the decisions on army policy. What had to be avoided at all costs was that two different General Staffs – those of the Wehrmacht and the army – should have a say in the running of the latter.

This was precisely what now appeared to have happened. Hitler and his O.K.W. not only decided what operations the army should conduct, but also when and how they should be conducted. O.K.H. was left to work out the appropriate orders whether or not it agreed with what it was being called on to implement. The Commander-in-Chief of the Army had been demoted from the status of military adviser to the Head of State to that of a subordinate commander pledged to unquestioning obedience. Before very long this was to be made only too plain by the creation of an 'O.K.W.' theatre of operations in Norway.

The explanation of how O.K.H. came to be brushed aside like this is to be found both on the personal plane and in the manner in which the question of continuing the war after Poland's defeat was handled.

HITLER – V. BRAUCHITSCH – HALDER

The main reason for the trend discussed above lay in the personality of *Hitler*, in his insatiable thirst for power and his excessive self-esteem, which was engendered by his undeniable successes and encouraged by the lick-spittling of his party bosses and certain members of his retinue. *Vis-à-vis* his military opponents he was greatly aided by the fact of being not only the Head of State but also, as Commander-in-Chief of the Wehrmacht, their military superior. Moreover, he had a genius for suddenly confronting his military collaborators with political and economic arguments which they could not immediately refute and of whose value, in any case, the statesman must perforce be considered the better judge.

In the last analysis, however, it was Hitler's lust for power which caused him to usurp the role of the supreme war leader in addition to being the Head of State and political chief. A conversation I had with him in 1943 proved most revealing in this respect. It was one of the many times I tried to induce Hitler to accept a rationalized form of command – in other words, to resign the direction of military operations in favour of a fully responsible Chief of the General Staff. On the occasion in question Hitler hotly denied having any desire to 'play the war lord' – though he was undoubtedly attracted by the glory that went with it. On the contrary, he contended, the really decisive thing was that he should have the *power* and exclusive authority to impose his will. Power was all he believed in, and he regarded his will as the embodiment of that power. Apart from this it is not unreasonable to suppose that after the Polish campaign Hitler feared the achievements of the Generals might impair his own prestige in the eyes of the people, and that that was why he treated O.K.H. so dictatorially from the outset regarding the conduct of the campaign in the west.

Such was the man – utterly unscrupulous, highly intelligent and possessed of an indomitable will – with whom Generals v. Brauchitsch and Halder had to contend. Not only was he acknowledged by the people as the Head of State: he also ranked as the most senior member of the Generals' own hierarchy.

Indeed, it would have been an unequal battle even if Hitler's military opponents had been different men.

The future *Field-Marshal v. Brauchitsch* was a very able officer. While not belonging to quite the same class as Baron v. Fritsch, Beck, v. Rundstedt, v. Bock and Ritter v. Leeb, he certainly ranked immediately after them and, as events have shown, also possessed all the requisite qualities of a Commander-in-Chief of the Army.

As far as v. Brauchitsch's character is concerned, his standards of personal behaviour were quite unassailable. Neither would I dispute his will-power, even though it tended in my own experience to be manifested in a somewhat negative inflexibility rather than in creative resolve. He preferred to have decisions suggested to him rather than to take and impose them on his own initiative. Indeed, he frequently evaded decision in the hope of being spared a struggle to which he did not feel equal. In many cases Brauchitsch put up a sturdy fight for the interests of the army – one example being his efforts to have Colonel-General v. Fritsch publicly rehabilitated by Hitler, although he was well aware how unpopular this would make him with the latter. The Order of the Day he published on the death of Fritsch was a sign of his courage. At bottom, however, he was no fighter. He was never really the sort of man to get his way by sheer force of personality. Colonel-General Beck, for one, complained most bitterly to me about the half-hearted way in which Brauchitsch had represented O.K.H.'s point of view at the time of the Czech crisis and left him, Beck, completely in the lurch. When, on the other hand, people like Herr v. Hassel, the former ambassador in Rome, blame v. Brauchitsch for wavering over the question of whether to resort to violence against Hitler, they forget the essential difference between plotting from behind a desk when one is no longer in a position of responsibility (as was the case with Herr v. Hassel) and committing oneself, as leader of the army, to a *coup d'état* which can imply civil war in peacetime and lead to the victory of one's external enemies in time of war.

Field-Marshal v. Brauchitsch, a man of elegant appearance who bore all the hallmarks of the aristocrat, was never anything but dignified in his bearing. He was correct, courteous and even charming, although this charm did not always leave one with an impression of inner warmth. Just as he lacked the aggressiveness that commands an opponent's respect, or at least compels him to go warily, so did he fail to impress one as a forceful, productive personality. The general effect was one of coolness and reserve. He often appeared slightly inhibited, he was certainly rather sensitive. Qualities like these might well ensure the support of his immediate collaborators, who respected the 'gentleman' in him, but they were not enough to assure him of the full confidence of the troops which a man like Baron v. Fritsch had enjoyed, nor could they impress a man of Hitler's type. Admittedly General v. Seeckt had been far colder, even to the extent of being unapproachable. But in this case everyone had sensed the inner fire that inspired him and the iron will which made him a leader of men. Neither quality had fallen to the share of v. Brauchitsch, nor had he been blessed with that soldierly boldness which – apart from his great qualities as a commander – had won v. Fritsch the hearts of his troops.

As far as v. Brauchitsch's relations with Hitler are concerned, I am convinced that he wore himself out mentally in his struggle with a man of such ruthless will. Disposition, origin and upbringing precluded him, in his encounters with Hitler, from resorting to the weapons which the latter, relying on his position as the Head of State, had not the least hesitation in using. Brauchitsch choked down his vexation and anger, particularly as he was no match for Hitler dialectically. And so it went on until a heart complaint finally compelled him to retire at a time most convenient to Hitler.

It is only fair to add that from the very start Brauchitsch found himself in a much more unfavourable position *vis-à-vis* Hitler than his predecessor had done. To begin with, ever since Blomberg had relinquished his post as Commander-in-Chief of the Wehrmacht, Hitler had not only been Head of State but also the supreme military authority. The final blow dealt to the army by War Minister v. Blomberg had been to suggest to Hitler that he should assume command of the Wehrmacht – though, of course, it is open to debate whether Hitler would not have arrived at this solution anyway, with or without Blomberg's advice.

Most of all, by the time v. Brauchitsch took office Hitler had acquired a very different attitude towards the army, and in particular towards O.K.H., from the one he had had in former years. There is no doubt that when he originally came to power he had shown the military leaders a certain deference and respected their professional abilities. It was an attitude he retained until the last in the case of a man like Field-Marshal v. Rundstedt, despite having twice relieved him of his command during the war.

There were two points in particular which led Hitler to change his view of the army in the last years of peace.

The first was the realization that under Colonel-General Baron v. Fritsch (as indeed under v. Brauchitsch) the army stuck firmly to its traditional notions of simplicity and chivalry and its soldierly conception of honour. While Hitler could certainly not reproach the army with disloyalty towards the State, it was quite obviously not going to throw its military principles overboard in favour of the National Socialist 'ideology'. It was equally clear, moreover, that this was the very thing about the army that made it all the more popular with wide circles of the people. Although Hitler had originally refused to listen to the calumnies against senior military figures served up to him from various party sources, the rabble-rousing campaign against the army, which was mainly the work of people like Göring, Himmler and Goebbels, ultimately bore fruit. Even War Minister v. Blomberg helped to arouse Hitler's mistrust, however unintentionally, by going out of his way to stress his task of 'marrying up the army with National Socialism'. The result of this agitation became evident when Göring, ostensibly as the 'senior officer of the Wehrmacht', addressed a group of high-ranking military leaders in spring 1939. In the course of his speech he quite brazenly upbraided the army, as distinct from the other two services, for maintaining an outlook that was steeped in tradition and did not fit in with the National-Socialist system. It was a speech which Colonel-General v. Brauchitsch, who was among those present, should on no account have tolerated.

The second source of tension in Hitler's relationship with O.K.H. consisted in what he later used to describe – to quote the least insulting of his epithets – as 'the everlasting hesitation of the Generals'.

The implication here was twofold. One thing he meant was O.K.H.'s very proper attempts to check the inordinate pace of rearmament, the steady acceleration of which was detrimental to the quality of the troops. Secondly, Hitler maintained that all his successes in the field of foreign policy had been achieved against the opposition of the Generals, who had in each case been too cautious to act. The answer to this is that Colonel-General v. Fritsch – i.e. O.K.H. – did not raise any objections to Hitler's plans regarding either the introduction of conscription or the occupation of the Rhineland.[1] Neither did General Beck object (v. Brauchitsch being absent from Berlin at the time) when Hitler decided to invade Austria. It was the War Minister, v. Blomberg, who first opposed general conscription, doing so for reasons of foreign policy which he presently discarded. It was also Blomberg who at the time of the march into the Rhineland advised Hitler – unbeknown to O.K.H. – to recall the German garrisons from the left bank of the river when the French ordered a partial mobilization. The fact that Hitler very nearly followed this advice, only being dissuaded from doing so by Foreign Minister v. Neurath's remark that this was not the time to lose one's nerve, may well have served – as a constant reminder of his own fit of weakness – to intensify Hitler's collective resentment against the Generals in future. And when O.K.H. repeatedly pointed out in the years of rearmament that the Army was still far from being ready for war, they did no more than their duty in issuing these warnings. Officially Hitler always agreed with them, yet they may well have increased his dislike of O.K.H.

The first time Hitler's foreign policy encountered formal opposition was at the conference with the Foreign Minister and three service chiefs on 5th November 1937, at which Hitler revealed his intentions towards Czechoslovakia. The fact that he clashed with the Foreign Minister, v. Neurath, as well as the War Minister, v. Blomberg, and the Commander-in-Chief of the Army, Baron v. Fritsch, was certainly one of his reasons for getting rid of these admonishers at the earliest opportunity.

It is widely believed today that the acceptance of Colonel-General Baron v. Fritsch's dismissal by Germany's Generals showed Hitler that he could treat O.K.H. just as he liked from then on. Whether this was the conclusion he drew at the time I should not care to say. If he did, he was certainly mistaken about the Generals' motives. Far from being a sign of weakness, their attitude was due to ignorance of the true facts of the case, their inability as decent soldiers to believe the

[1] *Zwischen Wehrmacht und Hitler* by General Hossbach. *Author.*

State leadership capable of such a base intrigue, and the practical impossibility in such circumstances of carrying out a *coup d'état*.

Finally, there can be no doubt that the party personalities I mentioned above were for ever harping on the theme of 'the everlasting objections of the Generals' in conversations with Hitler.

It is quite certain, therefore, that v. Brauchitsch found himself in an extremely difficult position from the start as far as Hitler was concerned. On assuming office, moreover, he was ill-advised enough to make a number of concessions affecting personnel, including the quite unjustified dismissal of a number of generals with excellent records and the appointment of General Keitel's brother as head of the *Heerespersonalamt*.[1] This was Brauchitsch's first fatal step.

The devastating blow to O.K.H.'s standing *vis-à-vis* Hitler came at the time of the Sudeten crisis, when, thanks to the tractability of the Western Powers, Hitler proved himself right in face of all the army's misgivings and objections. Von Brauchitsch's action in sacrificing his Chief-of-Staff on this occasion naturally weakened his position even further in Hitler's eyes.

The second O.K.H. personality who had to deal direct with Hitler after Beck's dismissal, *Colonel-General Halder*, was Field-Marshal v. Brauchitsch's equal as regards military qualifications. At all events, the two men worked together on terms of close confidence, and I am inclined to believe that when v. Brauchitsch agreed with Halder's recommendations he did so from conviction. Like most of the officers who had begun their careers on the Bavarian General Staff, Halder had a remarkable grasp of every aspect of staff duties and was a tireless worker into the bargain. A saying of Moltke's, 'Genius is diligence', might well have been his motto. Yet this man hardly glowed with the sacred fire that is said to inspire really great soldiers. While it speaks for his high sense of responsibility that he prepared for the Russian campaign by having an operations plan 'drawn up' by the *Oberquartiermeister I*, General Paulus, on the basis of studies made by the Chiefs-of-Staff of the Army Groups, the fact remains that the basic concept of a campaign plan should be born in the mind of the man who has to direct that campaign.

In his outward bearing Halder had not the elegance of v. Brauchitsch. He was incorruptibly objective in his utterances, and I myself have

---

[1] I.e. as Military Secretary. *Tr.*

known him put a criticism to Hitler with the utmost frankness. On the same occasion one also saw how fervently he stood up for the interests of the fighting troops and how much he felt for them when wrong decisions were imposed on him. Unfortunately, objectivity and moderation alone were not the qualities which could impress Hitler, and any feeling of sympathy for the troops left him completely cold.

What ultimately led to Halder's downfall, in my own opinion, was his divided allegiance. Even when he took over from Beck he was already a declared enemy of Hitler. According to Walter Görlitz, in his book *The German General Staff*, Halder told v. Brauchitsch on taking office that his only reason for accepting the post was to fight against Hitler. He is credited with numerous plans for Hitler's overthrow, though it is hard to say what real prospects of success these would have had in practice.

On the other hand, Halder was Germany's and later Hitler's Chief-of-Staff, after the latter had taken over command of the army. Now, although it may be given to a politician to play the dual role of responsible adviser and conspirator, soldiers are not usually fitted for this kind of thing. Above all, it is traditionally unthinkable in Germany that a Chief of the General Staff should not be on terms of confidence with his Commander-in-Chief. Even if, in the light of Hitler's actions, it is accepted as admissible for a Chief-of-Staff to plan the overthrow of the Head of State and Commander-in-Chief *in peacetime*, the dual role of Chief-of-Staff and plotter *in wartime* inevitably created an insoluble dilemma. As Chief of the General Staff, it was Halder's duty to strive for the victory of the army he was jointly responsible for leading – in other words, to see that the military operations of his Commander-in-Chief were successful. In the second of his roles, however, he could not desire such a victory. There cannot be the least doubt that Halder, when confronted by this difficult choice, opted for his military duty and did everything in his power to serve the German Army in its arduous struggle. At the same time his other role demanded that he should at all costs hold on to the position which, he hoped, would one day enable him to bring about Hitler's removal. To that end, however, he had to bow to the latter's military decisions, even if he did not agree with them. Certainly his chief reason for remaining was that he thought this his best hope of protecting the army from the consequences of Hitler's military blunders. But in doing so he had to pay the price of executing orders to which his military convictions prevented him from agreeing. The conflict was bound to wear him down inwardly and finally lead to his downfall. One thing is certain: it was in the interest of what was at stake, and not of his own person, that Colonel-General Halder stuck it out for so long as Chief-of-Staff.

I have endeavoured to give a pen portrait of the two personalities under whom, in autumn 1939, there culminated a process which can only be described as the eclipse of O.K.H. From what I have said it will be clear why neither of these officers, first-rate though they undoubtedly were, could be a match for a man like Hitler. At the same time, the fact that O.K.H.'s relegation to a purely executive organ was actually accomplished just after it had scored such brilliant victories in Poland was also due to the way in which Hitler and O.K.H. respectively approached the problem of how the war should henceforth be prosecuted.

Up till and immediately after the outbreak of war, Germany had quite naturally prepared only for defence in the west. Who could have guessed that the Western Powers would let Poland down so ignominiously after giving her a guarantee? Their feeble push into the forward zone of the Siegfried Line along the Saar – which was immediately followed by a withdrawal on to French territory – could not be regarded as even the preparatory step for any large offensive later on.

As long as such an offensive had been definitely expected, it had only been possible to wait and see whether we should succeed in halting it at the Siegfried Line or – in the event of its being launched towards the Ruhr through Luxembourg and Belgium – in delivering a counterblow once the necessary forces had been released from Poland. Now, however, an entirely new situation had been created by the inaction of the Western Powers. Even when allowance were made for French methods and the time the British took to act, the Western Powers could not be expected to take the offensive in the immediate future, now that Poland was beaten and the whole of the German Army available for the west. Poland's fate was sealed at the latest by 18th September, when the Battle of the Bzura was over and the Soviets had crossed her eastern frontier the previous day. This, then, should have been the deadline for an exchange of views between Hitler and the Commander-in-Chief of the Army on what action to take in the west. Yet, judging by the books published to date (notably those of General v. Lossberg, at that time the senior operations officer at O.K.W., and Ministerialrat Greiner, the O.K.W. war diarist), no such discussions took place.

It may be assumed that the reactions of Hitler and the O.K.H. leaders to the brilliant success in Poland and the unexpected inaction of the Western Powers were entirely different. Hitler undoubtedly interpreted the failure of the Anglo-French forces to take the offensive as a sign of weakness which would permit him to attack in the west himself. Furthermore, what had happened in Poland convinced him that henceforth there could be no task too big for the German Army to tackle. O.K.H., as will be seen, did not share this view by any means. On the other hand, it was permissible to infer from the attitude of the Western Powers that they had only entered the war to save their faces and that it must thus be possible to come to terms with them. Also, General Halder may have toyed with the idea of paving the way to such an understanding by removing Hitler, so that any German offensive in the west at that particular juncture would have been quite out of place.

Whatever the answer, O.K.H. could be certain that until then Hitler had never contemplated, even after the fall of Poland, the idea of an offensive in the west. I was given infallible proof of this in the winter of 1939–40. On one of the many occasions when Hitler issued the preparatory code-word to put the final troop movements into the assembly areas in train, I was visited by the Chief-of-Staff of the Air Fleet supporting Army Group A, General Sperrle, who told me that his formations would be unable to take off from the waterlogged airfields. When I objected that the Luftwaffe had had months in which to construct solid runways, Sperrle assured me that Hitler had on an earlier occasion strictly forbidden any kind of work associated with a future offensive. In the same connexion it may be noted that the ammunition production had not attained the level necessary for an eventual offensive in the west.

Obviously O.K.H. had misjudged Hitler's mentality in assuming that his viewpoint was immutable. Greiner tells us that during the second half of September, when the end was approaching in Poland, O.K.H. had had a paper on the further conduct of the war in the west prepared by General Heinrich v. Stülpnagel. The conclusion he reached was that the German Army would not be adequately equipped to break through the Maginot Line before 1942. He had not considered the possibility of going round through Belgium and Holland because the Reich Government had only recently assured these countries that their neutrality would be respected. In the light of this paper and Hitler's attitude hitherto, O.K.H. had evidently deduced that the policy in the west would continue to be defensive. At the end of the Polish campaign it accordingly ordered the army's defensive deployment in the west to be reinforced, manifestly without first obtaining Hitler's approval.

In the completely new situation created by the total collapse of Poland such a policy was tantamount to resigning the initiative to Hitler regarding any future plans. It was certainly not the right way for the military leaders to safeguard their influence on the further course of the war, whatever form this might take. Apart from that, the conclusions reached by v. Stülpnagel could not be regarded as an answer to the problem of Germany's future war policy. If we were to wait till 1942 to penetrate the Maginot Line, the Western Powers would in all likelihood have caught up with our lead in arms production. In addition, it would never have been possible to develop a decisive operation from a successful penetration of the Maginot Line. Against the minimum of 100 divisions available on the enemy side since 1939, this was no way to achieve decisive results. Even if the enemy committed powerful forces for the actual defence of the Maginot Line, he would still have been left with an adequate strategic reserve of between forty and sixty divisions with which immediately to intercept even a wide breakthrough of the fortifications. Without any doubt the struggle would have petered out inconclusively into trench warfare. Such could not be the aim of German strategy.

One cannot assume, of course, that Colonel-General v. Brauchitsch and his Chief-of-Staff thought they would achieve anything with a purely defensive strategy in the long run. Nonetheless they did pin their hopes initially on the possibility that the Western Powers would either still come to terms or take the offensive themselves in the end. Unfortunately they were not competent to take decisions in the former contingency, and their hope for an Allied offensive was, as will be shown, unrealistic. The fact of the matter was that from a military point of view the spring of 1940 was not only the earliest but also the latest occasion on which Germany could have hoped to fight a successful offensive in the west.

According to Greiner, Hitler was not informed of the Stülpnagel memorandum, but must still have been aware that O.K.H. was going to cling to a defensive policy in the west. Instead of the timely discussion on the future course of the war that should have taken place at the latest by mid-September, he now confronted the Commander-in-Chief of the Army with the *fait accompli* of his decision of 27th September and the O.K.W. directive which followed on 9th October. Without any previous consultation with the Commander-in-Chief, he not only ordered offensive measures in the west but even decided on the *timing and method* to be adopted. All of these were matters which should on no account have been settled without the concurrence of the Commander-in-Chief. Hitler required the offensive to be launched at the earliest possible date – in any event before the autumn was out. Originally, according to General v. Lossberg, he fixed 15th October as the deadline. At the latest this would have meant disengaging the armour and aircraft in Poland at the end of the Battle of the Bzura. Furthermore, Hitler had laid down *how* the proposed offensive operation should be conducted, namely by by-passing the Maginot Line by way of Belgium and Holland.

The Commander-in-Chief of the Army was to be left with merely the technical execution of an operation on which he had deliberately not been consulted and for which, in autumn 1939 at all events, he could certainly not guarantee any prospect of decisive success.

For those who wonder how the Commander-in-Chief of the Army could possibly accept such a *capitis diminutio* of his position by acceding to Hitler's intentions, Greiner has probably given the right answer in his book, *Die Oberste Wehrmachtführung*. He suggests that v. Brauchitsch, feeling that he was unlikely to achieve anything by immediate opposition, hoped that if he put up a show of goodwill at the beginning he would ultimately be able to talk Hitler out of his plan. Incidentally, the same view is advanced by General v. Lossberg on the strength of his own knowledge of Hitler and the latter's attitude at the time. Brauchitsch may also have been counting on the weather to make it impossible to carry out a late-autumn or winter offensive when the day came. If the decision could thus be delayed until the following spring, ways and means might be found of ending the war by a political compromise.

If these really were the thoughts of the Commander-in-Chief and his Chief-of-Staff, they certainly proved right as far as the weather went.

But the notion that Hitler could be 'talked out of' such a fundamental decision, even by General v. Reichenau, to whom O.K.H. duly entrusted the task of doing this, was to my mind quite futile. The only hope would have been if O.K.H. had been able to offer a better solution of its own which would impress Hitler.

As for there being any possibility of ending the war at that time by peaceful negotiation, none emerged. The peace offer made by Hitler to the Western Powers after the Polish campaign met with a flat rejection. Besides, Hitler would most probably not have accepted any reasonable settlement of the Polish question that would have made it possible to reach an understanding with the west. In any case, such a settlement was hardly conceivable now that Soviet Russia had swallowed the eastern half of Poland. Another very doubtful point is how Germany could have achieved an honourable peace *without* Hitler at that time. How was he to be overthrown? If General Halder had any fresh plan to take military action against Berlin in October 1939, all I can say is that he would have found even less support among the troops than in autumn 1938.

To begin with, then, Colonel-General v. Brauchitsch fell in with Hitler's intentions, and O.K.H. drafted 'Operation Order Yellow' in accordance with the policy Hitler had laid down. By 27th October, however, the Commander-in-Chief, backed by his Chief-of-Staff, was trying to persuade Hitler on military grounds to postpone the offensive till a more favourable time of year, by which he presumably meant spring 1940. According to Greiner, the same recommendation had been made to Hitler a few days previously by General v. Reichenau – probably at v. Brauchitsch's request. Though Hitler did not entirely reject the arguments put up to him, the date he had fixed as long ago as 22nd October for the start of the offensive – 12th November – continued to hold good.

On 5th November v. Brauchitsch made a fresh attempt to bring Hitler round. This was the day – assuming that the attack really did start on 12th November—on which the code-word had to be issued for the troops to begin moving into the assembly areas.

Though this conversation took place in private,[1] details of it leaked out, and its upshot was what I believe to have been an irreparable breach between Hitler and the Generals. According to what Greiner

---

[1] Keitel was not called in until later. *Author.*

gathered from Keitel, v. Brauchitsch read Hitler a memorandum comprising all his reasons for objecting to an offensive that autumn. Besides citing such incontrovertible facts as the state of the weather and the unpreparedness of the new formations, he advanced one argument which lashed Hitler into a white fury. It was a criticism of the performance of the fighting troops in the Polish campaign. Brauchitsch advanced the view that the infantry had not displayed the same aggressive spirit as in 1914 and that the discipline and staying power of combat units had not always been entirely up to standard as a result of the tempo of rearmament. Had v. Brauchitsch been talking to an audience of senior commanders they would have seen his point. Admittedly he was not justified in his charge that the infantry had not shown the same aggressiveness as in 1914 – at least as long as he expressed it in those generalized terms. This was due to a misunderstanding of the transformation through which the infantry attack had passed in the years between. The 1914 methods of attack were just not conceivable any longer. On the other hand, it could not be denied – and this occurs with untried troops at the beginning of every war – that individual units had occasionally shown signs of jitters, particularly when fighting in built-up areas. Furthermore, various higher formation headquarters had found it necessary to crack down on cases of indiscipline. These facts were not surprising if one considered that in the space of a very few years the Reichswehr of 100,000 men had been inflated to an army several millions strong, a large proportion of whom had only been with the colours since the general mobilization. But none of this – in the light of the victories in Poland – could be adequate reason for concluding that the army was unable to fight an offensive in the west. If only Colonel-General v. Brauchitsch had confined himself to emphasizing that the *newly-formed* divisions were still precluded by their lack of training and inner stability from going into action and that the offensive could not be carried out with the experienced divisions alone, he would have been on just as safe ground as he was with his objections to the season of the year. A generalization of the kind mentioned above, however, was the very last argument he should have advanced in any conversation with Hitler, who saw himself as the creator of that new Wehrmacht whose fighting qualities were now being called into question. Indeed, Hitler was right to the extent that if it had not been for his political audacity in pushing ahead with rearmament and for the part played by National Socialism in reviving the military spirit even among those social strata where it had been ostracized during the Weimar Republic, this Wehrmacht would never have attained the strength it possessed in 1939. What Hitler chose to overlook was that the achievements of the former Reichswehr were entirely on a par with his own. For had not the officers and non-commissioned officers who stemmed from the old Reichswehr devoted themselves so wholeheartedly to the preliminary planning and material preparations, Hitler would neither have come by the Wehrmacht he now regarded as his 'creation' nor could the victories in Poland have been won.

By raising such objections in the presence of Hitler, a dictator whose self-esteem was already inflated, v. Brauchitsch attained precisely the opposite of what he intended. Disregarding all v. Brauchitsch's factual arguments, Hitler took umbrage at the criticism he had presumed to direct against his – Hitler's own – achievements and brusquely broke off the interview. He insisted on adhering to 12th November as the operative date.

Fortunately the Weather God took a hand at this juncture and enforced a postponement – a process that was to repeat itself fifteen times before the end of January.

Therefore, even though O.K.H. had ultimately proved its point *vis-à-vis* Hitler regarding the possible date of the offensive, the upshot was a crisis of leadership whose consequences were to become appallingly obvious in the further course of the war. Its immediate effect was that Hitler and Brauchitsch ceased to meet. The G.S.O. I of the Operations Branch, the future General Heusinger, told me on 18th January 1940 that Brauchitsch had not seen Hitler since 5th November – a quite impossible situation with things as they were. A further consequence of the breach of 5th November was the talk given by Hitler to the commanders and chiefs-of-staff of all army groups, armies, and corps in the Reich Chancellory on 23rd November. I need not go into this fully, as it has already become known through other publications. Its essential points were Hitler's emphasis on his irrevocable decision to take the offensive in the west at the earliest possible date and the doubts which he even then expressed as to how long the Reich would remain free from an attack in the rear in the east.

As far as his factual explanation of the fundamental need to take the offensive in the west went, his remarks were well-considered and, I thought, convincing, except for the question of timing. Otherwise his speech constituted a massive attack not only on O.K.H., but on the Generals of the army as a whole, whom he accused of constantly obstructing his boldness and enterprise. In this respect it was the most biased speech I ever heard Hitler make. The Commander-in-Chief of the Army did the only possible thing and tendered his resignation. This Hitler refused to accept, though that was obviously no solution to the crisis. O.K.H. was still in the unhappy position of having to prepare for an offensive of which it did not approve. The Commander-in-Chief was still repudiated as an adviser on overall war policy and relegated to the status of a purely executive general.

Any inquiry into the reasons for such a development in the relationship between the Head of State and the army leaders will show the decisive factor to have been Hitler's thirst for power and his ever-growing self-conceit, both of which were augmented by the mischief-making of the Görings and Himmlers. Yet it must also be stated that O.K.H. made no small contribution towards its own elimination at Hitler's hands by the way it handled the problem of how the war should be prosecuted after the Polish campaign.

By deciding to remain on the defensive in the west, O.K.H. re-signed the initiative to Hitler – although it should unquestionably have been O.K.H.'s business in the first instance to recommend to the Head of State what steps were to be taken after the army, effectively supported by the Luftwaffe, had defeated Poland so swiftly.

O.K.H. was undoubtedly right to take the view in autumn 1939 that the time of year and the immaturity of the new formations made an offensive inadvisable at that stage. But neither this simple statement of fact nor the arrangements made to reinforce the defensive dispositions in the west provided an adequate answer to the problem of how to bring the war to a satisfactory conclusion in the military sense. This question had to be answered by *O.K.H.* if it were to assert its influence on overall strategy.

The Commander-in-Chief of the Army certainly had every right to recommend the course of political settlement with the Western Powers. But what was to happen if no prospect of such a settlement emerged? With a man of Hitler's type it was particularly necessary – even if an offensive in the west did not seem expedient at that moment

– that O.K.H. should indicate there and then the *military* way to end the war.

Consequently there were three questions to consider once the Polish campaign was over:

First, *could* the war be brought to a favourable conclusion by sticking to defensive tactics, or could this object be achieved only by a victorious German offensive in the west?

Secondly, if such an offensive proved necessary, *when* could it be launched with any prospect of decisive success?

Thirdly, *how* must it be conducted to ensure an effective victory on the Continent?

As far as the first question went, there were two possibilities.

One was that the Reich would reach a settlement with the Western Powers after the fall of Poland. O.K.H. was bound to regard this sceptically from the outset, partly because of the British national character, which made it fairly *improbable* that Great Britain would come to terms, and partly because Hitler was unlikely, once Poland had been defeated, to be prepared for a reasonable settlement of the German–Polish frontier question in the sense of a compromise. After all, in order to reach agreement with the Western Powers he had to re-establish Poland, and this he could not do after having made over her eastern part to the Soviets. That much was an accomplished fact which not even another German Government attaining power after Hitler's overthrow could have removed.

The other possibility of successfully ending the war by remaining on the defensive might occur if the Western Powers should decide, after all, to take the offensive. This would offer the Germans the prospect of attaining a victorious decision in the west in the course of delivering a *counterblow*. The same idea emerges in the book *Gespräche mit Halder*, where Halder is quoted as speaking of an 'operation on the rebound'. According to General Heusinger, however, O.K.H. only began to consider the project much later – i.e. some time in December – and not at the turn of September and October, the phase so vital for its own position.

Undoubtedly there was something very attractive about fighting an operation on the rebound, for the idea of saddling the enemy with the burden of an offensive against the Siegfried Line or the odium of violating the neutrality of Luxembourg, Belgium, and perhaps even

Holland was inevitably an extremely tempting one. But was this not really a case of wishful thinking, at least for the foreseeable future? Could it be supposed that the Western Powers – who had not dared to launch an offensive while the mass of the German forces were tied down in Poland – would attack now that the Wehrmacht faced them in full strength? I do not believe – and neither did I at the time – that any basis existed for a German 'rebound' operation.

This view has found clear corroboration in a 'war plan' drafted at the time on the orders of the Allied Commander-in-Chief, General Gamelin. The main train of thought reflected in this document, which later fell into the hands of German troops, was as follows:

Before *spring 1941* the Allied forces would not have amassed the material strength to take the offensive against Germany in the west. To attain a numerical superiority of ground forces, fresh allies would have to be won.

The British were *not* prepared to participate in a large *offensive* before 1941, except in the event of a partial collapse of Germany. (This remark, which obviously implies a hope of revolution, shows what we should have had to expect from a *coup d'état*.)

The *principal task* of the Western Powers in 1940 had to be to safe-guard the *integrity of French territory* and, of course, to hasten to the assistance of Belgium and Holland if they were attacked.

In addition, every effort would be made to create further *theatres of attrition* for Germany. Those named were the *Nordic States* and – if Italy remained neutral – the *Balkans*. Naturally the attempts to bring in Belgium and Holland on the side of the Allies would continue.

Finally, endeavours would be made to deprive the Reich of its *vital imports*, both by the already-mentioned creation of new theatres of war and by tightening the blockade through pressure on the neutral Powers.

From this 'war plan' it becomes palpably clear that the Western Powers intended to wage a *war of attrition* – in as many different theatres as possible – until such time as they had attained the clear pre-ponderance which would allow them – though in no case before 1941 – to launch an offensive in the west.

Although O.K.H. could not at the time in question know of this Allied war plan, it was only too likely that the Western Powers would fight a long-term war in the sense indicated.

In view of the bloody prospects an assault on the Siegfried Line would entail, the hope that the French and British peoples would tire of the 'phoney war' was hardly a realistic basis for any O.K.H. decisions. In no event could Germany wait until the enemy had built up his armaments (and in the light of Roosevelt's attitude, allowance must be made here for American aid) to a point where he was stronger on land and in the air as well as at sea. Least of all could she afford to do so with the Soviet Union at her back. The latter, having by this time obtained all it could hope for from Hitler, had hardly any more vital interests in common with the Reich, and the stronger the Western Powers grew, the more precarious the position of Germany would become.

As far as the military leaders were concerned, therefore, the situation after the Polish campaign was this: The answer to the first of the above three questions – i.e. whether the war could be brought to a *successful conclusion* by *remaining on the defensive* in the west – must be in the negative, unless the political leadership could still manage to reach a compromise with the Western Powers. The right of the Commander-in-Chief of the Army to advise Hitler to resort to compromise is beyond all doubt, if only because of the military risk a prolongation of the war would entail. Such action would, of course, involve accepting a *temporary* delay on the Western Front. Irrespective of that, however, it was both the duty and the right of the army leaders to give Hitler *military* guidance. *They* had to tell *him* what military steps were to be taken if no political solution of the conflict could be reached!

In other words, it was up to O.K.H. to present Hitler with an *alternative military plan* if it proved impossible to achieve the political compromise with the Western Powers for which even Hitler evidently hoped in the first instance. One must not assume that Hitler would continue as hitherto to reject an offensive in the west once Poland was beaten, nor must one wait until he took a military decision on his own account.

No military recommendation on the prosecution of the war could consist in maintaining the defensive in the west unless it were thought that Britain could be brought to her knees by aerial and submarine warfare – an assumption for which no real foundation existed.

On the *military* side, therefore, assuming that a political understanding proved unattainable, the only recommendation one could make was that the war in the west be conducted *offensively*. When such a recommendation was submitted, moreover, it was essential that O.K.H. should assure itself of the initiative in deciding on the timing and method.

As far as timing went, O.K.H. was in agreement with all the commanders on the Western Front that no decisive success could be gained from launching the offensive in the late autumn or winter.

The principal reason for this was the *season*. In autumn and winter the Wehrmacht would be prevented by weather conditions from playing its two big trumps, *armour* and *Luftwaffe*, to their fullest effect. In addition, the short period of daylight at this time of the year renders it virtually impossible to win even a tactical decision in the space of a single day, thereby cutting down the speed of operations.

The other reason was the still inadequate standard of training of all the *new formations* set up on the outbreak of war. The only troops really fit to go into action in autumn 1939 were the active divisions. None of the others had had enough experience of handling weapons or of operating as integral parts of a larger formation: nor did they as yet possess the requisite degree of inner stability. Furthermore, the refitting of the armoured formations following the Polish campaign was still not complete. If it were intended to start an offensive in the west before the end of autumn 1939, the mechanized divisions in Poland should have been released at an earlier date, but that was a point which had not occurred to Hitler. Over and above all this, serious deficiencies existed in the Luftwaffe.

Thus it was clear that an offensive in the west could not be justified before *spring 1940*. That this afforded time to seek a political solution of the conflict was welcome from the point of view of the military, little as it counted with Hitler after the rejection of his peace offer at the beginning of October.

Since the problem of *method*, namely the strategic preparation of an offensive in the west, is the subject of the next chapter, there is no point in going into it any further here.

Only this may be said in advance. The offensive plan imposed by Hitler on 9th October was a half-measure. Instead of being aimed at a *complete* decision on the Continent, it was – initially at any rate – concerned only with an interim objective.

This was the point that provided O.K.H. with its opportunity to bring home to Hitler that his military advisers had something better to offer than a partial solution not worthy of the stake involved. Always providing, of course, that O.K.H. itself believed that by launching an offensive it could achieve a complete decision on the Continent.

It is still not known what prompted the O.K.H. leaders to remain so non-committal on future policy in the west during those vital weeks after the Polish campaign that the military decision was actually placed in Hitler's hands. They may have been moved by a very proper desire to make him seek a political compromise. They may also have rightly shunned a repetition of the violation of Belgian neutrality and all that went with it. At the time, however, an outsider was left with the impression that the O.K.H. leaders considered it doubtful, to say the least, whether any German offensive would be *decisively successful.*

Be that as it may, O.K.H. left the initiative to Hitler to make the *military* decision. By further bowing to Hitler's will and putting out the orders for an operation with which its leaders privately disagreed, it *resigned* for all practical purposes as the authority responsible for land warfare.

When, shortly afterwards, the operational proposals put up by H.Q. Army Group A gave O.K.H. a chance to regain its lost position, it let the opportunity slip through its fingers.

By the time the western offensive, thanks to these same proposals, had achieved a degree of success exceeding even Hitler's original expectations, the latter regarded O.K.H. as a body which he could by-pass even in matters of grand tactics.

Hitler had taken over the functions which Schlieffen believed could at best be performed in our age by a triumvirate of king, statesman, and war lord. Now he had also usurped the role of the war lord. But had the 'drop of Samuel's anointing oil' which Schlieffen considered indispensable for at least one of the triumvirs really fallen on his head?

5

THE OPERATION PLAN CONTROVERSY

NOT UNTIL after the war did anything become generally known about the background of the plan which replaced O.K.H.'s original 'Operation Order Yellow' of 19th and 29th October 1939 as the basis of our offensive in the west – the plan by which so swift and decisive a victory was scored over the Anglo-French armies and the forces of Belgium and Holland. The first to disclose how this 'new' plan emerged was probably Liddell Hart,[1] who linked my name with it as a result of statements made to him by Field-Marshal v. Rundstedt and General Blumentritt, our chief of operations during the period in question.

Since I may be considered to have been the prime mover in this matter, it seems right that I should now make my own attempt, on the basis of the records at my disposal, to show how the plan came into being, especially as it has since acquired a certain significance. After all, the ideas behind the plan were mine, just as it was I who drafted all the memoranda to O.K.H. by which we sought to have the operation planned on the only lines conducive, in our opinion, to *decisive* success in the west. Finally it was I who – when already replaced as Chief-of-Staff of the Army Group – had an opportunity to expound to Hitler in person the ideas that our headquarters had so long failed to get accepted by O.K.H. Only a few days after this, O.K.H. put out a new Operation Order based on *our* recommendations!

At the same time I would stress that my commander, Colonel-General v. Rundstedt, and my collaborators Blumentritt and Tresckow, agreed with my view throughout and that v. Rundstedt backed our recommendations to the full with his own signature. Without his

[1] See *The Other Side of the Hill*, Cassell, 1948. *Tr.*

sanction we could never have kept up our attempts to change O.K.H.'s mind by these repeated memoranda.

The war historian or officer reading military history might well find it worth his while to study this intellectual tussle over an operation plan in its entirety. For the purpose of this book, however, I shall confine myself initially to outlining the O.K.H.'s plan and to explaining what I could not help regarding as the shortcomings of its (or, more precisely, of Hitler's) strategic conception. Next, by way of contrast to the O.K.H. plan, I propose to deal with the essential arguments on which the Army Group based its strategic considerations. Last of all, I shall briefly show how, after a long series of frustrations, the original operation plan was finally amended – undoubtedly on Hitler's instructions – to coincide with the views of our own headquarters.

THE O.K.H. (OR HITLER'S) PLAN

If asked to define, in the light of the Operation Orders issued by O.K.H., the basic strategy which that body (and Hitler) planned to adopt in the west, I would put it this way:

O.K.H. proposed – in accordance with Hitler's directive of 9th October – to send a strong right wing of the German armies through Holland into northern Belgium to defeat the Anglo-French forces it expected to encounter there together with the Belgians and Dutch. In other words, the decision was primarily to be sought by a strong thrust on the right wing. This assault wing consisted of Army Detachment N (an army detachment – *Armee-Abteilung* – being a small army of two or three army corps) and Army Group B (Colonel-General v. Bock) and was to assemble in the area of the Lower Rhine and the northern Eifel. Army Group B had three armies under command. Altogether the northern wing embraced thirty infantry divisions and the bulk of the mobile formations (nine armoured and four infantry divisions). Since the total number of German divisions available on the Western Front was 102, these therefore constituted almost half our aggregate strength.

While Army Detachment N's task was the elimination of Holland, the three armies in the Army Group were to attack through northern Belgium, passing north and south of Liège. The strong tank forces were intended to play a decisive role here in an attempt to overrun the enemy.

On 29th October this first Operation Order was amended to leave Holland out of the picture in the initial stages. This may have been due to representations from O.K.H.

Henceforth Army Group B was to attack round both sides of Liège with two armies up (Fourth and Sixth) and two (Eighteenth and Second) following through. Later, however, Holland was again in-

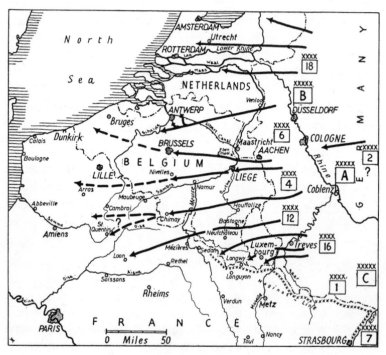

Map 3. The O.K.H. plan of Operations for German Offensive in the West.

cluded in the operation, her elimination being this time entrusted to Eighteenth Army.

The decisive thrust of Army Group B was to be covered on the southern flank by Army Group A. The latter, consisting of two armies (Twelfth and Sixteenth) and a total of twenty-two divisions (none of them with any mechanized troops) was to advance through southern Belgium and Luxembourg, after assembling in the southern Eifel and the Hunsrück. Twelfth Army was to follow through on the left of Army Group B, establishing a system of echeloned defence as it went in order to cover the further advance of Army Group B against enemy incursions.

Sixteenth Army was to wheel south after crossing Luxembourg in order to protect the deep flank of the whole operation by establishing a defensive position running closely along the north of the Maginot Line's westward projection between the Saar and the Meuse east of Sedan.

Army Group C was left with two armies and eighteen infantry divisions to hold the Siegfried Line from the Luxembourg frontier down to Switzerland. Seventeen infantry and two mobile divisions were available as army reserves.

The aim of this operation was defined in Paragraph 1 of the O.K.H. Operation Order of 19th October under the heading 'General Intention' (in pursuance of Hitler's O.K.W. Directive of 9th October). It was

'To defeat the largest possible elements of the French and Allied Armies and simultaneously to gain as much territory as possible in Holland, Belgium and Northern France as a basis for successful *air and sea operations against Britain* and as a broad protective zone for the Ruhr.'

Paragraph 2 of the Operation Order indicated that the first object of the two army groups' assault, which was to be co-ordinated under the Commander-in-Chief of the Army, v. Brauchitsch, must be

'While eliminating the Dutch armed forces, to defeat as many elements of the Belgian Army as possible in the vicinity of the frontier fortifications and, by rapidly concentrating powerful mechanised forces, to create a basis for the immediate prosecution of the attack with a strong right wing and the swift occupation of the Belgian coastline.'

In the afore-mentioned amendment to the Operation Order issued on 29th October, O.K.H. somewhat extended the aim of Army Group B's operation by re-wording the 'General Intention'. Henceforth this was to consist in

'Engaging and destroying the largest possible elements of the French Army in Northern France and Belgium, thereby creating favourable conditions for the prosecution of the war against Britain and France by land and air.'

In the paragraph headed 'Order of Battle and Tasks', O.K.H. set the Army Group the aim of

'Destroying the Allied forces north of the Somme and driving through to the Channel coast.'

The covering role of Army Group A, which continued to be mainly defensive, was broadened to the extent that its right-hand army (Twelfth) had now to be pushed over the Meuse opposite and south of Fumay and then to head through France's fortified frontier zone in the general direction of Laon.

The operational intention of both Operation Orders might best be expressed by saying that the Anglo-French elements we expected to meet in Belgium were to be floored by a (powerful) straight right while our (weaker) left fist covered up. The territorial objective was the Channel coastline. What would follow this first punch we were not told.

OBJECTIONS

Significantly enough, my first reaction to the plan laid down in these two Operation Orders was emotional rather than intellectual. The strategic intentions of O.K.H. struck me as being essentially an imitation of the famous Schlieffen Plan of 1914. I found it humiliating, to say the least, that our generation could do nothing better than repeat an old recipe, even when this was the product of a man like Schlieffen. What could possibly be achieved by turning up a war plan our opponents had already rehearsed with us once before and against whose repetition they were bound to have taken full precautions? For it was obvious to any military mind that the Germans would be even less keen – or able – to assault the Maginot Line of 1939 than they had the Verdun–Toul–Nancy–Epinal fortifications of 1914.

By this first rather emotional reaction of mine, however, I did O.K.H. an injustice. One reason was that the plan had come from Hitler; another was that it was actually far from being a repetition of Schlieffen's. The widespread view that this was so is correct in two respects only – i.e. it was intended in 1939, as in 1914, to place the main weight of the German offensive on the northern wing; and both plans also involved marching through Belgium. Otherwise the plans of 1914 and 1939 were widely divergent.

In the first place, the situations were entirely different. In 1914 it had still been possible – as Schlieffen did – to count on strategic surprise. Even if this did not include the march through Belgium, it certainly applied to the massing of Germany's forces on the extreme northern wing. In 1939 the corresponding intention on Hitler's part could not be concealed from the enemy.

Furthermore, there was reason in 1914 for hoping – as Schlieffen did – that the French would do us the good turn of launching a premature offensive into Lorraine. In 1939 no such development could be expected. The enemy would immediately throw in strong forces to meet our drive through Belgium and Holland, and these – in contrast to 1914 – would have to be tackled mainly head-on. Instead of taking the initiative prematurely in the centre of the front, the French were likely to strike a powerful back-hand blow at the southern flank of our main forces during their advance through Belgium. In other words, the Schlieffen Plan just *could* not be repeated.

Apart from this, I soon realized that neither O.K.H. nor Hitler had any intention of copying the Schlieffen Plan in the full magnitude of its conception. Schlieffen had drafted his plan with an eye to the utter and final defeat of the entire French Army. His aim was to outflank the enemy straight off in the north with a wide right hook and then, having cleared the whole of northern France, to drive down to the west of Paris and push the entire enemy army back against a front extending from Metz through the Vosges to the Swiss frontier, compelling it in the end to capitulate. To achieve this he had accepted the risk of initial reverses in Alsace, at the same time hoping that the enemy, by unleashing an offensive in Lorraine, would do their own bit towards making the Germans' big outflanking operation a complete success.

The 1939 operation plan, on the other hand, contained no clear-cut intention of fighting the campaign to a victorious conclusion. Its object was, quite clearly, *partial* victory (defeat of the Allied forces in northern Belgium) and *territorial gains* (possession of the Channel coast as a basis for future operations).

It may be that when the then Colonel-General v. Brauchitsch and his Chief-of-Staff were drafting the 1939 Operation Order they were reminded of what Moltke had written in his introduction to the General Staff's treatise on the War of 1870–71:

'No operation plan extends with any certainty beyond the first encounter with the main body of the enemy. It is only the layman who, as a campaign develops, thinks he sees the original plan being systematically fulfilled in every detail to its preconceived conclusion.'

If this thesis did inspire O.K.H.'s planning, it meant that the latter reserved the right to decide whether, and by what means, the offensive should be prosecuted once the first objectives – partial victory on the right wing in northern Belgium and the occupation of the Channel coast – were attained.

Judging by what I had heard when the Operation Order was handed to me in Zossen, however, I could only suppose that O.K.H. regarded the chances of achieving decisive results in the French theatre of war as extremely slender, if not non-existent. This impression was later reinforced during the many visits paid to our headquarters by the Commander-in-Chief of the Army and his Chief-of-Staff, neither of whom ever gave any serious attention to our repeated insistence on the need to strive after total victory. Similarly I doubt if Hitler himself then believed in the possibility of completely eliminating France in the course of the projected operation. Indeed, his primary concern was probably the recollection that when our offensive miscarried in 1914 we had found ourselves lacking even the necessary basis for submarine warfare against Britain. That was why he now attached such importance to winning that basis – in other words, to possession of the Channel coast.

Now it was perfectly clear that an operation aiming at the total defeat of France could no longer be executed at one stroke, as Schlieffen had planned to do. As has been explained above, the requisite conditions no longer obtained. Yet if it were proposed – once the partial victory envisaged by O.K.H. had been won – to proceed with a view to eliminating France entirely as an opponent, the present operation had at least to be related to this ultimate goal! In the first place, it had to bring about the total destruction of the enemy's northern wing, in order to establish decisive superiority for the second move, the aim of which would be to annihilate the remaining western forces in France.

In the second place, it had simultaneously to create a favourable strategic situation from which to launch this subsequent thrust.

To my mind, the operation as drafted offered no guarantee of fulfilling these two basic requirements.

When the German assault formation, Army Group B, which had a total strength of forty-three divisions, arrived in Belgium, it would run into twenty Belgian and – if Holland were brought in – a further ten Dutch divisions. However inferior these troops might be to the Germans in the qualitative sense, their prospects of resistance were favoured by strong fortifications (on both sides of Liège and along the Albert Canal) and natural obstacles (in Belgium the Albert Canal running down to the fortress of Antwerp, and the fortified line of the Meuse pivoted on Namur; in Holland the numerous waterways). Within a very few days, moreover, these forces would be joined by the Anglo-French armies (including all their tank and motorized divisions) already assembled on the Franco-Belgian frontier to meet a German invasion.

Thus the German assault wing would have no opportunity, as in 1914, of achieving strategic surprise by a grand-scale outflanking movement. With the arrival of the Anglo-French forces it would have to fight an opponent as strong as itself – and attack him more or less frontally at that. The success of this first blow must thus be achieved by tactical means, since there was no provision for it in the strategic dispositions for the offensive.

Were the enemy to show any skill in his leadership, he might conceivably succeed in evading an outright defeat in Belgium. Even if he did not manage to hold the fortified line Antwerp–Liège–Meuse (or Semois), he must still be expected to get back behind the lower Somme in reasonable order. Once there, he could draw on his powerful reserves to build up a new front. By this time the German offensive would be losing momentum, and Army Group A would be unable, either by the disposition or the strength of its forces, to prevent the enemy from forming a defence front from the end of the Maginot Line east of Sedan to the lower Somme. In this way the German Army would land in a situation similar to that of 1914 at the end of the autumn battles. Its only advantage would be possession of a broader coastal basis along the Channel. Consequently we should neither have achieved the destruction of the enemy forces in Belgium – which was essential if we were to have adequate superiority in the decisive phase – nor should we have been in a favourable strategic situation for these final battles. The operation planned by O.K.H. would bring partial victory, nothing more.

As it turned out, the enemy was overrun wholesale in Belgium in 1940, thanks to the skilful handling of Army Group B, with the result that the Belgian and Dutch armies were forced to capitulate. But however great our trust in German leadership and the striking power of our armour, these were not successes that could be counted upon in advance. Had the other side been better led, the story might have been a very different one.

The utter débâcle suffered by the enemy in northern Belgium was almost certainly due to the fact that, as a result of the changes later made to the operation plan, the tank units of Army Group A were able to cut straight through his lines of communication and push him away from the Somme.

Finally, there was one other thing that the O.K.H. plan failed to consider – the scope for manœuvre open to a bold and resolute enemy commander. One had no right to assume that such leadership would be lacking, particularly in view of the reputation General Gamelin enjoyed with us. He had certainly made an excellent impression on General Beck when the latter visited him before the war.

A bold enemy commander was in a position to parry the German drive expected through Belgium and simultaneously to mount a large-scale counter-offensive against the southern flank of the German northern wing. Even when the forces earmarked for support of the Belgians and Dutch had been thrown into Belgium, fifty or sixty divisions for such a counterblow could certainly be found in the Maginot Line, which could easily spare them. The further forward Army Group B advanced in the direction of the English Channel and Somme estuary, the better the enemy command could effect its thrust into the deep flank of the Germans' northern wing. Whether Army Group A, with its twenty-two divisions, would be strong enough to parry this was by no means certain. Whatever the answer, any developments on these lines would hardly be strategically conducive to a final solution in the western theatre.

ARMY GROUP A'S PLAN

The above objections, sketched out as they occurred to me when studying the O.K.H. Operation Orders, formed the basis of the proposals we set forth in a series of memoranda aimed at bringing the army leaders round to our own point of view. Since these proposals were inevitably somewhat repetitive, I shall merely summarize them

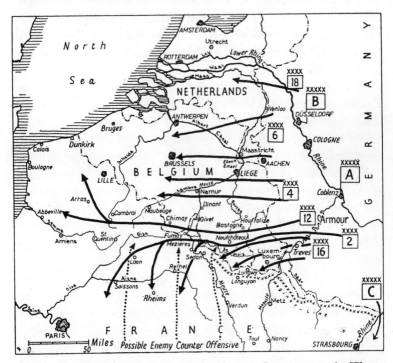

Map 4. Army Group A's Proposals for German Operations in the West.

here, at the same time indicating where they contrasted with the operational intentions of O.K.H.:

1. The *aim* of the western offensive, I submitted, must be to *force an issue by land.* To strive after the limited objectives set out in the O.K.H. Operation Orders justified neither the political hazards (violation of three countries' neutrality) nor the military stakes involved. The offensive capacity of the German Army was our trump card on the Continent, and to fritter it away on half-measures was inadmissible – if only on account of the Soviet Union.

2. The *main weight* of our attack must lie with Army Group A, not B. The proposed thrust by Army Group B would hit the waiting enemy more or less frontally; even if it achieved some initial success, it might well peter out on the Somme.

The real chance lay with Army Group A, and consisted in launching a *surprise attack through the Ardennes* – where the enemy would certainly not be expecting any armour because of the terrain – towards the lower Somme in order to cut off the enemy forces thrown into Belgium forward of that river. This was the only possible means of destroying the enemy's entire northern wing in Belgium preparatory to winning a final victory in France.

3. Besides offering the main *chance*, Army Group A also harboured the main *danger* for the German offensive.

If the enemy acted rightly, he would seek to elude an unfavourable contest in Belgium, possibly by withdrawing behind the Somme. Concurrently he would deploy all his available forces for a grand counter-offensive against our southern flank with the aim of surrounding the main body of the German Army in Belgium or forward of the Lower Rhine. Disinclined though one might be to credit the French High Command with such audacity, and certain though France's allies were to oppose so bold a solution, the possibility could still not be discounted.

If our offensive through northern Belgium were to halt on the lower Somme, the enemy would at least succeed in forming an unbroken defensive front with the reserves he had in hand. This front could start at the north-west end of the Maginot Line east of Sedan and, taking advantage of the Aisne and the Somme, run right down to the Channel.

To prevent this it was vital to smash *any enemy concentrations on our southern flank*, either on both sides of the Meuse or between the Meuse and Oise, before they could reach completion. The cohesion of the enemy front in this area must be destroyed from the outset with a view to turning the flank of the Maginot Line later on.

4. *Army Group A*, with which the operation's main effort must lie (even if initially, for reasons of space, more divisions could be accommodated with Army Group B), must be given three armies instead of two.

One army would drive through southern Belgium and across the

Meuse as already envisaged, but then it must thrust towards the lower Somme to take the enemy forces facing Army Group B in the rear.

Another army must be committed in a south-westerly direction with the task of taking *offensive* action against and smashing any enemy forces concentrating west of the Meuse to counter-attack against our southern flank.

A third army must, as envisaged, cover the deep flank of the overall operation from north of the Maginot Line between Sierk and Mouzon (east of Sedan).

In pursuance of this transfer of the main weight of the operation from Army Group B to Army Group A we duly called for:

(i) *one more army* (which, even if it could not be phased in until our offensive was under way, must be available from the very start) and

(ii) *strong armoured forces.*

These, very much condensed, are the main trends of thought constantly recurring in our Army Group's manifold memoranda to O.K.H.

THE STRUGGLE FOR ARMY GROUP A'S PLAN

Naturally I did not immediately find myself presented with a cut-and-dried operation plan in that October of 1939. Hard work and endeavour must always confront the ordinary mortal before he attains his goal. No ready-made works of art can spring from his brain as did Pallas Athene from the head of Zeus.

Nevertheless, the basic principles of the 'new' plan were contained in the Army Group's very first proposals to O.K.H. (dated 31st October 1939) on operational policy in the event of a German offensive.

To be more precise, there were two documents involved. The first was a letter from the Army Group Commander to the Commander-in-Chief dealing with the *fundamental problem* of carrying out a German offensive in the situation at that particular time.

Von Rundstedt began by emphasizing that the offensive planned in accordance with the Operation Orders of 19th and 29th October *could not have a decisive effect on the war.* The strength of Germany's forces in relation to the enemy's offered no basis for an all-out victory, nor did the operation, being entirely frontal in character, afford any prospect of turning the enemy's flank and taking him in the rear. The probable upshot would be a frontal battle on the Somme. At the same time v. Rundstedt pointed to the difficulties opposing the effective use of tanks and aircraft – our ace cards – in autumn and winter.

Nevertheless, an offensive must still be launched if its success would create the prerequisites for our fleet and air force to go into action against Britain. The experience of World War I had shown that it was not enough to possess only a part of the Channel coast: we must control the whole North French coastline as far as the Atlantic for this purpose.

To expend the offensive capacity of the German Army on a *limited victory* was, with the Soviet Union at our backs, indefensible. This offensive capacity was the decisive factor on the Continent, and the friendship of the Soviet Union would be ensured only as long as we had an army capable of offensive action.

For the time being our army's offensive capacity was invested solely in the regular divisions, and would remain so until the new formations had acquired the necessary degree of training and stability. A crucial offensive could not, however, be mounted with regular divisions alone.

It might be that the Western Powers could be made to take the offensive as the result of pressure by the Luftwaffe on Britain, though even if Britain were to demand such action it was not at all certain whether French fighting morale would stand up to the blood-letting this must entail. From our point of view it was desirable that the enemy should himself be saddled with the burden of attacking fortified positions and with the odium of violating Belgian (and Dutch) neutrality. At the same time one could not play a waiting game *indefinitely* and give Britain time to fill in the gaps in her armaments and aircraft production.

From the military point of view the war against Britain could be won only at sea and in the air. It could only be lost on the mainland if the army's offensive capacity were wasted on indecisive battles.

Von Rundstedt's letter thus amounted to a warning not to launch any German offensive *prematurely*—i.e. in the autumn or winter months. In this respect Army Group A and O.K.H. saw eye to eye. They did not agree, however, on the *method* to be adopted, and the Army Group Commander went on record against conducting the operations—for such was the implication of the O.K.H. Operation Orders – in a way which did not assure us of conclusive success.

Army Group A's second communication to O.K.H., dated 31st October and now put in the form of a staff letter, supplemented v. Rundstedt's appreciation by making definite recommendations on how we felt a German offensive should be conducted. This document, which already contained the essentials of the 'new' plan, stressed the necessity of:

(a) shifting the *main weight* of the operation as a whole on to the southern wing;

(b) committing *strong motorized forces* in such a manner that they could thrust up from the south into the rear of the Allied troops in northern Belgium;

(c) following up with *an additional army* responsible for warding off, by *offensive* action, any large-scale counter-attack against our southern flank.

One could hardly have expected this letter to evoke any response by 3rd November, the date on which we were visited by the Commander-in-Chief of the Army and his Chief-of-Staff, though it did enable me – acting on instructions from Colonel-General v. Rundstedt – to state our case direct. Colonel-General v. Brauchitsch, however, turned down the request I made for additional forces (the extra army and strong tank units) with the remark that he 'only wished he could spare them'. This made it clear enough that he still entirely refused to accept our point of view. Finally, however, he did promise us an armoured division and two motorized regiments from the army reserve.

Unfortunately our visitors also made it only too clear that they had strong reservations about the projected offensive in the west, specifically with regard to the chances of winning a decisive victory. Understandably enough they asked our army and corps commanders to report on the present condition of their formations, but the way they received the complaints – of which there were naturally many – about the state of the newly formed divisions left one with the impression that they personally set no very great store by the offensive.

To compensate for this impression, Colonel-General v. Rundstedt himself addressed the generals of the Army Group a few days later. By indicating the operational standpoint of his own staff, he showed them that there was actually every prospect of a victorious decision in the west, even if it were not expedient to take the offensive before the spring.

On 6th November, when replying to an O.K.H. request for a statement of our intentions in pursuance of the Operation Order, we put our recommendations up once again, but received no answer.

All this time Hitler's 'weather boffins', the Air Ministry meteorologists, were scampering merrily up and down their ladders. Every time they predicted even a brief spell of good weather, Hitler issued the code-word for the final troop assemblies. But on each occasion the boffins had to retract and the attack was called off.

On 12th November we were taken completely by surprise by the following teleprinter message:

'The Führer has now directed that a third group of fast-moving troops will be formed on the southern wing of Twelfth Army or in the sector allotted to Sixteenth Army, and that this will be directed against Sedan and the area to the east of it, taking advantage of the unwooded terrain on either side of Arlon, Tintigny and Florenville. Composition: H.Q. 19 Corps, 2 and 10 Panzer Divisions, one motorized division, the Leibstandarte and the Gross-Deutschland Regiment.

'The task of this group will be:

(a) To defeat mobile enemy forces thrown into southern Belgium and thereby to lighten the task of Twelfth and Sixteenth Armies;

(b) To gain a surprise hold on the west bank of the Meuse by or south-east of Sedan, thereby creating a favourable situation for the subsequent phases of the operation, specifically in the event of the armoured units under command of Sixth and Fourth Armies proving unsuccessful in their own sectors.'

The above was followed by an appropriate amplification of the O.K.H. Operation Order. It was apparent from the wording of the message that this allocation of 19 Corps to Army Group A had been made on Hitler's orders. What had caused him to do this? Possibly he conceived the idea following a recent interview with the commander of Sixteenth Army, General Busch. The latter was acquainted with my views and may have brought up our wish for armoured forces for a swift drive through the Ardennes. It is also possible that Hitler reached the decision on his own. He had a keen eye for tactical openings and spent much time brooding over maps. He may have realized that the easiest place to cross the Meuse was at Sedan, whereas the armour of Fourth Army further up would find the going much harder. Very likely he had recognized the Meuse crossing at Sedan as a promising spot (in the sense that it offered an opening on the river for the southern wing of Army Group A) and wanted – as he always did – to go for every tempting objective at once. In practice, pleased though we were at acquiring the panzer corps, it still entailed dispersing our armour, and for that reason the commander of 19 Panzer Corps, General Guderian, was at first none too happy about his formation's new role, his contention having always been that tanks should be used to 'punch hard' at one place at a time. Only when I had briefed him on our Army Group's operational motives for seeking to shift the main weight of the entire offensive to the southern wing and drawn his attention to the alluring target of the Somme estuary in the enemy's rear did Guderian show unbounded enthusiasm for our plan. Ultimately it was his *élan* which inspired our tanks on their dash round the backs of the enemy to the Channel coast. For me, of course, it was a great relief to know that my idea of pushing large numbers of tanks through such difficult country as the Ardennes was considered feasible by Guderian.

To come back once more to the allocation of 19 Panzer Corps, there is no doubt that Hitler envisaged it only as a *tactical* measure which would at the same time facilitate Army Group B's own crossing of the Meuse.

Nor did O.K.H.'s amplification to its Operation Order include any reference to setting new objectives. It had no notion whatever of seeking, or even paving the way for, a final decision by mounting an outflanking movement from Army Group A's sector in the direction of the Somme estuary.

On 21st November the Commander-in-Chief of the Army and his Chief-of-Staff paid us another visit in Coblenz. In addition to the army commanders of Army Group A, the commander of Army Group B, Colonel-General v. Bock, and his army commanders also attended.

It was a noteworthy occasion for one reason in particular. Von Brauchitsch had asked that the army group and army commanders should state their intentions, and what dispositions they had made, in pursuance of the O.K.H. Operation Order. Yet when our own turn came round, he announced that he only wanted the army commanders to speak. It was evident from this that he wished to obviate any risk of Army Group A's ventilating its disagreement with the Operation Order.

Consequently we had no choice but to hand the heads of O.K.H. a further memorandum we had prepared on our opinion of how the offensive should be conducted.

This, like its predecessors of 31st October and 6th November and the four that followed on 30th November, 6th December, 18th December and 12th January, set forth the principal considerations on which Army Group A's plan for the overall operation were based. Each of these memoranda propounded substantially the same concepts as have already been developed above, so I shall refrain from recapitulating them.

In the meantime, it seems, Hitler had been giving some thought to the employment of 19 Panzer Corps in the sector of Army Group A and to the problem of how to move up additional forces in support of it in case the thrust delivered by the armour still massed with Army Group B did not achieve the quick results expected of it. We are told by Greiner, who kept the O.K.W. war diary, that about mid-November Hitler asked O.K.H. whether, and by what methods, Guderian's armour could be reinforced should the need arise. Greiner also reports that about 20th November Hitler sent O.K.H. a directive instructing it to make provisions for a rapid switch of the offensive's main effort from Army Group B to Army Group A in the event of 'the latter's achieving quicker and more far-reaching results'.

Acting apparently on this directive, O.K.H. at the end of November moved up 14 Motorized Corps from east of the Rhine to locations behind Army Group A's assembly area. The corps still remained part of the army reserve, nonetheless, with O.K.H. retaining the express right to decide, in accordance with the situation, whether it would eventually be allotted to Army Group A or B.

It is not clear whether Hitler himself conceived the idea of shifting the main weight of the operation to Army Group A or whether he was even then aware of Army Group A's views.

On 24th November, the day after he had addressed the heads of the three services at Berlin, Hitler received Colonel-General v. Rundstedt and Generals Busch and Guderian. I gathered from Busch during the return journey to Coblenz that Hitler had shown great sympathy for the Army Group's viewpoint at the interview. If this is so, I think he must have been primarily concerned with the reinforcement of our Army Group's armour as a means of opening up the line of the Meuse at Sedan in the interest of Army Group B. I consider it most unlikely that v. Rundstedt used this occasion to present Hitler with our own draft plan, particularly as v. Brauchitsch's position was so precarious just then.

As for Greiner's statement that Hitler had heard of our plan as early as the end of October from his military assistant, Schmundt, this at least seems doubtful as far as the timing is concerned. However, Schmundt did come to see us on instructions from Hitler to ascertain whether an offensive really was precluded – as our reports claimed – by bad weather and the state of the ground. On that occasion Colonel Blumentritt, our Chief of Operations, and Lieutenant-Colonel v. Tresckow told Schmundt in confidence that the Army Group had sent O.K.H. a plan of attack which it considered to be better than the latter's own.

A few days later Blumentritt, with my consent (given only very reluctantly, though with v. Rundstedt's approval), sent Colonel Schmundt a copy of my last memorandum. Whether it was passed on to Hitler or even to Jodl I cannot say. At all events, when Hitler sent for me on 17th February 1940 to hear my views on an offensive in the west, he gave not the least hint that he had seen any of our memoranda to O.K.H.

It may be that Hitler's object at the end of November was to ensure that the main effort could be shifted from Army Group B to Army Group A when operations were *already in progress*. This still did not imply any deviation from the plan as it stood to date, nor did it mean that he had accepted our operational precepts. Despite the fact that 14 Motorized Corps had been moved up behind our assembly area, the Operation Order remained fully in force. Just as before, success was to be sought first and foremost by Army Group B's massed push through northern Belgium while Army Group A kept to its protective role. The only difference was that Hitler wanted to be in a position to switch the main effort of the offensive at a later stage if Army Group

B's successes did not come up to expectation or if Army Group A achieved quicker results.

This was made palpably clear by the reply I received from General Halder to a fresh memorandum I had submitted on *30th November*. It was, incidentally, the first acknowledgement of our recommendations to date.

The gist of our own remarks had been that a new point of attack – i.e. through Army Group A – now seemed to be emerging after all, and that provided the Ardennes breakthrough were successful, this must entail extending the scope of the operation just as we had suggested.

While conceding that our views largely coincided with those of O.K.H., Halder insisted that the latter's orders regarding 19 and 14 Corps did not establish a new focal point for the offensive, but merely provided for the *possibility* of creating one if the need were to arise. 'Owing to influences beyond our control,' he added, 'the decision as to where the main effort will be made has changed from a problem of planning to one of command during the operation itself.'

Two things could be gathered from the above. The first was that Hitler intended that his right to make the crucial decision should also cover the actual execution of the offensive. The second was that he intended making the location of the main effort dependent on how the offensive developed and that, for the time being at any rate, he was either unacquainted with our own plan or disinclined to adopt it.

The latter impression was confirmed by a reply given to me by Halder on the telephone on 15th December.

On 6th December I had sent him another personal letter recapitulating all the aspects favouring our operation plan. This letter actually contained the 'new' plan in its entirety. When Halder had still not replied by 15th December, I rang up General v. Stülpnagel, the *Oberquartiermeister I*, and asked him how much longer O.K.H. proposed to ignore our proposals. This produced the afore-mentioned telephone call from Halder. He assured me that the army leaders entirely agreed with us, but were under strict instructions to leave the main effort with Army Group B or, alternatively, to allow for a shift of this effort in the course of the offensive.

One might have assumed from this that the heads of O.K.H. had actually come round to our point of view and that they would have brought it to Hitler's notice in some form or other. However, I learnt at the same time from General Warlimont, Jodl's deputy, and from the Chief Operations Officer of the Wehrmacht Operations Staff, the future General v. Lossberg, that O.K.H. had never submitted any recommendations to Hitler on the lines suggested by us! It was all rather perplexing as far as we were concerned.

Whether or not O.K.H. was sincere in agreeing with us, the idea of not placing the main effort with Army Group A until after the offensive had started was in any case quite incompatible with the operations we at Army Group had in mind.

Admittedly, it was Napoleon who coined the phrase *on s'engage partout et on voit*. For the French this has become almost axiomatic, particularly since their Lorraine initiative in 1914 proved such a fiasco. It is also an axiom which the Allied High Command could undoubtedly have adopted in 1940. Since they wished to saddle us with the burden of taking the offensive, they would have been absolutely right to sit back and wait. Their duty lay in evading a test of strength in Belgium in order to deal a counterstroke against the southern flank of our offensive with the most powerful forces they could muster.

In our own case, however, there could be no question of waiting to see where and when we should play our trumps, for the operation plan of Army Group A was based on *surprise*. The enemy could hardly be expecting a strong armoured force to drive through the Ardennes with a whole army in its train. But this drive would attain its objective, the Lower Somme, only if any enemy forces thrown into southern Belgium were successfully overrun. We had to cross the Meuse at the same time as the remnants of these troops if we were subsequently to take the enemy forces facing Army Group B in northern Belgium in the rear.

Similarly, any attempt to smash the deployment of strong enemy reserves on our southern flank – between the Meuse and Oise, for example – before it could be completed, thereby creating a favourable jumping-off position for the 'second act', the destruction of the remaining enemy forces, could succeed only if we had enough forces down there to retain the initiative.

To wait and see 'which way the cat jumped' before deciding where to place one's main effort was tantamount to abandoning the chance of annihilating the enemy forces in northern Belgium by an outflanking movement from the south. At the same time it would mean allowing the enemy to deploy for that counterblow on our southern flank which constituted his own chance of victory. It was a chance, albeit, of which the enemy high command never availed itself.

As for the idea of waiting for adequate forces to be allocated to Army Group A and making the decision to deliver the main thrust there dependent on whether we managed to achieve surprise with inadequate forces, all one can do is to quote Moltke's dictum that 'an error in the first stages of deployment can never be made good'.

In short, one could not wait to see how our offensive developed – whether the massed drive of Army Group B would smash the enemy in Belgium or whether a lone 19 Panzer Corps would get through to Sedan. If Army Group A's plan were to be adopted, we must be given adequate armour and three armies *from the outset*, even if the third army could not be phased in until room for it had been found in the course of the advance. That was why, in my memorandum of 6th December, I had called for not two armies of twenty-two infantry divisions and only one panzer corps, but three armies of forty divisions and two mobile corps. (Incidentally, this was the actual number we secured after Hitler had intervened and our plan had been accepted.)

And so we had to go on with the struggle. Our prime concern from now on was to ensure that from the very first stage of the operation not only 19 Panzer Corps but also 14 Motorized Corps were utilized for the thrust through the Ardennes, across the Meuse at Sedan and on towards the Lower Somme. Furthermore, it was essential that the third army we had requested should be available from the outset to take offensive action against any enemy deployment on our southern flank west of the Meuse.

If we could get these two demands accepted – even if O.K.H. still would not accept our views as a whole – the offensive was bound to be guided into channels conducive to the *conclusive* victory for which we strove.

Admittedly, even our own operation plan would not – as Moltke put it – extend with any certainty beyond the first encounter with the main body of the enemy – least of all if a lack of adequate forces brought the attack to a standstill in its preliminary stages.

But in that very same context Moltke pointed out that the military commander must look past this first encounter 'and keep his eye fixed on the ultimate goal'. That goal, as we saw it, could be none other than total victory on the European mainland. Such must be the object of the German offensive throughout, even if two distinct phases were needed to achieve it.

The Napoleonic precept quoted above – which, in the last analysis, is exactly what Hitler's reservations regarding the location of the main effort boiled down to – might provide an admirable solution in other situations. In our own case it meant aiming short of absolute victory.

On *18th December*, my letter to the Chief-of-Staff on 6th December not having produced the desired effect, I submitted to v. Rundstedt a 'Draft Operation Order' for the western offensive based on our own conception of the operation. It was to serve him as a brief in interviews with the Commander-in-Chief of the Army and – if the latter agreed – with Hitler. The interview with v. Brauchitsch took place on 22nd December, but there was no meeting with Hitler. O.K.H. was also sent the above draft in writing, as I hoped that when expressed in this cut-and-dried form our views would have more chance of convincing the O.K.W. Operations Branch than the purely theoretical representations made hitherto. Only after the war did I find that the Operations Branch never received any of our memoranda from Halder.

The weather in the second half of December put any thought of an offensive out of the question. In any case, it seemed advisable to allow an interval to elapse before we again started pressing for a change in the operation plan, since we had supplied quite enough food for thought for the time being. As a result I was able to go home for Christmas. On my return to Coblenz from Liegnitz I looked in at O.K.H. in Zossen to find out what impression our draft had made. I was again assured by General v. Stülpnagel that they were much in agreement with our views, but that O.K.H. was bound by an order from Hitler to leave the decision open as to where the main effort should be made.

As before, it was not clear whether the Commander-in-Chief had made any mention of our recommendations to Hitler. It seemed improbable that he had done so, since I learnt from Lieutenant-Colonel Heusinger, then G.S.O. 1 of the Operations Branch, that v. Brauchitsch had not been near Hitler since 5th November.

In the New Year Hitler's weather boffins livened up again. The clear, frosty weather promised a fine spell which would enable the Luftwaffe to go into action, though the cold – accompanied by a thick blanket of snow in the Eifel and Ardennes – was by no means propitious to armour. At all events, Hitler again issued the code-word which set the troops moving into their final assembly areas for the offensive.

Undeterred by this, we sent O.K.H. one more memorandum on 12th January. It bore the title *Western Offensive* and again set forth the views we had so often expressed on the need to aim at a decisive victory. Although there could be no question of changing the Operation Order at that particular juncture, we felt that once the actual operation had started our views would still have to be taken into consideration. In any case, the order to start the offensive had been countermanded so many times already that it was reasonable to hope for a repetition that would still leave us time to get the plan fundamentally changed.

To achieve that, however, we had to remove the stumbling-block which to date had prevented our own plan from being accepted. Where did this lie? According to what O.K.H. had told us, it lay with Hitler. O.K.H. had repeatedly emphasized that though largely in agreement with our views, it was under orders from Hitler not to fix the focal point of the attack until the operations were under way. But had O.K.H. in fact ever apprised Hitler of our plan, which differed so radically from its own version? Would it not be possible to convince Hitler if only he could be shown a plan directed not merely at limited objectives but actually visualizing something which, as far as we could see, neither he nor the heads of O.K.H. had seriously considered to date – the possibility of conclusive victory in the west?

To get this clarified once and for all, the memorandum was accompanied by a letter from Colonel-General v. Rundstedt ending with the following sentence:

> 'Now that this Army Group has been informed that the Führer and Supreme Commander has retained overall control of the operations by reserving the right to decide where the main effort will be made (i.e. that O.K.H. is not free to make its own operational decision), I request that this memorandum be submitted to the Führer in person.
>
> (*signed*) V. RUNDSTEDT.'

This demand – which was made at my suggestion and to which the General had immediately been ready to append his signature – did, to a certain extent, contravene German military tradition, which prescribed that only the Commander-in-Chief of the Army or his Chief-of-

Staff were competent to make recommendations to the Supreme Commander.

However, if O.K.H. really agreed with our views, there was nothing to stop it taking up our operation plan and submitting it to Hitler on its own initiative. This would have given it an opportunity of impressing him, and possibly of rehabilitating itself as the ultimate authority in all matters affecting land operations. No one would have been more pleased to see this happen than myself, as one who had striven so much with Colonel-General v. Fritsch and General Beck to give O.K.H. this standing during my period of office as *Oberquartiermeister I*.[1]

If, on the other hand, O.K.H. had already made an unsuccessful attempt to get proposals in line with our own accepted by Hitler, the submission of a plan initiated by Colonel-General v. Rundstedt, of whom Hitler held so high an opinion, would have considerably strengthened its position.

Perhaps it would then still have been possible to dissuade Hitler from making the location of the main effort dependent on the course of operations. This – or so we had been led to believe by O.K.H. – was now the main obstacle to the realization of our policy.

The answer we received to this memorandum was disappointing. It said we were mistaken in supposing that O.K.H. sought only limited objectives, as others were to be fixed in due course. Provision had been made for assigning Army Group A extra forces and an additional army headquarters, but the actual timing must rest with the Commander-in-Chief of the Army. There was, we were told, no occasion to show Hitler our memorandum, with which the Commander-in-Chief was substantially in agreement.

This assurance of the Commander-in-Chief's agreement could still not close our eyes to his unwillingness to advocate to Hitler the fundamental changes which we recommended in the operation plan.

On the contrary, the Operation Order remained in force in its previous form. The outcome of the battle in Belgium was still to be sought by the frontal push of Army Group B, where the main effort would continue to be concentrated for at least the first phase of the offensive.

---

[1] That we at Army Group A never sought publicity as the progenitors of the new strategy is proved by the fact that it only became known after the war following Liddell Hart's talks with v. Rundstedt and Blumentritt. *Author.*

Army Group A remained responsible for protecting this operation. Nothing was done about broadening its task to include a drive towards the lower Somme and round the back of the enemy forces being tackled frontally by Army Group B in northern Belgium.

Any eventual shift in the main weight of the German offensive remained dependent on the progress of operations. Army Group A was not given the armour which, according to our own scheme of operations, must be *under command from the outset* if there were to be any hope of achieving surprise in southern Belgium and driving round behind the enemy in the direction of the Somme estuary. Neither was the Army Group to enjoy the security of having an additional army, necessary though this would be for any offensive action to cover our thrust against the anticipated enemy counterblow.

In other words, we were sticking to that 'irreparable error in the first stages of deployment'. Those responsible did not want to commit themselves to an operation which General Jodl described in February 1940 as 'a roundabout road on which the God of War might catch us'.

Quite unconsciously, the German and Allied High Commands had agreed that it was safer to attack each other head-on in northern Belgium than to become involved in a venturesome operation – on the German side by accepting the plan of Army Group A, on the Allied side by avoiding a conclusive battle in Belgium in order to deal a punishing blow to the southern flank of the German offensive.

Meanwhile something had occurred which many people have since held to be the decisive factor responsible for the fundamental changes which were later made to the operation plan to bring it into line with the recommendations of Army Group A.

The G.S.O. 1 of 7 Airborne Division had made an accidental landing on Belgian territory, as a result of which at least part of First Air Fleet's Operation Order fell into Belgian hands. One had to assume that the Western Powers would learn, through Belgium, of the operation plan existing to date.

In point of fact this misfortune did not lead to any alteration of the operation plan, though it may well have increased the readiness of Hitler and O.K.H. to entertain our Army Group's proposals later on. As it was, a Commander-in-Chief's conference in Bad Godesberg on 25th January of the generals commanding Army Groups A and B and their subordinate armies revealed no change in O.K.H.'s basic attitude. Though the meeting took place some considerable time after the mishap in question, the tasks of the army groups and armies remained the same as before. Army Group B's role was now merely expanded to allow for its Eighteenth Army to occupy the whole of Holland and not – as had previously been intended – only those parts of the country lying outside the so-called 'Fortress of Holland'. As far as Army Group A was concerned, everything remained as before. Though we were able to get Second Army H.Q. brought into our area, it remained, like 14 Motorized Corps, at the disposal of O.K.H. Despite my having pointed out, on my commander's instructions, that sending 19 Panzer Corps through the Ardennes on its own would not bring us success at Sedan now that the enemy had assembled considerable forces (Second French Army) on the Meuse, v. Brauchitsch still refused to place it under our command. This showed that the Supreme Command was just as determined as ever not to shift the main effort until it became clear what course the operations were taking. It also proved that the loss of the Operation Order to the Belgians had done nothing to change the minds of those at the top.

Nevertheless, Army Group H.Q. followed up these representations to O.K.H. on 25th January by a further memorandum five days later based on enemy intelligence we had received in the meantime. We pointed out that strong French forces – particularly mechanized units – could henceforth be expected to be thrown into southern Belgium. In these circumstances there was no point in hoping that 19 Panzer Corps would alone be strong enough either to overcome this enemy grouping or to force a crossing of the river.

Our view was corroborated by a sand-table exercise in Coblenz on 7th February at which we ran through the advance of 19 Panzer Corps and the two armies of our Army Group. It was only too plain from this how problematical the use of 19 Panzer Corps in isolation was going to be. I had the impression that General Halder, who attended the exercise as an observer, was at last beginning to realize the validity of our standpoint.

Meanwhile my own fate had taken a sudden turn. On 27th January I was notified that I had been appointed Commanding General of 38 Corps, the headquarters of which was about to be set up back at home. I learnt from Colonel-General v. Rundstedt that he had already been

informed of this in confidence by the Commander-in-Chief at the conference on 25th January. The reason given was that I could no longer
be passed over in any new corps appointments, as General Reinhardt,
who was my junior, was also being given a corps. Though there was
little or nothing about the move to distinguish it from the normal process of promotion, it still seemed strange to switch the Chief-of-Staff
of an army group just when a big offensive was impending. There were,
after all, other ways of solving the rank problem which supplied the
pretext for this change. It can hardly be doubted, therefore, that my
replacement was due to a desire on the part of O.K.H. to be rid of an
importunate nuisance who had ventured to put up an operation plan at
variance with its own.

At the close of the above-mentioned sand-table exercise, which I had
helped to run, v. Rundstedt thanked me in front of everyone present
for all I had done as his Chief-of-Staff. His choice of words on this
occasion reflected all the kindness and chivalry of that great commander.
It was a further source of satisfaction to me that the two army commanders of our Army Group, Generals Busch and List, as well as
General Guderian, not only deplored my removal but were genuinely
dismayed by it.

On 9th February I left Coblenz for Liegnitz.

My trusty colleagues Colonel Blumentritt and Lieutenant-Colonel v.
Tresckow, however, had no intention of throwing up the sponge and
treating my departure as the end of the struggle for our operation plan.

It was Tresckow, I imagine, who induced his friend Schmundt,
Hitler's military assistant, to fix an opportunity for me to talk to
Hitler personally about the way we thought the offensive in the west
should be conducted.

Be that as it may, on 17th February I was summoned to Berlin to
report to Hitler with the other newly appointed corps commanders.
Our interview was followed by a luncheon at which Hitler, as usual,
did most of the talking. He showed an amazing knowledge of technical
innovations in the enemy States as well as at home; and the reports of a
British destroyer's raid on the *Altmark* inside Norwegian territorial
waters prompted him to dwell at length on the inability of small States
to maintain their neutrality.

As we were taking our leave at the end of the meal, Hitler told me
to come to his study, where he invited me to outline my views on the

handling of the western offensive. I am not clear whether he had already been informed of our plan by Schmundt, and, if so, in what detail. In any case I found him surprisingly quick to grasp the points which our Army Group had been advocating for many months past, and he entirely agreed with what I had to say.

Immediately after this conversation I filed the following minute for the information of H.Q. Army Group A:

'When reporting to the Führer as Commanding General of 38 Corps on 17th February 1940, the former Chief-of-Staff of Army Group A had an opportunity to present the Army Group's viewpoint on the conduct of the operation in the west. The substance of his statements was as follows:

1. The *aim of the offensive* must be to *achieve decisive results on land.* The political and military stakes are too high for the limited objectives defined in the present Operation Order, i.e. defeat of the largest possible elements of the enemy in Belgium and occupation of parts of the Channel coast. Final victory on land must be the goal.

The operations must therefore be directed towards winning a final decision in France and destroying France's resistance.

2. This, contrary to what is laid down in the Operation Order, requires that the main point of effort be placed unequivocally on the southern wing from the start, i.e. with Army Group A; it cannot remain with Army Group B, nor can it be left open. Under present arrangements the best one can do is to attack the Anglo-French forces frontally as they advance into Belgium and to throw them back to the Somme, whereupon the operation may conceivably come to a standstill.

If the main effort is transferred to Army Group A in the south, the task of which is to drive through southern Belgium and over the Meuse in the direction of the *lower Somme*, the strong enemy forces expected in northern Belgium must, if thrown back by Army Group B in frontal attack, be cut off and destroyed. This will be possible only if Army Group A drives swiftly through to the lower Somme. That must be the first phase of the campaign. The second will be the envelopment of the whole French Army with a powerful right hook.

3. To fulfil this task, Army Group A must consist of *three armies*. Another army must therefore be inserted on its northern flank.

The northernmost army of the Army Group (Second) has the task of driving across the Meuse to the lower Somme to intercept the enemy forces retreating before Army Group B. To the south of it another army (Twelfth) must advance over the Meuse on both sides of Sedan and then swing south-west in order to smash *by attack* any French attempt to deploy in strength for a counter-attack west of the Meuse.

On the third army (Sixteenth) will devolve the initially defensive task of covering the southern flank of the operation between the Meuse and Moselle.

It is essential that the Luftwaffe smash the French troop concentrations at an early date, because if the French do attempt anything, it will be to carry out a large-scale counter-attack west or on both sides of the Meuse, possibly extending as far as the Moselle.

4. To send 19 Panzer Corps out on its own to force the Meuse at Sedan is to do things by halves. If the enemy comes to meet us with strong motorized forces in southern Belgium, the corps will be too weak to crush them quickly and get straight across the line of the Meuse. Conversely, if the enemy confines himself to holding the Meuse with the strong forces he has there at present, the corps will not be able to cross the river alone.

If motorized forces are to lead the advance, at least two corps must cross the Meuse simultaneously at Charleville and Sedan, independent of the armour directed against the Meuse at Givet by Fourth Army. Thus 14 Corps must be put alongside Guderian's corps from the outset; there can be no question of making its use with Army Groups A or B conditional on future developments.

The Führer indicated his agreement with the ideas put forward. Shortly afterwards the new and final Operation Order was issued.'

Unfortunately I no longer had access to this final Operation Order. I only know that its issue was ordered by Hitler on 20th February.

In its essentials it satisfied the demands for which I had fought so long. It provided for:

1. Two panzer corps (the 19th under General Guderian and the 14th under General v. Wietersheim) to lead the advance across the line of the Meuse between Charleville and Sedan. They were united under the newly created command of a 'panzer group' led by General v. Kleist.

2. The final allocation of H.Q. Second Army (previously with Army Group B) to Army Group A and the provision of the requisite forces. It would now be possible to insert this army immediately space became available between the Army Group boundaries after Sixteenth Army had wheeled south.

3. The placing of Fourth Army (previously with Army Group B) under command of Army Group A, to give the latter the necessary manœuvrability in its advance towards the lower Somme. (Army Group A had consistently called for at least the southernmost corps of this army in order to extend the boundaries of its own advance. Greiner is mistaken in putting the time of this change in the order of battle as far back as November. It was only implemented in pursuance of the new Operation Order.)

By these new instructions O.K.H. implied that it fully accepted the Army Group's point of view. The main weight of the operation as a whole was transferred to the southern wing to the fullest extent permitted by the breadth of the ground available to us north of the Maginot Line and the road network existing there. At the same time Army Group B remained strong enough, with three armies, to discharge its task in northern Belgium and Holland with the overwhelming success now known to us.

Army Group A, on the other hand, was now able to surprise the enemy by thrusting through the Ardennes and across the Meuse to the lower Somme. In this way it could prevent the enemy forces fighting in Belgium from withdrawing behind this river. It would likewise have been possible to deal effectively with any big counterblow against the southern flank of the German offensive.

As far as the *execution* of the German assault operation in May 1940 is concerned, I would say this:

The attack of Army Group B, thanks to the superiority of the German troops, and especially the armoured units, had a more decisive success than one might have expected in view of the strength of the Belgian fortifications and the fact that it was compelled to attack frontally.

Despite this, the really decisive reason for the Allies' utter defeat in northern Belgium was still the surprise thrust through the Ardennes, across the Meuse to the Somme estuary and ultimately against the Channel harbours. Apart from the energetic leadership of Colonel-General v. Rundstedt, this success is, I feel, primarily due to the tremendous verve with which General Guderian translated the Army Group's operational principles into action.

The success in northern Belgium was not as complete as it might have been. The enemy succeeded, according to Churchill's figures, in evacuating 338,226 men (26,176 of them French) from Dunkirk, though they lost all their heavy weapons and equipment in the process. This successful evacuation must be attributed to the intervention of Hitler, who twice stopped the onward sweep of our armour – once during its advance to the coast and again outside Dunkirk.

Three different reasons have been given for the latter order, the true effect of which was to throw a golden bridge across the Channel for the British Army. The first reason is that Hitler wished to spare the German armour for the second act of the French campaign, in which connexion Keitel is said to have told him that the ground around Dunkirk was bad tank country. Another reason offered is that Göring assured Hitler that the Luftwaffe was quite capable of preventing the escape from Dunkirk unaided. In view of Göring's thirst for prestige and his proclivity to boastfulness, I think it extremely probable that he did make some statement to this effect. Both arguments were wrong from the military point of view.

The third reason given is that Hitler – according to reports of a conversation between him and v. Rundstedt – deliberately allowed the British to escape because he believed it would facilitate an understanding with Britain.

Whatever the answer may be, Dunkirk was one of Hitler's most decisive mistakes. It hampered him in attempting the invasion of Britain and subsequently enabled the British to fight in Africa and Italy.

While Hitler accepted Army Group A's idea of cutting off the enemy in northern Belgium by driving through the Ardennes to the sea and allowed this to be carried out as far as the gates of Dunkirk, he did not entirely adopt its other idea of simultaneously creating a point of departure for the second phase. The German command was thus content to cover the dash of Army Group A's mechanized elements to the sea against counter-attack on either side of the Meuse by dropping off the succeeding divisions like a long string of pearls to defend the threatened southern flank. Apparently it was thought too risky that any enemy attempt to counter-attack in strength should be thwarted by immediately striking south to the west of the Meuse and thereby tearing apart the enemy front between the Meuse and Oise once and for all.

As was to be seen later on in the Russian campaign, Hitler had a certain instinct for operational problems, but lacked the thorough training of a military commander which enables the latter to accept considerable risks in the course of an operation because he knows he can master them. In this case, therefore, Hitler preferred the safe solution of defensive action to the bolder method suggested by Army Group A. It was his good fortune that the enemy commander did not mount any big counter-offensive, though in fact the latter could well have assembled some fifty divisions for this purpose on both sides of the Meuse – possibly extending as far east as the Moselle – even if it had meant temporarily abandoning everything in Holland and Belgium outside the fortified zones.

And so, after the first act of the German offensive had been completed, both opponents again found themselves facing each other on a continuous front running along the Maginot Line to Carignan and thence along the Aisne and lower Somme. The Germans' first task was to penetrate this front all over again. That the second phase of the German offensive so soon led to the total capitulation of the enemy is primarily due to his inability, after his losses in northern Belgium, adequately to man the whole of his front from the Swiss frontier to the sea. Another reason was that the morale of the French Army had already been badly dented – not to mention the fact that the enemy possessed nothing matching the quality of the German armoured formations. Had the Allied Commander-in-Chief acted as H.Q. Army Group A thought he should, he would have decided on a large-scale offensive on both sides of the Meuse. According to the plan of Army Group A, however, this would have been smashed while still in the assembly stage. If Army Group B, after simultaneously encircling the enemy in northern Belgium, had then wheeled forward over the lower Somme to envelop the rest of the French forces after the pattern of the Schlieffen Plan, we should have finished up fighting a battle in the rear of the Maginot Line with the fronts reversed.

In view of the fact that, with the exception of the British escape from Dunkirk, we ultimately gained a brilliant victory in the French theatre of war, the above observations may appear superfluous. Perhaps their only importance is to show that even if the enemy had displayed greater energy and better judgement, the 'new' plan would still have won the campaign – even allowing for the critical moments that might have occurred in the first phase between the Meuse and Moselle.

6

COMMANDING GENERAL,
38 ARMY CORPS

THE BYSTANDER

THE PART I subsequently played in the execution of the western offensive was so insignificant that I could well afford to leave it out of these memoirs altogether. My primary reason for including it is to pay grateful tribute to the bravery and extraordinary achievements of the troops who served under me at the time. Another is that the operations of 38 Corps following the Germans' successful breakthrough on the Somme will serve to illustrate a *pursuit* that was kept up right across the Seine and down as far as the Loire and never gave the enemy a moment's peace until his final collapse.

During the months in which others continued to work on the ideas for which I had fought, I initially had the modest task of watching my corps headquarters and the ancillary signals regiment assemble in Stettin. From time to time I received instructions to inspect new divisions in the process of being set up in Pomerania and Poznań.

On 10th May 1940 I learnt of the start of the German offensive in the west over the radio in Liegnitz, where I had gone for a short leave. It goes without saying that during the next few days all my wishes and most ardent hopes were with our troops as they drove through the Ardennes. Would they succeed in racing across Luxembourg and penetrating the Belgian defences on either side of Bastogne before strong French forces could close in? Would it be possible to maintain the momentum of the armour as it went over the Meuse at Sedan and created the basis for an encirclement of the enemy's northern wing?

The reader will appreciate that I was not feeling exactly grateful to the body which had banished me into the German hinterland at the very moment when the plan for which I had struggled so long and so doggedly was coming to fruition in the west.

On the evening of 10th May came the order to move H.Q. 38 Corps up to Brunswick. From there the next move took us to Düsseldorf,

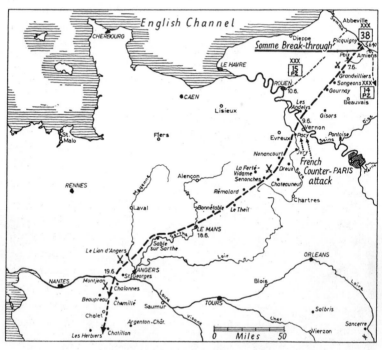

Map 5. 38 Corps' Advance from the Somme to the Loire.

where we came under command of Army Group B. For the next few days I had nothing else to do but 'swan' around inspecting the powerful Belgian positions which had fallen in the first assault on the Meuse at Maastricht and along the Albert Canal, as well as the very up-to-date fort of Eben-Emael, which had been taken in a surprise raid and was still under fire from Belgian batteries further back. I also visited Army Group B and Sixth Army to brief myself on the progress of the operations. I gathered that they still had no clear picture of what the enemy ultimately proposed to do. Neither, it seemed, had O.K.H., since it continued to cloak its future intentions in silence and confined itself to extending the boundary between the two army groups further to the north-west.

On 16th May our headquarters came under command of Army Group A, and the next day I reported to my erstwhile commander, Colonel-General v. Rundstedt, in Bastogne. I received a most cordial welcome from him, my successor, General v. Sodenstern, and the rest of my old staff, and here at last I learnt how well the operation through the Ardennes and over the Meuse had progressed. Our Corps was to go over to Twelfth Army, which would carry on with the westward drive towards the lower Somme, whereas the new Second Army was to be inserted between Twelfth and Sixteenth Armies with a front facing south-west.

Immediately on my arrival at H.Q. Twelfth Army I experienced a piece of interference by Hitler in the conduct of military operations. Acting on Hitler's instructions, O.K.H. sent down an order to the effect that Panzer Group Kleist must not go any further than the Oise for the time being and that Twelfth Army was to swing south-west and go over to the defensive. Second Army was now to be inserted between Fourth and Twelfth Armies to take over the further advance west. The reason given was that the Führer wished at all costs to avoid any German setback, however temporary, which would boost the already abysmally low morale of the French populace. He feared that such a setback might actually occur if Twelfth Army continued its envisaged drive westwards towards the lower Somme and got caught in the flank by a French counter-attack coming up west of the Meuse from the south.

In other words, the propagandist interests of the politician were already beginning to impinge upon the job of supreme commander. On the one hand it was clear that in halting Panzer Group Kleist on the Oise one risked losing the chance to destroy the very enemy forces in northern Belgium which the Panzer Group was supposed to take in the rear. At the same time the order that Twelfth Army was to go over to the defensive on the front facing south-west meant abandoning the initiative in the area between the Meuse and Oise. As it happened, there was no reason at the time for expecting any large-scale counter-attack in this sector. As Army Group A saw it, the enemy would need at least another week to bring up the forces necessary for a counter-offensive – if, indeed, he had any such plan in mind. The whole point was, however, that one of the basic propositions repeatedly put to O.K.H. by the Army Group during the winter had been that an *offensive* solution should be found for securing the southern flank of the thrust towards the lower Somme.

It was now apparent that Hitler, though not bold enough to accept a temporary risk on the southern flank of the German offensive, was already claiming the right to exercise a personal and detailed control of army operations.

The fact, however, that he was able at this juncture to plead the spectre of an even temporary German setback as grounds for intervening may perhaps have been due to O.K.H.'s failure – despite the advice given earlier by the Army Group – to insert Second Army into the front as soon as the first German forces had crossed the Meuse. It could go either between Fourth and Twelfth Armies to carry on with the drive for the lower Somme or between Twelfth and Sixteenth Armies for the *offensive* advance to the south-west between the Meuse and Oise. The reason for the omission cannot have been the lack of space for further divisions in the front line, since the important thing was to have an army headquarters in the line in time for the divergence which must now ensue in the direction of the thrusts. Room for more divisions would be found in due course when the zone of operations broadened out.

This example only serves to show once again that no operations plan will ever be implemented to the full extent envisaged by its originators, even when no cogent grounds exist for departing from it.

Even if on this occasion Hitler's interference did not seriously prejudice operations (as was subsequently the case when Panzer Group Kleist was halted outside Dunkirk), the defensive role he had allotted to Twelfth Army still enabled the enemy to build up a new front on the Aisne which had to be cracked all over again in the second phase of the French campaign at the cost of some very heavy fighting. The chance of finally putting an end by offensive action to any coherent French defence in this decisive stretch of front had been needlessly sacrificed. This very point – together with the encirclement of the enemy's northern wing – had been one of the cornerstones of our operational recommendations to O.K.H. in consideration of the inevitable second phase of the German offensive.

Meanwhile our headquarters had been moved as far forward as the picturesque little Luxembourg town of Clerf. At this stage we ceased to be onlookers and were put in charge of a number of the divisions following in the rear of Second Army. It was a somewhat uninspiring task to be given just when the decisive defeat of the enemy's northern wing was at hand.

About this time news reached me that my brother-in-law, Egbert v. Loesch, had been posted missing near Brussels as commander of a dive-bomber squadron. Egbert, my wife's youngest brother but one, had lived with us for several years in Dresden and Magdeburg when he was still at school. Always my wife's favourite brother, he had grown as dear to us as a son, and his young wife was now living with us in Liegnitz. For weeks to come she, her mother and my wife were tormented by worry and uncertainty, as no information was forthcoming on the fate of Egbert's aircraft and crew. The only thing known with any reasonable certainty was that they had crashed as Egbert's squadron was going in to the attack. Not until after the French campaign, was I able to have a proper investigation made, and after a long search the wreckage of the aircraft was located in the vicinity of Brussels. Inquiries with the inhabitants of a nearby village revealed that the aircraft had received a direct hit from an A.A. shell just as it went into its dive. Two members of the crew had managed to bale out, but both had been shot dead by Belgian troops, one while he was still floating down and the other after he had safely landed. My brother-in-law and the other man had died in the aircraft.

On 25th May my headquarters received orders to relieve H.Q. 14 Panzer Corps, which General v. Kleist had left behind with 9 Panzer and 2 Motorized Division to secure his rear on the lower Somme, in the Abbeville–Amiens sector. We took over on 27th May.

At this stage there was still no firm front on the lower Somme. 14 Panzer Corps' 2 Motorized Division (which was to be relieved by 57 Infantry Division) was holding a bridgehead around Abbeville on the left – or southern – bank of the river. 9 Panzer Division had the same task at Amiens. The intervening ground was merely being kept under surveillance.

So far the enemy, too, had been unable to bring up sufficient forces to form a new front along the lower Somme. Our Amiens bridgehead was apparently faced by a French colonial division and some British forces and the Abbeville bridgehead by a British division.

Our job was to hold both bridgeheads. Initially 9 Panzer Division and the 2 Motorized Division due to be relieved at Abbeville were to remain north of the Somme as mobile reserves. Shortly afterwards, however, they were quite rightly pulled up to the Channel coast to be used in the battle there.

General v. Wietersheim, Commanding General of 14 Panzer Corps, had told me at the hand-over that he did not anticipate any large-scale enemy activity. One hour after he left, reports came in that both bridgeheads were being violently attacked and that enemy armour had appeared in each place. However, both attacks were beaten off by the afternoon after several heavy French tanks had been knocked out at Amiens and thirty light and medium British ones at Abbeville. Of the latter, a gunner called Bringforth accounted for nine single-handed. He was the first private soldier I put up for the Knight's Cross.

Even so, I regarded these attacks as clear proof that the enemy was either hoping to get a relief force over the Somme to his hard-pressed northern wing or intending to set up a new front on the lower Somme. This confronted us with the same problem as I mentioned earlier in connexion with Hitler's order for Twelfth Army. Ought we in the same way to remain on the defensive on the lower Somme, or should we try to retain the initiative?

The defensive solution which 14 Panzer Corps had apparently been told to adopt would unquestionably allow the enemy to build up a strong new defence line along the lower Somme. Indeed, it was problematical whether we should even be able to hold the Amiens and Abbeville bridgeheads once the enemy brought up fresh forces. The two mechanized divisions provisionally left in reserve north of the Somme were most unsuitable for any battle for the bridgeheads, since they could neither be plugged into these to strengthen their defences nor could they be employed in a counter-attack role until the enemy had actually flattened the bridgeheads, wiped out the divisions inside them and come across the Somme.

The conclusion I drew from the above – and several times submitted to General v. Kluge, the commander of Fourth Army, of which we now formed part – was that we should use both mechanized divisions (or else both infantry divisions due to replace them) to carry out a surprise river-crossing between the two bridgeheads and deliver flanking attacks against the enemy forces assaulting them. What I had in mind was to fight a mobile action to the south – i.e. forward – of the river until such time as the battle in northern Belgium was over and the German northern wing could wheel forward across the Somme. Our aim should be to keep this open for it and to prevent the enemy from forming a continuous front. There was no denying, of course, that as long as the corps fought a lone action south of the river these tactics might land it in a difficult situation. It was a risk one had to accept if, in the interest of strategic continuity, we were to avoid the far-from-easy task of attacking a Somme front which the enemy had had time to stabilize and consolidate.

Unfortunately, however, the commander of Fourth Army paid no heed to our repeated representations and would not release the second-line divisions which were, in fact, available for a river-crossing. Whether this was a personal decision or due to instructions from O.K.H. I do not know. As a result, we had no choice but to carry on with the defence in the bridgeheads, while the enemy was left in a position to establish a continuous front along the river in between them. The fact of the matter was that people have normally only heard of defending a river from *behind* it or of keeping it open by means of fixed bridgeheads. The possibility of contesting a river-line by fighting a mobile action in *front* of it is not usually mentioned in the textbooks.

For the next few days the enemy kept up his attacks on the two bridgeheads and for a time the position around Amiens looked troublesome. A tour of the units there convinced me that everything was in order, however. A particularly prominent part in these defensive actions was played by 116 Infantry Regiment, then led by my old comrade from the Third Regiment of Footguards, the future General Herrlein.

At Abbeville, on the other hand, things took a critical turn on 29th May. Here, after a series of strenuous marches, 57 Infantry Division, which had so far no experience of action, had taken over from 2 Motorized Division. Shortly after its arrival an enemy attack supported by strong British armour broke into a number of German positions and caused heavy losses not only in killed and wounded, but also, as was later discovered, in prisoners. I myself had driven out to Abbeville just in time to meet a German battalion which, probably through having misunderstood its orders, had evacuated its positions and was now marching back through the town. I turned it straight round again, and in due course the division was master of the situation.

As General v. Kluge had actually authorized us to pull out of both bridgeheads if need be, he duly rejected a fresh request from us for permission to cross the Somme on both sides of Abbeville and take the enemy attacking there in a pincer. It was evident that the men at the top wished to avoid running the least risk until the battle in northern Belgium were concluded and an 'orderly' deployment could be carried out against the new front now being formed by the enemy.

It went without saying that the enemy would also make use of this interval to bring up his own reserves and establish a new front from the end of the Maginot Line in the Carignan area down to the mouth of the Somme. Once already, between the Oise and Meuse, Hitler had voluntarily surrendered the initiative, thereby enabling the enemy to form his front on the Aisne. Now all attempts to retain the initiative south of the Somme had been renounced as well.

ASSAULT MARCH TO THE LOIRE

While I had been fated to be little more than an onlooker for most of the first phase of the campaign in the west, at least the second was to bring me the experience of being able to play my full part as commander of a senior formation.

All our attempts to persuade our superiors to allow us to cross the Somme before the enemy organized a cohesive defence behind it had proved fruitless. The first few days of June were now devoted to preparing for the planned attack which Fourth Army was due to launch early on the 5th.

The sector on both sides of Abbeville was taken over by 2 Corps (General Count Brockdorff). Between this and 38 Corps, General Hoth's 15 Panzer Corps was sandwiched in at Ailly. The Amiens bridgehead, including 9 Panzer Division, was taken over by 14 Panzer Corps (General v. Wietersheim), which simultaneously came under command of the adjacent army. 38 Corps was thus left with a sector barely 30 miles wide on each side of Picquigny. For the first assault it had two divisions up – the 46 Sudeten Infantry Division (Major-General v. Hase) on the right and the 27 Swabian Division (Lieutenant-General Bergmann) on the left. The 6 Westphalian Division (Major-General v. Biegeleben) [1] was to be held in reserve to begin with, and

[1] Of these three well-tried divisional commanders, General v. Hase was executed after the attempt on Hitler's life on 20th July 1944, General Bergmann was killed in the east, and General v. Biegeleben died during the war. *Author.*

only committed to complete the break-through once the leading divisions had got across the river.

While the high ground on our own side undulated gently down towards the Somme and had no woods to provide any effective cover, the southern banks rose steeply and gave the enemy an ample view of our jumping-off positions. However, the actual valley of the river, which was only a few hundred yards wide, concealed the two opposing front lines from each other by virtue of the numerous thickets at the water's edge. On the southern side – still within the valley – were several villages, notably Breilly, Ailly and Picquigny, which the enemy appeared to have occupied in strength. Like most French villages, they had massive houses and walls that offered excellent strong-points to any defender. Up on the high ground behind the steep southern bank, in the rear of the enemy's defence zone, there were more villages and a number of sizeable woods affording the enemy useful centres of resistance and cover for his artillery.

Our corps was now faced by two French divisions – a negro colonial division and the 13 (Alsatian) Division. Intelligence reports indicated that the enemy's artillery was certainly no weaker than our own numerically, and possibly even stronger. In view of the type of ground and the ratio of forces involved, I felt our attack would best succeed if we utilized the element of surprise. Our own artillery was thus ordered to remain completely silent until the assault began. Only then was maximum fire to be put down on the southern bank and the villages down in the valley in order to eliminate all opposition to the actual river-crossing.

The infantry of both our divisions had been moved up into the riverside undergrowth the night before the attack, complete with rubber dinghies, pontoons and gangboards. Their mission was to effect a surprise crossing at first light and by-pass the villages.

The river-crossing at dawn on 5th June succeeded along the entire front, taking the enemy completely unawares. Then, however, his resistance came to life again up on the escarpment and in the villages by the river.

The enemy fought bravely – the negroes with their characteristic bloodthirstiness and contempt for human life, the Alsatians with the toughness one had to expect from this Alemanic people, who had furnished Germany with so many good soldiers in World War I. It was really tragic to meet these German lads as foes in the present fighting. When I talked to the prisoners, many of them told me – not without pride – that their fathers had served in the German Army, the Guards or the Imperial Navy. It all put me in mind of the numerous Alsatian recruits I had trained myself in the Third Foot Guards, most of them – like my range estimator of those days, Lance-Corporal Deschang – being excellent soldiers.

I had watched the start of the attack from my corps command post in a copse fairly near to the front. As soon as we were satisfied that the crossing had been generally successful, I went forward in my car. Now the struggle for possession of the commanding heights and the riverside villages started. One thing that struck us was the relative inactivity of the enemy artillery, which was quite out of proportion to the number of batteries we had identified. Obviously the French gunners were still far too Maginot-minded. Their shooting was not adaptable enough, and their speed in putting down strong concentrations of fire fell far short of the standard required in a war of movement. What was more, they had not developed forward observation technique to anything like the same extent as we had, nor were their specialists in this field of the same quality as our own observation battalions. As is so easy, the victor of 1918 had apparently been resting on his laurels much too long. It was, at all events, a pleasant surprise as far as we were concerned to find that the effect of the enemy artillery was not remotely comparable with that experienced in the static conditions of World War I.

All the same, my own crossing of the Somme flats proved somewhat ticklish, since the recently erected emergency bridge was still within range of the enemy in the village of Breilly. Nevertheless, I managed to get through quite safely to 63 Infantry Regiment of 27 Division, which, led by its excellent commander, Colonel Greiner, had just taken the opposing heights – though not without heavy losses. What struck me as particularly admirable was the composure of the wounded, who were having to wait in the dead ground for vehicles which could not evacuate them at this early stage. Next I went back over the Somme to make my way via another crossing point to 40 Infantry Regiment of the same division, which had gone in on the left wing of the corps. It was pinned down in front of Neuilly Wood, which fell largely within the sector of the neighbouring 14 Panzer Corps and was still held by the enemy. Here, too, I fear, quite considerable losses had occurred, since the regiment was under fire from behind from the village of Ailly, which was still in enemy hands. Despite this, the high ground commanding the valley had been captured here, too.

46 Infantry Division, on the right, had likewise made a successful crossing and was now in possession of the opposing heights. One could thus feel satisfied with the first day's results, even though the fighting for the riverside villages lasted well into the night.

As for the corps on each side of us, 15 Panzer Corps was also across the river, but could make no headway for some time, owing to the fact that the enemy was fighting hard for a large-sized locality called Arraines and thereby blocking the road indispensable to the armoured vehicles.

On our left, 14 Panzer Corps, which had attacked from the Amiens bridgehead after a preparatory bombardment, appeared to have met with a serious hold-up because of enemy minefields. For this reason it was directed to attack southwards, with the result that we were out of touch with it for the remainder of our advance.

The attack of 5th June had gained us so much space south of the river that it was possible to bring the first batteries over during the night. However, it was still not clear whether the enemy would admit his defeat or try to continue his tough resistance further back. In such situations there tends to be a complete lack of intelligence on a vital question like this. A veil of uncertainty – the one unvarying factor in war – had descended on the enemy's location and intentions. Any over-hastiness at such a time can lead to severe setbacks, whereas a delay of even a few hours may enable the enemy to build up a new front that will cause another round of heavy losses.

The field commander whose reaction here is to wait for unimpeachable intelligence reports to clarify the situation has little hope of being smiled upon by the Goddess of War. In the very early hours of 6th June, therefore, I drove out to the command post of 46 Division, which had meanwhile moved over to the south bank of the river. Finding everyone there obviously still half asleep after the strenuous events of the previous day, I pointed out the necessity of immediately taking up the pursuit, since the division appeared to have no direct contact with the enemy. With that I drove out to the division's forward areas, where, finding units of 42 Regiment without orders despite the audible din of combat out to their front, I set about getting them on the move. Next I paid a visit to the right-hand regiment of the corps. Though in fact ready to go forward, it was waiting to see what effect the artillery had on the village of Coisy to its front and the adjacent high ground and wood perimeter. Reconnaissance reports were not available. As I had the impression that neither the village nor the high ground and woods were any longer occupied, I ordered the regimental commander to start advancing on a broad front, but in well-dispersed groups. If there really were enemy still out there, they would duly show themselves and be beaten down by the artillery, which was being held in readiness. As long as it advanced in the pattern I had ordered, moreover, the regiment need have no fear of heavy losses. Since the commander evidently harboured strong doubts about my appreciation of the situation, I went on ahead in my *Kübelwagen*.[1] At the entry to Coisy we found the way barred by a barricade, but it was unmanned. From inside the village occasional shots could be heard, evidently fired by stragglers. After a brief observation, we drove into the village and found that it had indeed been evacuated, as had the high ground and the forward edge of the nearby woods. With this information in my pocket I returned to the regiment, which was now ready to advance, and suggested that they make arrangements to do their own reconnoitring in future. Although corps commanders are not meant to do the work of scouting patrols, I felt it necessary in the circumstances to set a drastic example, particularly as the fighting troops did not know me yet and I was convinced that the effectiveness of a pursuit depended on the initiative of the commanders. I was delighted to see how my A.D.C., Lieutenant v. Schwerdtner, and my young driver, Sergeant Nagel, enjoyed this unexpected reconnaissance trip.

During the afternoon I visited two regiments of 27 Division which were engaged in attacking the village of Saisemont. Somewhat unintentionally I found myself in the very front line, talking to a company commander. After briefing me on the situation, he apparently saw no reason why he should not take advantage of the presence of a high-ranking officer, and got me – flat on my belly – to spread out my big situation map and give him a detailed account of the battle as I knew it. Only after I had quenched his thirst for information could I start back for Corps, taking with me a wounded man who had likewise shown a

[1] A wartime variant of the *Volkswagen*, and the German equivalent of the Jeep. Tr.

burning interest in my account of the situation. Fortunately the return trip was quite short, my tactical headquarters having meanwhile been moved up into a small wood near the front.

On 7th June 6 Infantry Division, which had already been brought over the river the day before, was committed to battle on the corps' extreme right. These sturdy Westphalians – who have always been good soldiers – showed admirable *élan*, and when I drove out to see the division in the course of the afternoon I found the steep depression of the Poix sector – which could actually have served the enemy as a useful support – already captured, the small town of Poix in our hands and the regiment busy attacking a village on the far side of the sector. Nonetheless, Poix and the approach road which ran into it were under very uncomfortable fire from long-range artillery. Some light relief was provided when the driver of an ammunition lorry, finding himself halted by the shell-fire, chose to dive for cover under that very same vehicle, despite its cargo of shells!

That afternoon I was to see a regiment of 46 Division which was pinned down in front of the Poix sector. It, too, managed to cross by evening, after establishing the necessary liaison with the heavy weapons and artillery, which had presumably been lacking in the first instance.

27 Division, which had had to bear the brunt of the fighting, could now be assigned to the second line, for the pursuit was undoubtedly well into its stride. Its place on the left flank of the corps was to be taken by the newly allocated 1 Cavalry Division.

8th June saw a continuation of the pursuit, with the Westphalians still setting the pace. 46 Division reported a concentration of 100 tanks, against which a dive-bomber attack was ordered. Unfortunately nothing came of an order to the division to take advantage of this opportunity to seize the tanks. They vanished, although swift action would probably have produced the desired result.

The course of the fighting on 7th and 8th June left Corps H.Q. with the impression that our hard-hit opponent was no longer able to offer anything more than localized and temporary resistance in the open field. It could be assumed that he would try to get what forces he still possessed safely back behind the lower reaches of the Seine. There, with the help of any reserves he might have, he would in all likelihood renew his attempts to fight back. As far as the corps was concerned, therefore, everything depended on our moving in quickly to force our way across the river before the enemy had the time or opportunity to organize a defence. So although the corps was still about 45 miles from the Seine on the evening of 8th June, orders were given to the leading divisions to have their motorized spearheads not only up to the river but actually across it by the following day. The main body of infantry and horse-drawn artillery was to follow at the highest speed they could march so that they, too, reached the Seine on 9th June. 6 Division was directed towards the crossing at Les Andelys, 46 Division to that at Vernon.

This was an extraordinary feat to expect from troops who had been engaged in a running fight with the enemy for four days past, but there happen to be moments in war when a senior commander must impose the most severe demands if he is to avoid flinging away an opportunity for which his troops may have to fight all the harder later on.

In this case, moreover, the overall operation argued in favour of taking swift action. So far the French seemed determined to defend Paris. There were strong enemy forces stationed in the metropolitan defence system running from the Oise to the Marne far north of the city. If the Seine could be crossed below Paris, the defences in question would be lifted off their hinges and the forces manning them would have no alternative but to withdraw hastily from the city to avoid being cut off.

Thus the situation of the corps dictated high demands on the troops. It required commanders at all levels to display the utmost initiative and to act with the greatest possible speed. An opportunity as favourable as this must be seized with both hands.

From the early morning till the late evening of 9th June I was out on the road ensuring that the forward divisions of the corps reached the objectives assigned to them. It was a pleasure to note that despite what they had already been through, our infantry were cheerfully prepared to go to the limits of endurance to attain their goal, the Seine.

Naturally the usual frictions occurred, although in the case of 6 Division everything went off very smoothly. Early in the morning I had met the two divisional commanders and then paid a visit to 46 Division. When I subsequently arrived at 6 Division's crossing place by Les Andelys about noon I discovered that the reconnaissance battalion had by now reached the river and that the divisional staff were already preparing for the crossing, which was due to take place that afternoon. Unfortunately the bridge had been blown by the time the reconnaissance troops arrived. The picturesque little town of Les Andelys, perched high on a cliff, was burning from a dive-bomber raid which, since it gave advance notice of our arrival, we had not in the least desired.

One or two difficulties did crop up in the case of 46 Division, however. First of all, it had moved off three hours later than was expected. By the time I returned to it after visiting 6 Division it had lost all contact with its reconnaissance battalion, and the latter, wherever else it might be, was certainly not at the Seine, like that of 6 Division. There was nothing for it but to suggest to the commander of 46 Division that he meet me early that evening at Vernon, his crossing place. He might, I added, at least bring his missing reconnaissance battalion along with him.

Meanwhile I returned to Les Andelys, where I found 6 Division's crossing in progress at three points in the face of only weak opposition. The infantry and horse-drawn artillery had strained every nerve to reach the Seine in good time.

On returning to Vernon about seven in the evening, I found that the divisional commander and his reconnaissance battalion really had arrived. Here, too, unfortunately, the enemy had had time to destroy the bridge. As Vernon was under rather fierce machine-gun fire from the south bank of the river, I directed that the reconnaissance troops should cross at night under the cover of darkness.

During this turbulent chase I had been unable to employ 1 Cavalry Division – which had meantime arrived in the corps area – as I would have liked. It was still too far back, and the army had let me have it only on the express understanding that I committed it on the Oise to cover the army's left flank against any threat from Paris. Incidentally, the division reported that it had been attacked – still far to the rear of my advance divisions – by strong enemy armoured forces. These were clearly the tanks that had previously given 46 Division the slip and were now marauding in our extended flank.

When, after a short night's sleep, I returned to Vernon in the early hours of 10th June, 46 Division, too, had got its first elements across the river. Thus 38 Corps was the first to have established a firm foothold on the south bank. The troops had every right to be proud of the pursuit they had accomplished, and I, for my own part, was happy to know that swift action had probably spared the corps a hard struggle for the Seine crossings.

38 Corps' position was no enviable one, all the same. It stood alone on the south bank of the river. 15 Corps on its right had not reached the Seine until 10th June, and had then been diverted to Le Havre. 2 Corps, which was following behind, was still some distance away. On the left flank loomed the big question mark of Paris, where any number of the enemy might be hidden. What was more, 38 Corps needed another two days to lift all its forces over the river. The two weak pontoon bridges at Les Andelys and Vernon were the object of repeated attacks by the R.A.F., which did in fact succeed in putting the one at Vernon out of action for a time. If the enemy commander still had any reserves available on this wing and could bring himself to take the initiative, 38 Corps in its isolation south of the river would inevitably be their target.

The commander of Fourth Army, Colonel-General v. Kluge, had told me at the start of the offensive that the operational objective set him by O.K.H. was to 'gain bridgeheads south of the Seine'. Even if it were the Supreme Command's aim to decide this second phase of the French campaign not – as I had envisaged – by a strong north wing wheeling round to the west of Paris on the lines of the Schlieffen Plan but – most successfully, as it turned out – by a southward thrust of massed armour to the east of Paris, the mission allotted to Fourth Army still seemed a most inadequate one. For even if the thrust east of Paris were intended to be the decisive action, with Army Group C's breakthrough attacks on the Maginot Line and Army Group B's advance over the lower Somme ranking as perhaps only secondary undertakings, it was necessary that we retain the initiative. Army Group A did not start its drive across the Aisne until 9th June, and it still remained to be seen whether this would bring the decisive success expected of it. At the same time one had to assume that the enemy – also with the Schlieffen Plan in mind – would not overlook the danger of our executing an extensive outflanking movement across the lower Seine and would duly take his own counter-measures. This gave us all the more reason for retaining the initiative on the right wing of the German armies and not leaving the enemy any time to deploy here for either defence or counter-attack. If, then, Fourth Army's strategic role – as I saw it – gave reason for pressing on with the attacks south of the river, it seemed wrong to me that 38 Corps should sit in a bridgehead and wait for the enemy to amass what might prove to be superior forces against it.

I thus asked the army for permission to attack southwards as soon as my corps artillery were across the river, instead of holding the bridgehead which we had meanwhile expanded to the Eure. As a precaution, 27 Infantry Division, too, had been brought over to the south bank of the Seine. On 11th June, moreover, I requested approval to bring 1 Cavalry Division south of the Seine from its position on the Oise, where it had that very day scored a neat success against the enemy armour mentioned above. In the circumstances I found it entirely natural that the one cavalry division we possessed should form the spearhead of the pursuit. My intention was to use it to bar the railway lines and roads to Paris at the earliest possible date.

Unfortunately my proposals were turned down on the grounds that the army must first await instructions on its future actions. 1 Cavalry Division was then taken away from me and placed under command of 1 Corps in the second line of advance, with orders to continue guarding the Oise flank and in any case to remain north of the Seine. And so, to my intense regret, this fine division was deprived of the one role that would have corresponded to its special character.

Two incidents on the evening of 11th June served, in my opinion, to vindicate the requests we had made. 58 Infantry Regiment of 6 Division shot down an enemy pilot who was found to be carrying documents indicating that an extensive withdrawal had been ordered. Secondly, 46 Division reported that it was being subjected to a strong attack by the enemy's tanks – a sign that he found our presence south of the river most disagreeable. Further inactivity on our part could only improve the position as far as he was concerned.

46 Division beat off the attack the same evening, though the losses it suffered in the process were not inconsiderable. Early next day it reported that the enemy to its front was again preparing to attack (the number of tanks it named was 110) and urgently appealed for help. I resolved to go over to the attack on my own initiative with all three divisions. Hardly had the orders to this effect been issued, however, when the Army Commander himself appeared. While agreeing with my decision, he felt he must still bide his time in the absence of any fresh operational directives from O.K.H. His main anxiety was obviously

that I might set off with my corps on my own. Consequently he gave strict orders that the attack must not go beyond the line Evreux–Pacy. To make doubly sure, this was reiterated in army orders the same evening.

While the attack of 27 Division on the left made good progress, 46 Division reported that it was not yet able to get started because it had insufficient artillery, ammunition and rations on the south bank. Even so, it had repelled the tank attacks – though the number involved had proved to be not more than fifty or sixty.

The next few days were again a period of pursuit, 2 Corps crossing the Seine to our right on 13th June. That day we put up at a little château belonging to the well-known novelist Collette d'Arville, who was unfortunately away. I thus spent the night in Madame's bedroom: like the salon, it was most elegantly furnished, with a private entrance from the park presumably dating back to gayer days. The swimming-pool outside was a great boon to us all.

On 14th June we received a visit from the Commander-in-Chief. I was able to apprise him of the corps' successes to date, but while taking note of these, he revealed nothing about any future intentions.

On 15th June Colonel-General v. Kluge informed me that Fourth Army had now been given Le Mans as its objective, and stressed the need to go flat out for this without any regard for the formations on either flank. In our case, I feel, the advice was unnecessary.

On 16th June the divisions of the corps again encountered organized resistance along the line Ferté–Senoches–Chateauneuf. The forces involved were elements of 1, 2 and 3 Mechanized Divisions, which, after fighting in Flanders, had escaped through Dunkirk and disembarked again at Brest. Troops of two Spahi brigades and a Moroccan division were also identified. By evening enemy resistance was broken. Here, too, I was most impressed by the men of 6 Division when I visited the latter during my tour of the divisions.

That evening we received an army order fixing Le Mans–Angers as our axis of advance. 1 Corps was to be phased in on our left, taking 46 Division under command. 15 Panzer Corps, less one division earmarked to take Cherbourg, was to advance on the Lower Loire and 'form bridgeheads there'. This seemed to be the be-all and end-all of it.

On 17th June the resignation of Reynaud and the appointment of Marshal Pétain was announced. Was the old man to organize resistance afresh or did the politicians intend to leave it to this renowned veteran of the First World War to sign a capitulation?

An order from the Führer reaching us on 18th June called for a ruthless pursuit of the enemy – once again no novelty as far as we were concerned. It also ordered the occupation of 'the old Reich territories of Toul, Verdun and Nancy', the Creusot Works and the ports of Brest and Cherbourg. We made a forced march, one of our regiments covering almost 50 miles and a motorized reconnaissance battalion under Colonel Lindemann actually getting to a point west of Le Mans. I spent the night in the medieval castle of Bonnétable. With its moat and drawbridge, its four front towers with walls 9 feet thick, and its ceremonial gardens flanked by two more towers at the rear, it was, next to the Loire castles I was soon to see, probably the most impressive building of its kind I came across in France. The interior, too, was splendidly furnished, and even some of the domestic staff were still in occupation. The owner, M. de Rochefoucauld, Duke of Doudaigne, had unfortunately fled.

On 19th June I drove 30 miles out to Lindemann's reconnaissance battalion without seeing a single German soldier. At Le Mans, where my grandfather had made a victorious entry seventy years before, I went over the magnificent cathedral. En route we met bodies of unarmed French troops marching east and a whole artillery regiment which had surrendered to Lindemann, with its full complement of guns and vehicles. The enemy was obviously disintegrating. Despite this, I found Lindemann's battalion held up on the Mayenne sector at Lion d'Angers. Tanks had been spotted on the far bank and machine-guns had the bridge under fire. Lindemann was making vain efforts to drive off the enemy with the only artillery he had, a 10-cm. motorized battery. On going down to the most forward position by the river, some distance from the bridge, I discovered that except around the bridge itself the enemy was obviously not present in any great strength – if indeed he were there at all. Spotting a squadron commander who was apparently waiting on the bank to see whether the enemy would now give up the bridge voluntarily, I advised him to swim across further downstream. If he wished, I added, I should be glad to go with him. The offer worked. Shortly afterwards the entire squadron – naked as God made them – plunged into the river and reached the far bank unscathed. The bridge was ours – though by now, I fear, a number of

German dead lay around the approach to it from our side. I stayed with the reconnaissance troops till they had resumed their advance on the far side of the river, and then returned to my corps command post. In view of the fact that this reconnaissance force had been held up on the Mayenne for eight hours by only a few enemy tanks and machine-guns, I sent my senior aide, Lieutenant Graf, straight back to Lindemann with strict orders to cross the Loire that very night. Sure enough, Graf found the troops just about to settle down to rest – on our own side of the river. He carried his point, however, and the same night the battalion went over the river with Graf in command of the leading rubber dinghy.

During the hours of darkness Corps H.Q. heard from both divisions that they had their reconnaissance troops across the Loire. I immediately went forward, and could not help being impressed, on my arrival there, by the immensity of the river. At the western crossing point, Ingrades, there was a powerful current running, and the distance from bank to bank measured close on 600 yards. Two arches of the high bridge had been blown, and the intervening gap was to be closed by a pontoon bridge. To compensate for a difference in height of almost 30 feet, a steep ramp had to be installed. Since it proved hazardous enough to drive up this even in a *Kübelwagen*, all the heavy types of vehicles still had to be ferried across – no easy task in view of the breadth of the river, the strong current and the numerous sandbanks.

The position was simpler at Chalonnes, the other crossing point, for here the river split into three tributaries. The bridges over the two northern branches had fallen into our hands intact, leaving us only a stretch of 160 yards to span. At this spot I was to witness a most unusual duel. While the only French troops to be seen on the opposite bank during the morning had been unarmed, heavy tanks subsequently showed up there in the course of the afternoon. The forces we had ferried so far had been unable to halt them, since they still had no means of getting any guns across. So, from a position by the Chalonnes bridge, I saw an 88-mm. German AA gun and a heavy French tank come into position simultaneously on opposite sides of the river and open fire on one another at the very same instant. Unfortunately our own gun was immediately knocked out. The very next moment, however, its place was taken by a light anti-tank gun, which was lucky enough to score a direct hit on the one weak spot in front of the enemy 32-tonner. The latter immediately burst into flames.

That evening I moved into the castle of Serrant near Chalonnes. It was an imposing building of tremendous size, flanked by massive towers and arranged in the form of a horsehoe around ceremonial gardens. Round it all flowed a moat. The castle belonged to the Duc de la Trémouille, Prince de Tarent – one of the leading names of ancient France. The dukes had gained the latter title by marriage in about 1500 as the hereditary right of the Anjou family in Naples. They did not, however, win the Neapolitan throne, of which Ferdinand the Catholic took possession. Together with Bayard, a Trémouille had the sole right to the title of *chevalier sans peur et sans reproche*. In addition to the wonderful library, the castle contained a wealth of historical mementos, including many from the days when its masters were supporters of the Stuarts. The ground floor was closed, as this was one of the castles being used to store the furniture from the Palace of Versailles. I myself occupied an upstairs room in one of the towers, fully furnished for a *grand lever*, with a bed of state under a 25-foot-high canopy. Adjoining it was an equally splendid dressing-room with a wonderful coffered ceiling in barrel-vaulting. The castle, the outer walls of which were coated in white sandstone and the towers built of pebbles, lay in a huge park. A magnificent staircase under an arched Renaissance ceiling led up to the chambers on the first floor, a number of which were beautifully panelled and hung with paintings and the most delightful Gobelin tapestries. It goes without saying that here, as in all other quarters we occupied, the owner's property was respected and treated with the most scrupulous care.

By 22nd June we had succeeded in getting 6 and 27 Divisions over the Loire. Their reconnaissance units pressed a little further still to accept the surrender of countless French troops.

On 23rd June we learnt that an armistice had been signed in Compiègne the previous day. The French campaign was over. In a Corps Order of the Day I felt it proper to thank the divisions under my command – none of which, I pointed out, had enjoyed the benefits of armoured protection or mechanical propulsion – for their self-sacrifice, bravery and joint achievements. As the sequel to a successful assault operation they had made possible a 300-mile pursuit which had every right to be called 'the assault march to the Loire'!

The wheel had turned. The road from Compiègne 1918 to Compiègne 1940 had been a long one. Where would it take us from here?

7

BETWEEN TWO CAMPAIGNS

THE DAY the French laid down their arms erased one of the blackest memories in the minds of the Germans – that of the surrender of 11th November 1918, signed in Marshal Foch's railway-coach at Compiègne. Now France was having to sign her own capitulation at the same place and in that same coach.

22nd June 1940 marked the peak of Hitler's career. France, the threat of whose military might had hovered over Germany since 1918, was eliminated as an opponent of the Reich, just like her eastern satellites before her. Britain, even if by no means finally beaten, had been driven off the Continent. And although the Soviet Union – now a neighbour of the Reich – constituted a latent threat in the east despite the Moscow pact, she was hardly likely, in view of the German victories over Poland and France, to turn aggressive in the near future. If indeed the Kremlin had ever contemplated exploiting Germany's engagement in the west to carry out further expansion, it had apparently missed its chance. Evidently it had not allowed for the possibility of the Wehrmacht's winning so swift and decisive a victory over the Allied armies.

That the Wehrmacht had achieved such successes in Poland and France certainly did not mean that its leaders had been working for a war of revenge ever since that first day of Compiègne. Contrary to all the claims of hostile propagandists, the plain fact is that General Staff policy in the years between 1918 and 1939 – thanks to a sober appreciation of the dangers that would threaten the Reich in the event of hostilities – was not to wage a war of aggression or revenge but to safeguard the security of the Reich. Admittedly, the military leaders had ultimately allowed Hitler to outmanœuvre them, just as it may be said that they accepted the pre-eminence of politics – even politics they did not agree with, but could have prevented only by a *coup d'état*.

For the rest, the extent of the rearmament which Hitler had done everything possible to promote was far from being the only reason for the successes now attained. Certainly – considering the state of defencelessness dictated to Germany at Versailles – rearmament had been a prior necessity for the successful conduct of a war. But there could be no question of the Wehrmacht's having had anything like the preponderance which was later to be enjoyed by the Soviet Union on land and the Western Powers in the air. Indeed, as far as the number of formations, tanks and guns went, the Western Powers had been equal, and in some respects even superior, to the Germans. It was not weight of armaments that had decided the campaign in the west but the higher quality of the troops and better leadership on the German side. While not forgetting the immutable laws of warfare, the Wehrmacht had simply learnt a thing or two since 1918.

After the armistice O.K.H. started taking steps to demobilize a considerable number of divisions. At the same time certain infantry divisions were to become either armoured or motorized.

The headquarters of 38 Corps was initially moved into the region of Sanserre, on the middle reaches of the Loire, to handle the conversion of a number of these divisions. We thus exchanged the splendid castle of Serrant, filled with so many historical memories, for a smaller château built by the manufacturer of the world-famous Cointreau at the summit of a steep hill overlooking the Loire valley.

Our new home was supposed to represent an ancient stronghold and had all the hallmarks of bad taste usually found in imitations of this kind. The effect was not improved by a tower near the living-premises that had actually been built to look like a ruin. Nor did the little cannons along the terrace bear as much resemblance to war trophies as their owner, the liqueur manufacturer, might have hoped. The only beautiful thing about the place was the view from the top of the hill over the far-flung, fertile valley of the Loire.

One indication of the parvenu mentality of the owner could be found in a big picture hanging in his study. It depicted, ranged around a circular table, the crowned heads of Europe at the turn of the century – our own Kaiser, the old Emperor Franz Josef, Queen Victoria, and so forth. Unfortunately they all looked as if they had taken more

Cointreau than was good for them. On his feet beside the table was the owner himself, triumphantly brandishing a glass of his own liqueur. The removal of this monstrosity was the one change we made in that 'château'.

On 19th July all senior Wehrmacht commanders were summoned to Berlin to attend the Reichstag session at which Hitler announced the end of the campaign in the west. On the same occasion he expressed the gratitude of the nation by honouring a number of high military leaders, doing so on a scale which implied that he thought the war as good as won. Natural as the German people found it to honour meritorious soldiers, we army men felt the distinctions now bestowed overstepped the bounds of necessity both in character and scope.

Hitler's appointment of a dozen field-marshals and one grand-admiral simultaneously was bound to detract from the prestige of a rank which had previously been considered the most distinguished in Germany. Hitherto (apart from the few field-marshals nominated by Kaiser Wilhelm II in peace-time) one needed to have led a campaign in person, to have won a battle or taken a fortress to qualify for this dignity.

At the end of the Polish campaign, during which the Commander-in-Chief and both the army group commanders had fulfilled these requirements, Hitler had not seen fit to express his thanks to the army by making these men field-marshals. Yet now he was creating a dozen simultaneously. They included (apart from the Commander-in-Chief, who had fought two brilliant campaigns) the Chief of O.K.W., who had held neither a command nor the post of a Chief-of-Staff. Another was the Under-Secretary of State for the Luftwaffe, who, valuable as his feats of organization had been, really could not be ranked on a par with the Commander-in-Chief of the Army.

The most blatant indication of Hitler's attitude was the way he raised Göring over the heads of the army and navy Commanders-in-Chief by appointing him Reich Marshal and making him the sole recipient of the Grand Cross of the Iron Cross. In the circumstances this method of distributing the honours could only be regarded as a deliberate slight to v. Brauchitsch, and showed all too clearly what Hitler thought of O.K.H.

On the day of the Reichstag session I learnt that our Corps H.Q. was earmarked for a new role. We were moved to the Channel coast to prepare for the invasion of England, three infantry divisions being placed under our command. Our billets were in Le Touquet, an elegant seaside resort near Boulogne where a number of English people owned pretty villas. While the H.Q. took over one of the incredibly luxurious hotels, I and my immediate staff moved into a small villa belonging to a French shipowner. Though the owner had fled, he had left his domestic staff in possession, so we found someone already installed who could run the house and look after its furniture and other contents. In contrast to what happened later in Germany, it did not occur to us to act as lords and masters who could do as they pleased with enemy property. On the contrary, a strict check was kept on houses occupied by German troops, and the removal of whole sets of furniture or the appropriation of valuables as 'souvenirs' certainly had no place in the German Army's code of behaviour. When out riding one day, I passed a villa that had been left in a state of pretty average confusion by the German unit recently in occupation. The very next morning the sergeant-major of the company concerned had to move in with a fatigue party and personally ensure that order was restored.

As a result of the impeccable behaviour of our troops, nothing happened to disturb our relations with the civil population during my six months in France. The French, for all their politeness, maintained a dignified reserve which could only earn our respect. For the rest, I suppose everyone tended to fall under the spell of that blessed land, with its beautiful scenery and wealth of monuments to an ancient culture – to say nothing of the delights of a famous cuisine! And the things that were still to be had in the shops! Admittedly our purchasing power was limited, as only a percentage of a man's pay was issued in occupation currency. This regulation was strictly enforced where the army was concerned, thereby imposing a check on the natural urge to go shopping – a thing most desirable for Wehrmacht prestige. Still, one had enough to make an occasional trip to Paris and pass the day savouring the charm of that city.

Our stay on the coast enabled us to go bathing right up to the middle of November – a pleasure which my new aide, Lieutenant Specht, my faithful driver, Nagel, and my groom, Runge, enjoyed just as thoroughly as the opportunities for long gallops along the beach. On one occasion, however, we forgot about the unusual tides in the Channel, where there can be as much as 26 feet difference between high and low tide. This, incidentally, proved an extremely important factor when the possibility of a landing on the English coast and the times of embarkation in the invasion harbours came under discussion. As a result, when we were already far out to sea, the waves suddenly started lapping round our Mercedes on the beach. Only in the very nick of time did we succeed in getting a tractor to tow it out of the incoming tide, through sand that had already turned very soft.

But neither the joys and attractions of that beautiful country nor the period of rest after a successful campaign caused our troops to go soft – a fate to which occupation troops are usually exposed. Any tendency in that direction was counteracted by the need to train our formations for the projected invasion, a completely new task in itself. The troops had daily exercises in the dunes and neighbouring fenland, which in many respects resembled our intended landing-places. After the arrival of our ferrying equipment – converted Rhine and Elbe barges, small trawlers and motor-boats – we were able, in calm weather, to practise embarkation and disembarkation with the navy. As often as not, when a landing-craft beached clumsily, this spelt a cold bath for one or two of those taking part. The young midshipmen still had their own job to learn. One could not blame them for their lack of enthusiasm at having to command Elbe barges instead of serving on a smart cruiser or U-boat – particularly as it was not always easy to get along with the old salts who owned the barges and trawlers and stood beside them on the bridges of these rather fantastic invasion craft. Nevertheless, all personnel showed the utmost keenness in training for their unaccustomed task, and we were convinced that, like everything else, it could be mastered in due course.

OPERATION 'SEALION'

This seems to me to be a good place to include a few critical remarks on Hitler's invasion plan and the reasons that led him to abandon it.

If Hitler really believed he had already won the war after the defeat of France and that it was now merely a matter of bringing this home to Britain, he could not have been more wrong. The icy indifference of the British to his peace offer – which was anyway an extremely vague one – showed that neither the Government nor the nation were open to persuasion.

And so Hitler and O.K.W. found themselves wondering 'What next?'

Any statesman or supreme commander is liable to be faced with the same problem in wartime when an entirely new situation arises through a military setback or an unexpected development in the political field – the entry of another Power into the war on the side of the enemy, for example. In such circumstances he may have no choice but to throw the existing 'war plan' overboard. At the same time one may feel inclined to blame him for overestimating his own resources and underrating the enemy's or for committing an error of political judgement.

But when the head of a State or a war machine has to ask himself 'What next?' after his military operations have entirely fulfilled – or, as in this case, far exceeded – his expectations, leading to one enemy's defeat and causing the other to beat a retreat to his island fastness, one cannot help wondering whether such a thing as a 'war plan' ever existed on the German side.

Certainly no war goes off according to a firm programme set by one side or the other. But since Hitler accepted the risks of war with France and Britain in September 1939, it was his duty to consider beforehand how he should cope with these powers in various contingencies. It is quite obvious that prior to – or even during – the offensive in France, Germany's supreme command had no kind of 'war plan' to determine what measures should be taken once the victories it hoped for had been won. Hitler's hope was that Britain would give in. As for his military advisers, they clearly felt obliged to await a 'Führer's decision'.

The above state of affairs strikingly exemplified the inevitable outcome of the inexpedient military roof organization that had emerged in Germany when Hitler assumed supreme command without creating a Reich Chief-of-Staff responsible for grand strategy.

The plain fact is that, next to the Head of State who made the political decisions, there was no parallel military authority empowered to take responsibility for this overall strategy.

From its very inception Hitler had relegated O.K.W. to the status of a military secretariat. In any case, its chief, Keitel, would not have been in the least capable of advising Hitler on strategy.

As for the Commanders-in-Chief of the three armed services, Hitler allowed them practically no influence whatever on grand strategy. From time to time they were able to express an opinion on policy matters at personal interviews, but ultimately Hitler alone made the decisions on the basis of his own deliberations. So invariably did he insist on the right to initiate policy that – except in the case of Norway, where Raeder probably put up the first suggestion – I know of no instance in which a fundamental decision impinging on overall war policy can be placed to the credit of any of the three service staffs.

Since no one – least of all O.K.W. – was authorized to draft a 'war plan', the effect in practice was that everyone left things to 'the Führer's intuition'. Some, like Keitel and Göring, did so in credulous adulation; others, like Brauchitsch and Raeder, in a mood of resignation. The fact that all three service staffs certainly conducted their own internal studies of long-term policy made not a scrap of difference. (As early as the winter of 1939/40, for example, Grand-Admiral Raeder made the Naval Operations Staff examine the technical possibilities and requirements of a landing operation on the coast of England.) There was still no military authority or personality, in the sense of a real Chief of the General Staff, whom Hitler was prepared to regard not only as an expert or executive but also as being explicitly in charge of *overall* strategy.

In the event, the result of this pattern of command was, as I have already stated, that when the campaign in the west was finished, we were confronted with the problem of what to do next.

In addition to this, the German Supreme Command had two facts to contend with:

First, the existence of an unbeaten Britain which was palpably unwilling to come to terms.

Secondly, the danger of intervention by our new neighbour, the Soviet Union, however peace-loving it might be acting in the meantime. It was a threat which Hitler had indicated back in November 1939, when stressing the need to achieve a prompt decision in the west.

In the light of these two facts it was clear that the Reich's most pressing task must be to end the war with Britain at the earliest possible date. Only then could one hope that Stalin had finally missed his chance to exploit the discord of the European peoples for his own expansionist ends.

If no way to an understanding could be found, Germany must try to rid herself of her last opponent, England, by force of arms.

It is the tragedy of that brief period in which the fate of Europe was settled for so many years to come that neither side sought any means of coming to terms on a common-sense basis. What is certain is that Hitler would have preferred to avoid a life-and-death struggle with the British Empire because his real aims lay in the east.

The way he put over his far-too-vague peace offer at the Reichstag session after the campaign in France, however, was hardly conducive to favourable reactions. Apart from that, it is open to doubt whether Hitler, already drunk with a belief in his own infallibility, would have been ready to accept a peace based on reason and justice even if the opposing side had seriously suggested such a thing. What is more, he was now the prisoner of his own deeds. He had handed over half of Poland and the Baltic to the Soviet Union – an action he could reverse only at the cost of a new war. He had opened the way to Italy's covetous desire for territories under French sovereignty, and thereby landed himself in a state of dependency on his ally. Finally, since Prague, he had become untrustworthy in the eyes of the world and forfeited everyone's faith in whatever agreements he might subscribe to.

For all that, the mass of the German people would have wildly acclaimed him had Hitler presented them with a reasonable negotiated peace after the defeat of France. They were not eager to incorporate tracts of predominantly Polish territory into the Reich, nor did they feel any sympathy for those who, still dreaming of a distant past, based their claims to these lands on the fact that they had once formed part of the Holy Roman Empire. The idea of a Master Race whom it behoved to dominate Europe, or even the whole world, was never taken seriously in Germany except by a few party fanatics. Hitler had only to whistle his pack of propaganda enthusiasts to heel and the general approval for a reasonable peace would have been free to express itself.

On the other hand, though, it may be that the British national character, so impressively incorporated in the person of Winston Churchill, prevented Britain from entertaining any serious thought of a rational settlement at that or indeed any later stage of the war. There was that admirable tenacity of the British which impels them to go through with any struggle they have once embarked on, however threatening the situation of the moment may be. On top of this, in the bitterness of their 'unconditional' hatred for Hitler and his régime (and for 'Prussianism', too, in the case of several political leaders), came the inability to discern an even worse system, and an even greater menace to Europe, in the form of the Soviet Union. What also prejudiced

British policy was the traditional striving for a European balance of power, the restoration of which had been Britain's ultimate motive for entering the war, since it demanded the defeat of a Germany which had become too powerful on the Continent. British eyes were blind to the fact that the big need in a changed world would be to create a *world* balance of power in view of the might which the Soviet Union had attained and the dangers inherent in its dedication to the idea of world revolution.

In addition to all this, Churchill was probably too much of a fighter. His mind was too exclusively concerned with battle and ultimate victory to see beyond this military goal into the political future. Only several years later, when the Russians were approaching the Balkans, a neuralgic spot for Britain, did Churchill appreciate the danger of this development. By then, however, he could no longer get his way with Roosevelt and Stalin. Meanwhile he relied on the vitality of his people and the ability of the American President eventually to bring the United States into the war on Britain's side – disinclined though the American people might have been at that stage, for all their dislike of Hitler, to see this happen.

Furthermore, a man like Churchill was hardly going to overlook the latent danger which the Soviet Union represented for Germany. As far as the war was concerned, he booked it on the credit side for Britain. On the other hand, the idea of seeking a settlement with Germany on the premise that this would most probably be shortly followed by a struggle for power between the two totalitarian States appears to have found no place in his reasoning. This despite the fact that a sober assessment of the strengths and weaknesses of the two Powers would almost certainly have led him to deduce that neither could completely master the other and that they were much more likely to tie each other down, to their mutual debilitation, for some time to come. Such a situation would automatically have cast the Anglo-Saxon Powers as world umpires – to say nothing of the fact that the struggle between the two totalitarian States would probably have sealed the fate of their régimes.

In an age of dictatorships, ideologies and 'crusades', an age in which the emotions of the masses are whipped up by unbridled propaganda, the word 'reason' is, I fear, never spelt with a capital 'R'. And so, to both peoples' detriment and Europe's misfortune, it turned out that neither Britain nor Germany could see any practical alternative but to fight it out.

Thus the German Supreme Command's answer to the problem of what to do after the end of the campaign in the west was to continue the struggle against Britain. But the fact that, for the reasons discussed above, no war plan extending beyond the campaign in the west of the Continent had ever existed on the German side was to have grave consequences. When Hitler now conceived the plan (without actually making up his mind) to tackle Britain by invasion, no practical preparations whatever had been taken to this end. In consequence we threw away our best chance of taking immediate advantage of Britain's weakness. The preparations that were only now put in train used up so much time that the success of any landing became doubtful for reasons of weather alone.

This last fact, in addition to others to which we shall return in due course, gave Hitler his grounds – or rather his pretext – for dropping the invasion project and turning right away from Britain to strike at the Soviet Union. The outcome is well known.

Before I deal with the reasons for this decisive change of front, I feel I should review the chances that would have existed had Hitler been ready to carry through the fight with Britain to the last.

Three methods would have been open to us. The first would have been to try to force Britain to her knees by cutting off her supply lines from overseas. Germany's prospects here were favourable to the extent that she now had full possession of the coasts of Norway, Holland, Belgium and France as bases for air and submarine warfare.

The position regarding the resources to be used in this connexion was less favourable.

So far the navy had nothing remotely approaching an adequate number of U-boats – not to mention the heavy vessels, particularly aircraft-carriers, which would have had to co-operate with them. In addition, it was seen that Britain's anti-submarine defences would retain the upper hand as long as we failed to put the R.A.F. out of action. As for the Luftwaffe, the following are the tasks that would have devolved on it:

(i) to achieve mastery of the air at least to the extent of eliminating the R.A.F.'s ability to combat submarine warfare;

(ii) to paralyse the British ports;

(iii) to co-operate effectively with the U-boats in their attacks on enemy shipping.

In practice all this amounted to overcoming the R.A.F. and destroying its production centres.

That the Luftwaffe was still not strong enough to attain this object in 1940 is shown by the Battle of Britain. Whether the outcome would have been the same if weather conditions had not been so unexpectedly unfavourable in August and September and if the German command had not turned its attention from fighting the R.A.F. to attacking London at what might well have been a critical time for the enemy may be left undecided.

At all events, it was impossible in the summer of 1940, in the light of the very limited number of German bombers available and the lack of long-range fighters, speedily to fulfil the aim of overpowering the R.A.F. and destroying its production centres. Every battle that ever had to be fought out by sheer weight of material resources has always required more time and far more forces than were originally estimated. Quick decisions in battles between more or less equal opponents are usually reached only by superior leadership, and seldom by a test of strength, as would have inevitably been the case here.

We ought, therefore, to have prepared from the outset for a prolonged struggle. Just as the submarine fleet should first have been multiplied to guarantee success, so would similar steps have been necessary with regard to the Luftwaffe.

The fact must also be faced that the idea of quickly bringing a country as large as Britain to its knees by 'strategic air warfare' as conceived by General Douhet was – in those days, at any rate – still wishful thinking. The same thing may be said of the Allies' aerial warfare against the Reich later on.

In any case, once it had been decided to force Britain to the ground by cutting off her maritime traffic, the whole of the Reich's war production should have been given over to building up German submarine and air strength. A reduction of the army to free manpower for industry would have been indispensable in this connexion.

The very length of the struggle constituted its danger. No one could know how long the Russians would stay quiet. A reduction in Germany's land forces and the commitment of her entire air power against England would enable the Soviet Union, even if it did not enter the war, at least to exert political blackmail.

Another danger was the possibility that the Americans, who were hardly going to stand by and watch Britain slowly strangled, would intervene at an early stage. In a battle of air fleets and naval forces they could have intervened relatively quickly, whereas if an actual German invasion of England had been taking place they would certainly have come too late. Nevertheless – had the Reich had a real strategic policy – it would have been entirely conceivable that this course of action could have been taken with a prospect of success. Always bearing in mind, of course, the danger of intervention by the Soviet Union or the United States. And certainly only provided that the aim of destroying the R.A.F. and then cutting off Britain's supply lines at sea were strictly adhered to. Any digression into vague notions of striking at the morale of the enemy population by raids on the cities would only have endangered the chances of winning.

The second possible way of bringing down Britain I will call the struggle for the Mediterranean. Hitler – and, indeed, the German military leadership as a whole – are reproached with having been incapable of breaking free from the 'Continental' way of thinking and of never having recognized the significance of the Mediterranean as the life-line of the British Empire.

It is true, perhaps, that Hitler thought only in terms of the Continent. What is open to question, though, is whether, on the one hand, the loss of her position in the Mediterranean would really have compelled Britain to give up the fight and, on the other, what consequences the conquest of the Mediterranean zone would have had for the Reich.

It is indisputable that the loss of the Mediterranean would have been a serious blow for Britain. The possible effects with regard to India and the Near East, and thereby to oil supplies, might have been extremely grave. Furthermore, the final blocking of the sea to shipping would have substantially aggravated Britain's food problems.

But would this blow have been lethal? To my mind it would not. Britain would still have had her link with the Far and Middle East round the Cape of Good Hope, and this could in no event be cut, unless by a close blockade of the British Isles by the U-boats and Luftwaffe – in other words, by the afore-mentioned method. This, however, would have pinned down the Luftwaffe's entire resources, leaving nothing in hand for the Mediterranean! Painful though the loss of Gibraltar, Malta and her positions in Egypt and the Near East might well have been for Britain, it would certainly not have been fatal. Indeed, the British being as they are, it would presumably have served only to stiffen their national will. The British nation would have refused to accept these losses as final and would have gone on fighting all the more bitterly. In all probability it would have given the lie to the slogan about the Mediterranean being the life-line of the Empire. It is also most unlikely that the Dominions would have withdrawn their support.

The second question is what consequences the critical struggle for the Mediterranean would have had for the Reich.

The first point here is that though Italy might have made a good basis for operations, her armed forces could have provided only a very modest contribution to the contest. This did not need to be proved by events: it was already apparent.

In particular, the Italian Fleet could not have been expected to drive the British from the Mediterranean.

The main burden of the struggle would thus have to be borne by Germany, who would not be helped by the fact that her ally regarded the Mediterranean as his private reserve and would accordingly lay claim to the overall command.

If we were going to deprive Britain of her position in the Mediterranean in the hope of dealing her a mortal blow, Malta and Gibraltar would have to be taken and the British expelled from Egypt and Greece. There can hardly be any doubt that if Germany were to shift the focal point of her strategy to the Mediterranean, she would have had to solve this task in a *military* sense.

But that would not have been the end of it. The capture of Gibraltar could only have been carried out either with Spanish consent – which was in fact never obtained – or by bringing pressure to bear on the Spaniards. Either course would have meant the end of Spanish neutrality. The Reich would have been left with no other choice than to take over – with or without the agreement of Madrid and Lisbon – the protection of the whole Iberian coastline, as well as to guarantee the supply of that area. Resistance could have been expected from both countries – most of all from Portugal, who would have seen her colonies immediately occupied by England. Anyhow, the Iberian peninsula would have swallowed a considerable portion of the German Army in the long run, and the repercussions in the U.S.A. and Latin America to a forcible occupation of Spain and Portugal could have been disastrous.

If no real settlement were found with France, which was pretty well out of the question in view of the Italian and Spanish claims on her colonial territories, it would have ultimately become necessary to occupy French North Africa if a naval Power like Britain were to be prevented from one day retrieving a footing in the Mediterranean.

Once the British had been driven from Egypt – and from Greece, too, in the event of their moving in there – it seems likely that in the eastern Mediterranean the course of action considered here would inevitably have led on to the lands of the Near East, especially if one remembers that we should have needed to cut Britain's oil supplies. The view has been expressed that the creation of a base in the Near East would have offered Germany two advantages: one, the possibility of menacing India, and the other a flank position against the Soviet Union to deter it from intervening against Germany. I feel these arguments are unrealistic. Quite apart from the questionable effect the establishment of German troops in their countries would have had on the Near Eastern peoples, there are two other aspects to bear in mind.

Operations against India or the Soviet Union from the Near Eastern region could, for supply reasons alone, never have been executed on a scale guaranteeing real success. By virtue of being a naval Power, Britain had the bigger pull here.

The appearance of Germany in the Near East, far from dissuading the Soviet Union from action against Germany, would only have made her intervene all the sooner.

The crux of this whole Mediterranean problem, is, to my mind, as follows:

Britain's loss of her positions there would hardly have sealed her fate.

To go further, a decisive struggle for the mastery of the Mediterranean would ultimately have tied down such large German forces for so long that the temptation to the Soviet Union to come into the war against us would have increased beyond measure. This is all the more true if one considers that the spoils in which the Soviet Union might well have been interested – the Balkans and a dominating influence in the Near East – could henceforth have been won only by fighting it out with Germany.

To strive for Britain's downfall by way of the Mediterranean would, in fact, have constituted a détour comparable with that taken by Napoleon when he set out to strike a mortal blow at Britain in India by way of Egypt. It was a course entailing the long-term commitment of Germany's forces in a direction that could not be decisive. More than that, it would have enabled the British motherland to rearm and at the same time given the Soviet Union its really big opening *vis-à-vis* the Reich.

In point of fact the Mediterranean method would have implied evading the decision we felt unable to achieve against the British motherland direct.

This brings us to the third course at issue in 1940, that of an invasion of the island of Britain.

Before we pass on to this, it should be noted with regard to our Mediterranean strategy in its practical outcome that – as so often happened later on in Russia – Hitler never made the right forces available at the right time. It was in any case a cardinal error on his part to refrain from attempting to take Malta, the capture of which would almost certainly have been feasible in the early stages. His failure to do so can reasonably be regarded as a factor of decisive importance in the ultimate loss of North Africa and all that followed in its train.

At all events, in June 1940 Hitler conceived the plan of invading Britain (without, as I said, making any firm decision), and ordered the appropriate preparations to be started.

The operation was to be prepared under the code-name *Sealion*, but was to be put into execution only after certain prior conditions had been fulfilled. The manner in which the execution was planned and the interminable disputes which resulted – primarily between the army and navy staffs – have already been dealt with by others. So have the reasons – or pretexts – which were finally to justify the abandonment of the project.

All that will be done here, therefore, is to examine the three most important questions:

1. Would an invasion of England have compelled her to give up the struggle and would it, assuming that it had been successful, have finally decided the issue?

2. Could an invasion really have been expected to succeed, and what would have been the consequences of its failure?

3. What were the reasons that ultimately led Hitler to relinquish the plan (thereby giving up the idea of forcing an issue with Britain) and to turn against the Soviet Union?

The answer to the first question is that an invasion would have been the *quickest* way to overpower Britain. The two other ways discussed above could not bring a quick decision. But would this one have been final? The answer must be that there was every possibility – even probability – that even after the fall of the island the Churchill Government would have tried to continue the fight from Canada. Whether the other Dominions would have followed its lead cannot be told. Still, the conquest of the island itself still did not mean the complete defeat of the Empire.[1]

The cardinal point must surely be this: The conquest of the island by Germany would have deprived the other side of the very base that was indispensable – in those days, at any rate – for a sea-borne assault on the continent of Europe. To launch an invasion from over the Atlantic without being able to use the island as a springboard was beyond the bounds of possibility in those days, even if the United States came into the war. And it can hardly be doubted that with Britain occupied, the R.A.F. eliminated, the Fleet banished across the Atlantic and the island's war potential rendered nugatory, Germany would have been able to deal with the situation in the Mediterranean without further ado.

It must be stated, then, that even if the British Government had tried to fight on after the loss of the motherland, it would have had little further prospect of winning. Would the Dominions have continued to give their support in such circumstances?

Would the Soviet Union's latent threat to the Reich have been of any further consequence had the Russians no longer been able to count on a Second Front in the foreseeable future? Would not Stalin's

---

[1] Whether the British population – unlike the French – would have gone on resisting in the event of a successful invasion, or whether – as even Churchill has thought possible – a Government would have been found to sign a capitulation, is a purely hypothetical question which cannot be discussed here. (The same applies to whether, in the latter contingency, means could have been found, as in the case of Belgium in World War I, of feeding the British population.) *Author.*

reaction to this have been to turn his attentions – with Hitler's agreement – to Asia? Would the United States have undertaken their 'crusade' against the Reich had they known they must bear the brunt of the cost alone?

No conclusive answers to these questions can be found today, nor could they be found at the time.

Admittedly the Reich would have been just as unable to impose peace across the seas. Yet one thing is certain: its position following a successful invasion of Britain would have been an incomparably happier one than any to be found along the road taken by Hitler.

From the military point of view, then, an invasion of Britain in the summer of 1940, provided it offered a prospect of success, would undoubtedly have been the right solution. What steps should, or could, have been taken in the event of a German victory in order to bring about the negotiated peace which should always have been the aim of a rational German policy is outside the scope of this military study.

Let us rather turn to the military aspects again and seek to determine whether an invasion of Britain in 1940 would have had any chance of succeeding.

Opinions on this score will, I suppose, always remain divided. *Sealion* certainly involved tremendous risks.

Nevertheless, it is not enough to point to the vast amount of technical equipment required by the Allies for their invasion in 1944 in order to prove that a German invasion dependent on infinitely more primitive ferrying gear would have inevitably miscarried. Neither is it enough to refer to the Allies' absolute supremacy in the air and at sea in 1944, decisive though it was in both cases.

While Germany had none of these things to her credit in the summer of 1940, she had, on the other hand, the decisive advantage of not initially having to face any organized defence of the British coastline in the form of troops that were adequately armed, trained and led. It is a fact that as far as her land forces went in summer 1940, Britain was to a large extent defenceless. Her defencelessness would have been well-nigh complete had Hitler not allowed the B.E.F. to escape from Dunkirk.

The success of an invasion of England in the summer of 1940 depended on two factors:

1. Execution at the earliest possible date so that we could hit Britain while she was still undefended and take advantage of the summer weather. (In our own experience the Channel was almost invariably as calm as a mill-pond in July and August and at the beginning of September.)

2. Our ability to neutralize the R.A.F. and British Fleet in the Channel area for the duration of the crossing and the period immediately following it.

At the same time it is true that, with our uncertainty regarding the weather and the Luftwaffe's ability to gain air superiority over the Channel to at least the extent demanded, *Sealion* was bound to involve very big risks. In the light of these risks the responsible Wehrmacht staffs probably did go about the operation with some hesitation and various mental reservations.

That Hitler's own heart was not in it was clear even then. At all levels the preparations lacked that driving force from the top which was usually so apparent. General Jodl, Chief of the Combined Services Operations Staff, regarded any attempt at invasion as an act of desperation quite unwarranted by the situation as a whole.

The *Commander-in-Chief of the Luftwaffe*, Göring, whom the High Command had as usual failed to keep firmly in check, in no way regarded his air offensive against Britain as an integral part – vital though it was – of a concerted invasion undertaken by the Wehrmacht. On the contrary, the way he committed and ultimately squandered the Luftwaffe's resources points to his having regarded the air offensive against the island as a self-contained operation, which he conducted accordingly.

The *Naval High Command*, which had been the first authority to raise the question of an invasion of Britain, had at least concluded from its study of the practical problems involved that the operation would be feasible provided certain advance requirements were met. Despite this, it was probably more strongly affected than anyone else by its awareness of the inadequacy of its equipment.

The body taking the most positive view was undoubtedly the *High Command of the Army*, although it does not seem to have contemplated the idea of an invasion prior to the fall of France.

One thing is certain. Those who stood to risk their necks first and foremost if *Sealion* were put into execution – the army formations ear-marked to take part – were the very ones to display the greatest energy and assurance in their pursuit of the preparations. I feel entitled to say this because the formation under my own command, 38 Corps, was designed to go over in the first wave from between Boulogne and Etaples to the stretch of coast running from Bexhill to Beachy Head. Without underrating the dangers, we were confident of success. At the same time we may not have been sufficiently aware of the misgivings of the two other services, especially the navy.

It is well known that Hitler had two reasons – or pretexts – for finally dropping the *Sealion* plan.

One was the fact that the preparations took so long that the first wave could not have crossed till 24th September at the earliest. This was a date by which it would no longer be possible – even assuming that the first wave succeeded – to count on the continuing stretch of fine weather necessary for the follow-up.

The second and really decisive reason is the fact that even by this date the Luftwaffe had not attained the requisite air supremacy over British territory.

Even if these two facts are accepted as having in September 1940 been grounds for calling off the invasion, that still does not establish whether a German invasion would not have been possible had the German Command handled matters differently. This, however, must be the whole basis of any appraisal of Hitler's decision to avoid a fight to the death with Britain in order to turn on the Soviet Union.

The problem is, then, whether the two above-mentioned facts – the delay over the launching of *Sealion* and the inconclusive state of the Battle of Britain – were inevitable or not.

As far as the first is concerned – the postponement of the landing date till the end of September – this could most certainly have been avoided. The existence of a war plan focused on the problem of defeating Britain would have meant that a considerable part of the technical preparations for the invasion could have been tackled while the campaign in the west was still in progress. The existence of such a plan would have made it unthinkable for Hitler – whatever his motives – to allow the B.E.F. to escape from Dunkirk. At its worst the landing date would not have been retarded until well into the autumn had the German decision to invade Britain been taken at least at the time of the fall of France – that is, in mid-June – and not a whole month later, in mid-July. The invasion preparations, carried out as they were in pursuance of the order issued in July and within the limits of what was humanly possible at the time, were completed by the middle of September. A decision four weeks earlier would thus have made it possible to cross the Channel by the middle of August.

As for the unsatisfactory progress of the Battle of Britain that formed the second reason for the abandonment of *Sealion*, the following points come to mind:

The idea of gaining air supremacy over Britain by dint of an isolated aerial war commencing weeks in advance of the earliest possible invasion date was *an error of leadership*.

By gaining air supremacy *over* Britain *before* the invasion took place it was proposed to *guarantee* the success of the latter. All this achieved in the event was a premature dissipation of the Luftwaffe's strength in a battle fought under unfavourable conditions.

A sober assessment of its own strength in relation to the enemy's should at least have given the Luftwaffe staff strong doubts whether its own forces were *adequate* or *suitable* to carry the action against the R.A.F. and its production centres to a decisive conclusion above Britain herself.

First of all, the Luftwaffe leadership underrated the strength of Fighter Command and overestimated the effect of its own bombers, besides allowing itself to be surprised by the existence of an efficient radar system on the other side.

In addition, the range and penetration zone of the bombers, and even more so that of the fighters, were known to be below what was required. As a result the R.A.F. was able to dodge the annihilating blows that were aimed at it. Quite apart from this, the German fighters over England invariably had to operate under less favourable conditions than their opponents. The bombers, for their own part, had in a great number of cases to manage without proper fighter cover as soon as they outranged their escorts.

This consideration alone should have decided the Luftwaffe command against starting a showdown with the R.A.F. until the latter were compelled to join battle under similar conditions – i.e. over the Channel or its coastlines – in immediate operational conjunction with the actual invasion.

Finally, the German Command committed the further error of altering the operational target of its air offensive at the very moment when – despite the Luftwaffe's handicaps, some foreseeable, some unexpected, *vis-à-vis* the R.A.F. – the outcome was actually in the balance. On 7th September the main weight of the attacks was shifted to London – a target which no longer had any operational bearing on the invasion preparations.

Desirable though the attainment of air supremacy prior to the invasion always was, a careful review of all the factors involved should still have prompted the German Supreme Command to commit the Luftwaffe for its decisive blow only in immediate conjunction with the invasion.

One can, of course, object that on this basis the Luftwaffe's resources would have been called upon to perform too many tasks, namely:

> to attack British air bases in the south of England;
> to cover the embarkation in the French harbours;
> to protect the transports as they crossed the Channel;
> to support the first wave of invasion troops during their landing;
> and, in co-operation with the navy and coastal artillery, to prevent the British Fleet from interfering.

But not all these tasks would have been simultaneous, even if they had to be solved in close succession. For example, the British Fleet – apart from the light naval forces stationed in harbours in the south of England – could probably not have intervened until after the first wave of troops had landed.

Everything would have depended on the outcome of a big aerial battle which would have started over the Channel or southern England as soon as the army and navy began invading. The conditions experienced by the Luftwaffe in this battle would, nevertheless, have been immeasurably more favourable than in its raids on the interior of the country.

Naturally such a mode of action meant staking everything on one card. That, however, would have been the price one was bound to pay in the circumstances if the invasion were to be risked at all.

When Hitler, for the above-mentioned reasons, virtually discarded the plan for an invasion of England in September 1940, these reasons may indeed have been cogent enough at the time. The fact that they could emerge at all was due to the absence of any authority inside the German Supreme Command – except for Hitler the politician – that was responsible for *overall* strategic policy. There was no authority that could *in good time* have worked out a war plan to include Britain and been capable of effectively directing the invasion as a unified operation of all three services.

If the German Command thus cast away its chances of fighting the final bout with Britain to a successful conclusion, the reasons are to be sought not only in the shortcomings of the staff organization but substantially in Hitler's political thinking.

There can hardly be any doubt that Hitler always wished to *avoid a contest with Britain and the British Empire*. He stated often enough that it could never be in the Reich's interest to destroy the Empire. He admired this Empire as a political achievement. Even if one is unwilling to take such utterances at their face value, one thing at least is certain: Hitler knew that if the British Empire were destroyed, not he or Germany could be its heir, but the United States, Japan or the Soviet Union. Seen in this realistic perspective, his attitude to Britain does at least make sense. He had neither wanted nor expected war with Britain. Consequently he wished to *avoid* a showdown with her for as long as was possible.

This attitude, and doubtless also the fact that he had not expected such a staggering victory over France, explain Hitler's failure to adopt a war plan which aimed at defeating Britain, too, once France was overthrown. The point is that he did not *want* to land in Britain. His political concept was at odds with the strategic requirements that followed from the victory in the west. The disastrous part of it was that this concept of his encountered no sympathy in Britain.

Hitler's attitude towards the Soviet Union, on the other hand, was fundamentally different, despite the alliance he entered into with Stalin in 1939. He at once mistrusted and underrated the Russians. He feared their traditional urge for expansion – though he himself had opened the way to it in the west by signing the Moscow Pact.

One may assume that Hitler knew the two totalitarian Powers were bound to clash sooner or later after becoming next-door neighbours. Furthermore, he was for ever pre-occupied with 'Lebensraum' – the living space he felt obliged to secure for the German people. It was something he could find only in the east.

Though there was nothing about either of these lines of reasoning to prevent the ultimate clash with the Soviet Union from being put off until some later date, they were bound to acquire a special urgency for a man like Hitler when, after France's downfall, he seemed virtually the master of Europe. His feelings were reinforced by the menacing build-up of Soviet troops on Germany's eastern frontier – a trend which must in any event have given rise to misgivings about the Kremlin's future policies.

Hitler now faced the problem of invading England. He was aware of the high degree of risk such an undertaking then involved. If the invasion were to fail, the army and navy forces taking part would be forfeit, and even the Luftwaffe would emerge very much weakened. At the same time the failure of an invasion attempt would not, from the strictly military point of view, have irreparably impaired German military power. The more far-reaching effect would have been in the political field – on the one hand through the fillip any failure would have given to the determination of the British to go on with the war, on the other its impact on the attitudes of the United States and the Soviet Union. Most of all, though, a spectacular military failure of this kind would have gravely damaged the dictator's prestige, both in Germany and the world as a whole.

This was the one danger the dictator could not afford to run. Just as his general attitude towards the British Empire had always made him put any thought of a showdown behind him, and just as his false appraisal of the British mind had encouraged him to hope that it would still be possible to come to terms in the end, *so did he now recoil from taking the risk*. He wanted to *evade* the hazard of a decisive struggle with Britain. Instead of destroying her as a Power, he thought he could convince her of the need for settlement by trying – as he himself put it – to strike from her hand the last sword she might hope to point at Germany on the mainland of Europe.

But by thus recoiling from what was admittedly a pretty considerable military and political risk, Hitler, committed *his big error of judgement*. For one thing was certain. If Hitler jibbed at fighting the battle with Britain in the hour most favourable to himself, Germany must sooner or later land in an untenable situation. The longer the war with Britain dragged on, the greater the danger threatening the Reich in the east must become.

When Hitler did not venture to strike the decisive blow at Britain in the summer of 1940, and missed his unique chance of doing so, he could no longer play at seeing how long he could hold his breath. It was at this point that he was forced to venture the attempt to eliminate the Soviet Union by a *preventive war* while there was still no enemy in the west capable of menacing him on the Continent.

In reality this meant that because of his aversion to the risk of invading Britain, Hitler took on the far greater risk of a war on two fronts. At the same time, by taking so long over, and finally discarding the invasion plan, he wasted a year which should have brought Germany the final decision. It was a delay Germany could never make good.

With the cancellation of *Sealion* at the end of September, 38 Corps went back to normal training. The ferrying equipment that had been assembled for us was withdrawn from the Channel harbours, already imperilled by R.A.F. raids. Nothing was heard at this stage of Hitler's intentions regarding the Soviet Union, his final decision to attack it being taken much later. The first hints of what was to come did not reach me till the spring of 1941, when I was given a new appointment.

Part III

WAR IN THE EAST

8

PANZER DRIVE

A T THE end of February 1941 I handed over command of 38
Corps on the Channel coast in order to take over 56 Panzer
Corps, whose headquarters were about to be set up in Germany.
For me this fulfilled a wish I had cherished even before the campaign in
the west – to command a mechanized army corps.

As a corps commander, of course, I was not consulted on the
advisability and method of conducting a campaign against the Soviet
Union. Our own operation order was not received until a very late
stage – in May 1941, as far as I remember – and even then it covered
only the immediate commitments of the Panzer Group to which my
corps belonged.

Thus, as far as the actual conduct of operations against the Soviet
Union in 1941 is concerned, I cannot comment to anything like the
extent I have done regarding the western campaign, where I had
personally influenced the final shaping of the Operations Plan.

However, I think two factors may be said to have become generally
apparent since then.

The first was the mistake committed by Hitler, if by no one else, of
underrating the resources of the Soviet Union and the fighting qualities
of the Red Army. In consequence he based everything on the assumption that the Soviet Union could be overthrown by *military* means in
one campaign. Had this even been possible, it could have been achieved
only by bringing about the Soviet Union's simultaneous collapse from
within. Yet the policies which Hitler – in complete negation of the
efforts of the military authorities – pursued through his Reich Com-
missioners and Security Service (S.D.) in the occupied territories of the
east were bound to achieve the very opposite effect. In other words,
while his strategic policy was to demolish the Soviet system with the

utmost dispatch, his political actions were diametrically opposed to this. Differences between the aims of the political and military leaders have often arisen in other wars. In this case, with the military and political leadership united in Hitler's hands, the result was that his political measures in the east ran entirely counter to the requirements of his strategy, depriving it of whatever chance it may have had of a speedy victory.

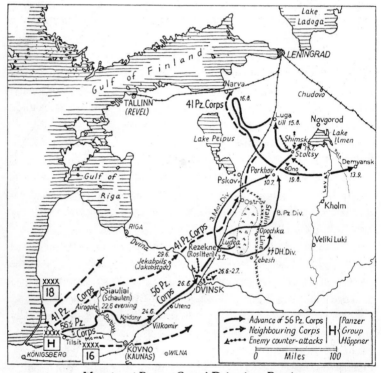

Map 6. 56 Panzer Corps' Drive into Russia.

The second factor was the failure to achieve a uniform strategic policy at the summit – i.e. between Hitler and O.K.H. This applied both to the planning of the overall operation and to its execution in the campaign of 1941.

Hitler's strategic aims were based primarily on *political* and *economic* considerations. These were: (*a*) the capture of Leningrad (a city he regarded as the cradle of Bolshevism), by which he proposed to join up with the Finns and dominate the Baltic, and (*b*) possession of the raw-material regions of the *Ukraine*, the armaments centres of the *Donetz Basin*, and later the *Caucasus oilfields*. By seizing these territories he hoped to cripple the Soviet war economy completely.

O.K.H., on the other hand, rightly contended that the conquest and retention of these undoubtedly important strategic areas depended on first defeating the Red Army. The main body of the latter, they argued, would be met on the road to *Moscow*,[1] since that city, as the focal point of Soviet power, was one whose loss the régime dare not risk. There were three reasons for this. One was that – in contrast to 1812 – Moscow really did form the political centre of Russia; another was that the loss of the armaments areas around and east of Moscow would at least inflict extensive damage on the Soviet war economy. The third and possibly most important reason from the strategic point of view was Moscow's position as the nodal point of European Russia's traffic network. Its loss would split the Russian defences in two and prevent the Soviet command from ever mounting a single, co-ordinated operation.

Viewed strategically, the divergence of views between Hitler and O.K.H. amounted to this: Hitler wanted to seek the issue *on both wings* (a solution for which, in view of the relative strengths involved and the vastness of the theatre of operations, Germany did not possess adequate forces), whereas O.K.H. sought it in the *centre of the front*.

It was on this divergence of basic strategy that the German conduct of operations ultimately foundered. Although Hitler agreed to the distribution of forces proposed by O.K.H., according to which the bulk of the army was to be committed in two army groups in the north and only one in the area south of the Pripet Marshes, the tug-of-war over strategic objectives continued throughout this campaign. The inevitable consequence was that Hitler not only failed to attain his aims, which were too far-flung anyway, but also confused the issue for O.K.H.

The 'General Intention' laid down by Hitler in his 'Barbarossa' Directive ('destruction of the bulk of the Russian Army located in western Russia by bold operations involving deep penetration by armoured spearheads; prevention of the withdrawal of battleworthy elements into the Russian interior') was in the last analysis nothing more than a strategic or even tactical formula. Admittedly, thanks to the superiority of German staff-work and the performance of the

---

[1] This appreciation was subsequently not fully confirmed by the actual distribution of the Soviet forces. *Author.*

combat troops, we achieved extraordinary successes that brought the Soviet armed forces to the very brink of defeat. But this 'formula' could never replace an operations plan over whose preparation and execution there should have been complete unanimity at the top and which, in view of the relative strengths of the opposing armies and the tremendous distances involved, accepted the premise that it might take *two* campaigns to destroy the Soviet armed forces.

In my capacity as a corps commander, however, I was not – as I have already said – briefed on the plans and intentions of the Supreme Command. For this reason I had no suspicion at the time of the momentous differences of a strategic nature existing between Hitler and O.K.H. Yet even at this level I soon began to feel their effect.

56 Panzer Corps was to attack from East Prussia as part of Fourth Panzer Group of Northern Army Group.

Northern Army Group (Field-Marshal Ritter v. Leeb) was assigned the task of driving forward from East Prussia to destroy the enemy's forces in the Baltic territories and then to advance on Leningrad.

The task of *Fourth Panzer Group* (Colonel-General Hoepner) in this connexion was to thrust forward to the Dvina opposite and below Dvinsk (Dünaburg) in order to seize all crossing points for a further advance in the direction of Opochka.

On the right of Fourth Panzer Group, *Sixteenth Army* (Colonel-General Busch) had to advance through Kovno (Kaunas); on the left, *Eighteenth Army* (General v. Küchler) was to move in the general direction of Riga.

I arrived in 56 Panzer Corps' assembly area on 16th June. Colonel-General Hoepner had issued the following orders for the advance of Fourth Panzer Group:

56 Panzer Corps (8 Panzer Division, 3 Motorized Infantry Division and 290 Infantry Division) was to break out in an easterly direction from the forest area north of the Memel and east of Tilsit and to gain the big road to Dvinsk north-east of Kovno. To its left *41 Panzer Corps* (General Reinhardt) (1 and 6 Panzer Divisions, 36 Motorized Infantry Division and 269 Infantry Division) was to advance towards the Dvina crossing at Jakobstadt. The SS Death's Head Division, also belonging to the Panzer Group, would initially follow along behind with a view to being sent in behind the corps making the fastest progress.

For the purpose both of cutting off all enemy forces forward of the Dvina and of forging ahead with Northern Army Group's operation, it was of decisive importance that the Dvina bridges should be captured intact, since this mighty river presented a formidable obstacle. The advance of Fourth Panzer Group would thus be a race to see which of the two corps could reach the Dvina first. 56 Panzer Corps was determined to be the winner, its advantage being that in the light of the available information it stood to encounter less resistance in the enemy rear than 41 Panzer Corps. For this very reason the latter had been given one armoured division more than our own corps. My suggestion that it would be better to make our main effort where we hoped to find the enemy weakest received no support from Panzer Group H.Q.

Before I describe the operations of 56 Panzer Corps, which are really conspicuous only for the fact that they were to develop into a panzer drive in the truest sense, some attention must be given to a matter which threw a revealing light on the gulf between soldiers' standards and those of our political leadership.

A few days before the offensive started we received an order from the Supreme Command of the Armed Forces (O.K.W.) which has since become known as the 'Commissar Order'. The gist of it was that all political commissars of the Red Army whom we captured were to be shot out of hand as exponents of Bolshevik ideology.

Now I agree that from the point of view of international law the status of these political commissars was extremely equivocal. They were certainly not soldiers, any more than I would have considered a *Gauleiter* attached to me as a political overseer to be a soldier. Neither could they be granted the same non-combatant status as chaplains, medical personnel or war correspondents. On the contrary, they were – without being soldiers – fanatical fighters, but fighters whose activities could only be regarded as illegal according to the traditional meaning of warfare. Their task was not only the political supervision of Soviet military leaders but, even more, to instil the greatest possible degree of cruelty into the fighting and to give it a character completely at variance with the traditional conceptions of soldierly behaviour. These same commissars were the men primarily responsible for the fighting methods and treatment of prisoners which clashed so blatantly with the provisions of the Hague Convention on land warfare.

Whatever one might feel about the status of commissars in inter-national law, however, it inevitably went against the grain of any soldier to shoot them down when they had been captured in battle. An order like the *Kommissarbefehl* was utterly unsoldierly. To have carried it out would have threatened not only the honour of our fighting troops but also their morale. Consequently I had no alternative but to inform my superiors that the Commissar Order would not be implemented by anyone under my command. My subordinate commanders were entirely at one with me in this, and everyone in the corps area acted accordingly. I need hardly add that my military superiors endorsed my attitude. It was only very much later, however, that all the efforts to get the Commissar Order rescinded were ultimately successful – when it had become clear, namely, that the order simply incited the commissars to resort to the most brutal methods to make their units fight on to the end.[1]

At 1300 hours on 21st June our H.Q. was notified that the offensive would begin at 0300 the following morning. The die was cast.

Because of the restricted space allotted to my corps in the forest area north of the Memel it was only possible to use 8 Panzer Division and 290 Infantry Division in the assault on the enemy frontier positions, which had been found to be occupied. For the time being 3 Motorized Infantry Division was kept south of the river.

In the immediate vicinity of the frontier we initially met with only weak resistance, probably from forward defended localities. Very soon, however, a hold-up was caused by a well-prepared pill-box system that was overcome only after 8 Panzer Division had broken through the enemy fortifications north of the Memel around noon.

On this very first day the Soviet Command showed its true face. Our troops came across a German patrol which had been cut off by the enemy earlier on. All its members were dead and gruesomely mutilated. My A.D.C. and I, who often had to pass through sectors of the front that had not been cleared of the enemy, agreed that we would never let an adversary like this capture us alive. Later on there were more than enough cases where Soviet soldiers, after throwing up their hands as if

---

[1] The fact that the rest of the army probably shared my view became apparent when I took command of Eleventh Army. The Commissar Order had not been carried out there either. The few commissars who were shot in spite of this had not been captured in action but picked up in the rear areas and sentenced as either the leaders or organizers of partisans' groups. Their cases were handled in accordance with military law. *Author*

to surrender, reached for their arms as soon as our infantry came near enough, or where Soviet wounded feigned death and then fired on our troops when their backs were turned.

It was our general impression that while those of the enemy in frontline areas were in no way surprised by our attack, the Soviet military command had probably not been expecting it – or not for a while, anyway – and for that reason never got as far as committing its powerful reserves in any co-ordinated form.

There has been a great deal of argument as to whether the Soviet troop dispositions were actually defensive or offensive in character. If one went by the strength of the forces assembled in the western parts of the Soviet Union and the powerful concentration of armour in the Bialystok area and around Lwow, it was possible to contend – as Hitler did in support of his decision to attack – that sooner or later the Soviet Union would take the offensive. On the other hand, the layout of the Soviet forces on 22nd June 1941 did not indicate any *immediate* intention of aggression on the part of the Soviet Union.

I think it would be nearest the truth to describe the Soviet dispositions – to which the occupation of eastern Poland, Bessarabia and the Baltic territories had already contributed very strong forces – as a 'deployment against every contingency'. On 22nd June 1941, undoubtedly, the Soviet Union's forces were still strung out in such depth that they could then have been used only in a defensive role. Yet the pattern could have been switched in no time to meet any change in Germany's political or military situation. With a minimum of delay the Red Army – each of whose army groups was numerically, if not qualitatively, superior to the German army group facing it – could have closed up and become capable of going over to the attack. Thus the Soviet dispositions did in fact constitute a latent threat, even though they remained formally defensive up to 22nd June. The moment the Soviet Union had been offered a favourable opportunity – military or political – it could have become a direct menace to the Reich.

Certainly Stalin would have preferred to avoid a clash with the Reich in summer 1941. But had international developments sooner or later led the Soviet leadership to believe that it could resort to political pressure, or even to the threat of military intervention against Germany, its provisionally defensive deployment could swiftly have taken on an offensive character. It was, precisely as I have said, a 'deployment against every contingency'.

And now let us return to 56 Corps.

If the corps were to fulfil its task of seizing the Dvinsk crossings intact, it had to concentrate on two things. On the very first day it had to thrust 50 miles into enemy territory in order to capture the crossing over the Dubissa at Airogola. I knew the Dubissa sector from World War I. What we should find there was a deep, ravined valley whose slopes no tank could negotiate. In the First War our railway engineers had laboured there for months on end to span the gap with a masterly construction of timber. If the enemy now succeeded in blowing up the big road viaduct at Airogola, the corps would be hopelessly stuck and the enemy would have time on the steep far bank of the river to organize a defence which would in any case be extremely difficult to penetrate. That we could thereafter no longer expect to make a surprise descent on the Dvinsk bridges was perfectly obvious. The Airogola crossing was indispensable to us as a springboard.

Excessive though Corps H.Q.'s requirements may appear to have been, 8 Panzer Division (General Brandenberger), with which I spent most of the day, still fulfilled its task. After breaking through the frontier positions and over-running all enemy resistance further back, it seized the Airologa crossing with a reconnaissance force by the evening of 22nd June. 290 Division followed, marching at record speed; and 3 Motorized Infantry Division, which had started moving over the Memel at noon, was directed towards a crossing south of Airogola.

The first step had succeeded.

The second condition for success at Dvinsk was that the corps should push straight through to that town regardless of whether the formations on its flanks kept abreast or not. The capture of those precious bridges depended entirely on our being able to take the enemy there completely by surprise. Naturally we were fully aware that this course of action involved considerable risks.

As it turned out – and as we had hoped – the corps had the good fortune to strike a weak patch in the enemy's defences. Despite repeated enemy counter-attacks, some of which entailed hard fighting, the divisions were able to break this resistance relatively quickly.

While on our left 41 Panzer Corps was temporarily held up by a strong enemy grouping dug in around Siauliai (Schaulen), and on our right the left wing of Sixteenth Army was fighting for Kovno, 56 Panzer Corps actually reached the Dvinsk highway by 24th June in the area of Wilkomierz. Already 105 miles deep into enemy territory, it had not only outdistanced the German formations on either flank, but had also left the Soviet forces in the frontier zone far behind it. Now there were a bare 80 miles to go to reach the coveted bridges at Dvinsk. But could we maintain the pace? The enemy was certain to throw in fresh reserves against us. At any moment, moreover, he was liable – at any rate temporarily – to patch up the breach behind us and cut off our supplies. But in spite of warnings from Panzer Group H.Q., we had no intention of letting the Goddess of Fortune elude us as a result of over-cautiousness on our part. Though 290 Infantry Division had naturally been unable to keep up with the rest of the corps, the fact that it was following in our train gave us a certain safeguard – particularly as it had already drawn the attention of strong enemy forces that would otherwise have attacked us in the rear. Meanwhile Corps H.Q. and the two mobile divisions – 8 Panzer moving up the highway and 3 Motorized Division, with rather more difficulty, along by-ways to the south of this – were striking out for the victory prize of Dvinsk. Both divisions were able to smash the enemy reserves thrown in to meet them. In these battles, some of which were extremely fierce, the enemy lost seventy tanks (about half the strength of our own armour) and numerous batteries. At this stage we had hardly the time or the men to spare for rounding up prisoners.

Early on 26th June 8 Panzer Division was outside Dvinsk, and at 0800 hours I was handed a report at its divisional headquarters that our dash to capture the two big bridges had succeeded. Fighting was still going on in the town on the far side of the river, but the big road-bridge had fallen into our hands completely intact. The sentries detailed to set off the demolition charges had been overrun a few yards from the entrance. The railway bridge had been only slightly damaged by a small explosion and was still fit for use. The following day 3 Motorized Infantry Division pulled off a surprise crossing of the river upstream from the town. Our aim was achieved!

Before the offensive started I had been asked how long we thought we should take to reach Dvinsk, assuming that it was possible to do so. My answer had been that if it could not be done inside four days, we could hardly count on capturing the crossings intact. And now, exactly four days and five hours after zero hour, we had actually completed, as the crow flies, a non-stop dash through 200 miles of enemy territory. We had brought it off only because the name of Dvinsk had been foremost in the mind of every officer and man, and because we

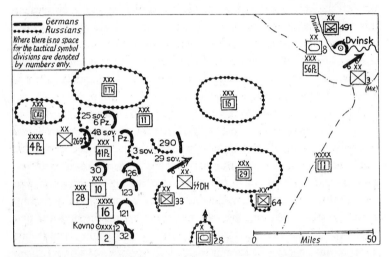

Map 7. Situation of Northern Army Group on 26th June 1941 after 56 Panzer Corps' Capture of Dvinsk.

had been ready to face heavy risks to reach our appointed goal. It gave us a tremendous feeling of achievement to drive over the big bridges into the town, despite the fact that the enemy had set most of it on fire before pulling out. It was an added satisfaction to know that we had not had to pay too high a price.

Naturally the corps' position – if only on the northern bank of the Dvina – was anything but secure. 41 Panzer Corps and the left wing of Sixteenth Army lay from 60 to 100 miles behind us. Between them and ourselves were several Soviet army corps, now withdrawing to the Dvina. Not only must we expect the enemy to do everything in his power to assail us on the northern bank: we also had to cover ourselves on the southern bank against those enemy formations approaching from the south. The precariousness of our position became further apparent when the Corps Q Branch was attacked from the rear in a wood not far from my own tactical headquarters.

However, we were less exercised by our present rather isolated position, which would not continue indefinitely, than by the problem of what the next move should be. Was the objective to be Leningrad, or should we turn towards Moscow? The Panzer Group Commander, who flew over to see us in a *Fieseler Storch* on 27th June, could tell us nothing. One might reasonably have expected the commander of a whole Panzer Group to be in the picture about future objectives, but this was obviously not the case. Instead, our enthusiasm was damped by an order to widen the bridgehead around Dvinsk and keep the crossings open. We were to wait for 41 Panzer Corps and the left wing of Sixteenth Army to move up, the former having been directed to cross the river at Jakobstadt.

While this was certainly the 'safe', staff-college solution, we had had other ideas. As we saw it, our sudden appearance so far behind the front must have caused considerable confusion among the enemy. He would obviously make every attempt to throw us back across the river, fetching in troops from any quarter to do so. The sooner we pushed on, therefore, the less chance he would have of offering us any systematic opposition with superior forces. If we drove on towards Pskov – while, of course, continuing to safeguard the Dvina crossings – and if, at the same time, Panzer Group H.Q. pushed the other panzer corps straight through Dvinsk behind us, it seemed likely that the enemy would have to keep on opposing us with whatever forces he happened to have on hand at the moment, and be incapable for the time being of fighting a set battle. As for the beaten enemy forces south of the Dvina, these could be left to the infantry armies coming up behind.

It goes without saying that the further a single panzer corps – or indeed the entire panzer group – ventured into the depths of the Russian hinterland, the greater the hazards became. Against this it may be said that the safety of a tank formation operating in the enemy's rear largely depends on its ability to keep moving. Once it comes to a halt it will immediately be assailed from all sides by the enemy's reserves.

But the Supreme Command did not share our view, and for this it certainly cannot be blamed. We should, after all, have been tempting Fortune more than somewhat had we tried to hold on to her coat-sleeve any longer, for there was always the possibility from now on that she would lead us over a precipice. And so, for the immediate future, the goal of Leningrad receded into the distance as far as we were concerned, leaving us to mark time at Dvinsk. As we had anticipated, the enemy was now moving up reinforcements – not only from Pskov, but from Minsk and Moscow as well. Before long we were having our work cut out to beat off the attacks he launched on the northern bank of the Dvina with an armoured division in support, and at a number of points the position became quite critical. In the course of a counter-attack made by 3 Panzer Division to recover some temporarily abandoned ground, our troops found the bodies of three officers and thirty men who had lain wounded in a field dressing-station captured by the enemy the previous day. Their mutilations were indescribable.

In the next few days the Soviet Air Force did everything possible to destroy the bridges which had been allowed to fall into our hands. With an almost mulish obstinacy one squadron after another flew in at treetop level, only to be shot down by our fighters or Flak. On one day alone they lost sixty-four aircraft in this way.

Finally, on 2nd July, we were able to move off again, after the SS Death's Head Division had joined the corps as its third mobile formation and 41 Panzer Corps had crossed the Dvina at Jakobstadt.

For its further advance Fourth Panzer Group had been allotted the axis Rezekne–Ostrov–Pskov. So Leningrad now beckoned, after all!

Nevertheless, six days had elapsed since the corps' surprise dash to Dvinsk. The enemy had had time to recover from the shock it must have given him to be suddenly confronted by German units on the northern bank of the Dvina.

A tank drive such as 56 Panzer Corps made to Dvinsk inevitably generates confusion and panic in the enemy communications zone; it ruptures the enemy's chain of command and makes it virtually impossible for him to co-ordinate his counter-measures. These advantages had now been waived as a result of Fourth Panzer Group's decision – however commendable its motives – to consolidate on the Dvina. Whether we should now be fortunate enough fully to regain that lead over the enemy was doubtful, to say the least. Certainly the only chance of doing so lay in the Panzer Group's being able to bring its forces into action as an integrated whole. As will be seen, however, this is precisely what it failed to do, even though the enemy's resistance remained insufficient to halt the advance.

To begin with, however, the Panzer Group moved off uniformly enough from the line Dvinsk–Jakobstadt in the direction of Pskov, 56 Panzer Corps proceeding along and to the east of the main road

Dvinsk–Rezekne–Ostrov–Pskov and 41 Panzer Corps to its left. The enemy's resistance proved tougher and more methodical than in the first few days of the campaign, but he was still being outfought over and over again.

The Panzer Group was now approaching the Stalin Line, a fortification which ran, in varying strength, along the original Soviet frontier from the southern extremity of Lake Peipus west of Pskov to what had once been the small Russian frontier fortress of Zebash.

At this stage Panzer Group H.Q. allocated the main road to 41 Panzer Corps to continue advancing on Ostrov, and swung 56 Panzer Corps hard east towards Zebash and Opochka. The intention was that we should break through the Stalin Line and outflank from the east a strong force of enemy armour believed to be based on Pskov. It was an excellent scheme if the force really existed and 56 Panzer Corps were able to execute the manœuvre with any speed. In our opinion, however, the former was not the case and the latter was not feasible, since in the direction it had been ordered to take, the corps had to negotiate extensive swamps lying forward of the Stalin Line. Our strong representations that both corps should be kept on the original line of advance towards Ostrov proved of no avail, and I regret to say that our misgivings regarding the swamps turned out to be fully justified.

8 Panzer Division did strike a timbered roadway leading across the swamps, but this was already completely blocked by the vehicles of a Soviet motorized division. It took days to clear the route and replace the blown bridges. When the division finally emerged from the swamps it ran into strong opposition which was broken only after relatively heavy fighting.

3 Motorized Division found only a narrow causeway, on which its vehicles could make no progress whatever. It had to be pulled out again and sent on to Ostrov behind 41 Panzer Corps.

Better ground – though it included a strong line of concrete fortifications – was struck by the SS Death's Head Division in its advance on Zebash. And now there emerged a weakness which was bound to be inherent in troops whose officers and N.C.O.s lacked solid training and proper experience. As far as its discipline and soldierly bearing went, the division in question undoubtedly made a good impression. I had even had reason to praise its extremely good march discipline – an important requirement for the efficient movement of motorized formations.

The division always showed great dash in the assault and was steadfast in defence. I had it under my command on frequent occasions later on and think it was probably the best *Waffen SS* division I ever came across. Its commander in those days was a brave man who was soon wounded and later killed.

None of these things, however, could compensate for deficient training in leadership. The division suffered excessive losses because its troops did not learn until they got into action what army units had mastered long ago. Their losses and lack of experience led them in turn to miss favourable opportunities, and this again caused unnecessary actions to be fought. I doubt if there is anything harder to learn than gauging the moment when a slackening of the enemy's resistance offers the attacker his decisive chance. The upshot of all this was that I repeatedly had to come to the division's assistance, without even then being able to prevent a sharp rise in casualties. After a matter of ten days the three regiments of the division had to be regrouped to form two new ones.

Yet, bravely as the Waffen SS divisions always fought, and fine though their achievements may have been, there is not the least doubt that it was an inexcusable mistake to set them up as a separate military organization. Hand-picked replacements who could have filled the posts of N.C.O.s in the army were expended on a quite inadmissible scale in the Waffen SS, which in general paid a toll of blood incommensurate with its actual gains. Naturally this cannot be laid at the door of the SS troops themselves. The blame for such unnecessary consumption of manpower must lie with the men who set up these special units for purely political motives, in the face of opposition from all the competent army authorities.

In no circumstances must we forget, however, that the Waffen SS, like the good comrades they were, fought shoulder to shoulder with the army at the front and always showed themselves courageous and reliable. Without doubt a large proportion of them would have been only too glad to be withdrawn from the jurisdiction of a man like Himmler and incorporated into the army.

Before returning to the fortunes of 56 Panzer Corps, I should like to give the reader a picture of how the command staff of a tank formation had to work during the last war.

As late as the Battle of St. Privat-Gravelotte, in the War of 1870–71, my grandfather assembled his staff on a hill from which he commanded a view of the entire battlefield and could personally direct the operations of his army corps. He was even able to ride over to the regiments as they deployed for the assault and, so the story goes, addressed some pretty harsh words to one battery for unlimbering too far from the enemy.

Such scenes are naturally a thing of the past. The staffs of World War I were forced further and further to the rear as the range of enemy artillery fire increased, and the breadth of the fronts rendered visual survey and personal command on the battlefield a sheer impossibility. Efficient telephone links were the decisive thing from then on, and Schlieffen's picture of the Supreme War Lord who sat behind his desk issuing stirring orders over the telephone duly became a reality.

World War II in its turn called for other methods of command, especially in the case of highly mobile formations. In the case of the latter, situations changed so rapidly, and favourable opportunities came and went so fast, that no tank-force commander could afford to bind himself to a command post any great distance to the rear. If he waited too far back for reports from his forward units, decisions would be taken much too late and all kinds of chances would be missed. Often, too, when a successful action had just been fought, it was necessary to counteract the only too natural phenomenon of battle fatigue and to instil new life into the men.

It was even more vital, in view of the unprecedented demands which our new war of movement made on the energies of officers and men, that higher commanders should show themselves as often as possible to the front-line troops. The ordinary soldier must never have the feeling that the 'top brass' are busy concocting orders somewhere to the rear without knowing what it looks like out in front. It gives him a certain satisfaction to see the Commanding General in the thick of it once in a while or watching a successful attack go in. Only by being up with the fighting troops day in and day out can one get to know their needs, listen to their worries and be of assistance to them. A senior commander must not only be the man who perpetually has demands to make in the accomplishment of his mission; he must be an ally and a comrade as well. Quite apart from anything else, he himself derives fresh energy from these visits to the fighting troops. Many's the time, when visiting a divisional headquarters, that I have heard anxieties voiced about the diminishing battle morale of the fighting troops and the excessive strain to which they were often unavoidably subjected. Such worries inevitably preoccupied commanders more and more as time went on, for it was they who ultimately bore the responsibility for the regiments and battalions. Yet once I had gone forward to the troops in the line, I was often overjoyed to find them more confident and optimistic than I had been led to expect – not infrequently because they had fought a successful action in the meantime. And then, as I smoked a cigarette with a tank crew or chatted with a rifle company about the overall situation, I never failed to encounter that irrepressible urge to press onward, that readiness to put forth the very last ounce of energy, which are the hallmarks of the German soldier. Experiences like this are among the finest things a senior commander can ask for. The higher one rises, unfortunately, the rarer they become. An army or army group commander is quite unable to mix in with the fighting troops to the same extent as the general commanding a corps.

Even the corps commander, of course, cannot be permanently on the road. A man who is constantly rushing around his forward areas, and can never be found when required, virtually hands over his command to his staff. This may be quite a good thing in many cases, but it is still not the role for which he was intended.

Everything ultimately hinges – particularly with highly mobile formations – on a rational organization of command duties, the continuity of which must be maintained at all costs.

It was indispensable that the Corps Q branch should usually remain stationary for several days at a time in order to keep the flow of supplies moving. The Commanding General and his operations branch, on the other hand, had to move their tactical headquarters forward once or even twice a day if they were to keep in touch with the mechanized divisions. This called for a high degree of mobility on the part of the headquarters. The only way to achieve it was to cut the tactical staff to a minimum – always a salutary measure where command is concerned – and to do without any of the usual comforts. Needless to say, the patron saint of Red Tape, who, apart from her other activities, I fear, likes to tag along behind armies in the field, used to have a pretty thin time when we were operating under conditions of this kind.

We did not waste time looking for accommodation. In France

castles and mansions had been ours for the asking. The small wooden huts of the east held little appeal, particularly in view of the ubiquity of certain 'domestic pets'. Consequently our tactical headquarters lived almost the whole time in tents and the two command wagons which, together with a few wartime *Volkswagen* and the vehicles of the wireless section and telephone exchange, carried our other ranks when we changed location. I myself slept in a sleeping-bag in the small tent I shared with my A.D.C., and do not remember having used a proper bed more than three times throughout this panzer drive. The one man with any objection to living under canvas was our senior military assistant, who preferred to sleep in his car. Unfortunately he had to leave his long legs sticking out through the door, with the result that he could never get his wet boots off after a rainy night.

We always used to pitch our little camp in a wood or a copse near the main axis of advance – if possible by a lake or stream so that we could take a quick plunge before breakfast or whenever we came back caked with dust and grime from a trip to the front.

While the Chief-of-Staff naturally had to stay behind the command post to deal with the work and telephone calls, I spent the days, and often part of the nights, out on the road. I usually left early in the morning, after receiving the dawn situation reports and issuing any orders that were necessary, to visit divisions and forward troops. At noon I would return to the command post for a while and then go out to visit another division, for as often as not it is just around eventide that success beckons or a fresh impetus is needed. By the time we returned to our tented camp, which would meanwhile have been shifted to a new location, we were dead tired and as black as sweeps. On such occasions it was a special treat to find that, thanks to the forethought of Major Niemann, my second assistant, we were to have a roast chicken or even a bottle of wine from his own small stock instead of the usual evening fare of rye bread, smoked sausage and margarine. I am afraid that however far forward we were, chickens and geese were very hard to come by, having as a rule been snapped up by other fanciers before we appeared on the scene. When, with the onset of the early autumn rains, it became rather too chilly to sit in the tents, we found it both pleasant and refreshing to use the sauna baths which, however primitive in form, were to be found on almost every farmstead.

Such flexible leadership on my part was, of course, possible only because I was able to take a wireless vehicle along with me on these trips under our excellent signals officer Kohler, who later became a General Staff major. Thanks to the admirable speed with which he could raise our tactical staff or any divisional headquarters on the air, I was kept continuously informed of the situation throughout the corps sector, and decisions taken by me on the spot could be passed back with the minimum of delay. I might add that during my imprisonment after the war Kohler proved a most unselfish friend and helper to my wife.

Apart from my faithful drivers Nagel and Schumann and two out-riders, my constant companion on these trips was my A.D.C., Lieuten-ant Specht. We called him 'Pepo' because of his short, wiry figure and his youthful freshness and happy-go-lucky nature. He was a young cavalry officer of the best type. Brisk, vigorous, somewhat irresponsible where danger was concerned, shrewd and quick on the uptake, he was always cheerful and slightly saucy. All these qualities had endeared him to me. He rode brilliantly (his father was a keen horse-breeder, his mother a first-class horsewoman) and had won several big events as a newly commissioned officer just before the war. He was game for any-thing, and would have liked nothing better than to take his Command-ing General out on skirmishing patrols. As long as we belonged to a panzer corps and could be daily at the scene of action, Pepo was con-tent with me and his lot, but when I became an army commander and could no longer be up at the front so often, he began to champ at the bit. It was a very proper attitude for a young officer, and I gave him his head on a number of occasions. In the Crimea he twice led a reconnais-sance squadron with great skill and dash. When we were in front of Leningrad I again sent him to a division, but this time he crashed while on his way there in a *Fieseler Storch*. The loss was a heavy blow to me.

Now let us return to 56 Panzer Corps. By 9th July it had become clear that Fourth Panzer Group's attempt to outflank the enemy forces it believed to be at Pskov by sending our corps round to the east had no hope of success on account of the marshiness of the ground and the strength of the enemy's resistance. There was nothing for it but to dis-continue the manœuvre and re-direct Corps H.Q. and 8 Panzer Division on to the original northern axis towards Ostrov, as had already been done with 3 Motorized Infantry Division. Still, since moving off from Dvinsk the corps had – according to intelligence reports available on 10th July – smashed four or five of the enemy's infantry divisions, one armoured division and one motorized division – forces far superior to its own numerically. Apart from the thousands of prisoners we had taken, our booty since crossing the Reich frontiers included sixty aircraft, 316 guns (including anti-tank and anti-aircraft), 205 tanks and 600 lorries. But the enemy, though pushed back to the east, was still not destroyed – as was very soon to become apparent.

Now that the Panzer Group was concentrated around Ostrov, we at 56 Panzer Corps hoped for a rapid, direct and uniform advance on Leningrad, with ourselves passing through Luga and 41 Panzer Corps through Pskov. In our view this offered the best chance not only of effecting the quick capture of the city but also of cutting off the enemy forces retreating through Livonia into Estonia before our Eighteenth Army. The task of safeguarding this operation on its open eastern flank would have had to devolve on Sixteenth Army as it moved up behind Fourth Panzer Group.

Presumably acting on directives from the highest level, however, Panzer Group H.Q. decided otherwise.

41 Panzer Corps was allotted the main road through Luga along which to advance on Leningrad.

56 Panzer Corps, once again pulling out to the east, was to advance through Porkhov and Novgorod to Chudovo in order to break communications between Leningrad and Moscow at the earliest possible date.

Important though the latter task was, these orders must once again have led to the two corps becoming widely dispersed, as a result of which each was liable to be deprived of the necessary striking power. The danger was increased by the fact that much of the country to be crossed this side of Leningrad was marshy or wooded and hardly suitable for large armoured formations.

A particularly regrettable step was the removal from 56 Panzer Corps of the SS Death's Head Division, which had meanwhile been relieved in the Zebesh–Opochka area by 290 Infantry Division. The SS Division was now retained south of Ostrov as the Panzer Group reserve. Thus, as had previously happened when we set off from the German frontier, the Panzer Group's main effort was again placed on its left wing – 41 Panzer Corps. 56 Panzer Corps was dispatched on its wide sweep round to Chudovo with only one armoured and one infantry division, thereby being denied the essential protection of its open south flank by the SS division following along in echelon on the right. It was a particularly risky move when one considered that even though the enemy forces engaged by the corps to date had been outfought, they were far from annihilated.

Be that as it may, we were still convinced that the corps would continue to find its safety in speed of movement.

3 Motorized Division, which only came back under command at Ostrov, had already taken Porkhov on 10th July after a hard struggle and was put on a minor road leading north. 8 Panzer Division was to drive through Zoltsy to seize the vital crossing point where the Mshaga ran into Lake Ilmen.

In a series of battles, most of them fierce ones, the advance was kept going for the next few days. Except for one attack on the corps command post on the north bank of the Shelon river in the early hours of 14th July – apparently carried out by enemy reconnaissance forces – the enemy had so far not made his presence felt on our open flank in the south. That same day, at my insistence, 8 Panzer Division, which had taken Zoltsy after a battle against an enemy well equipped with artillery and armour, pushed on to the Mshaga sector. It found the bridge already blown.

Meanwhile Panzer Group H.Q. had transferred the main effort of its advance even further west of the Luga road. It had moved 41 Panzer Corps' three mechanized formations northwards to bar the way to the enemy forces retiring through Narva, north of Lake Peipus, before Eighteenth Army. Only one infantry division of the corps (the 269th) had been left on the road to Luga.

Thus 56 Panzer Corps suddenly found itself even more isolated than before in its wide swing towards Chudovo. Accordingly we got on to Panzer Corps H.Q. to point out that if we were to carry out the Chudovo assignment our corps must have the immediate support both of the SS Death's Head Division and also of Sixteenth Army's 1 Corps, which was relatively close behind.

Before this appeal could be answered, however, 56 Panzer Corps was already in trouble. Early on 15th July we received a number of most unpleasant reports at the corps command post on the Shelon, west of Zoltsy. The enemy had launched a powerful attack from the north into the flank of 8 Panzer Division, now strung out to the Mshaga, and simultaneously driven up from the south over the Shelon. This meant that the bulk of 8 Panzer Division's fighting troops, who were located between Zoltsy and the Mshaga, were cut off from the division's rear echelons, in whose area corps H.Q. was located. But that was not all. The enemy had closed the trap behind ourselves, too, by pushing up strong forces from the south to straddle our supply route. At the same time 3 Motorized Division, advancing further northwards, found itself being attacked by superior enemy forces from the north and north-east at Maly Utogorsh.

It was obviously the enemy's intention to encircle 56 Panzer Corps while it was isolated. The failure to echelon the SS Death's Head Division along our rear right flank had enabled him to attack across the Shelon with those of his forces which lay south of us. At the same time the removal of 41 Panzer Corps from the Luga road had released the strong enemy forces there, and these were now attacking our northern flank.

Our corps' position at that moment was hardly an enviable one, and we could not help wondering whether we had taken rather too great a risk this time. Had we been carried away by our previous successes to the extent of paying insufficient heed to the enemy on our southern flank? Yet what other chance should we had have of carrying out our mission? As matters stood, the only course open to us was to pull 8 Panzer Division back through Zoltsy to escape the encirclement that now threatened. 3 Motorized Division had to be disengaged at the same time to give the corps back its freedom of movement. The next few days proved critical, with the enemy straining every nerve to keep up his encirclement and throwing in, besides his rifle divisions, two armoured divisions enjoying strong artillery and air support. 8 Panzer Division nevertheless managed to break through Zoltsy to the west and re-group, despite having to be temporarily supplied from the air. Before completing its own disengagement, 3 Motorized Division had to beat off seventeen successive attacks. In the meantime, after Panzer Group H.Q. had put the SS Death's Head Division under our command, it was possible for us to clear the corps supply route.

By 18th July the crisis was as good as over, the corps being by then firmly established around Dno on a front facing roughly east by north-east. The earlier danger on our open flank in the south was removed by the proximity of Sixteenth Army's 1 Corps, which was now drawing near Dno.

One consolation was afforded us by the capture from a courier aircraft of a letter bearing the signature of Marshal Voroshilov, whom I had

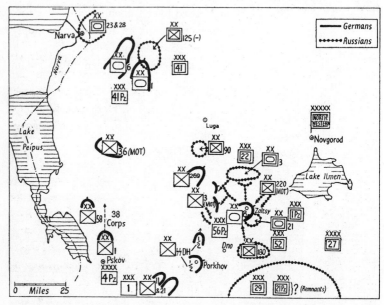

Map 8. Encirclement of 56 Panzer Corps at Zoltsy (15th–18th July 1941).

met in Moscow in 1931 and who now commanded the 'front' opposite us. This not only confirmed that very substantial elements of the Soviet armies had been wiped out, but in the same connexion referred specifically to the battles around Zoltsy.

As long as we had been surrounded, our only links with the rear had been at best by wireless or aircraft. The very moment our lines of communication were restored, however, the usual plethora of paper descended on us. One item deserving special mention was an ominous inquiry telegraphed through from the Supreme Command. Moscow radio, in somewhat premature celebration of our corps' encirclement, had reported the capture of certain top-secret data on our multiple rocket-launcher. The Soviets had obviously taken an intense dislike to this new weapon, with which we were able to fire missiles of flaming oil. Already the Soviet Army facing us had wirelessed a warning *en clair* that if we did not stop using it they would retaliate with gas – an empty threat, of course, in view of the complete inadequacy of their own chemical warfare defences. In these circumstances it was understandable that they should make such a song and dance about the capture of this information. Now we were being called upon to explain how a top-secret document could possibly fall into enemy hands. Obviously it had not been taken from the fighting troops, but from a transport column intercepted by the Soviets when they cut our supply route. This sort of thing was liable to happen to any armoured formation operating far ahead of its own army front. In response to the Supreme Command's inquiry we duly reported the facts of the case, adding that to avoid any further censure we would henceforth refrain from cruising around on our own some 60 miles behind the enemy lines.

On 19th July we had been informed by Panzer Group H.Q. that it now planned to send 56 Panzer Corps through Luga to Leningrad. 269 Infantry Division, which was assembled on the Luga road, had already been placed under our command. We still had no success with our proposal that the forces of the Panzer Group be at long last concentrated for concerted action – preferably up north with 41 Panzer Corps east of Narva (where there were four serviceable roads to Leningrad) rather than along the Luga axis, which ran through extensive woodlands.

For the rest, we were first to launch an attack eastwards with 1 Corps against the Mshaga sector, which we had already reached once before. Apparently the Supreme Command was still sticking to its plan for a wide outflanking movement and was even prepared to go round to the east of Lake Ilmen. For the time being, therefore, we and 1 Corps were involved in fresh battles, in the course of which the enemy was thrown back across the Mshaga.

On 26th July we had a visit from the *Oberquartiermeister I* of O.K.H., General Paulus. I put him in the picture about the battles we had fought to date and pointed out how run-down our Panzer Corps had become in country which was most unsuitable for the use of armoured troops. I also drew his attention to the disadvantages of scattering the Panzer Group's resources. The losses of our corps' three mobile divisions already amounted to 6,000 men, and both the troops and equipment were being subjected to excessive strain, even though 8 Panzer Division had been able, during a few days' rest, to bring the number of its serviceable tanks back from eighty up to the 150 mark.

I told Paulus that in my opinion the best thing to do would be to withdraw the entire Panzer Group from an area where a rapid advance was almost out of the question and to use it against Moscow. If, on the other hand, the idea of driving on Leningrad and executing a wide encircling movement through Chudovo were to be maintained, it was essential that infantry be made available. Once the wooded zone had been cleared, our own corps must be saved for the final thrust on the city, otherwise the mobile divisions would reach Leningrad in no fit state for fighting. In any case, I pointed out, such an operation would take time. If we wanted to gain swift possession of Leningrad and the coastline, the only thing to do was to concentrate the whole Panzer Group up north in the area east of Narva, whence it could drive straight for the city.

General Paulus entirely agreed with my views.

Initially, however, things turned out quite differently. While Sixteenth Army, consisting of 1 Corps and another corps which had just arrived, took over the Mshaga front west of Lake Ilmen, it was decided, after all, that 56 Panzer Corps should now carry out the thrust on Leningrad up the route through Luga. For this purpose we were allotted 3 Motorized Infantry Division, 269 Infantry Division and the newly-arrived SS Police Division.

This had the effect of dispersing the Panzer Group's mechanized forces further than ever. The SS Death's Head Division remained with Sixteenth Army by Lake Ilmen, and 8 Panzer Division was taken into reserve by the Panzer Group to be initially employed on clearing the communications zone of partisans – a role for which it was not only far too valuable but also quite unsuitable. The corps now had only one mobile division (3 Motorized) in the Luga area, while 41 Panzer Corps' own three were in action east of Narva. The maxim established by Colonel-General Guderian on the use of armour was '*klotzen, nicht kleckern*' – 'Don't spatter: Boot 'em!' In our own case the very opposite course seemed to have been taken. All our efforts to retain the three mobile divisions irrespective of which way our corps was sent proved unsuccessful. Experience has long shown that when forces run short, only very few commanders manage to maintain a tidy order of battle and avoid splitting their formations.

It would take up too much space here if I were to describe the battles around Luga. They proved very tough indeed. While the enemy had had only a very modest number of troops available in this area a few weeks previously, he had now brought his strength up to a full corps of three divisions supported by strong artillery and armour. To cap this, the country around Luga was a Russian training area with which, of course, the enemy was intimately acquainted, and in addition, he had had time to dig himself in properly.

While these battles were still in progress, our corps was given a new task. At long last it was to join up with 41 Panzer Corps in the north for the assault on Leningrad. Even now, however, only Corps H.Q. and 3 Motorized Division were involved: 8 Panzer and the SS Death's Head Division were to continue in their present role.

On 15th August we handed over at Luga to H.Q. 50 Corps under General Lindemann, an old friend of mine from World War I days, and began moving north. The route to our new command post on Lake Samro, 25 miles south-west of Narva, was so bad that we took eight hours to travel a distance of 125 miles. We had hardly reached Lake Samro late that evening when a telephone call was received from Panzer Group H.Q. ordering us to halt 3 Motorized Division, which was coming up behind us, and to drive straight down south again next morning to report to H.Q. Sixteenth Army in Dno. We, together with 3 Motorized Division and the SS Death's Head Division, which was being pulled over from Lake Ilmen, were now to join that formation. No one will pretend that we were particularly pleased at these peregrinations. The one admirable exception was our quartermaster, Major Kleinschmidt, whose cheerful equanimity was quite undaunted by the news that he would have to swing his supply and transport arrangements round through an angle of 180 degrees.

So, on 16th August, we moved back to Dno along the same dreadful route we had covered the day before. This time the distance was 160 miles, and we took thirteen hours to do it. Luckily, 3 Motorized had not come too far north and could be turned round in good time, but what the troops thought of it all I do not care to imagine.

The ultimate reason for the change was probably that our sum total of forces was inadequate and that the whole area between Leningrad, Pskov and Lake Ilmen was thoroughly unsuitable as tank country.

The picture we were given on our arrival at H.Q. Sixteenth Army was the following: 10 Corps, fighting on the right wing of the army south of Lake Ilmen, had been attacked and pushed back by far superior enemy forces (Thirty-Eighth Soviet Army, comprising eight divisions and cavalry formations). It was now fighting a difficult defensive battle south of Lake Ilmen on a front facing south, with the enemy obviously trying to outflank it in the west. 56 Panzer Corps was to provide the urgently needed relief.

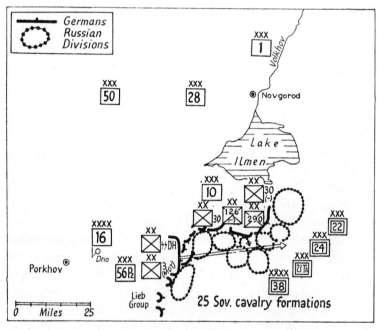

Map 9. 56 Panzer Corps' Drive into Flank of Thirty-Eighth Soviet Army on 19th August 1941.

What our corps had to do – if possible without attracting the attention of the enemy – was to introduce its two mechanized divisions into his western flank east of Dno in order to roll up the front while he was busy attacking our own 10 Corps in the north. The task confronting us was a pretty one, and it was gratifying to see how pleased the SS were to come back under our command. It was only a pity that we could not get 8 Panzer Division released for such a worth-while operation.

By 18th August the carefully concealed move of the two divisions into camouflaged assembly areas in the enemy's western flank had been

successfully completed, and when the corps unleashed its attack early
next day the enemy was obviously taken completely by surprise. Our
plan to roll up the enemy front from the flank proved entirely successful, and in the engagements that followed we and 10 Corps, which had
now returned to the attack, jointly succeeded in roundly defeating
Thirty-Eighth Soviet Army. By 22nd August we had reached the
Lovat south-east of Staraya Russa, despite the fact that in that sandy
terrain, with its almost complete absence of roads, the infantry of the
two motorized divisions had had to advance most of the way on foot.
During those few days 56 Panzer Corps alone captured 12,000 prisoners, 141 tanks, 246 guns and several hundred automatic weapons and
motor vehicles. The booty included two extremely interesting items.
One was a brand-new 8·8-cm. anti-aircraft battery of German manu-
facture from the year 1941. The other was the very first Soviet salvo
gun to fall into German hands. As I was most anxious to have the
latter evacuated, I was all the more indignant to find that it could not be
moved because somebody had helped himself to the tyres! The
offender proved to be none other than my second assistant, Major
Niemann, who had discovered that these tyres fitted our own command
wagon. He looked somewhat crestfallen when told to hand them back
for reassembly.

While the fighting troops, who once again had to exert themselves
to the utmost, were enjoying a brief rest on the Lovat, there was talk
of withdrawing 56 Panzer Corps for employment elsewhere, but then
Sixteenth Army's eastward advance south of Lake Ilmen was resumed,
after all. At the end of August, however, the first rains of that summer
set in, turning every road into such a quagmire that for a while both
motorized divisions were completely stuck. At the same time the enemy
moved up new forces. In lieu of his beaten Thirty-Eighth Army three
new armies appeared along the Kholm–Ilmen front opposite our own
Sixteenth Army – the Twenty-Seventh, Thirty-Fourth and Eleventh.
Fresh battles ensued, but to describe these in detail would take up too
much space. 56 Panzer Corps forced a crossing over the Pola and
pushed on to a point just short of Demyansk. Quite apart from the
fact that enemy resistance was stiffening, the painful effort of advancing
along roads several feet deep in mud imposed a particular strain on both
men and equipment. During this period the whole of my time was
spent out with my divisions, but even my sturdy *Kübelwagen* often had

to be towed by a tractor to make any headway on those so-called roads.

During this period even we came to feel the divergence between the aims pursued by Hitler (Leningrad) and O.K.H. (Moscow). The commander of Sixteenth Army, Colonel-General Busch, told me he intended to push east as far as the Valdai Heights so that he could later advance in the direction Kalinin–Moscow. It seemed that H.Q. Northern Army Group did not agree – principally because it was worried by the prospect of baring the army's eastern flank. While at the beginning of September, 57 Panzer Corps intervened in our operations from the area of Central Army Group in the south, we ourselves were told on 12th September that we would shortly be moved south with 3 Motorized Division to come under command of Ninth Army in Central Army Group. Even as a corps commander one could make neither head nor tail of all this chopping and changing, though I did form the impression that it was all ultimately due to the tug-of-war evidently going on between Hitler and O.K.H. over whether the strategic aim should be Moscow or Leningrad.

At all events, the battles which Sixteenth Army fought in those weeks with 56 Panzer Corps taking part were continuously successful, and on 16th September O.K.W. was able to announce the defeat of substantial elements of the Eleventh, Twenty-Seventh and Thirty-Fourth Soviet Armies. Nine enemy divisions were considered to have been destroyed and nine more badly battered.

We still failed to find any real satisfaction in these achievements, however, for no one was clear any longer what the actual aim of our strategy was or what higher purpose all these battles were supposed to serve. Whatever else might happen, the period of sensational advances of the kind we had made on Dvinsk was at an end.

My days at the head of 56 Panzer Corps were now numbered. On the evening of 12th September, under a steady downpour of rain, I was sitting in my tent with one or two officers of my staff. Ever since it had begun to get dark early we had taken to playing bridge to while away the time until the evening situation reports came in. Suddenly the telephone rang at my elbow and I was asked to take a call from my friend Busch, the army commander. A telephone message at this late hour did not usually bode anything pleasant, but on this occasion Busch read me out an order that had come over the teleprinter from O.K.H.:

*'General of the Infantry v. Manstein will leave forthwith for Southern
Army Group to assume command of Eleventh Army.'*

Every soldier will sense how proud and happy I felt at the prospect
of leading a whole army from now on. To me, at the time, this seemed
the peak of my military career.

Early next morning I took leave – only by telephone, unfortunately
– of the divisions under my command and then bade farewell to my
own staff. In doing so I had grateful memories of all that 56 Panzer
Corps and its staff had achieved in the past months, when the headquarters and divisions had grown into a thoroughly integrated unit.

Joyful though I was in taking over this new and bigger task, I was
nevertheless fully aware that probably the most satisfying phase of my
life as a soldier was now over. For three whole months I had lived close
to the fighting troops, sharing not only their trials and tribulations, but
also the pride of their successes. Time and again I had been able to
derive fresh energy from the very fact of this common experience, from
the cheerful devotion with which everyone went about his duty and
from the intimacy of comradeship. From now on my position would
prevent me from working among the troops to the extent I had done to
date.

It was unlikely that I should ever again live through anything comparable to the impetuous dash of 56 Panzer Corps in the first days of
the campaign – the fulfilment of all a tank-force commander's dreams.
I thus found the leave-taking extremely hard – most of all from my
experienced Chief-of-Staff, Colonel Baron v. Elverfeldt, a cool, high-
minded and never-failing counsellor. The same applied to my high-
spirited and talented Chief of Operations, Major Detleffsen, the head of
my Intelligence branch, Guido v. Kessel, and that indefatigable quartermaster, Major Kleinschmidt. Another of those I had to leave behind me
was the head of my adjutant-general's branch, Major v. d. Marwitz,
who had joined us only a few weeks previously and with whom I had
close ties of friendship dating back to the days we had spent together
in Pomerania and at the military academy.

When I left on the morning of 13th September to take formal leave
of my friend Busch, the only people I could take with me were my
A.D.C., Specht, and my two drivers, Nagel and Schumann. Not one of
them is alive today.

THE CRIMEAN CAMPAIGN

IF I NOW attempt to describe the battles fought in the Crimea by Eleventh Army and its Rumanian fellow-combatants, my main reason for doing so is to commemorate my comrades of the Crimean Army. At the same time I should like to give the men who survived those battles a general account of the events of which they could have had only an incomplete picture at the time.

These men put up a tremendous performance in the period 1941-2, fighting one battle after another against an adversary who almost invariably outnumbered them. In attack and pursuit their aggressive spirit was unparalleled; and when the situation appeared hopeless they would stand and fight unflinchingly. Often they may not have known what compelled us to make demands on them that seemed impossible to fulfil, or why they were flung from one action to another and from one front to the next. And yet they went to the very limit of endurance to carry out these demands, reciprocating the trust of those who led them.

But Eleventh Army's campaign in the Crimea also deserves attention outside the immediate circle of its participants, for it is one of the few cases where an army was still able to operate independently in a segregated theatre of war, left to its own devices and free of interference from the Supreme Command. It was a campaign which, in ten months of incessant fighting, included both offensive and defensive battles, mobile warfare with full freedom of action, a headlong pursuit operation, landings by an enemy in control of the sea, partisan engagements and an assault on a powerfully defended fortress.

Finally, the campaign is of interest because it was ought over the Black Sea peninsula which even today bears traces of the Greeks, Goths, Genoese and Tartars. Once before, in the war of 1854-6, this had been a focal point of history, and the names of places which played a role then – the Alma, Balaclava, Inkerman and Malakoff – will be heard here all over again.

Operationally, however, the war of 1854–6 can in no way be compared with the campaign fought in 1941–2. In the former case the Western Powers enjoyed naval supremacy and all the advantages this implies, whereas in the Crimean campaign of 1941–2 it was the Russians who controlled the Black Sea. Our Eleventh Army had not only to conquer the Crimea and Sevastopol, but also to contend with all the possibilities open to the Russians by reason of their mastery at sea.

THE SITUATION ON MY ASSUMPTION OF COMMAND

On 17th September 1941 I arrived at Eleventh Army H.Q. in Niko-layev, the Russian naval base at the mouth of the Bug, and took over command.

My predecessor, *Colonel-General Ritter v. Schobert*, had been buried in the city the day before. On one of his daily visits to the front he had landed on a Russian minefield in his *Fieseler Storch* aircraft, and both he and his pilot had been killed. In him the German Army lost an officer of great integrity and one of its most experienced front-line soldiers. His troops would have followed him anywhere.

H.Q. Eleventh Army, whose operations staff was later to form the headquarters of Don Army Group, was almost without exception a superb team of men, and I have grateful memories of the assistance I received from so many splendid officers in two and a half tough years of war. We got on extraordinarily well together, and when I relinquished my command in 1944 many of them did not want to remain on the staff.

The novelty of my new position did not end with the expansion of my sphere of command from an army corps into an army. I did not discover until I reached Nikolayev that in addition to Eleventh Army I was also to take over Third Rumanian Army, which was affiliated to it.

For political reasons the actual chain of command in this part of the Eastern Front had not been easy to arrange.

Command of the allied forces committed from Rumania – Third and Fourth Rumanian Armies and Eleventh German Army – had been entrusted to the Rumanian Head of State, Marshal Antonescu, but at the same time he was bound by the directives of Southern Army Group, commanded by Field-Marshal v. Rundstedt. H.Q. Eleventh Army had been acting as the connecting link between the Marshal and Army Group H.Q. and had advised him on operational matters.

By the time I arrived, however, the situation was such that Antonescu only retained control of Fourth Rumanian Army, which he had directed to attack Odessa. The other Rumanian army taking part in the campaign, the Third, had been placed under command of Eleventh Army, which henceforth took its orders direct from H.Q. Southern Army Group.

At the best of times it is embarrassing for an army headquarters to have to control another self-contained army in addition to its own, and the task was necessarily twice as difficult when the army in question happened to be an allied one. What made things harder still was that there were not only certain differences of organization, training and leadership between the two armies – as is always the case where allies are concerned – but also a noticeable contrast in their fighting qualities. From time to time this led us to take a firmer hand in our ally's handling of an operation than was usual with our own forces or desirable in the interest of good relations.

That we were able, despite these difficulties, to collaborate with the Rumanian headquarters staffs and fighting units without any real friction occurring was primarily due to the loyalty of the commander of Third Rumanian Army, General (later Colonel-General) Dumitrescu. The German liaison teams which we had attached to all Rumanian staffs down to divisional level also contributed by their tact, and when necessary by their firmness, to this co-operation.

The man most deserving of mention in this respect, however, is *Marshal Antonescu*. Whatever verdict posterity may pass on him as a politician, Antonescu was a real patriot, a good soldier and certainly our most loyal ally. He was a soldier who, having once bound up his country's destiny with that of the Reich, did everything possible until his overthrow to put Rumania's military power and war potential to effective use on our side. If this did not always work out quite as he had hoped, the reason was to be found in the internal circumstances of his State and his régime. At all events, he remained faithful to his allies, and I can only speak with gratitude of our work together.

As for the *Rumanian Army*, there is no doubt that it had considerable weaknesses. Although the Rumanian soldier – who was usually of peasant origin – was modest in his wants and usually a capable, brave fighter, the possibilities of training him as an individual fighting man who could think for himself in action, let alone as a non-commissioned officer, were to a great extent limited by the low standard of general education in Rumania. In cases where members of the German minority did come up to the necessary standard, Rumanian national prejudice tended to impede any advancement. Neither were such outmoded practices as flogging likely to improve the quality of the rank and file. Their effect was rather to make Rumanian soldiers of German stock do everything they could to join one of the German armed services or – since the latter were not allowed to accept them – the Waffen-SS.

One disadvantage as far as the inner stability of Rumanian troops was concerned was the absence of a non-commissioned officer corps as we know it. I am afraid people in Germany nowadays are all too ready to forget what a debt we have owed in the past to our excellent body of regular N.C.O.s.

Another factor of far-reaching importance was that a considerable proportion of the Rumanian officers holding senior and medium appointments were not up to requirement. Most of all, the Rumanians lacked that close link between officers and men which tends to be taken for granted in the German Army. Man management with them was entirely devoid of the 'Prussian' tradition.

Because they had no war experience, the combat training of the Rumanians fell short of the exigencies of modern warfare. This led to unnecessary losses, which in turn was bound to affect morale.

The military leaders, who had been under French influence since 1918, still thought in terms of World War I. Weapons and equipment were partly obsolete and also inadequate. This was particularly true of the anti-tank units, with the result that they could hardly be expected to hold their ground against Soviet tank attacks. Whether Germany could not have rendered more effective help in this respect is a question for others to decide.

One final drawback regarding the use of Rumanian troops on the Eastern Front was their terrific respect for 'the Russians'. In difficult situations this was liable to end in a panic. Indeed, it is a problem of which account must be taken in any war against Russia involving South-East European nations. In the case of the Bulgarians and Serbs the insecurity is increased by their sense of Slavonic affinity.

There was one other factor that could not be entirely disregarded in any assessment of the combat efficiency of Rumanian troops. At the time with which we are dealing Rumania had already attained her fundamental war aim, the reconquest of Bessarabia. Even 'Transnistria', the territory between the Dniester and Bug which she had been persuaded to accept by Hitler, did not really lie within the scope of Rumania's aspirations. It was understandable that the idea of pushing even further into the Russia they dreaded so much was none too warmly received by many Rumanians.

Despite all the defects and reservations mentioned above, however, the Rumanian troops performed their duty as best they could. Above all, they always readily submitted to German military leadership and did not, like other allies of ours, put matters of prestige before material necessity. Undoubtedly the soldierly mentality of Marshal Antonescu exerted a decisive influence in this respect.

To sum up, the verdict given me at the time by my advisers was that in the event of any substantial losses Third Rumanian Army would cease to be capable of offensive action and only be fit for defence if reinforced by German 'corset bones'.

The *sector* I had to command formed the southernmost wing of the Eastern Front. Broadly speaking, it embraced the Crimea and the part of the Dnieper bend south of Zaporozhye. There was no direct contact with the main forces of Southern Army Group advancing north of the Dnieper, which was all to the good as far as Eleventh Army's operational freedom was concerned. After the forest tracts of northern Russia in which I had last had to operate with a tank corps unsuited to that type of country, I now found myself in the vast expanses of the steppes, which were almost entirely devoid of natural obstacles, even if they did not offer any cover either. It was ideal tank country, but unfortunately Eleventh Army had no tanks.

The only variety was offered by the smaller rivers, the beds of which dried up in summer-time to form deep, steep-banked fissures known as *balkas*. Nevertheless, the very monotony of the steppes gave them a strange and unique fascination. Everyone was captivated at one time or other by the endlessness of the landscape, through which it was possible to drive for hours on end – often guided only by the compass – without encountering the least rise in the ground or setting eyes on a single human being or habitation. The distant horizon seemed like some mountain ridge behind which a paradise might beckon, but it only stretched on and on. The poles of the Anglo-Iranian telegraph line, built some years before by Siemens, alone served to break the eternal sameness of it all. Yet at sunset these steppes were transformed into a dazzling blaze of colour. In the eastern part of the Nogaisk Steppes, around and north-east of Melitopol, one came upon lovely villages with such German names as Karlsruhe and Helenental. They lay in the midst of rich fruit plantations, their well-built stone houses bearing witness to a past prosperity. The inhabitants still spoke the purest German, but they were almost all old men, women and children. The men had been deported by the Soviet authorities.

The *task* assigned to Eleventh Army by the Supreme Command inevitably committed it in two divergent directions.

On one hand, by advancing on the right wing of Southern Army Group, it was intended to continue pursuing the enemy as he withdrew eastwards. To this end the main body of the army was to be brought forward along the north coast of the Sea of Azov in the general direction of Rostov.

On the other hand, the army was also meant to take the Crimea – a task given special priority. One reason for this was the favourable effect the capture of the peninsula was expected to have on the attitude of Turkey. Another even more pressing one was the threat of the enemy's big Crimean air bases to the Rumanian oilfields, so vital to Germany. After the Crimea had been taken, the Eleventh Army's corps of mountain troops was to move over the Straits of Kerch towards the Caucasus, evidently to reinforce an offensive beyond Rostov.

At that time, therefore, the Supreme Command still had pretty far-reaching aims for the 1941 campaign. It was soon to become apparent that the dual role allotted to Eleventh Army was unrealistic.

At the beginning of September *Eleventh Army* had forced a crossing over the lower Dnieper at Berislavl – an exceptional feat of arms in which the main part had been played by 22 (Lower Saxon) Infantry Division. Nonetheless, it marked the point where the duality of the army's task inevitably brought about a cleavage in its axis of advance.

When I took command I found myself confronted by the following situation:

Two army corps – 30 Corps under General v. Salmuth (72 and 22

Infantry Divisions and the Leibstandarte Adolf Hitler) and 49 Mountain Corps under General Kübler (170 Infantry Division and 1 and 4 Mountain Divisions) – had continued their eastward pursuit of the enemy after his defeat on the Dnieper and were approaching the line from Melitopol to the Dnieper bend south of Zaporozhye.

One corps – the 54th under General Hansen – had been diverted to the approach to the Crimea, the Perekop isthmus. 50 Infantry Division, which had come from Greece, was partly under Fourth Rumanian Army before Odessa and partly engaged in mopping up the Black Sea coast.

Third Rumanian Army, comprising a mountain corps (1, 2 and 4 Mountain Brigades) and a cavalry corps (5, 6 and 8 Cavalry Brigades), was still west of the Dnieper, where it proposed to rest for a while. In doing so it was probably guided by a desire to avoid any advance beyond the river, since it had already exceeded Rumania's political aims in having to cross the Bug.

Faced with this dual mission of pursuing the enemy eastwards to Rostov and conquering the Crimea for a subsequent drive through Kerch to the Caucasus, Eleventh Army Headquarters had to decide whether to deal with the two divergent tasks simultaneously or in chronological order. A decision which was really the responsibility of the Supreme Command was thus left to an army.

It seemed quite certain that *both* tasks could not be solved simultaneously with the forces we had at our disposal.

The capture of the Crimea called for a considerably stronger force than 54 Corps, now facing Perekop. Although the Intelligence picture indicated that only three divisions of the enemy army were likely to have escaped from the Dnieper into the isthmus, it was not clear what forces the Russians had available in the Crimea itself, particularly at Sevastopol. Soon afterwards it emerged that the enemy could put not three but six divisions into action in the isthmus itself. These were later to be reinforced [1] by the Soviet Army then defending Odessa.

In view of the nature of the ground, however, a stubborn defence by even three enemy divisions would probably suffice to deny 54 Corps access to the Crimea or at least to cause it considerable losses in the fight through the isthmus.

The Crimea is divided from the mainland by the so-called Lazy Sea,

[1] I.e. rom the sea. *Tr.*

the Zivash. This is a kind of mud-flat or brackish swamp, almost impassable for infantry and an absolute obstacle to assault boats on account of its extreme shallowness. There are only two firm approaches to the Crimea – the isthmus of Perekop in the west and a neck of land running west of Genichesk in the east. The latter is so narrow in places as only to leave room for a causeway and railway embankment, both of which are interspersed with long stretches of bridges. For the purpose of an attack, therefore, it was quite useless.

As even the Perekop isthmus was less than five miles wide, the assault would have to be purely frontal and over ground quite devoid of cover. A flanking attack was ruled out by the proximity of the sea on either side. In addition to being already equipped with strong field defences, the isthmus was cut straight across the middle by Tartars' Ditch, an ancient earthwork anything up to 50 feet in depth.

Once the Perekop isthmus had been broken through, there was another bottle-neck to be tackled further south at Ishun, where salt lakes reduced the potential assault front to a mere two miles.

In view of these difficulties on the ground and the enemy's superiority in the air, we had to expect a hard and exhausting struggle. Even if we succeeded in breaking through at Perekop, it was doubtful whether the corps would still have the strength to fight a second battle at Ishun. In any case, two or three divisions would never be enough to conquer the whole of the Crimea including Sevastopol.

To ensure a swift occupation of the Crimea, therefore, the army had at all costs to detach strong additional forces from its pursuit group now heading eastwards. What remained should still suffice for the pursuit as long as the enemy continued to withdraw – though it would be too weak for an objective as remote as Rostov if he were to form a new front further back or actually bring up fresh forces.

Should it be considered crucial to advance on Rostov, the Crimea would have to be left behind for the time being. In that event, however, it would be difficult to tell when, if ever, the forces needed to conquer the peninsula could be made available. Besides, in the hands of an enemy with command of the sea the Crimea was liable to become a serious menace deep in the flank of the Eastern Front, quite apart from the fact that the air bases would continue to threaten the Rumanian oilfields.

If the attempt were made to conduct a far-reaching operation towards and beyond Rostov with two army corps and simultaneously to conquer the Crimea with one other corps, the only result could be that neither objective would be effectively attained.

Eleventh Army accordingly decided to give priority to the Crimea. At all costs we were determined not to tackle this task with insufficient forces. As a matter of course 54 Corps was given all the available army artillery, engineers and anti-aircraft guns, in addition to which it was to call forward 50 Infantry Division from its rear location at the latest in time for the second phase, the battle for the Ishun isthmus. But this was still not enough. It was imperative to have a second corps in order to conquer the Crimea quickly after the breakthrough – if indeed it were not actually needed to fight through the lakes at Ishun. We decided that this should be the German Mountain Corps, which the Supreme Command had anyway earmarked in its directives to be moved up through Kerch to the Caucasus later on. Meanwhile this formation of two divisions could be put to better use in the mountainous parts of the southern Crimea than out in the steppes.

Apart from all this, an attempt was to be made, once we had broken into the peninsula itself, to take the fortress of Sevastopol by a surprise thrust with motorized units. For this purpose the Leibstandarte was to assemble behind 54 Corps when it went into the assault.

These dispositions naturally entailed a considerable weakening of the army's eastern front. All that could be found to replace the forces there, apart from the elements of 22 Infantry Division being used on coastal defence north of the Crimea, was Third Rumanian Army. Despite the Rumanian inhibitions to which I alluded earlier, I was able to arrange in a personal talk with General Dumitrescu that his army should be moved quickly forward over the Dnieper.

It was perfectly clear that the measures taken by Eleventh Army would involve considerable risks if the enemy on its eastern front were to halt his retreat and try to regain the initiative there. This was the price that had to be paid if we were to avoid attempting the capture of the Crimea with inadequate forces.

BATTLE ON TWO FRONTS
BREAKTHROUGH AT PEREKOP AND THE BATTLE ON THE SEA OF AZOV

While supply difficulties caused the preparations for 54 Corps' attack on the Perekop isthmus to drag on till 24th September and our forces

were still regrouping on the lines already indicated, there were signs of
a change in the situation on the army's eastern front from 21st September onwards.

The enemy had taken up prepared positions along a front from west
of Melitopol to the Dnieper bend, with the result that the pursuit had
to be discontinued. Nonetheless, the army went ahead with the dis-

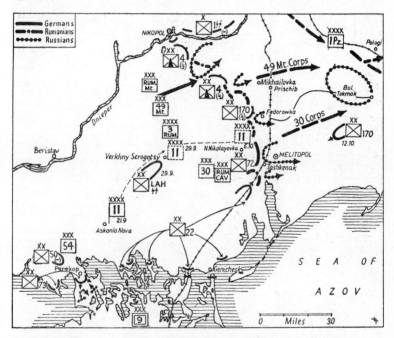

Map 10. Battle on the Sea of Azov and Breakthrough at the Isthmus
of Perekop (Autumn 1941).

engagement of the German Mountain Corps, giving orders for the remaining German formations to be mixed in with those of Third Rumanian Army in order to keep the risk down to a minimum. The
Rumanian cavalry corps in the southern sector of this front was incorporated into 30 German Corps, while Third Rumanian Army in the
north took over 170 German Infantry Division to bolster the
Rumanian mountain corps.

By 24th September 54 Corps was able to move in to the assault on
the Perekop isthmus. Though given maximum artillery support, 45
and 73 Infantry Divisions had the hardest possible conditions to fight

under, having to advance in blazing sunshine across salt steppes on which there was no trace of water or cover. The enemy had transformed the isthmus into a powerful, ten-mile-deep defence system, and he fought bitterly for every single trench and strong-point.

Nevertheless, after warding off strong enemy counter-attacks the corps took Perekop and crossed Tartars' Ditch on 26th September. Three more days' intensive fighting saw it through the rest of the enemy's defence zone and, after the capture of the strongly defended locality of Armyansk, out into more open country. The enemy fell back between the Ishun lakes, having suffered heavy losses in killed and left 10,000 prisoners, 112 tanks and 135 guns in our hands.

But the fruit of this hard-won victory, the final break-out into the Crimea, could still not be plucked. Although the enemy's losses had been heavy, the number of divisions facing the corps had meanwhile risen to six. In all likelihood any attempt to go straight ahead with the storming of the Ishun bottleneck would have been too much for our troops, in view of the relative strengths involved and the tremendous sacrifices it would have imposed on the German corps.

As for Eleventh Army's proposal to have reinforcements to hand at this juncture in the form of the Mountain Corps and the Leibstandarte, the enemy had already thwarted it. Obviously anticipating that we were intent on a speedy conquest of the Crimea, he had brought fresh forces up to his front between the Sea of Azov and the Dnieper.

Here, on 26th September, he had attacked our Army's eastern front with two new armies, the Eighteenth and Ninth, consisting of twelve divisions which were mainly new arrivals or recently rested. In the first assault he had admittedly failed to score any successes against our own 30 Corps – though even here the situation became pretty tense – but in the sector of Third Rumanian Army he had overrun the latter's 4 Mountain Brigade and torn a gap ten miles wide in the army front. The brigade in question had lost the bulk of its artillery and seemed to be at the end of its tether. Both the other Rumanian mountain brigades had also suffered severe losses.

We now had no choice but to make the German Mountain Corps, which was already on its way to the Perekop isthmus, do a right-about turn in order to set about restoring the position of Third Rumanian Army. Simultaneously, moreover, Eleventh Army was virtually deprived of the services of its one fast-moving formation, the Leib-

standarte, as we were now ordered by the Supreme Command to hold
it in hand for the drive on Rostov as part of First Panzer Group, to
which it would shortly be transferred. We thus had to abstain from
using the Leibstandarte to exploit the success in the isthmus, and it was
likewise ordered back to the eastern front.

In order to be close to the army's two fronts, the army operations
branch had on 21st September established a tactical headquarters at
Askania Nova in the Nogaisk Steppes, which had once been the
property of a German family, the Falz-Feins.

Formerly a model estate known all over Russia, it had now become
a collective farm. The manor buildings were sadly neglected, and the
retreating Soviet troops had destroyed all the machinery, just as they
had thrown petrol over the mountains of threshed wheat lying out in
the open air and set them on fire. The latter smouldered for weeks on
end without our being able to extinguish them.

The increasing gravity of the situation on the army's front impelled
us to move close up behind the danger spot with a small tactical staff on
29th September. This is always an expedient measure in times of crisis,
if only because it prevents subordinate staffs from pulling out early and
making a bad impression on the troops. On the occasion in question
it was particularly appropriate in view of the tendency of many
Rumanian headquarters staffs to change their locations prematurely.

The same day, the German Mountain Corps and the Leibstandarte
delivered a thrust into the enemy's southern flank where he had broken
into Third Rumanian Army but had failed to exploit his initial success
properly. While it was possible to restore the situation in this area, a
fresh crisis was brewing on the northern wing of 30 Corps, where a
Rumanian cavalry brigade had given way. I had to intervene vigorously
there and then to prevent its hasty withdrawal. The threatened breakthrough was then parried by swinging round the Leibstandarte to meet
it.

Tense though the situation on our eastern front had become as a
result of the events described above, it also had the makings of a
golden opportunity. By launching repeated attacks to frustrate our
intentions in the Crimea, the enemy had tied both his armies down on a
frontal basis and obviously now had no further reserves with which to
protect himself against the Dnieper crossings at Zaporozhye and Dnie-
propetrovsk, whence General v. Kleist's First Panzer Group could

break out against his northern flank. After I had made representations to Southern Army Group some days previously in favour of an intervention from this quarter, the appropriate orders were issued on 1st October. While Eleventh Army kept a tight hold on the still-attacking enemy, the panzer group steadily increased its pressure from the north. Now the enemy began to yield, and by 1st October it was the turn of 30 Corps and Third Rumanian Army to go over to the attack. In the next few days, in co-operation with First Panzer Group, we succeeded in encircling the mass of both enemy armies in the area Bol. Tokmak–Mariupol–Berdyansk or in destroying them as they retreated. Some 65,000 prisoners, 125 tanks and over 500 guns found their way into German hands on this occasion.

THE CONQUEST OF THE CRIMEA

Following the Battle of the Sea of Azov a change was made in the order of battle of the German southern wing. The Supreme Command seemed to have realized that no army could simultaneously fight one operation in the direction of Rostov and another in the Crimea, and from now on the advance on Rostov was entrusted to *First Panzer Group*, to which Eleventh Army was ordered to hand over 49 Mountain Corps and the Leibstandarte.

Eleventh Army was given the sole task of conquering the Crimea with its two remaining army corps. Of these, 30 Corps comprised 22, 72 and 170 Infantry Divisions, and 54 Corps was composed of 46, 73 and 50 Infantry Divisions (one third of the last-named being still outside Odessa).

Third Rumanian Army, which now reverted to the command of Marshal Antonescu, was merely to be responsible for coastal defence on the Black Sea and the Sea of Azov. After I had approached the Marshal direct, however, he agreed to let me take the headquarters of the Rumanian mountain corps, with one cavalry and one mountain brigade under command, into the Crimea to screen the eastern coastline.

Now that Eleventh Army's mission was reduced to the *single* aim of conquering the Crimea, however, the Supreme Command became all the more impatient for a corps to be put across the Straits of Kerch towards the Kuban at the earliest possible date.

Realizing from this demand how much Hitler was underestimating the enemy, Eleventh Army felt impelled to point out that the prior conditions for any such operation must be the complete clearance of the Crimea. The enemy would undoubtedly fight to the last for the peninsula and would abandon Odessa rather than Sevastopol.

Indeed, as long as the Soviets had even one foot in the Crimea there could be no question of throwing part of Eleventh Army – which had only two corps anyway – through Kerch to the Kuban. As it was, we took this opportunity to put in a bid for an extra corps of three divisions, and within the next few weeks – primarily, one would suppose, because of Hitler's above-mentioned requirement – the army was augmented by 42 Corps Headquarters and 132 and 24 Infantry Divisions. In consequence of the Russians' desperate efforts to hold on to the Crimea, these reinforcements were to prove indispensable for the peninsula battles alone.

THE STRUGGLE FOR THE ISHUN ISTHMUS

The immediate problem, however, was to resume the struggle for the approaches to the Crimea and to open up the way through Ishun. Just another assault operation, one might say. Yet that ten-day battle towers above the normal type of offensive action as a shining example of the aggressive spirit and self-sacrifice of the German soldier.

In it we lacked almost all the advantages which are generally regarded as prior necessities for an attack on fortified positions.

Numerical superiority was on the side of the Soviet defenders, not of the German attackers. Eleventh Army's total of six divisions was very soon confronted by eight Soviet rifle and four cavalry divisions, for on 16th October the Russians had evacuated the fortress of Odessa – until then the object of so many unsuccessful assaults by Fourth Rumanian Army – and transferred the defending army to the Crimea by sea. Despite the Luftwaffe's claim to have sunk 32,000 tons of shipping, the bulk of the convoys from Odessa had still made landfall at Sevastopol or harbours along the west coast of the peninsula. The first divisions of this Soviet army duly appeared at the battle-front shortly after the start of our offensive.

The German artillery was certainly superior to the enemy's and effectively supported the attacking infantry. But on the enemy side armour-plated coastal batteries were able to intervene from the north-west coast of the Crimea and the southern bank of the Zivash without

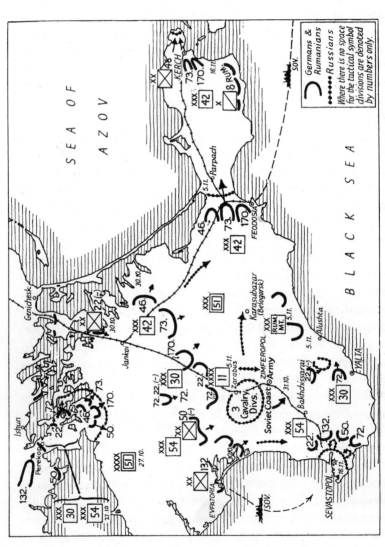

Map 11. Breakthrough at Ishun and Conquest of the Crimea (Autumn 1941).

the German guns initially being able to get to grips with them. And while the Russians had abundant armour to draw on for their counter-attacks, Eleventh Army did not possess a single tank.

Above all, senior commanders had hardly any opportunity to lighten the troops' arduous task by tactical manœuvre. In that situation it was quite impossible to take the enemy by surprise, since all he had to do was to sit in his well-constructed fieldworks and wait for the assault to develop. As had been the case at Perekop, the sea on one side and the Zivash on the other excluded any possibility of outflanking or even enfilading the enemy. On the contrary, it was necessary to carry the attack forward purely frontally along the three narrow strips of land into which the isthmus was divided by the lakes lying within it.

The breadth of these three strips allowed us to commit only the three divisions of 54 Corps (73, 46 and 22) in the first instance, 30 Corps being unable to go in until a certain amount of elbow-room had been gained further south.

The salt steppes of the isthmus, flat as a pancake and bare of vegeta-tion, offered no cover whatever to the attacker. Yet the air above them was dominated by the *Soviet* Air Force, whose fighters and fighter-bombers dived incessantly on any target they could find. Not only the front-line infantry and field batteries had to dig in: it was even neces-sary to dig pits for every vehicle and horse behind the battle zone as protection against enemy aircraft. Things got so bad that anti-aircraft batteries no longer dared to fire in case they were immediately wiped out from the air. Not until the last days of the offensive, after *Mölders* [1] and his fighter group had been called in to assist the army, could the sky be kept clear – and even then only in the hours of daylight. At night-time not even Mölders could help.

Under such combat conditions, and in the face of an opponent who stubbornly defended every inch of ground, the demands made on the attacking troops were bound to be abnormally high and their losses very considerable. Throughout this period I was constantly on the road to see for myself how things were going and what assistance could be rendered to the fighting units in their difficult struggle.

I was alarmed by the way fighting power deteriorated. The divisions carrying out this tough assignment had already made heavy sacrifices at Perekop or in the Azov battle, and the time came when one wondered

[1] Renowned fighter ace of World War II. *Tr.*

whether the struggle for the narrow corridors could possibly succeed or, assuming that we did manage to break through, whether our forces would still be equal to winning the Crimea from an enemy whose strength was constantly on the increase.

By 25th October the troops seemed too exhausted to go on with the attack. Twice already the commander of one particularly good division had reported that the regiments under his command were at the end of their strength. This was the hour that usually comes sooner or later in such a contest, when the outcome of the battle is on the razor's edge. It was the hour that must show whether the will of the attacker to exert himself to the very limit of physical endurance is stronger than that of the defender to go on resisting.

The struggle of deciding whether to call for a last supreme effort, at the risk of having ultimately demanded all that sacrifice in vain, is one that can only be fought out in the heart of the commander concerned. It would be pointless, however, were it not inspired by the confidence of the troops and their determination not to give up the fight.

Eleventh Army was not prepared, after all it had had to ask of the fighting troops, to throw victory away through its own weakness at what might be one minute to twelve. As it turned out, the unbroken aggressive spirit of the troops overcame even the enemy's grim resolution to hold out. After one more day of hard effort, 27th October brought the final success. On 28th October, at the end of ten days of the most bitter fighting, the Soviet defence collapsed. Eleventh Army could take up the pursuit.

PURSUIT

The chase which followed gave one more splendid example of the boldness and initiative of commanders at all levels and the self-denial of the fighting troops. The sight of those regiments, weakened by their heavy losses and well-nigh exhausted by the unprecedented demands of the campaign, yet racing towards the tempting goal of the South Crimean coast, put one in mind of the soldiers of another army who in 1796 stormed the fields of Italy promised them by Napoleon.

By 16th November the furious chase was over, and the whole of the Crimea except for the fortified area of Sevastopol was in our hands. The six divisions of Eleventh Army had wiped out the best part of two enemy armies totalling twelve rifle and four cavalry divisions. Of his initial strength of around 200,000 men, the enemy had lost over 100,000 as prisoners in the struggle for the two necks of land and the pursuit that followed, as well as 700 guns and 160 tanks. What troops had been able to escape across the Straits of Kerch or into Sevastopol were mere debris and without any heavy weapons. The fact that those taking refuge in the fortress could immediately be reformed into proper units was due to the enemy's command of the sea, which enabled him to bring in replacements and stores with a minimum of delay.

While the administrative branches of Eleventh Army H.Q. moved into Zimferopol, the largely Russianized capital of the Crimea lying in beautiful surroundings on the northern edge of the Yaila Mountains, our tactical headquarters went to Zarabus, a sizeable village north of the city, where we found very suitable accommodation in one of the new schools built by the Soviets in almost all the bigger country places. I personally lived with the Chief-of-Staff in the small farmhouse of the fruit-growing collective, where each of us had a modest room to himself. The furniture in my own consisted of a bed, a table and chair, a stool for the wash-bowl to stand on, and a few clothes-hooks. Naturally we could have obtained some furniture from Zimferopol, but our staff did not believe in indulging in comforts which the ordinary soldier had to do without.

Except for two brief stays at a command post on the Kerch front and the period in which the tactical headquarters was up in front of Sevastopol, we remained in these unpretentious quarters until August 1942. After the nomadic life we had led to date it was a complete change for all of us, though not necessarily a welcome one. Whenever a formation staff becomes static, the inevitable result is not only a settled day-to-day routine but also a return to the 'paper war'. I fought the paper war of that winter in my classroom between two little brick stoves we had built on the Russian pattern, the heating system having naturally been destroyed by the Soviets.

At this point I might touch on a problem which, even though it receded before the grave anxieties which the winter of 1941–2 was to cause us in the operational sphere, was always a matter of great concern to me. The man who commands an army is also its supreme arbiter, and the hardest task that can ever confront him is the confirmation of a death sentence. On one hand it is his inexorable duty to maintain discipline and, in the troops' own interest, to inflict severe penalties for delinquency in action. On the other, it is a grim thought to know that one can snuff out a human life by a mere signature. Of course, death claims thousands of victims a day in war, and every soldier expects to have to lay down his life. Yet there is a very big difference between falling honourably in battle and facing the muzzles of one's comrades' rifles to be ignominiously erased from the ranks of the living.

When, of course, a soldier had besmirched the honour of the army by some base action or culpably brought about the death of his comrades, there could be no mercy. But there were plenty of other cases caused not by sheer baseness of character but by some perfectly explainable human lapse. Even so, the court-martial concerned had to pass the death sentence according to the full rigour of military law.

In no case involving a death sentence was I ever content to base my final decision on the verbal elucidations of my army judges – admirable men though they were – but I always made a careful study of the files myself. When two soldiers in my corps were sentenced to death on the outbreak of war for raping and killing an old woman, they only received their just deserts. A very different case was that of a man who, after winning the Iron Cross in the Polish campaign, had been posted to a strange unit following a spell in hospital. On his very first day there his whole machine-gun crew was killed, whereupon he lost his nerve and fled. By law, it is true, his life was forfeit, but there still seemed grounds in this instance – even though the man had been guilty of cowardice and thereby of endangering unit morale – for applying a different yardstick. As I could not immediately quash the sentence passed by the court-martial, the procedure I adopted in this and other such cases was to consult the man's regimental commander and, subject to the latter's agreement, to suspend the sentence for four weeks. If the man redeemed himself in action during this time, I quashed the sentence. If he failed again, it was carried out. Of all the condemned men to whom this probationary period was granted, only one went over to the enemy. All the others either proved their worth or died like true soldiers in the heavy fighting in the east.

THE FIRST ASSAULT ON SEVASTOPOL

Eleventh Army's task now was to assault the enemy's last Crimean stronghold, Sevastopol. The sooner this was achieved, the less time the enemy would have to organize his defence and the greater would be the prospect of success. What was more, it reduced the likelihood of an intervention from the sea.

According to our calculations, the necessary troop movements and ammunition-dumping would be complete by 27th or 28th November. Consequently we made this the deadline for the start of the offensive.

At this point the Russian winter overtook us, its impact being all the more devastating by reason of the two different forms it took. In the Crimea itself the rains came, very soon rendering all the unpaved roads there quite unusable. The mainland in the north, on the other hand, was already in the grip of severe frosts which promptly immobilized four of the only five railway engines then available south of the Dnieper. In consequence Eleventh Army often found its supplies reduced to as little as one or two trainloads a day. Though there was ice on the Dnieper, it still would not hold, and so far no ice-free bridges existed.

And so the preparations for the assault dragged on. Instead of 27th November, the preliminary bombardment could not start until 17th December. At last, after a three-weeks delay which was ultimately to prove crucial, 54 and 30 Corps were able to launch their attacks against the northern and southern sectors respectively. Prior to this, however, Eleventh Army had had a difficult decision to make. On 17th October the critical turn of events around Rostov had caused the Army Group to order the immediate hand-over of 73 and 170 Infantry Divisions. Despite all our warnings that this would make it impossible to attack Sevastopol, we had only been allowed to keep 170 Division, which was still moving along the coast to join 30 Corps, and would not have reached Rostov in time anyway. This concession did not alter the fact that the removal of 73 Division deprived the assault on the northern sector of its necessary reserve element, and we had to make up our minds whether in these circumstances we could afford to attack at all. In the event, we decided to risk it.

It is not possible here to describe the course of the attack in detail. The first task was to drive the enemy, by a surprise thrust from the east, from his forward area between the Kacha and Belbek, and at the same time to capture his strong-points in the Belbek valley and along its southern elevation. Thereupon the assault would be carried forward through the actual fortress glacis south of the Belbek right up to Severnaya Bay. The main responsibility for the success of this battle lay with the valiant 22 (Lower Saxon) Infantry Division, under its outstanding commander, Lieutenant-General Wolff. It cleared the forward area between the Kacha and Belbek of the enemy, stormed the heights south of the Belbek valley with 132 Infantry Division and drove into the fortified zone proper to the south of the latter. But the spearhead of the attack was steadily narrowing, as 50 and 24 Infantry Divisions, whose task was to advance towards Severnaya Bay from the east, were not making any real progress in the difficult mountain country, parts of which were overgrown with almost impenetrable bush. The heavy fighting for the pill-boxes, which the enemy defended with stubborn determination, was sapping the strength of our troops, and the severe cold to which they were henceforth exposed taxed their energies to the utmost. Nevertheless, in the last few days of December – the struggle having continued all through Christmas – the tip of the spearhead drew near to Fort Stalin, the capture of which would at least have given our artillery visual command of Severnaya Bay. All we needed now were fresh troops – and the drive to the bay was bound to succeed. But these were just what we had lacked since handing over 73 Division, and not even by drastically packing the assault divisions into the spearhead of the attack could we make good the loss.

Such was the situation when the Soviet landings struck, first at Kerch and then at Feodosia. The threat was a deadly one, coming as it did at the very moment when the entire forces of the army, except for one German division and two Rumanian brigades, were in action around Sevastopol!

It was clear that we should have to throw forces from Sevastopol to the threatened points with the utmost speed. The slightest delay might prove fatal. But ought the attack on Sevastopol to be abandoned just when only one more push seemed necessary to gain command of Severnaya Bay?

Furthermore, it would almost certainly be easier to disengage forces from Sevastopol after a success on the northern front than if one were to let go of the enemy prematurely.

Eleventh Army accordingly decided to accept the risk involved in every further hour's postponement of the release of troops from Sevastopol. Initially only 30 Corps was ordered to halt its assault, and 170 Division was dispatched to the threatened Kerch peninsula. At the same time, with the agreement of the commander of 54 Corps and his divisional commanders, a final attempt was to be made on the northern front to reach the assault objective, Severnaya Bay.

As always, the troops gave everything they had, and 22 Division's vanguard, 16 Infantry Regiment, under Colonel v. Choltitz, actually penetrated the outer ring of Fort Stalin. By then everyone's strength had given out, and on 30th December the commanders of the assault divisions reported that no further attempts to carry on with the attack could be expected to succeed. After urgent representations by telephone through Army Group had convinced even Hitler that such action was necessary, Eleventh Army Headquarters issued orders for the attack to be finally stopped. Over and above this, it was reluctantly compelled to order the withdrawal of the northern front to the heights north of the Belbek valley. But for these measures the requisite forces could not have been released – to say nothing of the fact that the situation within the narrow confines of the spearhead would anyway have been untenable in the long run. Hitler's disapproval of this decision, which – though he could do nothing about it – clashed with the strict ban he had just placed on any voluntary withdrawals, weighed little in comparison with one's own responsibility to the troops who had sacrificed so much.

And so the first attempt to storm the fortress of Sevastopol had failed.

THE STALIN OFFENSIVE TO RE-CONQUER THE CRIMEA

The landing of Soviet troops on the Kerch peninsula, catching Eleventh Army just when the battle on the northern front of Sevastopol had entered its crucial phase, soon proved to be more than a mere diversionary measure on the enemy's part. Soviet radio stations proclaimed that this was an all-out offensive to re-conquer the Crimea, planned and commanded by Stalin personally, and that it would not end until Eleventh Army had been wiped off the map. That the threat was no empty one soon became apparent from the weight of enemy forces committed. Behind them, and in the utter ruthlessness with which they were expended, one sensed the brutal will of Stalin.

On 26th December, after crossing the Straits of Kerch, the enemy had begun by landing two divisions on either side of the city. Smaller landings followed on the northern coast of the peninsula. The position of 42 Corps (General Count Sponeck), which depended solely on 46

Infantry Division for the defence of the peninsula, was certainly not an enviable one. Count Sponeck accordingly requested permission to evacuate the peninsula in the hope that it could be sealed off at Parpach. Eleventh Army did not agree with him, for if the enemy succeeded in establishing a firm footing at Kerch, the upshot would be a second front in the Crimea and an extremely dangerous situation for the entire army as long as Sevastopol remained untaken. Consequently we ordered 42 Corps to strike while the enemy was still off balance after his landing and to hurl him back into the sea. At the same time, in order to keep the whole of 46 Division free for this task, we sent 4 and 8 Rumanian Mountain Brigades – of which the former was around Zimferopol and the latter engaged in guarding the eastern coast of the Crimea – to Feodosia to deal with any attempt the enemy might make to land at this critical spot. Simultaneously orders were given to the only regimental group of 73 Division still in the Crimea – i.e. the reinforced 213 Infantry Regiment – to move on Feodosia from Genichek.

By 28th December, 46 Infantry Regiment actually succeeded in eliminating both the enemy beach-heads north and south of Kerch, except for a small body of troops still fighting on the northern shore. In spite of this, Count Sponeck again asked permission to evacuate the Kerch peninsula. This we categorically forbade, still being convinced that any surrender of the Kerch peninsula might well lead to a situation which the army would be unable to master with the forces at its disposal.

Meanwhile, on 28th December, 54 Corps had moved off for its last attack on Sevastopol.

Yet the enemy was on the point of delivering a new blow. Early on 29th December we heard that he had carried out a night landing at Feodosia under cover of strong naval forces. Our own weak forces there (one engineer battalion, anti-tank troops and some coastal batteries – the Rumanians not having started to arrive until the following morning) had been unable to stop the landing. Our telephone link with 42 Corps Headquarters, which was located somewhere in the middle of the peninsula, was out of action, but at 1000 hours we were notified by radio that Count Sponeck had ordered the immediate evacuation of the peninsula because of the new landings at Feodosia. Though we immediately issued a countermand, it was never picked up by 42 Corps Signals. While fully appreciating the corps' anxiety not to be cut off by the enemy at Feodosia, we still did not believe that the situation would in any way be improved by a headlong withdrawal.

Simultaneously with countermanding the evacuation of the Kerch peninsula, Eleventh Army ordered the Rumanian Mountain Corps to throw the enemy forces disembarked at Feodosia straight back into the sea with the help of the two brigades mentioned earlier and a Rumanian motorized regiment now in the process of moving up. Although we had no illusions about the offensive capacity of these Rumanian formations, the enemy could still not be present at Feodosia in any real strength, and if we struck with real determination, it should be possible to catch him at a disadvantage. At the worst, we felt, the Rumanians would manage to contain the enemy in a narrow beach-head around Feodosia until German troops could get there.

DEVELOPMENT OF THE SITUATION ON THE KERCH PENINSULA

Even this hope was to prove illusory, however. Far from carrying home its attack on Feodosia, the Rumanian Mountain Corps actually allowed a handful of Soviet tanks to push it right back to a point east of Stary Krim.

By a series of forced marches 46 Infantry Division did in fact reach the narrow stretch of land at Parpach. In doing so, however, it had to abandon most of its guns on the ice-covered roads, and its troops arrived in a state of complete exhaustion. From the small beach-head still in his hands north of Kerch the enemy was immediately able to take up the pursuit, the speed with which his reinforcements arrived being due to the freezing-over of the straits. Had the Soviet commander pressed home his advantage properly by pursuing 46 Division really hard from Kerch and thrusting relentlessly after the Rumanians as they fell back from Feodosia, the fate of the entire Eleventh Army would have been at stake. As it happened, he did not know when to take time by the forelock. Either he did not realize what a chance he had, or else he did not venture to seize it.

And so it was possible, with the help of an exhausted 46 Division, 213 Infantry Regiment (which had meanwhile arrived from Genichek) and the Rumanians, to build up a protective front – albeit a perilously thin one – between the northern slopes of the Yaila Mountains near Stary Krim and the Zivash west of Ak-Monay. In order to stiffen the

Rumanian troops and safeguard their heavy weapons, all available German officers and men, including those who could be spared from Eleventh Army Headquarters, were attached to Rumanian units.

By 15th January, 30 and 42 Corps were ready to counter-attack on the Feodosia front. The decision to risk this attack was a hard one, for it had to be launched with three and a half weakened German divisions and a Rumanian mountain brigade against an opponent whose strength had meanwhile increased to eight divisions and one brigade. The enemy, moreover, had a limited number of tanks at his disposal, whereas we had none at all. The support of the Luftwaffe was more than doubtful, since bad weather had prevented it from flying any sorties against Feodosia for the last few days. Nevertheless, we had to take the chance and attack.

Thanks to the bravery of the troops, the attack succeeded, and by 18th January Feodosia was ours. In addition to 6,700 dead, the enemy had lost 10,000 prisoners, 177 guns and 85 tanks. It now emerged that the Luftwaffe had still done a good job in Feodosia harbour, in spite of the bad flying conditions, and had sunk a number of transport vessels.

Our success at Feodosia naturally led us to consider the possibility of immediately exploiting it to get the Soviet armies right out of the Kerch peninsula. But desirable though this would have been, Eleventh Army decided, after careful reflection, that it could not be done with the resources available, especially now that a tank battalion and two bomber wings originally promised to us – the very forces we should have needed for the task in question – had had to go to the Army Group.

Eleventh Army thus had to dispense with any sweeping exploitation of its achievements at Feodosia and to content itself with throwing the enemy back as far as the Parpach bottleneck, where the Kerch peninsula could be sealed off between the Black Sea and the Sea of Azov. There was certainly nothing pusillanimous about this decision: we simply realized that after everything the troops had gone through to date, it might cause very serious reverses to demand too much of them now.

THE 'STALIN OFFENSIVE' CONTINUES

Even though the recapture of Feodosia and the sealing-off of the Kerch peninsula at Parpach had temporarily banished a mortal danger, we did not let that lull us into a false sense of security. At that particular time the enemy was striving everywhere on the Eastern Front to make good his defeats of the previous summer and to regain the initiative. Why should he make an exception of the Crimea, where his mastery of the sea offered him such exceptionally good prospects? Success here could have decisive repercussions on the entire situation in the East – politically with regard to Turkey and economically through the recovery of a base for air operations against the Rumanian oilfields. Another point to consider was that Soviet propaganda had linked the offensive against the Crimea so closely with the name of Stalin that it was most unlikely to be called off.

And, sure enough, we soon discovered that the enemy was pushing reinforcements across to Kerch. Having possession of the frozen straits, he could put up with the loss of the port of Feodosia. Air photography continually showed the enemy to be concentrated in strength in his Black Sea harbours and the airfields in the area north of the Caucasus, and as early as 29th January Intelligence estimates of his strength on the Parpach front amounted to more than nine divisions, two rifle brigade groups and two independent tank brigades.

The Sevastopol front was also livening up again, particularly where the artillery was concerned.

After weeks of outward calm that were really loaded with tension, the enemy finally launched his big offensive on 27th February.

The heavy battles that followed on both the Parpach and Sevastopol fronts continued with unremitting violence until 3rd March. Then on both sides a period of exhaustion ensued. On the Parpach front we had eventually succeeded in containing the enemy breakthrough in the northern sector by making effective use of the marshlands there. Although the front was now a continuous one, however, it did recede quite a long way west in its northern part.

On 13th March the enemy began another mass attack, this time with eight rifle divisions and two independent armoured brigades 'up'. While we were able to knock out 136 tanks in the first three days, a number of crises developed. The bitterness of the fighting may be judged from the fact that the regiments of 46 Division, which bore the main brunt of the assault on this occasion, had to beat off anything from ten to twenty-two attacks between them during the same three days.

On 18th March 42 Corps had to report that it could no longer withstand any major attacks.

As the newly constituted 22 Panzer Division had arrived behind this front in the meantime, having been allocated to Eleventh Army by O.K.H., we decided that the extreme tenseness of the situation justified our employing it on a counter-attack. Our object was to regain the main fighting line we had originally held across the actual neck of the Parpach isthmus and thereby to cut off the two or three enemy divisions located in the northern salient.

Together with a very small tactical staff, I had moved into a command post close behind the threatened Parpach front in order to watch the preparations for the counter-attack being handled by 42 Corps Headquarters.

The attack, which took place on 20th March and was to be supported on either flank by 46 and 170 Infantry Divisions, proved a failure. The new armoured division ran straight into a Soviet assembly area in the early-morning mists. Obviously we had been wrong to throw it into a major battle before putting it through its paces in exercises with its parent formation. While this attack – despite its being directed at a relatively limited objective – miscarried, the same division came fully up to expectations only a few weeks later, after completing its training under warlike conditions as part of a larger formation. But what else could we have done in the circumstances but risk committing it to battle? At least it had given the enemy a severe shock and checked his preparations for another big attack at just the critical moment. When the latter did materialize on 26th March, it was beaten off by 42 Corps. This time the enemy had committed only four divisions, either because he had temporarily exhausted his other formations or because he preferred to limit his objective now that tanks had been seen on our side for the first time.

In the meantime, while 22 Panzer Division was out of the line for a rest and refit, the advance elements of 28 Light Division [1] also arrived behind the front. We could now face any new enemy attack with equanimity.

It came – and this was the enemy's last effort to reconquer the

---

[1] The new 'light' divisions, unlike their predecessors, were no longer a compromise between an armoured and a motorized division, but were closer, in structure and equipment, to a mountain division. They were later renamed 'pursuit divisions'. *Author.*

Crimea – on 9th April, launched by between six and eight rifle divisions and supported by 160 tanks. By 11th April it had been beaten off, with heavy losses to the enemy. With that the enemy's offensive capacity in this part of the theatre was finally spent.

The stout-hearted divisions which had seen this defensive battle through to a successful conclusion, despite the tremendous strains it imposed on them, were now able to relax, even though they could not be taken out of the line.

Army Headquarters, on the other hand, turned from an arduous winter of unprecedented trials and crisis to the next task it had to tackle – that of preparing its own offensive for the final expulsion of the Russians from the Crimea.

'OPERATION BUSTARD'
RECONQUEST OF THE KERCH PENINSULA

Between the penultimate and last defensive battle in the Kerch peninsula, Marshal Antonescu had come out to the Crimea and gone round with me on a tour of the Rumanian divisions and the Sevastopol front. In his soldierly way he made an excellent impression, and the senior Rumanian officers seemed to go in mortal fear of him. I was particularly grateful for his promise of two more Rumanian divisions, since apart from the two German divisions which had already arrived (22 Panzer and 28 Light), O.K.H. was unable to provide any further forces for the projected offensive.

According to O.K.H. directives, the final expulsion of the Soviets from the Crimea, including Sevastopol, was intended to preface the grand offensive which the Supreme Command planned to launch in the southern sector of the Eastern Front.

Eleventh Army's first concern was obviously to destroy the enemy in the Kerch peninsula. One reason for this was the impossibility of predicting how long an operation to clear Sevastopol would take. The most important one, however, was that the Kerch front, being the easiest to reinforce, continued to constitute the main threat to Eleventh Army. The enemy here could be given no time to recover from the losses of his abortive attacks. Sevastopol would have to be shelved until the Soviet forces in the Kerch peninsula had been wiped out.

The *relative strengths* of the Russian and German forces in the Crimea, however, gave no grounds for any great optimism regarding

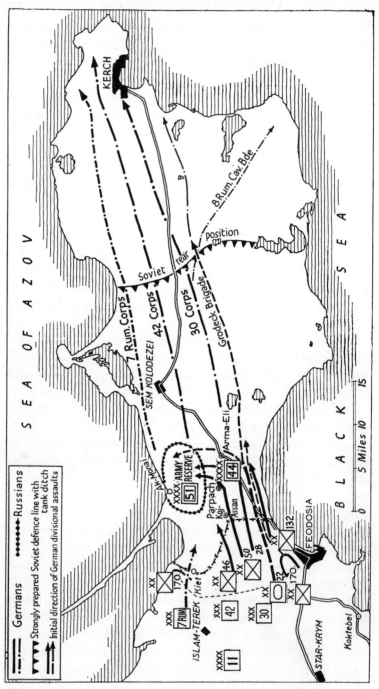

Map 12. Re-Conquest of the Kerch Peninsula (May 1942).

Germans

Russians

Strongly prepared Soviet defence line with tank ditch

initial direction of German divisional assaults

SEA OF AZOV

BLACK SEA

KERCH

8 Rum. Cav. Bde.

position

Soviet rear

7 Rum. Corps

42 Corps

30 Corps

Grodeck Brigade

SEM KOLODEZEI

Arma-Eli

Ak-monai

XXXX ARMY RESERVE 51

Parpach Koj-Assan

XXXX 44

50

28

170

46

30   42

7 RUM

132

22

170

FEODOSIA

ISLAM-TEREK (Kiet)

STAR-KRYM

Koktebel

XXXX 11

0   5   Miles   10   15

the outcome of these two big undertakings. The enemy had three armies in the Crimea, under command of a Crimean Front Head-quarters which appeared to have been only recently formed and was probably located in Kerch.

The Sevastopol fortress continued to be defended by the *Coast Army*, whose strength we had ascertained in February to be seven rifle divisions, one rifle brigade, two naval brigades and one dismounted cavalry division. During our Kerch offensive all we would have available to contain these forces on the northern and eastern fronts of the fortress were 54 Corps and the newly arrived 19 Rumanian Division, which had been put there to free 50 German Division for Kerch. The only force left on the southern front of Sevastopol would be 72 Infantry Division.

The Rumanian Mountain Corps, with only 4 Mountain Brigade under command, had to defend the entire south coast of the Crimea against surprise attacks from the sea. Thus Eleventh Army was having to strip the other fronts bare in order to attack at Kerch in the greatest possible strength.

On the Kerch front the enemy still had his *Forty-Fourth* and *Fifty-First Armies*. At the end of April 1942 they comprised seventeen rifle divisions, three rifle brigades, two cavalry divisions and four independent armoured brigades – an aggregate of twenty-six formations.

Against this formidable array we were able to commit merely five German infantry divisions (inclusive of 50 Division from Sevastopol) and 22 Panzer Division. These were augmented by the newly arrived 7 Rumanian Corps, consisting of 19 Rumanian Division, 8 Rumanian Cavalry Brigade and 10 Rumanian Division – the last-named having been moved over from the west coast. As the usefulness of these Rumanian forces in an offensive role was limited, the numerical disparity in the forthcoming offensive – now being planned under the code-name 'Bustard' – was increased still further.

It also had to be borne in mind that the attack through the Parpach gap must be a purely frontal one in the initial stages, as the seas on either side excluded any possibility of outflanking. What was more, the enemy had echeloned his defences in considerable depth. How were we in the circumstances, and in view of the enemy's superiority of at least two to one, to achieve our object of destroying both his armies?

One thing was clear: neither a frontal push against the two enemy armies nor even a simple breakthrough could get us anywhere. If, after losing his Parpach positions, the enemy should manage to re-form his front anywhere else, our operation would inevitably be halted. The broader the Kerch peninsula became as one went east, the more the enemy would be able to make his numerical superiority felt. Our total of six German divisions might suffice for an attack through a mere 11-mile gap at Parpach, where the enemy could not put in all his forces simultaneously, but how should we fare further east when it came to fighting on a 25-mile front? The object must be, then, not only to break through the enemy's Parpach front and achieve penetration in depth, but also to destroy either the main bulk, or at least a substantial part of his formations in the process of the first breakthrough.

In this respect the enemy himself offered us an opening. In his southern sector, between the Black Sea and Koy-Assan, he was, in the main, still sitting in the strongly prepared defences of his original Parpach front. His northern front, on the other hand, protruded well beyond the latter in a wide curve reaching as far west as Kiet and dating from the time when the enemy had overrun 18 Rumanian Division.

That the Soviet commander had considered the likelihood of our trying to cut off this bulge was clear from the way he had distributed his troops. According to our Intelligence reports he had massed two-thirds of his forces – both in the line and in reserve – in or behind his northern sector. In the south, however, there were only three divisions in the line and two or three in reserve. Quite likely the abortive attack by 22 Panzer Division earlier on, the aim of which had been to cut off the enemy front in the region west of Koy Assan, was the reason for these dispositions.

Such was the situation on which Eleventh Army based its assault plan for Operation Bustard. We intended to make our decisive thrust not immediately in the area where the front protruded west, but down in the southern sector, along the Black Sea coast. In other words, in the place where the enemy would be least expecting it.

This task was to devolve on 30 Corps, composed of 28 Light, 132 and 50 Infantry and 22 Panzer Divisions. Although 170 Infantry Division would have to remain in the central sector in the initial phase in order to deceive the enemy, it, too, would subsequently follow through in the south.

The plan was that 30 Corps should break through the Parpach positions with three divisions 'up' and exploit over the deep anti-tank ditch in an eastward direction to enable 22 Panzer Division to cross this obstacle. Once the latter had moved up, the corps would wheel north and drive into the flank and rear of the enemy forces concentrated in the northern sector. Then, in co-operation with 42 Corps and 7 Rumanian Corps, it would finally surround the enemy on the north coast of the peninsula.

The protection of 30 Corps' eastern flank against enemy attacks from the direction of Kerch was to be the responsibility of a mobile formation, Brigade Group Groddek, which was made up of German and Rumanian motorized units. It was to discharge its task *offensively* by advancing rapidly towards Kerch, since this would also serve to forestall any attempt by enemy elements in the rear to take evasive action.

In order to facilitate the difficult initial breakthrough at Parpach, Eleventh Army had made provisions for what was probably the first sea-borne assault-boat operation of its kind. A battalion travelling by assault boats from Feodosia was to be dropped in the rear of the Parpach positions at first light.

The decisive attack by the corps was to be supported not only by strong artillery but also by the whole of 8 Air Corps.

8 Air Corps, which also included strong anti-aircraft units, was by its structure the most powerful and hard-hitting Luftwaffe formation available for support of military operations. Its Commanding General, Baron v. Richthofen, was certainly the most outstanding Luftwaffe leader we had in World War II. He made immense demands on the units under his command, but always went up himself to supervise any important attack they made. Furthermore, one was constantly meeting him at the front, where he would visit the most forward units to weigh up the possibilities of giving air support to ground operations. We always got on extremely well together, both at Eleventh Army and later on at Southern Army Group. I remember v. Richthofen's achievements and those of his Air Corps with the utmost admiration and gratitude.

On the rest of the Parpach front 42 Corps and 7 Rumanian Corps had the task of simulating an attack in order to pin the enemy down. As soon as a breakthrough had been effected in the south, they were both to join in the main assault.

The success of the operation depended on two things. The first was our ability to keep the enemy thinking that our decisive attack would come in the north until it was too late for him to back out of the trap or throw his reserves into the southern sector. The second was the speed with which 30 Corps – and in particular 22 Panzer Division – carried out the northward thrust.

The first of these requirements was achieved by extensive deception tactics. Apart from wireless deception, these involved laying on a sham artillery preparation in the central and northern sectors and moving troops around in the same area. Apparently they were entirely successful, as the bulk of the enemy's reserves remained behind his northern wing until it was too late for them to move.

Immediately before the offensive began we lost our highly experienced Chief-of-Staff, General Wöhler, who had been such an invaluable support in the difficult days of the previous winter and played a leading role in the preparation of 'Bustard'. Both of us found it particularly hard to part just as we had at last gained the initiative ourselves. However, Wöhler had been appointed Chief-of-Staff of Central Army Group, and I obviously could not put anything in the way of his advancement.

Wöhler's successor was General Schulz, who was also to prove a sound counsellor and friend. He was an inestimable help to me in the most difficult phases of the 1943 winter campaign and throughout the time we were fighting to save Sixth Army. Apart from being a man of great personal courage, he had nerves of steel and a special awareness of the privations and needs of the fighting troops, as well as a most equable nature. Already, as Chief-of-Staff of a corps, he had won the knight's cross in a most difficult situation. Later, as a corps commander in Southern Army Group, he was to prove a tower of strength.

On 8th May, Eleventh Army moved off on 'Operation Bustard'.

30 Corps was able to cross the anti-tank obstacle and penetrate the enemy's most forward positions, and the assault-boat expedition, by virtue of the surprise it achieved, had rendered considerable assistance to our right wing in its advance along the coast. Nevertheless, it was no easy battle. The ground gained on the far side of the ditch was not sufficient for the armoured division to be moved over, and the subsequent attack by 42 Corps only progressed with difficulty. Neverthe-

less, we had already engaged ten enemy divisions and shattered the enemy's southern wing, and there was no indication that his reserves had moved away from the northern wing.

It was not possible to bring up and deploy 22 Panzer Division until 9th May, and before swinging north it had to fight off a strong tank attack. Then rain set in and continued all night, making it well-nigh impossible for the Luftwaffe's close-support units to co-operate or for the tanks to make any headway on the morning of 10th May. Though the weather cleared in the afternoon, the twenty-four-hour time-lag was liable to be our undoing in an operation so dependent on speed of movement. It was consoling to know that before the rain started Brigade Group Groddek had been able to move swiftly east – a fact which subsequently enabled it to frustrate every enemy attempt to form a front further back. Evidently the enemy had not anticipated such a bold drive into the depths of his communications zone. Unluckily the valiant brigade commander, Colonel v. Groddek, was severely wounded in the course of the operation and died soon afterwards.

From 11th May onwards the operations proceeded without any serious hold-up. 22 Panzer Division got through to the coast in the north, bottling up some eight enemy divisions as it went, and the army was able to give the order for the pursuit to start. The troops, Rumanians included, strained every nerve to carry it through successfully, and by 16th May Kerch had fallen to 170 Division and 213 Regiment. Even then a great deal more heavy fighting was needed to mop up the enemy remnants which had trickled back to the east coast.

Before the attack was launched I had once again moved into a command post close behind the front, and now I was out all day long visiting divisional staffs and the front-line troops. For a soldier there was something unforgettable about this tempestuous chase. All the roads were littered with enemy vehicles, tanks and guns, and one kept passing long processions of prisoners. The view from a hill near Kerch, where I had a rendezvous with General v. Richthofen, was quite breath-taking. Down below us, bathed in glorious sunshine, lay the Straits of Kerch – the goal we had dreamt of for so long. From the beach in front of us, which was crammed with Soviet vehicles of every possible description, enemy motor torpedo-boats made repeated attempts to pick up Soviet personnel, but they were driven off every time by our own gunfire. In order to spare our infantry any further sacrifices and bring about the surrender of the enemy elements still fighting back desperately along the coast itself, we had a mass artillery barrage laid down on these last pockets of resistance.

By 18th May the Battle of the Kerch Peninsula was over. Only small groups of the enemy continued to hold out in subterranean caves around Kerch for weeks to come under the pressure of a few fanatical commissars. According to the returns sent in, some 170,000 prisoners, 1,133 guns and 258 tanks had fallen into our hands.

Five German infantry divisions and one armoured, together with two Rumanian infantry divisions and one cavalry brigade, had annihilated two whole Soviet armies of twenty-six formations. Only negligible elements of the enemy had escaped across the straits of Kerch to the Taman Peninsula. A true battle of annihilation had been fought to a victorious finish!

'OPERATION STURGEON'

THE CONQUEST OF SEVASTOPOL

Eleventh Army still faced the hardest task of all: the conquest of Sevastopol.

I had already apprised Hitler of our intentions regarding the assault on the fortress during a visit to his headquarters in mid-April. It was the first time I had met him since submitting my views to him on the conduct of the offensive in the west in February 1940. Even at this second meeting I had the impression that he was not only extremely well informed on every detail of the battles fought to date, but also thoroughly appreciated the operational arguments expounded to him. He listened attentively to what I had to say and fully agreed with Eleventh Army's view on the way to conduct both the Kerch offensive and the assault on Sevastopol. He made not the least effort to interfere in our plans or, as was so often the case later on, to ramble off into endless recitations of production figures.

One vital question was not discussed on that occasion, however: whether, in view of the offensive planned in the Ukraine, it was right to commit the whole of Eleventh Army to an attack on the powerful Sevastopol fortress for a period that could not be predetermined with any real certainty, particularly now that the victory on the Kerch peninsula had removed the threat in the Crimea. The settlement of this problem was clearly a matter for the Supreme Command, not for our own headquarters. Speaking for myself, I believed at the time, and still do today, that the decision to make Eleventh Army take Sevastopol first was the correct one. Had we continued merely to invest the fortress, a good three or four German divisions, plus the Rumanian forces – in other words, half Eleventh Army – would have continued to be tied up in the Crimea.

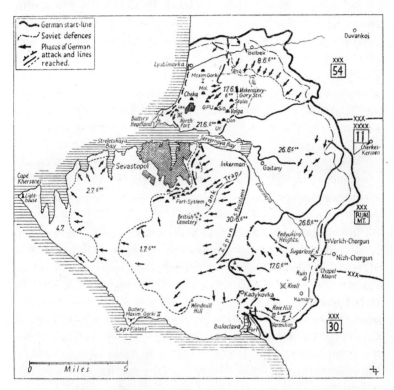

Map 13. Conquest of Sevastopol (June–July 1942).

What was undoubtedly a mistake, however, was the Supreme Command's decision, after Sevastopol's timely fall, to withdraw Eleventh Army from the southern wing of the Eastern Front for use at Leningrad and for patching up gaps in the line. After the fall of Sevastopol this army ought – as originally planned – to have been taken across the Straits of Kerch to the Kuban to intercept the enemy forces falling back on the Caucasus from the lower Don before Army Group A. Had the time factor not permitted this, it should at any rate have been taken into reserve behind the southern wing. The Stalingrad tragedy might then have been averted.

Immediately after the Kerch operation Eleventh Army began regrouping for the assault on Sevastopol.

42 Corps was made responsible for safeguarding the Kerch peninsula and the south coast of the Crimea. The only German troops left to it for this purpose were those of 46 Infantry Division, in addition to which it had 7 Rumanian Corps, comprising 10 and 19 Infantry Divisions, 4 Mountain Division [1] and 8 Cavalry Brigade. All other forces were forthwith dispatched to Sevastopol.[2]

There could be no shadow of doubt that the assault on the fortress would be even tougher than that of the previous December, the enemy having had half a year in which to tighten up his fortifications, bring his manpower up to strength and stock up with stores from across the sea.

The strength of the Sevastopol fortress consisted less in up-to-date fortifications – though a certain number of these did exist – than in the extraordinary difficulty of the ground, which was dotted with innumerable smaller defence installations. These formed a thick network covering the entire area from the Belbek valley to the Black Sea coast.

The whole of the ground between the Belbek valley and Severnaya Bay in particular constituted a strongly developed fortress belt.

The *northern front* ran south of the Belbek, though north of this, too, the enemy had an extensive strong-point around and northwards of the locality of Lyubimovka. The valley itself and the slopes rising away to the south were enfiladed by a 30·5-cm. battery housed in a thoroughly up-to-date armoured emplacement, known to us as 'Maxim Gorki I'. The slopes themselves were covered by a thick net of fieldworks 1 mile deep, some of which were concreted. Behind these came a series of strongly built, mainly concreted strong-points which our troops had nicknamed 'Stalin', 'Volga', 'Siberia', 'Molotov', 'G.P.U.' and 'Cheka', and which were mutually linked by a chain of dug-in positions. A final barrier to the northern shore of Severnaya Bay was formed by a defence zone of strong-points which included 'Donetz', 'Don', 'Lenin',

---

[1] Identical with the 4 Mountain Brigade mentioned earlier. The Rumanians had changed the designation of these mountain brigades without in fact increasing their strength to that of a division. *Tr.*

[2] 22 Panzer Division had to be handed over to Southern Army Group. *Author.*

the fortified locality of Bartenyevka, the old North Fort and the coastal batteries on 'Battery Headland'. Into the cliffs overlooking the bay the Russians had driven chambers for storing supplies and ammunition.

The *eastern front* branched off the northern one at a point about a mile and a quarter east of the village of Belbek, the hinge between the two being protected by the precipitous Kamyshly Ravine. The northern part of this eastern front ran through a stretch of the dense undergrowth with which the steep spurs of the Vaila Mountains in this area are covered. In this undergrowth there were countless small pockets of resistance – some of them nestling in holes blown in the rock – which an attacker could hardly touch with his artillery. This wooded northern sector of the eastern front ended in the steep cliffs south and south-east of the locality of Gaytany.

Though the woods petered out further south, the ground became increasingly difficult down towards the coast, where it resembled a range of rocky mountains.

Access to the southern fortress zone on both sides of the highway leading from the south coast to Sevastopol was barred in the first instance by a series of steep, dome-shaped summits which the Russians had converted into powerful strong-points. Crimea veterans will remember such names as 'Sugarloaf', 'North Nose', 'Chapel Mount' and 'Ruin Hill'. Then came the strongly defended village of Kamary, and finally the rocky massif north-east of the Bay of Balaclava. The enemy had been able to hold his own here when 105 Infantry Regiment achieved its bold capture of Balaclava Fort in autumn 1941. Penetration of this chain of fortified summits and cliffs was rendered all the more difficult by the fact that one hill always flanked the next.

Behind this forward defence zone in the south, north of the road from Sevastopol, rose the massif of the Feyukiny Heights, which was extended southwards to the coastal range by strong-points like 'Eagle's Perch' and the fortified village of Kadykovka. All these formed a sort of foreground to the strongest of the enemy's fortifications, which were established along the Zapun Heights. The latter are a range of hills with steep eastern slopes, beginning at the cliffs of Inkerman and dominating the valley of the Chornaya down to the south of Gaytany. There they turn south-west to bar the road to Sevastopol and finally link up with the sea through 'Windmill Hill', the western spur of the coastal range. The Zapun position, by virtue of its sharp drops and possibilities for mutual flanking fire, is extremely difficult for infantry to attack, and artillery observers up there command the entire fortress area as far as the eye can see. These Heights, incidentally, were the line held by the Western Powers during the Crimean War to cover the rear of their attack on Sevastopol against the Russians' idle relieving army.

But even when he had taken this commanding position, the attacker's troubles were still not over. Ranged along the coast were the coastal batteries, including 'Maxim Gorki II' in its armoured emplacement. There was also a wide semi-circle of continuous defences round the city itself, beginning at Inkerman on Severnaya Bay and rejoining the latter by Streletskaya Bay. It was composed of an anti-tank ditch, a barbed-wire obstacle and numerous pill-boxes, and included the British Crimean War cemetery south-east of Sevastopol, which the Russians had converted into a strong battery emplacement.

Finally there were a line of fortifications running hard along the periphery of the city and also several traverses screening the peninsula of Khersones towards the east. The Russians have always been known for their skill in laying out and camouflaging field defences, and at Sevastopol they had the added advantage of holding a stretch of country which offered them excellent opportunities for flanking fire. The rocky nature of the ground, moreover, made it possible to keep the cover for guns and mortars so narrow that they could practically only be destroyed by direct hits. And since we were dealing with Russians, it was a matter of course that extensive minefields had been laid not only along the front of the various defence zones, but also right inside them.

When considering how the assault on the fortress area should be conducted, Eleventh Army arrived at essentially the same conclusions as it had done the previous winter. We could not entertain any idea of using the central portion of the siege front for a decisive operation because artillery and air support – our two main trumps – could never become entirely effective in the wooded area there and our losses would be far too great. We thus had no choice but to attack once again from the north and north-east and in the south of the eastern sector.

This time, too – at least to begin with – the main punch was to be delivered in the north, for although the enemy fortifications were undoubtedly stronger and more numerous in the northern area of the fortress above Severnaya Bay than in its southern part, the going there was far easier. Above all, the artillery and Luftwaffe could be used to infinitely greater effect in the north than in the hilly country of the southern sector.

Of course, there still had to be an attack in the south as well. For one thing, it was important to split the enemy's defence by attacking from several sides at once. For another, he must be expected to hold out in the city itself and on the Khersones headland even after losing the fortified area north of Severnaya Bay. We had to remember that the task facing us at Sevastopol involved not only taking a fortress but also fighting an army which was certainly our match numerically even if it were inferior in material.[1]

The factor that had primarily guided our assault tactics in the winter – the need to gain command of the harbour at the earliest possible date – was no less important, however. As long as Eleventh Army had 8 Air Corps in support, the enemy would no longer be at liberty to supply himself by sea.

Such were the considerations on which Eleventh Army based its plan for 'Sturgeon', the code-name of the operation.

We intended to attack on the northern front and the southern part of the eastern front, while keeping the enemy pinned down in the central sector from Mekensia to Verkh-Chorgun. In the north the first objectives were the northern shore of Severnaya Bay and the heights around Gaytany, in the south the capture of the dominating heights of the Zapun position on both sides of the roads leading from the south coast and Balaclava to Sevastopol.

The *attack in the north* was to be carried out by *54 Corps*, comprising 22, 24, 50 and 132 Infantry Divisions (commanded by Generals Wolff, Baron v. Tettau, Schmidt and Lindemann) and a reinforced 213 Infantry Regiment. The corps' orders were to keep its forces rigidly concentrated in the main direction of assault on the high ground north of the eastern part of Severnaya Bay. All parts of the fortified zone bypassed in the first instance were to be pinned down with a view to taking as many of them as possible from the rear later on. The left wing of the corps was to gain possession of the heights of Gaytany and the

[1] According to the data available to Eleventh Army, the order of battle of the troops in the fortress at that time was as follows: H.Q. Coast Army (General Petrov); 2, 25, 95, 172, 345, 386 and 388 Rifle Divisions, 40 (dismounted) Cavalry Division, and 7, 8 and 79 Marine Brigades. (The badly battered Coast Army divisions which had escaped into the fortress earlier on were now believed to be fully up to strength again.) *Author*.

ground to the south-east of the latter in order to clear the way for the Rumanian Mountain Corps' subsequent advance further south.

The *attack in the south* was to be directed by H.Q. *30 Corps*, with 72 and 170 Infantry Divisions and 28 Light Division under command.[1] Its first job was to gain the starting line and artillery observation posts for the advance towards the Zapun Heights. To achieve this it had to capture the enemy's foremost defence zone based on the strong-points of 'North Nose', 'Chapel Mount', 'Ruin Hill', Kamary and 'High Cliff' south of Kamary and to eliminate flanking fire from the rocky heights east of Balaclava in the south. To solve this problem 72 Infantry Division was to advance along both sides of the highway to Sevastopol, while 28 Light Division – in accordance with its specialized role – had to capture the most northerly summits of the range of mountains east of Balaclava Bay. 170 Division was kept in reserve for the time being. Because of the peculiarly rugged terrain in this sector, the tasks in question could only be solved by carefully prepared local attacks.

Sandwiched between the two big assault groups, the *Rumanian Mountain Corps* was initially responsible for pinning down the enemy on its own front. In particular, 18 Rumanian Division was to carry out local attacks and an artillery bombardment to protect 54 Corps' left wing against enemy flanking action from the south. Further south, 1 Rumanian Mountain Division was to support 30 Corps' northern wing by capturing the Sugar Loaf.

In making its *artillery preparations* for the attack, Eleventh Army dispensed with the intensive barrage so popular with our opponents. In view of the peculiar nature of the ground and the endless number of enemy positions, this could not be expected to have any decisive effect nor should we have enough ammunition available. Instead, the preparations would start five days before the infantry assault, beginning with an air attack and all-out artillery strafe against supply lines and points where enemy reserves were known to be concentrated. In the five days that followed our gunners were to beat down the enemy artillery by steady *observed* fire and soften up positions in the enemy's foremost defence zone. Throughout this period 8 Air Corps would be making continual attacks on the city, harbour, supply installations and airfields.

[1] Commanded by Generals Müller-Gebhard, Sander and Sinnhuber respectively. *Author.*

And now a word about our artillery strength.

Eleventh Army had naturally called in every gun within reach for the attack, and O.K.H. had made available the heaviest pieces available.

In all, 54 Corps (artillery commander General Zuckertort) had at its disposal fifty-six heavy and medium batteries, forty-one light and eighteen mortar batteries, in addition to two battalions of assault guns. This made a total of 121 batteries, supported by two observation battalions.

The heavy siege artillery included batteries of cannon up to a calibre of 19 cm., as well as independent howitzer and heavy-howitzer batteries with calibres of 30·5, 35 and 42 cm. Furthermore, there were two special 60-cm. guns and the celebrated 80-cm. Big Dora. This monster had originally been designed for bombarding the most formidable section of the Maginot Line, but had not been finished in time. It was a miracle of technical achievement. The barrel must have been 90 feet long and the carriage as high as a two-storey house. Sixty trains had been required to bring it into position along a railway specially laid or the purpose. Two anti-aircraft regiments had to be constantly in attendance. Undoubtedly the effectiveness of the cannon bore no real relation to all the effort and expense that had gone into making it. Nevertheless, one of its shells did destroy a big enemy ammunition dump buried 90 feet deep in the natural rock on the northern shore of Severnaya Bay.

30 Corps' artillery was commanded by General Martinek, a particularly outstanding gunner officer who had previously held the same rank in the Austrian Army. Unfortunately he was later killed in the east as a corps commander.

Altogether the corps had twenty-five heavy and medium, twenty-five light and six mortar batteries, as well as one assault-gun and two observation battalions. Also assigned to it was 300 Panzer Regiment, whose tanks were remote-controlled and carried high-explosive charges.

The *Rumanian Mountain Corps* had twelve medium and twenty-two light batteries with which to perform its holding task.

A welcome addition to the assault artillery as a whole was provided by General v. Richthofen, Commander of 8 Air Corps, who turned over a number of his anti-aircraft regiments for use in a ground role.

At no other time on the German side in World War II can artillery ever have been more formidably massed – particularly as regards the high calibres used – than for the attack on Sevastopol. Yet how trifling this seems when compared with the masses of guns later considered indispensable by the Russians for a breakthrough in open country! At Sevastopol the attacker had 208 batteries (excluding anti-aircraft) at his disposal over a 22-mile front. This meant an average of less than ten batteries to every mile of front, though the ratio was obviously higher in the actual assault sectors. The Soviet offensives of 1945 were based on a ratio of 400 guns to every mile of assault front!

A few days before the attack I paid a brief visit to the south coast to take a closer look at 30 Corps' own preparations. Our command post down there was a charming little Moorish-style palace, perched on a steep cliff overhanging the Black Sea coast and formerly the property of a grand duke. On the last day of my stay I made a reconnaissance trip in our only naval vessel, an Italian E-boat, along the coast to a point off Balaclava, my object being to ascertain how much of the coastal road, up which the whole of the corps' reinforcements and supplies must pass, was visible from the sea and liable to come under observed bombardment from that quarter. In the event – presumably out of respect for our Luftwaffe – the Soviet Black Sea Fleet ventured no such action.

On the way back a calamity occurred just outside Yalta. Without any warning a hail of machine-gun bullets and cannon-shells began pumping into us from the sky. We were being strafed by two Soviet fighters which had swooped out of the sun, their sound having been drowned by the roar of our own powerful engines. In a matter of seconds seven of the sixteen persons on board were dead or wounded and the heat from the flames threatened to detonate the torpedoes slung alongside. The behaviour of the captain, a young Italian sub-lieutenant, was beyond all praise, and he showed immense presence of mind in the steps he took to save us and his ship. Disregarding the danger of mines, 'Pepo', my A.D.C., dived into the water and swam to the nearby shore, where – still stark naked – he stopped a passing truck. With this he dashed into Yalta and got the help of a Croatian motor-boat to tow us into harbour. It was a dismal journey. One Italian petty officer was dead and three sailors wounded. Captain v. Wedel, the port commandant of Yalta, had also been killed. But at my feet, severely wounded in the thigh, lay the truest comrade of all, my driver, Fritz Nagel. The Italian sub-lieutenant tore off his own shirt to use it as a makeshift bandage, but it was almost impossible to staunch the flow of blood from the artery.

Fritz Nagel came from Karlsruhe and had been my driver since 1938. We had seen and lived through so very much together, and he had already been wounded at my side once before during our time with 56 Panzer Corps. Throughout the years he had been a devoted comrade and in time had become a real friend to me. He had fine, frank brown eyes and not a trace of servility in his make-up. Sportsman-like and thoroughly decent by nature, he was a keen, cheerful soldier who had won the hearts of comrades and superiors alike. As soon as we touched land I took him straight to the field hospital. An operation was attempted, but he had already lost too much blood, and the same night his young light went out. We buried him alongside all our other German and Italian comrades in the Yalta cemetery high above the sea – perhaps one of the most lovely spots on the whole of that glorious coastline.

I sent Fritz Nagel's parents a copy of the words I spoke at his graveside.

But war waits for no man, not even for his thoughts. A few days later Eleventh Army's tactical headquarters, reduced to a bare minimum of personnel, set up a command post on the Sevastopol front at Yukhary Karales, a Tartar village nestling in a narrow valley among the cliffs. The Russians must have known that a command staff with its own signals section had moved in there, for every evening their 'duty pilot' flew over in an old Rata – known to the troops as a 'sewing machine' – to drop a stick of bombs, fortunately without ever doing the slightest damage. On a cliff-top above the village, in the Cherkess–Kermen mountains, where the Goths had once built their stronghold, we had established an observation post, and on the evening of 6th June we went up to watch the infantry assault go in along the entire front next morning. It was here, in a small dugout adjoined by an observation trench equipped with stereo-telescopes, that the Chief-of-Staff, the heads of the operations and intelligence branches, 'Pepo' and I spent the still hours of the night before the storm. Once again it was 'Pepo' who introduced a cheerful note into an otherwise pensive evening.

It had been suggested that I should issue an Order of the Day to the troops pointing out the importance of the impending battle. Generally speaking, I am not in favour of exhortations of this kind. Quite apart from the fact that they seldom get past the battalion orderly-rooms, our troops did not need reminding what was at stake. Since it was the usual thing to do on such occasions, however, I wrote out a few words on a sheet of paper and handed it to 'Pepo' for transmission to all corps headquarters. Shortly afterwards he returned to report: '*Herr General-oberst*, I've passed on the blurb.' It was a cheeky thing to say, but he was only expressing the ordinary soldier's view of such proclamations, and we all had a good laugh over it.

On the morning of 7th June, as dawn turned the eastern sky to gold and swept the shadows from the valleys, our artillery opened up in its full fury by way of a prelude to the infantry assault. Simultaneously the squadrons of the Luftwaffe hurtled down on to their allotted targets. The scene before us was indescribable, since it was unique in modern warfare for the leader of an army to command a view of his entire battlefield. To the north-west the eye could range from the woodlands that hid the fierce battles of 54 Corps' left wing from view right over to the heights south of the Belbek valley, for which we were to fight so bitterly. Looking due west, one could see the heights of Gaytany, and behind them, in the far distance, the shimmer of Severnaya Bay where it joined the Black Sea. Even the spurs of the Khersones peninsula, on which we were to find vestiges of Hellenic culture, were visible in clear weather. To the south-west there towered the menacing heights of Zapun and the rugged cliffs of the coastal range. At night, within the wide circumference of the fortress, one saw the flashes of enemy gunfire, and by day the clouds of rock and dust cast up by the bursts of our heavy shells and the bombs dropped by German aircraft. It was indeed a fantastic setting for such a gigantic spectacle!

At Sevastopol there was something more than an attacking army confronted by an adversary who was at least its numerical equal, something more than artillery and aircraft of the most modern design pounding away at fortifications embedded in steel, concrete and granite. Sevastopol was also the spirit of the German soldier – all his courage, initiative and self-sacrifice contending with the dogged resistance of an opponent whose natural elements were the advantage of terrain and the tenacity and steadfastness of the Russian soldier reinforced by the iron compulsion of the Soviet system. It is impossible to depict this struggle which was to go on for a round month in the most scorching heat (even early-morning temperatures being as much as 106° F.), in terms that would do justice to the feat of either attacker or defender. What our troops achieved in this battle would be worthy of an epic, but there is only space here for a brief account of a contest that must be almost unparalleled in its severity.

On its right wing 54 Corps had directed 132 Division to launch a frontal attack across the Belbek valley towards the commanding heights to the south of it, leaving out the enemy bridgehead of Lubyi-movka. To the left of it 22 Infantry Division had the task of opening the way across the valley for 132 Division by thrusting south of the Belbek from the east, over the Kamyshly gully. To the left of that, 50 Infantry Division, attacking through the locality of Kamyshly, was to join this thrust in a south-westerly direction. On the extreme left wing of the corps, in the mountainous woodlands, 24 Infantry Division was to work its way forward towards the heights of Gaytany, its left flank being covered by 18 Rumanian Division.

As a result of overwhelming support by the powerful assault artillery and the incessant attacks of 8 Air Corps, it was possible to cross the Kamyshly gully and Belbek valley on the first day and gain a footing on the commanding heights south of the latter.

Down in the south, 30 Corps' first job was to gain possession of the jumping-off positions for its own follow-up attack on both sides of the highway to Sevastopol, which was not to be launched until some days later.

The second phase of the offensive, lasting up to 17th June, was marked on both fronts by a bitter struggle for every foot of ground, every pill-box and every trench. Time and again the Russians tried to win back what they had lost by launching violent counter-attacks. In their big strong-points, and in the smaller pill-boxes too, they often fought till the last man and the last round. While the main burden of these battles was borne by the infantry and engineers, the advanced observation posts of our artillery still deserve special mention, since it was chiefly they who had to direct the fire which made it possible to take individual strong-points and pill-boxes. They, together with the assault guns, were the infantry's best helpmates.

On 13th June the valiant 16 Infantry Regiment of 22 Division, led by Colonel v. Choltitz, succeeded in taking Fort Stalin, before which its attack had come to a standstill the previous winter. The spirit of our infantry was typified by one wounded man of this regiment, who, pointing to his smashed arm and bandaged head, was heard to cry: 'I can take this lot now we've got the Stalin!'

By 17th June it had been possible, though at the cost of heavy losses, to drive a deep wedge into the fortified zone in the north. The positions of the second defence line, 'Cheka', 'GPU', 'Siberia' and 'Volga', were in our hands.

By the same date 30 Corps was likewise able to drive a wedge into the advanced defence zones in front of the Zapun positions. In the course of heavy fighting the fortified strongpoints of 'North Nose', 'Chapel Mount' and 'Ruin Hill' fell to 72 Division, while 170 Division took Kamary. To the north of the corps, after a series of fruitless charges, 1 Rumanian Mountain Division finally won the 'Sugar Loaf'. 28 Light Division, on the other hand, was advancing only very slowly over the rugged cliffs of the coastal range, 'Rose Hill' and 'Vermilion I and II', since the only mode of action to adopt in that maze of clefts and chasms was to leap-frog raiding parties from one point to the next, a process which entailed considerable losses.

Despite the price we had paid for these successes, however, the outcome of the offensive seemed to be very much in the balance for the next few days. The endurance of our own troops was visibly running out. In the case of 54 Corps it was found necessary to take 132 Division temporarily out of the line in order to exchange its sorely tried regiments for those of 46 Division in the Kerch peninsula. Its place was taken by 24 Division, which had to be released from the left wing of the corps for this purpose.

At the very same time Eleventh Army found itself under pressure from O.K.H. to release 8 Air Corps for the Ukraine offensive unless any prospect could be offered of Sevastopol's early fall. We, for our own part, insisted that the attack must at all costs go on until final success was achieved, which in turn depended on the continued presence of 8 Air Corps. In the end our view prevailed.

Yet who at that time, faced with the dwindling strength of our infantry, could have guaranteed the early fall of the fortress? Realizing that the strength of our own troops might give out prematurely,

Eleventh Army asked to be supplied with three extra infantry regiments – a request which O.K.H. duly approved. They were at least to arrive in time for the final phase of the struggle.

In the existing situation it was found expedient in the case of both assaulting corps to take advantage of an attacker's ability to switch the direction or main effort of his assault as he pleases, and thereby to take the enemy by surprise.

54 Corps turned west, committing 213 Infantry Regiment and 24 Division to battle as it did so. 213 Regiment, led by Colonel Hitzfeld, took the armour-plated battery 'Maxim Gorki I', one of whose guns had already been put out of action by a direct hit from a siege battery. The other was demolished by our engineers, who had succeeded in getting on to the top of it. However, the garrison of the fort, which went several storeys deep, did not surrender until our engineers had blown their way in through the turrets at ground level. In the course of one attempted break-out the commissar in command was killed, whereupon his men surrendered with the name of Christ trembling on their lips. After that 24 Division was able, by 21st June, to clear the rest of the northern sector along the west coast as far as the fortifications guarding the entrance to Severnaya Bay.

In the case of 30 Corps, too, a surprise alteration in the focal point of the attack brought about an important success by 17th June. The corps resolved to halt the advance across the northern chain of the coastal range east of Balaclava and to concentrate its forces on and immediately south of the main road for a surprise thrust. There was only artillery to counteract any flank action from the direction of the coastal range. 72 Division duly succeeded in over-running the enemy's positions south of the road, and its reconnaissance battalion, led by Major Baake, boldly exploited this initial gain by pushing straight through the floundering enemy as far as 'Eagle's Perch' in front of the Zapun line. In the early morning of 18th June the battalion managed to take the strongly defended 'Eagle' position and to remain in possession there until the division could move reinforcements up. This having been achieved, it was possible to extend our penetration of the enemy defence system northwards.

In the subsequent and third phase success was again achieved by sudden shifts in the focal point of the attack, particularly on the part of the artillery. In the north this meant the full attainment of the first

objective, Severnaya Bay, and in the south possession of our jumping-off
positions for the assault on the Zapun line.

In the northern sector the whole fire of the artillery was concentrated to permit 24 Division to take the peninsula forts dominating the
entrance to Severnaya Bay. The most formidable of these was the
antiquated but still powerful strong-point known as North Fort.

22 Division gained control along its whole front of the cliffs overlooking Severnaya Bay. There was extremely hard fighting for the railway tunnel on the boundary between 22 and 50 Divisions, out of
which the enemy launched a strong counter-attack with a brigade
that had recently arrived by cruiser. The tunnel was finally captured by
shelling its entrance. Not only hundreds of troops came out but an even
greater number of civilians, including women and children. Particular
difficulty was experienced in winkling the enemy out of his last hide-
outs on the northern shore of the bay, where deep galleries for storing
supplies and ammunition had been driven into the sheer wall of rock.
These had been equipped for defence by the addition of steel doors.
Since the occupants, under pressure from their commissars, showed no
sign of surrendering, we had to try to blow the doors open. As our
engineers approached the first of them, there was an explosion inside
the casemate and a large slab of cliff came tumbling down, burying not
only the enemy within but also our own squad of engineers. The
commissar in command had blown the casemate and its occupants sky-
high. In the end a second-lieutenant from an assault battery, who had
brought up his gun along the coastal road regardless of enemy shelling
from the southern shore, managed to force the other casemates to open
up after he had fired on their embrasures at point-blank range. Crowds
of completely worn-out soldiers and civilians emerged, their commissars having committed suicide.

Thirdly, 50 Division, which had some hard fighting to do in the
thicket-covered country of its own sector, was able to reach the
eastern end of Severnaya Bay and gain possession of the heights of
Gaytany dominating the mouth of the Chornaya valley.

To the left of it, the right wing of the Rumanian Mountain Corps
was fighting its way forward through wooded country over the hills
south-east of Gaytany. General Lascar, who later went into captivity
at Stalingrad, was the life and soul of this advance.

30 Corps, too, made gains by sudden changes in the direction of its

attack. Taking advantage of the capture of Eagle's Perch by 72 Division, it swung 170 Division round from the south to attack the Fedyukiny massif. The enemy, whose eyes were turned east and who was probably already expecting an attack on the Zapun Heights themselves, was taken completely by surprise, and it was possible to take the massif relatively quickly. This secured a firm base for the decisive assault on the Zapun line.

During the same few days some progress was also made by the left wing of the Rumanian Mountain Corps (1 Mountain Division).

Eleventh Army thus found itself in possession of almost the whole outer belt of the fortress by the morning of 26th June. The enemy had been thrown back into the inner fortified zone whose northern front was formed by the precipitous rock-face of Severnaya Bay's southern shore and whose eastern front ran from the heights of Inkerman along the Zapun range to the cliffs around Balaclava.

Eleventh Army now had to decide how to break open this inner ring of fortifications. It was taken for granted that the enemy in Sevastopol would continue to resist as bitterly as before – particularly as none of the statements issued by his immediate superiors, Crimean Front Headquarters, encouraged any hope of an evacuation.

On the other hand, the fact had to be faced that though the enemy's reserves might be largely expended, the offensive capacity of the German regiments was also virtually at an end.

In recent weeks I had spent all my mornings and afternoons visiting corps staffs, artillery commanders, divisions, regiments, battalions and gunner observation posts. I was only too well aware of the state of our units. The regiments had dwindled away to a few hundred men each, and I remember one company being pulled out of the line with a strength of one officer and eight men.

How, then, were we going to finish off the battle for Sevastopol, now that 54 Corps had Severnaya Bay before it and 30 Corps was facing the difficult assault on the Zapun Heights?

The ideal solution at this point would have been to switch the weight of the entire offensive to 30 Corps on the southern wing. In practice, however, this was just not possible. Moving the divisions alone was bound to take several days, and in this time the enemy would have an opportunity to recover his strength. In the frontal area the two sectors were linked by only one narrow road which we had taken immense trouble to build through the mountains the previous winter. In any case, it could not bear the weight of the heavy artillery, and the task of moving that quantity of guns round by way of Yalta and stocking them with ammunition when they reached the southern sector would have taken weeks to complete. An additional factor to bear in mind was the Supreme Command's intention of withdrawing 8 Air Corps from the Crimea at an early date.

Immediately after 22 Division reached Severnaya Bay, I had been down to visit its regiments in order to obtain a general view of the situation from an observation post on the northern shore. Before me lay a stretch of water between half a mile and 1,000 yards wide where whole fleets had once lain at anchor. On the far side, to the right, was the city of Sevastopol, and straight ahead a wall of cliff honeycombed with enemy positions. It occurred to me that from here – in other words, from the flank – one should be able to unhinge the Zapun fortifications, for the last direction from which the enemy seemed likely to expect an attack was across Severnaya Bay.

When I first discussed this plan of mine with 54 Corps and a number of subordinate commanders, there was a great deal of head-shaking and scepticism. How, they asked, could assault boats get across that broad stretch of bay in the face of the formidable array of guns and fortifications overlooking the southern shore? How, for that matter, were the assault boats even to be got to the shore and loaded with troops when the sole access to the water was down one or two steep ravines which could obviously be kept under fire by the enemy on the southern coast?

For the very reason that it appeared impossible, however, an attack across Severnaya Bay would take the enemy unawares and might well be the key to success. Despite all the objections raised, therefore, I stuck to my plan – hard though it was to order such a hazardous undertaking when one's own position prevented one from taking part.

Once the decision had been taken, everyone involved set about its execution with the utmost energy. In this connexion a special word of appreciation is due to the engineers, who had already given an excellent account of themselves alongside the infantry in the fighting for the pill-box positions.

The general offensive against the inner fortress area – 54 Corps crossing Severnaya Bay and 30 Corps assaulting the Zapun heights – was due to start early on the morning of 29th June. Already on 28th June 50 Division had succeeded in crossing the lower course of the Chornaya and taken the Inkerman. This was the scene of a tragedy that shows with what fanaticism the Bolsheviks fought. High above the Inkerman towered a sheer wall of cliff extending far away to the south. Inside it were enormous chambers which had served as cellarage for the Crimean champagne factories. Alongside the large stocks of wine the Bolsheviks had dumped ammunition, but now they were also using the chambers to accommodate thousands of wounded and refugees. Just as our troops were entering the Inkerman the whole cliff behind it shuddered under the impact of a tremendous detonation, and the 90-foot wall of rock fell in over a length of some 900 yards, burying thousands of people beneath it. Though the act of a few fanatical commissars, it was a measure of the contempt for human life which had become a principle of this Asiatic Power!

During those midnight hours of 28th–29th June in which the preparations for the crossing of Severnaya Bay were being made, a tremendous tension gripped everyone connected with the operation. In order to blanket all noise from the northern shore, 8 Air Corps kept up an incessant air raid on the city. The whole of the artillery stood by to begin a murderous bombardment of the cliff-tops on the southern shore the very moment any fire from there showed that the enemy had perceived what we were about. But everything remained quiet on the other side, and the difficult job of launching and loading the assault boats went off without a hitch. At one o'clock the first wave from 22 and 24 Divisions pushed off and headed for the opposite shore. The crossing, which obviously took the enemy absolutely by surprise, turned out a complete success, for by the time the enemy defences on the cliffside went into action our sturdy grenadiers had gained a firm footing on the shore below. Any enemy weapons showing themselves from now on were quickly knocked out by our troops as they scaled the cliffs to the plateau above. With that the dreaded Zapun position was unhinged from the flank.

At first light, however, our troops had also gone into action against the front of this position.

On the left wing of 54 Corps, 50 Division and the newly committed 132 Division (now composed of the infantry regiments of 46 Division) moved off from positions around and to the south of Gaytany to assault the heights between the Inkerman and a point to the south of it. The attack received supporting flank fire from the artillery on the north shore of Severnaya Bay and was joined by the right wing of the Rumanian Mountain Corps.

30 Corps likewise began its decisive push towards the Zapun line at daybreak, supported by the long-range batteries of 54 Corps and massed sorties by 8 Air Corps. While using its artillery to create the illusion that an attack on a broad front was pending, 30 Corps had assembled 170 Division as a task force in an extremely small area by the Fedjukiny Heights, and the latter, supported by assault guns, 300 Panzer Battalion and the direct fire of an anti-aircraft regiment, soon reached the high ground on both sides of the highway to Sevastopol. Taking advantage of the enemy's confusion, the division forthwith exploited far enough north, west and south for the corps to move its other divisions up to the crest.

After the successful crossing of the bay, the fall of the Heights of Inkerman and the penetration of the Zapun positions by 30 Corps, the fate of the Sevastopol fortress was sealed.

What now followed was a last desperate struggle that could neither stave off the defending army's utter defeat nor possibly benefit the Soviets as regards the overall operational situation. It would even have been superfluous from the viewpoint of military honour, for goodness knows the Russian soldier had fought bravely enough! But the political system demanded that the futile struggle should go on.

Now that they had captured the cliffs on the south shore of the bay, the divisions of 54 Corps which had carried out the crossing were already inside the wide outer ring of positions which encompassed the city. So while elements of the corps mopped up this ring in a southerly direction, the main body was able to turn west and deal with the peripheral fortifications and the city itself. With the fall of the famous Fort Malakoff, that bulwark which had cost so much blood in the Crimean War, the corps was into the defences of Sevastopol proper.

Meanwhile, before 29th June was out the two rear divisions of 30 Corps which had had the task of simulating a broad frontal attack – 28 Light Division and 72 Division – were pushed smartly through behind 170 Division.

Once they had reached the Zapun positions already taken by

the latter they were made to fan out to capture the Khersones peninsula.

28 Light Division broke through the outer ring of fortifications south-east of Sevastopol by taking the English Cemetery. The Russians had developed this into a main strong-point of their outer ring of fortifications, and the marble monuments once erected to British soldiers were now in ruins. The new dead of this battle were lying over graves torn open by shelling. Then the division thrust south of the city to take it from the west in case it should be defended; or, alternatively, to head off an enemy break-out.

170 Division's goal was the lighthouse on the extreme western tip of the Khersones peninsula – the spot from which Iphigeneia may have gazed, 'soulfully seeking the Grecian land'.

On 72 Division devolved the task of thrusting along the south coast. Rolling up the Zapun positions in a southward direction, it first took the dominant 'Windmill Hill', and thereby secured the main road to Sevastopol for the use of the corps. It was followed by 4 Rumanian Mountain Division, which set about flushing the defence system round Balaclava from the rear, taking 10,000 prisoners in the process.

After our experience of Soviet methods to date we were bound to assume that the enemy would make a last stand behind Sevastopol's perimeter defences and finally in the city itself. An order from Stalin had been repeatedly wirelessed to the defenders to hold out to the last man and the last round, and we knew that every member of the civil population capable of bearing arms had been mustered.

Our headquarters would have been neglectful of its duty to the soldiers of Eleventh Army had it failed to take account of this possibility. A battle within the city would cause more heavy losses to the attacker. In order to obviate them we directed the artillery and 8 Air Corps to go into action once more before the divisions resumed their assault. The enemy was to be shown that he could not expect to extract a further toll of blood from us in house-to-house fighting.

And so 1st July began with a massed bombardment of the perimeter fortifications and the enemy's strong-points in the interior of the city. Before long our reconnaissance aircraft reported that no further serious resistance need be anticipated. The shelling was stopped and the divisions moved in. It seemed probable that the enemy had pulled the bulk of his forces out to the west the previous night.

But the struggle was still not over. Although the Soviet Coast Army had given up the city, it had only done so in order to offer further resistance from behind the defences which sealed off the Khersones peninsula – either in pursuance of Stalin's backs-to-the-wall order or else in the hope of still getting part of the army evacuated by Red Fleet vessels at night from the deep inlets west of Sevastopol. As it turned out, only very few of the top commanders and commissars were fetched away by motor-torpedo boat, one of them being the army commander, General Petrov. When his successor tried to escape in the same way, he was intercepted by our Italian E-boat.

Thus the final battles on the Khersones peninsula lasted up till 4th July. While 72 Division captured the armour-plated fort of 'Maxim Gorki II', which was defended by several thousand men, the other divisions gradually pushed the enemy back towards the extreme tip of the peninsula. The Russians made repeated attempts to break through to the east by night, presumably in the hope of joining up with the partisans in the Yaila Mountains. Whole masses of them rushed at our lines, their arms linked to prevent anyone from hanging back. At their head, urging them on, there were often women and girls of the Communist Youth, themselves bearing arms. Inevitably the losses which sallies of this kind entailed were extraordinarily high.

In the end the remnants of the Coast Army sought refuge in big caverns on the shore of the Khersones peninsula, where they waited in vain to be evacuated. When they surrendered on 4th July, 30,000 men emerged from this small tip of land alone.

In all, the number of prisoners taken in the fortress was over 90,000, and the enemy's losses in killed amounted to many times our own. The amount of booty captured was so vast that it could not immediately be calculated. A naturally strong fortress, reinforced and consolidated in every conceivable way and defended by a whole army, had fallen. The army was annihilated and the entire Crimea now in German hands. At just the right time from the operational point of view, Eleventh Army had become free for use in the big German offensive on the southern wing of the Eastern Front.

I had spent the evening of 1st July with my immediate staff in our command post, a little Tartar dwelling in Yukhary Karales. The Soviet 'duty pilot' whose habit it had been to drop a few bombs in our valley around sundown had not shown up. Our thoughts went back to the battles of recent months and the comrades who were no longer with us.

And then, over the radio, came a triumphal fanfare heralding the special communique on the fall of Sevastopol. Shortly afterwards the following message came over the teleprinter:

'To the Commander-in-Chief of the Crimean Army
    Colonel-General v. Manstein

In grateful appreciation of your exceptionally meritorious services in the victorious battles of the Crimea, culminating in the annihilation of the enemy at Kerch and the conquest of the mighty fortress of Sevastopol, I hereby promote you Field-Marshal. By your promotion and the creation of a commemorative shield to be worn by all ranks who took part in the Crimean campaign, I pay tribute before the whole German people to the heroic achievements of the troops fighting under your command.

ADOLF HITLER.'

10

LENINGRAD–VITEBSK

WHILE THE divisions of Eleventh Army were recovering from the hardships of the recent fighting and I was on leave in Rumania, the various formation staffs were to work out plans for a crossing of the Straits of Kerch preparatory to the army's joining in the big offensive which had meanwhile been launched on the German southern wing. Throughout my leave I was kept posted on the preparations by the visits of my Chief of Operations, Colonel Busse. Unfortunately all this planning proved quite fruitless, as Hitler, who was as usual chasing after too many objectives at once, over-rated the initial successes of the offensive and gave up his original intention of including Eleventh Army in the operations.

Returning to the Crimea on 12th August I was disturbed to find a new directive from the Supreme Command awaiting me. The plan to take the army across the Straits had been dropped and replaced by an operation involving only H.Q. 42 Corps, 46 Division and certain Rumanian forces. Eleventh Army itself was earmarked for the capture of Leningrad, for which the artillery used in the assault on Sevastopol was already en route. Unfortunately three further divisions were detached from us. 50 Division was to remain in the Crimea. 22 Division, now converted back into an airborne division, was sent to Crete, where though one of our best formations – it was to lie more or less idle for he rest of the war. Finally, when we were already on the move, 72 Division was diverted to Central Army Group to deal with a local crisis there. Thus all that ultimately remained of Eleventh Army's original order of battle were H.Q.s 54 and 30 Corps, 24, 132 and 170 Infantry Divisions and 28 Light Division. Irrespective of what the Supreme Command's motives may have been, this dismemberment of an army in which the same corps and divisions had worked together for so long was deplorable. Mutual acquaintanceship and the trust that comes of fighting hard battles together are factors of the utmost importance in war and should never be disregarded.

But there was another aspect of even greater relevance. Could there be any justification for taking Eleventh Army away from the southern wing of the Eastern Front now that it was free in the Crimea and employing it on a task which was palpably less important – the conquest of Leningrad? On the German side, after all, the decisive results in that summer of 1942 were being sought in the south of the front. This was a task for which we could never be too strong, particularly as it was obvious even now that the duality of Hitler's objective – Stalingrad and the Caucasus – would split the offensive in two directions and that the further east it went the longer the northern flank of the spearhead must become.

Subsequent events showed how much better it would have been to keep Eleventh Army on the southern wing, irrespective of whether it had been moved forward over the Straits of Kerch to stop the enemy from falling back on the Caucasus or had initially followed up the attacking army groups as an operational reserve.

When I broke my flight north to call at Hitler's headquarters and talk over my new commitments, I discussed this problem in detail with the Chief of the General Staff, Colonel-General Halder. Halder made it quite clear that he completely disagreed with Hitler's proposal to try to take Leningrad in addition to conducting an offensive in the south, but said that Hitler had insisted on this and refused to relinquish the idea. However, when I asked if he thought it practicable to dispense entirely with Eleventh Army in the south he told me that he did. I myself remained sceptical, without of course being able to refute the Chief-of-Staff's opinion in advance.

On the same occasion I was appalled to find how bad relations were between Hitler and his Chief-of-Staff. One of the points brought up at the daily conference was the local crisis which had developed in Central Army Group's sector in consequence of a limited Soviet offensive there – the same crisis, in fact, that had necessitated the detachment of our own 72 Division. When Hitler took this as an occasion for indulging in a tirade against the men fighting on the spot, Halder emphatically contradicted him, pointing out that the strength of the troops had long been overtaxed and that the high loss of officers and N.C.O.'s in particular had been bound to have repercussions. Though couched in thoroughly objective language, Halder's strictures provoked an outburst of fury from Hitler. He questioned – in the most tactless terms – Halder's right to differ with him, declaring that as a front-line infantryman of World War I he was an infinitely better judge of the matter than Halder, who had never been in this position.

The whole scene was so undignified that I pointedly left the maptable and remained away till Hitler calmed down and asked me to return. Afterwards I felt compelled to mention the incident to the Head of the Personnel Office, General Schmundt, who was also Hitler's chief military assistant. I told him it was quite impossible for the Commander-in-Chief and the Chief-of-Staff of the Army to be on terms like this and that either Hitler must listen to his Chief-of-Staff and show him at least the respect that was his due, or Halder must take the only course remaining open to him. Unfortunately nothing of the sort occurred, until the break came six weeks later with Halder's dismissal.

On 27th August Eleventh Army headquarters arrived on the Leningrad front to investigate the possibilities of an attack in Eighteenth Army's sector and to settle on the plan for the assault on the city. It was intended that once this was done we should take over that part of Eighteenth Army's front which faced north, while the latter retained its eastern front on the Volkhov. The front earmarked for Eleventh Army was divided into three parts: the Neva sector from Lake Ladoga to the south-east of Leningrad; the actual assault front south of Leningrad; and the front containing the extensive bridgehead still held by the Soviets on the south shore of the Gulf of Finland around Oranienbaum.

In addition to powerful assault artillery, part of which had been brought up from Sevastopol, there were to be over thirteen divisions at the army's disposal, including the Spanish Blue Division, one armoured and one mountain division, and an SS brigade. Of these forces, however, since the Neva and Oranienbaum fronts would be requiring two divisions each, only nine and a half would be left for the attack on Leningrad. This was none too big a force considering that the enemy had an army there of nineteen rifle divisions, one rifle brigade, one frontier guard brigade and between one and two independent armoured brigades.

In view of these relative strengths it would naturally have been of tremendous assistance to us if the Finns, who had forces sealing off the Carelian Isthmus in the north of Leningrad, had participated in the offensive. However, when the question was put to the German liaison officer at Finnish headquarters, General Erfurth, it emerged that the Finnish High Command had declined to take part. The Finnish standpoint, according to the General, was that Finland had maintained ever since 1918 that her existence would never constitute a threat to Leningrad. This put any Finnish contribution to the offensive right out of the question.

Eleventh Army thus found itself thrown entirely on its own resources for the execution of its mission. We were well aware that the success of the operation was somewhat problematical, and the fact that it need not have been necessary at all hardly made it any more palatable to us. In the summer of 1941 there had probably been a very good chance of taking Leningrad by a *coup de main*. Though in those early days Hitler himself regarded the early capture of the city as a main priority, the opportunity was missed for some reason or other. Later Hitler thought he could starve Leningrad out. This the Soviets foiled by supplying the city over Lake Ladoga, in the summer by ship and in the winter by a railway line laid across the ice. What the Germans were left with today was a front from Lake Ladoga to the west of Oranienbaum which was a steady drain on their resources. While its removal was certainly most desirable, the advisability of attacking the city just now, when an attempt was being made to force the issue in the south of the Eastern Front, was a debatable point. As Schiller once said: 'What we omit from a single hour is lost to all eternity.'

Still, it was up to us to prepare as best we could for the attack we were called upon to make. To anyone reconnoitring along the front south of Leningrad the city seemed to lie within clutching distance, although it enjoyed the protection of a whole net of fieldworks distributed in depth. One could pick out the big Kolpino works on the Neva, which were still turning out tanks. The Pulkovo shipyards on the Gulf of Finland were also visible. In the distance were the silhouettes of St Isaac's Cathedral, the pointed tower of the Admiralty and the fortress of Peter and Paul. In clear weather it was also possible to see a battle-cruiser on the Neva that had been disabled by gunfire. She was one of the 10,000-ton vessels we had sold to the Russians in 1940. I was sad to learn that several of the imperial residences I knew from 1931 – the lovely Catherine Palace in Tsarskoe Selo, the smaller palace in the same place where the last Tsar lived, and the delightful Peterhof on the Gulf of Finland – had fallen victims to the war. They had been set on fire by Soviet shelling.

We realized from our reconnaissance that Eleventh Army must on no account become involved in any fighting inside the built-up areas of Leningrad, where its strength would be rapidly expended. As for Hitler's belief that the city could be compelled to surrender through terror raids by 8 Air Corps, we had no more faith in this than had Colonel-General v. Richthofen, the force's own experienced commander.

It was our intention, therefore, to begin by breaking through the front south of Leningrad with maximum artillery and air support, but not to carry the advance any further than the southern perimeter of the city. Thereupon two corps would turn east and quickly cross the Neva south-east of the city to destroy the enemy forces between there and Lake Ladoga, cut the supply route across the lake and isolate Leningrad from the east. Thereafter it should be possible to bring about the rapid fall of the city – like Warsaw before it – without any heavy house-to-house fighting.

Unfortunately Schiller's dictum was soon to prove only too true. Quite naturally the enemy had not failed to notice the German build-up in the Leningrad sector, and as early as 27th August he launched an attack against Eleventh Army's eastern front, forcing us to engage 170 Division just after its arrival. In the next few days it became clear that the Soviets were conducting a powerful relief offensive with the aim of forestalling our own attack.

On the afternoon of 4th September I received a telephone call from Hitler in person. He told me it was essential that I intervene on the Volkhov front to prevent a disaster there; I was to assume command myself and restore the situation by offensive action. That very day the enemy had effected a deep breakthrough over a wide stretch of Eighteenth Army's slender front south of Lake Ladoga.

Obviously it was somewhat embarrassing for us to relieve Eighteenth Army of command in its own sector just when a serious crisis had developed there. The headquarters staff had, quite understandably, been none too pleased to see us entrusted with so much as the attack on Leningrad. Even in the face of this open slight, however, it did everything possible to lighten our task in the absence of our own Q branch.

Instead of the projected attack on Leningrad, a battle now developed south of Lake Ladoga.

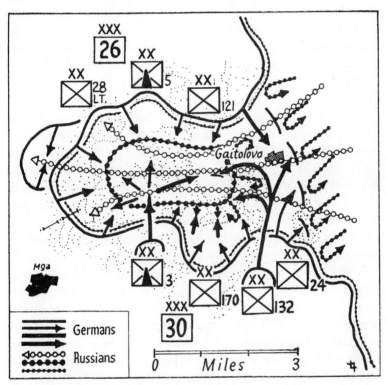

Map 14. Battle of Lake Ladoga (September 1942).

The enemy had succeeded in over-running a five-mile stretch of Eighteenth Army's front north of the railway line from Leningrad to the east and in penetrating some eight miles to a point above Mga, through which the line passed. The first problem was to halt the enemy with what forces Eleventh Army had available. At the cost of some hard fighting it was possible to do this in the next few days, and after assembling the rest of its divisions, which had arrived in the meantime, Eleventh Army was able to start its decisive counter-attack. This was launched from the two still-intact flanks in order to cut off the enemy spearhead at its root.

The drive from the south was performed by 30 Corps, comprising 24, 132 and 170 Infantry Divisions and 3 Mountain Division. From the north came 26 Corps, the formation originally responsible here, with 121 Infantry Division, 5 Mountain Division and 28 Light Division under command. By 21st September, after heavy fighting, the enemy bulge had been 'tied off'. In the next few days vigorous attacks by fresh enemy forces from the east were beaten off as they tried to relieve the encircled enemy spearheads. A similar attempt by the Leningrad Army, attacking with eight divisions across the Neva and from the front south of Leningrad, was equally unsuccessful.

At the same time, however, we had to dispose of the strong enemy forces still trapped between Gaitolovo and Mga. As usual, despite the hopelessness of his position and the utter futility – even from the viewpoint of operations as a whole – of continuing the struggle, the enemy had no thought of giving in. On the contrary, he tried again and again to break out of the pocket. As the entire area was thickly wooded (we, incidentally, would never have attempted such a breakthrough in country of this sort), any attempt on our part to get our infantry to grips with the enemy would have caused us excessive losses. Consequently Eleventh Army brought over the greatest possible concentration of artillery from the Leningrad front in order to subject the pocket to a round-the-clock bombardment. In the space of only a few days this shelling, supplemented by repeated attacks by the Luftwaffe, had turned the forest area into a pock-marked wilderness relieved only by the stumps of what had recently been giant trees. The captured diary of a Soviet regimental commander later gave us some idea of what effect we had achieved. It also showed just how ruthless the commissars had been in forcing the troops in the pocket to prolong their resistance.

By these methods we were able to end the fighting in the pocket by 2nd October. The enemy, Second Shock Army, had thrown no fewer than sixteen rifle divisions, nine rifle brigades and five armoured brigades into the battle, and, out of these, seven rifle divisions, six rifle brigades and four armoured brigades met their fate in the pocket. The remainder suffered extremely heavy losses in their fruitless attempts to batter a way through to the beleaguered force. Twelve thousand prisoners were taken, and over 300 guns, 500 mortars and 244 tanks were either captured or destroyed. The enemy's losses in dead many times exceeded the number of prisoners.

While the task of restoring the position on Eighteenth Army's eastern front was thereby fulfilled, our own divisions' casualties had also been heavy and a considerable amount of the ammunition intended for the attack on Leningrad had been used up. In view of this, there could be no question of immediately going over to the offensive. Nonetheless, Hitler was at first unwilling to give up the idea of taking Leningrad, although he was not prepared to set more limited objectives. This, of course, would still not have achieved our object, which was to iron out the position on the Leningrad front once and for all, and Eleventh Army duly insisted that it could not undertake an operation against the city without an adequate rest and refit, let alone with insufficient forces. While these discussions dragged on and one plan superseded another, October passed by.

It was more than frustrating to be stuck up here in the north when our offensive in the south of the front appeared to be petering out in the Caucasus and at the gates of Stalingrad. Not surprisingly, my A.D.C., Lieutenant Specht, once again felt the dissatisfaction which inevitably besets a young officer on a higher formation staff when there is nothing vital to occupy him. 'Pepo' began tugging at the bit and I, knowing how he felt, could not bring myself to deny him his wish. I sent him off to 170 Division, which was in action on the Neva and in whose ranks he had already fought for a time in the Crimea. The poor lad crashed in a *Fieseler Storch* while on his way to join his regiment, and we buried him on 25th October. His death was a sad blow to everyone, most of all to myself. Never again should we hear his clear voice and gay laugh. How I would miss this young comrade who had filled our many hours together with his merriment and been my companion on so many strenuous and dangerous trips, never once losing his brightness, self-confidence or drive! After my good comrade Nagel, he was the second of my immediate associates to be snatched away from us by the war in the east.

Just before Specht's burial I had to fly to the Supreme Headquarters to receive my field-marshal's baton. What a thrill it would have given him to have gone with me!

As had always been the case with me to date, Hitler went out of his way to be affable and spoke with warm appreciation of the way the troops of Eleventh Army had acquitted themselves in the battle of Lake Ladoga. I took this opportunity to impress my views on him regarding the excessive demands being imposed on our infantry. With such high losses as we were bound to have in the east when fighting an enemy as tough as the Russians, it was vitally important that the infantry regiments should always be brought back up to strength with the minimum possible delay. But when replacements never arrived on time – and none had ever done so since the Russian campaign began – the infantry had to go into action far below their proper strength, with the inevitable result that the fighting troops became more and more worn down as time went on.

Now, we were aware that the Luftwaffe, on instructions from Hitler, was in the process of setting up twenty-two so-called Luftwaffe Field Divisions, for which it was able to spare 170,000 men. There was nothing surprising in this. Göring had always done things on an extravagant scale in his own domain, not only where funds and installations were concerned, but also in regard to manpower. In the same vein the Luftwaffe had been established to take on operational commitments for which, as had since turned out, it was unable to find sufficient numbers either of air-crews or machines. This is not the place to inquire why things should have been allowed to come to such a pass. The essential fact was that the Luftwaffe had some 170,000 men to spare and could have spared them long ago, the dream of a strategic air war having ended, for all practical purposes, with the Battle of Britain.

These 170,000 men were now to be concentrated in the Luftwaffe's own private units to fight a war on the ground. Considering what a wide choice had been open to the Luftwaffe in making its selections for these divisions, they were doubtless composed of first-class soldiers. Had they been drafted to army divisions as replacements in autumn 1941 to maintain the latter at their full fighting strength, the German Army might well have been saved most of the emergencies of the winter of 1941–42. But to form these excellent troops into divisions within the framework of the Luftwaffe was sheer lunacy. Where were they to get the necessary close-combat training and practice in working with other formations? Where were they to get the battle experience so vital in the east? And where was the Luftwaffe to find divisional, regimental and battalion commanders?

I covered all these aspects in detail during that talk with Hitler and a little later set them out in a memorandum I drafted for his attention. He listened to my arguments attentively enough, but insisted that he had already given the matter his fullest consideration and must stick to his decision. Shortly afterwards the then Chief of Operations of Central Army Group, a man who was always well informed, on account of his friendship with Hitler's A.D.C., told me the reasons which Göring had given Hitler for wanting the Luftwaffe to set up its own divisions. Göring had claimed that he could not hand over 'his' soldiers, reared in the spirit of National Socialism, to an army which still had chaplains and was led by officers steeped in the traditions of the Kaiser. He had already told his own people that the Luftwaffe must make sacrifices, too, lest the army appear virtually to stand alone in this respect. Such were the arguments with which Göring had sold his scheme to Hitler!

Our Leningrad mission as such was now coming to an end. During my visit to Vinnitsa, Hitler said that my headquarters would probably be moved to Central Army Group in the Vitebsk region, where there were signs that a big enemy offensive was pending. If and when this materialized, our task would be to counteract it with an offensive of our own. At the same time, however, he told me that if he and his head-quarters should leave Vinnitsa, I was to be put in command of Army Group A. After removing Field-Marshal List from this appointment without valid reason, following a difference of opinion with him, Hitler had been commanding the Army Group himself as a sort of sideline – a quite impossible arrangement in the long run. More sur-prising still was what he had to say on this occasion in connexion with my eventual appointment as Commander-in-Chief of the Army Group. Next year, he told me, he was thinking of driving through the Caucasus to the Near East with a motorized army group! It was a measure of how unrealistically he still assessed the overall military situation and its strategic possibilities.

My last few days on the Leningrad front were marked by the hardest blow that could have befallen my dear wife, myself and our children in the last war – the death of our eldest son Gero. He fell for our be-loved Germany on 29th October, as a second lieutenant in the 51 Panzer Grenadier Regiment of my old 18 Division. I trust, as one under whose command so many thousands of youngsters gave their lives for Germany, that I may be forgiven for mentioning this purely personal loss here. The sacrifice of our son's life was certainly no different from that made by countless other young Germans and their fathers and mothers. But it will be appreciated that there must be a place in these memoirs of mine for the son who gave his life for our Fatherland. He shall stand here for all the others who trod the same road as he did, whose sacrifice was the same as his sacrifice, and who live on in the hearts of their dear ones just as our beloved son lives on in ours.

Our Gero, born on New Year's Eve 1922 and killed in his twentieth year, had been a delicate child from birth. He had suffered from asthma from childhood, and it was due only to the constant care of my wife that he grew up fit enough to become a soldier. Yet while his ailment deprived him of many things in his boyhood, it had also made him unusually mature and determined to do what life demanded of him despite all his handicaps.

Gero was a particularly lovable child – serious, thoughtful, but always happy. After taking his final school examination at the *Ritterakademie* in Liegnitz in 1940, he expressed the wish to become a soldier and to join my own arm, the infantry – known in Germany as the Queen of the Battlefield because it has from time immemorial borne the brunt of the fighting. It goes without saying that we, as his parents, understood this desire to follow in the footsteps of generations of ancestors, although neither of us had ever made any attempt to influence him in his choice of a profession. It was simply in his blood to become a regular officer – to be a trainer of German youth and to be at its head in times of stress.

So, having passed his school examinations, he joined 51 Panzer Grenadier Regiment in Liegnitz and went through the 1941 summer campaign in Russia as a private soldier. He was promoted corporal and won the Iron Cross for going back again with other volunteers to pick up a comrade wounded on patrol. In autumn 1941 he was sent home to the officers' school and in spring 1942 he received his commission.

After a serious illness and convalescent leave he came back to the regiment he loved, now in action on Lake Ilmen as part of Sixteenth Army. I had the joy of seeing him on his way out there when he visited me in my caravan at the front during the battle of Lake Ladoga. After that I saw him once more when I visited my friend Busch at Sixteenth Army Headquarters on 18th October. He had invited Gero up as well, so that we, Busch and our dear Specht, my A.D.C., were able to spend a happy evening together. Specht himself was killed only a few days later.

Early on 30th October 1942, after the morning situation reports had been handed in, my faithful Chief-of-Staff, General Schulz, the successor to Wöhler, brought me the news that our son Gero had been killed by a Russian bomb the previous night. As assistant adjutant of his battalion he had been on his way out to the front line to convey an order to a platoon commander.

We buried the dear boy on the shores of Lake Ilmen the following day. The padre of 18 Panzer Grenadier Division, Pastor Krüger, began his oration with the words:

'A Lieutenant of the Infantry.'

Our son would not have wished it otherwise.

After the funeral I flew home for a few days to be with my dear wife, for whom this boy had throughout the years been a special object of care and devotion. He had given us nothing but joy, for all the anxiety he had caused us by the ailment he had fought so bravely. We laid his soul in God's hands.

Gero Erich Sylvester von Manstein, as so many other young Germans, fell in action like the brave soldier he was. The officer's calling was his mission in life, and he fulfilled it with a maturity rare in one so young. If one can speak of a young aristocrat in this sense, then he was one indeed. Not merely in outward appearance – he was tall, slim and fine-limbed, with long, noble features – but most of all in character and outlook. There was not a single flaw in this boy's make-up. Modest, kind, ever eager to help others, at once serious-minded and cheerful, he had no thought for himself, but knew only comradeship and charity. His mind and spirit were perpetually open to all that is fine and good. It was his heritage to come of a long line of soldiers; but by the very fact of being an ardent German soldier he was at once a gentleman in the truest sense of the word – a gentleman and a Christian.

Whilst I was in Liegnitz after Gero's burial, Eleventh Army Headquarters was moved from Leningrad to Central Army Group's sector in the area of Vitebsk. There is nothing of importance to tell regarding the few weeks it spent there. Before any steps could be taken to use us in counteracting the anticipated offensive, events in the south of the Eastern Front led to our being given a new role.

On 20th November we received orders to assume immediate command of the sector on both sides of Stalingrad as the headquarters of a newly created 'Don Army Group'. I had just been on a trip to the front to visit v.d. Chevallerie's corps with my Chief of Operations, Colonel Busse, and had been delayed by the explosion of a mine under our train. In that territory the presence of partisans made it necessary to travel in armoured vehicles or specially protected trains.

Because the weather was too bad for flying, we had to leave Vitebsk by rail on 21st November, and were once again held up by a mine attack. We reached H.Q. Army Group B, which was still responsible for our future sector, on 24th November, my fifty-fifth birthday. What we learnt here about the situation of Sixth Army and the adjacent fronts of Fourth Panzer Army and Third and Fourth Rumanian Armies will be dealt with in the chapter on Stalingrad.

With members of the German minority in Siebenbürgen, accompanied by his son, Gero (standing beside author), and Lt. Specht (back to camera)

At H.Q. 50 Division in the Crimea

With Col.-Gen. Dumitrescu

Southern coastline in the Crimea

Maxim Gorki I

Sevastapol on fire

Russian Battery at entrance to Severnaya Bay

Crimean meeting with Marshal Antonescu

With Baron v. Richthofen at Kerch, May 1942 (author furthest left)

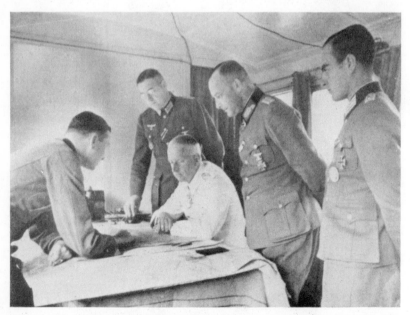

Caravan conference before Leningrad (*left to right:* Gen. Schulz, Col. Busse, the author, Major Eismann, and Lt. Specht)

Conference with Gen. Kempf and Gen. Busse, during 'Citadel'

H.Q. at Vinnitsa

II

HITLER AS SUPREME COMMANDER

MY APPOINTMENT as commander of Don Army Group brought me for the first time under Hitler's direct orders as Supreme Commander of the Armed Forces (Wehrmacht) and the Army (Heer). Only now did I find myself in a position to see how he tried to fulfil the duties of a supreme war leader besides those of a Head of State, for hitherto I had felt his influence on military decisions at best indirectly and from afar. Because of the strict secrecy surrounding all matters of an operational nature, I had been unable to form any valid opinion of my own.

During the campaign in *Poland* we had been unaware of any interference by Hitler in the leadership of the army. On his two visits to v. Rundstedt's army group he had listened sympathetically to our interpretations of the situation and agreed to our intentions without making any attempt to intervene.

As for the plan for the occupation of *Norway*, no outsider had known anything whatever about it. Hitler's attitude regarding the *offensive in the west* has already been discussed in detail. It was certainly both deplorable and alarming that he should have completely passed over O.K.H. in this matter, yet it had to be conceded that his view that the solution must be an offensive one was fundamentally correct from the *military* point of view, even if the same could not be said of his original timing. Admittedly he had laid down the outline of a plan which – as has already been pointed out – could hardly have produced a complete solution. At that stage he had probably not thought it possible to attain results on the scale ultimately achieved. Nevertheless, when the plan put up by Army Group A offered him this possibility, he had immediately grasped the idea and adopted it himself – even though he imposed certain limitations which betrayed his aversion to

273

risks. His fatal mistake of halting the armour outside Dunkirk had not at the time been apparent to an outsider, for the sight of beaches bestrewn with abandoned equipment tended to deceive anyone not yet aware how successful the British had been in getting their troops back across the Channel.

The absence of a 'war plan' permitting the timely preparation of an *invasion* did, however, reveal a failure of Wehrmacht leadership – in other words, on the part of Hitler himself. On the other hand, it was impossible for anyone not actually on the spot to judge whether or not the decision to turn on the Soviet Union was unavoidable for political reasons. The Soviet deployment on the German, Hungarian and Rumanian frontiers certainly looked menacing enough.

As commander of a corps and later of Eleventh Army I learnt just as little of Hitler's influence on the plan for an attack on the *Soviet Union* and the conduct of operations in the first phase of the campaign as I did of the plans for the summer offensive in 1942. There had certainly been no interference by Hitler in the handling of the Crimean campaign. Indeed, he had agreed to our intentions without hesitation when I went to see him in spring 1942 and had doubtless done everything to make our success at Sevastopol possible. I have already mentioned that I considered Eleventh Army to have been wrongly used after the fall of the fortress.

Now that I had come immediately under Hitler in my capacity as an army group commander, however, I was to get my first real experience of him in his exercise of the supreme command.

When considering Hitler in the role of a military leader, one should certainly not dismiss him with such clichés as 'the lance-corporal of World War I'.

He undoubtedly had a certain eye for operational openings, as had been shown by the way he opted for Army Group A's plan in the west. Indeed, this is often to be found in military amateurs – otherwise history would not have recorded so many dukes and princes as successful commanders. In addition, though, Hitler possessed an astoundingly retentive memory and an imagination that made him quick to grasp all technical matters and problems of armaments. He was amazingly familiar with the effect of the very latest enemy weapons and could reel off whole columns of figures on both our own and the enemy's war production. Indeed, this was his favourite way of side-tracking any topic that was not to his liking. There can be no question that his insight and unusual energy were responsible for many achievements in the sphere of armaments. Yet his belief in his own superiority in this respect ultimately had disastrous consequences. His interference prevented the smooth and timely development of the Luftwaffe, and it was undoubtedly he who hampered the development of rocket propulsion and atomic weapons.

Moreover, Hitler's interest in everything technical led him to overestimate the importance of his technical resources. As a result, he would count on a mere handful of assault-gun detachments or the new Tiger tanks to restore situations where only large bodies of troops could have any prospect of success.

What he lacked, broadly speaking, was simply *military ability based on experience* – something for which his 'intuition' was no substitute.

While Hitler may have had an eye for tactical opportunity and could quickly seize a chance when it was offered to him, he still lacked the ability to assess the prerequisites and practicability of a plan of operations. He failed to understand that the objectives and ultimate scope of an operation must be in direct proportion to the time and forces needed to carry it out – to say nothing of the possibilities of supply. He did not – or would not – realize that any long-range offensive operation calls for a steady build-up of troops over and above those committed in the original assault. All this was brought out with striking clarity in the planning and execution of the 1942 summer offensive. Another example was the fantastic idea he disclosed to me in autumn 1942 of driving through the Caucasus to the Near East and India with a motorized army group.

As in the political sphere (at all events after his successes of 1938), so in the military did Hitler lack all sense of *judgement* regarding what could be achieved and what could not. In autumn 1939, despite his contempt for France's powers of resistance, he had not originally recognized the possibility of attaining decisive success by a correctly planned German offensive. Yet when this success actually became his, he lost his eye for opportunity where conditions were different. What he lacked in each case was a real training in strategy and grand tactics.

And so this active mind seized on almost any aim that caught his fancy, causing him to fritter away Germany's strength by taking on several objectives simultaneously, often in the most dispersed theatres of war. The rule that *one can never be too strong at the crucial spot*, that one may even have to dispense with less vital fronts or accept the risk of radically weakening them in order to achieve a decisive aim, was something he never really grasped. As a result, in the offensives of 1942 and 1943 he could not bring himself to stake *everything* on success. Neither was he able or willing to see what action would be necessary to compensate for the unfavourable turn which events then took.

As for *Hitler's strategic aims* (at least in the conflict with the Soviet Union), these were to a very great extent conditioned by political considerations and the needs of the German war economy. This has already been indicated in the introductory remarks on the Russian campaign and will emerge again in connexion with the defensive battles of the years 1943–4.

Now, questions of a political and economic nature are undoubtedly of great importance when it comes to fixing strategic aims. What Hitler overlooked was that the achievement and – most important of all – the retention of a territorial objective presupposes the defeat of the enemy's armed forces. So long as this military issue is undecided – and this may be seen from the struggle against the Soviet Union – the attainment of territorial aims in the form of economically valuable areas remains problematical and their long-term retention a sheer impossibility. The day had yet to come when one could wreak such havoc on the enemy's armament centres or transport system with raiding aircraft or guided missiles that he was rendered incapable of continuing the fight.

While strategy must unquestionably be an instrument in the hands of the political leadership, the latter must not disregard – as did Hitler to a great extent when fixing operational objectives – the fact that the strategic aim of any war is to smash the military defensive power of the enemy. Only when victory has been secured is the way open to the realization of political and economic aims.

This brings me to the factor which probably did more than anything else to determine the character of Hitler's leadership – his overestimation of the *power of the will*. This *will*, as he saw it, had only to be translated into *faith* down to the youngest private soldier for the correctness of his decisions to be confirmed and the success of his orders ensured.

Obviously a strong will in a supreme commander is one of the essential prerequisites of victory. Many a battle has been lost and many a success thrown away because the supreme leader's will failed at the critical moment.

The will for victory which gives a commander the strength to see a grave crisis through is something very different from Hitler's will, which in the last analysis stemmed from a belief in his own 'mission'. Such a belief inevitably makes a man impervious to reason and leads him to think that his own will can operate even beyond the limits of hard reality – whether these consist in the presence of far superior enemy forces, in the conditions of space and time, or merely in the fact that the enemy also happens to have a will of his own.

Generally speaking, Hitler had little inclination to relate his own calculations to the probable intentions of the enemy, since he was convinced that his will would always triumph in the end. He was equally disinclined to accept any reports, however reliable, of enemy superiority, even though the latter might be many times stronger than he. Hitler either rejected such reports out of hand or minimized them with assertions about the enemy's deficiencies and took refuge in endless recitations of German production figures.

In the face of his will, the essential elements of the 'appreciation' of a situation on which every military commander's decision must be based were virtually eliminated. And with that Hitler turned his back on reality.

The only remarkable feature was that this over-estimation of his own will-power, this disregard for the enemy's resources and possible intentions, was not matched by a corresponding boldness of decision. The same man who, after his successes in politics up to 1938, had become a political gambler, actually recoiled from risks in the military field. The only bold military decision that may be booked to Hitler's credit was probably the one he took to occupy Norway, and even then the original suggestion had come from Grand-Admiral Raeder. Even here, as soon as a crisis cropped up at Narvik, Hitler was on the point of ordering the evacuation of the city and thereby of sacrificing the fundamental aim of the entire operation, which was to keep the iron-ore routes open. During the execution of the western campaign, too, as we have seen earlier, Hitler showed a certain aversion to taking military risks. The decision to attack the Soviet Union was, in the last analysis, the inevitable outcome of cancelling the invasion of Britain, which Hitler had likewise found too risky.

During the Russian campaign Hitler's fear of risk manifested itself in two ways. One – as will be shown later – was his refusal to accept that elasticity of operations which, in the conditions obtaining from 1943 onwards, could be achieved only by a voluntary, if temporary surrender of conquered territory. The second was his fear to denude secondary fronts or subsidiary theatres in favour of the spot where the main decision had to fall, even when a failure to do so was palpably dangerous.

There are three possible reasons why Hitler evaded these risks in the military field. First, he may secretly have felt that he lacked the military ability to cope with them. This being so, he was even less likely to credit his generals with having it. The second reason was the fear, common to all dictators, that his prestige would be shaken by any set-backs. In practice this attitude is bound to lead to the commission of military mistakes which damage the man's prestige more than ever. Thirdly, there was Hitler's intense dislike, rooted in his lust for power, of giving up anything on which he had once laid hands.

In the same context mention may be made of another trait of Hitler's against which his Chief-of-Staff, Colonel-General Zeitzler, and I both battled in vain throughout the period in which I was commanding Don Army Group.

Whenever he was confronted with a decision which he did not like taking but could not ultimately evade, Hitler would procrastinate as long as he possibly could. This happened every time it was urgently necessary for us to commit forces to battle in time to forestall an operational success by the enemy or to prevent its exploitation. The General Staff had to struggle with Hitler for days on end before it could get forces released from less-threatened sectors of the front to be sent to a crisis spot. In most cases he would give too small a number of troops when it was already too late – with the result that he usually finished up by having to grant several times what had originally been required. The tussle used to last for whole weeks when it was a question of abandoning untenable positions like the Donetz area in 1943 or the Dnieper Bend in 1944. The same applied to the evacuation of unimportant salients on quiet stretches of front for the purpose of acquiring extra forces. Possibly Hitler always expected things to go his way in the end, thereby enabling him to avoid decisions which were repugnant to him if only because they meant recognizing the fact that he must accommodate himself to the enemy's actions. His inflated belief in his own will-power, a certain aversion to accepting any risk in mobile operations (the *retour offensif*, for example) when its success could not be guaranteed in advance, and his dislike of giving up anything voluntarily – such were the factors which influenced Hitler's military leadership more and more as time went on. Obstinate defence of every foot of ground gradually became the be all and end all of that leadership. And so, after the Wehrmacht had won such extraordinary successes in the first years of war by dint of operational mobility, Hitler's reaction when the first crisis occurred in front of Moscow was to adopt Stalin's precept of hanging on doggedly to every single position. It was a policy that had brought the Soviet leaders so close to the abyss in 1941 that they finally relinquished it when the Germans launched their 1942 offensive.

Yet because the Soviet counter-offensive in that winter of 1941 had been frustrated by the resistance of our troops, Hitler was convinced that his ban on any voluntary withdrawal had saved the Germans from the fate of Napoleon's Grand Army in 1812. In this belief, admittedly, he was reinforced by the acquiescent attitude of his own retinue and several commanders at the front. When, therefore, a fresh crisis arose in autumn 1942 after the German offensive had become bogged down outside Stalingrad and in the Caucasus, Hitler again thought the arcanum of success lay in clinging at all costs to what he already possessed. Henceforth he could never be brought to renounce this notion.

Now it is generally recognized that defence is the stronger of the two forms of fighting. This is only true, however, when the defence is so efficacious that the attacker bleeds to death when assaulting the defender's positions. Such a thing was out of the question on the Eastern Front, where the number of German divisions available was never sufficient for so strong a defence to be organized. The enemy, being many times stronger than we were, was always able, by massing his forces at points of his own choice, to break through fronts that were far too widely extended. As a result, large numbers of German forces were unable to avoid encirclement. Only in mobile operations could the superiority of the German staffs and fighting troops have been turned to account and, perhaps, the forces of the Soviet Union ultimately brought to naught.

The effects of Hitler's ever-increasing predilection for 'hanging on at all costs' will be dealt with in greater detail in connexion with the defensive battles fought on the Eastern Front in 1943 and 1944. The reason for his insistence on it may be found deep down in his own personality. He was a man who saw fighting only in terms of the utmost brutality. His way of thinking conformed more to a mental picture of masses of the enemy bleeding to death before our lines than to the conception of a subtle fencer who knows how to make an occasional step backwards in order to lunge for the decisive thrust. For the *art* of war he substituted a brute force which, as he saw it, was guaranteed maximum effectiveness by the will-power behind it.

Since Hitler placed the power of force above that of the mind and, while having every regard for a soldier's bravery, did not rate his ability to the same extent, it is hardly surprising that, in the same way as he over-rated technical expedients, he was possessed of '*la rage du nombre*'. He would intoxicate himself with the production figures of the German armaments industry, which he had undoubtedly boosted to an amazing extent, even if he preferred to overlook the fact that the enemy's armaments figures were higher still.

What he forgot was the amount of training and skill required to render a new weapon fully effective. Once the new weapons had reached the front, he was content. It did not worry him whether the units concerned had mastered them or not, or whether a weapon had even been tested under combat conditions.

In just the same way Hitler was constantly ordering new divisions to be set up. Though an increase in the number of our formations was most desirable, they had to be filled at the cost of replacements for the divisions already in existence, which in course of time were drained of their last drop of blood. At the same time the newly established formations initially had to pay an excessively high toll of killed because of their lack of battle experience. The Luftwaffe Field Divisions, the unending series of SS divisions and finally the so-called People's Grenadier Divisions were the most blatant examples.

A final point worth mentioning is that although Hitler was always harping on his 'soldierly' outlook and loved to recall that he had acquired his military experience as a *front-line soldier*, his character had as little in common with the thoughts and emotions of soldiers as had his party with the Prussian virtues which it was so fond of invoking.

Hitler was certainly quite clearly informed of conditions at the front through the reports he received from the army groups and armies. In addition, he frequently interviewed officers who had just returned from the front-line areas. Thus he was not only aware of the achievements of our troops, but also knew what continuous overstrain they had had to endure since the beginning of the Russian campaign. Perhaps this was one of the reasons why we never managed to get Hitler anywhere near a front line in the east. It was hard enough to persuade him to visit our Army Group headquarters; the idea of going any further forward never occurred to him. It may be that he feared such trips would destroy those golden dreams about his invincible will.

Despite the pains Hitler took to stress his own former status as a front-line soldier, I still never had the feeling that his heart belonged to the fighting troops. Losses, as far as he was concerned, were merely figures which reduced fighting power. They are unlikely to have seriously disturbed him as a human being.[1]

[1] A former officer of O.K.W. who was transferred there after being badly wounded at the front and whose job brought him into almost daily contact with Hitler, mainly at the daily briefings but also at more private meetings, has written me the following note on this subject:

'I fully recognize the justification of this subjective feeling (i.e. that Hitler had no sympathy for the fighting troops and regarded losses as mere figures). That was how he appeared among a large body of people, but in reality he was almost the opposite. From a soldier's point of view he was possibly even *too* soft and certainly too dependent on his emotions. It was symptomatic that he could not stand any encounter with the horrors of war. He was afraid of his own softness and susceptibility, which would have hampered him in making the decisions that his political will demanded of him. Casualties which he was compelled to deal with personally or of which he was given realistic descriptions were a source of horror to him and obviously caused him as much suffering as the deaths of people he knew.

'On the strength of several years' observation I do not believe that this was play-acting but simply *one* side of his character. Outwardly, therefore, he assumed a deliberate air of indifference to avoid being distracted by the trait of which he himself was afraid. This is also the more deep-seated reason why he did not go to the front or visit any of the bombed cities. It was quite certainly not due to any lack of personal courage but to the fear of being horrified by what he would see.

'At private gatherings it was often noted in conversations about the efforts and achievements of the fighting troops that he had a great appreciation and sympathy for them.'

The opinion of this officer, who was not one of Hitler's supporters or admirers, at least shows what dissimilar impressions people could have of Hitler's character and mentality and how difficult it really was to get to the bottom of them. If – as is maintained above – Hitler actually was soft-hearted, how can one explain the brutal cruelty which became increasingly typical of his régime as time went on? *Author.*

In one respect, however, Hitler's outlook was entirely soldier-like—in the matter of war decorations. With these his first and foremost aim was to honour the brave among the fighting men, and the regulations he issued regarding the award of the Iron Cross at the beginning of the campaign were a model of their kind. This decoration, he decided, should be conferred only for deeds of bravery and outstanding leadership – which meant that, as far as the latter category was concerned, it could be won only by formation commanders and their senior staff officers. Unfortunately many of those responsible for awarding the decoration failed all along to observe this lucid and admirable ruling – partly, it must be admitted, as a result of the delay in creating a cross for meritorious war service, the *Kriegsverdienstkreuz*, which was intended for those who, though employed on duties rendering them ineligible for the Iron Cross, still deserved distinction. With Hitler it was always harder to secure a Knight's Cross for a deserving General than for an officer or man at the front.

As for the retrospective tendency to deride the many different badges and insignia that Hitler created in the course of the war, people should merely bear in mind what feats our soldiers accomplished during the many long years of its duration. Badges like the close-combat clasp (the *Nahkampfspange*) and the Eleventh Army Crimean Shield were at all events worn with pride. Besides, the number of medal ribbons worn by soldiers on the other side shows that the question of war decorations is not to be dismissed with a lot of silly talk about 'tin gongs'.

The deficiencies I have just described were bound to detract considerably from Hitler's fitness to play the self-appointed role of the supreme military leader.

They could still have been counterbalanced, however, if only he had been prepared to take advice from – and place genuine confidence in – an experienced and jointly responsible Chief of the General Staff. He did, after all, possess a number of the qualities indispensable to a supreme commander: a strong will, nerves that would stand up to the most serious crises, an undeniably keen brain and – as I said before – a certain talent in the operational field combined with an ability to recognize possibilities of a technical nature. If only he could have seen his way to compensate for his lack of training and experience in the military sphere – particularly as regards strategy and grand tactics – by utilizing the skill of his Chief-of-Staff, quite an efficient military leadership might have emerged despite all the shortcomings mentioned above. But this was precisely what Hitler would not accept.

Just as he considered the power of his will to be in every way decisive, so had his political successes – and, indeed, the military victories early in the war, which he regarded as his own personal achievement – caused him to lose all sense of proportion in assessing his own capabilities. To him the acceptance of advice from a jointly responsible Chief-of-Staff would not have meant supplementing his own will but submitting it to that of another. Added to this was the fact that he was imbued by origin and background with an insuperable mistrust of the military leaders, whose code and way of thinking were alien to him. Thus he was not prepared to see a really responsible military adviser alongside himself. He wanted to be another Napoleon, who had only tolerated men under him who would obediently carry out his will. Unfortunately he had neither Napoleon's military training nor his military genius.

I have already shown in the chapter dealing with the plan for the invasion of Britain that Hitler had so organized the Supreme Command that no one was vested with the authority to advise him on grand strategy or to draft a war plan. The Operations Staff (*Wehrmachtführungsstab*) of O.K.W., which was theoretically qualified to discharge such a task, in practice merely played the role of a military secretariat. Its only *raison d'être* was to translate Hitler's ideas and instructions into the terminology of military orders.

But there was even worse to come. Hitler's designation of Norway as an 'O.K.W.' theatre of operations in which O.K.H. had no authority was only the first step in the disruption of land operations. In due course all the other theatres were gradually turned over to O.K.W. Finally only the Eastern one remained as an O.K.H. responsibility, and even then it had Hitler at its head. Hence the Chief-of-Staff of the Army was left with just as little influence on the other theatres of war as were the Commanders-in-Chief of the two other services in matters of grand strategy. He had no say whatever in the overall distribution of the army's forces and often did not even know for certain what troops and material were being sent to the various theatres. In the circumstances it was inevitable that the O.K.W. Operations Staff and the General Staff of the army should clash. Indeed, Hitler probably created clashes deliberately in order that he alone should at all times have the decisive say. Naturally such faulty organization of the supreme military leadership was bound to contribute decisively to its breakdown. Another consequence of Hitler's over-estimation of his will-power and military ability was that he attempted more and more to interfere by separate orders of his own in the running of subordinate formations.

It has always been the special *forte* of German military leadership that it relies on commanders at all levels to show initiative and willingness to accept responsibility and does everything in its power to promote such qualities. That is why, as a matter of principle, the 'directives' of higher commands and the orders of medium and lower commands always contained so-called 'assignments' for subordinate formations. The detailed execution of these assignments was the business of the subordinate commanders concerned. This system of handling orders was largely the reason for the successes scored by the German Army over its opponents, whose own orders generally governed the actions of subordinate commanders down to the very last detail. Only when there was no other possible alternative left did anyone on our side encroach upon the authority of a subordinate formation headquarters by specifically laying down the action it should take.

Hitler, on the other hand, thought he could see things much better from behind his desk than the commanders at the front. He ignored the fact that much of what was marked on his far-too-detailed situation maps was obviously out of date. From that distance, moreover, he could not possibly judge what was the proper and necessary action to take on the spot.

He had grown increasingly accustomed to interfering in the running of the army groups, armies and lower formations by issuing special orders which were not his concern at all. While I had hitherto been spared such interference in my own sphere of command, I was forewarned of it by what Field-Marshal v. Kluge had to tell me when I met him on a railway station on my way from Vitebsk to Rostov. At Central Army Group, he said, he had to consult Hitler before any operation involving forces of a battalion or more could be mounted. Even if I personally did not experience such intolerable interference later on, there were still to be quite enough clashes with the Supreme Command as a result of Hitler's meddling.

In contrast to his passion for individual orders, which were usually nothing but a hindrance to command staffs and detrimental to operations, Hitler was loath to issue long-term operational directives. The more he came to regard the principle of 'holding on at all costs' as the alpha and omega of his policy, the less prepared was he to issue long-term directives which took account of the normally foreseeable development of a strategic situation. That such methods must ultimately have placed him at a disadvantage *vis-à-vis* the enemy was something he refused to see. His mistrust of his subordinate commanders prevented him from giving them, in the form of long-term directives, freedom of action, which they might put to a use that was not to his liking. The effect of this, however, was to do away with the very essence of leadership. In the long run even an army group could not get along without directives from the Supreme Command – certainly not when it formed part of a larger front and was bound to its neighbours on either flank. We often thought nostagically of our days in the Crimea, when we had been able to fight in a theatre all of our own.

It still remains for me to show – in as far as I can do so from personal experience – what pattern the disputes took which inevitably arose between Hitler and the army leaders as a result of his attitude to questions of military leadership. Many of the accounts on record depict him as foaming at the mouth and even taking an occasional bite at the carpet. Although he did undoubtedly lose all self-control on occasions, the only time he ever raised his voice or behaved badly when I was present was during the episode with Halder which I have already mentioned.

Hitler obviously sensed just how far he could afford to go with his interlocutor and what people he could hope to intimidate with outbursts of rage that may often have been simulated. I must say that as far as my own personal contacts with him went, he maintained appearances and kept things on a factual plane even when our views collided. On the one occasion when he did become personal, the extremely sharp retort it evoked was accepted in silence.

Hitler had a masterly knack of psychologically adapting himself to the individual whom he wished to bring round to his point of view. In addition, of course, he always knew anyone's motive for coming to see him, and could thus have all his counter-arguments ready beforehand. His faculty for inspiring others with his own confidence – whether feigned or genuine – was quite remarkable. This particularly applied when officers who did not know him well came to see him from the front. In such cases a man who had set out to 'tell Hitler the truth about things out there' came back converted and bursting with confidence.

In the various disputes I had with Hitler on operational matters in my capacity as an army group commander, what impressed me most was the incredible tenacity with which he would defend his point of view. There was almost invariably a tussle of several hours' duration before his visitor either attained his object or retired empty-handed, at best consoled with empty promises. I have known no other man who could show anything like the same staying power in a discussion of this kind. And while the maximum time involved in any dispute with a front-line commander would at worst be several hours, the Chief-of-Staff, General Zeitzler, often had to battle for days on end at the evening conferences in order to get Hitler to take the necessary action. Whenever one of these contests was in progress, we always used to ask Zeitzler what 'round' they had reached.

Besides, the arguments with which Hitler defended his point of view – and I include the purely military ones here – were not usually of a kind that could be dismissed out of hand. After all, in any discussion of operational intentions one is almost always dealing with a matter whose outcome nobody can predict with absolute certainty. Nothing is certain in war, when all is said and done.

Whenever Hitler perceived that he was not making any impression with his opinions on strategy, he immediately produced something from the political or economic sphere. Since he had a knowledge of the political and economic situations with which no front-line commander could compete, his arguments here were generally irrefutable. As a last resort all one could do was to insist that if he did not agree to the proposals or demands submitted to him, things would go wrong militarily and in turn have even worse repercussions in the political and economic fields.

On the other hand, Hitler frequently showed himself to be a very good listener even when he did not like what was being asked of him, and on such occasions he was quite capable of objective discussion.

Naturally no relationship of any intimacy could develop between this fanatical dictator – who thought only of his political aspirations and lived in a belief in his 'mission' – and the military leaders. The personal element obviously did not interest Hitler in the least. To him human beings were merely tools in the service of his political ambitions. From his own side there sprang no bond of loyalty to the German soldier.

The ever-more-apparent defects in Germany's military leadership, some of which arose from Hitler's character and others from the quite impossible organization of the Supreme Command outlined earlier on, naturally raised the question of whether anything could be done to bring about a change. I prefer to leave the political aspects aside here – as indeed I have done everywhere else in this book.

I made no less than three attempts, in the interest of a more rational conduct of the war, to persuade Hitler to accept some modification of the Supreme Command. From no other quarter, as far as I know, was the inadequacy of his military leadership ever put to him quite so bluntly.

I was fully alive to the fact that Hitler would never be prepared to relinquish the supreme command officially. As a dictator he could not possibly have done so without suffering what for him would have been an intolerable loss of prestige. In my opinion everything depended, therefore, on persuading Hitler – while nominally retaining the position of Supreme Commander – to leave the conduct of military operations in all theatres of war to *one* responsible Chief-of-Staff and to appoint a special Commander-in-Chief for the Eastern theatre. These attempts of mine, which unfortunately proved unavailing, will be discussed further when I come to deal with the events of the years 1943–4. For me they were a particularly precarious undertaking, for Hitler knew full well that I was the very man many people in the army would like to see in the position of a proper Chief-of-Staff or as Commander-in-Chief in the east.

It is not my intention here to go into the question of changing the leadership of the Reich by violent means, as exemplified by the events of 20th July 1944, although I may do so one day. Within the scope of these war memoirs it is enough to say that as one responsible for an army group in the field I did not feel I had the right to contemplate a *coup d'état* in wartime because in my own view it would have led to an immediate collapse of the front and probably to chaos inside Germany. Apart from this, there was always the question of the military oath and the admissibility of murder for political motives.

As I said at my trial: 'No senior military commander can for years on end expect his soldiers to lay down their lives for victory and then precipitate defeat by his own hand.'

In any case, it was already clear by that time that not even a *coup d'état* would make any difference to the Allied demand for unconditional surrender. At the time when I held a command we had not, to my mind, reached the point where such action had to be regarded as the only possible solution.

THE TRAGEDY OF STALINGRAD

'Stranger ! To Sparta say, her faithful band
Here lie in death, remembering her command.'

NEVER WILL these lines, telling of the heroism of the defenders of Thermopylae and ever after regarded as the song of praise to bravery, fidelity and soldierly obedience, be carved in stone at Stalingrad in memory of Sixth Army's martyrdom on the Volga. Nor is any cross or cenotaph likely to be raised over the vanished traces of the German soldiers who starved, froze and died there.

Yet the memory of their indescribable suffering, their unparalleled heroism, fidelity, and devotion to duty will live on long after the victors' cries of triumph have died away and the bereaved, the disillusioned and the bitter at heart have fallen silent.

The Battle of Stalingrad is understandably treated by the Soviets as the turning point of the war. The British ascribe similar importance to the Battle of Britain. The Americans are inclined to attribute the Allies' final success to their own entry into hostilities.

In Germany, too, many people feel constrained to regard Stalingrad as the decisive battle of World War II.

In point of fact not one of these individual events should really be rated as decisive. The outcome of the war was decided by a wealth of factors, the most significant of which was probably the hopelessly inferior position in which Germany ultimately found herself *vis-à-vis* her opponents in consequence of Hitler's policies and strategy.

Stalingrad was certainly a turning point to the extent that the wave of German offensives broke on the Volga, to recede like a breaker on the ebbing tide. But grave though the loss of Sixth Army undoubtedly was, it still need not have meant that the war in the east – and *ipso facto* the war as a whole – was irretrievably lost. It would still have been conceivable to force a stalemate if Germany's policies and military leadership had been adapted to such a solution.

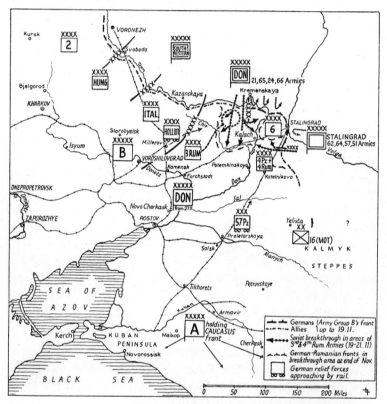

Map 15. Situation on German Southern Wing at end of November 1942: the Struggle to free Sixth Army.

THE WAY TO STALINGRAD

The cause of Sixth Army's destruction at Stalingrad is obviously to be found in Hitler's refusal – doubtless mainly for reasons of prestige – to give up the city voluntarily.

Yet the fact that Sixth Army could ever land in such a situation at all was due to the operational errors committed *beforehand* by the Supreme Command in the planning and execution of the 1942 offensive, most of all with regard to its final stages.

The plight in which the German southern wing found itself in the late autumn of 1942 as a result of these mistakes will be dealt with in the chapter on the winter campaign of 1942–3. All I propose to do here is to bring out the points which settled the fate of Sixth Army.

Thanks to the fact that Hitler's strategic objectives were governed chiefly by the needs of his war economy, the German offensive of 1942 had split into two different directions – the Caucasus and Stalingrad. By the time the German advance came to a halt, therefore, a front had emerged, to hold which there were not enough German forces available. To make things worse, no strategic reserve existed, the Supreme Command having squandered Eleventh Army in every conceivable direction immediately it became free in the Crimea.

Army Group A – with its front facing south – was located in the north of the Caucasus between the Black Sea and the Caspian. *Army Group B* held a front facing east and north-east which began on the Volga south of Stalingrad and bent back north of the city to join the Middle Don, along which it continued to a point north of Voronezh. Neither of the two army groups was strong enough to hold fronts of this length, particularly if one bore in mind that despite its heavy losses the enemy's southern wing had been able to avoid destruction and was not really beaten at all. Apart from this, the enemy had very strong strategic reserves in his other sectors, as well as in the hinterland. Last but not least, a gap 190 miles wide yawned between the two army groups in the Kalmyk Steppes, guarded only by the quite inadequate resources of one division (16 Motorized) based on Yelista.

The attempt to hold this over-extended front *for any length of time* constituted the *first* of the mistakes which were to plunge Sixth Army into its desperate situation at the end of November 1942.

The *second and even more fatal* mistake was that Hitler compelled Army Group B to tie down its principal striking force, *Fourth Panzer* and *Sixth Armies*, in the fighting in and around Stalingrad. The job of protecting the deep northern flank of this group along the Don was left to Third Rumanian Army, one Italian and one Hungarian army and, in the Voronezh sector, to the weak Second German Army. Hitler must have known that even behind the Don the allied armies could not stand up to a strong Soviet attack. The same was true of Fourth Rumanian Army, which he had entrusted with the task of guarding the open right flank of Fourth Panzer Army.

The attempt to gain control of the Volga by taking Stalingrad in a set battle after the original assault had been only partially successful would at best have been admissible on a very short-term basis. But to leave the main body of the Army Group at Stalingrad for weeks on end with inadequately protected flanks was a cardinal error. It amounted to nothing less than presenting the enemy with the initiative we ourselves had resigned on the whole southern wing, and was a clear invitation to him to surround Sixth Army.

A third mistake was the *utterly grotesque chain of command* on the German southern wing.

Army Group A had no commander of its own whatever. It was commanded by Hitler in what might be called a part-time capacity.

Army Group B had no fewer than seven armies under command, including four allied ones. No army group headquarters can cope with more than five armies at the outside, and when most of these are allied ones, the task inevitably becomes too much for it. H.Q. Army Group B had quite rightly established itself at Starobyelsk, behind the defensive front on the Don, in order to keep a better eye on the allied armies. The choice of this location, however, also meant that the headquarters was much too distant from the right wing of its sector. Another factor was that by his frequent interference in the conduct of operations Hitler largely deprived the Army Group Headquarters of control of Sixth Army.

It is true that O.K.H. had recognized these command problems and made plans to create a new Don Army Group under Marshal Antonescu. The new headquarters had not been set up, however, as Hitler first wished to see Stalingrad fall. This failure to use the Rumanian Marshal was a serious mistake. Admittedly his capacity for command was untried so far, but he was certainly a good soldier. In any case, his presence would have lent greater weight to our calls for further forces to guard the flanks of the Stalingrad front. He was, after all, a Head of State and an ally to whom Hitler had to pay greater heed than to German army group and army commanders. Above all, Antonescu's personality would have served to brace up the senior Rumanian commanders, who respected this man no less than they did the Russians.

It was clear from an impassioned letter he wrote me after my assumption of command that the Marshal had on several occasions called attention to the dangers of the situation in general and that of

Third Rumanian Army in particular. As long as he did not hold a responsible command at the front, however, these comments of his inevitably lacked the emphasis they would have carried if uttered by a Head of State simultaneously answerable for the sector that was threatened. It was equally clear that neither Army Group B nor Sixth Army had failed to give warning of the big offensive the enemy was preparing to launch against the covering fronts on each side of Stalingrad.

Finally, mention should be made of a fact which had grave repercussions on the position of Sixth Army and the entire southern wing. The whole of Army Group A, as well as Fourth Panzer and Sixth Armies, Third and Fourth Rumanian Armies and the Italian Army, were based on a single Dnieper crossing, the railway bridge at Dnepropetrovsk. The repair of the Zaporozhye railway bridge and the link across the Ukraine through Nikolayev and Kherson to the Crimea and thence across the Straits of Kerch had either been discontinued or was not yet complete. The north-to-south link behind the German lines was equally unsatisfactory. When it came to bringing up fresh troops or quickly switching forces behind the front, therefore, the German Supreme Command found itself at a permanent disadvantage *vis-à-vis* the enemy, who had much more efficient communications at his disposal in every direction.

Every Commander-in-Chief must run risks if he wants to succeed. The risk undertaken by the Supreme Command in the late autumn of 1942, however, should never have consisted in tying down the most hard-hitting forces of Army Group B at Stalingrad over a long period in which it was content to leave the Don front covered by such an easily destructible screen. One possible argument in the Supreme Command's favour is that it was quite unprepared for the allied armies to break down so completely. Yet the Rumanians, who were still the best of our allies, fought exactly as our experiences in the Crimea implied they would. Any illusions about the Italians' fighting capacities, of course, were inexcusable from the start.

The risk which the German command *ought* to have taken, after the summer offensive had merely won us more territory without bringing about the decisive defeat of the Soviet southern wing, consisted in *returning to mobile operations* between the Caucasus and middle reaches of the Don – with due advantage being taken of the large bend of the river – in order to *prevent the enemy from attaining the initiative*. But to substitute one risk for another was not in keeping with Hitler's mentality. By failing to take appropriate action after his offensive had petered out without achieving anything definite, he paved the way to the tragedy of Stalingrad!

DEVELOPMENT OF THE SITUATION AROUND STALINGRAD UP TO MY TAKE-OVER OF DON ARMY GROUP

The O.K.H. order received by Eleventh Army Headquarters on 21st November in the Vitebsk area laid down that for the purpose of stricter co-ordination of the armies involved in the arduous defensive battles to the west and south of Stalingrad, we were to take over command of Fourth Panzer Army, Sixth Army and Third Rumanian Army as '*H.Q. Don Army Group*'. Since we lacked a quartermaster-general's branch, we were to be joined by the one already formed for Marshal Antonescu. It was headed by Colonel Finkh, a General Staff officer whose soundness of character was matched only by his extraordinary talent for organizing supply and transport, and who in due course mastered all the supply difficulties with which the Army Group constantly found itself confronted. The airlift to Sixth Army, unfortunately, was outside his control. After my recall in April 1944 Colonel Finkh was transferred to the staff of the Commander-in-Chief in the west, where, I am told, he soon had supply and transport in a state as near perfection as the enemy's complete domination of the skies permitted. As one of the men implicated in the conspiracy against Hitler, he was executed after 20th July 1944.

Don Army Group's task, as defined in the O.K.H. order, was 'to bring the enemy attacks to a standstill and recapture the positions previously occupied by us'.

Initially the only reinforcements promised us were a corps headquarters and a division which were to be moved up to Millerovo, behind the future right wing of Army Group B.

It may be gathered from the wording of our task and the insignificance of the proposed reinforcements that when issuing this order O.K.H. still did not realize the danger of the situation around Stalingrad, although the ring had closed around Sixth Army that very day.

Further information was forthcoming in Vitebsk and during a train stop when I was able to talk to Field-Marshal v. Kluge and his Chief-of-Staff, General Wöhler. From this I gathered that the enemy had broken through *Third Rumanian Army*'s front on the Don north-west of Stalingrad in very great strength. Between one and two Soviet tank armies were involved, in addition to a great deal of cavalry – in all some thirty formations. The same thing had happened south of Stalingrad to *Fourth Rumanian Army*, which was under command of Fourth Panzer Army.

Before leaving Vitebsk, therefore, I sent the Chief of the General Staff a teleprinter message pointing out that in view of the magnitude of the enemy effort, our task at Stalingrad could not be merely a matter of regaining a fortified stretch of front. What we should need to restore the situation would be forces amounting to an army in strength – none of which, if possible, should be used for a counter-offensive until their assembly was fully complete.

General Zeitzler agreed with me, and promised to try to let us have an armoured division and two or three infantry divisions by way of addition.

I also teleprinted a request to Army Group B that Sixth Army be instructed to withdraw forces quite ruthlessly from its defence fronts in order to keep its rear free at the Don crossing at Kalach. Whether this instruction was ever passed to Sixth Army I have been unable to discover.

Not until we arrived at H.Q. Army Group B in Starobyelsk on 24th November did we obtain a clear picture of recent events and the current situation from the commander, Colonel-General Baron v. Weichs, and his Chief-of-Staff, General v. Sodenstern.

In the early hours of 19th November, after a tremendous artillery barrage, the enemy had broken out of his Don bridgehead at Kremenskaya and had also crossed the river further west to attack both the left wing of Sixth Army (11 Corps) and Third Rumanian Army (4 and 5 Rumanian Corps). Simultaneously he had launched a strong attack against Fourth Panzer Army (Colonel-General Hoth) south of Stalingrad, where it was intermingled with Fourth Rumanian Army. While the left wing of Sixth Army had held firm, the enemy had been able to overrun the Rumanians completely on both fronts. At each of the two points of penetration strong Soviet tank forces had immediately pushed through in depth – just as we had taught them to do. By an early hour on 21st November they had already linked up on the Don at Kalach, where the bridge so vital for the supply of Sixth Army had fallen into their hands intact. Since the forenoon of that day, therefore, the ring had been closed around Sixth Army and the German and Rumanian elements of Fourth Panzer Army which had been squeezed back into the pocket from the area south of Stalingrad. The encircled troops included five German corps totalling twenty divisions, two Rumanian corps, the mass of the army artillery not on the Leningrad front and large numbers of army engineer units. Even later on the Army Group was unable to obtain any exact data on the sum total of German soldiers trapped in the pocket. The returns sent in by Sixth Army fluctuated between 200,000 and 270,000 men, but it must be remembered here that the stated ration strengths included not only the Rumanian troops but also many thousand indigenous volunteers – the so-called 'Hiwis' – and prisoners-of-war. The most commonly quoted figure of over 300,000 is undoubtedly exaggerated. Various communications-zone troops were left outside the pocket, as were part of the B-echelon transport, a number of the wounded, and all ranks on leave. These residual elements, which later formed the cadres with which most of the Sixth Army divisions were reconstituted, still amounted to anything between 1,500 and 3,000 men per division. If one bears in mind that the divisions of Sixth Army had already fallen off in strength in November, the estimate that there were 200,000–220,000 men in the pocket, even allowing for the strong complement of army artillery and engineers, is probably fairly accurate.

The situation on 24th November was approximately as follows:

The only intact formations left to *Fourth Panzer Army* were 16 Motorized Division on its southern wing – widely extended across the steppes on both sides of Yelista – and 18 Rumanian Division on the northern side. All the other Rumanians had either been thrown back into Stalingrad or overrun. With what remnants of the Rumanian units it could scrape together, plus various German communications-zone troops, the army tried to hold an emergency defence line forward of Kotelnikovo and was not attacked again for the time being. What was left of *Fourth Rumanian Army* (including the headquarters) was placed under command of Colonel-General Hoth. After the Rumanian collapse, his 4 Corps, which had been part of the front south of Stalingrad, had swung back on to a front south and south-west of Stalingrad and had come under command of Sixth Army.

Sixth Army, consisting of 4, 8, 11 and 51 Army Corps and 14 Panzer Corps, was surrounded at Stalingrad. It had taken 11 Corps and elements of 8 Corps out of the front facing north on both sides of the Don and put them into the pocket's newly formed western front, the salient tip of which reached to a point east of the Kalach bridge. A new southern front had been formed out of reserves and those elements of Fourth Panzer (or Fourth Rumanian) Army which had been thrown back to Stalingrad. The pocket measured about 30 miles across from east to west and 25 miles from north to south.

Both wings of *Third Rumanian Army* had been broken through. In its centre a group of about three divisions under the same General Lascar who had distinguished himself at Sevastopol had put up a brave resistance, but they had since been surrounded and were now thought to have been captured.

48 Panzer Corps, which had been in reserve behind the front facing the Don bridgehead, had launched what appears to have been a belated counter-attack, but this had proved unsuccessful. Both its divisions were now encircled and under orders to fight their way out to the west. The corps commander, General Heim, had already been replaced on orders from Hitler and summoned to the latter's headquarters. There Hitler had him sentenced to death at a court-martial presided over by Göring, who was always available for tasks of this kind, on the ground that he, General Heim, was to blame for his corps' failure. Heim was later rehabilitated when it was found that his forces had indeed been too weak for the task confronting them. 48 Corps consisted of the newly formed Rumanian armoured division, which had had no battle experience whatever, and 22 Panzer Division, which had obviously not been up to standard from a technical point of view.

For all practical purposes Third Rumanian Army had only about three divisions still in existence. They were those of 1 and 2 Rumanian Corps, which had not been drawn into the battle and were located next to the Italians on the Don.

In the opinion of Army Group B, Sixth Army had at most two days' ammunition and six days' rations left. (These estimates were subsequently found to have been too low.) The airlift to date – insofar as the weather had permitted one to operate at all – had provided only one

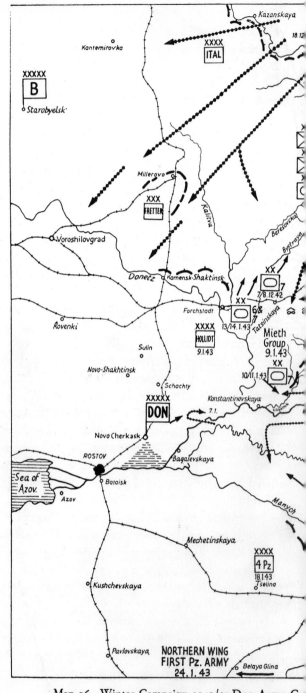

Map 16. Winter Campaign 1942/3: Don Army Gr

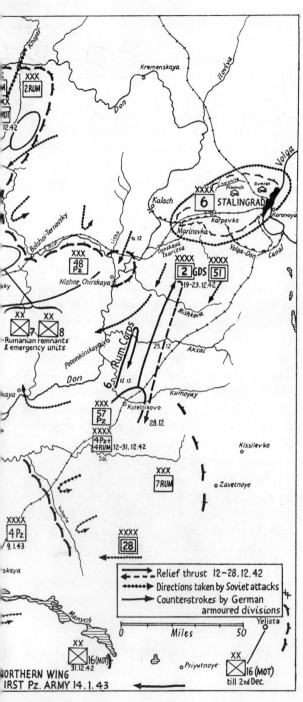

gle to keep Army Group A's rear free.

tenth of the army's requirements of ammunition and fuel. One hundred Junkers aircraft (equivalent to a working load of 200 tons less the inevitable losses) had been promised, and others were to follow.

Intelligence reports showed that the *enemy* had poured some twenty-four formations (i.e. divisions and armoured or mechanized brigades) through the gap he had torn in the front south of Stalingrad. These had then wheeled north against the southern flank of Sixth Army, which they were fiercely attacking.

From the point where he had penetrated *Third Rumanian Army*, the enemy had also pushed about twenty-four formations through towards Kalach in the rear of Sixth Army. About twenty-three more had been reported further west, advancing south and south-west towards the Chir. In addition, there were the Soviet troops in Stalingrad who had held out all along against Sixth Army's attacks and were now being reinforced across the Volga, as well as the superior forces still opposite the northern front of Sixth Army between the Volga and Don. Finally, there was no doubt that the enemy was continuously bringing up reinforcements by rail. Even by 28th November a total of 143 major formations (i.e. divisions, armoured brigades, etc.) had been identified in the operations area of the new Don Army Group.

The forces to form *Don Army Group* under my command were as follows. First there was Sixth Army, surrounded at Stalingrad by an enemy roughly three times as strong, and composed of twenty very tired German and two Rumanian divisions. Its stocks of ammunition, fuel and food were running low, and there was no steady inflow of supplies to build them up again. Quite apart from the fact that it was surrounded, the army enjoyed no operational freedom whatever, having received categoric orders from Hitler to hold fast to the 'fortress of Stalingrad'. Next came the remnants of Fourth Panzer Army and the two Rumanian armies. The best forces we possessed at present were one hitherto untouched German division (16 Motorized) – which could not be withdrawn from its defensive positions out in the steppes because it constituted Army Group A's only cover from the rear – and four still intact Rumanian divisions, whose combat value was unquestionably inferior to that of the Russians.

Sixth Army's subordination to H.Q. Don Army Group was more or less a fiction, however, for in practice it had hitherto come directly under O.K.H. It was Hitler who had tied it down at Stalingrad when it might still have been able to fight its own way out. Now, operationally speaking, it was immobilized. The Army Group could no longer 'command' it, but merely give it assistance. Besides, Hitler was still maintaining his direct control of Sixth Army by a General Staff liaison officer who was installed with his own signals section at Sixth Army Headquarters. Even in the matter of supplies Hitler had the final say, since he alone had the means at his disposal to maintain the army from the air. Strictly speaking, therefore, I should have been right to decline to have Sixth Army in my Army Group and to insist that it formally remain under the direct orders of O.K.H. I did not do so at the time because I hoped that I should be in a better position than O.K.H. to ensure the direct co-operation of the relieving forces with the encircled army. Why this co-operation did not materialize in the decisive phase will be shown later.

Apart from Sixth Army – which, being surrounded, was unusable in the operational sense – all that Don Army Group found awaiting it initially were mere remnants.

It was envisaged that the Army Group should receive the following new forces, to be allocated as below:

Forces	from	to	Role
H.Q. 57 Corps 23 Panzer Division Strong army artillery	Army Group A	Fourth Pz. Army	Relief drive on Stalingrad from south
6 Panzer Division (recently brought up to strength)	West		
One corps H.Q. Four/five divisions		Third Rum. Army (left wing)	To relieve Stalingrad by advance eastwards from Upper Chir as *Army Detachment Hollidt*

At H.Q. Army Group B I was shown a message which General Paulus, the commander of Sixth Army, had radioed to Hitler on – to the best of my recollection – 22nd or 23rd November. It stated that he and all his corps commanders considered it absolutely imperative that the army should break out to the south-west. To raise the forces needed for such an operation, however, he would have to shift certain formations around inside the army and, for the purpose of economizing in troops, take his northern front back on to a shorter line. The view taken at Army Group Headquarters was that even if Hitler had given immediate approval, no break-out could have started before 28th November.

However, Hitler had turned the request down and forbidden any retraction of the northern front. To make his point quite clear, he had entrusted General v. Seydlitz with command of the whole front in question.

The staff of Don Army Group had neither the time nor the opportunity to retrace past events in Sixth Army. Evidently General Paulus did everything possible, within the limits of Hitler's order binding him to Stalingrad, to extract forces from those of his army fronts which were not so seriously threatened in the first instance. By pulling in 4 Corps of Fourth Panzer Army he was able to assemble a new front on his open south flank. Furthermore, he tried to keep his rear free by throwing 14 Panzer Corps from the eastern to the western bank of the Don. Unfortunately it ran into superior Soviet forces west of the river. At the very same time 11 Corps – which was still holding its position west of the Don with a front facing north – was attacked in the rear. This situation led Sixth Army to pull both corps back into a bridge-head west of the Don and subsequently across the river to the east, so that it could form an all-round front between the Don and Volga.

Although these measures prevented Sixth Army from being plunged into the vortex of defeat which had engulfed its neighbours, they also inevitably led to its encirclement.

What must be made perfectly clear, on the other hand, is that it was the Supreme Command's business to issue an order affording Sixth Army the opportunity to acquire operational elbow-room and thereby to avoid being surrounded. A far-sighted leader would have realized from the start that to mass the whole of the German assault forces in and around Stalingrad without adequate flank protection placed them in mortal danger of being enveloped as soon as the enemy broke through the adjacent fronts. When the Soviets unleashed their big offensive across the Don and south of Stalingrad on 19th November, the German leaders must have known what was coming. From that moment onwards it was inadmissible to wait until the enemy had overrun the Rumanians, for even if their armies had not been carved up so quickly, it would still have been necessary to use Sixth Army in a mobile role in order to master the situation on the southern wing of Army Group B. By the evening of 19th November at the latest, therefore, O.K.H. should have given Sixth Army fresh orders allowing it freedom to manœuvre.

Without going into the details of the first few days of the Soviet offensive, one may safely say that the encirclement of Sixth Army could only have been prevented if the latter had attempted a break-out in the very early stages, either by crossing the Don to the west or by striking south-west along the east side of the river. The onus of ordering it to do so lay with the Supreme Command. While General Paulus should certainly have taken his own decision to disengage from Stalingrad, he could hardly have done so as early as O.K.H., not being briefed, as the latter was, on the situation in the neighbouring army areas. By 22nd or 23rd November, when he did ask for permission to break out, the vital hour may already have been missed. The fact that it was a serious psychological error to put this request to Hitler at all is another matter. Paulus had been acquainted with Hitler's views on the war in the east since the winter of 1941, when he had been *Oberquartiermeister I* at O.K.H. He was aware that Hitler credited himself with having saved the German Army from the disaster of a Napoleonic retreat that winter by ordering every foot of ground to be held. He must have realized that after Hitler's remarks about Stalingrad in his *Sportpalast* speech, the dictator would never agree to evacuation. The city's name was too closely bound up with his own military reputation. Thus the only solution would have been to confront him with the *fait accompli* of the army's disengagement from Stalingrad.

It is conceivable, of course, that such action might have cost Paulus his head. Yet no one must think that it was any fear of what might happen to him personally that kept Paulus from taking things into his own hands and doing what he believed to be right. It is more likely to have been loyalty to Hitler which impelled him to try to get the army's break-out authorized, particularly as he was in direct touch with O.K.H. by radio. And, as I have already pointed out, he can hardly have had a sufficiently clear picture of the overall situation. The difficulty of deciding to act on his own initiative may also have been increased by the fact that a break-out would *momentarily* have meant a bigger risk to the army than forming a hedgehog position in Stalingrad.

DON ARMY GROUP'S APPRECIATION OF THE SITUATION ON 24TH NOVEMBER

For the time being H.Q. Don Army Group was unable to take a hand in events by issuing any orders of its own. It could not take over its full responsibilities until such time as I arrived in Novocherkask, the place earmarked as our headquarters location, with a reasonably complete operations staff, and the necessary channels of communication had been established. Neither would be the case for some days yet. (For one thing, our aircraft had been grounded by a blizzard in the central sector, as a result of which we were having to continue the journey by train.)

Nonetheless, as the future commander of the Army Group, I had to make up my mind on one thing straight away on the basis of the situation report given to us on 24th November. Ought Sixth Army, if possible, to effect a break-out even at this late stage, or would it not be better, now that the first chance of doing so had undoubtedly been missed, to wait until a relief force could drive out to meet it?

After careful reflection, and in complete agreement with my Chief-of-Staff, General Schulz, and the Chief of Operations, Colonel Busse, I came to this conclusion:

The enemy would in the first instance do everything in his power to destroy the encircled Sixth Army. At the same time we had to bear in mind the possibility that he would try to exploit the collapse of Third Rumanian Army by pushing mechanized forces across the large bend of the Don towards Rostov, where he was offered the prospect of cutting off the rear communications not only of Sixth and Fourth Panzer Armies but also of Army Group A. The forces at the enemy's disposal – which he could doubtless augment by road and rail transport – would allow him to pursue the two aims simultaneously.

I further concluded that the Army Group's foremost task must in any case be the liberation of Sixth Army. On the one hand, the fate of 200,000 German soldiers was at stake. On the other, unless the army were kept in existence and ultimately set free, there could hardly be any hope of restoring the situation on the right wing of the Eastern Front. One thing was clear: even if we were able to raise the siege and re-establish contact, Sixth Army must on no account be left at Stalingrad. The city's prestige value as far as we were concerned was non-existent.

On the contrary, if we should succeed in getting the army out, it would be urgently needed to give the maximum possible help in stabilizing the situation on the southern wing sufficiently to bring us safely through the winter.

The immediate question, however, was whether Sixth Army, having once missed its real opportunity to break out, should try to do so at this particular moment. As two days had passed since General Paulus's request to Hitler, the attempt could not, according to Army Group B, begin before 29th or 30th November. By then the enemy would already have had more than a week in which to tighten his hold on the pocket.

The army would have the choice of only two escape routes, and in either case the enemy would be ready for it. One possibility was to break out towards the Don crossing at Kalach. But even if the army managed to pierce the encircling ring in this direction, there would still be the Don to bar its passage. Although most of the ammunition would have been expended on the original breakthrough, the army would now have to force a crossing against the powerful forces advancing west of the river towards the Lower Chir against negligible opposition. Its prospects of getting across, when it was short of ammunition and hard pressed by the enemy from north, east and south, seemed more than doubtful.

Conditions might be slightly better if Sixth Army were to try to break through to the remnants of Fourth Panzer Army by moving in a south-westerly direction east of the Don – though here, too, the enemy would be ready for it. The objection in this case was that even if the actual breakthrough were successful, the army could not count on there being any German forces to meet it in the first instance. On its heels would be the Soviet armies now opposite its eastern, northern, and western fronts around Stalingrad, while west of the river the enemy would be able to follow it southwards and forestall all its attempts to effect a crossing to the west. Most probably the army would sooner or later have no choice but to stand and fight out in the steppes without adequate supplies of ammunition, fuel, or food! Some elements, such as tank units, might possibly get away, but the fate of the army as a whole would be sealed. The Soviet forces it had been engaging till then would be released, and this in turn was likely to lead to the destruction of the German armies' entire southern wing – including Army Group A, which was still out in the Caucasus.

For the sake of both Sixth Army and the situation on the southern wing generally, our aim had to be to get the former out of the pocket intact and in fighting trim. This might have been done already if the Supreme Command had granted it operational freedom as soon as the danger of its encirclement became apparent. By now, however, it seemed too late for the army to break free and remain fit for further action without the extraneous help of relief forces.

On the other hand, it could be assumed that once the two relief groups moved off, Sixth Army's position would be substantially easier in the operational sense, even if not for the initial breakthrough. Once the enemy advancing west of the Don were engaged by other forces, Sixth Army would at least be spared the prospect of having to fight that particular opponent. And if, at the same time as Sixth Army moved off, the other relief group were to thrust into the rear of the Soviet siege front east of the Don, the enemy would be compelled to weaken the latter and thereby to facilitate the beleaguered army's initial breakthrough.[1]

At the same time the fact had to be faced that any delay was dangerous, since it would give the enemy time to consolidate his siege front. Such a risk could only be entertained if the Supreme Command guaranteed to supply Sixth Army by air for as long as was needed to liberate it.

Such was the premise for not now resorting to the desperate solution of an isolated break-out by Sixth Army but for awaiting a fresh opportunity. This would present itself as soon as the relief groups could go in.

In the light of the foregoing I informed the Chief-of-Staff of the Army by telephone that the Army Group's views were as follows:

A break-out by Sixth Army to the south-west was probably still possible even now. To leave the army at Stalingrad any longer constituted an *extreme risk*, in view of the ammunition and fuel shortage.

Nevertheless, since we considered that the best chance for an independent break-out had already been missed, it was preferable from the operational point of view at the present time to wait until the projected relief groups could come to the army's aid – always assuming

---

[1] Although the Hollidt relief group was finally never committed in that role, it did in fact tie down the Soviet forces operating west of the Don. The advance of Fourth Panzer Army, on the other hand, forced the enemy to weaken his front around Stalingrad considerably. *Author.*

that an adequate airlift could be counted upon. The latter factor, we emphasized, was *absolutely decisive*.

The relief operation could be launched with the forces due to arrive at the beginning of December. To achieve real effect, however, it would require a steady flow of further reinforcements, as the enemy would also be throwing in powerful forces on his own side.

An isolated break-out by Sixth Army might still become necessary if strong enemy pressure were to prevent us from deploying these new forces.

An absolute prerequisite for accepting the risk of not making an immediate break-out from Stalingrad was that Sixth Army should daily receive 400 tons of supplies by air.[1]

I made it perfectly clear in this conversation that unless the delivery of supplies could be guaranteed, one could not risk leaving Sixth Army in its present situation any longer, however temporarily.

Anyone who witnessed the subsequent tragedy of Stalingrad – Hitler's mulish determination to hold on to the city, O.K.H.'s deliberate failure to take the very last chance offered to it (a subject on which more will be said in due course), the delays which occurred in assembling the relief group of Fourth Panzer Army, and the Soviet breakthrough on the Italian front which rendered Army Detachment Hollidt incapable of any action to relieve Stalingrad – will conclude that it would have been better to insist on an immediate break-out by Sixth Army.

It is fair to assume that at least some elements of the besieged formation would have managed to fight their way through to the remnants of Fourth Panzer Army – certainly the tank units and probably a number of the infantry battalions, too.

On the other hand, it is unlikely that the army would have remained capable of operating as a formation. Things had already taken too ominous a turn by the earliest date at which a breakout could have been attempted.

Yet at the same time as the extricated elements of Sixth Army might have been joining Fourth Panzer Army, the entire enemy siege forces would have been released. With that, in all probability, the fate of the

---

[1] Four hundred tons daily was the army's minimum requirement of vehicle fuel and infantry and armour-piercing ammunition. After the ration stocks, etc., had been exhausted, this basic minimum rose to 550 tons. *Author.*

whole southern wing of the German forces in the east would have been sealed – including Army Group A.

I would nonetheless emphasize that the latter consideration played absolutely no part in shaping our appreciation of 24th November. Far from wanting to sacrifice Sixth Army in the interest of saving the southern wing, we hoped that it would have a better chance of escape when working in conjunction with the two groups earmarked for its relief than if it tried – at this late stage – to break out on its own.

My staff and I were actuated by the hope of extricating not mere military debris but a complete army which would still be fit for further operations. It goes without saying that the name of Stalingrad and the prestige factor cut no ice with us whatever.

That day, therefore, we refrained from presenting Hitler with a final demand for the break-out of Sixth Army or from ordering it on our own responsibility. One might add here that General Paulus, faced with the dilemma of whether to obey Hitler or the headquarters of his Army Group, would hardly have been able to opt for the latter.

For the rest, it was perfectly clear to us that even if the relief groups were able to get through to Sixth Army, the latter could not possibly be left at Stalingrad any longer. The essential thing to ensure was that it retained as much of its fighting power as possible in the meantime. It was much more likely to achieve this in the Stalingrad area – provided that it were properly supplied from the air – than if it were caught out in the steppes while trying to escape.

The criterion of whether Sixth Army could be freed in this way was twofold, however.

First, would the Luftwaffe be in a position to meet the army's vital needs? Secondly, could the Supreme Command furnish further relief forces – and if so, would it be prepared to do so? Both questions were clearly expressed in our message to O.K.H. Only Hitler, who as Commander-in-Chief of the Wehrmacht had power over all forces of the army and Luftwaffe in every theatre of war, was able to judge what the prospects were and take the appropriate decision. If the decision were an affirmative one, we should be justified in shelving the desperate measure of an isolated break-out and in leaving the army at Stalingrad.

Should Hitler, however, be unwilling to commit every available man to the relief of Stalingrad while there was still time, or should he indulge, against his better judgement, in illusions about the capacities of the Luftwaffe, he would be guilty of dire irresponsibility. The same may be said of those who – as it later turned out – awakened and fortified such beliefs in him or who would not understand that the fate of Sixth Army must have precedence over the demands of all other theatres.

That Göring would commit the supreme frivolity of promising an adequate airlift and then not even lay himself out to produce at least what he had available was something no soldier could foresee.

Neither, however, did we foresee to what extent Hitler would ignore all factual considerations in favour of his 'hold-or-bust' theory. Who could suppose that he would accept the loss of a whole army for the sake of the name of Stalingrad?

FIRST IMPRESSIONS AND DECISIONS

On the afternoon of 24th November we continued the journey from Starobyelsk to Novocherkask. Ten years before I had travelled down the same line to Rostov to attend the manœuvres of the Red Army in the Caucasus. On that earlier occasion all sorts of interesting impressions had lain ahead of me; today it was a mission as to the gravity of which my staff and I had no illusions. Time and again our thoughts went out to our beleaguered comrades at Stalingrad, despite the efforts of my A.D.C., Lieutenant Stahlberg, to divert us with good gramophone music and talk of other problems. He had joined our staff after the death of 'Pepo', having been brought to me by my former colleague Tresckow, whose nephew he was. Stahlberg remained my constant companion till the end of the war. Throughout those years he was a faithful assistant to me in all personal matters.

On the morning of 26th November I broke my journey in Rostov to see General Hauffe, the Head of the German Military Mission to Rumania, who had originally been designated as the German Chief-of-Staff of Antonescu's Army Group. He painted a most disagreeable picture of the state of the two Rumanian armies on the Stalingrad front. Of their twenty-two original divisions, he told us, nine were completely wiped out, nine had run away and could not be sent into action for the time being, and four were still fit for battle. Given time, however, he hoped to form a few extra formations out of the wreckage.

The antithesis to Hauffe's report was provided by a letter written to me by Marshal Antonescu. He had some bitter things to say about the Supreme Command, which he accused of not paying enough attention to his frequent warnings regarding the mounting danger in the Krementskaya bridgehead opposite Third Rumanian Army's front. He also complained of the way his own assumption of command had been repeatedly postponed.

With every justification, moreover, the Marshal pointed out that of all Germany's allies, Rumania and he personally had done most for the common cause. Of his own accord he had made twenty-two divisions available for the 1942 campaign and – unlike Italy or Hungary – had unreservedly placed these under German command, despite not being bound to the Reich by any obligation of a contractual nature.

His letter voiced the justified disillusionment of a soldier who sees his troops lost through the mistakes of others.

Inwardly I could not dispute the justness of the Marshal's criticisms. I wrote to tell him that as one who had not previously been involved in the events in question, I was unable to comment on his strictures myself and had passed his letter on to Hitler – at whom, of course, I knew them to be aimed. It could certainly do Hitler no harm to have to read such unvarnished criticism by his most loyal ally. Besides, the letter touched on a political question: that of confidence between allies. Antonescu mentioned that his mortal enemy, the leader of the Iron Guard, had been put beyond his reach by Himmler and was now being kept in Germany 'for a rainy day'. The Iron Guard, a radical political organization, had earlier staged a *putsch* against the Antonescu régime and initially succeeded in surrounding the Marshal's official residence. Though the Marshal had ultimately been able to put down the rising, the Iron Guard leader had escaped abroad. It was understandable that Antonescu should consider himself disloyally treated when Himmler now held a protecting hand over this man. Such underhand tactics were hardly conducive to the strengthening of an alliance.

Antonescu's original reason for writing to me was to complain that German officers and men, in both their official and unofficial capacities, had been guilty of roughly handling Rumanian soldiers and passing defamatory remarks about them. Although such occurrences could be accounted for by recent events and the poor showing made by many Rumanian units, I naturally took immediate action. However much one might sympathize with the indignation of German troops who had been left in the lurch by neighbouring units, incidents of this kind could only damage our common cause.

I have already shown what could and could not be expected of Rumanian troops in various situations. But they were still our best allies and did fight bravely in many places.

On 26th November we arrived at our new headquarters in Novocherkask. The only guard unit available was a battalion of Cossack volunteers, who obviously considered it a special honour to do sentry duty in front of our office building. As our main channels of communication were ready the next night, we were able to take over command of Don Army Group on the morning of 27th November.

The task confronting us was a two-sided one. Its chief feature, and the one on which everything depended, was the relief and rescue of Sixth Army. Apart from being a priority in the humane sense, this was also vital from the operational point of view, first and foremost because there could be hardly any hope of restoring the situation on the southern wing of the Eastern Front – or, indeed, in the eastern theatre as a whole – unless the forces of Sixth Army were preserved.

The other side of the task – and this had to be borne in mind throughout – was *the already existing danger that the entire southern wing of the German armies would be destroyed.* If this were allowed to happen, it would most probably be the end of the struggle in the east and consequently lose us the war. Should the Russians succeed in tearing through the flimsy screen – for the moment consisting mainly of Rumanian remnants and German B-echelon troops and emergency units [1] – which, leaving aside the so-called Fortress of Stalingrad, constituted the sole protection of the whole operational area between the rear of Army Group A and the still-existing Don front, not only Sixth Army's position would be hopeless. That of Army Group A, as well, would become more than critical.

It was thanks to the Commander of Fourth Panzer Army, Colonel-General Hoth, and the recently appointed Chief-of-Staff of Third Rumanian Army, Colonel Wenck, that we ever succeeded at all, in the

[1] *Ad hoc* units formed from non-combat units, headquarters staffs, Luftwaffe troops and Army personnel who had been on the way back to their parent units from privilege or sick leave. These 'emergency units' lacked cohesion, seasoned officers and weapons (especially anti-tank protection and artillery), and most of them had had little or no battle experience or training in close combat. Their fighting value was therefore low. Nonetheless, after being welded together for a period in action they often fought outstandingly well. *Author.*

critical days at the end of November, in raising the screens which, by covering the enormous gaps between Sixth Army, Army Group A and the Don front, prevented any exploitation of the situation by the Russians. Had the enemy been able at that time to thrust a fast-moving army down to the lower Don at Rostov – which he was undoubtedly strong enough to do – the loss of Army Group A as well as Sixth Army would have become quite conceivable.

But even though this mortal threat to the southern wing remained constantly present, the Army Group did not allow one single man or round of ammunition needed for the rescue of Sixth Army to be diverted from that task. As long as there was the remotest prospect of success, it went to the very limit of its powers and resources to bring off the attempted relief. To do so it had to accept the greatest imaginable risks.

The fact that we ultimately failed in our mission was primarily due to the extraordinary preponderance of the enemy's forces and the deficient strength of our own. Further handicaps were created by weather conditions, which greatly hampered the activities of the Luftwaffe, particularly in supplying Sixth Army, and by the transport position, which did not permit the relief forces to be brought into action quickly enough.

Furthermore, we now experienced for the first time the inhibitions which emanated from the German Supreme Command and had their origin in Hitler's personality, opinions and character. These have already been described in the chapter on Hitler's military leadership. Their effect in this case was that the Supreme Command would not run the risk of setbacks on other fronts in order to put everything it had into the relief operation. Furthermore, they caused repeated delays in the taking of priority decisions, although the trend of the situation could be clearly foreseen and had repeatedly been pointed out to Hitler by our own headquarters.

Of the two different tasks I mentioned as confronting the Army Group on its assumption of command, the first – that of extricating Sixth Army – was virtually all over by Christmas 1942, when it was clear that Fourth Panzer Army could no longer succeed in effecting a link-up. With Hitler still clinging to Stalingrad, H.Q. Sixth Army backed down at the decisive hour – contrary to the Army Group's instructions – from taking what was possibly the very last chance of salvation. With that the army's fate was as good as settled. Hitler's ideal of still being able to relieve it at a later date by bringing up an SS panzer corps from Kharkov in January was illusory from the first.

What followed in the Stalingrad pocket after Fourth Panzer Army's attacks had come to a standstill was indeed the death-struggle of Sixth Army. Yet in view of the fact that the other part of the Army Group's mission was still to prevent the destruction of the southern wing as a whole, it was not until this struggle had reached its closing stages that we could justifiably attempt to cut it short – and thereby curtail the losses and suffering of the doomed army – by recommending a capitulation.

The battles to save Sixth Army were, of course, closely bound up with developments on the whole of the German southern wing. My object in considering the latter separately in a later chapter is to give greater clarity to the various operational considerations involved.

SITUATION AT THE TIME OF THE TAKE-OVER

The situation facing the Army Group on its assumption of command differed very little from that of 24th November.

The *enemy* had obviously committed his main forces primarily in the ring enclosing Sixth Army. Of the 143 Soviet formations reported in the Army Group area, some sixty at least had been employed all along on the encirclement of the army. The latter's southern front was subjected to a heavy attack on 28th November, but this the army managed to beat off. On all its other fronts at the end of November there was only localized fighting, in the course of which the defences became more firmly established. Nevertheless it was clear that any attempt to break out just then would have run into powerful opposition, and the stocks of ammunition and fuel still available in the pocket would inevitably have been used up. Even if the initial breakthrough had come off, the army would have reached the Don without ammunition or fuel at a time when there could be no relief group at hand.

Otherwise the enemy was busy feeling his way forward against the thin screens being thrown across the gaps to the south and west of Stalingrad, behind which the relief forces were to complete their assembly.

The Army Group's immediate problem was to obtain the clearest possible picture of *the condition and intentions of Sixth Army*. What it had been able to discover from O.K.H. and Army Group B at a distance of several hundred miles was obviously not enough.

As early as 26th November I had been handed a letter from General Paulus by an officer who had flown out of the pocket.[1] In it Paulus stressed the necessity of having 'freedom of action in an extreme emergency', since a situation calling for an immediate break-out to the south-west was liable to arise any day or hour. The information which this letter neglected to give on the army's supply position was provided in a report furnished by General Pickert, a Luftwaffe officer who had himself just flown out of the pocket, having been detailed by the commander of Fourth Air Fleet, Colonel-General Baron v. Richthofen, to organize the airlift.

According to Pickert the army had enough rations – albeit on short issue – for twelve days. Ammunition stocks were at 10–20 per cent of the normal scale, which corresponded to the amount which would be expended in one day's intensive fighting! The vehicle fuel was only enough for minor troop movements and would not suffice to concentrate the tanks for a break-out. If these figures were correct, one could only wonder how Sixth Army had proposed to implement the break-out plan of which it had given notice four days previously.

In the light of this information I resolved to fly into the pocket and talk to Paulus myself. However, my Chief-of-Staff and Chief of Operations finally prevailed on me to abandon the idea, as it seemed more than likely, from the state of the weather, that I should be detained there for two days or more. To be away for all that time was inadmissible in view of the tense situation and the need to keep O.K.H. constantly aware of the Army Group's views, so I dispatched my Chief-of-Staff, General Schulz, instead, and on a later occasion my Chief of Operations, Colonel Busse.

Schulz's mission was primarily to gain a first-hand impression of the situation and condition of Sixth Army and its command staff and to brief the army commander on the plans for raising the siege. In this way the latter was to be given an opportunity to comment on the prospects and timing of the operation. Everything depended on harmonizing Paulus's views with our own, as it was clear that in the absence of telephone lines or any reliable means of written communication the Army Group could exert only a limited influence on Sixth

[1] See Appendix I.

Army's decisions. The need for complete understanding was increased by the existence of the O.K.H. liaison officer, whose presence at the Army Headquarters kept it under the constant sway of Hitler's thoughts and orders.

Apart from revealing his deep but only too understandable depression over a situation for which not he but the Supreme Command was responsible, Paulus's letter seemed to me, in the desire it expressed for 'freedom of action in an extreme emergency', to indicate that he intended breaking out of the pocket if the position there became *untenable*. This might either be because the enemy had already penetrated or even broken through one or more of the army's fronts – so that the tactical situation had become untenable – or else because the strength of the troops was giving out. In either case, to my mind, an attempted break-out could end only in catastrophe. In the situation that now prevailed two things were of fundamental importance. First there must be a stubborn defence to keep the army in existence. Next must come a breakthrough – not launched as a forlorn hope, but deliberately timed to take place when the army still had the strength to carry it out, and also to coincide with relief operations from outside the pocket.

Such were the views which Schulz had to put over to Paulus.

The overall impression he brought back with him – and this was later confirmed by Colonel Busse – was that Sixth Army, provided it were properly supplied from the air, did not judge its chances of holding out at all unfavourably. (That such an attitude could also be dangerous would be seen later on.)

With that I come to the question of whether an *airlift to Sixth Army* could really be contemplated.

In our report to O.K.H. from Starobyelsk on 24th November I had been at pains to point out how crucial this was. Only if a guarantee of air supplies were given, I had said, could we afford to delay a break-out until the intervention of relief forces improved the army's chances of escape.

By refusing to sanction Paulus's request for a break-out the day before my telephone conversation, Hitler had to all intents and purposes already given that guarantee. His refusal had been based on an assurance from Göring, whose staff was indeed the sole authority competent to assess the Luftwaffe's ability to keep Sixth Army supplied at Stalingrad.

On assuming command of Don Army Group, I was told by Colonel-General v. Richthofen, whose Fourth Air Fleet was in support of us and responsible for supplying Sixth Army from the air, that he did not think an adequate airlift could be flown under the prevailing weather conditions. Even if the weather improved, he said, he still did not believe it would be possible to maintain the lift for any length of time, and had already told Göring as much. Of course, he added, he was in no position to judge the extent of Göring's other resources.

The Army Group immediately reported v. Richthofen's opinion to O.K.H., but its only reaction was to refer us to forthcoming increases in the strength of the transport squadrons. The same answer was given to our daily reports that the loads flown into the pocket were coming nowhere near the quotas envisaged. These new squadrons arrived right enough, and their crews did their duty with great self-sacrifice, but although the Luftwaffe lost 488 aircraft and about 1,000 men at Stalingrad, it never succeeded in providing Sixth Army with anything like its minimum requirements.

It is thus established that the promise Göring gave to Hitler on 23rd November – or possibly even earlier – was entirely unwarranted. Whether it was due to a false appreciation of Luftwaffe potentialities or frivolously given in a desire to show off or humour Hitler, I cannot tell. In any event the responsibility is Göring's. Nevertheless, Hitler should still have checked up on the reliability of his statements. Besides knowing what sort of person Göring was, he was also well aware of the strength of the Luftwaffe.

Unlike Hitler, neither the Army Group staff nor the chief of Fourth Air Fleet were in a position to verify the facts. Nor had they any immediate reason for seeing anything wildly impracticable in a *short-term* airlift. After all, in the winter of 1941–2 the Luftwaffe had provided 100,000 men in the Demyansk pocket with everything they needed.

Although in fact twice that number were surrounded this time, it could only be a matter – to our mind – of keeping supplies going for a few weeks or so. As soon as the relief groups drew near to the pocket, Sixth Army must in any event break out. To leave it at Stalingrad for a longer period was quite out of the question.

All the Commander-in-Chief of the Luftwaffe had to do in effect was to make a straightforward calculation.

Sixth Army's minimum requirement of all types of supplies totalled

550 tons per day or at least 400 tons until all ration dumps in the pocket were exhausted.

In order to lift 550 tons – if each aircraft made one run daily – we should need 225 Ju-52s (or correspondingly more He-111s, which could carry only 1·5 tons at the outside).

The distances to be flown from the air-bases of Morosovsky and Tatsinskaya were 110 and 135 miles respectively, though in either case only the last 30 miles would be over enemy territory. (Neither of these airfields was lost to the enemy until Christmas 1942, when the fate of Sixth Army was already decided.) In favourable weather conditions the aircraft could be expected to make two trips each in twenty-four hours. On the days when this happened the number of machines needed would be reduced by half.

These figures formed the preliminary basis on which the Commander-in-Chief of the Luftwaffe had to assess the possibility of supplying Sixth Army by air. In addition, however, he had the following factors to consider:

First, there was the probability in winter that the squadrons working the airlift would be grounded by weather. The resultant deficit would have to be made up by lifting an extra tonnage on flying days – i.e. the number of aircraft must be proportionately increased. While it was difficult to predict to what extent the weather would prejudice flying, the Luftwaffe meteorologists should be able to turn up certain records from the previous winter.

The second factor to be taken into account was that not all machines are ever airworthy at any one given time. This could be seen from statistics. To a large extent the number of aircraft out of commission depended on what ground-crews and maintenance facilities were available at the air bases. This is a subject to which I shall return later.

Finally it had to be remembered that a certain percentage of the transport machines would be shot down or crash. The rate of losses by enemy action was again largely dependent on how much fighter cover the Luftwaffe could provide.

The Commander-in-Chief of the Luftwaffe thus had to weigh two questions with the utmost care before giving any firm promises about an airlift.

Had he any prospect whatever of immediately assembling 550 tons of carrier space, bearing in mind the extra demands imposed by bad weather and the non-availability of aircraft for technical reasons?

Could he maintain this figure by a continuous flow of replacements, and above all by providing an appropriate number of fighter and pursuit aircraft to combat the air defences anticipated on the enemy's side, until such time as Sixth Army was likely to be relieved?

Göring was the only man in a position to give completely satisfactory answers to these questions. Only he was able to tell whether the requisite number of aircraft could be found and whether their use here was defensible in the light of the Luftwaffe's other commitments. If neither were the case, it was his duty to tell Hitler so point blank when the decision regarding Sixth Army was taken – i.e. around 22nd–23rd November.

It was Göring's further duty, once Hitler had ordered the army to remain at Stalingrad, immediately to throw in the Luftwaffe's very last reserves of carrier aircraft, fighters and repair shops.

It is doubtful whether Göring did everything he could have done in this field, and at the beginning of January, as a result of the Army Group's constant references to the inadequacy of the airlift, Hitler ordered Field-Marshal Milch to take it over. As the latter had all the forces and resources of the Luftwaffe in Germany at his disposal, he was certainly in a position to improve the airlift's basic efficiency.

By now, unfortunately, it was too late from the operational point of view for him to do any good. The same went for the airlift as such, for in the meantime the two above-named bases had been lost and the supplies had to be flown over much longer stretches.

As if his original promise of 22nd–23rd November had not been frivolous enough, Göring proceeded to make things even worse by not exhausting all the possibilities open to him in the first vital weeks of the siege. For that was the time when the bid to save Sixth Army might still have had some chance of success.

The more debatable and confused the airlift issue became, the more important it was to relieve Sixth Army at the earliest possible date. According to details passed to the Army Group by O.K.H., the latter was to make the following forces available for this purpose:

(a) In the framework of *Fourth Panzer Army*: 57 Panzer Corps under General Kirchner (to be moved over from Army Group A) with 6 and 23 Panzer Divisions and 15 Luftwaffe Field Division under command. These forces were scheduled to arrive in the Kotelnikovo area by 3rd December.

(b) Deploying in the sector of Third Rumanian Army: a new formation to be known as *Army Detachment Hollidt*, consisting of 62, 294 and 336 Infantry Divisions; 48 Panzer Corps (General v. Knobelsdorff) with 11 and 22 Panzer Divisions; 3 Mountain Division; and 7 and 8 Luftwaffe Field Divisions. This group was to be ready to become operational on the Upper Chir around 5th December.

All told, the Army Group expected to have relief forces amounting to four armoured divisions, four infantry or mountain divisions and three Luftwaffe field divisions. It was assumed from the start, of course, that the Luftwaffe divisions could at best be employed in some defensive role, such as shielding the flanks of the assault elements.

The forces indicated – assuming that they did become available in this strength and at the times stated – might conceivably suffice to make temporary contact with Sixth Army and to restore its freedom of movement. In no event, however, could they administer a defeat big enough to enable us – as Hitler had put it in the jargon of static warfare – to 'reoccupy the positions held prior to the attack'.

On 27th November the Army Group received a teleprinter message from O.K.H. replying to the appreciation of the situation we had submitted three days previously. It appeared from this that Hitler was still prejudiced by the ideas already referred to. The reason he gave for deciding to hold fast to Stalingrad was that if we abandoned it now we should have to try all over again next year, at an even greater cost, to regain what we had sacrificed so much to win in 1942.

Quite apart from whether a repetition of the 1942 offensive would be at all expedient or feasible when the time came, the question simply did not arise at the present moment. The real problem was whether the least possibility existed of somehow or other restoring the situation on the southern wing of the Eastern Front. Unless Sixth Army were saved, there seemed to be almost no hope of doing so.

On 28th November, therefore, I sent Hitler a detailed appraisal of the position, appending a table which showed the strengths of enemy forces (in all, 143 major formations) operating against us. I also gave a clear picture of the situation and condition of Sixth Army, noting in particular that it would shortly be deprived of the use of its artillery through lack of ammunition and loss of mobility.

In the circumstances, I said, it was doubtful whether one could afford to wait for all the relief forces to arrive, particularly Army Detachment Hollidt. Presumably the relief group of Fourth Panzer Army would now have to move off ahead of it. Naturally nothing decisive could be achieved by this, for everything depended – as we had already pointed out on 24th November – on the provision of additional forces. The best one could hope to do was to cut a corridor to Sixth Army through which to replenish its fuel and ammunition stocks and thereby restore its mobility. After that, however, the army *must* be fetched straight out of the pocket, as it could not possibly survive the winter out in the open steppes.

Above all, I told Hitler, it was strategically impossible to go on tying down our forces in an excessively small area while the enemy enjoyed a free hand along hundreds of miles of front. What we must regain at all costs was our manœuvrability, as the solution applied in the case of the Demyansk pocket the previous year was now out of the question.

The above appraisal was fully confirmed by later events.

It was 3rd December before we received a reply on this fundamental question of operational policy – just one more example of the way Hitler loved to defer answers which were not to his taste.

The reply did state, however, that Hitler agreed with our views. There were only two points on which he had any qualifications to make. In the first place, he did not wish the northern front of Stalingrad to be pulled back or shortened for the purpose of finding extra forces. Secondly, while not disputing the *number* of enemy formations listed in my appreciation, he nonetheless contended that the *strength* of the Soviet divisions had been reduced and that the enemy command would have trouble in maintaining supplies and proper control as a result of its unexpected successes.

He was possibly right regarding the reduction of divisional strengths. This was more than offset, however, by the extent to which our own forces had been weakened in several months' heavy fighting – a subject on which the Army Group had reported in no uncertain terms. That the Soviets were already having supply difficulties was unlikely, and the supposition that they had any control problem was mere hypothesis.

At any rate – and this was of paramount importance – it could be assumed from Hitler's general endorsement of our views that he accepted the three essential points:

(i) Even in the event of our being able to fight a way through to Sixth Army, the latter could not be left at Stalingrad for any length of time.

(ii) The army must receive a daily average of supplies by air.

(iii) As the Army Group had been constantly emphasizing since 21st November, a continuous flow of reinforcements was needed.

It will be seen in due course that Hitler really had not the slightest intention of releasing Sixth Army from Stalingrad. Neither were the other two prerequisites for the success of the operation to be fulfilled.

The first thing we discovered was that the *strength* of the forces being provided by O.K.H. for the relief of Sixth Army, as well as the *timing* of their availability, were by no means in keeping with what we had gathered from the promises made to us in Starobyelsk.

To begin with, there were considerable delays in transporting the troops to their new areas. In the case of Army Detachment Hollidt this was due to the low efficiency of the railways, and in that of Fourth Panzer Army's relief group to the fact that while the steppes around Stalingrad were in the grip of an icy frost, a thaw had set in down in the Caucasus. Consequently the wheeled elements of 23 Panzer Divisions were unable to move by road as scheduled and had to go by rail instead.

At the slow rate of progress this involved, 57 Panzer Corps' operational deadline was put off by several days – in a situation where every single day counted.

The *strength* of the relief groups proved more unsatisfactory still. 15 Luftwaffe Field Division, which was due to join 57 Panzer Corps, had not even been established yet – a process which took several weeks to complete. When finally ready, the division had to be committed to battle at the height of an emergency (at a time, incidentally, when the relief problem had long been decided in the negative sense) and disintegrated during its first few days in action. The army artillery to be handed over by Army Group A, except for one regiment of smoke troops, never arrived at all. Of the total of seven divisions earmarked for the *Hollidt* relief group, we found that it had already been necessary to commit two infantry divisions (62 and 294) on the front of Third Rumanian Army to provide it with at least a modicum of stability. Their withdrawal would have led to the immediate collapse of 1 and 2 Rumanian Corps' battle-fronts. Both divisions were thus excluded from the relief operation from the start. Another of the promised formations which failed to put in an appearance was 3 Mountain Division. The first half of it, which had already entrained, was diverted by O.K.H. to Army Group A to deal with a local crisis; the second was retained by Central Army Group for a similar purpose. 22 Panzer Division, which had been thrown in with Third Rumanian Army at the beginning of the Soviet offensive, proved to be a complete wreck incapable of any offensive action after the losses it had suffered in the November battles. Since it was impossible to employ the Luftwaffe divisions in an offensive role, practically the only striking forces left for the relief operations of Fourth Panzer Army and Army Detachment Hollidt respectively were 57 Panzer Corps (with a strength of two armoured divisions) and 48 Panzer Corps (11 Panzer Division and 336 Infantry Division, the first of which was still moving up). 17 Panzer Division and 306 Infantry Division, which O.K.H. subsequently brought in to replace the divisions which had failed to arrive, could neither fully compensate for the deficiency of strength nor be ready to go into action as early as the relief operation demanded.

In the circumstances, the original idea of relieving Sixth Army from two different directions – Fourth Panzer Army from the Kotelnikovo area east of the Don and Army Detachment Hollidt from the Middle Chir towards Kalach – would be invalidated by a shortage of forces. The most we could hope to do now was to assemble sufficient strength at one spot. As things stood, this left only Fourth Panzer Army eligible for the attack. It had a shorter mileage to cover to Stalingrad and did not have an obstacle like the Don to negotiate. It was also reasonable to hope that the last quarter from which the enemy would expect a relief offensive was anywhere east of the Don, as the whole situation made it extremely risky for the Germans to assemble large forces in that area. For the very same reason he had initially put out relatively weak forces in the direction of Kotelnikovo for protection of his siege front. Here, for the time being, Fourth Panzer Army was faced with only five enemy divisions, whereas the enemy on the Chir had already fifteen divisions in the line.

The order issued by the Army Group on 1st December for Operation 'Winter Tempest' thus envisaged the following:

On a date still to be fixed (but in any case not earlier than 8th December), Fourth Panzer Army was to attack east of the Don with the bulk of its forces, moving off from the area of Kotelnikovo. Once it had thrust through the enemy's covering forces, its task would be to attack and roll up the southern and/or western siege front encircling Stalingrad.

A smaller force provided by Army Detachment Hollidt's 48 Panzer Corps was to thrust from the Don–Chir bridgehead of Nizhne Chirskaya into the rear of the enemy covering forces. Should the enemy opposite Fourth Panzer Army north of Kotelnikovo be conspicuously reinforced prior to the attack, or should the situation of Fourth Rumanian Army, whose job was to cover Fourth Panzer Army's long eastern flank, take another critical turn, the following alternative plan would come into operation. The armoured divisions of Fourth Panzer Army would make a surprise move northwards along the west bank of the Don and launch the main thrust from the Nizhne Chirskaya bridgehead. It was also envisaged that a less powerful shock group should thrust up at Kalach from out of the Don–Chir bridgehead west of the Don in order to cut the enemy's communications there and open up the Don bridge for Sixth Army.

As regards *Sixth Army*, the orders laid down that on a date after Fourth Panzer Army's attack still to be fixed by the Army Group it would initially break through to the south-west in the direction of the Donskaya Tsarytsa, its aim being to link up with Fourth Panzer Army and to take a hand in rolling up the southern and western siege fronts and capturing the Don crossing.

On express instructions from Hitler the army was to continue to hold its existing positions in the pocket. That this would not be possible in practice when it broke out to the south-west to meet Fourth Panzer Army was perfectly obvious, for when the Soviets attacked on the northern or eastern fronts it would have to give way step by step. In the event, undoubtedly, Hitler would have had no choice but to accept this fact, as he did on later occasions. (Not that we could say so in the operation order, of course, as Hitler would have learnt of it through his liaison officer at Sixth Army Headquarters and immediately issued a countermand.)

During the first few days after my take-over everything remained fairly quiet on the Army Group front. Evidently the enemy was preparing a concentric assault on Sixth Army. On the other hand, he apparently did not care to venture an immediate thrust on Rostov with strong armoured forces, nor did he even try to go for the Army Group's vital Donetz crossings or the railway junction of Likhakha. Probably he thought he could save himself the risk attaching to a tank drive of this kind, since his preponderance of forces in the large bend of the Don promised to assure him of success in any event. Yet he undoubtedly sacrificed a big opportunity in this way, for at the end of November and in early December the forces we should have needed for intercepting such a thrust simply did not exist.

ENEMY ATTACKS ON SIXTH ARMY

On 2nd December the enemy made his first attack on Sixth Army. Like those which followed on the 4th and 8th of the month, it was bloodily repulsed by the courageous troops in the pocket. Fortunately the supply position now appeared more favourable than we had originally dared to expect, for on 2nd December the army reported that by existing on a reduced scale of rations and slaughtering a large proportion of the horses, it could – reckoning from 30th November – manage with its present stocks for twelve to sixteen days. At the same time the state of the weather encouraged us to hope for an improvement in the rate of air supplies, a record load of 300 tons being flown into the pocket on 5th December. (Unfortunately this was to remain an all-time high.) Nonetheless it was clear that no time must be lost in making contact with Sixth Army on the ground and fetching it out of the pocket.

As far as this went, the only thing in our favour to date was that the enemy had not ventured to exploit his chance of severing the Army Group's rear communications at the Donetz crossings or at Rostov (where he could have simultaneously cut off Army Group A). Otherwise the position deteriorated badly in the sectors from which the relief thrusts were to be made.

In the case of *Fourth Panzer Army* the arrival of 57 Panzer Corps from the Caucasus was delayed for the reasons already stated. The assembly date, originally 3rd December, was put off till 8th and then till

12th December. Naturally the enemy was not going to remain inactive over so long a period. On 3rd December he pushed forward in strength towards Kotelnikovo, 57 Panzer Corps' main railhead, obviously with a view to clearing up the position there. The following day he was driven back by 6 Panzer Division, which had meanwhile become operational. From 8th December onwards there were signs of a major enemy force gathering on Fourth Panzer Army's northern front (north-east of Kotelnikovo), where a new Soviet army (Fifty-First) was identified. On the other hand, things remained quiet on the Panzer Army's eastern front, which was manned mainly by the troops of the subordinate Fourth Rumanian Army. The same applied to 16 Motorized Division around Yelista. With a view to setting the Rumanians' minds at rest, we made this division dispatch a light motorized force up north to reconnoitre in the rear of the Soviet front facing them. It established beyond all possible doubt that for the time being the enemy had no forces assembled in any great strength west of the Volga.

CRISIS ON THE CHIR FRONT

Events took a much more serious turn in the area of *Army Detachment Hollidt* (*Third Rumanian Army*'s sector). Here, on the *Lower Chir*, from its junction with the Don to a point some 45 miles upstream, the only troops on the ground, apart from a few anti-aircraft groups, were alarm units which had been set up from B-echelon elements and Sixth Army men returning from leave. These were later augmented by the two Luftwaffe divisions which, after originally being earmarked for Army Detachment Hollidt, had been found to be only conditionally employable owing to their complete lack of battle experience and shortage of trained officers and N.C.O.s.

The rent torn between the bend in the Chir at Bolshoi Ternovsky and the still intact Don front when the Russians broke through Third Rumanian Army in November had been patched up by bending back the right wing of the Third Rumanian Army elements on the Don (1 and 2 Rumanian Corps) and by bringing in the badly battered 22 Panzer Division and remnants of the over-run Rumanian divisions. In fact, however, the infantry divisions destined for Army Detachment Hollidt should also have been committed here in order to afford this 75-mile stretch of front a minimum degree of stability. By the beginning of December there were ominous signs of an impending major offensive on the Chir front, and two days later strong enemy artillery was identified along the lower reaches of the river. It was here, on 4th December, that the Russian attacks began, striking without respite at one point after another. The more the enemy persisted in his attempts to break through, the more critical the situation became. It was absolutely vital that we should continue to hold this stretch of river, as our bridgehead in the angle between the Chir and Don, including the Don bridge at Nizhne Chirskaya, was of fundamental importance for the relief of Sixth Army. Apart from that, an enemy breakthrough over the Chir would have cleared the way to the Morosovsky and Tatsinskaya airfields, which were only 25 and 50 miles away, as well as to the Donetz crossings and Rostov. In the circumstances the Army Group had no choice but to agree that 48 Panzer Corps (whose 11 Panzer and 336 Infantry Division had arrived by this time) should temporarily be used to bolster up the front on the Lower Chir. The corps found itself playing the role of a veritable fire-fighter, dashing from one spot to the next to intervene every time the thin screen of alarm units threatened to collapse. Naturally this temporarily deprived Army Detachment Hollidt of the only divisions it could have employed in an offensive relief role from this direction. As soon as the situation permitted, however, it was still intended to bring the corps across the Nizhne Chirskaya bridge to co-operate with the relief group of Fourth Panzer Army.

On 9th December the attacks against Sixth Army, in the course of which the enemy had come in for some very rough treatment, started to slacken off. This probably meant that forces were already being released to head off any German attempt to lift the siege.

On the Chir front the enemy kept up his pressure unremittingly, but on Fourth Panzer Army's northern front, after the failure of his Kotelnikovo operation, he displayed a certain degree of restraint.

THE VAIN FIGHT FOR DECISIONS

I need hardly say that in this critical situation I was in constant telephonic communication with the Chief-of-Staff of the Army, General Zeitzler. He entirely agreed with my forecast of developments and the inferences I drew. But whether he would be able to get Hitler to take appropriate – and timely – action was quite a different matter.

Apart from our constant demand for reinforcement of the Luftwaffe transport squadrons working the airlift to Sixth Army, there were two outstanding issues:

The first was that even if Sixth Army could be relieved, *it must on no account be left in the Stalingrad area* any longer. Hitler himself still wanted to hang on to the city – just as he had insisted on doing with the Demyansk pocket the previous winter – and to keep the army supplied there by means of a land corridor.

Don Army Group, on the other hand, was as convinced as ever that this was entirely the wrong solution and that it was essential to become operationally mobile again if disaster were to be avoided. This tug-of-war continued until the very last chance of saving Sixth Army had been thrown away.

The second issue was the *reinforcement of the relief forces*. Ever since the discovery that of the seven divisions originally promised us for Army Detachment Hollidt's relief bid we could at best expect to get 48 Panzer Corps with a strength of two divisions, it had been vital to strengthen Fourth Panzer Army. Anyone could see that the latter was not going to reach Stalingrad with only 6 and 23 Panzer Divisions.

There were two possible ways of effecting this reinforcement.

Don Army Group repeatedly asked to be given Army Group A's 3 Panzer Corps of two armoured divisions, which should not have been used in mountainous country anyway. On each occasion the request was refused because Army Group A claimed it could not release the corps unless it were allowed to evacuate a salient projecting far into the Caucasus – a measure which Hitler, in turn, would not countenance. We were just as unsuccessful in our attempts to get an Army Group A regiment to relieve 16 Motorized Division at Yelista, where it was covering the deep flank of First Panzer Army. By the time anything was done about this it was too late to make any difference at Stalingrad.

The second possible way of reinforcing Fourth Panzer Army in time for its thrust to Stalingrad lay in the provision of new forces by O.K.H. At the time in question 17 Panzer Division and the newly established 306 Infantry Division were – in that order – on their way to Don Army Group. In consequence of the delay involved in assembling 57 Panzer Corps at Kotelnikovo, the former of the two could have arrived just in time to move off with it to Stalingrad. Unfortunately O.K.H. had the division detrained as its own reserve behind the left wing of the Army Group because – not without reason – it feared a large-scale attack was impending there. Yet O.K.H. could not have it both ways: success for Fourth Panzer Army *and* security against a crisis which – if it did arise – 17 Panzer Division could not master anyway. While we preferred success for Fourth Panzer Army, Hitler opted for the security he hoped to achieve by his retention of 17 Panzer Division. The upshot was that when Hitler did release the division after 306 Infantry Division had caught up, it arrived too late for the first phase of the relief operation. Possibly this was where the decisive opportunity was thrown away!

To enhance the effect of my telephone calls on Zeitzler, and also to strengthen his hand in the daily battles he had to fight, I felt obliged to have frequent appreciations of the situation teleprinted through to him, or even direct to Hitler.

One of these 'appreciations' – that of 9th December 1942 – is given in Appendix II to show what pains we took to keep Hitler and O.K.H. in the picture at all times. It also affords impressive evidence of the numerical preponderance confronting the Army Group and shows the type of forces with which – except for the few newly arrived divisions – it had to conduct the battles outside the Stalingrad pocket. Last but not least, it demonstrates how the Army Group strove to bring home the gist of all operational problems to the Supreme Command.

For the benefit of critical readers, two comments on this appreciation might be interpolated here.

Some people may object to our having included any reference whatever to ways and means of continuing the battle in the event of Sixth Army's being kept at Stalingrad after a corridor had been cut through to it. The answer to this is that it would have been quite pointless to try to convince a man like Hitler of the futility of leaving an army in the city even assuming that supply by such a corridor were possible. Only by indicating the reinforcement problems which would beset him if he attempted to retain his hold on the city could one hope to make him see the need to disengage Sixth Army. Unfortunately even this appeal to reason failed to shake his obstinacy where prestige was concerned. At the time, however, we still cherished the hope that Hitler would bow to the inevitable when it came to the point.

Secondly, it may seem surprising, in view of the number of enemy formations confronting the Army Group, that we still continued to believe in the possibility of relieving Sixth Army at all. We might well be reproached with having under-rated our opponent.

The crux of the matter as far as we were concerned, however, was that the maximum risk had to be accepted if we were to bring our comrades of Sixth Army a chance of salvation. Events have shown that we came near enough to opening their way to freedom. The fact that we were fated to fail in the end was due to causes which I shall discuss in due course.

A RACE FOR LIFE OR DEATH

We and the enemy now set off on a race for life or death. Our own goal was to save the life of Sixth Army. But to do so we staked the very existence not only of Don Army Group but also of Army Group A.

It was a race to decide whether the relief group of Fourth Panzer Army would manage to join hands with Sixth Army east of the Don before the enemy forced us to break off the operation. This he might achieve by over-running our weak front on the Chir or the left wing of the Army Group (and possibly the right wing of Army Group B as well) and putting himself in a position to cut all the rear communications of Don Army Group and Army Group A.

To mount and maintain an assault operation east of the Don while the danger outlined above grew increasingly acute from one day to the next meant incurring a risk that can seldom have been run before. I cannot believe that Hitler realized its full import at the time, otherwise he would almost certainly have taken more radical measures, at least to the extent of reinforcing Fourth Panzer Army for a speedy relief of Stalingrad. Instead, as General Zeitzler himself expressed it, he 'did nothing but put spokes in our wheel'. Two examples of this were his retention of 17 Panzer Division in the wrong spot throughout the crucial phase of the operation and his failure to release 16 Motorized Division until it was too late. Many was the time Hitler declared that generals and General Staff officers could only 'compute' and would not take chances. There can hardly be any more striking rebuttal of his claim than the risk run by Don Army Group when it ordered Fourth Panzer Army's drive on Stalingrad and kept this going till the last possible moment in a situation which threatened to destroy the whole southern wing of the German armies.

This race with death, which began on 12th December, when Fourth

Panzer Army struck out for Stalingrad, can only be sketched in broad outline here, as it is not possible to depict the lightning changes of situation which occurred in 57 Panzer Corps' battles against an enemy who never ceased to throw in fresh forces – tanks first and foremost.

The versatility of our armour and the superiority of our tank crews were brilliantly demonstrated in this period, as were the bravery of the panzer grenadiers and the skill of our anti-tank units. At the same time it was seen what an experienced old armoured division like 6 Panzer could achieve under its admirable commander General Rauss and the tank specialist Colonel v. Hünersdorff (who, I am sorry to say, was later to be killed at the head of this same division) when it went into action with its full complement of armoured vehicles and assault guns. How hard, in contrast, was the lot of 23 Panzer Division (commanded by General v. Vormann, a former colleague of mine in the O.K.H. Operations Branch who had been five times wounded in World War I), which had a bare twenty tanks to work with!

Let us now try to follow at least those features of the battle that were material to its outcome.

While 57 Corps finished assembling *east of the Don* around Kotelnikovo, strong enemy forces had again been attacking our front on the Lower Chir since 10th December. It was now clear that there could be no further question of releasing 48 Panzer Corps on this front for it to break out of the Chir–Don bridgehead and co-operate with 57 Panzer Corps.

This made it more urgent than ever that 57 Panzer Corps should get on the move. After smashing an enemy attempt to over-run it while it was still in the process of detraining and final assembly, the corps was able to cross the start line on 12th December. Its flanks were covered against the Volga in the east by 7 Rumanian Corps and up to the Don in the west by 6 Rumanian Corps. The attack evidently surprised the enemy, who did not appear to have expected it quite so soon, and initially the corps made good progress. Far from sticking to defensive tactics, however, the enemy hastened to bring up fresh forces from the Stalingrad area and counter-attacked again and again in attempts to re-capture ground already won by our tanks or to surround small numbers of the latter with his own numerically superior armour. In spite of having wiped out one strong group after another, 57 Panzer Corps had still achieved nothing decisive by 17th December, the date on which

17 Panzer Division was at last able to intervene east of the Don. O.K.H. had finally released it from its detraining area behind the left wing of the Army Group in response to demands from my head-quarters. Before it could take a hand east of the river, however, the division still had to accomplish the long haul up to and across the Don bridge at Potemkinskaya.

While 57 Panzer Corps was striving for decisive results on the east bank of the river, the enemy redoubled his efforts to the west of it in order to bring about the collapse of the German front on the Chir. Above all, he had obviously grasped the significance of the bridgehead we were holding in the angle of the Chir and Don, together with the Don bridge contained therein, for ever since 12th December these had been the constant target of massed Soviet attacks. On 14th December we were forced off the bridge, and had to blow it up. By 15th December it was apparent that the battle on the Lower Chir front had only a few more days to run.

At the very same time, however, a new danger loomed up in the large bend of the Don. On 15th December there were obvious signs of an enemy attack being prepared in front of the left wing of Don Army Group and the right wing of Army Group B, and the following day local attacks were launched. Initially it was not entirely clear whether the enemy was following his frequent practice of feeling out the front prior to a decisive breakthrough, or whether he was seeking to prevent us from transferring any forces from this sector to the battlefield east of the Don. Then, however, our radio monitors identified a new army (Third Guards), which implied that a breakthrough with some such far-reaching objective as Rostov was impending.

The Army Group could not afford a decisive battle on its left wing as long as it had to fight for the liberation of Sixth Army east of the Don. It had to hold off here if it could. So that the responsible head-quarters, *Army Detachment Hollidt*, might find the necessary reserves for a delaying action, Army Group made it pull back on to a shorter front further to the rear, bearing in mind the need to preserve con-tinuity with the right wing of Army Group B.

December 18th proved a day of crisis of the first order.

East of the Don, despite the arrival of 17 Panzer Division, 57 Panzer Corps had still not fought things to a point which offered any prospect of its being able to thrust swiftly into the vicinity of Stalingrad and create the conditions needed for Sixth Army's break-out. On the contrary, it looked as though the corps would be forced on to the defensive, since the enemy was continuing to throw forces in its path from the siege front round the city.

On the *Lower Chir* heavy fighting was still in progress, although the enemy had not so far succeeded in penetrating our front. On the *left wing of the Army Group*, on the other hand, a most serious crisis was taking shape, the enemy having begun a major attack against Army Detachment Hollidt and the Italian army forming the right wing of Army Group B.

In the case of *Army Detachment Hollidt* the two Rumanian corps proved unequal to the onslaught, and there was some doubt whether even the German divisions would attain their alternative position in any semblance of order after being abandoned wholesale by their allies.

What made things worse still was that the enemy had been able to over-run the *Italian Army* in the first assault, thereby tearing open the flank of Don Army Group.

The same day the Army Group called on O.K.H. to take immediate steps to initiate the break-out of Sixth Army towards Fourth Panzer Army. There was still a chance that once 17 Panzer Division had made its presence fully felt, 57 Panzer Corps could win further ground in the direction of the pocket. In other words, one could still hope for a favourable outcome of the struggle east of the Don. Yet how much earlier this could have been achieved if only 17 Panzer and 16 Motorized Divisions (of which the latter was still tied up at Yelista) could have been available for Fourth Panzer Army's relief operation from the very outset!

Notwithstanding our insistence on the urgent need for a decision that would allow Sixth Army to break out of Stalingrad, Hitler declined to sanction this – although his Chief-of-Staff had simultaneously to inform us that all forces still in the process of moving up were being directed to Army Group B on account of the plight of the Italian Army. The fact that we were asked in this same connexion whether Stalingrad could still be held showed what little idea the Supreme Command had – or was prepared to have – of the seriousness of the situation.

Hitler's refusal to disengage the army from Stalingrad at this stage did not deter the Army Group from at least preparing for the inevitable. On 18th December I sent my chief Intelligence officer, Major Eismann, into the pocket to give Sixth Army our views on the break-out operation which would undoubtedly become necessary in the very near future.

The following were the salient points of what he had to say:

The critical situation on the Chir front, and even more so on the Army Group's left wing, meant that Fourth Panzer Army's battle to free Sixth Army east of the Don could only continue for a limited period. Furthermore, it was doubtful whether the Panzer Army could maintain its drive right up to the actual siege front because the enemy was constantly throwing in fresh forces from here to meet it. For this same reason, however, Sixth Army's chances of breaking through the siege ring were at present better than they had ever been. A link-up between Fourth Panzer and Sixth Armies depended on the latter's taking an active part in the battle from now on. As soon as it set about breaking out of the pocket towards the south-west, the enemy would be unable to weaken his siege front any further, and this in turn would enable Fourth Panzer Army to resume its advance towards the pocket.

The task allotted to Sixth Army in the orders for 'Winter Tempest' which it had received on 1st December – i.e. to hold itself in readiness to thrust south-west as far as the Donskaya Tsarytsa in order to make contact with Fourth Panzer Army – would probably have to be extended. The army might now have to continue beyond the limited objective laid down for it in the 'Winter Tempest' operation and keep pushing south-west until it actually joined the Panzer Army. While 'Winter Tempest' laid down that Sixth Army should still hold the Stalingrad area in accordance with Hitler's orders, the new alternative plan would mean evacuating it sector by sector in keeping with the progress of the breakthrough to the south-west.

Major Eismann was also to point out that while the Army Group had made every possible effort in this direction, it did not believe the airlift could be improved far enough to allow Sixth Army to hold out at Stalingrad for any length of time.

The outcome of Major Eismann's mission, which had been intended to harmonize the views of the two headquarters, was not encouraging.

Paulus himself had not been unimpressed by what Eismann told him, though he did not fail to emphasize the magnitude of the difficulties and risks which the task outlined to him would imply. The Army's Chief of Operations and Quartermaster-General likewise stressed these difficulties to Major Eismann, but both men also declared that in the circumstances it was not only essential to attempt a break-out at the earliest possible moment but also *entirely feasible*.

What ultimately decided the attitude of Sixth Army Headquarters was the opinion of the Chief-of-Staff, Major-General Arthur Schmidt. He contended that it was quite impossible for the army to break out just then and that such a solution would be 'an acknowledgement of disaster'. 'Sixth Army,' he told Eismann, 'will still be in position at Easter. All you people have to do is to supply it better.' Schmidt obviously assumed that it was the business of the Supreme Command or Army Group to get the army out of a situation in which it had landed through no fault of our own and to keep it adequately supplied from the air in the meantime. It was an understandable point of view, and one which in theory he had every right to hold. Unfortunately circumstances had proved stronger. Eismann pointed out that although the Army Group was doing everything in its power to maintain supplies, it was not to blame when the weather brought the airlift to a virtual standstill, nor was it in a position to produce transport machines out of a hat. But all his remonstrances were like water off a duck's back as far as Schmidt was concerned. Even when Eismann sought to show that a break-out by Sixth Army was necessary in the interest of operations as a whole, the Chief-of-Staff still would not budge.

While the army commander was probably a better-trained tactician and a clearer thinker, it looked as if his Chief-of-Staff was the stronger personality of the two.[1]

And so the upshot of the talks was that General Paulus himself ended by pronouncing the break-out a sheer impossibility and pointing out that the surrender of Stalingrad was forbidden 'by order of the Führer'!

While Major Eismann's mission had certainly made Sixth Army Headquarters fully aware of the situation and the Army Group's inten-

---

[1] Disastrous though Schmidt's obstinacy was in this particular case, the same quality did him great credit in captivity later on. Judging by all that one has heard, he gave an admirable account of himself as a soldier and comrade, getting himself sentenced to twenty-five years' forced labour in the process. Justice compels us to pay tribute to his behaviour. *Author.*

tions, it had still not achieved any identity of views on the task intended for Sixth Army. Could we expect an army headquarters staff to execute an extremely difficult operation successfully when the army commander and his Chief-of-Staff harboured doubts as to its feasibility?

At any other time such a divergence of opinions would have been regarded as grounds for requesting a change in the army command. In the present critical situation, however, there could be no justification for such action. Any successor to the commander or the Chief-of-Staff would have needed time to 'play himself in', and when every day was vital this just could not be spared. In any case, it would have been hopeless to try to obtain Hitler's approval for such a change, since it would have affected the very men who recommended holding out at Stalingrad.

In spite of everything, Don Army Group was not willing to let slip the one remaining chance of saving Sixth Army, no matter how many difficulties and dangers the undertaking were to involve. It would entail issuing a formal order freeing the army commander of all responsibility for both the hazard of a break-out and the abandonment of Stalingrad. This was a step we were fully prepared to take.

The reasons why this order was not ultimately implemented by Sixth Army will be discussed later in their proper context. They were the subject of numerous conversations which Paulus and I and our respective Chiefs-of-Staff conducted on a newly established ultra-high-frequency wavelength, as well as of discussions between my own headquarters and the Supreme Command.

The next day, *19th December*, encouraged us to hope that the situation east of the Don would shortly reach a stage where the projected co-operation of the two armies might lead to the successful extrication of the one now at Stalingrad.

On this particular day *57 Panzer Corps* scored a gratifying success. It managed to cross the Aksai river and thrust northwards as far as the Mishkova, its spearhead actually coming within 30 miles of the southern siege front! *The moment for which we had longed since the take-over, when the approach of relief forces would offer Sixth Army its chance to break free, had arrived.* If Sixth Army now began its break-out while Fourth Panzer Army either continued to attack northwards or at least drew off further forces from the siege front, the enemy in between would find himself between two fires, and there would at least be a prospect of establishing enough contact to provide Sixth Army with the fuel, ammunition and food it needed for continuing its break-through. For this purpose the Army Group had assembled transport columns loaded with 3,000 tons of supplies behind Fourth Panzer Army, in addition to tractors for mobilizing part of the Sixth Army artillery. They were all to be rushed through to the beleaguered army as soon as the tanks had cleared a route, however temporary.

The situation on the Army Group's front *west of the Don* on 19th December likewise indicated that the troops there should be able – at least for as long as Sixth Army needed to fight a way through to the south-west – to stall off any decisive developments compelling us to break off the operation east of the river.

Meanwhile, our front on the *Lower Chir* was still holding.

Although the Army Group found it necessary to intervene with *Army Detachment Hollidt* to safeguard the latter's withdrawal opera-tion, there was every prospect that its alternative positions would be occupied as planned. On the other hand, the threat to the Army De-tachment's open left flank was still present.

The race with death on either side of the Don had entered its final and decisive phase!

Would the Army Group succeed in preserving the situation in the large bend of the Don for a few days longer, until Sixth Army had availed itself of what was undoubtedly its *last* opportunity? Certainly it could only do so if not a single hour were wasted!

At noon on 19th December, therefore, the Army Group sent the Supreme Command an urgent appeal by teleprinter to let Sixth Army finally disengage from Stalingrad and drive south-west to join Fourth Panzer Army.[1]

When this message, too, failed to evoke any immediate response, an order was issued to Fourth Panzer and Sixth Armies at 1800 hours,[2] in which the latter was directed to *commence breaking through to the south-west forthwith*. The first phase of the operation was to be the 'Winter Tempest' attack detailed on 1st December. It would, if necessary, con-tinue beyond the Donskaya Tsaritsa for the purpose of making contact with Fourth Panzer Army and enabling the supply convoy to pass through.

---

[1] See Appendix III. *Author.*   [2] See Appendix IV. *Author.*

At the same time the order envisaged a second phase of the break-through which would, if need be, follow directly on the 'Winter Tempest' attack. On receipt of the code-word 'Thunderclap', Sixth Army was to proceed with its advance towards Fourth Panzer Army and simultaneously begin to evacuate the Stalingrad area sector by sector. The reservation imposed on the issue of this code-word arose from the need to synchronize the assault operations of both armies, as well as from the question as to whether it would be possible to co-ordinate the passage of the transport convoy with these operations. Above all, the Army Group had to try to persuade Hitler to rescind his order to Sixth Army to hold Stalingrad at all costs, for although the responsibility for not complying with it would rest with the Army Group as soon as it gave the signal for 'Thunderclap', the commander of Sixth Army would still feel his hands were tied as long as it remained in force.

FORFEITURE OF THE CHANCE TO SAVE SIXTH ARMY

If there had ever been a chance to save Sixth Army since the end of November, when Hitler refused Paulus permission for an immediate break-out before the enemy had consolidated his siege ring round Stalingrad, that chance came on 19th December. The Army Group had given the order to take it in spite of the difficulties Sixth Army's breakthrough might entail and the perilous situation that had meanwhile developed on the rest of the Army Group's front. The risk we were running in the latter respect will be discussed in due course. The immediate problem – that is, from 19th till 25th December – was whether Sixth Army would actually be able and willing to carry out the order issued to it.

Hitler did in fact agree to the army's attacking in a south-westerly direction for the purpose of joining up with Fourth Panzer Army. Yet he continued to insist that it should hold its northern, eastern, and western fronts around the city. He was still hoping that it would be possible to cut open a 'corridor' through which the army at Stalingrad could be supplied on a really long-term basis. There were two very obvious objections to this:

First, the situation of the Army Group as a whole, particularly with regard to developments in the neighbouring area of Army Group B, no longer allowed two armies – Sixth and Fourth Panzer – to be tied down east of the Don. By this time not only the fate of Sixth Army was at stake but also that of Don Army Group and Army Group A, both of which, if the enemy took resolute action, were liable to be cut off from their communications zones.

Secondly, it was a sheer impossibility for Sixth Army to mobilize all its remaining offensive power for a breakthrough to the south-west and still hold its present fronts around Stalingrad. It might conceivably be able to do so for one or two days longer, until such time as the enemy had grasped its intentions, but there could never be any question of its making a long stand in the city and simultaneously maintaining a link with Fourth Panzer Army.

While Hitler's reasons for opposing the execution of the plan laid down in the Army Group order of 19th December were unrealistic, the objections raised by *Sixth Army Headquarters* were not of a kind that could be dismissed out of hand. They showed how great were the risks which must necessarily be incurred if the Army Group order were carried out.

When the army declared that it could not undertake the break-out as long as Hitler insisted on the retention of Stalingrad, it was perfectly right. That was why the Army Group had explicitly ordered the evacuation of the fortified area on receipt of 'Thunderclap'. However, the army commander still had to decide whom to obey – Hitler or the commander of the Army Group.

Furthermore, the army thought it would need six days to prepare for the break-out. In our own view the estimate was much too high and unacceptable in the present situation, even if due allowance were made for all the difficulties facing the army in consequence of its great loss of mobility. To wait six days more seemed impossible to us, if only because of the situation on the Army Group's left wing. Most of all, the enemy forming the siege front around the city was not going to sit doing nothing for all that time, while the break-out preparations went on under his very nose. It might perhaps be possible to conceal these preparations – and the consequent thinning-out of Sixth Army's other fronts – for a limited period. But if the assembly of forces for the break-through on the south-western front were going to take six whole days, the enemy would already have started attacking on the other fronts before the breakthrough gained momentum. This must be avoided at all costs.

The army also doubted its ability even to disengage the forces ear-marked for the breakthrough from their present fronts, as the latter were already being subjected to local attack. Here, too, speed would be all-important. Provided that the army started its break-out in good time, it would be spared the trouble of combating any enemy incursions on its other fronts and need merely fight delaying actions to cover a step-by-step withdrawal.

The army rightly emphasized in the teleprinter conversations be-tween General Paulus and myself and our respective Chiefs-of-Staff that the code-word 'Thunderclap' must follow immediately upon 'Winter Tempest' and that it would not be possible to pause, for ex-ample, on the Donskaya Tsarytsa. This was a point on which we were completely unanimous, the Army Group order having in fact already foreshadowed that 'Thunderclap' would be linked directly to 'Winter Tempest'.

What undoubtedly weighed heavily with the commander of Sixth Army was the fact that the general debility of the troops and the re-duced mobility of units following the slaughtering of horses for food made it most unlikely that such a difficult and risky undertaking – par-ticularly when carried out under conditions of extreme cold – could possibly succeed.

It was the fuel position, however, which finally decided Sixth Army against attempting to break out and persuaded the Army Group that it could not insist on its order being implemented. General Paulus re-ported that he had only enough petrol to take his tanks – of which about 100 must still have been serviceable – a maximum distance of 20 miles. This meant that he could not move off until either an adequate supply of fuel (and rations) were guaranteed or Fourth Panzer Army had advanced to within 20 miles of the enemy siege front. Now no one could dispute the inability of Sixth Army's tanks – which represented its essential offensive power – to bridge a gap of some 30 miles with fuel stocks that were only sufficient for 20. On the other hand, one could not possibly wait until the army's fuel stocks were brought up to the level it demanded (4,000 tons) – quite apart from the fact that we were aware from practical experience of the utter impossibility of lifting such quantities by air. Any such delay would have meant wasting the time that could still be spared for the army's breakthrough.

One had to be prepared to live from hand to mouth and to go into action with what one had – including, of course, the quantities of fuel which could be flown in during the next few days, while the army was still assembling. Beyond that one could only hope that stocks could be constantly replenished from the air in the course of the breakthrough.

A point worth remembering here is that troops always have more fuel in hand than they care to admit in official returns. But even if this were not taken into account, one could still hope that things would develop on the following lines. The moment Sixth Army launched its attack towards the south-west things would become easier for Fourth Panzer Army, for henceforth the enemy would no longer be able to keep throwing out fresh forces from the Stalingrad siege front to meet it. Fourth Panzer Army, whose further progress over the Mishkova was by no means a certainty on 19th December, would doubtless be able to accomplish the outstanding 12 miles once the pressure were relieved by the action of Sixth Army.

It was obviously risky to include this in our calculations, but without it we simply could not expect to save Sixth Army.

But the really crucial reason why this fuel question was ultimately decisive in bringing about the retention of Sixth Army at Stalingrad lay in the fact that Hitler had a liaison officer in the pocket. By this means he learnt of Paulus's contention that the fuel situation made it impossible for him not only to launch a breakthrough operation but even to move up to the start-line.

I spent some considerable time on the telephone trying to make Hitler allow Sixth Army to break out and abandon Stalingrad. 'I fail to see what you are driving at,' was all he would say. 'Paulus has only enough petrol for 15 to 20 miles at the most. He says himself that he can't break out at present.'

And so the Army Group had to contend on one hand with the Supreme Command, which made any attack by Sixth Army to the south-west dependent on its simultaneous retention of the remaining Stalingrad fronts, and on the other with the command staff of Sixth Army, which declared that the fuel situation rendered it incapable of complying with the Army Group order. In support of his decision Hitler was able to invoke the army commander who would be called upon to tackle this difficult task. Had he not had this pretext to hand, he might still have been forced by the pressure of events to give up his demand that the city continue to be held even when the breakthrough was in progress. But then, in all probability, General Paulus would likewise have seen the whole problem with different eyes, since he would no longer have been acting against an express order from Hitler.

The fact that I have dealt in such detail with the Sixth Army commander's motives in not seizing the last opportunity to save his army is due to my belief that I owe this to him irrespective of anything connected with his personal character or subsequent conduct. As I have already stated, none of the reasons he advanced for his decision could be turned down as inadmissible. Yet the fact remained that this was our one and only chance of saving the army. Not to utilize it – however great the risks – meant to resign all hope of salvation. To take it implied staking everything on one card. In the view of the Army Group, this was now imperative.

It is easy to criticize the attitude of the future Field-Marshal Paulus in those vital days. Certainly there was more to it than mere 'blind obedience' to Hitler, for there can be no question that Paulus had grave conscientious doubts as to whether he should mount an operation which must inevitably lead – in direct contravention of the wish clearly expressed by Hitler – to the surrender of Stalingrad to the enemy. In the same connexion, however, it should be noted that when it occurred as the result of overwhelming enemy pressure, even this surrender would have been justifiable in relation to Hitler's order, and that since the Army Group had ordered the evacuation, it was the latter's own responsibility.

Apart from this conflict of conscience, however, the army commander was faced with a tremendous gamble if he obeyed the Army Group order. While a break-out certainly offered the army a chance of rescue, it could equally well lead to its destruction. Should the first attempt to break through the enemy's siege front prove unsuccessful, should Sixth Army get stuck half way while Fourth Panzer Army were unable to make any further progress, or should the enemy manage to over-run the German troops shielding the break-out from the rear and flanks, then Sixth Army's fate would be sealed in no time at all. The task confronting it was an incredibly formidable one and hazardous in the extreme. Like a square fighting in all four directions at once, it had to move out to meet Fourth Panzer Army under the constant threat of being fought to a standstill in its attack to the south-west or alternatively of having its rearguard and flank protection overrun.

Furthermore, this task would have had to be performed with troops already worn down by hunger and greatly restricted in their mobility. It is not unlikely, however, that the hope of regaining their freedom and eluding death or captivity would have helped them to accomplish an apparent impossibility.

When General Paulus let the last opportunity slip, when he hesitated and finally decided against the venture, he certainly did so on account of the responsibility he felt on his own shoulders. Although the Army Group strove by its order to absolve him of that responsibility, he still felt unable to acquit himself of it, either *vis-à-vis* Hitler or before his own conscience.

In the week that followed the Army Group's order for an immediate break-out, the fate of Sixth Army was decided.

For six whole days the Army Group ran every conceivable risk in order to leave the door open to Sixth Army to fight its way back to freedom in conjunction with Fourth Panzer Army. Throughout this period the Army Group was constantly threatened by the danger that the enemy – resolutely exploiting his breakthrough in the area of the Italian Army – would either drive across the open Donetz crossings to Rostov, where he could strike at the life-line of our whole southern wing, or else that he would wheel round into the rear of the left wing of Don Army Group, Army Detachment Hollidt.

We had to see the attempt through even at the risk that the thin protective screen serving us as a front on the Lower Chir (Third Rumanian Army) and in the area of Army Detachment Hollidt might finally disintegrate.

In spite of everything, the Army Group left Fourth Panzer Army in its exposed position east of the Don as long as it was possible to hope that Sixth Army would avail itself of its last opportunity of escape. The time limit was reached when developments on the left wing of the Army Group left us no choice but to throw forces in there from the eastern bank of the Don and when, on 25th December, the position of 57 Panzer Corps on the Mishkova became untenable.

Let us now briefly survey the dramatic events of that week.

It all began on the left wing of the Army Group, or, more precisely, on the left flank of Army Detachment Hollidt.

Exactly what happened to the Italians was not known. It seemed that only one light division and one or another of the infantry divisions had put up any resistance worth mentioning. Be that as it may, on the morning of 20th December the German General commanding the corps on the Italians' right wing came in to state that the two Italian divisions under his command were at that moment beating a rapid retreat, evidently because of a report that there were already two enemy armoured corps deep in their flank. As a result the flank of Army Detachment Hollidt was completely exposed.

When the Army Group Headquarters was informed of this situation by General Hollidt (who actually came under Army Group B), it directed him to use every means at his disposal to halt the Italian divisions. The Army Detachment under his command received orders to hold its position on the Upper Chir and to cover its left flank by an echeloned defence.

In the course of the day, however, the Army Detachment's own flimsy front was penetrated in two places. 7 Rumanian Division carried out an unauthorized withdrawal, and H.Q. 1 Rumanian Corps abandoned its command post in a panic.

By the evening of 20th December the situation in Army Detachment Hollidt's deep flank was utterly obscure. No one could tell whether the Italians who had been in action next to it were still offering any resistance, and if so, where. The enemy's armoured spearheads were reported everywhere in the rear of Army Detachment Hollidt, even as far back as the important Donetz crossing of Kamensk-Shakhtinsky.

During the next two days the position of *Army Detachment Hollidt* became increasingly acute. With even its front penetrated, it presented a no longer protectable flank and rear to the enemy armour, which now enjoyed a completely free hand in the sector where the Italians had been over-run. Before long this perilous situation was bound to have its effect on the Third Rumanian Army front on the Lower Chir.

Army Detachment Hollidt first had to do its best to establish a new front roughly level with that of Third Rumanian Army in order to cover both the latter's flank and the Morosovsky and Tatsinskaya airfields that were so indispensable to the Stalingrad airlift. Everything possible also had to be done to keep the important Donetz crossings of Forchstadt and Kamensk-Shakhtinsky open.

That such temporary expedients could contain the situation on the

Army Group's left wing for at most two or three days longer was only too evident. As early as 20th December the Army Group had sent O.K.H. a teleprinter message stating point blank that if the enemy acted decisively following his breakthrough on the Italian front, he would bear down on Rostov and seek a major decision against Don Army Group and Army Group A. It was characteristic of the state of affairs prevailing at the Supreme Command that even the Chief-of-Staff of the German Army was unable to take this message in to Hitler on that particular day because the latter – with only O.K.W. representatives in attendance – was busy negotiating with an Italian delegation. The only reply we got was an O.K.H. directive received on 22nd December, assigning Army Detachment Hollidt a defence line which had long been overtaken by events. On the very same day it was actually touch and go whether the German and a handful of Rumanian formations which the Army Detachment had fighting out in front would ever get back to form a new line at all.

Clearly the Army Group could not expect any effective measures from the Supreme Command to stabilize the position in the gap torn in our front with Army Group B by the Italian débâcle. It had even refused to allow the quick transfer of an infantry division from Army Group A to ensure the immediate protection of Rostov. All we could do, therefore, was to draw on our own resources – a decision rendered particularly painful by the fact that it could only be carried out at the expense of the Army Group's right wing – i.e. the forces now in action east of the Don. Yet there was no room for any delay, for *on 24th December the crisis at Army Detachment Hollidt reached its climax*. Three enemy tank and mechanized corps had driven through the breach in the front where the Italians and 3 Rumanian Division had been. Two of them (25 Tank and 50 Mechanized Corps) were already approaching the vital airlift bases at Morosovsky and Tatsinskaya, while the third (8 Tank Corps) was round behind those elements of the Army Detachment which were still fighting on either the middle or upper reaches of the Chir.

While the situation on the left wing of the Army Group, particularly on its open western flank, became increasingly grave, we continued to strive for the break-out of Sixth Army, which still depended on Hitler's renunciation of Stalingrad and on the army's readiness to take the plunge.

Fourth Panzer Army was meanwhile doing everything in its power to accomplish the last lap to Stalingrad, hoping at the same time that Sixth Army would make its task easier by starting to attack to the south-west.

In the days following its arrival at the Mishkova on 19th December, the relieving army had become imbroiled in heavy fighting against the never-ending waves of forces thrown in by the enemy from Stalingrad to halt its advance. Despite this, 57 Panzer Corps had succeeded in gaining a foothold on the north bank of the river and, after a series of ding-dong engagements, in forming a bridgehead there. Mass attacks by the enemy brought him nothing but bloody losses. Already, on the distant horizon, the leading troops of the corps could see the reflection of the gunfire around Stalingrad! Success seemed to be within striking distance if only Sixth Army would create a diversion by going over to the attack and at least prevent the enemy from constantly throwing fresh forces in the path of Fourth Panzer Army. For reasons which have already been stated, however, Sixth Army's attack never materialized.

On the afternoon of 23rd December the Army Group was regretfully compelled to take account of the situation on the left wing, which was more than critical by this time, by shifting forces to that area. Third Rumanian Army on the Lower Chir was directed to release H.Q. 48 Panzer Corps and 11 Panzer Division to restore the position on the Army Group's western wing, and to make good this loss Fourth Panzer Army had to give up one armoured division, without which the Lower Chir front could not possibly be held.

The very next day showed how imperative this measure had been. Tatsinskaya airfield was lost, and with it went a means of supplying Sixth Army by air. It could not be recaptured until 28th December.

The Army Group had only taken this agonizing decision to deprive the Fourth Panzer Army relief group of a whole division when it became clear that Sixth Army could no longer be expected to break out in time. Even now it could have put off doing so if only 16 Motorized Division had been already available. On 20th December, admittedly, O.K.H. had yielded to the promptings of my own headquarters and finally given orders for this division to be relieved at Yelista by the Viking Division from Army Group B, but unfortunately the process was to take ten days to complete. As it happened, ten days was the exact period which had elapsed since the Army Group's first request for 16 Motorized Division's release! Had approval been given forthwith, the division could have been immediately available for action on the Chir front on 23rd December and 57 Panzer Corps need never have been deprived of an armoured division. As was so often the case, the decision bore the stamp of Hitler's dilatoriness.

Although Hitler now promised to let the Army Group have 7 Panzer Division, it was bound to arrive too late for the relief operation already in progress. At the same time he hoped to see events take a turn for the better now that the first battalion of Tigers was due to arrive, but this was to prove equally fallacious. Apart from the fact that some considerable time was to pass before the Tigers showed up, they had never been tested under active-service conditions and were afflicted with so many growing pains that they could not initially render any worthwhile assistance. This, incidentally, was typical of the way Hitler over-rated the power of new weapons.

And so, in the battleground east of the Don, too, the hour now came for the initiative to pass to our opponents.

On 27th December 57 Panzer Corps was attacked in the Mishkova sector, where a steady enemy build-up had been going on, and was pushed back to the Aksai. It became clear in the next few days that the Soviet intention was to envelop the Corps from the east and west.

Two Soviet armies (Fifty-First and Second Guards, comprising three mechanized, one tank, three rifle and one cavalry corps) were identified on the northern and eastern fronts of Fourth Panzer Army. A large proportion of these forces had been drawn from the Stalingrad siege front, though reinforcements had also come from over the Volga.

Within a day or two the enormous preponderance of forces now amassed by the enemy compelled Fourth Panzer Army to withdraw as far as Kotelnikovo, whence it had originally begun to drive to Stalingrad on 12th December. What rendered this withdrawal quite inevitable was the inability of the Fourth Rumanian Army units under command to rise to the task of giving flank protection to the troops of 57 Panzer Corps in their hard battle on the Aksai. The troops of both 7 Rumanian Corps, which was to have held the army's eastern flank towards the Volga, and of 6 Rumanian Corps, which was meant to safeguard the ground between 57 Panzer Corps and the Don, had lost all will to fight – due in part, no doubt, to the scant efforts of either of the command staffs to maintain morale. For all his assurances that he was doing everything possible to rally his troops to fresh resistance, the commander of Fourth Rumanian Army proved powerless in the face of such disintegration. We were left with no choice but to pull these units out of the line and send them home to Rumania.

The attempt to relieve Sixth Army undertaken on 12th December had failed, at least for the time being.

Could there, judging by the way things had developed since, be any hope of renewing it?

Today, with one's retrospective knowledge of the turn events took in the area of Army Group B, the reply to this question must be in the negative. At the time, though, it could not be foreseen that the catastrophe suffered by the Italian Army would be followed, before January was out, by an even greater one in the Hungarian Army's sector on the Don.

And so, despite all the objections which existed, the Army Group still did not feel able to abandon its policy of getting help through to Sixth Army. With this in mind, it submitted the following proposals to O.K.H. on 26th December.

In order to maintain the position on the *left wing of the Army Group*, where the enemy was threatening to break through towards Rostov, for at least a limited period, we called for the earliest possible intervention of an army-sized battle group (*Armeegruppe*) which O.K.H. had already begun assembling in the Millerovo area, just behind the right wing of Army Group B. In addition, we wanted an infantry division of Army Group A's Seventeenth Army moved quickly over to Rostov for the purpose of affording it direct protection. Likewise 7 Panzer Division, which had provisionally been promised to the Army Group and would be arriving too late to be committed east of the Don, must now take a hand in the battle on the left wing of the Army Group.

The worst that need be expected in the *centre of the Army Group front* was a withdrawal to the Don–Donetz line. Besides, the situation on the Lower Chir had relaxed somewhat in the last few days, as the enemy had obviously concentrated his forces further west to capture our airfields at Tatsinskaya and Morosovsky.

The question of whether a second attempt to raise the Stalingrad siege could be made or not depended on our ability to assemble enough forces east of the Don to enable Fourth Panzer Army to beat the enemy now pursuing it. To this end Don Army Group called on O.K.H. – as it had been doing repeatedly since 18th December and even before that – immediately to transfer 3 Panzer Corps and an infantry division from First Panzer Army to reinforce Fourth Panzer Army. These forces, when combined with 16 Motorized Division (whose arrival must likewise be expedited), would have sufficed, in the Army Group's opinion, for Fourth Panzer Army to renew its advance on Stalingrad. We reckoned, moreover, that they could be made available to the latter within six days. The same period must suffice to fly in Sixth Army's urgent requirements of fuel (1,000 tons) and food (500 tons), the Supreme Command having meanwhile promised more squadrons of transport aircraft. Tatsinskaya and Morosovsky would be free again in a day or two. It goes without saying that at the same time we repeatedly demanded freedom of movement for Sixth Army. Even though the latter might consider it hopeless to attempt a break-out at the present juncture, the Army Group Headquarters insisted that there was no alternative, since it was quite impossible to keep the army supplied inside the pocket. In view of the general situation and the state of Sixth Army's troops, however, we considered that the latest possible date for a break-out must be around the New Year, by which time Fourth Panzer Army – always provided that its reinforcements arrived – could have started attacking towards the pocket again. Admittedly, even if the break-out were a success, one could now hardly expect Sixth Army to reach Fourth Panzer Army as an intact formation. Nonetheless, a considerable number of its troops would presumably have an opportunity to fight their way through.

The question was whether First Panzer Army could spare the above-mentioned forces at this time. Both Hitler and Army Group A Headquarters contended that it could not.

Whether this refusal was justified must be left for others to decide. At all events, on 27th December Don Army Group sent O.K.H. (for Hitler's attention) a statement of comparative strengths indicating that the transfer of the three divisions we had asked for was perfectly feasible. According to the figures given, the ratio of German to enemy forces in the area of Army Group A was unquestionably a more favourable one than that existing in the case of Don Army Group. The latter's formations, moreover, had been involved in some extremely heavy fighting in the last month and a half and were correspondingly run down. Don Army Group was having to fight in open country, whereas ever since the Caucasus offensive petered out the armies of Army Group A had been holding positions which must by now be reasonably strong. But even if First Panzer Army had been unable, after handing over the three divisions in question, to withstand a more powerful enemy attack, it could still have employed elastic tactics to delay the enemy's advance until the battle to save Sixth Army had been settled one way or the other. Hitler, however, would not admit this possibility at the time, although our own headquarters had pointed out several times already that even if we could get Sixth Army out, it would not be possible to hold the Caucasus front permanently. The 'grand solution' advocated by us – which meant taking Sixth Army out of Stalingrad and going over to mobile operations throughout the areas of Don Army Group and Army Group A – was something which Hitler would not accept.

His refusal to weaken Army Group A may, apart from his fundamental unwillingness ever to surrender anything, have had yet another reason. He evidently believed he had another possibility in hand of bringing assistance to Sixth Army, even though not till a later date.

According to an O.K.H. directive received by us on 31st December, Hitler had resolved to move the SS Panzer Corps, which had had a rest and refit and consisted of the 'Leibstandarte', 'Death's Head' and 'Reich' Panzer Grenadier Divisions, over from the Western to the Eastern theatre. The corps was to concentrate around Kharkov and from there carry forward a relief offensive against Stalingrad. On account of the limited capacity of the railways, however, its assembly in the Kharkov area could not be completed before mid-February. How Sixth Army was to be kept alive in the meantime was not stated. Even though it was not yet possible to foresee the same sort of disaster in the Hungarian sector which had just befallen the Italians, the provision of the SS Panzer Corps was still necessary in view of the ever-increasing gravity of the situation between Army Group B and Don Army Group. However, there was no basis whatever for assuming that the forces of the SS Panzer Corps would ever suffice to carry an offensive as far as Stalingrad. What might well have been achieved over the relatively short distance of 80 miles from Kotelnikovo to Stalingrad in December, when the reinforcement of Fourth Panzer Army had been entirely feasible, could only be regarded as sheer fantasy in February, when it was a matter of covering 350 miles from Kharkov. If Hitler really did believe such a drive possible, it merely substantiates what was said about him in an earlier chapter.

When Hitler rejected all Don Army Group's requests for the speedy reinforcement of Fourth Panzer Army at the end of December, the fate of Sixth Army was finally sealed. In vain had we staked the last available man and the last available shell on the liberation of Sixth Army! In vain had we striven till the last possible moment to get the relief operation carried out and thrown the fate of the whole Army Group into the balance to do so!

From the beginning of January onwards, events in the area of Don Army Group could be more or less divided into two parallel phases, i.e.:

> *Sixth Army's final battle around Stalingrad*
> and
> the *struggle to preserve the entire southern wing*, embracing Army Groups A, B and Don.

While the latter must be dealt with separately for reasons of operational continuity, the former is covered in the last part of this chapter. Therein will be seen what an immense bearing Sixth Army's last battle was to have on the preservation of the southern wing of the German armies.

SIXTH ARMY'S LAST BATTLE

The death-struggle of Sixth Army, which began around the turn of the year, is a tale of indescribable suffering. It was marked not only by the despair and justified bitterness of the men who had been deceived in their trust, but even more by the steadfastness they displayed in the face of an undeserved but inexorable fate, by their high degree of bravery, comradeship and devotion to duty, and by their calm resignation and humble faith in God.

If I refrain from dwelling on these things here, it is certainly not because we at Army Group Headquarters were not intensely affected by them. Respect for a heroism which may never find its equal renders me incapable of doing full justice to these happenings at Stalingrad.

There is one question, however, which I feel both impelled and qualified to answer as the former commander of Don Army Group. Was it justifiable or necessary – and if so, for how long – to demand this sacrifice of our soldiers? In other words, did Sixth Army's final battle serve any useful purpose? To answer the question properly, one must examine it against the background of the current situation, and the stern exigencies this imposed, rather than in the light of Germany's ultimate defeat.

On 26th December the commander of Sixth Army sent us the message reproduced below. We passed it straight on to O.K.H., our policy all along having been to present the Army's position in a quite unembellished form. (From this moment onwards the only reports we received on the position inside the pocket came by radio or from officers flown out as couriers. We had been unable to maintain the ultra-high-frequency radio link by which it was possible to hold teleprinter conversations over a brief period.)

The message from Colonel-General Paulus ran as follows:

'Bloody losses, cold, and inadequate supplies have recently made serious inroads on divisions' fighting strength. I must therefore report the following:

1. Army can continue to beat off small-scale attacks and deal with local crises for some time yet, always providing that supply improves and replacements are flown in at earliest possible moment.

2. If enemy draws off forces in any strength from Hoth's [1] front and uses these or any other troops to launch mass attacks on Stalingrad fortress, latter cannot hold out for long.

3. No longer possible to execute break-out unless corridor is cut in advance and Army replenished with men and supplies.

'I therefore request representations at highest level to ensure energetic measures for speedy relief, unless overall situation compels sacrifice of army. Army will naturally do everything in its power to hold out till last possible moment.

'I have also to report that only 70 tons were flown in today. Some of the corps will exhaust bread supplies tomorrow, fats this evening, evening fare tomorrow. Radical measures now urgent.'

[1] I.e. Colonel-General Hoth, commanding Fourth Panzer Army. *Tr.*

The contents of this message confirmed how wrong Paulus's Chief-of-Staff had been only a week before when he asserted that the army could hold out till Easter if properly supplied.

The message also showed that when the Army Group had ordered Sixth Army to break out of the pocket one week previously, this – in view of the approach of Fourth Panzer Army – had not only been its *first* chance of being rescued but – as could be seen from the state the army was in – its *last* one, too.

Otherwise, except for local attacks, there was relative calm on the Sixth Army fronts around the end of December and beginning of January. This was either because the enemy wished to munition his artillery for a grand assault or because he was putting all the forces he could spare into an attempt to destroy Fourth Panzer Army and to score the success he was after in the large bend of the Don.

On 8th January General Hube appeared at Army Group Head-quarters on his way back from seeing Hitler. The latter had had Hube flown out of Stalingrad to Lötzen to brief him on the situation of Sixth Army. Hube told me that he had given Hitler a completely un-varnished picture of things in the pocket. (This cannot, in fact, have differed in any respect from the one already available to Hitler from the Army Group's daily situation reports, but presumably he was not prepared to credit our own version without further evidence.)

Nevertheless, it was remarkable how Hube's stay in Lötzen had impressed him and to what extent he had been influenced by Hitler's display of confidence – genuine or otherwise. Hitler had declared that everything would be done to *supply Sixth Army for a long time to come* and had drawn attention to the plan for its relief at a later date. With his confidence thus restored, Hube returned into the pocket, only to be flown out again on instructions from Hitler to take over the running of the airlift from outside. Not even he was able to improve it, however, its low efficiency being due to the prevailing weather and the inade-quate resources of the Luftwaffe and not to any shortcomings in the actual organization. One statement of Hube's which touched me per-sonally concerned a rumour circulating in Sixth Army that I had sent them the signal: 'Hang on – I'll get you out: Manstein.' While I left no stone unturned to extricate Sixth Army from Stalingrad, it has never been my custom to promise the troops anything which I was not cer-tain of fulfilling and did not rest with me alone.

General Hube, who was a fearless man, had tried to bring home to Hitler how damaging such events as the encirclement of Sixth Army must be to his prestige as Head of State. By this means he wished to suggest that Hitler should hand over command – at least on the Eastern Front – to a soldier. In view of the fact that Hube had called in to see us on his way to Lötzen, Hitler doubtless supposed that Hube's *démarche* had been inspired by me. This was in fact not the case.

When, after the fall of Stalingrad, I myself proposed a change in the supreme military command to Hitler, he was already forewarned and flatly refused to consider such a thing. Otherwise – especially as he was then still under the impression of his responsibility for the loss of Sixth Army – he might have proved more receptive to my ideas.

On 9th January the enemy called upon Sixth Army to capitulate. On Hitler's orders, the demand was rejected.

I do not think I can be reproached with ever having taken an uncritical view of Hitler's decisions or actions in the military sphere. Yet I entirely support the decision he made in this instance, for however harsh it may have been from the humanitarian point of view, it was still necessary at the time.

I do not propose to deal here with the purely soldierly viewpoint that no army may capitulate as long as it still has any strength left to fight. To abandon it would mean the very end of soldiering. Until we reach the happy era when states can do without armed might and soldiers no longer exist, this conception of soldierly honour will have to be maintained. Even the apparent hopelessness of a battle that can be avoided by capitulation does not in itself justify a surrender. If every Commander-in-Chief were to capitulate as soon as he considered his position hopeless, no one would ever win a war. Even in situations apparently quite bereft of hope if has often been possible to find a way out in the end. From General Paulus's point of view, at all events, it was his soldierly duty to refuse to capitulate. An exception could only have been made if the army had had no further role to play and could serve no useful purpose in prolonging its struggle. And this in turn brings us to the crucial point which justifies Hitler's order to refuse to capitulate and also barred the Army Group from intervening in favour of such action at that particular time. No matter how futile Sixth Army's continued resistance might be in the long run, it still had – as long as it could conceivably go on fighting – a decisive role to fulfil in the over-all strategic situation. It had to try to tie down the enemy forces oppos-ing it for the longest possible space of time.

At the beginning of December an approximate total of sixty enemy formations (i.e. rifle divisions, armoured and mechanized brigades etc.) had been identified in the siege ring around the army. Some of them had doubtless been temporarily drawn off by the attack of Fourth Panzer Army, but new ones had been brought up to replace them. By 19th January, ninety of the 259 formations reported to be facing Don Army Group were committed around Sixth Army. What would have happened if the bulk of these ninety formations had been released through a capitulation of Sixth Army on 9th January is plain enough in the light of what has already been said about the Army Group's position and the consequent threat to the southern wing as a whole.

The army was still capable of fighting, even though this was ulti-mately futile from its own point of view. Yet its ability to hold out was of decisive importance for the situation on the southern wing. Every extra day Sixth Army could continue to tie down the enemy forces surrounding it was vital as far as the fate of the entire Eastern Front was concerned. It is idle to point out today that we still lost the war in the end and that its early termination would have spared us infinite misery. That is merely being wise after the event. In those days it was by no means certain that Germany was bound to lose the war in the military sense. A military stalemate, which might in turn have led to a similar state of affairs in the political field, would have been entirely within the bounds of possibility if the situation on the southern wing of the German armies could in some way have been restored. This, however, depended first and foremost on Sixth Army's continuing the struggle and holding down the enemy siege forces for as long as it possessed the slightest capacity to resist. It was the cruel necessity of war which compelled the Supreme Command to demand that one last sacrifice of the brave troops at Stalingrad. The fact that the self-same Supreme Command was responsible for the army's plight is beside the point in this context.   .

Following Sixth Army's refusal to capitulate on 9th January, the Soviet attack, preceded by intensive artillery preparation and sup-ported by a large number of tanks, broke loose on all fronts. The main pressure was directed against the salient which protruded furthest west by Marinovka, and the enemy was able to break in at several points.

On 11th January the situation became even more critical, and because of the lack of ammunition and fuel the army could no longer restore it to any appreciable extent. The loss of the positions in the Karpovka Valley – and in particular of the inhabited localities there – deprived the troops on the western front of what protection they had hitherto enjoyed against the cold. Furthermore, the state of the weather ruled out any hope of an airlift.

This aggravation of Sixth Army's plight was made clear in a special report of 12th January which the Army Group immediately forwarded to O.K.H.

'Despite the troops' heroic resistance,' the army stated, 'the heavy fighting of the last few days has resulted in deep enemy penetrations which could so far be contained only with difficulty. Reserves are no longer available; nor can any be formed. Heavy weapons now immobilised. Severe losses and inadequate supplies, together with cold, have also considerably reduced troops' powers of resistance. If enemy maintains attacks in present strength, fortress front unlikely to hold more than a few days longer. Resistance will then resolve itself into localised actions.'

On 12th January weather again stopped the airlift and also prevented the Luftwaffe from flying any sorties in support of the army's hard defensive battles.

That evening General Pickert, the man responsible for controlling the Luftwaffe's side of the airlift, came out of the pocket. He painted a shocking picture of the position and set a limit of two to four days on the army's capacity for continued resistance – an estimate that was to prove inaccurate by reason of the bravery and self-sacrifice of the troops. In Pickert's opinion not even an improvement of the airlift could make much difference from now on, as the army's resources no longer sufficed to patch up the points where the enemy had broken in.

The following information on the tactical situation inside the pocket emerged from a report brought out to us by Pickert from Paulus (who had meanwhile been promoted Colonel-General):

On the north-western front the enemy had attacked with a force of between ten and twelve divisions. Parts of 3 and 29 Motorized Infantry

Divisions had been outflanked from the north and smashed, with the result that it no longer seemed possible to rebuild a defence line here. The two gallant divisions had knocked out 100 tanks between them, but the enemy still appeared to have fifty intact.

On the southern front of the pocket, in spite of heroic resistance by 297 Infantry Division, the enemy had succeeded in breaking in after two days of intensive artillery bombardment. Here, too, there were no more forces available to close the gap. Of over 100 Soviet tanks taking part in this assault, forty had been knocked out.

The eastern front of the pocket was still holding at present, though here, too, heavy enemy pressure was being exerted.

On the north-eastern front the enemy had penetrated deeply in several places. 16 Panzer Division's fighting strength was exhausted.

Paulus further stated that the army would stand and fight to the last round. Any reduction in the size of the pocket as now suggested by Hitler to General Hube [1] would only serve to hasten the collapse, as no heavy weapons could now be moved. Since the airlift had been inadequate all along, no improvement could help matters now. The length of time the army could continue to resist depended entirely on the intensity of the enemy's attacks.

That same day the Pitomnik airfield was lost. Henceforth the only one left to us in the Stalingrad pocket was that at Gumrak.

During the night, however, Paulus reported that there might still be some prospect of continuing to defend the city if several battalions of troops were flown in forthwith with their full scale of weapons. He had already asked us repeatedly to fly in several thousand men to make good his losses, but the Army Group had been unable to comply because it possessed neither the necessary replacements nor, indeed, a single uncommitted battalion. Nor would it in any case have acceded to these requests from Sixth Army once Fourth Panzer Army's rescue drive had become bogged down, if only because there could be no justification for dispatching any reinforcements or replacements into the pocket from then on. It was already quite bad enough to have to fly unit commanders and General Staff officers back into the pocket on their return from leave. But apart from the fact that the army urgently needed them, these officers – some of whom bore such old military

---

[1] At the time when it was vitally necessary to accumulate forces for the break-out Hitler had issued an order expressly forbidding such action. *Author.*

names as Bismarck and Below – themselves insisted on returning to their troops, thereby proving that the tradition of self-denial and comradeship could withstand the hardest of tests.

On 13th January Colonel-General Paulus's senior aide, Captain Behr, an exemplary young officer who had already won the Knight's Cross, flew out to see us, bringing the army's war diary with him. He told us how bravely the troops were still fighting and what fortitude all ranks had shown in coming to terms with the cruelty of their fate.

Behr carried letters from Paulus and his Chief-of-Staff to Schulz and myself – letters reflecting the courage, integrity and decency that govern the German soldier's way of thinking. They fully recognized that the Army Group had done everything humanly possible to get Sixth Army out. On the other hand, of course, one detected their bitterness at the fact that the promises about air supplies had not been kept. All I can say to this is that neither Colonel-General v. Richthofen nor I had ever made such promises. The man responsible for them was Göring.

On 16th January there was again heavy fighting on all the army fronts. For a time it was impossible for any more aircraft to land, following the excessive losses inflicted by the enemy's ground and fighter defences earlier in the day. In the main it was now only possible to fly supplies in at night or drop them from the air. Inevitably a considerable volume of stores delivered by the latter method went astray.

The same day Hitler put Field-Marshal Milch in charge of the airlift. On 17th January the army radioed that the Gumrak airfield was usable again, but the Luftwaffe did not agree. The Army Group, however, insisted that an attempt be made to land there.

On 19th January I had my first talk with Milch, who had been slightly injured the day before when the car in which he had been coming to see me collided with a railway engine. I impressed on him the urgent need for a radical improvement of the airlift notwithstanding the hopelessness of Sixth Army's position. Apart from the fact that we owed it to our comrades at Stalingrad to maintain their supplies until the very last hour, I said, the army was performing a vital operational task in continuing to tie down ninety Soviet formations. In view of the critical situation on the rest of the Army Group's front and its open flank by Army Group B, every extra day we could keep Sixth Army in action might well be of decisive value. Milch promised to release all possible resources from the home front, including the last reserves of transport aircraft and technical personnel for maintenance and repair work. The latter were particularly important now, as the Morosovsky and Tatsinskaya airfields had by this time fallen into enemy hands and the airlift was having to operate from Novocherkask and Rostov and bases even further to the rear.

From what Milch told me it was clear that if he had been called in several weeks earlier he might have been able to ease matters considerably, since he had access to many resources back at home which were not available to v. Richthofen. This meant that Göring was all the more to blame for not having ensured that the resources in question were tapped at the right time.

On 24th January the following communication reached us from the Chief-of-Staff of the Army, General Zeitzler:

'The following radio message has been received here:

"Fortress can be held for only a few days longer. Troops exhausted and weapons immobilised as a result of non-arrival of supplies. Imminent loss of last airfield will reduce supplies to a minimum. No basis left on which to carry out mission to hold Stalingrad. Russians already able to pierce individual fronts, whole stretches of which are being lost through men dying. Heroism of officers and men nevertheless unbroken. In order to use this for final blow, shall give orders just before final break-up for all elements to fight through to south-west in organized groups. Some of these will get through and sow confusion behind Russian lines. Failure to move will mean end of everyone, as prisoners will also die of cold and hunger. Suggest flying out a few men, officers and other ranks, as specialists for use in future operations. Appropriate order must be given soon, as landing facilities unlikely to exist much longer. Please detail officers by name, obviously excluding myself.

PAULUS."

'The following reply has been sent:

"Message received. Identical with recommendation put up by me four days ago. On my resubmission, Führer has directed:

1. Re break-out: Führer reserves right of final decision. Please send further signal in case.

2. Re flying-out of personnel: Führer has refused for time being. Please send Zitzewitz here to restate case. I shall take him to see Führer.

ZEITZLER." '

As regards Colonel-General Paulus's request to have individual members of his army flown out, I would offer the following comment.

Seen purely from the viewpoint of military expediency, it would naturally have been desirable to save the highest possible number of essential specialists – always bearing in mind, of course, that they must be selected quite irrespective of rank. From the humanitarian point of view, it goes without saying that one should try to get every single man out. Yet there was also an aspect of soldierly ethics to consider – the one which dictated that the very first to be flown out should be the wounded. (This, in fact, we did succeed in doing on a quite remarkable scale.) The evacuation of specialists, however, could only have been achieved at the expense of leaving wounded men behind. Besides, the majority of specialists to be flown out would inevitably have been officers, for the simple reason that an officer's training renders him more important in war than the private soldier, unless the latter happens to have some very special qualification as a technician or scientist. But in a situation like Sixth Army's, the German military code demands that when lives are at stake, the officers must take second place to the men. It was for this reason that the Army Group made no move to get the Sixth Army commander's proposal accepted by Hitler.

As for any attempt to break through the enemy lines in small groups at the last moment, Hitler's 'final decision' never materialized.

Nonetheless, the Army Group did try to create a basis of survival for successful groups of evaders by dropping food at various points behind the enemy front and sending out reconnaissance aircraft in search of them. But none reached the Army Group Front, nor were any sighted by our pilots.

At all events, Paulus's message shows that up to the very last those members of Sixth Army who still had any strength left did not lose their will to fight. Indeed, we were aware that some of the younger officers and men, whose resistance was not yet exhausted, were resolved whatever happened to try to fight their way through the enemy's siege-ring when the time came. This was why we took the measures described above, fruitless though they proved.

On 22nd January the Russians reached the Gumrak airfield, with the result that supplies could no longer be delivered by landing aircraft. Having reported that he could no longer seal the gap in the front there and that his ammunition and rations were coming to an end, Paulus now sought Hitler's permission to begin surrender negotiations. In this connexion I had a long argument with the latter by telephone. I urged him to authorize a capitulation, my belief being that though every day's reduction of the army's resistance must aggravate the Army Group's situation as a whole, the time had now come to put an end to this valiant struggle. In bitter fighting the army had expended its last ounce of strength to hold a far stronger enemy, thereby decisively contributing to the salvation of the Eastern Front that winter. From now on the army's sufferings would bear no relation to any advantage which could be derived from continuing to tie down the enemy's forces.

In a long and violent dispute Hitler rejected the request made by Paulus and myself and ordered the army to fight on to the end. His grounds for doing so were that every day the enemy's Stalingrad divisions were prevented from being committed elsewhere represented a vital saving. Yet the situation was critical enough now that the Russians had also overrun the Hungarian Army on the Don and virtually wiped Army Group B off the map. From Voroshilovgrad on the Donetz up as far as Voronezh on the Don there was a gaping void within which the enemy was advancing in strength and had almost complete freedom of movement. Whether, in this situation, Don Army Group and Army Group A, which was now withdrawing from the Caucasus, could be saved at all seemed more than doubtful.

Hitler contended that even if Sixth Army were no longer able to form a coherent front, the fight could still be continued in smaller pockets for some time yet. Finally he declared that capitulation was futile, as the Russians would never keep any agreements anyway.

That the second prediction was correct in essence, if not in the strictly literal sense, is shown by the fact that of the 90,000 prisoners who finally fell into Soviet hands, not more than a few thousand can be alive today. It must be emphasized here, moreover, that the Soviets had intact railways running close up to Stalingrad and that, given good-will, it must have been possible for them to feed and evacuate the prisoners. Inevitable though the high loss of life from cold and exhaustion may well have been, the death rate in this case still appears quite excessive.

When Hitler turned down my request for Sixth Army's capitulation, I was naturally faced with the personal problem of deciding whether to register my disagreement by resigning command of the Army Group.

It was not the first time that I had contemplated doing so. The problem had particularly oppressed me during those Christmas days of 1942 when I had failed to persuade Hitler to let Sixth Army break out. And I was often to encounter it again in the months ahead.

It is, I think, understandable that one should have wished to be released from responsibilities rendered almost unbearable by the interminable, nerve-racking battles that had to be fought with one's own Supreme Command before it would accept the need for any urgent military action. The extent to which this wish preoccupied me at that time is apparent from a remark made by my G.S.O. I, the then Colonel Busse, to the chief engineer of Sixth Army just after Christmas 1942. According to the latter, Busse's words were: 'If I had not kept begging him (Manstein) to stay for the troops' sake, he'd have chucked the job back at Hitler long ago.' This impulsive utterance by the man who was then my closest collaborator is the best indication of my attitude and position.

But let me make a few general remarks here on the question of a senior commander's resignation in the field. The first point is that a senior commander is no more able to pack up and go home than any other soldier. Hitler was not compelled to accept a resignation, and would hardly have been likely to do so in this case. The soldier in the field is not in the pleasant position of a politician, who is always at liberty to climb off the band-wagon when things go wrong or the line taken by the Government does not suit him. The soldier has to fight where and when he is ordered.

There are admittedly cases where a senior commander cannot reconcile it with his responsibilities to carry out an order he has been given. Then, like Seydlitz at the Battle of Zorndorf, he has to say: 'After the battle the King may dispose of my head as he will, but during the battle he will kindly allow me to make use of it.' No general can vindicate his loss of a battle by claiming that he was compelled – against his better judgement – to execute an order that led to defeat. In this case the only course open to him is that of disobedience, for which he is answerable with his head. Success will usually decide whether he was right or not.

This was my reason on 19th December for giving Sixth Army that order immediately to break out to the south-west contrary to an express directive from Hitler. The fact that the order did not achieve anything is due to the failure of Sixth Army Headquarters to carry it out. It will hardly ever be possible to decide conclusively whether the latter was right to forgo this one remaining chance of salvation, as no one can tell whether the break-out would have succeeded or not.

On later occasions, too, I acted contrary to Hitler's orders whenever it was absolutely necessary to do so. Success proved me right, and Hitler had to tolerate my disobedience. (Unauthorized action was not admissible, however, when it would have landed the adjacent army groups in trouble.)

This question of resignation has another aspect, however, besides the one mentioned above. I refer to the feeling of responsibility which a senior commander must have towards his soldiers.

At the time in question I had not only Sixth Army to consider. The fate of my entire Army Group was at stake, as well as that of Army Group A. To throw up my task at this moment, however justifiable the human motives might be in the light of Hitler's attitude over the capitulation of Sixth Army, struck me as a betrayal of those brave troops who were also involved in a life-and-death struggle outside the Stalingrad pocket.

The fact that Don Army Group subsequently succeeded in mastering one of the most difficult situations of the war served, in my own opinion, to justify my decision that day not to resign out of sheer disgust.

Just how vital Sixth Army's bitter resistance had been may be gathered from a short sketch of developments in the areas of Don Army Group and Army Groups A and B in January 1943.

On *29th December* O.K.H. had finally given in to the insistence of Don Army Group and ordered the withdrawal of Army Group A from the Caucasus, initially by taking its left wing – First Panzer Army – back on to the Kuma line Pyatigorsk–Praskoveya (155 miles southeast of Salsk). Because of the time needed to salvage equipment, the move proceeded extraordinarily slowly and no forces became free for the time being.

By *9th January*, the date of *Sixth Army's rejection of the surrender call*, First Panzer Army had still not reached the Kuma line.

Fourth Panzer Army, whose task was to cover the rear of Army Group A south of the Don and simultaneously to keep its communications through Rostov open, had been pushed back to the west through Kotelnikovo after some heavy fighting against a much superior enemy (three armies strong) south of the Don. By 9th January it was fighting hard defensive battles along the Kuberle, between the Sal and the Manych, and we could see that the enemy intended to envelop it from both flanks. His 3 Guards Tank Corps, on the Don around Konstantinovka, was swinging south-east and driving on Proletarskaya in the rear of Fourth Panzer Army. Similarly, along the Manych, the Soviet Twenty-Eighth Army, newly arrived from the Kalmyk Steppes, was trying to execute an out-flanking movement to the south.

Army Detachment Hollidt, after some heavy fighting in the large bend of the Don, had had to retire to the Kagalnik sector. Even here the enemy had already broken into the southern flank of its positions, a small enemy force having crossed the Don north-east of Novocherkask (the location of Army Group Headquarters) on 7th January. On the northern wing of the army detachment 7 Panzer Division was trying to delay the enemy's approach to the Donetz crossing at Forchstadt by local shock tactics. The crossing at Kamensk could only be covered by emergency units and the few Rumanians who had not disappeared from the battlefield.

North-west from this point stretched the enormous gap left by the disintegration of the *Italian Army*. Fighting around Millerovo, for a time almost completely surrounded, was the weak *Fretter-Pico Battle Group* belonging to Army Group B.

On 24th January, the day Sixth Army finally crumbled into three tightly packed groups in and around Stalingrad and could no longer tie down any Soviet forces worth mentioning, the situation on the rest of the front was as follows:

The northern wing of *Army Group A* was still around Belaya Glina and, even further south, east of Armavir, which meant that it was 100–125 miles from Rostov. The withdrawal of the bulk of First Panzer Army through Rostov had now been finally approved by O.K.H.

Of *Don Army Group*, *Fourth Panzer Army* was fighting desperately south-east of Rostov to keep the Don crossing clear for First Panzer Army, which I envisaged throwing on to the left wing of my Army Group to hold the Donetz from Voroshilovgrad upwards.

Army Detachment Hollidt was defending the Donetz from its junction with the Don up to a point above Forchstadt.

The *Fretter-Pico Battle Group* (consisting of two dilapidated divisions) was guarding the Donetz on both sides of Kamensk.

Since 19th January, in consequence of the disintegration of the *Italian* and *Hungarian* Armies (the latter, too, having meanwhile been over-run on the Don), there had been a gap some 200 miles wide from Voroshilovgrad on the Donetz to Voronezh on the Don. On 23rd January the 'front' as far as Starobyelsk had been placed under Don Army Group. Practically the only troops left there were those of 19 Panzer Division, which was already pretty battered after giving up Starobyelsk in the face of three Soviet army corps.

When the last resistance of Sixth Army ceased on *1st February*, the enemy was threatening to cross the Donetz in the Voroshilovgrad area with a group of three tank, one mechanized and one rifle corps and appeared to have thrown another group of three or four tank corps and one rifle corps against the line of the river from Lissichansk to Zlaviansk.

There would seem to be little point in discussing how the situation would have developed between 9th January and 1st February, or what might have happened subsequently, had not the enemy been tied down so long at Stalingrad by the heroic resistance of Sixth Army!

Now let us return to the army's final struggle.

On 24th January the front broke down into three small pockets, one in the centre of Stalingrad and the other two on its northern and southern perimeters.

On 31st January the army commander, meanwhile promoted Field-Marshal, was taken prisoner with his staff.

On 1st February the last of the fighting came to an end when what was left of 11 Corps also surrendered in the north of the city.

The struggle of Sixth Army was over!

Soviet captivity was to finish off a process of decline begun by the utter ruthlessness of the fighting, pitiless hunger and the icy cold of the

Russian steppes. The soldiers who suffered it had surrendered only when their arms were powerless to bear weapons and their hands too frozen to operate them, when the exhaustion of their ammunition left them defenceless in the face of an overwhelming foe! Thanks to the self-sacrifice of the German aircrews, however, it had still been possible to evacuate some 30,000 wounded from the pocket.

Anyone seeking to fix the responsibility for the tragedy of Stalingrad already has the answer from Hitler's own lips. On 5th February I was summoned to Supreme Headquarters, all my pleas to Hitler to come and see the situation on our front for himself, or at least to send the Chief-of-Staff or General Jodl, having failed to move him.

Hitler opened the interview with roughly these words:

'*I alone* bear the responsibility for Stalingrad! I could perhaps put some of the blame on Göring by saying that he gave me an incorrect picture of the Luftwaffe's potentialities. But he has been appointed by me as my successor, and as such I cannot charge him with the responsibility for Stalingrad.'

It was certainly to Hitler's credit that he accepted responsibility unreservedly in this instance and made no attempt whatever to find a scapegoat. On the other hand, we are confronted by his regrettable failure to draw any conclusions for the future from a defeat for which his own errors of leadership were to blame.

Yet there is one fact which overshadows the question of responsibility and all that the ruthlessness of captivity, brain-washing and justified bitterness may have subsequently done to affect the attitude of many an individual member of the sacrificed Army:

By their incomparable bravery and devotion to duty, the officers and men of the army raised a memorial to German arms which, though not of stone or bronze, will nonetheless survive the ages. It is an invisible memorial, engraved with the words prefacing this account of the greatest of soldiers' tragedies.

The following are the headquarters staffs and formations of Sixth Army which perished at Stalingrad:

H.Q. 4, 8 and 11 Corps and H.Q. 14 Panzer Corps;

44, 71, 76, 79, 94, 113, 295, 297, 305, 371, 376, 384 and 389 Infantry Divisions;

100 Rifle (Jäger) Division and 369 Croatian Regiment;

14, 16 and 24 Panzer Divisions;

3, 29 and 60 Motorized Divisions;

as well as numerous army and army-group troops, anti-aircraft units and ground units of the Luftwaffe.

Finally, there were 1 Rumanian Cavalry Division and 20 Rumanian Infantry Division.

13

THE 1942-3 WINTER CAMPAIGN IN SOUTH RUSSIA

'Strategy is a system of stop-gaps.'

MOLTKE

WHILE THE eyes of all Germany were on Stalingrad at the turn of 1942–3, and anxious hearts prayed for the sons who fought there, the southern wing of the Eastern Front was simultaneously the scene of a struggle even greater than that being waged for the lives and freedom of Sixth Army's gallant two hundred thousand.

The issue was no longer the fate of a single army but of the entire southern wing of the front and ultimately of all the German armies in the east.

This struggle was spared the tragedy of defeat, being ultimately marked – for the last time in World War II – by a brief glimpse of victory. But it embraced, quite apart from its initial association with the trials of Sixth Army, such a wealth of unprecedented tensions and well-nigh fatal crises that the campaign may be regarded as one of the most exciting of the war. On the German side there could no longer be any question of this being one last bid for the palm of final victory. Indeed, thanks to the errors of leadership in the summer and autumn campaigns of 1942, the principal aim – at least to begin with – could only be, in the words of Schlieffen, 'to bring defeat underfoot'. In the face of an enemy whose manifold superiority offered him every chance of victory, the German command had to improvise again and again, and the fighting troops to perform unparalleled feats.

Though its end was marked by neither the fanfares of victory nor the muffled drum-beats which accompanied Sixth Army's death-march,

367

this battle still deserves recording. As a withdrawal operation it must inevitably be devoid of glory. Yet the fact that, far from ending in defeat, it offered the Supreme Command one more chance of achieving at least a military stalemate was possibly something more than an ordinary victory.

STRATEGIC BASIS OF THE WINTER CAMPAIGN

In order to appreciate the significance of this decisive campaign on the southern wing and the magnitude of the dangers it involved, we must briefly consider the operational position at its inception.

In the winter of 1941–2 Russia's military resources had only sufficed to halt the German attack on Moscow, and with it the German campaign as a whole. Then, in the summer of 1942, the tide had surged eastwards again, finally to ebb on the Volga and in the Caucasus.

But now – in the winter of 1942–3 – the enemy at last felt strong enough to wrest the initiative from us. The question henceforth was whether that winter would bring the decisive step towards Germany's defeat in the east. Momentous and distressing though the Stalingrad disaster undoubtedly was, it could not, in terms of World War II, effect such a blow on its own, whereas the annihilation of the German armies' entire southern wing might well have paved the way to an early victory over Germany. There were two reasons why the Soviet High Command could hope to attain this goal in the south of the Eastern Front. One was the extraordinary numerical superiority of the Russian forces; the second was the favourable position it found itself in operationally as a result of the German errors of leadership associated with the name of Stalingrad. It undoubtedly strove after this goal, even if it did not succeed in reaching it.

Let me first give a short account of the strategic situation at the start of this winter campaign in South Russia.

The *German front* in November 1942 formed a wide arc curving far out to the east in the area of the Caucasus and eastern Ukraine. The right wing of this arc touched the Black Sea at Novorossisk and continued along the front of *Army Group A* (Seventeenth Army and First Panzer Army) through the northern Caucasus without actually linking up with the Caspian Sea in the east.

The deep open flank of this front, which faced southwards, had only 16 Motorized Division to cover it in the direction of the Lower Volga in the east. The division was located in the Kalmyk Steppes east of Yelista.

The continuous front of *Army Group B* only began at a point south of Stalingrad. From Stalingrad it receded to the Don and then ran along the latter as far as Voronezh. In it were Fourth Rumanian Army, Fourth Panzer Army, Sixth Army, Third Rumanian Army, one Italian and one Hungarian army and then Second German Army. The bulk of the German forces had for months past been bunched around Stalingrad, while the rest of the front, in particular the line of the Don, was entrusted mainly to allied armies. There were no reserves worth speaking of behind the fronts of either Army Group A or B.

The enemy, whose armies formed a 'Caucasus Front', a 'South-West Front' and a 'Voronezh Front', had not only superior forces in the line but also powerful reserves behind these army groups and the central or Moscow sector of the Eastern Front, as well as in the hinterland.

In order to grasp the true danger of this situation and the full extent to which it benefited the enemy, one must try to picture one or two distances of strategic significance.

The distance to the Don crossing at *Rostov* from the Don sector in which Third Rumanian Army was over-run on 19th November (i.e. opposite and west of the Russians' Don bridgehead at Kremenskaya), as well as from that occupied by the Italian Army on each side of Kasanskaya, amounted to only a little more than 185 miles. Through Rostov ran the rear communications not only of the whole of Army Group A but also of Fourth Rumanian and Fourth Panzer Army. Yet the left wing of Army Group A was at least 375 miles from Rostov, while Fourth Panzer Army, in its location south of Stalingrad, was some 250 miles away.

Further back the lines of communication of the German armies' southern wing led across the *Dnieper crossings* of Zaporozhye and Dnepropetrovsk. The connexion through the Crimea and across the Straits of Kerch was not a very efficient one. These vital Dnieper crossings in the rear of the German southern wing lay some 440 miles from Stalingrad and more than 560 miles from the left wing of the Caucasus front. On the other hand, they were only about 260 miles from the enemy front on the Don, measuring either from Kasanskaya to Zaporozhye or from Svoboda to Dnepropetrovsk!

What this situation could mean in practice I knew only too well from personal experience, having in summer 1941 covered the odd 190 miles from Tilsit to Dvinsk in four days with 56 Panzer Corps. I had done so, moreover, against opposition that was certainly tougher than anything the Italian and Hungarian Armies could offer on the Don. At that time the Russians had also had very many more reserves behind their front than were available to us in the winter of 1942.

Added to this strategic advantage was the Russians' immense preponderance of numbers. The ratio of forces at the beginning of Don Army Group's struggle has already been shown in the chapter on Stalingrad. How it developed in the course of the winter may be gathered from two figures. In March 1943 the number of divisions at the disposal of Southern (formerly Don) Army Group on the 435-mile front from the Sea of Azov to north of Kharkov was thirty-two. Facing this sector, either in or behind the line, were 341 enemy formations, consisting of rifle divisions, armoured or mechanized brigades, and cavalry divisions.

Thus the conditions under which Don Army Group had to fight were constantly governed by two factors:

First, an *overwhelming superiority* of numbers. Even when the Army Group, augmented by the bulk of First Panzer Army and new forces supplied by O.K.H., consisted of three, and later four, *German* armies, the ratio of German to enemy forces was still 1 : 7. (This allows for the numerical inferiority of certain Russian formations when compared to German divisions.)

Secondly, there was a *strategic danger* inherent in the fact that an enemy who was stronger than ourselves, and who for a time enjoyed complete freedom of action following the collapse of the allied armies, had *shorter distances to travel to the life-lines* of the German southern wing – Rostov and the Dnieper crossings – than we had.

Taken in conjunction with one another, these two factors implied a danger that the southern wing, once cut off from its supplies, would be pushed back against the coast of the Sea of Azov or Black Sea and ultimately destroyed, as the Soviet Black Sea Fleet was just as capable as ever of imposing a blockade. After the destruction of Don Army Group and Army Group A, however, the fate of the entire Eastern Front would have been sealed sooner or later.

KEYNOTES OF OPERATIONAL POLICY

By virtue of the initial strategic situation outlined above, the whole battle on the southern wing in the winter of 1942–3 – and it was destined to be *the* battle in the east that winter – boiled down to the same question on both sides. Would the *Soviets* succeed in trapping the German southern wing, thereby accomplishing the decisive step towards their final victory, or would the *German* command be able to avert such a catastrophe?

The operational plan for the *Russians* to adopt was obvious enough. It had been offered them on a silver platter when the German Supreme Command allowed the front to petrify in the final phase of the summer offensive. Nothing was more natural than that the Soviets should first seize their chance to trap Sixth Army as it lay bunched around Stalingrad.

In the further course of operations, the enemy was to be expected to cash in on his knock-out successes in the Rumanian, Italian and Hungarian sectors and to try, by striking again and again in ever-increasing strength and scope, to outflank the German southern wing to the north and west. His object had to be to amputate this wing from its communications zones and ultimately to box it in on the sea-coast. It was a strategic concept which derived every possible encouragement from the situation in which the German southern wing had been left for far too long by the Supreme Command.

On the *German side* there was the much harder problem of deciding how to escape from the danger in which we had been landed by our own omissions and the enemy's first unexpected successes on both sides of Stalingrad. In view of the overall strategic situation, however, our Supreme Command should have realized from the first day of the enemy attack how things would develop and, in particular, how dangerously exposed was Army Group A in the Caucasus.

Broadly speaking, the *German Supreme Command* had to choose between two courses. The first would have been to disengage Sixth Army from the Volga immediately after it had begun to be attacked and before it could be tightly surrounded, and then to try to restore the situation in the *large bend of the Don* with the help of strong reinforcements. At the same time it would have been necessary to shore up the allied-occupied Don sectors with German forces. Obviously, however, the Supreme Command neither had the necessary troops available for this solution nor could it, in view of the low capacity of the few existing railways, have brought them up in time. To take Sixth Army away from Stalingrad was something it could not make up its mind to do. Indeed, not many weeks after the start of the Soviet offensive it was clear that the army was to be lost for good and that the best it could do within the framework of the operation as a whole was to tie down the largest possible body of forces for the longest possible period. It was a task which the gallant army fulfilled till the end and for which it ultimately sacrificed itself.

Nevertheless, even after events had taken such an ominous turn as a result of the obstinate way in which Hitler clung to Stalingrad, and after all hope of extricating Sixth Army had proved illusory, there was still a second course open to the Supreme Command. At the cost of surrendering the territory won in the summer campaign (which could not be held anyway), *a grave crisis could have been turned into victory!* To this end it would have been necessary to withdraw the forces of Don Army Group and Army Group A from the front's eastward protuberance according to fixed timings, taking them first behind the Lower Don or Donetz and subsequently to the Lower Dnieper.

In the meantime, any forces that could possibly be made available – including those divisions of either army group which became disengaged through the shortening of the front – would have had to be concentrated, let us say, somewhere around Kharkov. On them would have devolved the task of driving into the flank of the enemy as he pursued the retiring army groups or attempted to cut them off from the Dnieper crossings. In other words, the idea would have been to convert a large-scale withdrawal into an envelopment operation with the aim of pushing our pursuer back against the sea and destroying him there.

Don Army Group proposed this solution to O.K.H. when there was no longer any prospect of relieving Sixth Army and as soon as it became plain that Army Group A's position in the Caucasus was untenable and that the enemy breakthrough on the Italian front threatened to cut off the entire southern wing.

But Hitler was not the man to embark on a course which initially committed him to relinquish the conquests of summer 1942 and would unquestionably have entailed considerable operational hazards. Such a step was entirely out of keeping with the personality I have already analysed in the chapter on Hitler as a Supreme Commander. With his lack of experience in operational matters, he may even then have hoped to restore the situation on the southern wing by throwing in the SS Panzer Corps which was moving up to Kharkov.

As far as Don Army Group Headquarters was concerned, the first of the above-mentioned courses had already been ruled out before it arrived on the scene, for by that time Sixth Army had been completely surrounded. Neither the battered remnants handed over to us as 'Don Army Group', nor the thin trickle of reinforcements we were getting, could possibly suffice to fight a battle in the large bend of the Don with any prospect of success – even less so after the reinforcements had been held up in Army Group B's sector following the defeat of the Italian Army. As for the second course, that of turning a large-scale withdrawal operation into a counterblow against the enemy's northern flank as he inevitably exposed this in the course of his pursuit, Don Army Group lacked the absolute authority to take it. To do so we should have required power of command over the whole southern wing of the Eastern Front and freedom to do what we liked with the O.K.H. reserves.

Instead, the Army Group was committed to deal in turn with the tasks which presented themselves in its allotted sphere of command. It had to devise one stop-gap after another to meet a danger which arose from the original strategic situation and grew increasingly acute as time went on: *the danger that the entire southern wing would be tied off.*

The *first task* confronting the Army Group was the relief of Sixth Army. Initially this had to take precedence over all other operational considerations.

Once this task had proved insoluble for the reasons already related in the chapter on Stalingrad, the Army Group had to tackle the problem of preventing the even greater catastrophe of the loss of the whole southern wing. As the forces still available as reserves to O.K.H. were not enough to keep the southern wing's lines of communication over the Lower Don and Dnieper open, the only course left to us was to gather in the eastern wing of the Army Group and throw the forces thus released over to the western wing. Everything depended, then, on our always thinking far enough ahead to switch forces from our eastern to our western wing in time to intercept the enemy's outflanking movements as they gradually extended further and further west. It was a task rendered all the more difficult by the fact that the neighbouring formation in the north, Army Group B, was slowly but surely disappearing from sight as a result of the loss of the allied armies. On the other hand, it was not possible to shift forces to the western wing in sufficient numbers without calling on forces from Army Group A, which was not under Don Army Group's orders.

Though conceived on a larger scale and extending over a longer period, it was the same task that had confronted General Paulus at Stalingrad between 19th and 23rd November. This time, too, it was a matter of moving forces promptly and regardless of local repercussions to *the* places on which the survival of our rear communications depended and simultaneously of maintaining our operational mobility. The only difference was that in General Paulus's case the decision had been compressed into a few days, or perhaps even hours, and that he could count on no reinforcements whatever to begin with. In our own case, however, this idea was to govern our whole approach to operations and involve us in months of conflict with the Supreme Command.

In essence, the idea of leap-frogging from east to west to parry the enemy's attempts to 'tie off' the southern wing was an extremely simple one. In war, however, it is so often the simple things which prove hardest to carry out, the real difficulties lying not so much in the taking of a decision as in its unswerving execution. In the present instance any withdrawal of forces from the eastern wing was bound to create a danger there which no one could be sure of surviving. Above all, if these shifts of forces were to have a timely effect, they must be initiated some time – if not several weeks – before the danger of being cut off had become so acute as to be acknowledged by Hitler. Last but not least, developments in Army Group A's sector, as will be seen later, long prevented us from putting the 'leap-frog' plan into practice.

And so, simple and self-evident though it was, this basic approach of ours proved difficult to implement consistently in the face of the increasing gravity of the situation. The same difficulty was experienced in getting it accepted by the Supreme Command – at least in time for it to have any useful effect – since the latter's views were diametrically opposed to our own. Hitler persisted in the principle of holding rigidly on to his gains, whereas we considered operational mobility – at which our operations staffs and fighting troops had the advantage of the enemy – to be the real key to victory.

The situation which confronted it at the time of its take-over, combined with the restrictions imposed on it by the Supreme Command and its far-reaching dependence on the actions and attitudes of the neighbouring army groups, led Don Army Group to adopt a 'system of stop-gaps' without, at the same time, ever sacrificing the basic formula.

In the light of the foregoing, Don (later Southern) Army Group's winter campaign of 1942–3 may be broken down into four successive phases:

The *first* was the struggle for the *relief of Sixth Army*, on which the Army Group staked everything it could possibly afford.

The *second phase* was the Army Group's struggle to *keep the rear of Army Group A free* while it was being disengaged from the Caucasus front.

The *third phase* consisted in the actual battle to *keep open the lines of communication* of the German armies' southern wing and to prevent it from being 'tied off'.

This led to the final, *fourth phase* in which the Army Group succeeded – if on a smaller scale than it would have liked – in delivering the *counterblow* culminating in the battle of Kharkov.

FIRST PHASE: THE STRUGGLE TO FREE SIXTH ARMY

The attempt to relieve Sixth Army, or rather to enable it to break out of the Stalingrad pocket, has already been recounted.

In an all-out effort to make this attempt succeed, Don Army Group went to the very limits of what could be risked. Right up to the time when the fate of Sixth Army was sealed, i.e. the end of December 1942, it endeavoured to manage with a minimum of forces in the centre and on the left of the Army Group front, which only amounted to a thin protective screen as it was. Its object was to delay any decisive developments in these sectors until Fourth Panzer Army's battle east of the Don had successfully opened up the beleaguered army's way to freedom.

Only after all hope of linking up Fourth Panzer and Sixth Armies had had to be abandoned, and the simultaneous defeat of the Italian Army had laid bare Don Army Group's western flank and thrown open the enemy's road to Rostov, did the Army Group concede precedence to the problem of maintaining the whole southern wing of the Eastern Front.

All that remains for me to do in this context is to give a brief account of how Don Army Group's situation came to deteriorate as a result, on one hand, of Sixth Army's decision not to attempt the break-out and, on the other, of the way things developed on the right wing of Army Group B (the Italian Army).

The difficult position in which *Fourth Panzer Army* had landed on the eastern wing of the Army Group as the enemy threw in increasingly strong forces from the Stalingrad siege-front to meet it has already been indicated. In the battles between the Aksai and Kotelnikovo, as well as in the fighting for the latter as a spring-board for Fourth Panzer Army's relief offensive, 57 Panzer Corps suffered considerable losses after being left alone on the battlefield by the Rumanians. 23 Panzer Division, which had been severely weakened before this, was particularly badly hit. The non-appearance of reinforcements from Army Group A made it unlikely that Fourth Panzer Army would even hold its own sufficiently to prevent the enemy from swinging strong forces into the rear of First Panzer Army.

The trend of events on the rest of the Army Group front was not a whit less serious. In what had been the sector of *Third Rumanian Army*, the fact that Fourth Panzer Army was falling back east of the Don enabled the enemy to cross the ice-covered river around Potemkinskaya, and a little later at Tsymlyanskaya, and to threaten the Chir positions in the flank and rear. On this front, General Mieth had meanwhile assumed command in place of Third Rumanian Army Headquarters. Since the Russians were coming over the Don from the east and south, we had no choice initially but to order the Mieth Group to make a fighting withdrawal behind the Kagalnik.

On the left wing of the Army Group the position looked even more critical. Admittedly *Army Detachment Hollidt* had succeeded, notwithstanding the loss of the Rumanian divisions, in bringing its forces back southwards from the Upper Chir. Without any justification, however, a newly arrived, recently formed division which was to have taken over the defence of the Army Detachment's flank on the Bystraya Gnilaya gave up the crossing point at Milyutinsky. This opened the enemy's way into Hollidt's flank and also to the important air-base at Morosowsky.

Far more serious still was the fact that, thanks to the disintegration of the Italian Army and the almost complete elimination of the

Rumanians from the battle (1 and 2 Rumanian Corps on what had been the left wing of Army Detachment Hollidt), the enemy was able to make for the Don crossings of Forchstadt, Kamensk and Voroshilovgrad almost unopposed. Only at Millerovo, where the newly formed *Fretter-Pico Group* on the right wing of Army Group B stood like a solitary island amid the red flood, was any resistance being offered. In any case, the enemy was free to wheel east into the rear of Army Detachment Hollidt or the Mieth Group, or alternatively to keep heading south to Rostov.

Don Army Group's situation was serious enough, therefore. Had it been acting quite independently, the only correct way to solve the crisis would have been to put the 'leap-frog' principle into effect forthwith, regardless of any other considerations. *Fourth Panzer Army* could have been pulled back to Rostov in one single movement and thereafter used to fight off the threat to the Army Group's left flank and its communications to the west. The forces of the *Mieth Group* and *Army Detachment Hollidt* still in action in the large bend of the Don would have had to come back to the Donetz.

The objection to this solution lay in the fact that Army Group A was still lodged as firmly as ever in its positions in the Caucasus. To expose its rear by shifting Don Army Group's forces over to the western wing was out of the question. On the contrary, it was Don Army Group's duty not only to cover the rear of Army Group A, but also to keep open its lines of communication through Rostov.

For the time being, then, the idea of basing the Army Group's operations on the principle of switching their main effort westwards to balk the enemy's attempts to cut off the whole wing of the German armies could still not take effect. During the first few weeks after the take-over, indeed, the Army Group had deliberately shelved it in the interest of Sixth Army. Now – in the second phase – it found itself compelled, in spite of the steadily growing threat to its western flank, to embark on a desperate struggle to keep the rear of Army Group A free.

SECOND PHASE: THE FIGHT TO KEEP ARMY GROUP A'S REAR FREE

The German Supreme Command should really have been aware from the start that Army Group A could not stay in the Caucasus if the battle to free Sixth Army did not immediately succeed – in other words, if there were no clear possibility of somehow establishing a reasonably secure situation within the large bend of the Don. But when the enemy tore a gap on the right wing of Army Group B which opened his way to Rostov, it should have been palpably evident to anyone that there could no longer be any question of holding the Caucasus front. Unless, of course, Hitler had been able or willing to bring in large bodies of troops from other theatres.

As early as 20th December, the day when the flight of two Italian divisions had exposed the flank of Army Detachment Hollidt and cleared the Russians' way to the Donetz crossings, I had pointed out to General Zeitzler that by advancing in the direction of Rostov the enemy would now have his chance to strike the decisive blow against the whole of the German southern wing.

On 24th December I had again drawn attention to the fact that it was now no longer the fate of Don Army Group alone that was at stake but of Army Group A as well.

I have already mentioned the rejection of my demand for the release of forces from Army Group A to Rostov and Fourth Panzer Army. Even if one no longer envisaged renewing the attempt to extend a rescuing hand to Sixth Army, it was still in Army Group A's interest that Fourth Panzer Army should be reinforced, since its defeat would have given the enemy access to the Army Group's rear. Since Army Group A – quite understandably – did not want to hand any units over, it was the business of the Supreme Command to *order* the equalization of forces so urgently needed between the two Army Groups. One possible reason for Army Group A's refusal to let us have the divisions we asked for (see the Chapter on Stalingrad) may well have been the quite perplexing degree to which its formations and units had been shuffled around and intermingled with one another. Undoubtedly the disengagement of the larger ones would have been a difficult and at best time-consuming task. This state of affairs was in part the inevitable outcome of a need – in the absence of adequate re-serves – to patch up the gaps caused by enemy penetrations. However, it was also due in equal measure to the Army Group's having for months on end been without a commander of its own to keep things in order. At the best of times, many military commanders are unable to appreciate that units must be left in their normal order of battle if one is to achieve maximum efficiency and preserve manœuvrability. When, as in this case, there was no responsible commander whatever for a considerable period, it was hardly surprising if the troops became disorganized.

In response to the insistence of Don Army Group, Hitler finally decided on 29th December to order the withdrawal of the eastern and most exposed wing of Army Group A, First Panzer Army, to the Kuma sector of Pyatigorsk–Praskoveya. Yet he still had no intention of giving up the Caucasus front as a whole. Evidently he still hoped that by bending back Army Group A's eastern wing to the Kuma he would be able to pivot it upon the Manych flats, thereby stabilizing the situation between the Manych and Don and simultaneously keeping the communications of the southern wing open across the Lower Dnieper. Thus the 'balcony' which had been formed in November by pushing the front out into the Caucasus and up to the Volga and which had led to the unfavourable situation we were in at present was not to be eliminated, but merely reduced in size. Where, on the other hand, the forces were to be found to compensate for the loss of the Rumanian and Italian armies – and before very long the Hungarian one as well – remained a complete mystery. This, in due course, was what caused the remainder of the Caucasus front to be abandoned.

In this second phase of its struggle Don Army Group was confronted with *the following tasks*:

Instead of acting as the situation really demanded and radically shifting the main point of effort to its western wing to remove the danger of being cut off, the Army Group was compelled, in the face of a mounting crisis, to *fight for time*.

South of the Lower Don it had to *protect Army Group A's rear* and at the same time to *keep its communications through Rostov open*. It was a dual commitment with which the weak forces of Fourth Panzer Army were unlikely to cope in view of the wide expanse of territory they had to control between the Caucasus and Don and the strength of the enemy operating there.

In the *large bend of the Don* and *forwards of the Donetz* it was the job of *Army Detachment Hollidt* to retard the enemy's advance north of the Lower Don to such an extent that he could not cut off Fourth Panzer Army, and with it Army Group A, by a swift thrust on Rostov from the east. In addition, it had to prevent the enemy from crossing

the Donetz line Forchstadt–Kamensk–Voroshilovgrad and thereby
deny him access to Rostov from the north.

Finally, the Army Group had to find ways and means of keeping
open the lines of communication running to the Lower Dnieper in the
west, either with its own resources or else with the assistance of what
meagre reserves O.K.H. was able to send us.

All this had to be done with troops who had long been subjected to
overstrain and were faced by an enemy many times stronger than
themselves.

Difficult though this task, or series of tasks, was in itself, the paramount danger lay in Army Group A's inability to disengage swiftly
from the Caucasus. It was just one more example of the hardening-up
process which inevitably sets in whenever mobile operations degenerate into static warfare. If only for the sake of economizing one's forces,
immovable weapons have to be dug in and rations and ammunition
accumulated. Various facilities are installed to ease the lot of the troops
– a particularly important measure when a shortage of reserves prevents them from being taken out to rest. As the horses cannot usually
be fed in a static battle zone, they have to be accommodated further
back, and this in turn tends to immobilize the fighting units. (The
state of the roads during a Russian winter, particularly in mountainous
country, only added to these difficulties.)

The upshot is always that troops and formation staffs lose the knack
of quickly adapting themselves to the changes of situation which daily
occur in a war of movement. Inertia and stagnation gain the upper
hand, for every change involves difficult reliefs, movement of forces,
inconveniences and often danger. The inevitable process of accumulat-
ing weapons, equipment and stores of all kinds ties down assets which
one feels unable to do without for the rest of the war. The result is that
when the command staff in question is faced with the necessity of a
major withdrawal, it begins by asking for a long period of grace in
which to prepare for the evacuation. It may even reject the idea of a
withdrawal out of hand because of the equipment and stores it has come
to regard as indispensable. It will be remembered that when the German
offensive came to a standstill in 1918, even such a notable commander
as Ludendorff could not bring himself, by a boldly conceived withdrawal, to precipitate the war of movement in which Germany's last
hope of victory then lay. In the final analysis he felt unable to write off

all the matériel committed on and behind the German front, or else could not make up his mind to abandon territory which it had cost such sacrifices to win.

The situation on Army Group A's front was a similar one. A talk with the Chief-of-Staff of First Panzer Army revealed that this formation could not begin moving back until 2nd January, but after we had helped out with petrol it was finally able to start on New Year's Day. Even then, Army Group A announced a few days later that First Panzer Army would have to fall back on to the Kuma line sector by sector in the interest of getting equipment out and evacuating the wounded from the mountain resorts in the Caucasus. For these purposes, it was stated, the army would require 155 trains (twenty per division) and would not (on account of the low rail capacities) be in position along the Kuma line for another twenty-five days. So although it should have been realized since the end of November that at least the rear of Army Group A would be endangered sooner or later, it was obvious that nothing had been done to prepare for an evacuation. One reason for the omission was undoubtedly that Hitler had forbidden such preparations or was expected to do so if he learnt of them. But an equally important one, I am sure, was the Army Group's lack of a responsible commander in recent months.

O.K.H. had been considering the idea of placing Army Group A, which had now been taken over by Colonel-General v. Kleist, under my command. Generally speaking, it is not a good thing to put an army group or army under a headquarters of equal status. In the present critical situation, however, this would probably have had its advantages – provided, of course, that no strings were attached. Any possibility of interference by Hitler or of Army Group A's invoking his decisions in opposition to my own had to be expressly barred. Hitler, however, was unwilling to accept my conditions, and Army Group A consequently remained autonomous. All that Don Army Group could do was to keep on pressing for a speed-up of Army Group A's evacuation measures with a view to effecting the earliest possible release of the forces whose intervention south of the Don and later on the western wing of Don Army Group would be of decisive importance. Everything depended on cutting down this second phase of the winter campaign to the utmost in order to get the position on the German southern wing finally stabilized. The only hope of doing so lay in smashing the enemy forces which were trying to envelop that wing to the west. In the event, it did prove possible to get the *deadlines for the Caucasus evacuation* considerably curtailed.

The hindrances mentioned above were due partly to what appeared to be the inevitable outcome of static warfare conditions and the difficulties encountered in a mountainous theatre, and partly to the Supreme Command's aversion to surrendering anything voluntarily. The fact that they committed Don Army Group to a battle in the Don area lasting from the end of December to early February was bound – in view of what was happening to Army Group B – to intensify the danger that the whole southern wing would be cut off.

It would hardly be possible to find a better illustration of Moltke's definition of strategy than in this battle fought by the two armies of Don Army Group. The reason why we succeeded, despite a series of crises, in mastering the tasks already outlined is that the army and army group staffs adhered firmly to two well-established German principles of leadership:

(i) Always conduct operations elastically and resourcefully;
(ii) Give every possible scope to the initiative and self-sufficiency of commanders at all levels.

Both principles, admittedly, were greatly at variance with Hitler's own way of thinking. While the first will find expression in the account of the battle fought by our two armies, I should like to say a few words on the second one now.

It has always been the particular forte of German leadership to grant wide scope to the self-dependence of subordinate commanders – to allot them *tasks* which leave the method of execution to the discretion of the individual. From time immemorial – certainly since the elder Moltke's day – this principle has distinguished Germany's military leadership from that of other armies. The latter, far from giving the same latitude to subordinate commanders on the tactical plane, have always tended to prescribe, by means of long and detailed directives, the way orders should actually be carried out or to make tactical action conform to a specific pattern. On the German side this system was considered a bad one. It would, admittedly, appear to reduce the risk of failure in the case of a mediocre commander. Yet it only too easily leads to the executant's having to act against the exigencies of the local situation. Worst of all, in its preoccupation with security it waives the opportunity that may occur through the independent action of a subordinate commander in boldly exploiting some favourable situation at a decisive moment. The German method is really rooted in the German character, which – contrary to all the nonsense talked about 'blind obedience' – has a strong streak of individuality and – possibly as part of its Germanic heritage – finds a certain pleasure in taking risks. The granting of such independence to subordinate commanders does, of course, presuppose that all members of the military hierarchy are imbued with certain tactical or operational axioms. Only the school of the German General Staff can, I suppose, be said to have produced such a consistency of outlook. Nevertheless, there are plenty of occasions when the senior commander in the field is faced with the problem of whether or not to take a hand in the operations of the armies or other formations under his command. The more complex the situation and the smaller the forces with which he has to manage, the more often is he tempted to meddle in the business of his subordinates.

As far as my own Headquarters was concerned, I think I can say that we only intervened in the operations of our armies when it was quite imperative to do so. This was particularly true whenever the Army Group's operational intentions involved the assumption of responsibilities which it would have been unreasonable to expect the army headquarters in question to accept. On the other hand, we refrained on principle from proffering off-the-record 'advice', which kills all initiative and hides responsibility.

That Hitler showed little understanding for the old-established German principle of leadership and repeatedly sought to meddle in the operations of subordinate headquarters by issuing specific orders of his own has already been mentioned earlier on. Nothing could be done about such orders when they related to the movements of adjacent army groups or the action to be taken with formations which were still O.K.H. reserves. However, in the many cases when they directed that a particular line was to be held to the last man and the last round, the force of circumstances usually proved stronger in the end.

Something which has also been discussed already and was even harder to overcome was Hitler's dilatoriness in the taking of urgently needed decisions. We could not, after all, compel him to give an order.

In such cases one had no choice but to report that in default of an O.K.H. directive by such-and-such a time or such-and-such a day, we should act at our own discretion.

In contrast to the above, I doubt very much whether any of the armies under our command during this or any later campaign ever had reason to complain that we were slow to take decisions. Whenever they put an inquiry or recommendation up to my headquarters, they always received an immediate reply. Only in difficult situations did the Army Group ever delay a decision for a very limited period – at most for a few hours or until the following morning.

On the whole – apart from Stalingrad – the Army Group always managed in the end to get the requisite action taken in the face of Hitler's interference or procrastination.

FOURTH PANZER ARMY'S BATTLES SOUTH OF THE LOWER DON

Fourth Panzer Army had two different tasks to fulfil if it was to keep the rear of Army Group A free.

It had to prevent the enemy now on its heels from moving in against the rear of First Panzer Army until such time as the latter had wheeled back from the Caucasus on to a front facing east.

At the same time, it had to ensure that the enemy did not thrust down the lower reaches of the Don to Rostov and cut off both Fourth Panzer Army and Army Group A from their communications zones.

It was clear that the army had not enough forces to deny the enemy the whole area between the lower course of the Don and the northern spurs of the Caucasus. Since the loss of the Rumanians all it had up around Kotelnikovo was 57 Panzer Corps, consisting only of two seriously weakened divisions (17 and 23 Panzer). 15 Luftwaffe Field Division was still not ready to go into action, and 16 Motorized Division had still not been relieved at Yelista by forces from Army Group A.

All Don Army Group's efforts to get the army reinforced in good time were unavailing. The provision of 3 Panzer Corps by Army Group A had already been turned down by O.K.H., and now 7 Panzer Division, which Don Army Group had intended to use with Fourth Panzer Army, was retained by Hitler at Rostov to cover this crossing-point to the north following the collapse of the Italian Army. In essence this was not a bad idea, except that the infantry division we had requested from Army Group A (i.e. from Seventeenth Army) would have done just as well. But this, as I have said, Hitler had refused to let us have because he feared that its withdrawal from the Novorossisk sector would cause the Rumanian divisions there to give way.

An acute threat materialized in the rear of First Panzer Army when strong elements of the enemy which had been following Fourth Panzer Army turned south against First Panzer Army just as it was swinging backwards. Although 16 Motorized Division was able to launch a successful attack and bar the way to the enemy from behind the Manych, it was delayed still further from taking part in the struggle of Fourth Panzer Army, which it now did not join until the middle of January.

A measure which the Army Group had intended taking in its own area to reinforce Fourth Panzer Army was thwarted by the enemy. We had envisaged bringing 11 Panzer Division out of the large bend of the Don to join the army. Just when it was about to come over the Lower Don, however, the enemy himself crossed the river at two different places to drive from the south and south-east into the rear of the Mieth Group, which was still holding the Lower Chir on a front facing north. To parry this thrust and to enable the Mieth Group to swing back into a front facing east behind the Kagalnik, 11 Panzer Division had to be committed north of the Don and was lost to Fourth Panzer Army in consequence.

In the end, therefore, the only forces to augment the two above-named armoured divisions of 57 Panzer Corps were the Viking SS Division, which had already been released earlier by Army Group A, and – in mid-January – 16 Motorized Division.

By this time Fourth Panzer Army was under pressure through Kotelnikovo from two Soviet armies, Second Guards and Fifty-First, which between them comprised one tank, three mechanized, three rifle and one cavalry corps. Shortly afterwards a third army (Twenty-Eighth) made its appearance further south from the Kalmyk Steppes.

It could safely be assumed that these three armies were bent not merely on tying down Fourth Panzer Army from the front, but ultimately on by-passing it to the north and south in order to encircle it completely.

If Hitler thought he could order us, in the face of that preponderance of forces and with such an expanse of territory to cover, to make the army hold some 'line' or other, or else to obtain his approval before undertaking any withdrawal, he was seriously mistaken. As an obstacle, a hard-and-fast line was likely to prove about as effective as a cobweb in Fourth Panzer Army's situation. Nonetheless, he still made repeated attempts to restrict our operational freedom by orders of this kind and stuck to his refusal to reinforce Fourth Panzer Army. By 5th January, therefore, I felt I must ask to be relieved of command of Don Army Group and sent the Chief of the General Staff a teleprinter message which stated *inter alia*:

'Should these proposals not be approved and this headquarters continue to be tied down to the same extent as hitherto, I cannot see that any useful purpose will be served by my continuing as commander of Don Army Group. In the circumstances it would appear more appropriate to replace me by a "sub-directorate" of the kind maintained by the Quartermaster-General.'

(The Quartermaster-General's 'sub-directorates' at army groups were headed by older staff officers who ran their formations' supply and transport services in accordance with direct instructions from the central directorate.)

As things now stood, Fourth Panzer Army's object was not to offer inadequate resistance along an over-extended line, but to keep its forces close together. Only thus could it offer *strong* opposition at vital spots or deal the enemy a surprise blow whenever an opportunity presented itself. At times it would obviously have to denude parts of its area completely and be content to cover others with only a flimsy defence screen.

Colonel-General Hoth, supported by his admirable Chief-of-Staff, General Fangohr, went about this difficult task with a calm resolution matched only by the versatility of his leadership. He skilfully retarded the progress of the enemy pressing hard on his front without exposing himself to danger by holding any one position too long. Furthermore, by rapidly assembling forces on both his wings, he repeatedly dealt the enemy sharp jabs which foiled every attempt to outflank him.

Though unable to let the army have sufficient forces to discharge its difficult task, the Army Group did reserve the right to relieve it of responsibility for at least its most intricate problem by the issue of specific orders. As I have said, Fourth Panzer Army actually had to deal with two tasks at once. It had to prevent any of the three enemy armies following it from taking First Panzer Army in the rear before the latter had completed its swing back from the Caucasus on to a front facing east and was ready to look after its own defence. At the same time it had to counter any attempt by the enemy to drive on Rostov along the lower arm of the Don. If this were successful, the three armies fighting south of the Lower Don would be cut off.

Fourth Panzer Army was only capable of solving *one* of these tasks at most. Which of them should have priority was a matter that only the Army Group could decide. Admittedly the threat to Rostov was the greater danger in the long run. Yet should the enemy succeed in encircling First Panzer Army as it wheeled back into its new position, there could be no further point even in holding Rostov, and the three German armies south of the Don would be doomed. If, on the other hand, the withdrawal of First Panzer Army were successfully accomplished, ways and means would be found to avert a crisis at Rostov.

The enemy did try to exploit the two opportunities indicated above. It has already been mentioned that 16 Motorized Division had just been in time to intercept the Soviet elements which had turned off to take First Panzer Army in the rear. Yet, with the same operational aim in view, the enemy made repeated attempts to envelop Fourth Panzer Army to the south and thereby to introduce himself between the latter and First Panzer Army. At the same time he endeavoured to drive along the Lower Don through Konstantinovka in the direction of Rostov. On 7th January a smallish enemy force turned up on the northern bank of the Don some 12 miles from the Army Group Headquarters' location at Novocherkask, after the Cossacks and frontier troops guarding that stretch of river had given way. We had to dislodge this domestic invader with a few tanks fetched out of workshops for the purpose. Subsequently the tank corps of which this enemy force formed part was turned off towards Proletarskaya in the rear of Fourth Panzer Army, which meant that we were rid of the threat to Rostov for at least the next few days. Fourth Panzer Army, for its own part, was duly able to cope with this threat on its northern flank.

By 14th January First Panzer Army had completed its withdrawal movement, having been able to speed it up after all in the meantime. It now had its left wing established on a line running from Cherkask to Petrovskoye. This meant that at least a measure of operational co-operation was now possible between First and Fourth Panzer Armies, even if a wide gap still yawned between Petrovskoye and Proletar-skaya. (This, admittedly, was partly covered by the mud-flats of the Manych.)

The first part of *Fourth Panzer Army's* task, which had been to keep the rear of Army Group A free in the area south of the Don, was thus fulfilled. There still remained the second part – that of holding open this Army Group's lines of communication through Rostov.

In the face of the enemy's many times greater strength, the accom-plishment of the second part was complicated by the fact that First Panzer Army was initially to remain several days in the line it had reached in order to prepare the further evacuation of its rear areas. Indeed, Fourth Panzer Army's task was to come dangerously near to not being fulfilled at all, for even now Hitler could still not make up his mind to abandon the Caucasus entirely. The question of whether First Panzer Army was to be pulled back on to the northern bank of the Don or whether the whole of Army Group A should remain in the Kuban still hung in the balance.

THE BATTLES OF ARMY DETACHMENT HOLLIDT

While Fourth Panzer Army was carrying out its task south of the Don during the first half of January, *Army Detachment Hollidt* had a no less difficult job to do in the large bend of river. As was stated in the chapter on Stalingrad, the enemy had spent the past few weeks making repeated attacks in infinitely superior strength on the Army Detach-ment's front along the Chir.

At General Hollidt's disposal, on a front extending some 125 miles from the Don at Nizhne Chirskaya as far as Kamensk-Shakhtinsky, were – and this included the Mieth Group, now under command – four infantry divisions (62, 294, 336 and 387) which had already been very badly worn down in the fighting to date. Also helping to hold the front were some 'alarm units' and – a valuable buttress, these – anti-aircraft units commanded by the seasoned General Stahel. As for the Army Detachment's two Luftwaffe field divisions, what little was left of them inevitably had to be incorporated into army formations. The main strength of the Army Detachment was constituted by 6 and 11 Panzer Divisions, augmented by the newly arrived 7 Panzer. The badly battered 22 Panzer Division had to be disbanded.

With these forces General Hollidt had to prevent the enemy in the north from moving down on the lower reaches of the Don (i.e. into the rear of Fourth Panzer Army) and – most important of all – from breaking through to Rostov for as long as Fourth Panzer Army and Army Group A were in the area south of the Don. Furthermore, it was the Army Detachment's job to see that the enemy opposite its left wing did not push through to the Donetz crossings between Forchstadt and Voroshilovgrad, thereby opening the way to Rostov from the north-west. At the same time, however, the Army Detachment found itself threatened on both flanks – in the west as a result of the disappearance from the battlefield of the Italians (in whose place the Fretter–Pico Group was slowly fighting its way back from the Millerovo region towards the Donetz), and in the east because several enemy army corps now had crossed the Don, first at Potemkinskaya and then at Tsymlyanskaya. They could only be stopped, as was noted earlier, by throwing in 11 Panzer Division and bending the Mieth Group back on to a front facing east from behind the Kagalnik.

Like Fourth Panzer Army, Army Detachment Hollidt reflected firm yet versatile leadership in mastering its task amid heavy fighting and incessant crises. Here, too, however, the Army Group assumed ultimate responsibility by ordering it, at great – if not immediate – risk to the spots thus laid bare, to bunch its armour together for short offensive thrusts.

The fact that the Army Detachment succeeded in finally halting the enemy on the Donetz, and thereby in saving Fourth Panzer Army and Army Group A from being cut off south of the Don, must be ascribed first and foremost – while not forgetting the way its staff handled operations – to the bravery with which the infantry divisions and all other formations and units helping to hold the line stood their ground against the enemy's recurrent attacks. Yet their defence could never have been maintained had not our armoured divisions time and again shown up at danger spots at just the right moment. On one hand they intervened to ward off the impending encirclement of the Army Detachment's right wing as it wheeled back on to the Kagalnik and later to intercept a threatened breakthrough in that sector. On the other, they surprised the enemy by driving straight into his assembly positions as he was about to attack the Army Detachment's northern front forward of the Donetz. While it was the business of the Army Detachment itself to mount such close counterblows as part of its defensive role, the actual responsibility for risking them usually lay with the Army Group. The latter had to relieve the Army Detachment of responsibility for any emergencies which might arise whenever, on Army Group instructions, it concentrated its armour in one spot and thereby imperilled the remaining sectors of the front.

THIRD PHASE: THE STRUGGLE TO KEEP THE SOUTHERN WING'S COMMUNICATIONS OPEN

OPERATIONAL POSITION AT MID-JANUARY 1943

By the middle of January 1943 the operational situation on the southern wing of the Eastern Front had come to a head. Its seeds had been laid in the late autumn of 1942, when our military command had allowed the front to solidify into a line which was operationally untenable from a long-term point of view. What had clearly been shaping up since Christmas Week 1942, when the last opportunity for Sixth Army to break out was missed, had now come to pass. Only the desperate struggle waged by the German fighting troops and command staffs had so far staved off an even worse crisis.

Sixth Army was doomed. The best it could do now, with what little strength it still possessed, was to render its comrades in the Don bend and the Caucasus the last supreme service of tying down strong enemy forces for just a short while longer.

It was clear that after the loss of Sixth Army the *Caucasus region* could not even be held on a reduced scale.

Now, however, thanks to the doggedness and dexterity with which *Fourth Panzer Army* had been fighting in the area south of the Don, there was at least a chance that when the Caucasus went, *Army Group A* need not be lost with it. Its eastern wing, which had been in the greatest danger of all, was now safely retracted. And even though *First Panzer Army* was still 190 miles from the river-crossing at Rostov, it was nonetheless out of the mountains and no longer threatened from the rear. If things came to the worst, it could fight its own way back from now on.

In the *area between the Don and Donetz* it had so far been possible

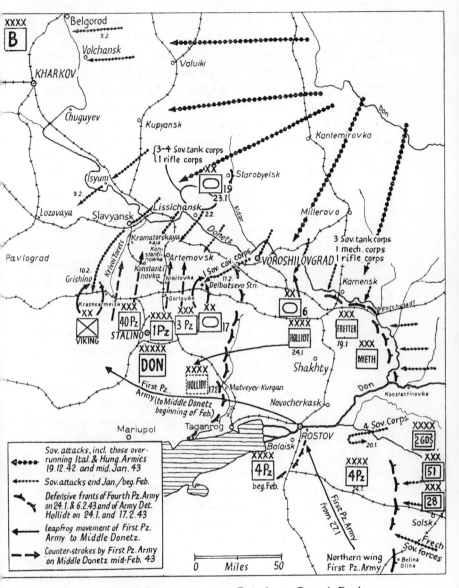

Map 17. Winter Campaign 1942–3: Don Army Group's Battles to keep Communications Zone free.

to deny the enemy access to Rostov and prevent him from closing the trap from the north behind the three armies standing south of the lower arm of the Don.

But it was evident that neither *Army Detachment Hollidt* nor the *Fretter-Pico Group* (now fighting around Millerovo and consisting of H.Q. 30 Corps with 3 Mountain and 304 Infantry Divisions under command) could prevent the enemy from crossing the Donetz upstream from Kamensk-Shakhtinsky once he was strong enough to reach so far round to the west. From then on he would be at liberty to drive on Rostov from the north-west or straight down to the Sea of Azov.

Worst of all, about this time the *Army Group B* sector held by the *Hungarian Army* on the Middle Don collapsed before a fresh enemy offensive. The connecting front in the north was also caught up in the disaster. Army Group B wanted to take its forces back behind the Aidar as far up as Starobyelsk, which meant leaving open the Donetz downstream from Voroshilovgrad. For all practical purposes, however, this wing of the Army Group was to cease to exist within a few days. A wide gap opened up from Voroshilovgrad to the north in which only isolated German battle groups of Army Group B were offering desperate local resistance. The Hungarians – like the Italians – had disappeared from the battlefield.

It seemed certain that O.K.H. could not hope to plug this hole with the reserves now on the way.

In any case, as far as *Don Army Group* was concerned, the time had obviously come to 'leap-frog' strong forces from the area south of the Don to the Middle Donetz if the enemy were to be prevented from tying off Don Army Group and Army Group A.

The *German Supreme Command* still did not agree, however. Either it was unable to foresee what turn events would inevitably take if nothing effective were done to make us strong in the *crucial area* between the Donetz and Lower Dnieper, or it simply *would not* see the dangers of the situation.

Hitler was still not disposed to give up the Caucasus region. He still thought he could somehow maintain a front south of the Don which would at least safeguard his possession of the Maikop oilfields. His minimum requirement was the retention of an extensive bridgehead in the Kuban from which he proposed at a later date to renew his grab for the Caucasus oil.

And so, in the weeks that followed, our Army Group was compelled to continue its desperate struggle on both sides of the Don in the interest of a systematic withdrawal of Army Group A. All this time it was having a fierce dispute with the Supreme Command over the idea of 'leap-frogging' forces to the Donetz area. This concerned not only the acceptability of the principle as such but also the question as to how many of Army Group A's forces should be brought back through Rostov to the decisive battleground. To tie up substantial elements of Army Group A in a Kuban bridgehead amounted, in our opinion, to sheer wishful thinking from the point of view of operations as a whole.

THE BATTLES IN THE SECOND HALF OF JANUARY

By 14th January, the day on which First Panzer Army reached the line Cherkask–Petrovskoye and established a front facing eastwards, another crisis was brewing in the area of *Army Detachment Hollidt*.

On that day an enemy tank corps succeeded in breaking through towards the Donetz on the right wing of Army Group B, in the area of the *Fretter–Pico Group* south of Millerovo. Although O.K.H. provided the group with a new infantry division (302), this alone could not possibly suffice to stabilize the situation on the river.

When, on 16th January, O.K.H. placed the Fretter-Pico Group under command of Don Army Group (while simultaneously extending the latter's front to the Aidar), it was still not even certain whether the group would get back behind the Donetz at all. It had meanwhile emerged that the enemy intended to throw three or four mechanized corps against the Donetz on either side of Kamensk-Shakhtinsky in the Fretter-Pico Group's own area.

Fortunately, thanks to a neat success scored a few days previously by Army Detachment Hollidt when two of its armoured divisions had struck a surprise blow on the Kalitva, an enemy attack had been wiped out there while still in the preparation stage.

We therefore ordered the Army Detachment to execute its planned withdrawal into the Donetz positions in such a way as to have an armoured division available at the earliest possible moment for mobile defence of the Donetz sector of Forchstadt-Kamensk. For operations in the newly acquired Kamensk–Voroshilovgrad sector of the river, however, there was nothing to hand – except for the Italians who had streamed back there as stragglers. In other words, there was a danger that Don Army Group's Donetz front would shortly be outflanked to the west.

At the same time, it became evident that the enemy intended to envelop Army Detachment Hollidt from the east as well. In the gap between its right wing, where the Donetz joined the Don, and *Fourth Panzer Army*, which was still having to cover First Panzer Army's northern flank against a far superior enemy forward of Salsk on the Manych, two enemy corps were identified in the angle between the Sal, Don and Manych. These could be expected to attempt to cross the Don for an advance on Rostov or else to thrust into the rear of Army Detachment Hollidt's Donetz positions.

Don Army Group accordingly proposed that it now be allowed to shift Fourth Panzer Army over to its western wing (while leaving one division temporarily forward of Rostov to keep the crossing open for First Panzer Army). This would naturally have necessitated O.K.H.'s issuing simultaneous orders for the withdrawal of Army Group A – with First Panzer Army moving back on Rostov and Seventeenth Army into the Kuban.

Once again it was impossible to get a quick decision from Hitler. Neither would he countenance the Army Group's proposal that Army Group A's armoured divisions be concentrated in the area of Fourth Panzer Army for a short offensive stroke to facilitate First Panzer Army's withdrawal and thereby to speed up the release of Fourth Panzer Army.

Not until 18th January did O.K.H. finally concede Fourth Panzer Army *freedom of movement* to the extent that the latter no longer had to cover the northern flank of First Panzer Army on the Manych north-eastwards of Salsk. On the other hand, Don Army Group still had to safeguard Army Group A's use of the Rostov–Tikhorets railway line until eighty-eight supply trains had passed safely through to stock up the Kuban bridgehead. Whether First Panzer Army would now be withdrawn towards Rostov or into the Kuban was still anybody's guess.

The time being taken to decide whether to allow forces to be 'leapfrogged' westwards inside the German southern wing could only benefit the enemy, of course. It enabled him to exploit the collapse of the Italian and Hungarian sectors of Army Group B's front and to assemble powerful forces with which to advance over the Middle

Donetz towards the coast of the Sea of Azov or the Dnieper crossings – forces to which, for the moment, we had nothing to offer in the way of opposition. The enemy was also given opportunity to concentrate his formations for a direct assault on Rostov and to envelop Army Detachment Hollidt's western wing through Voroshilovgrad.

On 20th January the enemy in the area of *Fourth Panzer Army* launched an attack over the Lower Manych towards Rostov with four corps he had concentrated for this purpose. His tanks reached the Rostov airfield. Though 16 Panzer Division, which Fourth Panzer Army had thrown over to this northern wing, had been delaying the enemy's progress between the Don and Manych by repeated thrusts into his flank from the southern bank of the latter, it had naturally been unable to halt all four corps on its own.

By simultaneously attacking the army's 57 Panzer Corps, which was now gradually falling back on Rostov from the Middle Manych, the enemy endeavoured to detain Fourth Panzer Army's main forces forward of Rostov until he had possession of the Rostov crossing in their rear.

Furthermore, the enemy was hitting hard at the front of *Army Detachment Hollidt*. Here, too, he obviously aimed to pin down our forces until he had encircled them by the capture of Rostov and an envelopment movement across the Middle Donetz. By launching these attacks against General Mieth's Corps in the angle between the Don and Donetz as well as on either side of Kamensk, he was presumably also trying to prevent the release of any forces from this front which could be thrown against him on the Middle Donetz.

Once again the Army Group's problem was which threat to tackle first. Two armoured divisions (7 and 11 Panzer) were standing by in Army Detachment Hollidt's area to be switched to the western wing on the middle Donetz. But however great the danger there might become in the long run, the Army Group felt it was even more urgent at this moment to avert the threat to Rostov. Everything possible had to be done to get not only Fourth but at least the whole of First Panzer Army back through the city. Otherwise there would not be the slightest prospect of ever assembling sufficient forces on the Army Group's western wing to counteract the danger of the entire southern wing's being surrounded on the sea-coasts.

For this reason Don Army Group resolved that, in order to prevent the capture of Rostov, the two above-named armoured divisions should in the first instance be used to deliver a sharp blow at the enemy attacking over the lower Manych in the direction of the city. However, because of petrol shortage (all the supply trains at that time were going to the Kuban bridgehead by way of Rostov!) and the impossibility of obtaining air support for our attack under the prevailing weather conditions, this counterblow took longer to effect than was admissible in the existing situation. For time was pressing more and more. Since Sixth Army's resistance was now coming to an end, we had to expect to have most of the enemy's Stalingrad forces about our ears within two or three weeks. I had already told General Zeitzler on 22nd January that I should not be surprised to see them turn up in the Starobyelsk area, i.e. in the broad gap between Don Army Group and Army Group B.

The same day Hitler finally decided that a part, at least, of *First Panzer Army* should not be taken into the Kuban bridgehead, but be brought back through Rostov – that is, into what was later to be the decisive battleground. This, though only a compromise solution in our own eyes, was nonetheless welcome in the sense of the Army Group's own conception of operations.

It was, however, of the utmost importance that this withdrawal should be performed at maximum speed, so that Fourth Panzer Army, in its turn, could be transferred to the Army Group's western wing at the earliest possible moment. The rapidity of First Panzer Army's withdrawal through Rostov depended entirely on the ability of Army Group A's other components to adapt their speed of movement accordingly. Yet it was clear that even now the Army Group was still unable to increase its speed to the extent the situation demanded. I have never been able to elicit a satisfactory reason for this. At all events First Panzer Army maintained after coming under my command that had it not been repeatedly halted on instructions from above, it could in fact have moved much more smartly from the very start. Both Army Group A and O.K.H. disputed this. Whatever the answer, the fact remains that Army Group A had so timed the move of its left wing – which was still around Belaya Glina, 30 miles east of Tikhorets on 23rd January – that it would not reach Tikhorets until 1st February!

On 23rd January Don Army Group came into another 'legacy' – this time the southern part of Army Group B's front between the

Donetz and Starobyelsk. As usual, the liabilities far outweighed every-thing else. They consisted of about 40 extra miles of front and at least three enemy corps now on the advance in that sector – one of them armoured and the other mechanized. The only asset we acquired – now that the Italians could no longer be counted upon – was 19 Panzer Division, at that moment located around Starobyelsk. The very next day, however, it was forced to yield Starobyelsk to the enemy. It was an exceptional achievement on the part of this valiant division, so out-standingly led by Lieutenant-General Postel, that it was ever able to fight a way through to the west at all. The enemy's action in swinging south across the Donetz was something it could not prevent.

On 24th January Hitler decided that if possible the whole of *First Panzer Army* should be withdrawn through Rostov from now on. Since its southern wing was still at Armavir, this naturally meant tying down Fourth Panzer Army south of the Don even longer in order to keep Rostov open. Whether the army could still be thrown over to the western wing of the Army Group in time thus became increasingly doubtful.

There were, nonetheless, two gratifying facts to record.

Army Group A, which had been understandably reluctant to see one of its armies disappear across the Don, had realized after all that its own fate, too, would be decided on the Donetz and not in the Kuban. Be-sides, it was becoming more and more unlikely that a force of any strength in the Kuban could be supplied across the Straits of Kerch. Henceforth Army Group A, as well, came out in favour of withdraw-ing the largest possible number of forces through Rostov.

The second fact was that on 25th January the above-mentioned attack of two of our armoured divisions on the enemy advancing across the Lower Manych finally produced the success we had hoped for. With that, the immediate threat to the Rostov crossings was eliminated for the time being.

Instead, the situation on *Fourth Panzer Army*'s southern wing took another critical turn. Bringing up fresh forces which appeared to have been drawn from the Soviet armies pressing after Army Group A, the enemy attempted to get between Fourth Panzer Army and the northern wing of First Panzer Army in order to envelop the former from the south and force the latter away from Rostov. Don Army Group accordingly presented Army Group A with a final demand that it should join in this battle with an armoured division and also step up First Panzer Army's withdrawal on Rostov with every means at its disposal.

At last, on 27th January, at least the northern half of First Panzer Army came under command of Don Army Group, with the result that the latter was now itself able to order the measures to which I have just referred.

At the same time, since Fourth Panzer Army still had to keep the Rostov crossing open for the time being, Don Army Group decided that H.Q. First Panzer Army, which could be released sooner south of the Don, should be the first to move over to the Middle Donetz. It was to be followed there by its divisions as they were fed through Rostov, as well as by forces of Fourth Panzer Army as they became available.

By 31st January things had reached a point where First Panzer Army could be expected to come back through Rostov – though whether it would arrive at the Donetz in time to stop the enemy breaking across the river to the sea-coast was quite another matter. The unfortunate thing was that even now not all of the army's formations could be got to the decisive battleground. Thanks to Hitler's hesitation in deciding whether to bring the army back towards Rostov or to move it into the Kuban, 50 Division (one of the well-tried formations of the former Crimean Army) had not been in time to join in the move to Rostov and had gone over to Seventeenth Army. Furthermore, after days of indecision, Hitler at the last moment re-allocated 13 Panzer Division to Army Group A for use in the Kuban after we had striven to the last to preserve a gap through which to slip it to Rostov. Thus both these divisions were withheld from the crucial battleground while some 400,000 men lay virtually paralysed in the Kuban. Admittedly the latter served to tie down the powerful enemy forces who were vainly striving to do away with the bridgehead. But they never achieved the operational effect which Hitler sought, and ultimately the enemy was left free to decide what size of force he should leave there. Not even Hitler's argument that a large force must be kept in the Kuban in order to deny the enemy the naval port of Novorossisk held any water. He still had to give it up in the end.

On 29th January our headquarters moved from Taganrog, where it had gone on the 12th, to Stalino, as the Army Group's main point of effort now had to shift from the Don to the Donetz.

During the battles in and south of the large bend of the Don, the aim of which had been to cover the withdrawal of Army Group A from the *Caucasus*, but in which the larger issue was whether the German southern wing could be preserved at all, a fresh problem was already emerging. The question was whether this southern wing would be able to maintain the *Donetz area*.

This area, which lies between the Sea of Azov, the Don estuary and the Lower and Middle Donetz and is roughly bounded in the west by the line Mariupol–Krasnoarmeiskoye–Isyum, had played a fundamental part in Hitler's operational calculations as far back as 1941, for he considered possession of it to be of vital importance to the outcome of the war. On the one hand he contended that we should not get through the war *economically* without its vast coal deposits, while on the other he considered that the loss of these had dealt a telling blow to the Soviet war effort. Donetz coal, he declared, was the only kind the Russians had (at least in European Russia) that was suitable for coking, and sooner or later the lack of it must paralyse their tank and munitions production. While I do not propose to discuss the pros and cons of these assertions, the fact remains that the Russians managed to produce thousands of tanks and millions of shells in the years 1942–3 without recourse to this Donetz coal.

The real question was whether we could remain the military masters of the Donetz basin or not. From the point of view of our war economy it was unquestionably desirable that we should retain it – with the one qualification that while we extracted substantial quantities of Donetz coal for our own use, all the bunker coal for the railway supplying this vast territory had to be brought out from Germany because Donetz coal did not suit our locomotives. As the *Reichsbahn* had to run several coal-trains a day to cover its own requirements, the proportion of troop trains fell off accordingly.

Be that as it may, Hitler maintained that the German war economy could not possibly do without the Donetz basin. (A year later he said exactly the same thing about the manganese output of Nikopol.) And yet our possession of the area was in doubt from the moment the Hungarian front collapsed south of Voronezh, throwing open the enemy's road to the Donetz and across it to the Dnieper crossings or the Sea of Azov.

The first time the question of our fighting to hold the Donetz basin came up was in a telephone conversation I had with General Zeitzler on 19th January. He wanted to hear my views on the subject, having 'broached' it to Hitler – albeit without success – the day before. This was the day on which the danger appeared of a breach in the whole front from Voroshilovgrad to Voronezh. I told Zeitzler that however important this area might be, even from the economic point of view, the question was relatively simple to answer. If it were to be retained in its entirety, strong forces must be assembled with a minimum delay and as far east as was feasible – forward of Kharkov, if possible. Should we be unable to do this because it was thought that Central and Northern Army Groups could not spare any more forces, because the new drafts at home were not ready, because O.K.W. would not release any forces from other fronts or, finally, because such a sudden deployment would be too much for the railways in their present state, we should simply have to accept the consequences. The southern wing of the German Armies could not close the gap with its own forces if it re- mained on the Lower Don. Nor could it go on fighting there in isola- tion if the expected reinforcements took a long time to arrive and de- ployed far to the rear – i.e. out of all relation to the operations of the southern wing. The battle being fought by the southern wing and the deployment of the new forces must be so attuned to one another in a spatial sense as to become operationally coherent. Either the new forces must be made to deploy swiftly and relatively far to the east, in which case it would be possible for the Army Group to remain on the Lower Don and Donetz, or else they could not, and the Army Group would have to be pulled back to join them. If one of these two courses were not taken, the enemy would have an opportunity to cut off the whole southern wing before any reinforcements could make their presence felt. General Zeitzler agreed with me.

It was certain in any case that the SS Panzer Corps due to assemble around Kharkov by the middle of February would not have the necessary strength to close the gap now being torn open from Voro- shilovgrad to Voronezh. Nor could it be made operational in time to launch an offensive thrust north of the Donetz for the purpose of free- ing the flank of the southern wing in the event of its remaining on the Lower Don and Donetz.

The next few days served to increase the Army Group's alarm at the trend of events in its deep flank.

As early as 20th January we had noticed two enemy corps trying to outflank the Army Group's left wing (the Fretter-Pico Group at Kamensk) by a movement in the direction of Voroshilovgrad. At the same time the enemy was feeling his way forward against the Italian remnants behind the Donetz east of Voroshilovgrad. Otherwise his main forces apparently aimed to drive west on Starobyelsk in the first instance, obviously with the object of gaining some initial elbow-room. As soon as the enemy had attained these aims, however, it could be assumed that he would not only strive to envelop the Fretter-Pico Group, but also, by throwing strong forces further round to the west, to advance over the Donetz towards the Dnieper crossings or the coast of the Sea of Azov.

Only four days later, on 24th January, there were already reports of enemy cavalry south of the Donetz in the region of Voroshilovgrad – though it was always possible that a false alarm had been sounded by some jumpy town major in a rear area.

On 31st January I sent O.K.H. a teleprinter message re-stating my views on the problem of holding the Donetz basin.

The prior condition for retaining it, I said, was that a *timely* attempt be made from the direction of Kharkov to relieve the pressure on us and that the enemy in the area north-east of the city be beaten before the muddy season set in. If, as unfortunately seemed to be the case, neither of these should prove practicable, there would be no possibility of holding the basin – at least not to its full extent in the east. Any attempt to remain on the Lower Don and Donetz would thus be a mistake from the operational point of view.

A second factor which must not be overlooked, I went on, was that our present forces would not alone suffice to hold the whole Donetz area if – as seemed certain – the enemy were to bring up further reinforcements from the Caucasus and Stalingrad. It was just not good enough to pin one's hopes on the enemy's becoming exhausted (great though his losses might well have been in attacks on *German* troops) or on his operations being brought to a premature halt by difficulties of supply. (These were the arguments which Hitler constantly produced to General Zeitzler whenever the latter drew his attention, on the strength of the basically accurate intelligence reports he received from us, to the tremendous numerical superiority of the enemy. Undoubtedly there was some justification for what Hitler said. Yet it had to be borne in mind that the enemy's attacks on *allied* armies had cost him very little and that he was *far less dependent* on supply and transport than we Germans were in enemy territory.) The very next few days confirmed the Army Group's appreciation of the enemy's intentions. It became clear that he was out to crush our front on the Donetz and simultaneously to outflank us to the west.

On 2nd February he crossed the Donetz east of Voroshilovgrad without encountering any serious opposition from the Italians there. The *assault group* he had assembled consisted of *three tank corps, one mechanized and one rifle corps* – obviously part of the forces which had previously over-run the Italians on the Don. The objectives of this grouping could be taken to be Rostov or Taganrog.

After ejecting 19 Panzer Division from Starobyelsk, the enemy had swung another strong force of *three or four tank corps and a rifle corps* south-west against the line Slavyansk–Lisichansk. It was plain that he planned a movement to outflank our wing further west. This – if one ignored the residue of Italians – he could expect to find around or even east of Voroshilovgrad.

Except for the measures the Army Group was able to take in its own sphere of command with the ultimate object of flinging First Panzer Army over to the Middle Donetz, therefore, the period following the end of January was taken up with wrangles between the Army Group and O.K.H. on how to proceed with the operations as a whole.

As has been stated, I had already emphasized to General Zeitzler on 19th January that the *whole* of the Donetz basin could only be held on condition that strong forces intervened swiftly and effectively from the Kharkov direction. As no prospect of this existed, I asked for permission to reduce the echeloning of our eastern wing at least far enough to release the forces which the Army Group would need if it were to prevent the amputation of the southern wing with its own resources and the reinforcements it had been promised.

We had already dispatched First Panzer Army to the Middle Donetz to counteract the threat of envelopment that had now become acute there.

What had to be done now was to get *Fourth Panzer Army*, too, out of the 'balcony' on the Lower Don and Donetz. This was the only timely way to meet the danger of an enemy attempt to cut us off from the Dnieper crossings by advancing across the Isyum–Slavyansk line. Further up the Don, moreover, the enemy must always be expected to bring even more troops over the river towards the Lower Dnieper than had already been reported at Slavyansk. Apart from 1 Division of the SS Panzer Corps, which had meanwhile arrived at Kharkov, there were nothing but battered remnants to oppose him anywhere in the area of Army Group B. These alone could not prevent him from wheeling into our deep flank. But Fourth Panzer Army could only be released if a considerable reduction were made in the length of the Army Group front. Instead of continuing to hold the extensive arc formed by the Lower Don and the Donetz from Rostov as far as the region west of Voroshilovgrad, the right wing of the Army Group must be taken back, as it were, on to the string of the bow. This 'string' was the system of defences which the German southern wing had held in 1941 after the first withdrawal from Rostov – a line running behind the Mius and continuing northwards as far as the Middle Donetz. Taking the front back into this position naturally meant abandoning the eastern part of the Donetz coalfields.

In order to justify this withdrawal, I made an attempt to bring home my conception of the long-term conduct of military operations to the Supreme Command. The following is roughly how I expressed it in a teleprinter message addressed for Hitler's personal attention:

To hold the Don–Donetz salient for any length of time was not possible, even in a purely defensive context, with the forces at the Army Group's disposal. In the event of the Supreme Command's having to remain on the defensive in 1943 on account of the loss of Sixth Army and its twenty divisions, an all-out attempt to defend the entire Donetz basin would mean committing all the forces there that could possibly be made available. That, however, would give the enemy a free hand to take the offensive with far superior forces at any point he cared to pick on the remainder of the front. While the present danger was that Don Army Group would be bottled up on the Sea of Azov (and Army Group A consequently lost in the Kuban), we could safely assume that even if this could be avoided and the whole Donetz area held, the enemy's later aim would be to encircle the whole southern wing of the Eastern Front on the Black Sea.

If, on the other hand, the Supreme Command felt able to seek a solution by renewed offensive action in 1943, it could again only do so on the southern wing – but on no account from out of the Don–

Donetz salient because of the now familiar supply difficulties and the flanking threat to which any attack from this 'balcony' projection would be exposed from the outset. The only means of achieving an offensive solution – always assuming that this were in the least feasible – consisted in the first place in drawing the enemy westwards towards the Lower Dnieper on our southern wing. Having once achieved this, we had to launch a powerful attack from the Kharkov area and smash the Russian front connecting there in order to turn south and surround the enemy on the Sea of Azov.

Hitler, however, was apparently unwilling to entertain any ideas of this kind. He had already been told by Zeitzler himself – so the latter informed me – that the only question now was whether to abandon the Donetz area by itself or to lose Don Army Group along with it. Hitler's answer had been that although his Chief-of-Staff was probably right from the operational point of view, the surrender of the Donetz area was impossible for economic reasons – not so much because of any loss of coal to ourselves as because a German withdrawal would put the enemy back in possession of the supplies so vital to his own steel production. As an interim solution, Hitler had directed that the SS 'Reich' Division, the first of the SS Panzer Corps' formations to have reached Kharkov, should launch a thrust from that area into the rear of the enemy forces advancing against our Donetz front.

Quite apart from the fact that this solitary division could never suffice for such a far-ranging operation (it would have had to over-run six enemy divisions for a start) and that there would be nothing available to cover its ever-lengthening northern flank, its commitment to battle would have meant splitting up the only striking force – the SS Panzer Corps – which could be expected to join us in the foreseeable future. If it came to that, the 'Reich' Division was no longer free for such an operation, Army Group B having already had to throw it in to meet the rapid advance of the Soviets towards Kharkov. At that very hour it was tied up in a pretty unpromising defensive action at Volchansk, north-east of the city.

During the next couple of days (4th and 5th February) the situation on Don Army Group's front deteriorated visibly, the enemy bringing sharp pressure to bear on *Fourth Panzer Army* as it covered the flow of First Panzer Army through Rostov. Two armies from his former Caucasus front, Forty-Fourth and Fifty-Eighth, had now joined the three already facing Fourth Panzer Army – a sure sign that the 'threat' which Army Group A's Seventeenth Army in the Kuban was supposed to constitute in the flank of the Russians had not deterred them from transferring substantial forces to the decisive battleground. Before long Don Army Group would have to expect a massed attack on both Rostov itself and the Don front each side of Novocherkask.

In addition, a strong motorized force was found to be moving from Stalingrad towards the Don.

On the Army Group's left wing, too, the situation was becoming increasingly grave. East of Voroshilovgrad, 6 Panzer Division, which Army Detachment Hollidt had rushed up to the Middle Donetz in pursuance of the Army Group order of 14th January, had not succeeded in flinging the enemy back across the river. All it could do for the time being was to bottle him up in the bridgehead he had gained there.

Further west, the enemy had been able to cross the Donetz on a broad front, there being practically no forces whatever to defend it. He was now outside Slavyansk and had taken Isyum.

Even now, therefore, it appeared doubtful whether the withdrawal of *Army Detachment Hollidt* into the Mius positions would still be at all feasible. The Army Group had intended to have it on the Novocherkask–Kamensk line by 5th January, but in fact it had been tied down on the Don and Donetz through Hitler's refusal to let us take the front back to the Mius. If the enemy were to push swiftly south-eastwards from Slavyansk, he would unhinge the Mius defences from the start.

Even though H.Q. First Panzer Army and the forces we had allocated to it were by this time on the road from Rostov to the Middle Donetz, it would inevitably be several days yet before the army could take an effective hand there. What made things worse was that the saturated roads in the coastal area greatly hampered the progress of the armoured divisions, whereas the ground further north was still frozen solid and in no way affected the Russians' mobility.

In view of these ominous developments, the Army Group not only renewed its call for an immediate withdrawal of its right wing to the Mius, but also presented O.K.H. with a series of specific demands which were intended to underline the perilousness of the situation. It called for the concentration of 7 AA Division, which was engaged on anti-aircraft defence in the communications zone, to provide both air and ground protection for the supply route running through

Dnepropetrovsk. It called for the immediate preparation of an airlift in case the enemy were to cut its rear communications.

It called for a ruthless increase in the transport capacity of the railway at the expense of supplies to Army Group B, which had hardly any more troops to feed anyway.

It demanded that unless the promised attack by the SS 'Reich' Division had achieved complete success – which must mean reaching Kupyansk – by 6th February, the SS Panzer Corps should attack *south* of the Donetz towards Isyum as soon as the increase in trooptrains enabled it to assemble around Kharkov.

Finally, the Army Group called for the immediate transfer of the combat troops of 13 Panzer Division and two infantry divisions of Seventeenth Army to the Lower Dnieper, where they would be furnished with new weapons and take over the B-echelon transport and supply columns of Sixth Army located there.

Even if Hitler shut his eyes to our more long-term view of operations, these demands would in any case bring the urgency of the position home to him.

And sure enough, as a result of this teleprinter message, a Condor aircraft touched down on our airstrip on 6th February to fetch me to General Headquarters for an interview with Hitler. His decision to give me a personal hearing may have been partially due to a visit paid to us at the end of January by his senior military assistant, Schmundt, to whom we had expressed our views very forcibly on the present situation and the way in which things were being handled at the top.

The *conference of 6th February 1943* between Hitler and myself made it possible to forestall the disaster threatening to overtake the German southern wing and to give the Supreme Command one more chance at least to obtain a stalemate in the east.

Hitler opened the talks – as I have already reported in the chapter on Stalingrad – with an unqualified admission of his exclusive responsibility for the fate of Sixth Army, which had met its tragic end a few days previously. At the time I had the impression that he was deeply affected by this tragedy, not just because it amounted to a blatant failure of his own leadership, but also because he was deeply depressed in a purely personal sense by the fate of the soldiers who, out of faith in him, had fought to the last with such courage and devotion to duty. Yet later on I came to doubt whether Hitler had any place whatever in his heart for the soldiers who put such boundless trust in him and remained true to him till the end. By then I wondered if he did not regard all of them – from field-marshal down to private soldier – as mere tools of his war aims.

Be that as it may, this gesture of Hitler's in assuming immediate and unqualified responsibility for Stalingrad struck a chivalrous note. Whether deliberately or unconsciously, he had thus shown considerable psychological skill in the way he opened our discussion. He always did have a masterly knack of adapting his manner to his interlocutor.

For my own part, I had made up my mind to discuss two questions with him.

The first was that of the future conduct of operations in my own area, which depended on getting Hitler's consent to the abandonment of the eastern part of the Donetz basin. It was essential to elicit this from him that very day.

The second question I wished to bring up was that of the Supreme Command – i.e. the form in which it had been exercised by Hitler ever since the dismissal of Field-Marshal v. Brauchitsch. The outcome of this style of leadership – Stalingrad – gave me adequate reason for raising it.

To dispose of the second question first, let me say quite briefly that no satisfactory conclusion was reached. Realizing that a dictator like Hitler would never bring himself to resign as Commander-in-Chief, I tried to get him to accept a solution which would not damage his prestige and yet guarantee a salutary military leadership for the future. I asked him to ensure the uniformity of this leadership by appointing *one* Chief-of-Staff whom he must trust implicitly and at the same time vest with the appropriate responsibility and authority.

But Hitler was clearly not willing to treat the matter impartially. He kept resorting to the personal aspects of the case, complaining of the disappointments he had suffered with v. Blomberg the War Minister and even with v. Brauchitsch. He quite bluntly declared, moreover, that he could not possibly put anyone in a position that would virtually set him above Göring, who would never subordinate himself to the guidance of a Chief-of-Staff even if the latter were acting in Hitler's name. Whether Hitler was really reluctant to offend Göring or merely used this as a pretext, I cannot say.

This brings us back to the first question, that of the future of operations in the area of Don Army Group.

I began by giving Hitler a picture of the Army Group's present situation and went on to list the conclusions to be drawn from it. I pointed out that our forces would on no account suffice to hold the area of the Don and Donetz. However highly Hitler cared to rate its value to either side, the only real question was whether, in trying to hang on to the whole of the Donetz basin, we wanted to lose the latter *plus* Don Army Group (and in due course Army Group A as well) or whether, by abandoning part of it at the right moment, we could avert the catastrophe that threatened to overtake us.

Passing on from these manifest aspects of the present situation, I endeavoured to make Hitler see what would inevitably happen later if we persisted in remaining in the Don–Donetz 'balcony'. The enemy would be free, now that Army Group B was almost completely out of action, to turn the strong forces advancing through the latter's area down towards the Lower Dnieper or the coast and thus to cut off the entire southern wing. What happened down on this southern wing, I emphasized, would decide the outcome of the whole war in the east. It was certain that the enemy would continue to draw on his still strong reserves (particularly from around Stalingrad) to ensure that his struggle to slice off the German armies' southern wing fully achieved its object. For this reason no counter-thrust by the SS Panzer Corps could be considered adequate to intercept the wide outflanking movement which the enemy would make. He would be quite powerful enough to carry out this envelopment and screen it off to the west around Kharkov simultaneously. Even the sum total of possible German reinforcements would still not be enough to stop this enemy thrust. It was absolutely essential, therefore, that First Panzer Army, now on its way to the Middle Donetz, should be immediately followed by Fourth Panzer Army to intercept the still not acute, but nonetheless inevitable threat of an enemy envelopment between the Donetz and Dnieper. Only then would it be possible, in co-operation with the approaching reinforcements, to restore the situation on the German southern wing of the Eastern Front – i.e. the entire stretch of front from the coast of the Sea of Azov to the right wing of Central Army Group. Unless Fourth Panzer Army were pulled back from the Lower Don, this would not be possible. Yet to take it away from there automatically implied withdrawing from the Don–Donetz salient into the Mius positions along its base. There was not a day to lose over this. Indeed, it was already doubtful – thanks to the delay in taking a decision – whether Army Detachment Hollidt, now saddled with the defence of the whole front from the coastline to the Middle Donetz, would ever get back to the Mius in time. Consequently I had to receive permission that very day to give up the eastern part of the Donetz area as far as the Mius.

This statement of mine – to which, incidentally, Hitler listened with the utmost composure – was followed by a dispute on the Donetz basin issue lasting several hours. Even during the second part of our talks, when I discussed the whole problem of leadership with him in private, Hitler kept coming back to it.

As was to be my experience on similar occasions, he avoided any real discussion of what I had to say on operational matters. He did not even try to propound a better plan of his own or to refute the assumptions on which I had based my arguments. Nor did he dispute that the situation would develop in the way I felt bound to anticipate. He treated every statement not bearing directly on the most pressing needs of the moment as sheer hypothesis which might or might not become reality. Now, all considerations of an operational nature are ultimately based – especially when one has lost the initiative to the enemy – on appreciations or hypotheses regarding the course of action which the enemy may be expected to take. While no one can prove beforehand that a situation will develop in such-and-such a way, the only successful military commander is the one who can think ahead. He must be able to see through the veil in which the enemy's future actions are always wrapped, at least to the extent of correctly judging the possibilities open to both the enemy and himself. The greater one's sphere of command, of course, the further ahead one must think. And the greater the distances to be covered and the formations to be moved, the longer is the interval that must elapse before the decision one has taken can produce tangible results. This long-term thinking was not to Hitler's taste, however – at least not in the operational field. Possibly he disliked the prospect of being confronted with conclusions which did not conform to his wishes. Since these could not be refuted, he avoided becoming involved in them wherever possible.

And so this time, too, he mainly drew his arguments from other fields. He began by dwelling on his understandable aversion to any voluntary surrender of hard-won territory so long as it could not be proved – as he thought – that no alternative method existed. It was a viewpoint which every soldier will appreciate. In my own case, particularly, it went right against the grain on this and so many later occasions to have to goad Hitler into giving territory up. I should have much preferred to be able to submit plans for successful offensives instead of for the now inevitable withdrawals. But it is a well-known maxim of war that whoever tries to hold on to everything at once, finishes up by holding nothing at all.

Another argument which Hitler kept advancing was that any shortening of the front such as I had proposed for the purpose of making additional forces available would release an equivalent proportion of enemy forces which could then be thrown into the scale at a crucial spot. This, in itself, was also quite a tenable argument. The constantly decisive factor in any such shift of forces, however, is which of the two opponents gains the lead – in other words, which of them is offered the opportunity, by his own timely action, to seize the initiative at the crucial spot and thereafter to dictate his own terms to the more slow-moving enemy, even when the latter is collectively the stronger. In the case of any attempt to hold the Don–Donetz salient, moreover, the excessive length of the fronts virtually cancelled out the superiority in strength usually enjoyed by a defender over his attacker. In conditions of this kind the attacker has a chance to pierce the over-extended front at a spot of his own choosing, using relatively small forces and suffering no great losses. Since the defence lacks reserves, he is able to demolish the whole structure.

Hitler also argued that if one fought bitterly for every foot of ground and made the enemy pay dearly for every step he advanced, even the Soviet armies' offensive power must one day be exhausted. The enemy had now been attacking for two and a half months without a break. His losses were high and he must soon be at the end of his tether. As he drew further away from his starting lines, moreover, his supply difficulties would halt any far-flung outflanking movement he might be planning.

There was certainly a great deal of truth in all that Hitler said. Undoubtedly the enemy had had very big losses, at least when attacking sectors held by the Germans, and these would have made large inroads on his offensive power. Yet he had had correspondingly easy successes in sectors where there was not the stubborn resistance of German troops to contend with. It was also true that the losses of the Soviet troops – the infantry first and foremost – had greatly lowered their quality, otherwise we could not have held our own against such odds. But however much the enemy divisions' losses might reduce their combat efficiency, there were always new ones to take their place. As for Soviet supply difficulties, these could indeed be expected to increase the further the enemy's operations took him. But in this age of motor transport the distances from the armies' railheads to the Sea of Azov or the Lower Dnieper were not big enough to frustrate the impending Soviet drive to lop off the German southern wing.

During World War I it had still been accepted that no army could normally put more than 95 miles between itself and its railhead. That this figure no longer held good in World War II had been adequately proved by our own operations in both east and west. In addition, the Russians were masters at the rapid reconstruction of railways, which presented relatively few engineering problems on those vast expanses of plain. In any case, it was entirely wrong to base our own measures on the vague hope that the enemy would soon reach the limit of his strength or mobility. When all was said and done, our own divisions, long overtaxed and severely bled, were themselves not far from exhaustion. In this respect I must emphasize that Hitler was fully aware of the condition and casualties of our own troops. What he did not care to admit was that the newly established divisions initially had to pay far too high a toll in blood on account of their lack of combat experience. On the other hand, he did agree that the Luftwaffe field divisions had proved a fiasco, and even confessed that they had been brought into existence as a concession to Göring's thirst for prestige.

All Hitler actually had to say about the operational position was to express the belief that the SS Panzer Corps would be able to remove the acute threat to the Middle Donetz front by a south-easterly thrust from the Kharkov region in the direction of Isyum. His one reservation was that by the time the corps' second division, the 'Leibstandarte', arrived, the 'Reich' Division should have dealt with the enemy at Volchansk. (A third division could not come until later.) His faith in the penetrating power of this newly established SS Panzer Corps was apparently unbounded. Otherwise, however, his statements showed that he still did not, or would not, realize the dangers of the less immediate future, especially when the enemy's Stalingrad formations appeared on the new battlefield.

But the most decisive argument repeatedly put forward by Hitler was the present impossibility, as he saw it, of giving up the Donetz area. He feared the repercussions on Turkey, for one thing. Most of all, he stressed the importance of the Donetz coal to our own war economy and the effect on the enemy of continuing to be deprived of it. Only by regaining this coal, he said, would the Russians be able to maintain their steel production and thereby keep up their output of tanks, guns and ammunition. When reminded that they had turned out plenty of tanks and ammunition to date despite having lost the Donetz basin, Hitler replied that they were simply living off their existing stocks of steel. If they did not get the coalfields back, he insisted, they could not keep up their previous production, which in turn would prevent them from mounting any more big offensives. Now no one would deny that the enemy must be having production trouble in consequence of the loss of the coking coal and the steel and other plant of the Donetz basin. One proof, in my own opinion, was the fact that he had so far not succeeded in replacing the mass of the artillery he had lost in 1941. It was this which had enabled us to defend the patchwork Chir front earlier on. That winter he did in fact have enough guns to commit an overwhelming concentration of them on limited sectors of front – as, for example, during the three successive breakthroughs on the Don – but he obviously still had not enough to equip all his divisions with fully mobile artillery. This discussion on the economic importance of the Donetz area, by the way, gave Hitler an opportunity to display his quite astonishing knowledge of production figures and weapon potentials.

In this conflict of views on the advisability or otherwise of trying to hold on to the Donetz basin, I was ultimately left with only one trump card in my hand. Shortly before my flight to Lötzen we had had a visit at my headquarters from Paul Pleiger, President of the *Reichsvereinigung Kohle*, the German coal cartel. When questioned on the real importance of the Donetz area to the German and Russian war economies, he had assured me that the mines around Shakhty – i.e. in that part of the basin which lay east of the Mius – were in no way vital, as the coal there was unsuitable for coking or locomotive combustion. This disposed of Hitler's objections from the standpoint of economic warfare!

But anyone who supposes that he would now admit his defeat is underestimating the man's pertinacity. As a means at least of delaying the evacuation of the Don–Donetz salient, he finally resorted to the weather. As luck would have it, an unusually early thaw had set in during the last few days. The road across the ice of Taganrog Bay could no longer be used with complete safety, and although the Don and Donetz were still frozen over, it was always possible that the ice would soon start breaking up if the milder weather continued.

Hitler now used all the eloquence at his command to persuade me that in only a few days' time the broad valley of the Don might well be an impassable obstacle over which the enemy could not possibly attack before summer. Conversely, our own Fourth Panzer Army would get bogged down in the mud if it moved west. The least I could do in the circumstances, he said, was to wait for a short while longer.

When I still would not budge and refused to stake the fate of my Army Group on the hope of a quite unseasonable change of weather, Hitler finally agreed to the withdrawal of the Army Group's eastern front to the Mius. If one included the discussion on the command problem, we had been in conference for four whole hours.

The extent of Hitler's perseverance is shown by a small thing which happened just after I had taken leave of him. Having given what amounted to final approval of my operational intentions, he called me back again as I was about to leave his room. He said that while he naturally had no wish to alter a decision once it had been agreed upon, he would still urge me to consider just once more whether I could not wait for at least a little longer. A thaw in the Don basin might even yet enable us to remain in the Don–Donetz salient. I still stood firm, however. All I would promise him was not to issue the withdrawal order until I reached my headquarters at noon next day, provided the situation report sent up that evening did not necessitate immediate action.

I have given all this space to my interview with Hitler not only on account of the decisive effect it had on the outcome of the campaign that winter, but also because I find it in many respects typical of his attitude and of the difficulty of getting him to accept anything which did not conform to his own wishes.

DEVELOPMENT UP TO THE END OF FEBRUARY

It would be wrong to suppose, just because we had succeeded, after a long tussle, in obtaining Hitler's agreement to the evacuation of the east of the Donetz basin – which in turn enabled us to throw Fourth Panzer Army over to our western wing – that the menace to the German southern wing as a whole was already eliminated. The process of 'leap-frogging' *Fourth Panzer Army* from east to west was bound to take about two weeks, in view of the distance involved and the state of the roads. Furthermore, it was by no means certain whether *Army Detachment Hollidt* would reach the Mius positions safely, considering that the enemy in its deep flank around Voroshilovgrad was already south of the Donetz. It was still uncertain, moreover, whether *First Panzer Army* could hold, or restore to any reasonable extent, the front on the Middle Donetz. Above all, the situation in the area of *Army Group B* – i.e. in the region of Kharkov – was shaping so ominously that all sorts of opportunities were opening up to the enemy. Not only could he drive through to the Dnieper crossings at Dnepropetrovsk and Zaporozhye and cut off Don Army Group's communications there; it was even possible for him to cross the river further upstream and block it from the west. Besides shifting Fourth Panzer Army over to the western wing of the Army Group, therefore, it would be necessary to form a new grouping of forces to replace Army Group B's allied armies, which had by now gone almost completely to pieces.

At noon on 7th February I arrived back at my headquarters at Stalino. The situation on the Don had been aggravated by the capture of Bataisk, a suburb of Rostov on the south bank of the river. Immediately upon my return the Army Group gave orders to fall back behind the Don and begun moving *H.Q. Fourth Panzer Army*, together with whatever divisions it could make available, over to the western wing. *Army Detachment Hollidt* received instructions to retire to the line Novocherkask–Kamensk in the first instance.

On 8th February further emergencies arose at Rostov and Voroshilovgrad, where the enemy broke out of the bridgehead he had gained earlier on. The position of First Panzer Army, now involved in the fighting on the Middle Donetz, was just as critical inasmuch as the success we had hoped it would score against the enemy advancing across the stretch of river between Lisichansk and Slavyansk had so far not materialized.

Around Kharkov, in the area of *Army Group B*, a new army detachment was just being formed under General Lanz. The SS Panzer Corps, which was still in the process of arriving, had been placed under its command. We learnt that the SS 'Reich' Division, which was to have smashed the enemy at Volchansk preparatory to thrusting south-east towards Isyum, had in fact come nowhere near doing so. On the contrary, it had retired behind the Donetz. In the circumstances it was certain that nothing would come of the thrust which Hitler had proposed making with the SS Panzer Corps – of which the 'Reich' Division was the only formation so far available – to relieve the pressure on our western flank.

On 9th February the enemy had taken Belgorod and Kursk, in Army Group B's area north of Kharkov. He was also advancing west from the Donetz bend around Isyum. In the gap between the Dnieper and the right wing of Central Army Group, which only began some considerable distance north of Kursk, there was practically nothing but Army Detachment Lanz (whose assembly at Kharkov was already imperilled) and Army Group B's badly battered Second Army west of Kursk.

In view of the fact that the enemy could now carry out a wide outflanking movement across the Dnieper upstream from Dnepropetrovsk, it was clear that despite the steps taken to shift Fourth Panzer Army to the western wing, Don Army Group would in the long run be unable to guarantee the security of its rear communications with its own forces alone. Something radical had to be done. I accordingly sent General Zeitzler a teleprinter message calling for the deployment within the next fortnight of a new army of at least five or six divisions in the area north of Dnepropetrovsk, as well as of another army behind Second Army's front – i.e. west of Kursk – for a thrust to the south. To do this, I said, there must be a basic improvement in the efficiency of transport, as the slow trickle of divisions which had been coming through to date could not possibly help matters in the present situation.

General Zeitzler did hold out the prospect of really effective assistance from now on. He hoped that he could at last release six more divisions from Central and Northern Army Groups and get these to us faster than had been the case hitherto. The daily number of trains he envisaged was thirty-seven, which meant that we could count on having one of the six promised divisions every other day. In view of the breadth of the gap torn in the German front, of course, even these forces would be no more than a stop-gap to tide us over the worst dangers until the muddy season set in, and whether they would arrive in time depended on developments around Kharkov, on which our own Army Group had no influence. In any case, the German southern wing remained overshadowed by the mortal danger that either before or immediately after the muddy season the enemy would push through to the Sea of Azov or, by striking even further west, to the Black Sea.

While the Army Group's deep flank thus constituted its main source of anxiety, the trend of events on its own fronts was also far from encouraging.

First Panzer Army (commander, General v. Mackensen; Chief-of-Staff, Colonel Wenck), the task of which was to throw the enemy who had crossed the Middle Donetz back across the river, had to contend with two superior enemy forces. The first, which had come over the Donetz at Voroshilovgrad, was trying to drive in between *Army Detachment Hollidt* as it fell back on the Mius and First Panzer Army as it moved up to the Donetz from the south. The other was the force which had crossed the Donetz along the Lisichansk–Slavyansk line and was now striving to shift its main effort to its western wing on both sides of the Krivoi Torets. First Panzer Army, which was liable to be enveloped from both flanks, had to try to tackle the two groups of enemy successively. The Army Group's own view was that it should deliver the first punch on its western wing and dispatch the enemy at Slavyansk before turning on the force at Voroshilovgrad. Unfortunately the army had initially been compelled to tie up part of its forces with the latter group, with the result that it was no longer strong enough to beat the enemy at Slavyansk. This, in turn, meant that there could not be enough forces south of Voroshilovgrad to block the enemy's thrust to the south-west.

As is so often the case in times of crisis, the large-scale emergencies were intensified by irritations of a localized character. On the basis of a reconnaissance carried out before it dispatched 40 Panzer Corps to destroy the enemy force advancing from Slavyansk, *First Panzer Army* had decided that it was impossible for tanks to outflank the enemy over the ground west of the Krivoi Torets because the deep fissures criss-crossing this particular stretch of country were buried in snow. Consequently 40 Panzer Corps put in its attack more or less frontally along and eastwards of the river valley. As the intense cold of the Russian winter makes it virtually impossible for troops to remain in the open country at night, most of the fighting inevitably took place around the inhabited localities in the Krivoi Torets valley, the first main objective being possession of the big factory town of Kramatorskaya. In a battle of this kind, however, there was no hope of gaining the quick decision we so urgently needed against the enemy force at Slavyansk, and 11 Panzer Division, which was leading the attack, progressed only with great difficulty.

While the Army Group's intention of cutting the enemy off from the Donetz by enveloping him from the west had thus been rendered nugatory, the latter pushed a strong force of armour through the allegedly impassable country west of the Krivoi Torets on the night of 11th February, penetrating as far as Grishino. Once again it was seen that the western conception of impassability had only limited validity where the Russians are concerned – partly, of course, because the wider tracks of Soviet armoured vehicles made it considerably easier for them to negotiate the mud or deep snow which held up our own tanks. At Grishino the enemy was now not only deep in the flank of First Panzer Army but also blocking the Army Group's main railway line from Dnepropetrovsk to Krasnoarmeiskoye. Only the railway through Zaporozhye remained open, and even in this case efficiency was reduced by the fact that the big Dnieper bridge destroyed by the enemy in 1941 was still not open to traffic. As a result all goods had to be reloaded, and tank-wagons carrying petrol could not go through to the front.

While supplies to the battle front, especially petrol, were thus endangered and *First Panzer Army* was faced with the threat of being outflanked from the west, the enemy simultaneously tried to turn its flank from the east with the forces which had broken through by way of Voroshilovgrad. In particular, one enemy cavalry corps had managed to penetrate as far as the important rail junction of Debaltsevo, which lay not only far to the rear of the army's right wing but even behind the position due to be occupied by Army Detachment Hollidt on the Mius. Although it was possible to surround this corps at Debaltsevo, its destruction proved a difficult and lengthy business on account of the tough resistance it put up in the villages. As a result 17 Panzer Division, which was urgently required on the army's western wing, remained tied down here for the time being.

On the eastern front, Soviet armoured forces just back from a rest and refit pressed hard behind *Army Detachment Hollidt* as it fell back on the Mius. As a result we were temporarily unable to pull out the armoured divisions still with the Army Detachment. (The Army Detachment did, nonetheless, succeed in reaching the Mius positions on 17th February and in organizing a defence there.)

On the western wing it had meanwhile proved possible to halt the enemy armour at Grishino by throwing in the 'Viking' Division as it arrived from the Don. The latter was unable to dispose of the enemy with any speed, however. Apart from having been considerably weakened in the recent heavy fighting, it was suffering from an acute shortage of officers. The division was composed of SS volunteers from the Baltic and Nordic countries, and its losses had been so severe that there were no longer enough officers available with a command of the appropriate languages. Naturally enough this had an adverse effect on the fighting efficiency of what was intrinsically a useful body of troops.

In the meantime *Fourth Panzer Army* was still moving by road and rail from the Lower Don to the western wing, its progress being considerably delayed by the bad state of the roads. Thus, apart from the fact that the enemy was already in First Panzer Army's deep flank at Grishino and able to send in fresh forces to reinforce those temporarily held up there, the danger in the yawning gap between the left wing of First Panzer Army and the Kharkov region remained as desperate as ever. In this area the enemy had complete freedom of action.

These critical developments in the Army Group's own area were primarily the result of the excessive length of time it had had to leave its forces forward on the Don and Donetz to cover the withdrawal of Army Group A. Henceforth our headquarters also watched Army Group B's sector with growing alarm.

The enemy was capable – while ensuring that he was covered in the direction of Kharkov – of moving down on Pavlograd with the forces reported to be advancing westwards from Isyum. From Pavlograd he could go on to the Dnieper crossings of Dnepropetrovsk and Zaporozhye, thereby severing the Army Group's communications across the river. He could, moreover, try to over-run Army Detachment Lanz, which was still in the process of assembling. If he succeeded, his way across the Dnieper would be open on both sides of Kremenchug, and he would subsequently be able to block the approaches to the Crimea and the Dnieper crossing at Kherson. The result would be the encirclement of the entire German southern wing. Even if the onset of the muddy season, which usually came about the end of March, were to interrupt such a far-reaching operation, the enemy could still be expected to continue pursuing this objective once it was over.

In the light of these reflections, I sent O.K.H. a fresh appreciation of the situation on 12th February for submission to Hitler. Basing myself on the operational considerations outlined above, I laid special emphasis on two points:

First, the *ratio of forces*. I pointed out that although the enemy had quite obviously been trying for almost three months past to precipitate matters on the Eastern Front by either demolishing or isolating our southern wing, the distribution of forces on our own side still took not the least account of this fact. Even if one allowed for the large number of divisions which had been sent to Don Army Group in recent months, the ratio of German to Soviet forces here and in Army Group B was still at least 1 : 8, whereas in the case of Central and Northern Army Groups it stood at 1 : 4. Now it was quite understandable that O.K.H. should hesitate to create new crisis spots by taking forces away from these two Army Groups. Furthermore, O.K.H. had probably been quite right when it pointed out, in reply to previous representations from me on the subject, that almost the whole of the available replacements of troops and weapons were being sent to Don Army Group, as a result of which the fighting potential of Central and Northern Army Groups was lower than our own. To all this, however, we could retort that the divisions of Don Army Group had been involved in incessant and very heavy fighting for months on end, which was not so in the case of the two Army Groups in the north. Besides, our divisions were fighting in open country, while Central and Northern Army Groups were established in timbered dug-outs.

The crucial factor, in any case, was that the enemy's decisive effort was directed not against the central or northern sectors of the German armies but against their southern wing, and that it was inadmissible that we should continue to be left at such a numerical disadvantage.

It could be taken for granted that even if we succeeded in averting the danger of being cut off from the Dnieper crossings, the enemy would still not lose sight of his more far-reaching aim of destroying the southern wing by surrounding it on the sea-coast. For this reason there must at all costs be a radical improvement in the ratio of forces on the German southern wing, even if it involved making concessions on other parts of the front or in other theatres of war.

In addition to ventilating this fundamental question of the overall distribution of forces, I also stated my views to O.K.H. on the *subsequent conduct of operations on the German southern wing*. This will be dealt with in the chapter on Operation Citadel.

During the night of 12th February the Army Group – which had meanwhile been renamed *Southern Army Group* – moved its headquarters to Zaporozhye with a view to having the best possible control of the battle at what would shortly become the decisive spot.

On the night of 13th February a directive was received from O.K.H. which was obviously the sequel to my proposals of 9th February. It ruled, in accordance with these proposals, that a new army should deploy on the line Poltava–Dnepropetrovsk and another behind the southern wing of Second Army. In the event, however, neither army was ever formed. The one which was due to deploy behind Second Army did not arrive at all. While Second Army did receive a few reinforcements, they were given to it at the cost of those promised to ourselves. The army which was to deploy on the line Poltava–Dnepropetrovsk was Army Detachment Lanz, already committed at Kharkov. It was subsequently placed under command of Southern Army Group, together with the sector of Army Group B inclusive of Belgorod. Second Army went over to Central Army Group, and H.Q. Army Group B was finally withdrawn from the Eastern Front order of battle.

FOURTH PHASE: 'THE GERMAN COUNTERSTROKE'

And so, around the middle of February 1943, the acute crisis in the area of Southern Army Group reached a new climax. With it the danger that the entire southern wing of armies would be encircled by an extensive flanking movement from the neighbouring sector in the north threatened to take shape sooner or later. And yet, paradoxically, it was in this very culmination of the crisis that the germs of a counterstroke lay.

Initially, however, the picture became gloomier still.

It was undoubtedly a hazardous step to withdraw Army Group B at this particular moment from command at the cleft in the front. Although, apart from Second Army, it now had nothing but the battered remains of various units at its disposal, it still constituted an essential link in the chain of command on the Eastern Front. Its removal was bound to cause the front to burst open at the seam between Central and Southern Army Groups.

In point of fact, moreover, H.Q. Southern Army Group could not yet assume command of the Kharkov sector now apportioned to it (i.e. that held by Army Detachment Lanz), as no signals links had been established. Before we could take over, Kharkov was due to be lost. The fact that the take-over could take place as quickly as it did was due to the consistently high performance of the Army Group signals regiment and the purposeful way in which our Chief Signals Officer, General Müller, handled our communications. As usual we got liberal assistance from my friend General Fellgiebel, the chief of the Corps of Signals.

But although the removal of H.Q. Army Group B complicated the handling of operations at the most delicate spot on the Eastern Front, it still served one useful purpose. By bringing Army Detachment Lanz under Southern Army Group, it enabled our headquarters to exercise *exclusive* command at the decisive place and the decisive time. In effect this contributed substantially to the final success of the winter campaign of 1942–3.

Meanwhile the Kharkov area was to become a fresh source of anxiety or the Army Group, even if Army Group B – or rather Hitler, by dint of his personal interventions – remained in command there for a few days yet.

Army Detachment Lanz had been ordered by Hitler to hold Kharkov at all costs, which now threatened to become a prestige issue like Stalingrad before it. With the object of relieving the pressure on Southern Army Group's left flank, moreover, the Army Detachment was to thrust in the direction of Losovaya with the SS Panzer Corps as its nucleus. Of the latter's three armoured divisions, there were still only two to hand.

Clearly the Army Detachment could fulfil only one of these two tasks with the forces at its command. It could either fight around

Kharkov or else lend a hand on the left wing of Southern Army Group. I therefore suggested to Hitler that Army Detachment Lanz should forgo Kharkov for the time being and try instead to beat the enemy south of the city. By this means the danger of the Army Group's being enveloped across the Dnieper on both sides of Kremenchug would be temporarily eliminated. On the other hand, it was reasonable to suppose that by throwing in Fourth Panzer Army, we could cope on our own with the enemy making for the Dnieper crossings at Zaporozhye and Dnepropetrovsk. Once Lanz had dealt with the enemy south of Kharkov he could turn his attention to recapturing the city.

This solution, however, did not suit Hitler, for whom Kharkov, as the fourth biggest city in the Soviet Union, had already become a symbol of prestige, and on 13th February he again passed a strict order to Army Detachment Lanz, through Army Group B, to hold Kharkov at all costs.

Thereupon I demanded to be informed by O.K.H. whether this order would remain in force after Lanz had come under my own command and whether we should adhere to it even if the SS Panzer Corps were threatened with encirclement in Kharkov. I also requested an answer to the general appreciation which I had sent to Lötzen the previous day. In reply General Zeitzler told me that Hitler had described it as 'much too far-reaching'. To this I retorted that I considered it only right for an army group to think four to eight weeks ahead – unlike the Supreme Command, which never seemed to look any further than the next three days.

As for the situation at Kharkov, circumstances proved stronger than Hitler's will. The SS Panzer Corps, which really was in danger of being surrounded there, evacuated the city on 15th February – incidentally against the orders of General Lanz. This accomplished fact was reported to us by Army Group B, which finally relinquished its command about this time. Had the evacuation of Kharkov been ordered by a general of the army, Hitler would undoubtedly have had him court-martialled. But because this action had – quite rightly – been taken by the SS Panzer Corps, nothing of the sort occurred. All the same, the commander of Army Detachment Lanz was replaced a few days later by General Kempf on the grounds that Lanz was a mountaineer, while Kempf was a tank specialist.

While the situation around Kharkov was manifestly deteriorating during the period in which Army Group B handed over the area to Southern Army Group, the possibility of the latter's being cut off from its communications across the Dnieper also became acute.

It was reported on 16th February that the enemy – as we had been expecting him to do for some time past – was advancing in strength towards Pavlograd and Dnepropetrovsk from the area west of Isyum. If he succeeded in reaching Losovaya junction or Pavlograd (or alternatively the station of Sinsinikovo hard to the south-west of Pavlograd), the railway link through Poltava would be severed.

At the same time the speed of arrival of the reinforcements promised by O.K.H. slackened off again. Instead of the scheduled thirty-seven troop-trains per day, only six had come through on 14th February.

Furthermore, *Central Army Group* announced that at present it lacked the necessary forces to make any serious attempt to co-operate with Southern Army Group along the line of cleavage between us. Apparently it would be more than happy if it succeeded in halting Second Army, which was falling back into a concavity which already extended far west of Kursk.

The situation had become so critical that Hitler decided to visit me at my headquarters. Presumably my various comments had set him thinking. Much as I welcomed the prospect of putting my views to him personally and of letting him see the seriousness of our position for himself, it was naturally difficult to guarantee his safety in a sizeable factory town like Zaporozhye (on which the enemy was advancing) – particularly as he had expressed the intention of staying for some days. He and his suite, which included the Chief of the General Staff and General Jodl (and, as usual, his private cook), were accommodated in our office building, the whole vicinity of which had to be hermetically sealed off. Even then the situation was not very reassuring, for Hitler's arrival had not passed unnoticed. As he drove into Zaporozhye from the airfield he was recognized by soldiers and Party officials in the streets. Practically the only troops we had available were our own defence company and a few anti-aircraft units, and before long enemy tanks were to get so close to the town that they could have fired at the airfield lying east of the Dnieper.

Hitler arrived at my headquarters at noon on 17th February. I began by giving him the following review of the situation:

Army Detachment Hollidt had reached the Mius positions that same day, closely pursued by the enemy.

First Panzer Army had halted the enemy at Grishino, but not yet finished him off. In the Kramatorskaya area, likewise, the battle against the enemy forces which had come over the Lisichansk–Slavyansk line was still undecided.

Army Detachment Lanz, having evacuated Kharkov, had withdrawn south-west towards the Mosh sector.

I then went on to inform Hitler of my intention to take the SS Panzer Corps right out of Kharkov, leaving only the balance of Army Detachment Lanz in occupation.

The SS Panzer Corps was to thrust south-eastwards from the Krasnograd area in the general direction of Pavlograd, thereby coming into concert with Fourth Panzer Army as it moved up there. The job of these forces would be to smash the enemy advancing through the broad gap between First Panzer Army and Army Detachment Lanz. As soon as this had been achieved and there was no further danger that Army Detachment Hollidt and First Panzer Army would be cut off, we should proceed to attack in the Kharkov area.

Hitler at first refused to discuss the sequence of the operations I was proposing. He would not admit that there really were powerful forces advancing through the area between First Panzer Army and Army Detachment Lanz. He also feared that the operations I envisaged between the Dnieper and the Donetz would become bogged down in the mud. As the winter was already quite far advanced, this was naturally a possibility to be reckoned with. But the main reason for Hitler's negative reaction was most probably the wish to recapture Kharkov at the earliest possible date, which he hoped would be when the SS Panzer Corps had assembled its full complement of divisions. In fact the situation was such that a prior condition for any stroke in the direction of Kharkov was the removal of the threat to the Dnieper crossings. Unless the communications across this river were kept open, neither First Panzer Army nor Army Detachment Hollidt could remain alive. For the stroke at Kharkov, moreover, the co-operation of at least a part of Fourth Panzer Army would be needed. Since it was certain that when the thaw finally put an end to operations, it would do so in the region between the Donetz and Dnieper before it affected the country around and north of Kharkov, one could reasonably hope that we should still have time to attack at Kharkov after we had beaten the enemy now advancing between First Panzer Army and Army Detachment Lanz. On the other hand, it was more than doubtful whether the two operations could be carried out the other way round.

Because of the obstinacy with which Hitler invariably clung to his point of view, another interminable discussion ensued. I finally put an end to it by pointing out that as the SS Panzer Corps must in any case first assemble on the Kharkov–Krasnograd road, which it could not do before 19th February at the earliest, the final decision on whether to go north or south need not be taken till then. This dilatory approach of mine was made possible by the reflection that Fourth Panzer Army could not be available before 19th February either. I also felt justified in assuming that Hitler would be brought to reason by the course of events which he was now experiencing at first hand.

On 18th February I saw Hitler again. The enemy had attacked in strength on the Mius and penetrated at several places into the as yet unconsolidated front of *Army Detachment Hollidt*. Furthermore, it had still not been possible to destroy the enemy cavalry corps encircled behind this front at Debaltsevo. I submitted to Hitler that in spite of this it was still urgently necessary to withdraw motorized units from here to the western wing, even if it were not possible at that particular moment. The enemy mechanized corps in the deep flank of First Panzer Army at Grishino was not yet defeated either, so that the forces committed there were still tied up.

On the other hand, there was now incontestable evidence that the enemy in the gap between *First Panzer Army* and *Army Detachment Lanz* was indeed advancing in force against the Dnieper crossings. His 267 Rifle Division had been identified south of Krasnograd, and he had taken Pavlograd with 35 Guards Division, which included a tank battalion. An Italian division located there (one left over from the former Italian Army) had hurriedly pulled out on the approach of the enemy.

Army Detachment Lanz had reported that the wheeled-vehicle units of the 'Death's Head' SS Panzer Division were completely bogged down between Kiev and Poltava. This washed out the northwards stroke to retake Kharkov which had been Hitler's primary concern. If the SS Panzer Corps had not even been able to hold the city without the 'Death's Head' Division, it was less likely than ever to recapture it when the latter's availability date could not be anticipated for the time being. The only thing we could do, therefore, was to strike south-eastwards and destroy the enemy advancing through the gap between Army Detachment Lanz and First Panzer Army. Since the thaw must be expected in that area, too, in the very near future, there was no time to lose. In the circumstances Hitler agreed to my idea of immediately committing the 'Reich' Division, as the first available formation of the SS Panzer Corps, in the direction of Pavlograd. The 'Leibstandarte' Division was to provide Fourth Panzer Army's operation with cover against the enemy pushing hard southwards from Kharkov. At all events it was now to be hoped that Fourth Panzer Army, reinforced by the 'Reich' Division, would be successful.

Following this decision, I put my view to Hitler on the situation generally. I pointed out that even if we managed – and it was far from certain that we should – to avoid any unfavourable developments until the muddy season set in, I still had to think ahead. The mud would not give us a break of more than a few weeks. After that the Army Group would have a front of 470 miles to hold, for which, inclusive of the forces of Army Detachment Lanz, there were thirty-two divisions available. On the other hand, it could be taken for granted that once the muddy season was over, the enemy would again direct his main effort against the German southern wing and go all out to encircle it on the Black Sea.

A front of 470 miles defended by only about thirty divisions, I told Hitler, could be pierced by a stronger enemy at any point he liked. Above all, no one could prevent him from steadily outflanking the Army Group to the north until he reached the Sea of Azov or the Black Sea.

Once the muddy season finished, therefore, the Army Group must not remain stationary until the enemy broke through somewhere or outflanked it in the north. It could only afford to stay where it was if O.K.H. were able to launch a well-timed offensive stroke to relieve the pressure on the front which still projected a long way eastwards.

My purpose in putting forward these ideas was to persuade Hitler to consider operations on a long-term basis for once. It was obvious, however, that he had no intention whatever of committing himself. While admitting that the Army Group's forces would be too weak to defend that front in the coming year, he would not accept the ratio of strengths I had given him. He did not dispute the presence opposite us of the 341 enemy formations we had identified, but contended that they were no longer of any value. When I objected that our own divisions were also at the end of their tether, he replied that they would be brought fully up to strength and issued with new weapons during the muddy season (which in point of fact they were). He would not recognize, however, that during that same period the enemy would bring his 1926 class of one and a half million men to the front. Neither would he admit that with the number of tanks the enemy could produce in two months (i.e. the approximate duration of the muddy season) he could refit about sixty armoured brigades. Instead, Hitler was at pains to emphasize the decisive importance which the Donetz area would have for Soviet tank production if it were once to fall back into enemy hands. As for Germany's own conduct of operations in the east in 1943, he could not take the forces for a large offensive from any of the other theatres, nor could he find them from newly drafted units. On the other hand, he did think that it would be possible to take limited and localized action with the help of new weapons. This brought Hitler right back to the subject of weapons and weapon production, and it proved impossible to pin him down on his intentions regarding the coming summer campaign.

We lived, it seemed, in two entirely different worlds.

On 19th February a further conference took place, and this time Field-Marshal v. Kleist had been asked to attend. Apparently Hitler's stay at my headquarters had quite impressed him after all as to the dangers on the German southern wing, for he announced that Army Group A was henceforth to transfer whatever forces it could possibly spare to Southern Army Group. In his own words, Army Group A would henceforth be regarded as an 'adjacent reservoir of forces' for the Southern Army Group front, which presumably meant that his plan for bringing the Kuban bridgehead back into the operational picture at some later date was now on the shelf. The future was to show, unfortunately, that this 'reservoir' was not to be exploited on anything like the scale which the transport facilities over the Crimea would have allowed. The Kuban bridgehead was to go on living its isolated existence. Experience has long taught that nothing is more difficult than to get forces released from a place once they have been wrongly tied up there.

That day tension mounted even higher when the enemy, apparently in considerable strength, reached the railway station of Sinsinokovo. As a result of this he not only temporarily blocked the main supply line to the centre and right wing of the Army Group but was also less than 35–40 miles away from the headquarters in which the Führer of the Reich was staying! As there were no troops whatever on the intervening ground, I was most relieved when Hitler flew home the same afternoon. It was quite conceivable that by the following day the enemy tanks could have denied us the use of our airfield lying east of the Dnieper.

The last point I had made to Hitler was that I should need almost all the armoured divisions for the blows I intended delivering on the western wing, which meant they would have to be taken away from the Mius positions. If it had been possible to hold the latter until now, the only reason was that the main body of the enemy forces advancing on them had to pass through the Rostov bottleneck and had not yet arrived. The possibility that the Donetz area would be taken from the east, therefore, was one which could not be ignored. Nothing could be done to prevent it until we had first removed the danger of the Army Group's being cut off from its rear communications. This Hitler seemed to grasp.

In any case, I had the impression that Hitler's visit to my headquarters had helped to bring home to him the danger of encirclement which immediately threatened the southern wing of the Eastern Front and would continue to do so for some time to come. In spite of this, a story was soon afterwards circulated by O.K.W. or General Schmundt that the real purpose of Hitler's trip had been 'to put some backbone into the Army Group'. I am not aware that my headquarters was ever in need of this. Even if we were not prepared to do what Hitler demanded and fight stolidly for every foot of ground regardless of the consequences of 'holding on at all costs', I do not think it would be easy to find another headquarters which, in the teeth of so many crises, clung more stubbornly than our own to its will for victory. In this respect there was never the slightest divergence between my staff and myself.

THE BATTLE BETWEEN DONETZ AND DNIEPER

On 19th February the Army Group ordered *Fourth Panzer Army* to deploy for its counter-attack against the enemy who had come over the line Pereshchepino–Pavlograd–Grishino to cut off the Army Group from the Dnieper.

On 20th February the picture of the enemy's operational intentions became completely clear and proved to be exactly as we had anticipated.

On our eastern front the enemy attacked *Army Detachment Hollidt*'s positions on the Mius, breaking through at three main points.

To cut our communications over the Dnieper he appeared to have committed – in addition to the forces held up by us at Grishino and Kramatorskaya – an army with a strength of three rifle divisions, two tank corps and some cavalry.

Simultaneously he was trying to break through the weak front of *Army Detachment Kempf* (General Lanz having now been relieved by General Kempf) to the west and south-west of Kharkov. Furthermore, he was making a bid to envelop this Army Detachment on its north-western wing and – by reaching further north – to outflank it completely.

In the face of these developments the *Army Group* had two different things to accomplish. It must try to hold the eastern front on the Mius to the best of its ability – though whether it could do so with such limited forces and without any reserves was an open question.

Secondly, it must use *Fourth Panzer Army* to bring about the quick defeat of the enemy in between *First Panzer Army* and *Army Detachment Kempf* in order to prevent its own isolation from the Dnieper crossings. If it failed in this, most of the Army Group's forces would shortly be immobilized through a lack of motor fuel.

Once it had been possible to beat the enemy force between the Donetz and Dnieper, it would depend on how the situation had developed in the meantime whether we could immediately thrust northwards with all our mobile forces in order to restore the position of *Army Detachment Kempf*. On the other hand, it might first be necessary for *Fourth Panzer Army* to fight another action in the area of *First Panzer Army* if the latter had still not succeeded in dealing on its own with the enemy at Grishino and Kramatorskaya.

In any case we must hold off on our northern wing, i.e. in *Army Detachment Kempf*'s area, for the time being. All that the latter could be given to do at present was to bar the way to the Dnieper, be it through Krasnograd to Dnepropetrovsk or through Poltava to Kremenchug, by putting up the toughest possible resistance. Should the enemy by

Map 18. Winter Campaign 1942–3: German Counterstroke, the Battle between Donetz and Dnieper.

any chance be aspiring to reach Kiev (and the many signs that he was were making Hitler increasingly apprehensive), we could only wish him a pleasant trip. Such a far-flung outflanking movement was hardly likely to achieve any positive results before the muddy season set in.

21st February brought us the first hints of relief on what at present were the Army Group's most vital stretches of front.

The *eastern front on the Mius* had held. The remnants of the enemy cavalry corps long surrounded behind it at Debaltsevo were finally compelled to surrender. An enemy tank corps which had been encircled after breaking through the Mius front at Matveyevkurgan was also doomed to destruction.

On the right wing of *First Panzer Army* the enemy was maintaining his pressure on the Fretter-Pico Group, obviously with the object of next unhinging the Mius position or outflanking the northern front of First Panzer Army. Opposite the latter everything remained quiet. Monitored wireless messages made it clear that the Soviet force engaged on the western front of *First Panzer Army* at Grishino and in the Kramatorskaya area (i.e. the Popov group) was faring badly. Evidently its supplies had broken down.

Fourth Panzer Army had taken Pavlograd, and there was reason to hope that its last formations would have closed up with the main body before the roads softened. The fact that a not very powerful enemy tank force had thrust close up to Zaporozhye did not now imply any great danger. It ran out of petrol some 12 miles from the town and was duly destroyed piecemeal. Unfortunately a new division destined for Pavlograd (332) was diverted to the right wing of Central Army Group by O.K.H. while already on its way up to us. Though Second Army's position was probably not at all rosy, Southern Army Group had a prior claim now that we were finally on the way to regaining the initiative. Whether the enemy made any progress towards Kiev in the meantime was comparatively unimportant.

That the enemy did harbour such intentions was shown by the fact that Soviet forces were advancing in considerable strength from the Belgorod direction towards Akhtyrka, clearly with a view to getting round the northern flank of Army Detachment Kempf.

In the next few days *Fourth Panzer Army*'s counterstroke achieved the success for which we had been hoping. With that the initiative in this campaign at last passed back to the German side.

For a start, the army smashed the forces advancing towards the Dnieper crossings – i.e. those in the area around and south of Pavlograd. What Hitler had refused to accept was now substantiated, in that there did prove to be two tank, one rifle and one cavalry corps involved. Immediately afterwards it was possible, in co-operation with *First Panzer Army*, to defeat the four enemy tank and mechanized corps opposite its western front.

By 1st March it was clear that by reason of his defeats between the Donetz and Dnieper the enemy was also beginning to soften up opposite the northern front of First Panzer Army and that the latter would regain the Donetz line in this sector. One felt a strong temptation to chase the enemy across the still frozen river and take him in the rear in and west of Kharkov.

To have our hands free to advance across the Middle Donetz, however, it was first necessary to knock out the southern wing of the enemy's Kharkov group, which was present in force on the Berestovaya, south-west of the city. Whether this could still be done in view of the imminent thaw was more than doubtful. Consequently the Army Group had to content itself initially with seeking out and defeating the Kharkov enemy west of the Donetz.

In the southern strip of the Army Group's operational area, near to the coast, it had already started to thaw. At the end of February the enemy on the *Mius front* had given up his attempt to break through with armoured and other mobile formations and sent in rifle divisions instead. Evidently he wanted to have at least some bridgeheads west of the river before the mud came. After even this broad assault had failed, his offensive finally degenerated into fruitless local attacks.

By 2nd March the Army Group was able to survey the results of its first counterblow, delivered by *Fourth Panzer Army* and the left wing of *First Panzer Army* against the enemy between the Donetz and Dnieper. In the course of this attack and *Army Detachment Hollidt*'s successful defensive on the Mius, the armies of the enemy's 'South-West Front' had received such a beating that they were temporarily incapable of further offensive action. Particularly heavy punishment had been meted out to the forces which had driven forward against the left wing of First Panzer Army and into the gap between the latter and Army Detachment Kempf – the Soviet *Sixth Army*, the *Popov Group* which had fought at Grishino, and *First Guards Army*. The enemy's

25 Tank Corps and three rifle divisions could be written off completely, while 3 and 10 Tank Corps and 4 Guards Tank Corps, one independent armoured brigade, one mechanized brigade, one rifle division and one ski brigade were known to have had a severe battering. In addition, heavy losses had been suffered by 1 Guards Tank Corps and 18 Tank Corps, as well as by six rifle divisions and two ski brigades.

According to reports received from our own troops, the enemy had left some 23,000 dead on the *Donetz–Dnieper battlefield*, and the booty included 615 tanks, 354 field-pieces, 69 anti-aircraft guns and large numbers of machine-guns and mortars. The figure of 9,000 prisoners appeared small in comparison. The reason for it was that our own forces, most of which were armoured, had not been able to form an unbroken ring round the enemy. Because of the cold – particularly at night – the troops tended to bunch together in and around the villages, with the result that individual Soviet soldiers and units which abandoned their vehicles were left with plenty of room to slip away over the intervening countryside. It had not been possible to block the Donetz in the enemy's rear, as it was still ice-bound and entirely passable to lightly armed troops moving on foot.

Apart from the enemy losses already mentioned, 4 Guards Mechanized Corps, which had been encircled behind the Mius front, and 7 Guards Cavalry Corps were also wiped out.

THE BATTLE OF KHARKOV

After thus regaining the initiative by the victory between the Donetz and Dnieper, Southern Army Group proceeded to deliver the stroke against the '*Voronezh Front*' – i.e. the enemy forces located in the Kharkov area – in accordance with an order already issued on 28th February. The intention was to attack these forces in their southern flank with the aim either of turning the latter or – if at all possible – of later driving into the enemy rear from the east. Our object was not the possession of Kharkov but the defeat – and if possible the destruction – of the enemy units located there.

Hence the first priority was to smash the enemy's southern wing, which consisted of *Third Soviet Tank Army* on the Berestovaya south-west of the city. This was achieved by *Fourth Panzer Army* by 5th March. Of Third Tank Army, 12 and 4 Tank Corps, a cavalry corps and three rifle divisions were partly cut to pieces and partly captured in a small pocket at Krasnograd. While there were once again relatively few prisoners, our own troops put the number of enemy dead at 12,000 and reported the capture of 61 tanks, 225 guns and 600 motor vehicles.

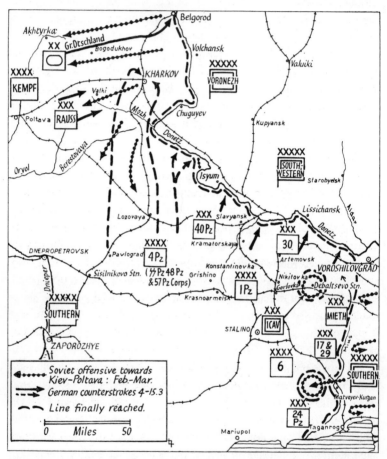

Map 19. Winter Campaign 1942–3: German Counterstroke, the Battle of Kharkov.

A turn in the weather prevented the Army Group from now moving against the rear of the enemy harassing Army Detachment Kempf at Akhtyrka and Poltava in order to make him fight a battle with reversed front. This would have necessitated Fourth Panzer Army's crossing the Donetz downstream from Kharkov, but the ice was liable to break up at any time and no pontoon bridges would have held against the drift-ice. Even to launch a smaller-scale flanking movement by crossing the Mosh and taking the city – through which the enemy's rear communications ran – from behind hardly seemed feasible now that the ground was thawing out. Thus an attempt had to be made to roll up the enemy from the flank and to force him away from Kharkov in the process.

With this aim in view, *Fourth Panzer Army* – including the SS Panzer Corps, the last formation of which, the 'Death's Head' Division, had meanwhile arrived complete – attacked in a northward direction from the Krasnograd area on 7th March. *Army Detachment Kempf* joined in as soon as the enemy began to relax his pressure on its own front.

The attack made good progress in the days that followed. By this time, however, the enemy had recognized the threat to his Voronezh Front. Our radio monitors ascertained that he was moving what appeared to be several tank and mechanized corps from the Voroshilovgrad area to Isyum, presumably for use against the flank of Fourth Panzer Army as it drove north of Kharkov. These, however, no longer achieved any notable impression, either because they had expended their offensive capacity in the preceding battles around Voroshilovgrad or on the Mius, or else because the thawing of the Donetz hindered their intervention. All the enemy could do was to win a minor bridgehead north-west of Isyum on the south bank of the river. He also fetched 2 Guards Tank Corps up to Kharkov from the east and pulled certain of his forces which had been harassing Army Detachment Kempf's northern wing and Second Army back to Bogodukhov. As Second Army was too weak to go over to the offensive itself, it seemed doubtful whether we should succeed in preventing the forces which had pushed a long way west towards and north of Akhtyrka from escaping eastwards. Whatever happened, though, we wanted to try to force the enemy facing Army Detachment Kempf further south away from Kharkov or alternatively to cut him off from the Donetz crossings east of the river. If this came off, Kharkov could be taken by a *coup de main*. At all costs the Army Group wished to avoid Kharkov's becoming a second Stalingrad in which our assault forces might become irretrievably committed.

It was inevitable, however, that the name of Kharkov should act as a magic stimulus on the fighting troops and less senior command staffs.

The SS Panzer Corps, wishing to lay the recaptured city at 'its Führer's' feet as a symbol of victory, was eager to take the shortest route there, so that the Army Group had to intervene vigorously on more than one occasion to ensure that the corps did not launch a frontal assault on Kharkov and become tied down there while enemy elements still fighting to the west of the city were able to make good their escape. In the end it was possible to bring the SS Panzer Corps round to the east. The city fell without difficulty, and we succeeded in cutting off the retreat of considerable numbers of the enemy across the Donetz.

As has been seen, the enemy had been compelled by developments in the area around and south of Kharkov to thin out his forces opposite *Army Detachment Kempf* when they were already near to Poltava and in possession of Akhtyrka further north. Subsequently he had to move them back towards Kharkov and Belgorod, with *Army Detachment Kempf* in close pursuit.

On 10th March Hitler paid our headquarters a further visit. In addition to briefing him on the current situation, I dealt in particular with our view of how operations should be conducted at the end of the muddy season, which was now setting in. This will be covered in the next chapter.

On 14th March Kharkov fell to the SS Panzer Corps. At the same time, on the northern wing of *Army Detachment Kempf*, the 'Gross-Deutschland' Division moved swiftly on Belgorod. The enemy once again threw in strong armoured forces to oppose it, but these were wiped out at Gaivoron.

The capture of Kharkov and Belgorod marked the conclusion of Army Group's second counterblow, as the increasing muddiness of the ground did not permit any further operations. As a matter of fact the Army Group would have liked to wind up by clearing out, with the help of Central Army Group, the enemy salient extending some distance westwards of Kursk in order to shorten the German front. The scheme had to be abandoned, however, as Central Army Group declared itself unable to co-operate. As a result the salient continued to constitute a troublesome dent in our front which left certain openings to the enemy and at the same time cramped our own operations. Nevertheless, the Army Group was now securely in possession of the entire Donetz front from Belgorod down to where the Mius positions branched off from it. These Donetz and Mius fronts together formed the very same line as had been held by German troops in the winter of 1941–2.

RETROSPECT

If, in conclusion, we cast a final glance at the full course and outcome of the 1942–3 winter campaign in South Russia, we must begin by acknowledging the successes attained on the Soviet side, the magnitude of which was incontestable. The Russians had contrived to encircle and destroy the German Sixth Army, the strongest we had in the field. They had, moreover, swept four allied armies clean off the map. Many brave members of the latter had fallen in battle, and considerable numbers had gone into captivity. What allied troops remained had disintegrated and had sooner or later to be withdrawn for good from the zone of operations. Even though it was possible to reconstitute the majority of Sixth Army's divisions from residual units and replacements and for Army Detachment Hollidt to assume the designation of Sixth Army in March 1943, the loss of the bulk of the fighting troops of twenty divisions, besides a considerable proportion of the army artillery and engineers, was quite irreparable. And limited though the fighting efficiency of the allied armies might be, their loss was still a considerable one, depriving us as it did of a substitute for German forces on quiet sectors of the front.

Yet despite the disappearance of five whole armies from the German order of battle, no one can say that this alone need have decisively influenced the outcome of the war. It was accompanied by the loss of the whole of the immense territories we had won in the 1942 summer offensive, together with their natural resources. The grab for the Caucasian oilfields, one of the fundamental aims of that offensive, had failed to come off – and here we may note that this economic goal, on which Göring had been so insistent, decisively contributed to the offensive's split. In their pursuit of this economic objective people had forgotten that its attainment and retention always depended on defeating the main body of the enemy forces. All the same, it had still been possible to hold the part of the Donetz basin that was essential to the conduct of the war.

But great though their gains undoubtedly were, the Russians had still not succeeded in winning their decisive victory over the German southern wing, the destruction of which could probably never have been made good by our side. By the end of the winter campaign the initiative was back in German hands, and the Russians had suffered two defeats. Though not decisive in character, these did lead to a stabilization of the front and offer the German command a prospect of fighting the war in the east to a draw. Nevertheless, we could clearly bury any hope of changing the course of the war by an offensive in the summer of 1943. Our loss of fighting power had already been far too great for anything of that order.

The obvious inference for the Supreme Command to draw was that it must strive with every means at its disposal to come to terms with at least one of Germany's opponents. Similarly it must realize the need to base its subsequent conduct of the war in the east on a policy of sparing its own forces – particularly by avoiding the loss of entire armies, as at Stalingrad – while seeking to wear down the offensive capacity of the enemy's. To that end, resolutely ignoring all secondary aspirations, it must switch the main effort to the Eastern theatre for as long as Germany's Western adversaries were unable to land in France or to deliver a critical blow from the Mediterranean area.

If we now return to the 1942–3 winter offensive and its outcome, the next question to ask is why the Soviet command, despite its big successes in this campaign, did not achieve the *decisive* success of annihilating the whole of the German southern wing? After all, with that overwhelming number of formations and the operational advantages it possessed at the outset, it had the highest possible trumps to play.

It must be emphasized for a start that the Soviet command showed no lack of aggressive spirit and engaged its troops without the least regard for casualties in order to attain its objectives. The troops themselves, as was almost invariably true of the Russians, fought with great bravery and at times made unbelievable sacrifices. Nonetheless, there was an unmistakable fall-off in the quality of the infantry, and the losses of artillery in 1941–2 had still not been made good. Since the beginning of the war the Soviet leaders had unquestionably learnt a great number of lessons, especially regarding the organization and use of large armoured formations. Although the enemy had possessed large numbers of tanks as early as 1941, he had not known then how to use them as individual members of a united whole. By now he had them properly organized in his tank and mechanized corps and had also taken over the German technique of penetration in depth. In spite of this we almost always succeeded – except in the situation of November 1942 – in ultimately beating or destroying these tank and mechanized formations, even when they had already driven deep into the German forward areas. After the encirclement of Sixth Army, on the other hand, they were never again able to drive through to vital spots with such speed and in such strength as to fulfil the aim of cutting off the German southern wing, whether on the Don, the coast of the Sea of Azov or the Lower Dnieper. Except for Stalingrad, where Hitler gave it the opportunity, the Soviet command was never able to bring about a battle of encirclement as we had done on various occasions in 1941, taking several thousand prisoners in the process. This held good in spite of the Russians' enormous preponderance of forces in the winter of 1942–3 and the fact that the opening situation and the collapse of the allied armies afforded them a free passage into the rear of the German front. We, on the other hand, had had to fight a mainly frontal battle in 1941.

So let us take a look at the Soviet leadership at the top. In view of the operational situation that existed at the end of the German summer offensive, the strategic aim of encircling the German southern wing was so palpably evident that it could not possibly be overlooked. The idea of breaking through the fronts of the allied armies was also a very obvious move. In other words, not very much genius was required on the Soviet side to draft an operations plan in the late autumn of 1942.

The first stroke – the encirclement of Sixth Army – was undoubtedly correct. If it succeeded – and the German Supreme Command did everything to see that it did – the strongest striking force the Germans had would be eliminated.

It would have been better if this first blow had been co-ordinated with the offensive against the fronts of the Italian and Hungarian Armies, in order that every effort should be made from the start to cut off the German forces at Rostov or on the Sea of Azov in one unified and large-scale assault operation. Clearly the available artillery was not equal to the task, and for this reason, presumably, the breakthrough operations had to be staggered. It is also conceivable that the transport situation did not allow the sum total of assault forces to be assembled and supplied simultaneously.

However, the unexpectedly swift and complete collapse of the allied armies on our own side compensated the Soviets to a great extent for the inconveniences which this staggering of the three breakthrough offensives entailed. When the Soviet command failed to accomplish its mission of tying off the German southern wing on the Lower Don, the Sea of Azov or, in the last instance, the Dnieper, the reason was certainly not that its offensive was necessarily bound to get bogged down in that extensive zone of operations. When considered by the standards of modern warfare, the distances to be covered by the Soviet assault groups to their various objectives were by no means excessive. Nor were the German reserves which were thrown in to meet them so strong that the Soviet offensive need have come to a standstill short of its decisive objectives and have ultimately ended in a serious reverse.

On the contrary, one must say that, with the exception of Stalingrad, the Soviet command never managed to co-ordinate *strength* and *speed* when hitting a decisive spot.

In the first phase of the winter campaign it undoubtedly tied down unnecessarily large forces against Sixth Army in order to make doubly sure of its prize. In doing so, it let slip the chance to cut off the German southern wing's supply lines on the Lower Don. The forces that attacked the Chir front were certainly strong, but they did not act in concert.

After the breakthrough on the Italian front the Soviet command similarly failed to stake everything on quickly crossing the Donetz and reaching Rostov. With such far-reaching objectives involved, there was admittedly a danger that the Russians would later be attacked in the flank themselves, but they should have expected to derive the necessary protection here from the offensive due to be launched on the Hungarian front immediately afterwards. Risky, I agree. But anyone who is not prepared to take such risks will never achieve decisive and – as was essential in this case – speedy results.

Even after the successful breakthrough against the Hungarian Army, which tore open the German front from the Donetz to Voronezh, the Soviet command still failed to press on with sufficient speed and strength in the decisive direction – towards the Dnieper crossings. Instead of putting all its eggs in one basket and simply leaving a strong, concentrated shock group to provide offensive protection to the west, it squandered its forces in a series of far-ranging unco-ordinated thrusts at Akhtyrka and Poltava by way of Kursk, against the Dnieper and across the Donetz line Slavyansk–Lisichensk–Voroshilovgrad. In this way it enabled the German command to be stronger at the decisive spots when the time came.

Schlieffen once said that both sides in a battle or campaign, the loser just as much as the winner, contribute to the outcome by the various actions they take. The German Supreme Command's share of responsibility for the loss of Sixth Army – and indeed for the whole crisis which arose on the southern wing of the Eastern Front in the winter of 1942–3 – has already been plainly stated. It is thus only fair to mention what contribution the German side made to the Russians' ultimate failure to encircle the German southern wing.

In this respect only one thing need be said: but for the almost superhuman achievements of the *German troops* and their commanders in facing up to an enemy many times their superior in numbers, the Army Group could never have succeeded in 'bringing its defeat underfoot'. This winter campaign could never have been fought had not our brave *infantry divisions* – unlike the troops of our allies, and often without adequate anti-tank defences – stood firm before the assaults of the enemy's armoured formations and, by closing the front behind his tanks whenever they broke through, ensured their ultimate destruction. A similar debt was owed to our *panzer divisions*, which fought with unparalleled versatility and more than doubled their effectiveness by the way they dodged from one place to the next. The German fighting troops, convinced of their superiority as soldiers, stood their ground in the most desperate situations, and their courage and self-sacrifice did much to compensate for the enemy's numerical preponderance.

One thing must not be forgotten. It was the valiant *Sixth Army* which, by loyally fighting on to the last, snatched the palm of an annihilating victory against the German southern wing from the enemy's hand. Had it, instead of resisting till early February, given up the struggle as soon as its position became hopeless, the Russians could have thrown in such an extra weight of forces at the crucial spots that their aim to encircle the whole southern wing of the German front would most probably have been achieved. Such was Sixth Army's vital contribution to our success in once more stabilizing the situation on the Eastern Front in March 1943. Though the self-sacrifice of the men of Sixth Army may have been in vain so far as the final outcome of the war was concerned, this can never annul its moral worth.

That is why, now that we have come to the end of the chapter, the name of Sixth Army is to shine forth for one last time. This army fulfilled the highest demand that can ever be made on a soldier – to fight on to the last in a hopeless situation for the sake of his comrades.

14

OPERATION 'CITADEL' *Kursk.*

THE PRECEDING chapter has shown that the winter campaign of 1942–3, which had started with the Russian breakthrough on the Don and Volga on both sides of Stalingrad, did not ultimately bring the Soviet command the decisive operational success for which it might have hoped.

The question now was how the German side should continue the struggle the following summer. Obviously, after so many major formations had been lost, there would no longer be the forces available to mount another crucial offensive on the scale of 1941 and 1942. What did still seem possible – given proper leadership on the German side – was that the Soviet Union could be worn down to such an extent that it would tire of its already excessive sacrifices and be ready to accept a stalemate. At the time in question this was far from being wishful thinking. On the other hand, such an aim could not be realized by going over to purely defensive, static warfare. For one thing, there were not enough German divisions to defend the far-flung front from the Baltic to the Black Sea decisively. For another, it was unlikely that the Soviets would take any action until the Western Allies landed in Europe – the danger of which had become all the more acute in the light of recent events in North Africa.

The German command thus had very little time left in which to force a draw in the east. It could only do so if it succeeded, within the framework of a – now inevitable – *strategic defensive*, in dealing the enemy powerful blows of a localized character which would sap his strength to a decisive degree – first and foremost through losses in prisoners. This pre-supposed an operational elasticity on our part which would give maximum effect to the still-superior quality of the German command staffs and fighting troops.

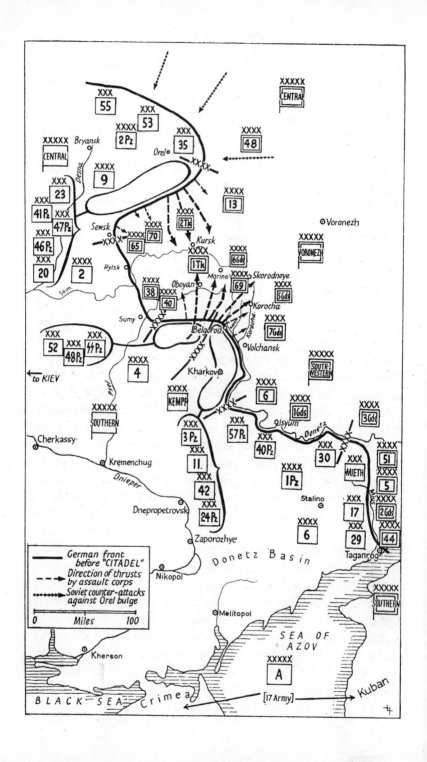

XXXX
55

XXX
53

XXXXX
CENTRAL

XXXX
2 Pz

XXX
35

XXXX
48

XXXXX
CENTRAL

Bryansk

Orel

XXXX
9

XXXX
13

XXX
23

XXX
41 Pz

XXX
47 Pz

Sewsk

XXXX
70

XXX
2 Tk

XXXX
66 ds

Kursk

○ Voronezh

XXXXX
VORONEZH

XXX
46 Pz

XXXX
65

XXX
1 Tk

XXX
20

XXXX
2

Rylsk

XXXX
38

Oboyan

40

Marino

XXXX
69

Skorodnoye

XXXX
5 Gds

Seim

Sumy

Belgorod

Korocha

XXXX
7 Gds

Volchansk

XXX
52

XXX
48 Pz

XXX
ᛋᛋ Pz

XXXX
4

Kharkov

XXXXX
SOUTH-
WESTERN

to KIEV

XXXX
KEMPF

XXXX
6

Donetz

XXXX
16 ds

Isyum

XXXX
3 Gds

XXX
3 Pz

XXX
57 Pz

Cherkassy

XXX
11.

XXX
40 Pz

XXX
30

XXX
MIETH

XXXX
51

Kremenchug

XXX
42

XXX
1 Pz

XXXX
5

Dnieper

XXX
24 Pz

Dnepropetrovsk

Stalino

XXX
17

XXXX
2 Gds

XXXX
6

XXX
29

XXXX
44

Zaporozhye

Taganrog

German front
before "CITADEL"

Direction of thrusts
by assault corps

Soviet counter-attacks
against Orel bulge

Donetz Basin

XXXXX
SOUTHERN

Nikopol

0   Miles   100

○ Melitopol

SEA OF
AZOV

Kherson

XXXXX
A

BLACK SEA Crimea

[17 Army]   ➔ Kuban

We naturally had to consider what action the Soviet command would take once the muddy season was over. Would Stalin wait until his allies had met his repeated demands for a landing on the European mainland? Though it seemed very natural that he should do so, there were still many arguments against it. Soviet self-confidence had undoubtedly increased since the big successes late in the previous autumn. Could the Soviet leaders possibly afford, from a psychological point of view, to call a halt to their loudly advertised 'liberation of the holy soil of Russia'? Must the Kremlin not be anxious to beat its allies to the Balkans, the traditional target of Russian expansionism?

Assuming that the enemy resumed the offensive as soon as he had made good his losses, therefore, it seemed certain that he would continue to direct the main pressure of his attacks against the southern wing of the German front, i.e. against Southern Army Group.

The bulge in the German front, which ran down the Donetz and Mius from a point below Kharkov, embracing the valuable coal-mining and industrial region south of that city, was just begging to be sliced off. Should the enemy succeed in breaking through around Kharkov or even across the Middle Donetz, he could still achieve his aim of the previous winter and destroy the German southern wing on the Black Sea coast. (At this time Army Group A was still in the Kuban bridgehead!) By the same stroke he would regain possession of the precious Donetz area and the granaries of the Ukraine, in addition to opening the way to the Balkans and Rumanian oilfields, with all the political consequences this would have entailed in regard to Turkey. In no other sector of the Eastern Front was the Soviet Union offered such immense opportunities in the military, economic or political fields. The decisive thrust, then, would be delivered against Southern Army Group – a fact which, in view of the Russians' numerical superiority, naturally did not exclude the possibility of smaller-scale offensives in other parts of the front.

Southern Army Group had on a number of occasions brought these considerations to the notice of O.K.H. and Hitler. What the latter ultimately had to decide was whether the overall situation allowed us to wait for the Russians to start an offensive and then to hit them hard '*on the backhand*' at the first good opportunity, or whether we should

Map 20. Operation 'Citadel' (July 1943).

attack as early as possible ourselves and – still within the framework of a strategic defensive – strike a limited blow '*on the forehand*'.

The Army Group preferred the former solution as one offering better prospects operationally, and had already submitted a tentative plan to Hitler in February. It envisaged that if the Russians did as we anticipated and launched a pincer attack on the Donetz area from the north and south – an operation which could sooner or later be supplemented by an offensive around Kharkov – our arc of front along the Donetz and Mius should be given up in accordance with an agreed time-table in order to draw the enemy westwards towards the Lower Dnieper. Simultaneously all the reserves that could possibly be released – in particular the bulk of the armour – were to assemble in the area west of Kharkov, first to smash the enemy assault forces which we expected to find there and then to drive into the flank of those advancing in the direction of the Lower Dnieper. In this way the enemy would be doomed to suffer the same fate on the coast of the Sea of Azov as he had in store for us on the Black Sea.

The plan did not meet with Hitler's approval, however. He was still pre-occupied with the economic aspects of the Donetz basin and apprehensive about the possible repercussions of an even temporary evacuation on the attitudes of Turkey and Rumania. But what probably did most to prejudice him was his belief that we must fight for every foot of the ground he had won from Stalin in the winter of 1941 and which had in his view 'saved the German Army from a Napoleonic retreat'. Besides this, however, he undoubtedly shrank from the risks which the proposed operation would assuredly entail. Inwardly, perhaps, he did not trust himself to cope with them, for in spite of having a certain eye for tactics, he still lacked the ability of a great captain.

Consequently our minds now turned to the idea of a '*forehand*' *stroke*. An attempt must be made to strike the enemy a blow of limited scope before he could recover from his losses in the winter campaign and resuscitate his beaten forces.

A suitable target was presented by the Soviet salient which protruded far into our own front line around the city of Kursk. The Russians facing the boundary between Central and Southern Army Groups had been able to retain this when the muddy season set in, and it now formed a jumping-off position for any attacks they might be contemplating against the flanks of the two German army groups. The appreciable Soviet forces inside the salient would be cut off if our attack were successful, and provided that we launched it early enough we could hope to catch them in a state of unpreparedness. In particular, the enemy would have to commit the armoured units which had been so severely battered towards the end of the winter campaign, thereby giving us a chance to punish them wholesale.

And so we come to Operation 'Citadel' – the last major offensive operation undertaken by the Germans in the east. For this attack against the Kursk bulge, *Southern Army Group* provided two armies, Fourth Panzer and Detachment Kempf, comprising eleven armoured or panzer grenadier divisions and five infantry. In order to do so, of course, it had to thin out the Donetz and Mius fronts considerably.

For the attack from the north, *Central Army Group* provided Ninth Army, consisting of six armoured or panzer grenadier divisions and five infantry. The principal danger here lay in the army's having to assemble in the salient jutting out to the east around Orel, where the enemy might attack it in the rear from the east and north.

Operation 'Citadel' was timed to start in the first half of May, when the ground could be expected to have dried out sufficiently and the enemy would still not have finished refitting – especially his armour.

At the beginning of May, however, Hitler decided – against the advice of the two army group commanders – to postpone 'Citadel' till June, by which time, he hoped, our armoured divisions would be stronger still after being fitted out with new tanks. He stuck to his decision even after it had been pointed out to him that the unfavourable developments in Tunisia could mean that if 'Citadel' were put off any longer, there would be a danger of its coinciding with an enemy landing on the Continent. Nor would he recognize that the longer one waited, the more armour the Russians would have – particularly as their tank output undoubtedly exceeded that of Germany. As a result of delays in the delivery of our own new tanks, the Army Group was not ultimately able to move off on 'Citadel' until the beginning of July, by which time the essential advantage of a 'forehand' blow was lost. The whole idea had been to attack before the enemy had replenished his forces and got over the reverses of the winter. At the same time it was certain that the longer we took to launch the operation, the greater must be the threat to those of Southern Army Group's armies in the Donetz–Mius salient which had had to hand over all their available forces and, most of all, to the Orel bulge as the jumping-off base of Central Army Group's Ninth Army.

On 5th July the German armies were finally able to attack. Though every deception and camouflage measure had been taken, we could no longer expect to catch the enemy unawares after a delay of that length.

On the assault front of *Central Army Group*, Ninth Army succeeded in penetrating the enemy fortifications to a depth of about 9 miles in the first two days. After heavy fighting in which it had to beat off counter-attacks by enemy reserves, it managed to deepen this penetration by a few more miles up till 9th July, but then it came to a halt before a built-in system of positions on a dominant height to the rear of the front. Its intention of resuming the attack in a few days' time was frustrated by the enemy, who attacked the Orel bulge in strength from the north and north-east on 11th July. To support Second Panzer Army in holding this front, the Army Group found itself compelled to throw strong mobile forces from Ninth Army into the Orel battle.

The offensive in *Southern Army Group*'s area developed more favourably. Here, too, the attack through the enemy's deeply echeloned defences proved difficult enough and made only slow progress. However, by 11th July it had been possible to break through the last position into the area of Prokhorovka and Oboyan. During this time hasty counter-attacks by the enemy's mobile reserves were beaten off, in the course of which ten tank or mechanized corps were either smashed or severely battered. By 13th July the enemy facing Southern Army Group had lost 24,000 men as prisoners, 1,800 tanks, 267 field-pieces and 1,080 anti-tank guns.

On 13th July, when the battle was at its climax and the issue apparently at hand, the commanders of the two army groups concerned were summoned to Hitler. He opened the conference by announcing that the Western Allies had landed in Sicily that day and that the situation there had taken an extremely serious turn. The Italians were not even attempting to fight, and the island was likely to be lost. Since the next step might well be a landing in the Balkans or Lower Italy, it was necessary to form new armies in Italy and the western Balkans. These forces must be found from the Eastern Front, so 'Citadel' would have to be discontinued.

Thus the very thing had come to pass of which I had warned Hitler in May.

The commander of Central Army Group, Field-Marshal v. Kluge, reported that Ninth Army was making no further headway and that he was having to deprive it of all its mobile forces to check the enemy's deep incursions into the Orel salient. There could be no question of continuing with 'Citadel' or of resuming the operation at a later date.

Speaking for my own Army Group, I pointed out that the battle was now at its culminating point, and that to break it off at this moment would be tantamount to throwing a victory away. On no account should we let go of the enemy until the mobile reserves he had committed were completely beaten.

Nonetheless, Hitler ruled that 'Citadel' was to be called off on account of the situation in the Mediterranean and the state of affairs in Central Army Group. The only concession he would make was that Southern Army Group should continue the attack until it had achieved its aim of smashing the enemy's armoured reserves. As a matter of fact not even this could be accomplished, for only a few days later the Army Group was ordered to hand over several armoured divisions to Central Army Group. The assault groups of both formations had to be withdrawn to their original start-lines.

And so the last German offensive in the east ended in a fiasco, even though the enemy opposite the two attacking armies of Southern Army Group had suffered four times their losses in prisoners, dead and wounded.

15

THE DEFENSIVE BATTLES OF 1943-4

WHEN 'CITADEL' was called off, the initiative in the Eastern theatre of war finally passed to the Russians. Now that we had failed to encircle strong forces of the enemy in the Kursk salient and had even had to cut short the action against his mobile reserves before anything decisive could be achieved, his preponderance of numbers was bound to make itself felt. Indeed, his attack on the Orel bulge was only the prelude to a grand offensive.

Henceforth Southern Army Group found itself waging a defensive struggle which could not be anything more than a system of improvisations and stop-gaps. Being too weak, on that widely extended front, for purely passive defence against an enemy so many times stronger than itself, it had to concentrate its efforts – even at the risk of repercussions in sectors temporarily less threatened – on punctually assembling forces wherever there was a Soviet breakthrough to intercept or a chance of inflicting a blow on the enemy. What had to be avoided at all costs was that any elements of the Army Group should become cut off through deep enemy breakthroughs and suffer the same fate as Sixth Army at Stalingrad. To 'maintain ourselves in the field', and in doing so to wear down the enemy's offensive capacity to the utmost, became the whole essence of this struggle.

FIRST BATTLE OF THE DONETZ

As had been expected, the enemy's first blow was directed against the front embracing the Donetz area.

On 17th July a powerful offensive was launched against Sixth Army on the Mius and First Panzer Army on the Middle Donetz. While achieving considerable penetration, however, the enemy was unable to force a breakthrough.

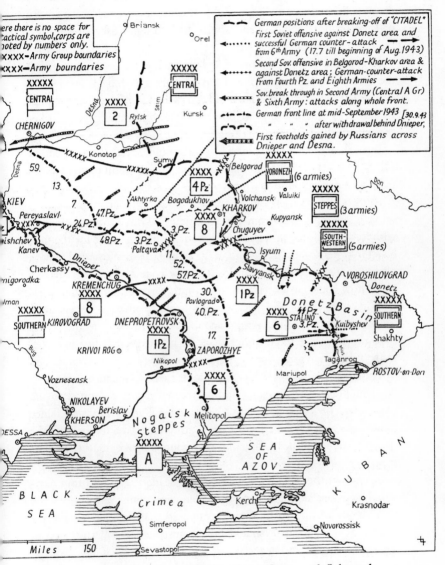

ere there is no space for
tactical symbol, corps are
noted by numbers only.

xxxx—Army Group boundaries
xxxx—Army boundaries

Legend:

— German positions after breaking-off of "CITADEL"
- First Soviet offensive against Donetz area and
  successful German counter-attack
  from 6th Army (17.7 till beginning of Aug.1943)
- Second Sov. offensive in Belgorod-Kharkov area &
  against Donetz area; German-counter-attack
  from Fourth Pz. and Eighth Armies
- Sov. break through in Second Army (Central A Gr)
  & Sixth Army; attacks along whole front.
- German front line at mid-September 1943 [30.9.43
  " " " " after withdrawal behind Dnieper,
- First footholds gained by Russians across
  Dnieper and Desna.

Map 21. Battles Fought by Southern Army Group 17th July–30th
September 1943.

Sixth Army, by committing both the mechanized formations left as reserves in the Donetz area, was able to halt the attack after the enemy had won a bridgehead 12 miles wide and 10 miles deep on the west bank of the Mius north of Kuibyshev.

In the case of *First Panzer Army* the enemy succeeded in crossing the Donetz south-east of Isyum on roughly a 20-mile front, but by throwing in both the divisions of 24 Panzer Corps moving up from Kharkov, it was possible to prevent him from gaining any further ground south of the river.

Even though we were able to halt these Soviet attacks by the end of July, however, the situation in the Donetz area was still hardly tenable from a long-term point of view.

And so, having itself had to call off the 'Citadel' operation for good on 17th July on orders from Hitler, Southern Army Group decided to withdraw a substantial weight of armour from that wing for the time being in order to iron things out in the Donetz area. We hoped to have given the enemy so much punishment in the course of 'Citadel' that we could now count on a breathing space in this part of the front.

Without a doubt this decision was a disastrous one in regard to subsequent events on the Army Group's northern wing, as the enemy took the offensive there earlier than we had expected. But mistaken though the move proved to be, the fact remains that it was conditioned by Hitler's insistence on holding the Donetz area. In practice, moreover, the temporary weakening of the northern wing was limited to the withdrawal of H.Q. 3 Panzer Corps and 3 Panzer Division, since Hitler again put the SS Panzer Corps, now earmarked for Italy, at the Army Group's disposal for this one counterstroke in the Donetz area.

In view of the fact that the two corps headquarters and four armoured divisions destined for the Donetz area could only arrive one after the other, the Army Group proposed that the two leading divisions of the SS Corps should first deliver a short, sharp punch to straighten out First Panzer Army's position south of the Donetz. Thereupon the whole of our armour would be used to wipe out the big enemy bridgehead in Sixth Army's sector and to restore the Mius front. Hitler, however, promptly banned any action in First Panzer Army's area, although there was not the least reason why this need have protracted the stay of the SS Corps. Since there had already been a case of interference in the Army Group's handling of operations during 'Citadel' (i.e. when Hitler had stopped 24 Panzer Corps from being used with Army Detachment Kempf), I felt compelled to protest to O.K.H. This is what I wrote to General Zeitzler:

'If my misgivings about coming developments are disregarded, and if my intentions as a commander, which aim merely at removing difficulties for which I am not responsible, continue to be frustrated, I shall have no choice but to assume that the Führer has not the necessary confidence in this Headquarters. I am far from believing myself infallible. Everyone makes mistakes – even great captains like Frederick and Napoleon. At the same time I would point out that Eleventh Army won the Crimean campaign under very difficult conditions and that when faced with an almost hopeless situation at the end of last year, Southern Army Group still mastered it.

'If the Führer thinks he can find any army group commander or headquarters staff with better nerves than we had during the past winter, with more initiative than we showed in the Crimea, on the Donetz or at Kharkov, with greater powers of improvisation than were displayed by us in the Crimean or winter campaign, or with the ability to foresee the inevitable more clearly than we have done, I am fully prepared to hand over to them!

'As long as I remain at this post, however, I must have the chance to use my own head.'

July 30th saw the start of the counter-attack launched in Sixth Army's area by the armour brought over from the northern wing of the Army Group. It resulted in the complete restoration of the situation on the Mius front. The ratio of forces involved in this battle was indicative not only of the situation obtaining at the time but also of the superior quality of the German troops. In his bridgehead the enemy had no less than sixteen rifle divisions, two mechanized corps, one armoured brigade and two anti-tank brigades. The German counter-attack was performed by four armoured, one panzer grenadier and two infantry divisions.

In the course of this counter-attack and the Soviet attacks preceding it, the enemy lost some 18,000 men as prisoners, 700 tanks, 200 field-guns and 400 anti-tank guns.

THE BATTLE WEST OF BELGOROD AND THE FIGHT FOR
KHARKOV

Having thus succeeded in restoring the situation in Sixth Army's sector, we were still left with the festering wound on First Panzer Army's Donetz front. It could no longer be cauterized because of the storm now brewing over the Army Group's northern wing.

From the moment when Army Detachment Kempf and Fourth Panzer Army were withdrawn to their pre-'Citadel' positions, the enemy had been putting them under steady pressure. Around the turn of the month our radio monitoring and air reconnaissance showed him to be assembling a strong concentration of armour in the Kursk salient, obviously by bringing fresh forces over from the centre of the Eastern Front. Other offensive preparations were also noticed in the Donetz bend south-east of Kharkov.

On 2nd August we informed O.K.H. that we were expecting an immediate offensive against the Army Group's northern front west of Belgorod. This, we thought, would probably be supplemented by an attack south-east of Kharkov with the aim of taking our forces round the town in a pincer movement and opening the enemy's way to the Dnieper. We asked for the return of the two armoured divisions which had been handed over to Central Army Group and for permission to retain the SS Panzer Corps for use on our northern wing. Apart from this, we directed that 3 Panzer Corps and 3 Panzer Division be lifted back from the Donetz area to Kharkov.

On 3rd August the first enemy attack broke loose against Fourth Panzer Army and Army Detachment Kempf's front west of Belgorod. The enemy managed to effect a breakthrough on the inter-army boundary, and in the next few days he extended it considerably in breadth and depth. Fourth Panzer Army was pushed back to the west and Army Detachment Kempf in a southerly direction towards Kharkov. Even by 8th August there was a gaping hole 35 miles wide between the two armies in the area north-west of the town. The enemy seemed free to drive through to Poltava and onwards to the Dnieper.

The Army Group had ordered 3 Panzer Corps [1] over to Kharkov in order that Army Detachment Kempf should fling it into the eastern

---

[1] Consisting of the two SS armoured divisions which Hitler had finally allowed us to retain, plus 3 Panzer Division. *Author.*

flank of the enemy's breakthrough spearhead. Simultaneously Fourth Panzer Army was to thrust into the spearhead's western flank with the two armoured divisions returned from Central Army Group and another panzer grenadier division.

It was clear, however, that no action by these forces, nor indeed by those of the Army Group as a whole, could provide any long-term answer to the problem. Our divisional casualties were already alarmingly high, and two divisions had broken down completely as a result of continuous overstrain. During the rapid advance of the enemy, moreover, a large number of our tanks had been lost while in workshops.

In contrast to all this, the enemy had apparently made up the losses incurred during 'Citadel' more quickly than we had expected. Above all, he had drawn strong new forces from other fronts.

As one might have anticipated, it emerged beyond any possible shadow of doubt that the enemy was now resolved to force an issue against the German southern wing. Not only was he constantly bringing up fresh forces to the breakthrough front, but an attack was also imminent on our front east and south-east of Kharkov. At the same time there were signs that a fresh offensive was planned on the Donetz–Mius front.

When the Chief of the General Staff came to see us on 8th August I told him quite plainly that from now on we could no longer confine ourselves to such isolated problems as whether such-and-such a division could be spared for Southern Army Group or whether the Kuban bridgehead should be evacuated or not. The vital thing was that we should do everything in our power to frustrate what was obviously an enemy bid to destroy the German southern wing. There were two possible ways of doing this. One was to evacuate the Donetz area forthwith in order to release forces for the Army Group's northern wing and at least to hold the Dnieper in the south. The other was that O.K.H. should swiftly transfer at least ten divisions from other fronts to those of Fourth Panzer Army and Central Army Group's Second Army adjoining it in the north, and set a further ten in motion towards the Dnieper. But this time, too, despite the Army Group's repeated demands, no effective action was taken.

Meanwhile the position was growing steadily worse. While the enemy pushed Fourth Panzer Army further west, it became clear that he simultaneously intended to outflank Army Detachment Kempf through the gap he had torn and to encircle it at Kharkov. On 12th August he also attacked our front east and south-east of the town. The divisions there, being far too widely extended, gave way, and the danger that the Army Detachment would be enveloped around the city became imminent.

As usual – but this time for political reasons first and foremost – Hitler demanded that the town be held at all costs, pointing out that its fall could have an unfavourable effect on the attitudes of Turkey and Bulgaria. However true that might be, the Army Group had no intention of sacrificing an army for Kharkov.

On 22nd August Kharkov was abandoned to obtain forces for the two threatened wings of Army Detachment Kempf and prevent its encirclement. In the meantime it had been re-designated Eighth Army and taken over by my erstwhile Chief-of-Staff, General Wöhler. Although I had got on well with General Kempf, I did not oppose the change – the proposal for which came from Hitler – as Wöhler's cautiousness and sang-froid, which had stood up to such severe tests in the Crimea, would be of particular value in the present situation.

Otherwise 22nd August was very much a day of crisis.

In the Donetz area the enemy had attacked again. Though able to halt a threatened breakthrough, Sixth Army's forces had not sufficed to restore the situation. First Panzer Army had brought another major attack to a standstill, but it, too, was coming to the end of its strength. While Eighth Army was able to get out of Kharkov unscathed, Fourth Panzer Army had to face heavy fighting, although it did succeed in winning one defensive action on its southern wing.

Nevertheless, by 23rd August it was possible, by throwing in the armour that had come back from the Donetz area and Central Army Group, to stop the enemy breakthrough towards Poltava for the time being. A front, however thin and incomplete, had been re-established in the sectors of Fourth Panzer and Eighth Armies from a point hard south of Kharkov to south-west of Akhtyrka. While Fourth Panzer Army had been able to maintain contact with the right wing of Central Army Group, there was still a wide gap in the army's front south-west of Akhtyrka. This was closed at the end of the month in the course of an attack to straighten out the front.

The Intelligence picture of 23rd August shows with what odds the two armies had to contend. Against Fourth Panzer Army alone the enemy had committed his 'Voronezh Front', with three armies (two rifle and one tank) assaulting and a fourth one apparently following up. Opposite Eighth Army was the 'Steppes Front', consisting of no less than six armies, of which one was armoured.

An even clearer idea of the Army Group's position as a whole may be gathered from a breakdown of comparative strengths (including the breadths of front involved) which we submitted to O.K.H. on 20th–21st August:

Own Formation	Breadth of Front	Number of Divisions	Approx. Fighting Power	Number of Enemy Formations (Excluding those withdrawn to date)
Sixth Army	155 miles	10 infantry 1 armoured	Equiv. to 3½ divs. „ „ ½ div.	31 rifle divisions 2 mechanized corps 7 armoured brigades 7 armoured regiments (total complement of tanks about 400)
First Panzer Army	155 miles	8 infantry 3 armoured (or panzer grenadier)	„ „ 5½ divs. „ „ 1¼ divs.	32 rifle divisions 1 tank corps 1 mechanized corps 1 armoured brigade 6 armoured regiments 1 cavalry corps (total complement of tanks about 220)
Eighth Army	130 miles	12 infantry 5 armoured	„ „ 5¾ divs. „ „ 2⅓ divs.	44–45 rifle divisions 33 mechanized corps 3 tank corps 11 armoured brigades 16 armoured regiments (total complement of tanks about 360)
Fourth Panzer Army	170 miles	8 infantry 5 armoured	„ „ 3 divs. „ „ 2 divs.	20–22 rifle divisions 1 mechanized corps 5 tank corps 1 armoured brigade 1 armoured regiment (total complement of tanks about 490)
Southern Army Group	610 miles	38 infantry 14 armoured	„ „ 18 infantry „ „ 6 armoured	

When estimating the fighting power of the enemy's forces, we had assumed that in the case of most of the rifle and armoured formations it lay somewhere between 30 and 50 per cent. In the case of a small number of still fresh divisions and individual tank or mechanized corps it was conceivably still between 70 and 80 per cent. Undoubtedly, then, the enemy, too, had had very heavy losses, since the depreciation of his fighting power was more or less the same as our own.

What we could do nothing to offset was the higher number of the

Soviet formations, particularly as the enemy was to bring up fresh forces from the Orel front in the next few days.

The above comparisons also show the extent to which the enemy had concentrated his forces – armour first and foremost – against the Army Group's northern wing. The way he was massing forces in front of Eighth Army and the right wing of Fourth Panzer Army clearly revealed his intention of forcing a breakthrough in the direction of the Dnieper. Subsequently, by bringing up even more reinforcements, he extended this to an attempt to outflank Fourth Panzer Army in the north and push it away from Kiev.

What also emerges from our breakdown of strengths is that in contrast to the enemy's own build-up since the beginning of 'Citadel' (fifty-five rifle divisions, two tank or mechanized corps and numerous armoured brigades etc.), Southern Army Group's increment of formations had been quite insignificant – nine infantry and one armoured division up to the end of August. Of these, four infantry divisions fell to 7 Corps, which had come over to Fourth Panzer Army from the right wing of Central Army Group. Since this army's front was thus prolonged by 75 miles, the four divisions in question constituted no real increase.

Nonetheless, we did have five extra infantry divisions and one armoured. Had we received them prior to 'Citadel', they could at least have speeded up the Army Group's first offensive success and influenced the course of the battle very much in our favour. There can be no doubt that they could have been released more easily before 'Citadel' than after it, for since then the situation had become more strained all round.

THE CONFLAGRATION SPREADS

While the re-establishment of a fairly continuous front from Kharkov to Sumy had by 27th August brought about a relaxation – however brief – in the tension on the Army Group's northern wing, the position in the Donetz area became more perilous than ever.

Consequently the Army Group submitted a categorical demand that its southern wing *either* be provided with *further forces* – without change of assignment – *or else* be given *freedom of movement* to halt the enemy on a shorter line further back.

As a result Hitler finally made up his mind to come out to South

Russia for a short conference. It took place in Vinnitsa, where his own headquarters had formerly been.

During the talks my army commanders and I, as well as a corps and a divisional commander, gave Hitler a very clear picture of the situation, with special reference to the condition of the troops, who had long been suffering from overstrain. I drew particular attention to the fact that for a casualty total of 133,000 men there had been only 33,000 replacements. Even though the enemy's fighting power might be considerably weakened, I said, the large number of formations he possessed would still allow him to keep on throwing in divisions capable of offensive action. Apart from this, he would continue to bring in forces from other sectors of the Eastern Front.

Summing up the present situation, I insisted that while the Donetz area could not be held with the forces now available, the far greater danger for the German southern wing as a whole lay on the northern wing of our Army Group. Eighth and Fourth Panzer Armies would be unable in the long run to prevent the enemy from breaking through to the Dnieper.

I presented Hitler with the clear alternative:

Either of *quickly providing the Army Group with new forces* – in any case not less than twelve divisions – and exchanging our tired divisions with others from quiet stretches of front;

Or of *abandoning the Donetz area* to release forces within the Army Group.

Hitler, who remained entirely objective throughout this discussion, though he persisted in trying to ramble off into all sorts of technical details, agreed that the Army Group must be afforded vigorous support, and promised to provide whatever formations could possibly be spared from the sectors of Northern and Central Army Groups. The possibility of exchanging worn-out divisions with others from quieter sectors, he said, would be clarified in a day or two.

The very next day showed that nothing would come of these promises.

The Russians had attacked the left wing of Central Army Group (Second Army), achieving a local breakthrough which compelled the army in question to fall back to the west. Another local crisis in the same Army Group had been caused by a successful Soviet attack in the sector of Fourth Army.

Following a visit by Field-Marshal v. Kluge to General Headquarters on 28th August, nothing further was heard of any release of forces from his sector. Northern Army Group, too, now claimed that it could not spare a single division. As far as the other theatres of operations were concerned, Hitler first wanted to await developments and see whether the British would now land in Apulia or the Balkans or tie their forces down in Sardinia – a contingency which was just as improbable as it was unimportant.

Unfortunately the Russians paid not the slightest heed to this desire of Hitler's to put off his decision. They went on attacking, and the situation became increasingly critical.

Sixth Army was penetrated, and the corps it had fighting on the coast threatened to be encircled by the enemy. Since the divisions which O.K.H. had brought into the Donetz area against the wishes of the Army Group, which had wanted them for the northern wing, did not suffice to restore the situation, orders were issued to Sixth Army on 31st August to fall back on a prepared position in the rear known as a testudo. This meant that the first step in the evacuation of the Donetz area was already taken. The same evening Hitler finally gave the Army Group freedom gradually to withdraw Sixth Army and the right wing of First Panzer Army – 'provided,' he said, 'that the situation absolutely demands it and there is no other possible alternative.' At the same time instructions were given to destroy all installations of military importance in the Donetz area.

If only it had been given this freedom of movement a few weeks earlier, the Army Group would have been in a position to fight the battle on its southern wing more economically. It could have freed formations for the vital northern wing and still halted the enemy advance on a shortened front, possibly even forward of the Dnieper. Now, however, freedom of movement served only to preserve the southern wing from defeat. Even so it remained doubtful whether a proper front could still be established forward of the river.

While *First Panzer Army*, except for that part of its right wing which had to be pulled back in conjunction with Sixth Army's withdrawal to new positions, was able to hold on the Middle Donetz, the situation on the northern wing of the Army Group was again deteriorating.

Eighth Army, now being attacked from the north and east in the area south of Kharkov, was able to forestall an enemy breakthrough only by pulling back – fortunately no great distance – and shortening its front.

Fourth Panzer Army had been compelled by the withdrawal of its northern neighbour, Central Army Group's Second Army, to bend back its left wing. This had the effect of extending its front, which was already much too thinly held, farther than ever. The further fact that ineptitude in the leadership of Second Army's southernmost corps – 13 – caused it to retire into the Panzer Army's area saddled the latter not only with four fairly battered divisions, but also with another 56 miles of front, this time facing north. One could foresee that once the enemy – whose assault power had temporarily slackened – resumed the offensive, the army was unlikely to hold him. This danger was rendered greater still by the new threat to the army's northern flank.

The increasing gravity of the situation, and even more the absence of any decision from Hitler regarding reinforcements, caused me to fly to General Headquarters in East Prussia on 3rd September. I asked Field-Marshal v. Kluge to accompany me, as I wished to act conjointly with him in getting our forces distributed in a way which would take account of what the enemy so obviously had in mind. At the same time we wished to broach the need for rationalizing the overall leadership – i.e. for getting rid of O.K.W.–O.K.H. duplication in the Eastern theatre of war. The previous day I had written General Zeitzler a letter demanding that something finally be done to effect a real concentration of effort at the decisive point on the Eastern Front. In view of developments on the adjacent wings of Southern and Central Army Groups, I had said, it was essential that we take the precaution of *assembling a strong army forward of Kiev*. If the arrival of reinforcements from other theatres were delayed until our Western opponents committed themselves by a landing on the Continent, we should be too late in the east. In any case, it should not be too difficult to guess the Western Powers' general intentions from the disposition of their naval forces and shipping space. Zeitzler told me that when he showed the letter to Hitler, the latter had fumed with rage and averred that all I was interested in doing was conducting ingenious operations and justifying myself in the war diary. A pretty naïve contention, I felt.

I am sorry to say that the talk v. Kluge and I had with Hitler proved quite profitless. Hitler declared that no forces could be spared either from other theatres or from Northern Army Group. His reaction to the idea of creating a unified command by transferring responsibility for all theatres of war to the Chief of the General Staff was equally negative, his contention being that even the latter's influence could make no difference or improvement to the overall conduct of the war. Hitler, of course, was fully aware that the ultimate object of proposing a Chief-of-Staff who would be *responsible* for *all* theatres of operations was that he (Hitler), while continuing to have the final say, should relinquish the conduct of operations as such. He was just as much opposed to this as he was to renouncing the command in the east by appointing an actual Commander-in-Chief for that theatre.

As O.K.H. still took no measures in the next few days to accommodate itself to the situation in Southern Army Group, I sent off a further teleprinter message on 7th September in which I again reviewed the position on the Army Group front. I pointed out that the enemy had already committed fifty-five divisions, two tank corps etc. against us, and that these came not only from his reserves but largely from other sectors of the Eastern Front. Furthermore, others were on the way. Once again I insisted that decisive action must be urgently taken if the Army Group were to remain in control of the situation.

The upshot of this was that Hitler appeared at our headquarters in Zaporozhye the very next day, having also summoned Field-Marshal v. Kleist, commander of Army Group A, and General Ruoff, whose Seventeenth Army was still in the Kuban, to meet him there.

All I could do at this conference was once again to stress the seriousness of the Army Group's situation, the state of its troops, and the consequences which would result not only for ourselves but also for Army Group A if our northern wing were defeated.

I emphasized that the position on the Army Group's right wing could not be restored *forward of the Dnieper*. On the northern wing of Sixth Army the enemy had succeeded in tearing a 28-mile gap in our front in which only the remains of two divisions were still fighting. With the small amount of armour at our disposal, the counter-attack we had already launched could not hope to close it. Whether we liked it or not, therefore, we should be compelled to retire behind the Dnieper, particularly in view of the possible repercussions of the exceptionally tense situation on the Army Group's northern wing.

In order to find the necessary forces to sustain this northern wing, I proposed that Central Army Group should be withdrawn to the Dnieper line *forthwith*. This would cut its front by one third and result in such a saving of forces that it would at last be possible to acquire sufficient strength at the vital spot on the Eastern Front.

Hitler now accepted in principle the need to take the right wing of the Army Group back on to the Melitopol-Dnieper line, though he still hoped to avoid doing so by bringing up new S.P. assault-gun battalions. As usual, he thought the use of technical resources was sufficient to halt a development which in fact could only have been averted by throwing in several divisions.

As for acquiring forces from Central Army Group by taking it back to the Upper Dnieper, however, Hitler maintained that it was impossible to withdraw that distance at such short notice. The muddy season would be upon us before a movement of those dimensions could be completed, and, as had already happened in the evacuation of the Orel salient, too much equipment would be lost in the process. The best one could hope for was to withdraw to some intermediate line. This, of course, would not have achieved the man-power economy we were after.

It was all a question of operational flexibility, and this was something on which our own views – based as they were on the experiences of the Crimea and the 1942-3 winter campaign – differed fundamentally from those of O.K.H. and even of the other army groups. During the campaigns in question we had always had to operate with speed and mobility and never had time for long-winded planning and preparation. Hitler and the other army groups, on the other hand, did not think it permissible to initiate and execute extensive troop movements so swiftly. Admittedly the rapid evacuation of fronts which had long been static was complicated by an order of Hitler's that all armies should accumulate a three-month stock of rations and ammunition so as to stand firm whenever their supplies were temporarily interrupted.

But though he could not bring himself to approve anything so radical as my proposal for shortening Central Army Group's front, Hitler did recognize the necessity of decisively strengthening Southern Army Group.

At the suggestion of the Chief of the General Staff, he directed Central Army Group immediately to assemble a corps of two armoured and two infantry divisions on its boundary with Fourth Panzer Army.

The purpose of this was to forestall the envelopment of our northern wing.

In addition, he promised to meet my demand for more divisions to safeguard the Dnieper crossings. Last of all, in order to make more forces available, he decided to evacuate the Kuban bridgehead, which had long since ceased to be of any operational value. According to Field-Marshal v. Kleist, this operation could be completed by 12th October.

Unfortunately we were not able to get the appropriate orders issued straight away – i.e. direct from my headquarters. But when I saw Hitler off at the airstrip he repeated his promise of reinforcements before getting into his machine.

On the afternoon of the same day we issued orders to Sixth and First Panzer Armies to go over to a mobile defensive, conducting it in such a way that the stability of the troops was maintained and as much time as possible gained for the withdrawal.

As far as the fronts of Fourth Panzer and Eighth Armies were concerned, the Army Group hoped that once Hitler had fulfilled his promise, the situation on Fourth Panzer's northern wing could be restored through a counter-attack by the corps which Central Army Group was due to hand over to us. We should be able to buttress the front with the divisions now moving to the Dnieper. It would then still be possible to halt the enemy forward of the river – somewhere up around Poltava.

Unfortunately the next day brought us a fresh disappointment. The order for the movement of four divisions into the Dnieper line, which Hitler had firmly promised to issue when he left me, did not go out. Furthermore, the assembly of a corps on our right wing by Central Army Group was delayed. There was still some doubt as to whether, when and in what strength it would really be available.

I asked the Chief of the General Staff to tell Hitler that in these circumstances we must accept the possibility of the enemy's breaking through to the Dnieper crossings, including the one at Kiev. In view of the fact that the Supreme Command had repeatedly put off taking decisions and failed to keep promises on which the Army Group had already had to base measures of its own, I considered it necessary to insert a paragraph which could only be conveyed to Hitler in writing on account of its bluntness. I quote it here verbatim because it clearly reveals the divergence of views between the Supreme Command and Southern Army Group:

> 'The Army Group has been reporting ever since the end of the winter battles that it would not be able to defend its front with the forces at its disposal and has repeatedly called, without success, for a radical adjustment of forces within the Eastern Front or between the latter and other theatres of war. In view of the importance of the territory being defended by Southern Army Group and the clearly foreseeable fact that the Russians would direct the main effort of their offensive against the latter, this adjustment was absolutely imperative.
>
> 'Instead, the Army Group was divested of forces after "Citadel" and never provided with adequate or timely reinforcements when a crisis occurred.
>
> 'My motive in making these statements is not to fix ex post facto responsibility for developments in the east but to ensure that in future the necessary action is taken in good time.'

Yet Hitler could evidently not bring himself to accept what we now regarded as the inevitable and to withdraw Central Army Group to the Dnieper line of his own free will, thereby disengaging sufficient forces to retain control of the situation on the German southern wing. Neither the appeals of his Chief-of-Staff nor a fresh memorandum from Southern Army Group could do anything to move him. In this latest memorandum we expressed the view that the Soviet offensive which Hitler feared was about to be launched against Central Army Group would only amount to holding attacks aimed at preventing any radical concentration of forces on our own northern wing. Neither the operations nor the war economy, we added, would be seriously prejudiced by a withdrawal of Central Army Group to the Dnieper line.

When still no action was taken to ensure that Central Army Group finally set about grouping the forces which we had been promised on our northern wing, against which the enemy was steadily bringing up new formations, the danger arose that Fourth Panzer Army would be enveloped from the north and pushed away from Kiev to the south. Such a development would not only preclude the establishment of a new front behind the Dnieper, but also put the Army Group in imminent danger of encirclement.

In a report outlining this situation to O.K.H., the Army Group announced on 14th September that it would be compelled the following day to order even its northern wing to retire behind the river on both sides of Kiev. Eighth Army had already been given instructions to go over to mobile tactics. The idea of possibly halting the enemy forward of the Dnieper on a shorter front somewhere around Poltava had been rendered futile by Hitler's dilatoriness.

In reply we received a message instructing us not to issue the order until Hitler had had another talk with me on 15th September. My answer to this was that any such meeting would be pointless unless I could speak to him privately with only the Chief-of-Staff in attendance.

On this occasion I again told Hitler how things had deteriorated on our front since his last visit and emphasized that the crisis which had come about on the northern wing of my Army Group might well prove fatal not only to ourselves but eventually to the Eastern Front as a whole. This crisis, I added, was the consequence of Central Army Group's failure to hand over forces to us. In view of the fact that Southern Army Group had always loyally obeyed any O.K.H. orders of this kind, we did not see why other army groups should not do the same – particularly as the forces in question could not help Central Army Group to hold its own front if Fourth Panzer Army collapsed. To me, I said, it seemed quite intolerable that a transfer of forces which the Supreme Command itself had acknowledged to be urgently necessary could not be enforced. What was to become of us if Army Group commanders did not do what they were told? *I*, at any rate, was confident that I could get my own orders carried out! (The reason why Hitler had not got his way with Central Army Group in this case was, of course, that he had failed to give timely consideration to the need to shorten the front there and had not demanded prompt execution in spite of all the objections raised.)

I closed my remarks by saying that it was very doubtful at the moment whether Fourth Panzer Army would get back over the Dnieper. While the Army Group would naturally do everything in its power to ensure that this operation ran smoothly, we had to insist that all four available railways should simultaneously be used to bring over one division each from Central Army Group to our own northern wing for as long as was necessary to restore the situation there. (That this would inevitably necessitate withdrawing Central Army Group on to the

Dnieper line was self-evident.) The fate of the whole Eastern Front was at stake here, I said, and the only possible solution was to bring strong forces up into the Kiev area forthwith.

Although Hitler accepted my implicit criticism of his leadership calmly enough, he doubtless derived small satisfaction from the interview. Nevertheless, this meeting did result in the immediate issue of an order to Central Army Group to move four divisions off at top speed to Southern Army Group, starting on 17th September and using all four railway lines at once. We were also promised infantry units and replacements from the west to bring our divisions up to strength – in all, thirty-two battalions.

On my return to Army Group Headquarters an order was issued to all our armies on the evening of 15th September to retire on to a line running from Melitopol along the Dnieper to a point above Kiev and thence along the Desna.

The reader may have gained the impression that throughout the weeks the Army Group was fighting forward of the Dnieper the activities of its headquarters staff were largely devoted to disputes with Hitler. Indeed, our constant attempts to persuade the Supreme Command to take necessary measures in good time (and unavoidable ones before it was too late) did cost us a great deal of effort and nervous energy. Mine was a staff accustomed to taking quick decisions, and I personally was hardly one to enjoy continually repeating the obvious. In the last analysis this struggle to get operational needs recognized in time was the decisive feature of the 1943-4 campaign on the German side.

THE WITHDRAWAL BEHIND THE DNIEPER

The Army Group order issued on 15th September after my return from General Headquarters laid down that the armies' rate of withdrawal to the Dnieper line should be entirely subjected to the need to maintain the fighting strength of the troops. It expressly stated that 'all orders and decisions must give priority to the principle that as long as units remain intact they will overcome every difficulty, whereas no withdrawal can be carried out with troops who have lost their fighting strength or stability'. Wherever possible the armies were to let the enemy expend his energies in the assault in order to gain time for the withdrawal.

Sixth Army had to pull back its two southern corps into the prepared positions between Melitopol and the Dnieper bend south of Zaporozhye. Its northern corps was to retire into the Zaporozhye bridgehead. While this corps sector now came under the orders of First Panzer Army, the rest of Sixth Army went over to Army Group A, whose Seventeenth Army was being brought back from the Kuban to the Crimea.

First Panzer Army had to cross the Dnieper at Zaporozhye and Dnepropetrovsk in order to take over the front from Zaporozhye to a point 20 miles east of Kremenchug. Once the east–west crossings had been completed the Dnepropetrovsk bridgehead was to be abandoned, whereas that of Zaporozhye had to be held on the express orders of Hitler. The right wing of Eighth Army, which was likewise to be withdrawn on to Dnepropetrovsk, came under command of First Panzer Army.

The army was also instructed to take immediate steps to assemble 40 Panzer Corps (with a strength of two armoured divisions, one panzer grenadier division and the SS Cavalry Division) south of the Dnieper for transfer to the Army Group's left wing. This measure was, however, thwarted by Hitler's order to hold the Zaporozhye bridgehead. The consequences will be discussed later.

Eighth Army was to change banks in the sector flanked by the bridgeheads of Kremenchug and Cherkassy, attaining the latter crossing by dint of concentrating strong armoured forces on its left wing. Since the army had to hold a front behind the Dnieper reaching to a point 20 miles south of Kiev, it was to take over Fourth Panzer Army's 24 Panzer Corps as soon as the latter crossed the river.

Fourth Panzer Army's task was to get the last-named corps over the Dnieper at Kanev and the main bulk of the army at Kiev, as well as to ensure that behind the river contact was re-established to the north with the right wing of Central Army Group.

The withdrawal into the Melitopol–Dnieper positions which was set in motion by this order and executed in the face of unremitting pressure from a far superior opponent probably represents the most difficult operation performed by the Army Group throughout the 1943–4 campaign.

On the right wing, in Sixth Army's area, the manœuvre proceeded with relative ease, as the army was able to pull its forces back frontally into the consolidated positions north of Melitopol and the bridgehead of Zaporozhye. The main danger in this sector lay in the superior strength of the pursuer – particularly of his armour, which was able to thrust into the midst of our forces while they were actually on the move.

On the other hand, exceptional difficulty was experienced in getting the other three armies back behind the river. From a front 440 miles in length they had to converge on a maximum of five Dnieper crossings. Having once crossed the Dnieper, however, they had to form another defensive front as wide as their previous one and be fully deployed again before the enemy could gain a foothold on the southern bank. It was this very process of concentrating the entire forces of each army on to one or at most two crossing points that gave the enemy his big chance. Apart from anything else, he could exploit the period in which the Germans were having to be fed back through the Dnepropetrovsk, Kremenchug, Cherkassy, Kanev and Kiev crossing points in order to take the river in his stride in between.

What made the withdrawal even more complex was that neither of the Army Group's central elements, Eighth Army and the left wing of First Panzer Army, could withdraw along an axis perpendicular to the Dnieper. Instead they had to move north of – and very nearly parallel to – the river to reach the crossings through which they must pass. Eighth Army actually had to fight its way back to its own crossing-place, Cherkassy, while on the left wing of the Army Group there was a danger that Fourth Panzer Army would be pushed right away from Kiev as a result of developments on the southern wing of Central Army Group.

The fact that this extraordinarily difficult withdrawal succeeded in spite of numerous local crises was due to the versatile leadership of the army commanders and the magnificent attitude of the troops. Only commanders and formation staffs who felt superior to their counterparts on the other side, only troops who had no feeling of being beaten even when they were pulling away from the enemy, could have brought off this feat. The enemy did not manage to hinder the movement of the armies towards the few crossings available to them. Neither was he able, despite his strength, to take advantage of their convergence on these crossing points to push strong forces across the river at any other spot and in this way to unhinge its defence from the outset. The fact that he did succeed in getting on to the western bank of the Dnieper in one or two places was inevitable in the absence of any German forces to safeguard the river in advance. I shall come back to this in due course.

SCORCHED EARTH

The extremely difficult conditions under which these movements had to be carried out made it imperative that we should take every possible measure likely to impede the enemy. It was essential to ensure that when he reached the Dnieper he could not immediately continue his offensive while still enjoying the advantages of pursuit.

Consequently it was now necessary for the Germans, too, to resort to the 'scorched-earth' policy which the Soviets had adopted during their retreats in previous years.

In a 15-mile zone forward of the Dnieper everything which might enable the enemy to go straight over the river on a broad front was destroyed or evacuated. This included anything affording cover or accommodation for Soviet troops in an assembly area opposite our Dnieper defences and anything which might ease their supply problem, particularly in the way of food.

At the same time, in pursuance of instructions specially promulgated by Göring's economic staff, the zone was to be emptied of all provisions, economic goods and machinery which could assist Soviet war production. In the case of my own Army Group, this measure was confined to essential machinery, horses and cattle. Naturally there was no question of our 'pillaging' the area. That was something which the German Army – unlike certain others – did not tolerate. Strict checkpoints were set up to ensure that no vehicle carried misappropriated goods. As for the effects and stocks of factories, warehouses and *Sovkhozes*, these were in any case the property of the State and not of private individuals.

Since it was Soviet policy, whenever any territory was recaptured, immediately to embody all able-bodied males under sixty into the armed forces and to conscript the whole of the remaining population for work of military importance, often in the battle zone itself, the Supreme Command had directed that the civil population would also be evacuated. In practice, this coercive measure was applied only to men of military age, who would have immediately been re-enlisted.

On the other hand, a considerable proportion of the Russian population joined our withdrawal quite voluntarily in order to escape the dreaded Soviets, forming big trek columns like those we ourselves were to see later in eastern Germany. Far from being forcibly abducted, these people received every possible help from the German Armies and were conducted into areas west of the Dnieper in which the German authorities had arranged to feed and accommodate them. They were allowed to take along everything, including horses and cattle, which could possibly accompany them, and wherever we could manage to do so we put our own vehicles at their disposal. Although the war caused these people a great deal of misfortune and hardship, the latter bore no comparison to the terror-bombing suffered by the civil population in Germany or what happened later on in Germany's eastern territories. In any case, all the measures taken on the German side were conditioned by *military necessity*.

One or two figures may serve to show what an immense technical achievement this withdrawal operation was. To begin with, there were 200,000 wounded to evacuate. About 2,500 trains were needed to shift German equipment and stores and requisitioned Soviet property. And the Russian civilians who had attached themselves to us alone numbered many hundreds of thousands. Despite the extra difficulties involved in having only a few crossing points at our disposal, the withdrawal was completed in a relatively short space of time, thereby proving – contrary to what others might think – that even operations of this kind can be executed quickly.

By 30th September every army in the Group was back on the Melitopol–Dnieper line.

THE FIGHT FOR THE DNIEPER LINE

By crossing the Dnieper the Army Group had undoubtedly put a strong natural obstacle between itself and the enemy – at least as long as the summer was with us. Yet it could not expect the decrease in tension to last for long.

We were convinced that the *enemy* would continue to seek a showdown in *this* sector of the Eastern Front and nowhere else, for operationally, economically and politically it was here that the most tempting prizes lay. Consequently he could be expected to exploit the supply potential of his southern wing to the utmost in order to keep throwing fresh forces – either from his reserves or from other sectors of the front – into the struggle against Southern Army Group. Obviously he would not be debarred from launching holding attacks or limited offensives in other parts of the front, but even if they produced local successes, these would not be of decisive importance when compared with the events on the southern wing.

What prospects did Southern Army Group have of holding its ground? Was there a chance that the enemy might finally bleed himself white in attacks on the Dnieper line?

These questions could have been answered much more confidently in the autumn of 1943 if the Dnieper line had been a strongly prepared system of fortifications. This, unfortunately, was far from being the case.

It is true that as early as the winter of 1942–3 the Army Group had called on O.K.H. to fortify the Dnieper line with the least possible delay. It was unable to do so itself because at that time the river was still outside its zone of operations. However, Hitler had turned down the request – partly because he was opposed to rear-area defences on principle as an encouragement to retreat, and partly also because he wished to put all his labour and materials into the Atlantic Wall. As the fighting drew nearer to the Dnieper in the early months of 1943, however, the Army Group had on its own initiative taken steps to convert Zaporozhye, Dnepropetrovsk, Kremenchug and Kiev into bridgeheads so that the enemy would in any event be prevented from cutting the communications to the rear at these vital crossing points. With the final transition to defensive warfare after the end of 'Citadel' we had set about enlarging and extending the Dnieper fortifications with the help of requisitioned civilian labour. Even then only light fieldworks could be built, as the Army Group was dependent on O.K.H. for construction machinery, concrete, steel, barbed wire and mines and on the Reich Commissariat in the Ukraine for timber, while Hitler was still giving priority to the Atlantic Wall. So although the Dnieper could be considered a formidable obstacle so long as it did not freeze over, it would be effective only if its defences were occupied in sufficient strength to compensate for their lightness of structure.

But this was just where our weakness lay. German formation strengths had fallen off to a frightening degree in the incessant fighting of the past two and a half months, and the replacements of personnel and weapons – especially tanks – came nowhere near filling the gaps. To a very large extent this was due – as I said earlier – to Hitler's persistence in setting up new divisions back at home.

Even before completing the withdrawal, the Army Group gave O.K.H. a plain statement of the strength position, from which it appeared doubtful whether the Dnieper line could be held for any length of time. We pointed out that the defence of the river itself must be carried out by the infantry divisions, the armour being retained as a mobile reserve ready to intervene wherever the enemy attempted to cross in force.

In the same connexion we had to report that for the immediate defence of a 440-mile Dnieper front, the three armies left to the Army Group had a total of thirty-seven infantry divisions at their disposal. (This figure included three which were at present on their way out to us. Five divisions whose fighting power was completely spent had been absorbed into other formations.) In other words, every division would be responsible for some 12 miles of front. As against this, the average number of soldiers fit for *front-line combat duties* per division was now only about 1,000 – a figure which would not rise above 2,000 even after the promised replacements had arrived. Obviously no decisive defence could function on this basis, even from behind the Dnieper.

As for the seventeen armoured or panzer grenadier divisions now available to the Army Group, we said, hardly one of them had any real punch left, and the number of tanks had dropped just as sharply as the manpower of the panzer grenadier regiments.

The Army Group accordingly demanded that more infantry divisions should follow the three at present moving up to join it. This was additionally justified, we felt, by the fact that Central Army Group's front was being reduced by one third as a result of its withdrawal to the Dnieper. Furthermore, Central Army Group (or its southern wing, at any rate) was unlikely to be the target of any decisive offensive, as the enemy would merely land himself in the Pinsk Marshes in the process.

In equal measures we emphasized the importance of giving priority to the formations of Southern Army Group in the replacement of troops and equipment, since it was they who would continue to bear the brunt of the fighting on the Eastern Front, just as they had done to date. Nor must there be another ammunition shortage like the one which had already occurred during the withdrawal.

It would quite definitely depend on the fulfilment of these demands, we said, whether the enemy offensive in the struggle for the Dnieper line could be frustrated or not.

Ultimately, therefore, the question was whether the German Supreme Command still had the forces and means available to win the struggle in the part of the Eastern Front where the enemy was intent on bringing matters to a head in 1943.

At the time one could not possibly say that this would be hopeless from the start in view of the *overall* superiority of the Soviet forces. Even if the enemy were willing to stake everything this year on gaining a decisive victory on the southern wing, the supply problem still imposed certain limitations on the number of forces he could commit in this part of the front. It was thus of paramount importance that the German Supreme Command should anticipate the enemy onslaught which seemed likely to be launched here by massing its own forces in *good time* and *adequate strength* in the same area. Obviously it could do so only if it made up its mind to accept considerable risks in other sectors of the Eastern Front and other theatres of operations. Provided that such action were taken, an abortive Soviet offensive against Southern Army Group would probably wear down the enemy's attacking power to a conclusive degree – a success which might decisively influence the further course of the war.

This question of timely and adequate support for the southern wing of the German armies continued to be the bone of contention between Southern Army Group and the German Supreme Command. As I would rather not retail the innumerable arguments it caused, I will merely point out that the Chiefs of the General Staff and the Operations Branch entirely agreed with us. On 3rd October, for example, General Heusinger told me that he had proposed an evacuation of the Crimea and the withdrawal of Northern Army Group on to a shortened line in order to release forces for Southern Army Group within the framework of the Eastern Front. Likewise he had suggested the construction of a proper *Ostwall*[1] somewhere well to the rear. (Hitler had recently been using the term *Ostwall* to describe the Dnieper fortifica-

---

[1] Lit. 'Eastern Rampart' – in other words, a system of fortifications similar to the Siegfried Line, or Westwall. *Tr.*

tions originally built against his wishes.) The Führer had turned down both proposals. Though the possibility of bringing in formations from other theatres was under consideration, said Heusinger, this would produce only a few divisions at the most.

Now let us return to the position on the Dnieper.

By the end of September it had become clear how the enemy intended to prosecute his offensive over and beyond the river.

Powerful forces had followed Sixth Army (under command of Army Group A since the middle of the month) as it moved back into the Melitopol–Dnieper positions.

Three enemy armies (two up and one in reserve), comprising twenty rifle divisions and two tank or mechanized corps, were pursuing First Panzer Army towards the Zaporozhye bridgehead.

Two armies of fifteen divisions, followed by a tank army of three corps, were advancing on the Dnieper between Dnepropetrovsk and Kremenchug.

Two armies of about twelve rifle divisions, two tank and one mechanized corps, followed by a tank army of three more corps, were moving towards the Dnieper between Cherkassy and Rzhishchev.

On the other hand, the only Soviet forces initially identified as moving on Kiev and the sector of river north of the city were three rifle and one mechanized corps. Obviously the enemy wanted to direct the main effort of his operations against the Dnieper bend in the first instance. In point of fact, the sector of river north and south of Kiev was just where he could move forces most speedily from the Central Front.

Although the Army Group succeeded, under the difficult conditions already outlined, in getting its forces back across the Dnieper by 30th September, it still could not prevent the enemy from gaining a footing on the southern bank at two places.

Half way between Dnepropetrovsk and Kremenchug, by making use of the islands there, he managed to cross the river on both sides of the boundary of First Panzer and Eighth Armies. The far bank was too weakly held to stop him. Unfortunately 40 Panzer Corps, which the Army Group had previously ordered to assemble south of the Dnieper as a mobile reserve, was not on hand to throw the enemy back across the river in an immediate counter-attack. It was still in the Zaporozhye bridgehead. As has already been noted, Hitler had given orders

during the withdrawal that the bridgeheads of Zaporozhye, Dnepropetrovsk, Kremenchug and Kiev were to be held. It was a measure to
which there could have been no possible objection if only the Army
Group had had enough forces to hold them. As this was not the case,
it had provided for their evacuation on completion of the east-to-west
crossing – an arrangement which Hitler tacitly accepted as far as the
last three were concerned. On the other hand, despite all representations to the contrary, he had expressly ordered the retention of the
bridgehead of Zaporozhye, which was to be even further enlarged.
Apart from referring to the need to keep control of the big Dnieper
dam and its power-station, he had pointed out that the enemy would
hardly dare to attack Sixth Army's Melitopol front as long as we held
the bridgehead. Operationally speaking, the latter viewpoint was quite
a sound one – except that Hitler was again pursuing too many aims at
once. The upshot of the order to hold Zaporozhye was that First
Panzer Army could not release 40 Panzer Corps in time. This disposed
of any possibility of counter-attacking to destroy the enemy between
Dnepropetrovsk and Kremenchug before he had got across the river
in sufficient strength to establish a wide bridgehead.

The enemy had also effected a crossing at the end of September by
exploiting the narrow loop in the Dnieper south of Pereyaslavl (west
of the Kanev bridge). Evidently he was planning a major crossing at
this spot, since he brought no less than four tank and one mechanized
corps up to the river on both sides of it. Having dropped several parachute brigades south of the Dnieper, he soon had eight rifle divisions
and a tank corps inside the loop.

A further emergency arose on the extreme north wing of the Army
Group. Up here, on the boundary between Fourth Panzer Army and
Central Army Group, the enemy had been able to cross the Desna,
which was meant to be held in the first instance. According to orders
issued earlier by O.K.H., Second Army should have had forces
assembled to meet this very contingency, but no such assembly had
taken place.

In mid-September the Army Group had moved its headquarters from
Zaporozhye to Kirovograd, a town of some importance forming
the centre of the industrial area in the Dnieper bend. From there I had
visited the crisis spots developing on the Dnieper front held by First

Panzer and Eighth Armies, and also the front at Kiev. The impression I formed at the time was that while Fourth Panzer Army's front would probably hold, it was no longer likely that the trouble on the boundary between the two other armies could be completely eradicated.

At the beginning of October the Army Group then moved into what had formerly been General Headquarters in Vinnitsa, which was more favourably placed for conducting operations on the Army Group front as a whole. It was situated in a wood, where immense trouble had originally been taken to provide it with its own water, light and power supplies for the benefit of Hitler and the O.K.W. staff. The offices and living quarters were in wooden huts, simply built but tastefully furnished. One astonishing feature of the place was a network of underground sentry-posts running through the entire wood. Apparently Hitler had wanted to be guarded, but preferred those who guarded him to remain invisible. We, fortunately, had no occasion to take such safety precautions. Vinnitsa was a large health resort lying amid picturesque scenery on the Bug. All its hotels and other establishments were now being used as military hospitals, which I visited as soon as my work permitted.

October 1943 found Southern Army Group already involved in the decisive struggle for the Dnieper Line. While the late autumn usually plunged the northern sectors of the Eastern Front into a period of rain and mud which made it difficult even for the Soviets to undertake any major offensive operations, this was not so in the south, where the fighting continued unabated.

In accordance with the enemy order of battle which we had already identified at the end of September, four main targets of enemy pressure emerged in the Army Group area:

(i) the *Zaporozhye bridgehead*, the removal of which the enemy apparently regarded as a prior necessity for continuing his offensive against the adjacent Sixth Army in the south;

(ii & iii) the *two Dnieper sectors* in which the enemy had already succeeded in gaining a footing on the southern bank;

(iv) the northern wing of Fourth Panzer Army *north of Kiev*.

Although the Zaporozhye bridgehead was able to beat off strong Soviet attacks at the beginning of October (which meant, of course,

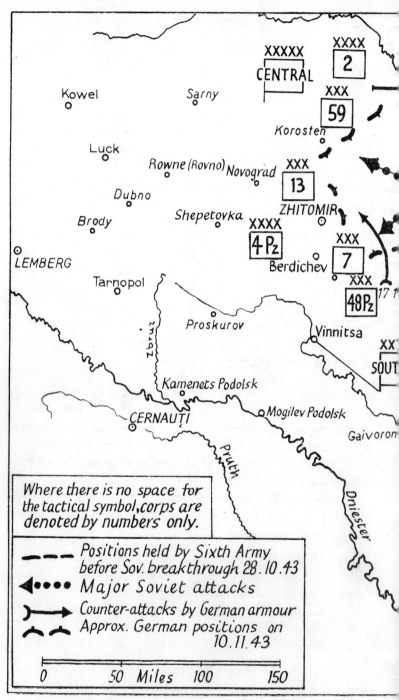

Kowel

Sarny

XXXXX
CENTRAL

XXXX
2

XXX
59

Korosten

Luck

Rowne (Rovno) Novograd

XXX
13

Dubno

Shepetovka

ZHITOMIR

Brody

XXXX
4 Pz

LEMBERG

XXX
7

Tarnopol

Berdichev

XXX
48 Pz

17 1

Zbrucz

Proskurov

Vinnitsa

XX
SOUT

Kamenets Podolsk

Mogilev Podolsk

CERNAUTI

Gaivoron

Pruth

Dniester

Where there is no space for
the tactical symbol, corps are
denoted by numbers only.

- - - Positions held by Sixth Army
before Sov. breakthrough 28.10.43

◄•••• Major Soviet attacks

➤— Counter-attacks by German armour

⌣⌣ Approx. German positions on
10.11.43

0   50   Miles   100   150

Map 22. The Fight fo

BLACK SEA

the Dnieper Bend.

that 40 Panzer Corps did not become free in time to eliminate the
enemy bridgehead between Dnepropetrovsk and Kremenchug), the
enemy paused only to bring up reinforcements before renewing his
assault. By laying down a barrage of shellfire bigger than anything we
had seen to date (it was here that entire 'divisions' of artillery appeared
for the first time) and throwing in no fewer than ten divisions strongly
supported by armour, he succeeded in breaking into the bridgehead.
After heavy fighting, the latter had to be abandoned. Although we still
managed to get the defending troops back over the river and to blow up
both the dam road and the railway bridge which we had finished repairing only a few months before, the divisions which had been fighting
in the bridgehead were severely weakened, and it was doubtful whether
they would still be fit to defend the river itself. In any case, we had
been made to pay far too dearly for Hitler's insistence on holding the
bridgehead.

While it had been possible to bring the enemy to a temporary halt
at his point of penetration half way between Dnepropetrovsk and Kremenchug by calling on the mobile reserves of First Panzer and Eighth
Armies, he could not be made to release his hold on the southern bank
of the river and was steadily building up his forces there to extend the
bridgehead in both breadth and depth. More will be said later on developments in this quarter, which were to have a decisive effect on
future operations in the Dnieper bend.

At the same time the enemy was making every possible effort to en-
large the bridgehead he had gained on the left wing of Eighth Army in
the Dnieper loop at Pereyaslavl. However, mobile forces from Fourth
Panzer and Eighth Armies succeeded in repulsing his attempts to
cross the river on a broad front and in destroying what forces had
already been put over. The same fate overtook the Soviet parachute
brigades dropped here and south-west of Cherkassy. Thus the enemy
in this narrow bridgehead south of Pereyaslavl, which was extremely
difficult to break out of, remained to a large extent under our control.

In *Fourth Panzer Army's area* the enemy succeeded in the course of
October in establishing a foothold on the western bank of the Dnieper
immediately north of Kiev. He was also able to cross on a broad front
opposite the northernmost corps of the army after scoring a success
against the right wing of the neighbouring Second Army. At this point
a danger emerged which invariably lurks on the boundaries of two

different spheres of command. Just as before, the measures whereby the Army Group had intended to iron out the situation on the boundary with its northern neighbour could not be accomplished because Second Army had failed to carry out O.K.H.'s orders to assemble and hand over forces for this purpose. Even after I had lodged a sharply worded protest with O.K.H., it was still unable to get its orders obeyed. Nevertheless, Fourth Panzer Army did manage to hold the ridge some miles west of the Dnieper in the area of the two corps in action north of Kiev. For all that, the situation remained a dangerous one, as we had to expect the enemy to wheel round on Kiev from the north as soon as he had acquired reinforcements.

The most alarming feature of all was that this initial fighting had already led us to commit all the Army Group's mobile formations. Their fighting power was being whittled down just as fast as that of the infantry divisions in the line. This made it increasingly difficult to form fresh mobile reserves and placed us in even more urgent need of reinforcements.

BATTLE OF THE DNIEPER BEND

The Army Group had to continue to regard its northern wing as the more decisive of the two, for if the enemy were to succeed in finally smashing it, he would be at liberty to execute an extensive outflanking movement against both Southern Army Group and Army Group A. In fact, however, he devoted his main efforts in October to attaining a success in the Dnieper bend itself. This, coupled with the fact that Hitler insisted on holding the Crimea for economic and political reasons, compelled the Army Group to accept a decisive battle there.

Throughout October the 'Steppes Front', whose headquarters seemed to be by far the most active on the enemy side, brought more and more forces into the bridgehead south of the Dnieper on the boundary of First Panzer and Eighth Armies. By the end of the month it had more than five armies (one of which was entirely armoured) in there – in all, sixty-one rifle divisions and seven tank or mechanized corps with an estimated strength of over 900 armoured fighting vehicles. Neither of the German army wings could hold its ground against these odds, and each was compelled to wheel back to the east or west as the case might be. A wide gap opened up between the two armies, leaving the enemy free to drive deep into the Dnieper bend towards

Krivoi Rog and Nikopol, the retention of which Hitler considered essential to the German war effort.

Worst of all, any further advance on the enemy's part was bound to lead to the isolation of First Panzer Army in the eastern part of the Dnieper bend. This last danger was the paramount one in the eyes of the Army Group, which was on no account prepared to let the army become encircled.

Meanwhile, our persistent calls for reinforcements had at least impelled O.K.H. to provide us with two refitted armoured divisions (14 and 24) and one infantry division. Three more armoured divisions (1 Panzer and the Leibstandarte, both back from a rest and refit, plus the new 25 Panzer) were also promised to us, though their final allocation and date of arrival were still unsettled.

How different things might have been if these five armoured formations had been at the Army Group's disposal four weeks earlier, when it reached the Dnieper! Even if this could not have been managed for reasons of refitment, what very different chances the Army Group would have had operationally if it could have counted on these forces well in advance and also enjoyed freedom of movement on its southern wing!

With things as they were, however, we could not even wait until all five armoured divisions had arrived, for by that time the fate of First Panzer Army might already be sealed.

Hence we had to resign ourselves to delivering a counterblow with the forces immediately available, 2 Panzer and 1 Infantry Division. Moving forward under command of 40 Panzer Corps from the area into which Eighth Army's wing had fallen back, these forces were to drive from the west into the flank and rear of the enemy advancing in the direction of Krivoi Rog. First Panzer Army, for its own part, had to throw in all its available infantry and armour in order to keep its vital communications through Krivoi Rog open. To enable it to do so, the Army Group had ordered it to leave only safety screens out along the Dnieper in the area where 30 Corps was holding the river on both sides of Dnepropetrovsk. The main bulk of the corps' forces were to be taken back on to a shortened front running from the north of Zaporozhye to north of Krivoi Rog in order to release formations for action at the decisive spot. Hitler had to put up with this surrender of part of the Dnieper bank whether he liked it or not.

Thanks to the exemplary manner in which the two armies co-operated (40 Panzer Corps went over to First Panzer Army in the course of the operation), the counterblow delivered at the end of October north of Krivoi Rog – which already had the enemy at its gates – ended in a neat success. The enemy, instead of cutting off First Panzer Army in the eastern part of the Dnieper bend, as he had intended, suffered a severe setback. According to reports received from the armies, some 10,000 enemy were killed, apart from which 350 tanks, more than the same number of guns and 5,000 prisoners fell into our hands. These figures, when compared with earlier records of captured booty and personnel, showed the extraordinary increase in the material equipment of the Red Army in relation to its manpower. At all events, it could be presumed that two or three tank or mechanized corps and eight rifle divisions had received a severe beating and that several more were badly mauled. Furthermore, it had been possible to re-establish a continuous front between First Panzer and Eighth Army. With the odds still as much against us as ever, however, our forces had not been sufficient to throw the enemy back on to the northern bank of the Dnieper. This was something which would have to wait until the arrival of the three armoured divisions which we had been promised – always assuming that no fresh emergencies arose elsewhere in the meantime. But that was exactly what did happen, almost at once.

While the immediate threat to First Panzer Army was now removed, a new and perhaps even more dangerous one emerged in the rear of it. On 28th October a far superior enemy force had attacked Sixth Army, which was holding the front between the Dnieper and the coast of the Sea of Azov in the area of Army Group A. The depth of penetration was considerable, and Sixth Army – with an alacrity which surprised us – was thereupon withdrawn westwards. In the process its northern wing (4 and 29 Corps) wheeled back into an extended bridgehead south of the Dnieper, which meant that the rear of First Panzer Army and also the Nikopol area were at least covered for the time being. The rest of the army withdrew further to the west in the direction of the Dnieper crossing of Berislav and the lower reaches of the river – though in fact the Nogaisk Steppes offered no basis whatever for quickly forming a new front.

This development in Sixth Army's area constituted a serious threat to First Panzer Army in the eastern part of the Dnieper bend, for although it had temporarily been possible to stabilize the latter's position by 40 Panzer Corps' counterblow against the Soviet forces thrusting at Krivoi Rog, the enemy had by no means suffered a decisive defeat. The main blow planned by the Army Group could not be delivered here before mid-November, as that was the earliest we could expect the three extra armoured divisions to arrive. By that time Sixth Army's southern wing would probably have been flung behind the Lower Dnieper, Seventeenth Army would be cut off in the Crimea, and the enemy would be able to move against the rear of First Panzer Army from the south, coming over the Dnieper on either side of Nikopol. The position of First Panzer Army, which was even now confined to a narrow, hose-shaped area reaching as far east as Zaporozhye with its front facing north and east, would then become more than precarious. If this development could not be prevented, there would be nothing for it but to pull First Panzer Army out to the west from the eastern part of the Dnieper bend. This would have meant more or less abandoning the latter area – in any case losing Nikopol with its stocks of manganese ore and leaving the Crimea to its fate.

To forestall any such development, and in particular to obviate any threat to the rear of First Panzer Army, I suggested the following operational expedient to O.K.H.:

Immediately on disengaging from the battle north of Krivoi Rog, 40 Panzer Corps should launch a surprise attack with two – if possible three – armoured divisions from the bridgehead still held by Sixth Army south of Nikopol, driving into the flank of the enemy forces which were pursuing Sixth Army through the Nogaisk Steppes towards the Lower Dnieper. The purpose of this thrust would be to enable Sixth Army to form a front forward of the Dnieper and to maintain contact with Seventeenth Army in the Crimea. At the same time the threat to First Panzer Army's rear would be eliminated.

By 12th November at the latest the corps should again be available north of the Dnieper to take part in the projected stroke in the area of First Panzer Army, together with the three extra armoured divisions now due to arrive. Should this meet with the decisive success for which we hoped, it might even be possible to effect a further intervention in Sixth Army's area with a view to recapturing the Melitopol–Dnieper front.

This proposal naturally received enthusiastic approval from Hitler, presenting him as it did with the prospect of keeping Nikopol and the Crimea.

Nonetheless, it never came to fruition, as Sixth Army's withdrawal behind the Lower Dnieper proceeded so fast that a sally by 40 Panzer Corps from the Nikopol bridgehead had no further hope of success. After that, events on the northern wing of the Army Group ruled out any possibility of using the three armoured divisions still on their way to us in the Dnieper bend.

It would have been pointless to mention this plan here at all had it not contained one all-important lesson – that even when forced to resort to operational expedients, one should never for a moment disregard the fundamental idea on which one's own conduct of operations is based.

The Army Group had continually emphasized the decisive significance of its northern wing, where the enemy could be expected to launch another major attack in the near future. It would thus have been in line with our general conception of things to take steps to prevent any enemy success at this spot. To that end we should have had to take 40 Panzer Corps out of the Dnieper bend after its successful stroke at Krivoi Rog and put it behind the northern wing of the Army Group, where arrangements would also have had to be made to commit the three extra armoured divisions still moving up.

In view of the trend in Sixth Army's area, however, this would inevitably have meant withdrawing First Panzer Army out of the eastern part of the Dnieper bend, which would in turn have necessitated the abandonment of Nikopol and the evacuation of the Crimea.

It is quite certain that Hitler, who had let the Army Group have all five armoured divisions for the express purpose of restoring the situation in the Dnieper bend, would never have agreed to such a scheme of operations. He would have continued to insist that an attempt be made to hold the Dnieper bend and the Crimea. This does not alter the fact that the Army Group still ought to have acted in the way indicated above.

The proposal made by me, though justified in regard to the threat to First Panzer Army, was nevertheless a mistake as far as the Army Group's operations as a whole were concerned. As a result, 40 Panzer Corps was left pinned down in the Dnieper bend.

There were two reasons why I thus acted against my own basic conception of the way the operations should be conducted. One was the hope that while in possession of the Dnieper line on each side of Nikopol we could deal the enemy surprise blows in quick succession on both banks of the river and, if successful, restore the position on the southern wing. The other reason was that if we did not venture this operation, we should have no choice but to give up the Crimea – a particularly painful prospect for those of us who had once conducted Eleventh Army's bitter struggle for the peninsula. It would still have been more correct, however, not to disregard the principle that the Army Group's northern wing was operationally the more important.

THE BATTLE FOR KIEV

At the beginning of November the enemy again attacked the northern wing of the Army Group, Fourth Panzer Army's Dnieper front, with strong forces. It was not clear whether this was an offensive with far-reaching aims or whether the enemy first intended to win the necessary assembly space west of the river. It soon became evident that the formations of Fourth Panzer Army would be unable to hold the Dnieper against the far stronger Russians, and by 5th November it could be seen that Kiev would be lost.

The Army Group concluded from this that it would now be necessary to fling all the forces that could be made available in its area, especially the three armoured divisions still on their way up, on to its northern wing. Since Hitler had released these divisions expressly for use in the Lower Dnieper area, the agreement of O.K.H. had to be obtained. If the latter could not supply Fourth Panzer Army with further strong forces, there would be no alternative but to give up the Dnieper bend. As no decision was forthcoming on this fundamental question, I flew to General Headquarters on 7th November.

At the meeting Hitler declared that he was not prepared to let slip 'this first unique opportunity' offered by the Army Group's proposal to take a hand in Sixth Army's area for the sake of preserving the Crimea. No success we might score at Kiev, he said, could be so effective that the armour up there would become free in time to help the southern wing. Neither the Crimea nor the defences on the Lower Dnieper would hold out as long as that.

To this I replied that by adhering to the plan for operations in the Dnieper bend and Sixth Army's area we should be running far too great a risk on our northern wing, which would in turn affect the entire position of Southern Army Group and Army Group A. Much as I disliked forgoing the stroke south of the Lower Dnieper, it was now absolutely essential that we intervene at Kiev with all three of the armoured divisions now arriving.

Hitler retorted that there were both military and political reasons why we must achieve the success now offered to us in the area of the Lower Dnieper. For one thing, the army must be made conscious that it was still capable of striking successful blows. For another, it was vitally necessary to our war economy that we retain the manganese deposits of Nikopol. Furthermore, the enemy must not be allowed to regain the Crimea as a basis for aerial warfare against the Rumanian oilfields.

While thoroughly appreciating Hitler's motives, I insisted that the risk on our northern wing was now becoming too great. If things went wrong with Fourth Panzer Army, the fate of Southern Army Group and Army Group A would be sealed sooner or later.

Hitler admitted the magnitude of the risk, but declared that it was one which must be accepted in our present situation and that he was prepared to shoulder the responsibility.

I did succeed, nevertheless, in getting him to agree to send our northern wing the so-often-promised 4 Panzer Division of Second Army (incidentally, it did not come this time either), the 'Nordland' SS Brigade and – at a later date – 2 Parachute Division. In due course, moreover, he even reconciled himself to seeing not merely one of the three new armoured divisions (25 Panzer) used with Fourth Panzer Army instead of in the Dnieper bend, but the two others as well (1 Panzer and the Leibstandarte). On the other hand, the two armoured divisions of 40 Panzer Corps (14 and 24) had to remain with First Panzer Army, where the door was still to be left open for a blow in Sixth Army's area later on. In any case, they could not have been taken away as long as Hitler was not ready to withdraw First Panzer Army to the west from its perilous position in the Dnieper bend, thereby renouncing Nikopol and the Crimea.

In the next few days the situation of Fourth Panzer Army took a rapid turn for the worse. Its eleven infantry divisions, almost all of which were now down to regimental strength, were no longer a match for an opponent who had committed between seventeen and twenty fully manned rifle divisions, three or four tank corps and one cavalry corps in the very first wave of his offensive. Even the two armoured divisions at the army's disposal as a mobile reserve were too weak to stop the enemy's breakthroughs.

After heavy fighting, Kiev had to be evacuated in order that 7 Corps should not be surrounded in the city. The latter was thrown back to the south, and could only halt the enemy advance some 30 miles away. On the western wing of 7 Corps, almost 40 miles south-west of Kiev, the railway junction of Fastov, so essential for detraining reinforcements and supplying Eighth Army, fell to the Russians.

Both corps on the Dnieper north of Kiev were thrown back to the west – 13 Corps to Zhitomir and 49 Corps to Korosten. Each of these junctions, both of which were important for communication with Central Army Group and supplies to Fourth Panzer Army, was reached by the enemy.

Fourth Panzer Army was now torn into three widely separated groups. The only ray of hope in this gloomy situation consisted in the fact that the enemy's assault was also split in two different directions – one south and the other west. The Soviet elements advancing westwards would be of no direct consequence as long as they were unable to swing south and perform a large-scale outflanking movement round the Army Group. To prevent them from doing so until the reinforcements brought up by the Army Group could intervene was the job of the two corps which had been pushed back to the west.

Yet we were to pass through some critical days before the Army Group's counter-measures could take effect from mid-November onwards. These were to consist in a counterblow by the three fresh armoured divisions (25, 1 and the Leibstandarte under command of 48 Panzer Corps, which had been specially released for this purpose by the Army Group) against enemy armour advancing in a south-westerly direction from Kiev. At the moment this was the most menacing enemy force in operation. Afterwards the panzer corps was to wheel west and smash the enemy pursuing 13 Corps towards Zhitomir.

After a success in this quarter it might yet be possible to drive into the rear of the enemy attacking southwards along the Dnieper. In order to reinforce Fourth Panzer Army still further, the Army Group moved over two extra armoured divisions (3 and 10), two panzer grenadier divisions (20 and the SS 'Reich' Division) and 198 Infantry

Division from Eighth Army. Admittedly this unduly weakened Eighth Army's front, but the Army Group had no choice but to thin out temporarily less important stretches of front in favour of the decisive spot of the moment.

Unfortunately, as 48 Panzer Corps could not be assembled before mid-November and the situation south-west of Kiev was becoming progressively more grave, the Army Group unexpectedly had to release the first available armoured division, 25 Panzer, for a limited attack at Fastov aimed at keeping the Panzer Corps' assembly area free. Once again we saw what price a newly drafted division had to pay for its initiation into war conditions in the east. In addition, the divisional commander, who had hastened on in front with his reconnaissance battalion, was put out of action the moment it made contact with the enemy. Instead of leading to the recapture of the Fastov junction, therefore, this undertaking caused a psychological setback to troops who were fighting their first action in the east. Nonetheless, by actually making the attack and committing the forces brought over from Eighth Army, it was possible to halt the enemy on the front south of Kiev and to prevent the Dnieper front from being outflanked any further.

On 15th November 48 Panzer Corps was able to deliver the projected counterblow. The first aim was reached with the defeat of the enemy tank corps advancing south-westwards from Kiev. Thereupon the pressure on 13 Corps was relieved by a swing to the west, and Zhitomir was duly retaken. However, the Panzer Corps' ultimate thrust eastwards along the big Zhitomir–Kiev road into the rear of the Soviet front south of Kiev came to grief in the mud. But even though this meant that the enemy could not be cleared from the western bank of the Dnieper, it had still been possible initially to overcome Fourth Panzer Army's crisis by the beginning of December. The army now held a front running northwards from a point 25 miles south of Kiev to the area north of Zhitomir. 49 Corps, still in its isolated position around Korosten, had been able to recapture the town and thereby to clear the railway link with Central Army Group. According to Fourth Panzer Army, the enemy's losses in dead amounted to some 20,000 men. The fact that only 5,000 prisoners had been taken, as against the 600 tanks, 300 field-guns and over 1,200 anti-tank guns reported to have been either captured or destroyed, once again showed the steady rise in the Red Army's scale of equipment.[1] Of all the Soviet forces encountered on the Kiev front, two-thirds of the infantry divisions, as well as four tank, one mechanized and one cavalry corps, could be regarded as seriously weakened.

Unfortunately the initially rapid retirement of Fourth Panzer Army's corps to the south and west had given Hitler the idea that the command of the army must be placed in other hands. Although I insisted that the loss of the Dnieper front had been due to the superior strength of the enemy and the run-down state of our own divisions rather than to errors in the leadership of the army, Hitler took the view that Colonel-General Hoth needed a rest after the excessive strain of the last few years, and he was accordingly transferred to the Reserve of Officers. I deeply regretted his removal, but at least obtained an assurance that he would be given an army in the west after he had had some leave. Hoth was succeeded by a former Austrian officer, General Rauss, who had made his name in the Army Group as commander of 6 Panzer Division and later of 11 Corps.

THE SECOND BATTLE OF THE DNIEPER BEND

While the fighting was still in progress on Fourth Panzer Army's front, the enemy had already recovered in mid-November from his setback at Krivoi Rog. With the help of fresh forces, he had launched another major attack in the Dnieper bend against the northern front of First Panzer Army and the adjacent right wing (on a front facing east) of Eighth Army. On First Panzer Army's eastern front he also tried to cross the river south of Zaporozhye and attacked Eighth Army's Dnieper front on both sides of Cherkassy. Later he extended his offensive still further by an attack from the south on the bridgehead of Nikopol. (The corps of Sixth Army in here had been placed under command of First Panzer Army.) The enemy's obvious intention now was finally to encircle First Panzer Army in the east of the Dnieper bend and to destroy it there.

This turn of events in the second half of November impelled the Army Group to approach O.K.H. regarding the further conduct of operations.

A memorandum we submitted on 20th November was based on the

---

[1] Obviously these returns were always open to duplication. But even when due allowance has been made for this, they still give a representative picture. *Author*.

premise that in spite of his present mass engagement of troops on the Army Group front, the enemy still had powerful strategic reserves at his disposal. According to available intelligence, we pointed out, forty-four rifle divisions and a large number of armoured brigades set up by the Soviets in 1943 had still not been committed to battle. In addition, it could be assumed that thirty-three rifle divisions and eleven tank or mechanized corps were now being rested and refitted behind the enemy front. Hence the enemy must be expected to go on with his offensive against the southern wing of the Eastern Front throughout the winter, exerting his main pressure on the northern wing of Southern Army Group. Even if our current counterstroke in Fourth Panzer Army's sector should turn out favourably, the enemy would still be able to maintain an adequate assembly area west of the Dnieper from which to resume his offensive later on. For this reason there could be no question of releasing forces from the Army Group's operationally decisive northern wing for a supporting action in the Dnieper bend.

Should it nevertheless be possible, we said, to ward off the enemy offensive now in full swing in the latter area and simultaneously to stabilize the situation in Fourth Panzer Army's sector, things would still develop on the following lines.

The Army Group would have to get through the winter holding a front which far exceeded the resources of its almost completely exhausted divisions. It would not have enough reserves to take effective action against any major enemy attacks, particularly if called upon to do so at several places at once.

Operationally, therefore, the Army Group would remain completely at the enemy's mercy – a particularly dangerous state of affairs in view of the reduced fighting power of its own formations. No battle fought on this basis would have the effect of decisively diminishing the enemy's offensive capacity. The fact that the Soviets would continuously be in a position to dictate our actions to us, while we ourselves were unable to form reserves in time to ward off or anticipate his blows, would cause us excessive losses not only of ground but also of weapons and manpower.

The prior condition for successfully prosecuting this struggle, we insisted, was a *sufficiency of hard-hitting reserves*. If these could not be transferred from other theatres, they must be created by radically shortening the front on the German southern wing (including a seaborne withdrawal of Seventeenth Army from the Crimea). The Army Group could not last the winter if it had to fight without reserves.

Up to the end of November the situation on the southern wing of the Eastern Front developed as follows.

South of the Lower Dnieper (Army Group A), *Sixth Army*'s right wing had vanished behind the lower arm of the river, leaving only a narrow bridgehead at Kherson. Seventeenth Army was cut off in the Crimea and barring the approaches to the peninsula.

On the other hand, it had proved possible to maintain the bridgehead forward of Nikopol in its entire breadth, despite the fact that Fourth Ukrainian Front, the responsible Soviet formation in the south, had committed its main forces – eighteen divisions and strong armour – to the attack here.

For the time being the enemy had called a halt in front of the lower arm of the Dnieper and the Crimean approaches.

In the *Dnieper bend* he had been able to cross the river on a narrow front south of Zaporozhye and to form a small bridgehead. Otherwise *First Panzer Army*'s defensive tactics had been entirely successful, for although it had been pushed back slightly in some places as a result of the enemy's unremitting attacks, the latter had nowhere forced a breakthrough. Nonetheless, the fighting had compelled the army to commit its last reserves. At the end of November it was holding a continuous front which ran from north of Zaporozhye to north-west of Krivoi Rog, where it bent round to the north to join up with Eighth Army.

Eighth Army's own position had become very ticklish – partly, of course, because of the loss of the one infantry and four mobile divisions which it had had to hand over to Fourth Panzer Army to cope with the situation at Kiev at the beginning of November. The enemy had been able to extend his firm base south of the Dnieper in the Kremenchug sector so far upstream that he now had control of the Kremenchug crossing point. South-west of the town, moreover, he had punched a hole – however narrow it might be at the moment – in the army front facing east.

On Eighth Army's northern front on the Dnieper the enemy had made a successful crossing on both sides of Cherkassy. Not having any reserves left, the army had been forced to abandon some 60 miles of river bank and to set up a new – though extremely thin – defensive front behind a marshy water-course which ran parallel to the Dnieper about 30 miles south of it.

Although the Army Group had let Eighth Army have two mobile formations from both First and Fourth Panzer Armies as soon as their positions permitted it to do so, it was doubtful whether Eighth Army could close the gap in its eastern front and regain control of the situation at Cherkassy. This gives some idea of the extent to which the Army Group had to rush its armoured formations to and fro. Each attempt to restore the situation at one point by the use of mobile divisions inevitably provoked a crisis in the army area from which they had come.

By the end of November, at all events, the line of the Dnieper from north of Zaporozhye to west of Cherkassy, and also from south of Kiev right up into Central Army Group's sector, was in enemy hands.

On *Southern Army Group's northern wing*, in the area of *Fourth Panzer Army*, the tension had temporarily relaxed after 48 Panzer Corps' successful counterstroke. Yet there could be no doubt whatever that the enemy was going to assemble fresh forces here and then deliver the decisive thrust into the deep flank of the Army Group. Despite this, the urgent need to continue the struggle for the Dnieper bend had made it imperative to return the two afore-mentioned mobile formations to Eighth Army.

At the beginning of December, Fourth Panzer Army still had its right wing on the Dnieper, where its 24 Panzer Corps [1] was in contact with the left wing of Eighth Army upstream from the Kanev crossing. Some 30 miles south of Kiev the front swung sharply away from the river to the west and described a continuous line (48 and 7 Panzer Corps and 13 Corps) as far as the region north of Zhitomir. Some distance away, with a front facing east, was 59 Corps around Korosten.

A BATTLE ALL ALONG THE LINE

The Soviet attempts to *force an issue in the Dnieper bend* continued throughout December. Except for occasional pauses to substitute fresh formations for those which had grown battle-weary or to throw additional forces into the struggle, the enemy subjected this eastern bastion

---

[1] At that time our panzer corps were by no means entirely made up of armoured divisions. They consisted of a panzer corps headquarters with either infantry or armoured divisions under command, according to the prevailing situation. *Author.*

of ours to an unending succession of assaults which unquestionably caused him extremely heavy casualties.

In the actual bend of the river, *3 Ukrainian Front* repeatedly attacked the northern front of First Panzer Army (30 Corps and 57 Panzer Corps), but in spite of its immense preponderance of numbers it did not achieve any success worth mentioning.

Simultaneously *2 Ukrainian Front* (hitherto known as the 'Steppes Front') put in no fewer than six rifle armies and one tank army in order to over-run the left wing of First Panzer Army and the Eighth Army front facing east. The enemy clearly intended, by employing a massive concentration of armour, to break through to the south-west in the area north-west of Krivoi Rog, on the boundary between the two German armies. Having once achieved this, he would be able to encircle First Panzer Army in the east of the Dnieper bend by driving on towards the lower arm of the river. A second area on which this offensive appeared to be focused was the northern part of Eighth Army's eastern front south of the Dnieper. The enemy's aim here was presumably to bring about the encirclement of Eighth Army in conjunction with a sudden push from the bridgehead he had won at Cherkassy.

At the same time three armies of *4 Ukrainian Front* attacked the Nikopol bridgehead – which automatically included the rear of First Panzer Army – from the south.

While these attacks were beaten off, the overwhelming superiority of 2 Ukrainian Front's attack on the left wing of First Panzer Army inevitably brought the enemy certain successes against Eighth Army. On two occasions he succeeded in breaking through in considerable depth at the two main points of effort mentioned above. As a result, our front had to fall back gradually between Krivoi Rog (which could still be held) and the Dnieper.

In both cases the Army Group was able – though only by seriously weakening sectors which were temporarily less threatened – to assemble a panzer corps of several divisions at the spot in question and, by counter-attacking the enemy breakthrough, to prevent it from affecting the operations as a whole. Yet it was unavoidable in this heavy fighting that the German formations should show increasing signs of battle fatigue. The infantry divisions were no longer getting a moment's respite, and the armoured forces had to be rushed like fire-fighters from one sector of the front to the next. While the enemy's own losses in killed and wounded were undoubtedly many times greater than our own, he was still able to replace them. On the other hand, none of the Army Group's attempts to convince the Supreme Command that it was operationally incorrect to use our forces in the Dnieper bend produced any real results. O.K.H. could not find the necessary replacements of personnel and matériel to compensate for the loss of fighting power, and Hitler refused to agree to a timely surrender of this bastion for the purpose of extracting forces to use on the operationally far more important northern wing. All our warnings that the present successes in defending the Dnieper bend could not remove the danger of First Panzer Army's ultimate encirclement, as long as the enemy continued to bring up reinforcements, fell on deaf ears. So did our attempts to point out the urgency of forming reserves in the south by shortening the front. On the contrary, we had ultimately had no choice – as I have already mentioned – but to throw two divisions into the Dnieper bend from the Army Group's northern wing, where they would have been far more usefully placed.

It needed a desperate crisis on this northern wing before Hitler would face up – and even then most reluctantly – to these operational necessities.

The reason which he continued to give for hanging on to the Dnieper bend was the importance of Nikopol and the Crimea to our war effort. Even now he had not relinquished the hope that once the enemy attacks in the Dnieper bend had been beaten off it would be possible to strike another blow southwards to free the Crimea. What also influenced him here was doubtless the belief that the enemy would finally bleed to death so long as he (Hitler) insisted on holding every foot of ground just as he had done outside Moscow in 1941. Every time a shortening of the front was advocated, moreover, he repeatedly fell back on the quite irrefutable argument that this would release enemy formations as well. What Hitler chose to overlook was that although an attacker may bleed to death before an adequately defended front, any attempt to hold one which can at best be manned on the scale of a safety screen will merely cause the meagre defending forces to be expended at an excessive rate. Assuming, that is, that the enemy does not simply over-run them.

On the *northern wing of the Army Group*, admittedly, the strokes delivered by Fourth Panzer Army's 48 Panzer Corps had created a breathing space, but there could not be the slightest doubt that the enemy would resume the offensive there as soon as he had made good his losses. Fourth Panzer Army's task must be to postpone that moment as long as possible by continuing to weaken its opponent. Furthermore, as the main forces of the army were now disposed along a front facing north between the Dnieper and the region north of Zhitomir, there was as much danger as ever that the enemy would try to outflank its western wing – a manœuvre which 59 Corps, isolated around Korosten, was in no position to prevent.

As Fourth Panzer Army's forces were in any case insufficient to dislodge the enemy completely from the western bank of the Dnieper by an attack towards Kiev, the Army Group felt it must at least try to create a margin of safety for the army's western wing. The longer it was possible to retain the initiative regained there by 48 Panzer Corps, the better it would be.

Fourth Panzer Army was accordingly directed to exploit the situation on the now open western wing in the Zhitomir–Korosten area with a view to launching further offensive blows against limited objectives. On Army Group instructions, 48 Panzer Corps was taken out of the front facing north and, by the use of extensive camouflage and deception tactics, moved by night into the open western flank of the enemy's Sixtieth Army north of Zhitomir. In the surprise attack that followed, the latter was rolled up from the west. Immediately afterwards the corps struck another blow at an enemy force in the process of grouping south-east of Korosten, in the course of which at least three mechanized corps were badly mauled.

Eventually, then, it was possible not only to smash parts of the new offensive group before it could finish forming west of the Dnieper but also to re-establish a certain degree of control over the area opposite Fourth Panzer Army's left wing.

This did not alter the fact that another serious storm was brewing on the same wing of the Army Group. It broke loose on 24th December.

I received the first reports of the start of an enemy attack on both sides of the Kiev–Zhitomir road while I was visiting 20 Panzer Grenadier Division, which was in reserve behind the threatened front. I was there to attend the Christmas celebrations of its regiments. At first the news did not sound any too serious, the only area where things looked at all precarious being that of 25 Panzer Division south of the road. However, the evening situation reports which I saw on arriving back at our headquarters in Vinnitsa indicated that the enemy was attempting a large-scale breakthrough towards Zhitomir.

In the next few days the following intelligence picture emerged:

1 Ukrainian Front in the Kiev sector had concentrated very powerful forces west of the town for a broad breakthrough along and south of the Zhitomir road. In this main assault group were Thirty-Eighth, First Guards and First Tank Armies, initially embracing over eighteen rifle divisions and six tank or mechanized corps. Within the next few days Eighteenth Army was also identified.

This main attack was extended southwards by Fortieth Army south of Fastov.

On the northern wing of the assault front the recently beaten Sixtieth Army, since brought up to strength, and further north Thirteenth Army, were advancing on Korosten with at least fourteen rifle divisions and one cavalry corps under command. While some of these forces had been severely weakened in the afore-mentioned attack by our 48 Panzer Corps, Third Guards Tank Army, with a strength of no less than six tank or mechanized corps, appeared to be busy assembling behind them. Admittedly three or four of these corps, too, had been badly hit in the recent fighting, but the hydra lost no time in sprouting new heads. Anyway, this concentration of mobile formations implied that the enemy intended to supplement the breakthrough towards Zhitomir with a far-flung outflanking movement by way of Korosten.

It is true that 48 Panzer Corps, consisting of two hard-hitting armoured divisions, 168 Infantry Division and 18 Artillery Division (newly formed in the Army Group area), was being held in readiness around Zhitomir, behind the most badly threatened sector of front (now commanded by 42 Corps). It was open to doubt, however, whether these forces would suffice to halt a thrust by an enemy so many times stronger than themselves. And even if they should do so, there would still not be enough forces to meet the threat of an enemy thrust through Korosten, followed by an envelopment of the Army Group's northern wing.

On 25th December, therefore, the Army Group sent O.K.H. a teleprinter message outlining our own position in relation to the enemy's and pointing out what inferences were to be drawn. With the forces it

had at present, we reported, Fourth Panzer Army could not stop the
enemy offensive, which meant that it could not fulfil its task of covering
the deep flank of Southern Army Group and Army Group A. Consequently the army must be *radically* reinforced. If O.K.H. had no more
forces for this purpose, the Army Group would be compelled to detach
at least five or six divisions from its right wing. In that event the latter
obviously could not remain its present position in the Dnieper bend,
and we must accordingly request that it be granted freedom of action.

At the same time Fourth Panzer Army was directed in the first instance to use all its available forces to stop the main Soviet assault
group from breaking through towards Zhitomir in 42 Corps' sector.
Its northern wing (13 and 59 Corps), the army was told, must engage
the enemy in such a way that he was prevented from turning down on
Zhitomir. 17 Panzer Division, already released from Sixth Army
(which had temporarily reverted to the Army Group's command) on
the Lower Dnieper, was moved over to Fourth Panzer Army.

In reply to a further inquiry from O.K.H. which – doubtless at the
instance of Hitler – was again directed at obtaining a compromise solution in the Dnieper bend, the Army Group reported that 'the time for
attempting to master the situation on the Army Group's northern wing
by such isolated measures as the transfer of single divisions is now
past'!

To judge from the size of the force which the enemy had committed
up there, we said, not even a temporary stoppage of his offensive could
make any difference now, particularly as he would certainly be throwing further elements of his winter reserves into the battle. *In fact the
position was such that developments in the area Korosten–Zhitomir–
Berdichev–Vinnitsa–south of Kiev in the next few weeks would decide
whether or not the southern wing of the German armies in the east would
be cut off and forced away to the south-west.*

It was imperative that energetic measures be taken to counteract this
danger. The situation was similar to that in which the Army Group
had found itself during the winter of 1942–3, when the only possible
means of repairing the front had been to leap-frog First and Fourth
Panzer Armies from the right to the left wing. What must be done now
was to release First Panzer Army from the Dnieper bend and shift it
over towards Berdichev with at least five or six divisions. This could
only be achieved by giving up the eastern part of the Dnieper bend and

taking the front there back into prepared positions on a line running from the knee of the Dnieper west of Nikopol to Krivoi Rog.

By shortening the front in this way, we explained, we should be saving twelve divisions. Six of them, as already stated, were to be sent to First Panzer Army on the Army Group's northern wing. The remainder were to be left to Sixth Army – which was to take over what had hitherto been First Panzer Army's sector – for the purpose of establishing a defence on the Lower Dnieper.

The forces to be thrown over to the northern wing of the Army Group were as far as possible to be directed from the east against the enemy spearhead breaking through to Zhitomir.

In addition, O.K.H. would have to send further forces to the northern wing of the Army Group to intercept the enemy outflanking movement which threatened there. Later, if possible, these forces would be used from the west to supplement First Panzer Army's attack on the main assault group.

We also pointed out that while the present situation in the Dnieper bend, where the enemy's attacks had temporarily slackened off, would permit this regrouping to take place without any great risk, the proposed withdrawal of the front was liable to prove difficult if we waited until the enemy was again ready to attack there.

In view of the above, as well as of Fourth Panzer Army's own position, we concluded, it was essential that the Supreme Command make a *quick* decision.

When, despite promptings from us, there was still no decision on this proposal by 28th December but merely the promise of one or two divisions for Fourth Panzer Army, the Army Group issued the appropriate orders on 29th December. *H.Q. First Panzer Army* was to hand over its present sector to Sixth Army by 1st January and, by 3rd January at the latest, to take over Fourth Panzer Army's (i.e. 24 Panzer and 7 Corps') front running from the Dnieper to a point some 27 miles south-east of Berdichev. Behind the left wing of this front 3 Panzer Corps was to assemble with four divisions drawn from the Dnieper bend or Sixth Army – 6 and 17 Panzer Divisions, 16 Panzer Grenadier Division and 101 Light (Jäger) Division. Other divisions would follow. One reason why this switch of First Panzer Army was not initiated on an even larger scale was the limited availability of transport. Another, however, was that the Army Group could not order the evacuation of the eastern part of the Dnieper bend without Hitler's consent, as it was bound to have direct repercussions on the position of Army Group A. Even at army group level, unfortunately, the possibility of taking decisions independently of the Supreme Command ends where the power to co-ordinate operations *between* the army groups begins.

To the stretch of front remaining to *Fourth Panzer Army* were to come the forces put at its disposal by O.K.H. (H.Q. 46 Corps, with 16 Panzer Division, 1 Infantry Division and 4 Mountain Division under command).

It remained doubtful, however, whether these would suffice for the two counterblows planned against the flanks of the main enemy assault group driving towards the south-west. The first thing, in any case, was to bring the enemy to a standstill.

On 30th December the Army Group reported the steps it had taken to O.K.H., and the following day Hitler belatedly gave his consent. On the other hand, he continued to evade the urgently needed decision to give up the eastern part of the Dnieper bend and with it the bridgehead of Nikopol.

While the transfer of forces ordered by the Army Group was being set in motion, the situation in Fourth Panzer Army's sector became increasingly ominous by 31st December.

The main enemy assault group had achieved a wide breakthrough to the south-west in the direction of Vinnitsa. Although the army's front south of Kiev (24 Panzer and 7 Corps) was still holding, it had had to bend back its western wing considerably. Beyond it, in the area where 3 Panzer Corps was supposed to assemble, there was a gaping void 50 miles wide. Not until a point less than 30 miles south-east of Berdichev did another thin front belonging to Fourth Panzer Army begin, and even this, running hard east of the road from Berdichev to Zhitomir, petered out again north of the latter. Fighting around Zhitomir, with a front facing north and east, was 13 Corps. Between it and 59 Corps, which had been pushed back to the west of Korosten, yawned another 50-mile gap in which, some distance to the rear, 26 Panzer Corps was to concentrate.

Fortunately, the opposing forces were temporarily engaged against the disconnected groups of Fourth Panzer Army described above. As for the broad gaps between them, the enemy had so far not fully exploited – or else entirely failed to appreciate – the chances they offered his mobile elements of driving straight through to the Army Group's rear areas or else of surrounding Fourth Panzer Army.

At the beginning of *January* the position of the Army Group as a whole grew progressively worse.

In the *Dnieper bend* (and this also applied to the Nikopol bridge-head), a fresh offensive was being prepared against Sixth and Eighth Armies. Should it break loose before the eastern part of the river-bend had been relinquished in accordance with the Army Group's demand, the situation of this wing could become extremely grave. Worst of all, it would no longer be possible to disengage the armoured divisions which were to follow *H.Q. First Panzer Army* to the northern wing as a second wave and whose release had already been ordered by the Army Group. A major enemy attack did in fact materialize east of Kirovograd on 3rd January, and the two divisions there were stuck for the time being.

All this time it was becoming increasingly urgent that the northern wing should be supplied with further forces, the enemy having meanwhile recognized the big opportunity offered to him by the gaps torn in Fourth Panzer Army's front.

In what was now the area of *First Panzer Army*, the headquarters of which had assumed command in the sector south and south-west of Kiev with effect from 3rd January, the enemy pushed southwards to a point some 30 miles north of Uman. Here he was provisionally halted by the arrival of 3 Panzer Corps' forward elements.

A particularly serious situation had arisen in Fourth Panzer Army. Faced with the danger of having both wings outflanked, it had by 4th January been compelled to fall back on to a front which began less than 40 miles east of Vinnitsa and ran north towards Berdichev (for which a battle was already in progress), finally ending about 40 miles west of the town on the former Soviet–Polish frontier.

In the broad gap between ourselves and Central Army Group further north, 59 Corps had gone back to the former frontier along and north of the highway from Zhitomir to Rovno.

These developments during the first few days of the month impelled me to fly to Hitler's headquarters on 4th January to try to persuade him once and for all of the need for a radical transposition of forces from the right to the left wing of the Army Group.

I began by describing the new danger threatening us in the Dnieper bend and the exceedingly critical state of affairs in the area of Fourth Panzer Army.

Next I gave a detailed explanation of our plan to take the enemy harassing this Army in his flanks by attacking with First Panzer Army's 3 Panzer Corps from the east and with 26 Panzer Corps, now arriving behind Fourth Panzer Army's northern wing, from the north-west.[1] At the same time I warned Hitler that the most these projected counter-attacks could do would be to provide a purely temporary relief from the immediate danger which threatened. From a long-term point of view they offered no solution to the situation on the Army Group's northern wing. If the position here were not cleared up once and for all, the entire southern wing of the Eastern Front would be in mortal peril, and Southern Army Group and Army Group A would ultimately meet their end in Rumania or on the Black Sea.

If the Supreme Command, therefore, did not provide substantial reinforcements, it would no longer be possible to put off withdrawing the southern wing of the Army Group – which would mean abandoning Nikopol and, *ipso facto*, the Crimea – for the purpose of extracting forces for the decisive northern wing.

I ought to point out at this stage that the Army Group regarded a withdrawal from the east of the Dnieper bend as only the first step towards transposing the main effort to the northern wing on a scale consistent with the overall situation.

In order to regroup to that extent, it would be necessary to shorten the front in the south far more radically.

For this reason the Army Group had already taken the precaution of having a defence line further west reconnoitred and developed – a fact of which Hitler was naturally aware. Taking advantage of favourable stretches of river, this line ran in a more or less northerly or north-westerly direction from the lower reaches of the Bug to the southern extremities of the area in which the battles of the Army Group's northern wing were at present raging. Occupation of this line would roughly halve the length of front being held by Sixth and Eighth Armies, which had now been stretched to 560 miles through the continued retention of the Dnieper bend. By cutting our frontage as

[1] Hitler showed sound judgement on this occasion, for he doubted our ability to strike on both wings of Fourth Panzer Army. Subsequent events proved him right. *Author.*

drastically as this and saving really substantial forces (coupled with the transfer of Seventeenth Army from the Crimea to the mainland), we should at last be able to shift our main effort to our northern wing. At the same time the southern wing would still be left with enough forces to hold the afore-mentioned line against a far superior opponent. On the other hand, in view of the damage we had done to his railway network, the enemy would scarcely be capable of shifting forces from his own southern wing into the area west of Kiev at the same speed and on the same scale as we could.

The basis for such a sweeping withdrawal of the German southern wing, of course, first had to be created by the evacuation of the Dnieper bend. To have demanded it straight off would have been most inexpedient in view of what we knew Hitler's attitude to be. He just was not the man to recognize the need for a far-sighted operational policy.

On the contrary, Hitler even now categorically refused to evacuate the Dnieper bend or to give up Nikopol, as he contended that the resultant loss of the Crimea would provoke a change of heart in Turkey, as well as in Bulgaria and Rumania.

He went on to declare that he was in no position to let the Army Group have any further forces for its northern wing, as he would at best be able to take these from Northern Army Group, and then only by pulling it back to Lake Peipus. This might lead to the defection of Finland, which would in turn lose us mastery of the Baltic. Thereafter it would no longer be possible to bring ore from Sweden, and our U-boats would be deprived of a vital training area.

As for giving us forces from the west, said Hitler, he could not do this until an enemy landing had first been beaten off or the British did as he expected and tied themselves down in Portugal. What he must do was to play for time until things clarified in the west and our new formations were ready to go into action. From May onwards, moreover, submarine warfare would begin to make its effect felt.

There were so many disagreements on the enemy side, Hitler added, that the coalition was bound to fall apart one day. To gain time was therefore a matter of paramount importance. While he took just as grave a view as I did of the threat to my Army Group, he had to accept a risk here until he had more forces at his disposal. It was quite futile to attempt to refute Hitler's arguments, since he would merely retort – as he could usually do in such cases – that I lacked an overall perspective.

All I could do was to keep referring to the gravity of the situation on our northern wing and to emphasize that the counter-measures being taken by the Army Group could not possibly offer a final solution to the crisis. It was absolutely imperative that in some way or other a *new army* be swiftly assembled behind the northern wing of the Army Group, *roughly in the region of Rovno*, to meet the threat of a large-scale envelopment by the enemy.

As there could be no point in prolonging this discussion with Hitler in front of the large number of people who attended the daily conference, I asked to see him privately, with only the Chief-of-Staff present. Obviously wondering what I was going to bring up this time, Hitler reluctantly gave his consent, and the emissaries of O.K.W. and Göring, the various aides, Hitler's historiographer and the two stenographers duly departed. (Normally the stenographers had to take down every word at these daily meetings. Having no maps in front of them, however, they often could not grasp the sense of all that was said.)

I had flown to General Headquarters with the firm intention of raising the question of the top-level military leadership again, in addition to discussing the position of my Army Group.

As soon as everyone but General Zeitzler had left the room, I asked leave to speak quite openly.

'Please do,' said Hitler. His manner, if not actually icy, was certainly distant.

'One thing we must be clear about, *mein Führer*,' I began, 'is that the extremely critical situation we are now in cannot be put down to the enemy's superiority alone, great though it is. It is also due to the way in which we are led.'

As I spoke these words, Hitler's expression hardened. He stared at me with a look which made me feel he wished to crush my will to continue. I cannot remember a human gaze ever conveying such will-power. In his otherwise coarse face, the eyes were probably the only attractive and certainly the most expressive feature, and now they were boring into me as if to force me to my knees. At the same moment the notion of an Indian snake-charmer flashed through my mind, and I realized that those eyes must have intimidated many a man before me. I still went on talking, however, and told Hitler that things simply could not go on under the present type of leadership. I must, I said, revert to the proposal I had made to him twice already. To handle grand strategy he needed one *thoroughly responsible* Chief-of-Staff on whose advice alone he must rely in all matters of military policy. The logical effect of this arrangement on the Eastern Front must be – as was already the case in Italy and the West – the appointment of a Commander-in-Chief enjoying full independence within the framework of grand strategy.

As had happened on the two previous occasions when I had approached Hitler about the need for a radical change in his handling of military affairs (amounting in practice, if not formally, to his relinquishment of command), he reacted entirely negatively, asserting that he alone could decide what forces were available for the various theatres of war and what policies should be pursued there. In any case, he said, Göring would never submit to another man's orders.

As regards the proposed appointment of a Commander-in-Chief for the Eastern theatre of war, I have already quoted Hitler's retort that no other man would have the same authority as he had. 'Even I cannot get the Field-Marshals to obey me!' he cried. 'Do you imagine, for example, that they would obey you any more readily? If it comes to the worst, I can dismiss them. No one else would have the authority to do that.'

When I replied that *my* orders were always carried out, he made no further comment and brought the meeting to a close.

Once again, then, I had failed in a well-disposed attempt to persuade Hitler to change the system of command at the top in such a way as to satisfy the exigencies of the war without outwardly affecting his prestige. His unwillingness to hand over to a soldier was probably due in part to his exaggerated faith in his own powers. Not even in private would he admit to having made mistakes or to being in need of a military adviser. Another cause was probably the mistrust which made the dictator determined to keep the army under *his* control against any contingency.

On the other hand, I was well aware that any attempt to settle the matter by force would lead to the collapse of our armies in the field. As far as I was concerned, the prospect of the Russians' getting into Germany excluded the use of violent means just as much as the Anglo-Saxon demand for unconditional surrender.

And so I had to return to my headquarters without having been able to get the Army Group's position alleviated or to bring about a rational organization of command at the top. On no account, however, were we going to abandon our efforts to gain freedom of movement for our right wing in the Dnieper bend and to reinforce our wing in the north.

In view of the negative outcome of the conference at Hitler's headquarters, the Army Group was left with no choice but to carry on with the struggle in the Dnieper bend. On its northern wing operations had to be conducted in such a way as to prevent the enemy from encircling Fourth Panzer Army and breaking through to the south, which would result in the severance of all the southern wing's rear communications.

Throughout January the enemy in the *Dnieper bend* continued to pit all his strength against the bastion we were still having to hold there. In doing so, he assailed Eighth Army's eastern front with particular fury – though the sector now commanded by Sixth Army also had to fight off repeated attacks. The latter were directed not only against the front facing north inside the river bend but also from the south against the Nikopol bridgehead.

Thanks to the heroism of the German troops and the numerous stop-gaps devised by the two army commands, the enemy in this combat area continued to have only limited success, despite the fact that he was now many times stronger in numbers and matériel. Although Eighth Army's front was pushed back a little to the west and Kirovograd was abandoned, the enemy still did not accomplish a decisive breakthrough for the purpose of trapping our forces in the Dnieper bend.

On *the Army Group's left wing*, on the other hand, the situation was becoming more and more difficult.

Fourth Panzer Army, unable to withstand the intensive enemy pressure, found itself compelled to give up Berdichev and – in order to preserve a minimum degree of continuity on the main part of its front – to fall back further still to the west and south-west. But that was not the worst of it.

What constituted an infinitely greater danger was that around 6th January the enemy had realized what opportunities were offered to him by the gap between First Panzer Army and the right wing of Fourth Panzer Army, as well as by the wide open space which had appeared between Fourth Panzer Army and Central Army Group. Inside the latter a weak, solitary 59 Corps was making a fighting withdrawal towards Rovno.

It became clear that the enemy had now halted along the front of Fourth Panzer Army in order to exploit his chances in its exposed flanks.

While he sought to demolish Fourth Panzer Army's northern wing with three armies (Eighteenth, First Guards and First Guards Tank), he dispatched his Sixtieth and Thirteenth Armies on a pursuit to Rovno further north.

At the same time strong Soviet forces (First Tank and Fortieth Armies) drove further southwards in the gap between our own First and Fourth Panzer Armies. Their spearheads got to about 20 miles north of Uman, the supply base of First Panzer Army, and close to Vinnitsa, where Army Group Headquarters had previously been. The latter had been transferred to Proskurov a few days earlier when the signals links with the Army Group's right wing were endangered by the sudden Soviet push. Eventually enemy armour even succeeded in temporarily blocking the most important of the Army Group's railway supply lines at Zhmerinka. (Those further south ran through Rumanian territory and had a lower efficiency.)

In this situation the Army Group had to choose between two courses. Should it take steps to counteract a further enemy thrust in its almost wide open northern flank, where there was an inherent possibility of a far-flung outflanking movement round its northern wing later on? Or was it more important to prevent the enemy's final breakthrough in the gap between First Panzer and Fourth Panzer Armies? There were insufficient forces available to discharge both tasks at once.

We resolved to tackle the second danger first, as the more pressing of the two. If the enemy were allowed to drive through this gap in strength and to head south towards the Upper Bug, Eighth and Sixth Armies would face an imminent threat of being cut off.

Conversely, a continuation of the enemy's advance in the Army Group's northern flank would not constitute a direct threat to our existence until some time in the less immediate future. Up here a certain relief would ultimately be provided by the forces which Hitler would sooner or later be compelled to bring up.

If, on the other hand, the two armies of the southern wing were once cut off, there would no longer be any possibility of extricating them. The only correct solution – an extensive withdrawal of the Army

Group's southern wing for the sake of gaining forces to overcome the crisis on the northern one – was still categorically vetoed by Hitler.

In the light of these considerations we decided first of all to concentrate all the forces that could possibly be spared for a stroke against the enemy advancing southwards in the gap between First Panzer and Fourth Panzer Armies.

This gap was rendered even more dangerous by the fact that the enemy's breakthrough in the direction of Uman had forced First Panzer Army to bend its western wing in the area south-west of Kiev back to the south. It now stood back to back, so to speak, with Eighth Army, which had its front facing eastwards in the Dnieper bend. As the inner wings of both armies still held the Dnieper on either side of Kanev, the German position formed a sort of sack, of which the top was hitched to the Dnieper in the north and the two sides formed the above-mentioned fronts of the two armies, facing east and west respectively. If the enemy in the gap north of Uman were successful, it would be only too easy for him to isolate this 'sack' in the south. The most sensible thing, of course, would have been to evacuate it, since forces were being unprofitably used on its defence. But here, too, Hitler was on no account prepared to see the Dnieper bank abandoned voluntarily. He was still hoping that by using this salient as a springboard he would one day be able to recapture the eastern part of the Dnieper bend. And so the 'sack' remained in existence. Not very long afterwards it became the Cherkassy pocket.

The Army Group intended that the blow to be struck at the enemy advancing between Fourth and First Panzer Armies should take the form of a three-pronged pincer attack.

From the *east* – out of First Panzer Army's sector – 7 Corps had to thrust into the enemy's flank. It was released from the above-mentioned salient by an Army Group order laying down that only a weak defensive screen should remain on the Dnieper. This measure paid off insofar as the corps was not caught in the Cherkassy pocket later on.

From the *west*, 46 Panzer Corps was to drive into the other flank. At this moment it was still on its way over from France.

From the *south*, 3 Panzer Corps, released by the Army Group from the Dnieper bend, was thrown in to meet the enemy. Its task was to hold him down by mobile fighting until the two other corps were ready to attack.

By the second half of January everything was set for the counter-blow. Because of the small number of formations available, however, it had to be carried out in two phases, the gap between Fourth and First Panzer Armies having meanwhile widened to almost 45 miles.

In the first instance, 7 Corps and 3 Panzer Corps defeated Fortieth Soviet Army in the eastern part of the gap. Thereafter, as the result of another concentric attack by 3 and 26 Panzer Corps in which 1 Infantry Division, 4 Mountain Division and 18 Artillery Division played a substantial part, appreciable elements of the enemy's First Tank Army were surrounded and smashed in the west of the gap. During the latter attack – I no longer possess the figures for the first one – approximately 5,000 Soviet troops were killed, and though only 5,500 were taken prisoner, the enemy lost 700 tanks, more than 200 field guns and around 500 anti-tank guns. Fourteen Soviet infantry divisions and five tank or mechanized corps had been affected by the two strokes, though the enemy had doubtless managed to save at least a part of his troops from encirclement.

While all this was taking place, of course, the controversy between Army Group and O.K.H. on the question of future operations continued. Time after time we stressed the importance of finally granting freedom of movement to our right wing and ceasing to clamp it down in the Dnieper bend, which had long been an improper policy from the operational point of view. In a letter submitted through the Chief of the General Staff, I took Hitler up on the arguments he had given me on 4th January for holding fast to the Dnieper bend. The attitudes of Turkey, Bulgaria and Rumania, I told him, would depend less on the Crimea than the presence of an intact German southern wing forward of the eastern frontier of the two last-named countries.

The Army Group was also at pains to emphasize that the final issue on the whole of the German southern wing would depend on the timely assembly of a strong army around Rovno behind the Army Group's left wing – whether this was done by disengaging forces from the right wing after pulling it back on to a shortened front, by transferring formations down from Northern Army Group or by evacuating Seventeenth Army from the Crimea. Only if we could assemble this army around Rovno in good time, we said, could the enemy be prevented from executing a wide envelopment movement in our northern flank and thereby from forcing the entire southern wing of our Eastern

Front away to Rumania. While the Chief-of-Staff entirely concurred
with our views and made repeated efforts to get Hitler to listen to them,
the latter stuck to his principle of stubbornly holding on at all costs. It
was impossible to obtain a directive on how he proposed to conduct
operations on a longer-term basis – i.e. further than holding on for the
next twenty-four hours.

What made this sort of leadership more irrational than ever was the
fact that even O.K.H. credited the enemy with still having powerful
strategic reserves at his disposal which he must be expected to commit
sooner or later. How could anyone exercise proper command in the
field when Hitler did not even tell the army groups how he conceived
the future of operations generally? How, if those enemy reserves
actually did exist, was their intervention to be anticipated with any
degree of foresight? This impossible state of affairs was the subject of a
letter in which I stated the following:

> 'If any leadership is to be successful, it must be based on a har-
> monious co-ordination of policy at all levels, which is dependent on
> clear directives from the top and a unanimous appreciation of the
> situation obtaining on the enemy's side. The Army Group cannot
> merely think from one day to the next. It cannot make do with a
> directive to hold on regardless when at the very same time it sees the
> enemy preparing to force the issue by an outflanking movement
> which it has no means of opposing.
>
> 'I must therefore request O.K.H. either to accept the Army
> Group's views on the basis of the appreciations already submitted
> or else to refute them by passing down its own appreciation of future
> developments.
>
> 'If the Supreme Command remains dumb as well as deaf to the
> conclusions drawn by the Army Group in its own limited sphere of
> activity, a co-ordinated policy will be quite out of the question.'

When there was no reply to this either, I wrote a long letter to
Hitler personally. Once again I pointed out the situation of the Army
Group, the operational possibilities open to the enemy, and the state
of our own troops. I left no room for doubt as to how the overall
situation must develop if no action were taken in accordance with the
Army Group's recommendations. In particular, I underlined the vital
necessity of assembling forces with the least possible delay behind the

Army Group's northern wing to counteract the enemy's palpable intention of outflanking it, with all the far-reaching consequences this would entail. Considering the urgency of this, as well as the danger lying in the eventual isolation of the Army Group's southern wing in the Dnieper bend, I closed with the words:

> 'Allow me to say this in conclusion, *mein Führer*: as far as we are concerned, it is a matter not of eluding a danger but of taking steps to overcome one which we may shortly be compelled to face.'

This communication was to play its part in a clash I had with Hitler a few days later.

On 27th January he summoned all army group and army commanders on the Eastern Front, in addition to a large number of other senior officers, to General Headquarters. He wished to address us in person on the need for National-Socialist education inside the army. The more difficult the military situation became, the greater importance he attached to 'faith' as a guarantee of victory. It was an attitude which he sought to apply more and more in the selection of senior officers for posts down to divisional commander.

Even in his greeting at the simple luncheon which preceded the meeting, one sensed that he had not forgiven me for the criticism implicit in my comments of 4th January.

Now, in his address, he actually went so far as to throw the following words in the faces of the men whose armies had accomplished so much:

'If the end should come one day,' he said, 'it should really be the Field-Marshals and generals who stand by the flags to the last.'

I have never been one to put up with insults. Furthermore, Hitler's words were bound to strike any soldier as a deliberate snub to the army leaders whose courage and will to fulfil their soldierly duty to the bitter end were now being called into question.

Being accustomed to listen to a superior in silence, all those present held their peace. But I personally felt the implied insult so strongly that the blood rushed to my head, and when, by way of emphasis, Hitler repeated his remarks, I called out: 'And so they will, *mein Führer*!'

This exclamation of mine naturally had nothing whatever to do with my attitude towards the National-Socialist system. It was merely intended to show that we were not going to accept imputations of that sort from anyone, including Hitler. I was told afterwards that my comrades, who found Hitler's words just as provocative as I did, had sighed with relief when I spoke.

Hitler, however, had probably never experienced an interruption before when making a speech as Head of State – in this case, as supreme war leader into the bargain. The years when he had heard heckling at public meetings were long past. He obviously lost the thread of what he was saying and, with an icy glare in my direction, called out to me: 'Thank you, Field-Marshal v. Manstein!' Thereupon he brought his address to a somewhat abrupt conclusion.

While I was taking tea with Zeitzler, there was a telephone call to say that Hitler wished to see me in the presence of Keitel. 'Field-Marshal,' he told me when I went in, 'I cannot allow you to interrupt me when I am addressing the generals. You yourself would not tolerate such behaviour from your own subordinates.'

Since there was no answer to this, I did not reply. Then Hitler, who was obviously extremely annoyed, made a mistake.

'By the way,' he said, 'a few days ago you sent me a paper on the situation. I suppose your idea was to justify yourself to posterity in the war diary.'

This was really too much. 'Letters I write to you personally,' I retorted, 'do not get filed in the war diary. You must excuse me if I use an English expression in this connexion, but all I can say to your interpretation of my motives is that *I* am a gentleman.'

Silence. Hitler, after a short pause: 'Thank you very much.'

At the evening conference, to which I was specially summoned, Hitler's manner towards me was again thoroughly amiable. He even consulted me on the possibility of defending the Crimea, on which General Jänicke, commander of Eleventh Army, had just been reporting. I knew, of course, that he would not forgive me for the retort I had made earlier. But I had much more important things to worry about than my personal relations with the Supreme Commander.

During the month of *February* three sectors in particular were to be very much in the news. They may be distinguished by the names of Nikopol, Cherkassy and Rovno.

THE LOSS OF NIKOPOL

With effect from 6th February, Sixth Army reverted to Army Group A, on orders from Hitler. The reason he gave General Zeitzler for this decision was a significant one. Hitler wanted to send two of Sixth Army's divisions to the Crimea, which was even then a forlorn hope. He now explained that he was putting Sixth Army under Army Group A because he would not get these divisions from Southern Army Group.

In one way, the latter regarded the handover of Sixth Army as a welcome relief, for we had quite enough worries in any case! However, it meant losing a reservoir of forces on which we should have been able to draw had we been free to pull the army out of the east of the Dnieper bend and the Nikopol bridgehead in good time. But this was just what Hitler had prevented. Now the enemy was to force him to surrender the areas in question.

On 31st January heavy new enemy attacks had started against the northern front of Sixth Army east of Krivoi Rog and against the Nikopol bridgehead from the south. The upshot was the penetration of the bridgehead. After three days' fighting, the enemy also achieved a decisive breakthrough on the army's northern front, where, despite the fact that the number of divisions was only 2 : 1 in favour of the Soviets, 30 Corps received a severe battering from twelve rifle divisions and two tank corps. Although there had been six infantry divisions in the line and two armoured ones behind it, the former were so short of replacements and weapons that they really only amounted to battle groups, while the armoured divisions had only five serviceable tanks left! Even with these brave troops, constant overstrain was bound to tell sooner or later.

As Sixth Army was by now already removed from Southern Army Group's control, I cannot deal with the further course of the fighting in this sector. The fact is, at all events, that once the enemy had broken through Sixth Army's northern front, the two corps fighting there, like the other two in the Nikopol bridgehead, were well-nigh cut off. It was a development which the Army Group had predicted on numerous occasions. This time even Hitler had to agree to the abandonment of the east of the Dnieper bend and the Nikopol bridgehead. Sixth Army did in fact manage, after heavy fighting, to extricate its corps from the noose, but only at the cost of considerable losses in equipment. Had this bastion been given up at the proper time, it would not only have been possible to withdraw all the forces inside it in good order, but also to free divisions for the far more important northern wing of the Army Group. Instead, Sixth Army's formations had been expended in the wrong place operationally, and one doubted whether they could ultimately withstand the pressure of the pursuing enemy.

THE CHERKASSY POCKET

In the *middle of the Army Group front*, having dealt their successful counterblow against Fortieth Soviet Army in the east of the gap there,

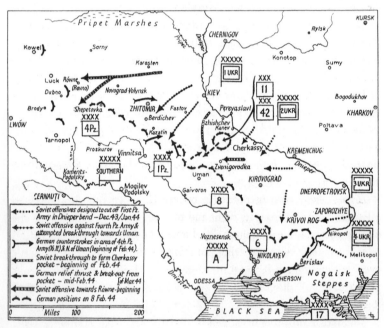

Map 23. Battles Fought by Southern Army Group up to mid-February 1944.

the mobile formations of First Panzer Army had passed on to their second 'leg' in the western part. Immediately our armoured divisions left the first battle-ground, however, the enemy hydra grew more heads.

At the end of January strong enemy forces, including several tank and mechanized corps, broke into the north-western section of the projecting arc of front which the inner wings of First Panzer and Eighth Armies were still having to hold by the Dnieper upstream from Cherkassy. His thrust took the enemy in between 7 and 42 Corps and as far south as the Zvenigorodka area.

Simultaneously the enemy had attacked the Eighth Army front facing east in the area south-west of Cherkassy and broken through it with fresh forces of Fourth Guards and Fifth Guards Tank Armies. These succeeded in driving so far westwards that they were able to join hands with the enemy troops which had broken through First Panzer Army from the north-west towards Zvenigorodka. This meant that the salient described earlier was cut off, and with it First Panzer Army's 42 Corps and Eighth Army's 11 Corps.

Such was the situation which awaited me when I arrived back at Army Group Headquarters on 28th January. Decisive measures were instantly taken to clear an escape route for the encircled corps.

First Panzer Army received orders to end the battle against the forces of First Soviet Tank Army on its left wing as soon as possible and to release 3 Panzer Corps with the utmost speed. It was to be thrown over to the new crisis spot with 16 and 17 Panzer Divisions, the Leibstandarte and the heavy Panzer Regiment Baeke, which had already distinguished itself in the battle mentioned above. 1 Panzer Division was to follow as soon as it could.

Eighth Army was instructed to release H.Q. 47 Panzer Corps and 3 Panzer Division from its front and to form them up in the direction of the point of breakthrough. 24 Panzer Division was also ordered over from Sixth Army to reinforce this group. When it arrived, however, Hitler ordered it to be returned to Army Group A because the position in the Nikopol bridgehead was already turning critical. In fact it got there too late to do any good.

The Army Group's orders were that the two corps – First Panzer Army's from the west and Eighth Army's from the south – were to attack the flank and rear of the enemy forces which had surrounded 42 and 11 Corps.

The number of divisions employed by the Army Group to get the two corps out was a relatively large one. It appeared necessary, however, in view of the fact that the enemy had crammed no less than twenty-six rifle divisions and between seven and nine tank or mechanized corps into this battle-ground from the north-west and east. The reason for their plurality, it is true, was that Soviet divisional strengths were also well down by now, except where fresh or recently refitted formations were concerned.

The task of our two assault groups was first to cut the rear communications of these numerous enemy formations and then to destroy them by concentric attacks.

Unfortunately their assembly was delayed, first by snow and then by the mud which followed. Once they could move off, however, they succeeded in getting to grips with and administering wholesale punishment to a substantial portion of the enemy forces which had isolated the Cherkassy pocket. Between them, the two corps reported the capture of more than 700 tanks, over 600 anti-tank guns and about 150 field-pieces, but only just over 2,000 prisoners. This indicated that the enemy forces had been largely made up of motorized formations. Eventually impenetrable mud or snow put an end to the advance. 3 Panzer Corps' spearhead had got within eight miles of the south-western front of the pocket, while 47 Corps had probably drawn off a substantial proportion of the enemy forces.

The Army Group operations staff had gone to Uman in our command train to supervise the co-operation of the two armies in this battle. The headquarters of First Panzer Army was at Uman itself and that of Eighth Army was easily accessible from the same place. While in Uman I made two attempts to reach the fronts of both assault groups, but each time my car became hopelessly stuck in mud or snow. From one day to the next the weather vacillated between blizzards and thaws. Once again it was seen that the broad tracks of the Soviet tanks made them better than our own at moving over snow-covered ground or a saturated subsoil.

As there was no further prospect of getting the armour right up to the pocket, I gave orders for the two encircled corps to break out to the south-west. In the meantime they had been crowded together from all sides by recurrent enemy attacks, and the space now left to them measured only about 30 miles from north to south and 10–12 miles from east to west. The Russians had already called on them to capitulate on 4th February.

Under command of their Commanding Generals, Stemmermann and Lieb, the two corps commenced their break-out during the night of 16th–17th February. As they set off towards 3 Panzer Corps, it made one last effort to get at least a few tanks through the bottomless mud to meet them. The corps in the pocket had instructions from the Army Group to use their entire artillery and ammunition in support of the break-out. Being unable to move through deep mud across country devoid of roads, the batteries had to stay put after they had fired off their ammunition. Rearguards equipped with a small number of guns covered the break-out against the enemy now moving in from the north-east and south.

It can be imagined with what mixed feelings of hope and anxiety we sat in our command train waiting to hear whether the break-out had succeeded. At 0125 hours on the morning of 17th February we received the gratifying news that the first contact had been established between the escaping troops and the spearheads of 3 Panzer Corps. The enemy in between them was literally over-run. By 28th February we knew that between 30,000 and 32,000 men would come out of the pocket. Considering the drop in the strength of the fronts and the fact that six divisions and one brigade had been surrounded, this figure must be taken to represent the bulk of the fighting troops.[1] One most distressing factor was that the majority of the wounded could not be brought out. General Stemmermann was killed during the fighting.

It had thus been possible to spare both corps the fate suffered by Sixth Army at Stalingrad. In this case, too, Hitler had called for the pocket to be held, but in the end he had consented retrospectively to the break-out preparations ordered by the Army Group. The latter had then issued the order for the actual break-out without previously notifying Hitler in order to avoid any possibility of a countermand.

Naturally the bulk of the guns and heavy weapons had stuck fast in the mud on the way out, only a small number being extricated as a result of the almost superhuman efforts of the troops. The six and a half liberated divisions obviously had to be pulled out of the line for the time being. However, this loss of fighting power, though it further compli- cated the Army Group's position, was to a great extent counter-balanced by the joy of having saved at least the fighting men of the two corps.

First Panzer and Eighth Armies still had the task of firmly reuniting their fronts and releasing armour for the mobile reserve as soon as possible.

After I had visited units of the divisions which had participated in the break-out, my operations staff returned to Proskurov. This was rendered urgently necessary by the situation on the Army Group's left wing.

---

[1] The ration strength of both corps before their encirclement had totalled 54,000. Some of the rear units, however, had evaded the trap. *Author.*

ROVNO

For the reasons stated earlier, the Army Group had done everything in its power during the month of February to prevent the enemy from finally breaking through the centre of its front. It had been able to forestall the threatened isolation of its right wing when the latter was still held fast in the Dnieper bend. Thereupon it had been faced with the necessity of fetching the two encircled corps out of the Cherkassy pocket. Once this had been achieved, our attention inevitably became riveted on developments in the north of the Army Group area.

By this time *Fourth Panzer Army* was on a front facing north-east which actually ran fairly continuously from north-east of Vinnitsa to the west of the small town of Shepetovka. The latter lies some 50 miles due north of Proskurov, where Army Group Headquarters was located. At Shepetovka the army's continuous front came to an end. For a front some 150 miles in length there were at present only nine weakened but still battle-worthy divisions available under three corps commands – five being infantry, two armoured and two panzer grena- diers. For the moment the pressure on the army front had relaxed, the enemy having presumably had to pause in his advance. Nevertheless, it was clear that Fourth Panzer Army would hardly be able to hold out with the above forces against a far superior enemy.

But there was also another danger with far graver implications for the position of the Army Group as a whole.

In front of the western wing of Fourth Panzer Army, extending right up to the southern boundary of Central Army Group in the north, there was now a wide open space practically devoid of German forces. From this area, sooner or later, the enemy was liable to launch a large-scale flanking movement against Fourth Panzer Army, which would be synonymous with outflanking the whole of Southern Army Group. Even though the northern part of this vacuum – the Pinsk Marshes – was automatically excluded from any major operations, there was still an east-to-west bridge of land about 40 miles in breadth immediately above Fourth Panzer Army's front. Through it ran the highway leading from Kiev to Rovno via Zhitomir and further west- wards to Lwòw and Lublin in the Government-General.

In order to block this bridge of land, the Army Group had shifted 13 Corps on to the extreme north wing. The latter was led with great dash by my former Chief-of-Staff at 38 Corps, General Hauffe, who was unfortunately killed at the head of his troops in March 1944. With the few forces at his disposal, Hauffe held up the enemy advance on either side of the highway through February and March, again and again evading the pincer movements of his far stronger opponent. Further north, already within the region of the Pinsk Marshes, a group of police units was guarding the big railway from Kiev to Poland.

Against such odds, of course, the solitary 13 Corps could do no more than delay the enemy advance. As early as the beginning of February the town of Rovno was lost, in consequence of which 13 Corps had to retire westwards towards Dubno.

The Reich Commissioner for the Ukraine, Gauleiter Koch, who resided in Rovno, had naturally lost no time in making himself scarce – though not before enjoining the civil administrators and police forces under his jurisdiction to fight to the last. He was to decamp from East Prussia in exactly the same way later on. Hitler, on the other hand, demanded the head of the general responsible for the loss of the town. According to Zeitzler, even Keitel advocated the immediate shooting of the senior German commander there. When Zeitzler energetically opposed this, averring that Hitler would in any case wish to hear his generals' views, Göring put his oar in. 'Oh no, you don't,' he said. 'Where would we be if that happened every time? Anyway, it isn't the job of a Head of State.' Quite apart from the fact that the affair was no concern whatever of Göring's, he was just about the last person with any right to damn others for alleged dereliction of duty. His utterance was one more example of his notorious hatred of the generals, and the army as a whole. Hitler did not, in fact, accept the recommendations of Keitel and Göring, but ordered a court of inquiry, as a result of which sentence of death was passed not upon the officer originally accused, but on the divisional commander responsible for the Rovno area. This was subsequently quashed by Hitler, who accepted the appeals put up by myself and the army commander in view of the reasons which had led to the loss of Rovno. The 'mobile courts martial', which had power to pass summary judgement over the heads of local commanders, had still not been instituted in my day.

But let us return to Fourth Panzer Army.

Even though, as I have said, there was no immediate threat to the army front, it was perfectly clear that that wide expanse of territory to the north, guarded as it was by a mere handful of forces, would shortly become the basis of an enemy offensive. This might be directed at Lwów in the west or against Fourth Panzer Army in the south in the form of an outflanking movement round its western wing.

It will be recalled that in anticipation of this danger the Army Group had on a number of occasions called for the assembly of an army in the area of Rovno. No such assembly had taken place. The Supreme Command had neither released forces elsewhere for this purpose (i.e. by detaching them from Northern Army Group or evacuating the Crimea), nor had it enabled Southern Army Group to do so by granting it freedom of movement on its southern wing.

It goes without saying that on completion of the Cherkassy battle the Army Group had drawn strong armoured forces from the centre of its front over to the left wing, where they were in position by 15th March. But as we emphasized to O.K.H., these forces would at best suffice to maintain a certain degree of stability on Fourth Panzer Army's front in the event of another major attack. They would on no account be adequate to cope with a wide outflanking movement against the army's western wing. As the issue was as destined as ever to be settled on the northern wing, it was absolutely essential that the latter be provided with additional forces. For the present, however, nothing decisive was done by the Supreme Command in this respect.

Clearly Hitler assumed the enemy's offensive power to be already exhausted. In addition, he was expecting the muddy season to set in shortly and put a stop to any large-scale activity on the part of the Soviets.

It was true that the attack we had launched in mid-February to free the two corps from the Cherkassy pocket had become bogged down as a result of the spells of mud with which the blizzards had been interspersed. Yet it was still too early to count on the actual muddy season to start.

As for the hopefully awaited exhaustion of the enemy's offensive power, it was only permissible to consider this within the context of our own diminished formation strengths. For O.K.H.'s consideration, the Army Group submitted a series of figures which gave a graphic picture of the respective losses and replacements on both sides of the front.

We had deduced from numerous prisoner-of-war interrogations that in the period from July 1943 to January 1944 the enemy formations facing our front must have received about 1,080,000 men as replacements. This figure could be taken to correspond with the losses suffered by the enemy in the same period. On the other hand, Southern Army Group's casualties in dead, wounded and missing during the same space of time had amounted to 405,409 men. The corresponding number of replacements in this case was 221,893. So although the enemy's formations had suffered far more heavily than our own and the combat value of his infantry in particular was declining at an ever-increasing rate, it was still evident from the figures in question that the ratio of forces had shifted very much to our disadvantage.

The present position with armoured formations was that the Soviet tank corps in the line possessed an average of 50-100 tanks each (except for one isolated case in which there were only twenty), as against a planned establishment of 200-250. In contrast to this, the average number of tanks which our own armoured divisions could send into action was at best just over thirty. Only the armoured divisions recently sent to the Army Group were in any better shape, but with others the position was even worse. In all, the enemy opposite our front had received approximately 2,700 new tanks during the period under review, whereas we – and this included self-propelled assault guns – had had only 872. In producing these figures, we took no account of the large number of reserve formations at the enemy's disposal.

A characteristic picture is offered by the following breakdown of data supplied by the armies under our command. There may, of course, have been occasional duplication, specifically in the case of knocked-out tanks. According to these returns, the enemy losses had been as follows:

	Prisoners	Tanks	Field-Guns	Anti-tank Guns
January:	17,653	2,873	588	2,481
February:	7,700	1,055	200	855

One thing these figures show is the extraordinarily high scale of equipment enjoyed by the Red Army even at that stage. The time was past when it had been compelled to throw masses of men into battle. On the other hand, the figures revealed a striking discrepancy between the number of prisoners taken and the amount of material captured or destroyed. Either the Soviets had often been able to avoid capture by abandoning their heavy weapons (which could possibly indicate a deterioration of battle morale) or they must have been suffering exceptionally bloody losses.

As for Hitler's own attitude – in the light of the above figures – regarding the future conduct of operations and the possibility of a perilous turn of events on the Army Group's northern wing, a telephone conversation I had with General Zeitzler on 18th February proved most informative.

In pointing out the danger which could be foreseen on our northern wing, I had drawn attention to the ratio of forces and mentioned that the figure in our own case was still unfavourable in comparison with the other army groups. I will now quote from a transcript of the conversation made by one of my staff officers:

Zeitzler: 'I've had another long talk to the Führer on that subject, as well as on the consequences involved, but got no change.'

Myself: 'How does he envisage our future operations, then?'

Zeitzler: 'He says the Russians are bound to stop attacking some time. They have been attacking non-stop since last July and can't go on for ever. So I said, "*Mein Führer*, if you were a Russian now, what would *you* do?" "Nothing at all," he said. "Well," I told him, "*I* should attack, and I should go for Lwów!" '

Hitler, however, obviously went on counting on exhaustion and the weather to put an end to the enemy's offensive operations. By May – as he had told me earlier – he would have new divisions at his disposal. Had he only put the personnel and equipment they required into our own battle-tested divisions, things might have turned out very differently.

THE DAY OF RECKONING

In March 1944 it was time to foot the bill for the Supreme Command's cardinal error of never having been willing to give anything up (either in the east itself or some other theatre) for the sake of being stronger than the enemy at the decisive spot. What we had to pay for, first and foremost, was Germany's failure to stake *absolutely everything* on bringing about a *showdown in the east* in 1943 in order to achieve at least a stalemate or to exhaust the Russians' offensive power before a real second front emerged in the west.

Then there was the mistake of having persisted to the very last in keeping the southern wing of the Eastern Front clamped down in bastions jutting far out to the east – first in the Donetz basin and the Kuban, and then in the Dnieper bend and the Crimea, thereby offering the enemy every chance to cut these forces off. In doing so the Supreme Command had overlooked the fact that ultimately the issue would not be decided in the struggle for these bastions, but in the place from which the enemy could proceed to push the entire southern wing of German armies away towards the Black Sea or Rumania. Ever since 'Citadel' this decisive spot had been the northern wing of Southern Army Group.

Now it was too late! The crucial year of 1943 had slipped by without the achievement of so much as a stalemate. Whether this could ever be accomplished now depended on the outcome of the invasion which would certainly come in 1944.

But first the account had to be settled on the southern wing of the Eastern Front!

Hitler now proved to have been premature, to say the least, in voicing the hope at the end of February that the exhaustion of Soviet strength and the onset of the muddy season would halt the enemy offensive.

It was perfectly true that, thanks to the spirit displayed by the German troops, the enemy's hard-won gains had cost him extraordinary sacrifices. It was also apparent that the quality of his infantry formations, into which he had relentlessly pressed all the able-bodied male inhabitants of reconquered territories, was steadily deteriorating. But the plain fact remained that he still had abundant formations of fresh or rested troops on which to draw. Even if the number of tanks in his tank and mechanized corps had fallen off in consequence of the high losses mentioned earlier, it was still many times greater than that of the German armoured divisions. On the German side even a rigorous comb-out of units in the rear areas had failed to make good the shortage of replacements. Already we had enlisted hundreds of thousands of indigenous volunteers in our B-echelon units and supply columns. These men – mainly Ukrainians and Caucasians – did their duty with the utmost loyalty, preferring to fight in the German Army (in spite of the policy pursued by the Party authorities in the occupied territories) rather than to go back under Bolshevik domination.

The *muddy season*, though interrupted by spells of frost, set in at the beginning of March. Initially, however, it affected us far more unfavourably than it did the Russians. It has already been remarked that the Soviet tanks were more mobile than ours in snow and mud, thanks to their wider tracks. At the same time, however, enormous numbers of American trucks made their appearance on the enemy side. As they were still able to drive over open country when our own were already tied to the few firm roads, the enemy was also able to move the infantry element of his tank and mechanized corps quickly. In addition, the worse the mud became, the more the lack of tractors was felt on the German side. Consequently our mobile formations could only be moved long distances at the cost of considerable delays, and tended to get the worst of the struggle against a more mobile opponent.

Until such time as mud put a temporary stop to the enemy's offensive operations, and also for the later period when the struggle could be resumed, the Army Group was faced with the necessity of preserving a strong northern wing.

The enemy would, of course, also continue to attack Army Group A (i.e. Sixth Army) and our own Eighth Army. He had just as good a prospect as ever of smashing this wing, which was still echeloned well out to the east, and of pushing it back against the Black Sea, or at all events of winning the crossings over the Bug and later over the Dniester. Here lay the chance of recapturing Bessarabia and opening the route to Rumania and the rest of the Balkans! The area, incidentally, which Roosevelt was so keen to cede to 'Uncle Joe'.

Nonetheless, the German side was still capable of effecting an elastic withdrawal on this wing and saving considerable forces from Sixth Army's front, which could be very much shortened in the process. It would still be possible – either behind the Bug or the Lower Dniester (in any case, therefore, still forward of the old Rumanian frontier) – to bring the enemy to a definite standstill on a front adequately manned for a decisive defensive.

So when signs of fresh offensive preparations were noticed opposite the southern wing of Eighth Army as early as 22nd February, the Army Group asked that the army should be given freedom to take evasive action. We were neither able nor inclined to supply this part of the front with forces which were far more urgently needed on the left wing of the Army Group. Eighth Army's ability to adopt elastic tactics depended, of course, on whether its southern neighbour, Sixth Army, which was echeloned even further to the east, could co-operate in the movement we suggested. This was our reason for seeking O.K.H.'s prior agreement.

Not surprisingly, Hitler would not give it. On the contrary, the Army Group was subsequently made to hand over more forces (3 and 24 Panzer Divisions) to launch an attack in support of Sixth Army when a new setback ensued on its much-too-extended front.

Operationally, however, far greater chances than those offered to the enemy by advancing along the Black Sea coast against Army Group A would present themselves if he were to achieve a decisive success opposite the northern wing of Southern Army Group. If, by throwing in a maximum concentration of forces, he should manage – perhaps even before the muddy season began – to over-run the front of Fourth Panzer Army, he would in the first place gain possession of the railway line which ran from Lwów through Zhmerinka into the Southern Ukraine and was vital for the supply of the whole of the German southern wing. Subsequently, by continuing to advance southwards, the enemy would get into the deep flank and rear of the southern wing.

Over and above this it was certain that he would make use of the gap which had opened up between the northern wing of Southern Army Group and the southern wing of Central Army Group in order to assemble another powerful assault force. Its task would be to go round the Army Group's left wing or carry out the drive on Lwów which General Zeitzler had foreshadowed to Hitler. The recent appearance of H.Q. 1 Belorussian Front in this area at the end of February provided an unmistakable pointer to such intentions. With its left wing outflanked in this way, the Army Group would inevitably be pushed away to the south, perhaps while still east of the Carpathians. Through Lwów, on the other hand, the Soviets would be free to drive into Galicia or Poland proper.

Any development of this nature had to be forestalled at all costs.

As soon as the struggle to liberate the two corps surrounded near Cherkassy was over and contact had been re-established between the fronts of First Panzer and Eighth Armies in this area, the Army Group had ordered a radical shift of forces to its left wing. In the sectors of

First Panzer and Eighth Armies H.Q. 3 Panzer Corps was released with 1, 11 and 16 Panzer Divisions. They were to be followed as early as possible by 17 Panzer and the Artillery Division to an assembly area around Proskurov, behind Fourth Panzer Army. Also transferred to the latter from the above-named armies were 7 Panzer Division, the Leibstandarte and a battalion of heavy tanks (305). Fourth Panzer Army was to assemble these latter formations around Tarnopol under H.Q. 48 Panzer Corps. While 3 Panzer Corps' task would be to foil an enemy breakthrough on the front north of Proskurov, 48 Panzer Corps was to prevent an envelopment of the western wing by way of Tarnopol. Three infantry divisions granted by O.K.H. (68, 357 and 359) were also moved into Fourth Panzer Army's area.

The disengagement of these divisions from the fronts of their parent armies naturally took time. On top of that, the state of the roads and transport no longer permitted any rapid moves. As a result, they could not reach their appointed destinations before the middle of March.

At the beginning of that month the Army Group also ordered its army areas to be extended over towards the left wing. The object here was to enable Fourth Panzer Army to take charge of the area now acquiring special importance between Tarnopol and Dubno. The army handed over its present front, which ended at Shepetovka, to First Panzer Army and assumed command in the area from east of Tarnopol to Dubno. The only forces available there at the time, however, were 48 Panzer Corps, which was busy assembling around Tarnopol, 13 Corps, which was in action around Dubno, and a group of police units at Kovel.

First Panzer Army in turn surrendered its sector of front north of Uman to Eighth Army. On orders from O.K.H., the corps on the latter army's right wing went over to Sixth Army.

At the beginning of March the Army Group moved its headquarters first to Kamenec-Poldolsk and later to Lwów, in order to be behind the vital left wing. We had instructions from Hitler not to enter Rumanian territory, inside which our vantage point could have been behind the centre of the Army Group front.

It was still debatable whether the measures outlined above would suffice to intercept any enemy offensive launched before the muddy season set in. For the period which followed it, as the Army Group repeatedly emphasized to O.K.H., it would in any case be essential to bring forces with an equivalent strength of two armies, comprising between fifteen and twenty divisions, up to Lwów. Only then could we prevent a large-scale outflanking of the Army Group's left wing, with all the consequences already described. (It could be assumed, however, that the newly drafted forces of which Hitler had spoken, but of whose numbers the Army Group was told nothing, would be inadequate for this purpose. It was imperative to acquire forces by further shortening the fronts of both Northern Army Group and Sixth Army, as well as by evacuating the Crimea.)

It goes without saying that the freeing of forces within the Army Group's own area on the scale already indicated implied a big risk for Eighth and First Panzer Armies, since the enemy would continue to attack them, too, as long as the ground and weather gave him the least opportunity of doing so. His object in this case would be to break through in the direction of the Middle Bug and its crossings at Vinnitsa and Voznessensk.

With things as they now were, however, the Army Group had to choose between two evils. In terms of the overall situation, the lesser evil was undoubtedly that the enemy would come forward in the area of First Panzer Army's right wing and opposite Eighth Army. The operational effects of such an advance could still be counteracted by withdrawing the neighbouring Sixth Army behind the Bug or at worst behind the Dniester. On the other hand, the operational consequences of a decisive enemy success against the Army Group's left wing would be irreparable. To prevent it, and at all costs to bar the Russians's way into the deep flank of Southern Army Group and Army Group A or to Lwów, must now be Southern Army Group's operational aim until the muddy season became fully effective. The possibility that its right wing – and consequently the whole of Army Group A – might be forced to withdraw further westwards was a risk which it had to accept.

THE STRUGGLE CONTINUES – DESPITE THE MUD

Although the weather prevented our air reconnaissance from telling what movements or troop concentrations were taking place on the other side, the Army Group was able to assess the enemy's intentions as follows by the end of February:

The recently identified *1 Belorussian Front* would assemble forces in the Rovno area to envelop the Army Group's western wing.

1 Ukrainian Front was expected to attack the front facing north on both sides of Proskurov, now under command of First Panzer Army.

2 Ukrainian Front, we assumed, would renew its attacks on Eighth Army and the right wing of First Panzer Army and – if it succeeded in crossing the Bug – head for Czernowitz (Cernauţi).

3 and 4 Ukrainian Fronts would continue their attempts to score a success against Sixth Army and the right wing of Eighth Army.

On 3rd March the assault broke loose against the Army Group's left wing in the area of Fourth and First Panzer Armies. Superior enemy forces, including a tank corps, seized hold of 13 Corps around Dubno and tried to envelop it. The main thrust, which was carried out by two tank armies plus Sixtieth Soviet Army, was aimed at a breakthrough to the south across the line Proskurov–Tarnopol, the enemy's intention obviously being to cut the Army Group's most important communication line and – provided that the weather still permitted – to drive right through to the Dniester. Simultaneously Eighteenth Soviet Army was attempting to force the right wing of First Panzer Army away to the south-east.

The survey given below gives some idea of the relative strengths during this period:

Enemy Forces on 9 Mar. 44		*Own Forces as on 29 Feb. 44*	*Sectors Held by Own Forces*
Opposing *Sixth Army:* (Army Group A)	62 rifle divs. 3 tank/mech. corps 1 cav. corps 1 tank corps (resting)	18 inf. divs. (approx.) 3 arm. divs.	
Opposing *Eighth Army:*	57 rifle divs. 11 tank/mech. corps	5 inf. divs. 4 arm./pz. gren. divs. }	95 miles
Opposing *First Panzer Army:*	37–40 rifle divs. 11 tank/mech. corps	8 inf. divs. 1 art. div. 1 arm. div. }	112 miles
Opposing *Fourth Panzer Army:*	18 rifle divs. 5 tank/mech. corps 1 cav. corps	8 inf. divs. 1 defence div. 1 police form. 9½ arm./pz.gren. divs. }	320 miles

Westward shift of army boundaries within Army Group at end of March resulted in the following transfers of forces:

From	*To*	*Forces Transferred*	*Lengths of Front Involved*
First Panzer Army	Eighth Army	3 inf. divs.	37 miles
Fourth Panzer Army	First Panzer Army	5 inf. divs. 3½ arm./pz. gren. divs.	125 miles

When I visited the front line at Shepetovka on 4th March, 59 Corps' position there was already extremely serious. The enemy had penetrated our fronts on either side of it and was preparing to entrap the corps by means of enveloping attacks from east and west. To eliminate this danger it had to be pulled back – a manœuvre which duly succeeded thanks to the firm, unflurried leadership of the Commanding General, my erstwhile Chief-of-Staff, Schulz, and the intervention of 1 Panzer Division, which had just arrived on the scene. Nonetheless, the enemy maintained his efforts to encircle the corps by pursuing it towards Proskurov.

Both of the panzer corps which had been brought up behind this wing of the Army Group now went into action. 3 Panzer Corps was thrown to the north-west from Proskurov to smash the enemy advancing in the gap between First and Fourth Panzer Armies. 48 Panzer Corps was directed to attack the enemy armour driving on Tarnopol.

By 7th March the enemy had committed a total of twenty-two to twenty-five rifle divisions and seven tank or mechanized corps in this sector.

At the beginning of March the enemy also started an offensive against the left wing of Eighth Army, having within two weeks managed to replace the losses inflicted by our panzer corps in their thrust to free the Cherkassy pocket. Hardly had we withdrawn the two corps from that sector to bring them behind the left wing of the Army Group when he began his offensive in the direction of Uman. Having staked no less than twenty rifle divisions on his breakthrough, he succeeded in smashing 7 Corps, and by 9th March he was at the gates of the town.

In the area of Army Group A (Sixth Army) the enemy likewise resumed his offensive and achieved a breakthrough towards Nikolayev at the mouth of the Bug.

In a situation report to O.K.H. on 7th March the Army Group had stated that it had no alternative but to fight on as best it could until mud put a stop to the enemy's operations. At the same time, however, it had emphasized the decisive importance of having sufficient forces available in the Tarnopol–Luck–Lwów area at the end of the muddy season to prevent a breakthrough towards the last-named town or to drive into the enemy's flank if he should try to advance southwards from Tarnopol.

The Army Group's prime consideration just now, therefore, must be to *fight for time* and to do its utmost – even at the cost of giving up further ground – to keep its formations in fighting trim until the mud forced the enemy to call off his attacks. Unfortunately a great deal of time was to elapse before then.

At this stage of operations Hitler thought he had found a new means of bringing the enemy's advance to a standstill. Henceforth places which had acquired tactical significance as nodal points of road or rail traffic were to be declared 'strongholds'. Each was allotted an *ad hoc* commander, or *Kampfkommandant*, who was in honour bound to defend the locality in question and answered for it with his head. The armies in whose sectors Hitler had personally selected such 'strongholds' were responsible for stocking them up at early date and providing adequate garrisons. Hitler assumed that by blocking important roads or diverting Soviet forces, these places would serve to delay the advance. In fact it was clear from the outset that they would achieve no such thing. In practice they required more troops to defend them than was worth devoting to their retention. Since 'strongholds' without proper fortifications or adequate garrisons must inevitably fall to the enemy sooner or later without fulfilling their intended purpose, the Army Group in every case but one contrived to get them abandoned before they were hopelessly surrounded. The exception was Tarnopol, where in the end only remnants of the garrison were able to break out. Later in 1944 this method of Hitler's led to considerable losses.

In line with its policy of fighting for time and preserving the armies from encirclement, the Army Group on 11th March had to order *Eighth Army* to move back after the enemy had broken through the front on its left wing. Two days later, for the same reason, the right wing of First Panzer Army was withdrawn behind the Bug.

On its left wing *First Panzer Army* had to go on fighting in the Proskurov area so as to restore contact with Fourth Panzer Army and relieve the pressure on its right wing.

Fourth Panzer Army's task was to prevent the enemy armour east of Tarnopol from breaking through to the Dniester in the south and forcing First Panzer Army away to the south-east. At the same time, by throwing in the O.K.H. divisions mentioned earlier, it was to clear the lines of communication from Lwów via Tarnopol to Proskurov.

From now on, however, things moved increasingly fast. By 15th March the enemy succeeded in almost completely destroying the left wing of *Eighth Army*, causing a broad gap to appear between Uman and First Panzer Army at Vinnitsa. Continuing his south-westerly advance, he was able to get the leading elements of five armies, including an armoured one, across the Bug in Eighth Army's area. While the latter threw over all detachable forces from its right to its left wing to attack the enemy now across the river, it was clear that they could only impede him on a purely local basis and had no hope of gaining the Bug as a defence line over a sector of this breadth or of restoring contact with First Panzer Army. On the contrary, the strong enemy forces now crossing the river would be in a position to push Eighth Army off to the south and get to the Dniester before it.

On *First Panzer Army*'s right wing, too, the enemy had achieved a breakthrough which took him to the Bug south of Vinnitsa. Although Hitler immediately proclaimed the town a 'stronghold', there was never any question of its being able to put up a protracted defence, since this would have called for at least three divisions. And where were they to be found?

On the army's left wing, west of Proskurov, there were indications of an enemy envelopment by Third Guards Tank Army, which had three tank corps under command.

In *Fourth Panzer Army*'s sector a successful attack by the infantry divisions supplied by O.K.H. made it possible to restore the situation in the Tarnopol area for the time being. In contrast to this, 13 Corps was threatened with encirclement as it retired in the direction of Brody.

It was plain from the overall picture that there was no further possibility of regaining and holding the Bug on the Army Group's right wing. As early as 16th March it emerged that the enemy forces which had crossed the river were heading west with a tank army towards the nearest Dniester crossings. Three other armies, one of them armoured, were turning south against the northern flank of *Eighth Army*. At the same time both wings of *First Panzer Army* were in danger of being enveloped. Despite the success at Tarnopol it was doubtful whether *Fourth Panzer Army* could in the long run prevent the enemy from advancing on Lwów or turning off to the south.

Such was the tense situation prevailing when I was summoned to the Obersalzberg. A few days previously Hitler's military assistant, General Schmundt, had been out to see me to obtain my signature to a rather curious document. This was by way of being a declaration of loyalty to Hitler by all field-marshals in view of the propaganda disseminated by v. Seydlitz, the general taken prisoner at Stalingrad. The idea had probably come from Schmundt himself, who thought it might strengthen Hitler's trust in the army. Since every field-marshal but myself had already signed (significantly enough Schmundt had included Model among the signatories, although his rank at the time was still Colonel-General), I had no choice but to follow suit. Refusal to do so would have implied that I sympathized with Seydlitz's activities. All the same, I told Schmundt that I considered the declaration quite unnecessary from a soldier's point of view, as it was perfectly obvious that German troops would pay no attention to the propaganda of the Free Germany Committee. I might mention in this connexion that leaflets dropped over the Cherkassy pocket earlier on had completely failed to achieve their purpose – as, of course, had a letter from Seydlitz to General Lieb, the man in command there. About the same time another letter which gave every impression of being genuine had found its way on to my own desk. It had been handed in to us after being picked up by a Ukrainian partisan.[1]

On 19th March the document I mentioned above was ceremoniously handed over to Hitler by Field-Marshal v. Rundstedt in the presence of numerous senior members of the three armed services. Hitler appeared deeply moved by the occasion. Yet how little it really accorded with a soldier's code of values!

In view of Hitler's negative response to all my recommendations in the past and his persistent refusals to recognize irrevocable necessities, this call for a demonstration of loyalty makes it pertinent to ask why I still remained at my post.

---

[1] While there had been hardly any sign of partisans in the Eastern Ukraine (where the administration was solely in the hands of the German military authorities), the movement was all the more active in the western parts of that territory. One reason for this was that the large forests provided partisan groups with safe hide-outs and made it easier for them to attack roads and railways. The other, however, was that the rule of Reich Commissioner Koch had driven the population straight into their arms. There were, by the way, three different categories of partisans. The Soviet variety fought against the Germans and terrorized the peaceful population. The Ukrainians fought the Soviet partisans, but usually released any Germans after first disarming them. Finally there were bands of Polish partisans who fought both Germans and Ukrainians. This largely applied in the Lwów district, which was already in Galicia. Here the urban population was largely Polish and the rural communities mainly Ukrainian. The Lwów area – unlike the rest of the Government-General – was wisely administered. While giving preferential treatment to the Ukrainians, the man responsible, District Commissioner Wächter, still protected the interests of the Polish minority. Ultimately he was able to raise a complete division of Ukrainian volunteers. *Author.*

[handwritten marginalia at top: "such a perceptive man could not, see?"]

[handwritten marginalia at right: "Ich das glaube nicht"]

As regards the more general implications of this question, I can only say that it was not granted to me – as one who had for several years past been engrossed in arduous duties at the front – to perceive Hitler's true nature, or the moral deterioration of the régime, to the extent to which we can obviously do today. Rumours of the kind that circulated at home hardly penetrated to the front, perhaps least of all to ourselves. The anxieties and problems which the fighting brought us left little time for reflection on matters of wider interest. In this respect our position was entirely different from that of soldiers or politicians in Germany or occupied territories where no fighting was taking place.

In the military sphere, however, I could not overlook the faults of Hitler's leadership. My grounds for not believing it possible to remove him by violent means in wartime have already been stated.

As for the reasons which impelled me to remain at my post, I often used to wish that I could leave it. On many an occasion, when Hitler refused to accept my recommendations or tried to meddle in the affairs of my headquarters, I had told the Chief of the General Staff that he (Hitler) had better find someone else to take over Southern Army Group. But apart from the pleas of my immediate staff, what always dissuaded me from resigning my command was not the desire – so often advanced as a motive in such cases – to 'prevent worse things from happening'. It was rather the conviction that no other headquarters but ours would be capable of mastering the tasks which confronted a commander in our decisive sector of the front. My departure would have meant more than a change in the person of the Army Group Commander.

Something told me that I had no right to leave my troops in the lurch. Unless, of course, some impending disaster compelled me to tender my resignation as a last resort in order to force Hitler's hand. This very contingency was shortly to arise in connexion with the fate of First Panzer Army.

The meeting on the Obersalzberg afforded me an opportunity to make the following proposals to Hitler by reason of the ever-increasing gravity of the situation:

(i) *Immediate withdrawal of Sixth Army* behind the Dniester. This formation was still situated in a salient extending well east of the Lower Bug and requiring far too many forces. The Commander of Army Group A, Field-Marshal v. Kleist, had himself recommended the same action.

(ii) *Rapid northward switch of the strong forces thus released by Sixth Army* into the *area between the Dniester and Pruth* (which formed the old Rumanian frontier) in order to prevent Eighth Army from being forced away from the Dniester to the south-east.

(iii) A clear decision laying down that the task of *covering Rumania*, either on the Dniester or the Pruth, should henceforth devolve on *Army Group A* in conjunction with Rumanian forces.

(iv) *Quick assistance for Southern Army Group's northern wing* to prevent the enemy from forcing it back into the Carpathians or driving through to Lwów.

This solution, I added, would initially mean putting up with a gap between Army Group A and Southern Army Group if a strong front were to be formed north of the Carpathians. Should the enemy later attempt to get through this gap to the Balkans by way of Hungary, we should be able to thrust into his rear from the north as soon as we received the reinforcements which Hitler had promised to let us have in May.

Hitler, however, declined to consider any such far-reaching conceptions. He directed that Army Group A should remain on the Bug and announced only small-scale assistance for the Southern Army Group's northern wing.

In a detailed appreciation of the situation sent to General Zeitzler on 22nd March, I repeated the above proposals, basing them on both the state of the fighting troops and the fact that the existing situation no longer allowed us to close the front between Eighth and First Panzer Armies. It was of the utmost importance, I said, that Army Group A – which must now take *Eighth Army* under command – should cover Rumania while Southern Army Group prevented an enemy advance westwards in the area north of the Carpathians. To this end it was essential that *Fourth Panzer Army* should be able to hold its present positions, which meant that it must at all costs be reinforced. *First Panzer Army*'s main commitment must be to link up with Fourth Panzer Army again and prevent itself from being pushed away to the south. The Carpathian passes between the two army groups could be held by Hungarian forces.

The Hungarians, who had been more or less coerced into the war, still had their eyes on Siebenbürgen, which they had lost to Rumania in 1918. Our Rumanian and Hungarian allies were known to view each other with such mistrust that they were holding crack troops ready in their respective countries to use against one another if the need arose. After the defeats on the Don in Winter 1942-3 the two Rumanian armies, and later the Hungarian army, had been taken out of the front.

However, Marshal Antonescu had again made forces available for coastal defence on the Sea of Azov. He also allowed the Rumanian formations forming part of Seventeenth Army to remain in the Kuban bridgehead and later in the Crimea. Now he was providing new armies for the defence of Rumania as part of Army Group A.

After the withdrawal of their army from the battle front, the Hungarians had left only a few divisions behind in the Ukraine. It was expressly laid down that these should not become involved in any fighting with the Soviets, so that whenever the front line drew closer we had to pull them back in good time. Their duties were confined to guarding roads and railways against partisans in the communications zones.

Now the situation was becoming critical for Hungary, too, and to defend the Carpathians and the area up to the Dniester we had to have the services of the intact army she had on home territory. At the same time, however, the attitude of her Government had become dubious, and on 15th March General Lindemann came down from O.K.H. with instructions for the swift disarmament of the Hungarian forces behind our front in the event of Hungary's defection. Fortunately we were spared the necessity of carrying out such a task. Following Horthy's visit to the Obersalzberg, First Hungarian Army was placed under our command on 23rd March. Each of its two corps comprised one motorized and four infantry divisions, but all of them had first to mobilize! Apart from this, the scale and quality of the Hungarians' weapons did not meet the requirements of warfare against Soviet armoured units. Nonetheless, these forces could be expected to hold their own against the Soviets in the Carpathians, as we felt that the Russians would only be able to put their armour to very limited use in the mountainous terrain. We were reinforced in this belief by the recollection of how bravely the Honved had defended the Carpathian passes against the Russians in World War I. Everything would depend, of course, on energetic leadership on the Hungarian side. In this connexion we were not encouraged by a visit paid to us on 28th March by General Lakatos (who, as far as I remember, was then Chief-of-Staff or Minister for War) and the commander of First Hungarian Army. All these two men did in response to our demands was to plead the unpreparedness of their troops (in March 1944, of all times!) and their shortage of anti-tank weapons. We could not escape the impression that certain highly-placed circles in the Hungarian Army were not disposed to defend the frontiers of their homeland with any real vigour. What could they possibly be expecting of the Russians?

It had already been clear from the evening situation report sent through to me at the Obersalzberg on 19th March that the situation of Southern Army Group had taken a further turn for the worse.

It appeared that *Eighth Army*, in spite of having thrown all available armour on to its left wing, would no longer be able to prevent the latter from being outflanked to the west and forced away in a southerly direction. Since Hitler would not agree to the solution we had suggested (i.e. that of throwing forces over to this spot from Sixth Army simultaneously with a withdrawal of the latter), all we could do was to try to persuade Marshal Antonescu to place forces at our disposal even at this early stage in order to prolong Eighth Army's front to the north-west. In point of fact the Marshal had only envisaged using them to defend the Pruth.

Apart from this aggravation of Eighth Army's position, an even more ominous development occurred on the Army Group's northern wing.

Up here, having been unable to maintain its right wing on the Bug, *First Panzer Army* now held a front facing north-east and extending roughly from the Dniester (north-west of Mogilev-Podolsk) to the Zbrucz, which formed the frontier with Poland.

Further west, as has already been noted, *Fourth Panzer Army* had temporarily restored the situation east of Tarnopol by a counter-attack with some newly-arrived divisions.

On 20th March, however, after committing two tank armies (First and Fourth) for this purpose, the enemy had achieved a breakthrough on both sides of the inter-army boundary and headed southwards in the direction of the Upper Dniester. On 23rd March the spearheads of First and Fourth Tank Armies were already approaching the Dniester crossings north of Czernowitz and south of Kamenec-Podolsk. This put the enemy squarely across First Panzer Army's lines of communication. The moment the danger became apparent, the Army Group had ordered First Panzer Army to take its front back on to a shortened line in order to acquire forces with which to fight its rear free. The army had also been given control of a group from Fourth Panzer Army commanded by General Mauss which had continued to stand like a solitary pillar in the rear of First Panzer Army after everything else in that area had been driven away by the two enemy armies. The task of General Mauss's force was to halt the main body of the enemy behind the armoured spearheads, thereby cutting the latter off from their supplies.

Obviously these measures could not restore the situation on the Army Group's northern wing. Although, for the moment, the enemy had nothing but armour straddling the communications deep in First Panzer Army's rear (as a result of which its headquarters had already arranged for an airlift), there was every indication that the army would shortly be surrounded in the fullest sense of the word. If a front of any durability were still to be established north of the Carpathians, it was imperative that First Panzer Army be extricated forthwith.

On 23rd March the Army Group had asked O.K.H. for the speedy provision of forces to free First Panzer Army's rear communications. (These, we considered, could be released from Hungary, which had meanwhile been occupied.)

On 24th March we received an answer to the effect that First Panzer Army was not only to hold its present extended front but also to prolong it as far as Tarnopol in the west, as well as to clear its communications zone of the enemy.

Thereupon the Army Group reported at noon the same day that it would order First Panzer Army to break out to the west if it did not receive a directive appropriate to its earlier request by 1500 hours.

At 1600 hours we received the Solomon-like reply that the Führer agreed to the fundamental idea of First Panzer Army's clearing its communications to the west but still insisted that it should mainly continue to hold the present front between the Dniester and Tarnopol. Where the army was to find the forces to drive west and clear its communications zone of the enemy was quite beyond us. It was exactly the same as at Stalingrad in December 1942, when Hitler had likewise been ready to let Sixth Army attempt to break-out in the direction of Fourth Panzer Army. In that case, too, he had demanded the simultaneous retention of the city, which simply meant that Sixth Army could not assemble any forces for a break-out.

When I rang up General Zeitzler to point out once again how utterly

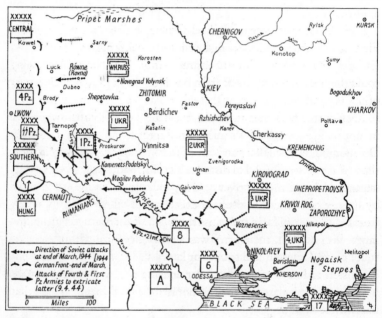

Map 24. Developments on Southern Wing of Eastern Front at end of March 1944.

impossible Hitler's demand was, he replied that the latter just did not grasp the full gravity of the situation. Nevertheless, I still received a summons late that evening to report to General Headquarters the following day.

Concurrently with this controversy, another was going on between myself and the Commander of First Panzer Army, Colonel-General Hube.[1] While Hube agreed with us that First Panzer Army's situation had become untenable and that it must without fail evade the encircle-

---

[1] Hube, a one-armed infantryman of World War I, took over this command from Colonel-General Mackensen in October 1943 when the latter was given an army in Italy. Earlier on he had commanded a panzer corps at Stalingrad. He was killed in an air crash in 1944. *Tr.*

ment which now threatened it, he did not want it to break through to the west but to be taken back southwards over the Dniester.

This was certainly the easier course at that particular moment. If the army took the western route it would have to fight its way to freedom against two Soviet tank armies, whereas at present it could escape across the Dniester without becoming involved in any really serious fighting.

I still could not accept Colonel-General Hube's view, however. First of all, it was indispensable that First Panzer Army should re-establish contact with Fourth Panzer Army in the west. How else could the enemy be prevented from breaking through to Galicia north of the Carpathians? The best that could happen if the army took the southern route was that it would finish up being forced away into mountains. Yet even this was uncertain. Superficially, the way across the Dniester looked the less hazardous of the two. But closer examination showed that it would lead to disaster. The army possessed no bridging materials for crossing the river on a broad front. Any attempt to cross by the few secure bridges now in existence would expose it to attack from the enemy air force and cause the loss of most of the heavy equipment. Worst of all, the enemy was already advancing from the east south of the Dniester, and sooner or later First Panzer Army must become sandwiched between the latter and the two tank armies which, having just cut its rear communications, were now preparing to cross the river behind it.

I therefore made it quite clear to General Hube that the Army Group would not permit his army to retire towards the south bank of the Dniester but would *order a breakthrough to the west*. Even before I flew to the Obersalzberg, he was given a warning order to link up initially with the group of German forces on the Zbrucz by a thrust to the west.

Having taken off from Lwów early on the morning of 25th March, I reached the Berghof in time for the midday conference.

In describing First Panzer Army's situation to Hitler, I emphasized that its eastern and northern fronts were under strong enemy pressure, to which the long-overtaxed divisions – particularly in view of the in-adequacy of the airlift – would not be equal in the long run. In the deep western flank of the army, I added, the enemy was across its rear communications, with the spearheads of one tank army already making for the south bank of the Dniester and those of another aiming south-east at Kamenec-Podolsk in the army's rear. South of the river, too, the enemy was advancing from the east to bar the Dniester in the army's rear.

In this situation, I said, there was no alternative but to strike through to the west with the army's tank formations, clear its supply lines and restore contact with Fourth Panzer Army. By such tactics it might even be possible to paralyse the supplies of the two enemy armies operating in First Panzer Army's rear. This westward thrust must obviously be covered off to the east and north-east by the army's remaining forces. Although they would not be able to do so on their present extended fronts, the army's southern wing must still remain resting on the Dniester.

On no account, I said, could I agree to General Hube's proposal to take his army on to the southern bank of the Dniester. First, because operations made it necessary to concentrate First and Fourth Panzer Armies north of the Carpathians. Secondly, because any withdrawal to the south of the river would probably result in First Panzer Army's being encircled all over again and ultimately annihilated.

The success of the proposed breakthrough, I added, would depend on a simultaneous drive by Fourth Panzer Army from the west. For this reason the latter must be reinforced immediately.

Hitler replied that he was unable to release any forces for this purpose. As long as he had to expect an invasion in western Europe, he said, no formations must be taken away from that theatre. In similar vein he contended that our divisions in Hungary were indispensable there for political reasons. Furthermore, he still refused to acknowledge that a breakthrough by First Panzer Army to the west inevitably necessitated a corresponding withdrawal of its front in the east.

A sharp exchange took place between Hitler and myself when he tried to hold me responsible for the unfavourable position in which Southern Army Group had landed. Some days previously I had gathered from General Zeitzler that Hitler had accused the Army Group of having frittered away the numerous forces supplied to it over a period of months. I had asked Zeitzler to tell Hitler from me that the Army Group had had no other choice but to commit these divisions in driblets, as they had only been given to us sporadically and in most cases too late. Had Hitler ever held out any prospect of our getting the strong forces we had so often demanded for our northern wing – even if only for some date in the future – or else granted us operational freedom on our southern wing, he would have had nothing to complain about today! Zeitzler had entirely agreed with me. Indeed, this very factor had done more than anything else to influence the trend of events since 'Citadel'.

Now Hitler asserted that all we (i.e. the Army Group) were ever interested in doing was 'playing at grand tactics'.[1] Last autumn, he said, he had been told that the Dnieper would be held. Hardly had he given his reluctant approval for us to retire behind that river when the need for a further withdrawal had been announced on account of a break-through at Kiev. I retorted that things had been bound to turn out that way. *He* was the person who had detained our forces on the southern wing to hold the Donetz and Dnieper areas instead of letting us strengthen our northern wing.

Next Hitler declared that according to the Luftwaffe there were very few enemy tanks to be seen, but that whole German units were running away from them, thereby causing the front to be constantly pulled back. As the only Luftwaffe reports Hitler received came from its High Command, I assumed that Göring had once again been giving vent to his hatred for the army.

I replied with some asperity that if the fighting troops could no longer hold out in some places, this must be attributed to constant overstrain, physical exhaustion and the extent to which unit strengths had dwindled away. If ever proof were needed that over-leniency was not one of our failings, it could be found in the number of senior commanders we had replaced. All of these men, I emphasized, were actually brave and experienced soldiers, but not one had been able to check the decline in the troops' powers of resistance. The fact that the two newly-drafted divisions sent to Fourth Panzer Army had now been over-run by enemy tanks was the result of inadequate training and deficient battle experience. This was another aspect which we had covered often enough in our reports.

As there was nothing to be gained from all this wrangling, I sought to clinch matters by stating that I assumed we agreed on the need for First Panzer Army to concentrate its armour and break through to the west for the purpose both of regaining contact with Fourth Panzer Army and of freeing its own communications at the rear. I also assumed,

[1] *'immer nur operieren'. Tr.*

I said, that the balance of the army's forces would be covering the operation to the north and east – though on what line they could do so would be seen later. The order to First Panzer Army, I insisted, must be issued by me that very same day. I reiterated that no success could be expected unless Fourth Panzer Army were put in a position to drive towards First Panzer Army from the west.

Hitler, however, again rejected this demand and ordered a resumption of the talks at the evening conference. Despite the sharpness of our disagreements, by the way, he had maintained the normal courtesies throughout.

After leaving the familiar conference-room with its glorious outlook towards Salzburg, I sent a message in to General Schmundt that I should like to speak to him outside. I asked him to inform Hitler that I considered it futile to remain in command of the Army Group unless he accepted my recommendations. If he could not see his way to approving my actions, I said, I wished the command of Southern Army Group to be entrusted to somebody else.

That afternoon a telephone call from my Chief-of-Staff, General Busse, was put through to my quarters in Berchtesgaden. He informed me that General Hube had again made an urgent request for permission to head south across the Dniester instead of breaking through to the west. In the evening I was sent a further signal from the army describing the western breakthrough as impracticable and insisting that the correct solution was to head southwards. General Busse, who had already sent a negative reply to the first request, now asked for my final decision. I directed that the breakthrough be carried out as ordered.

When I appeared at the evening conference Hitler's mood had completely changed. His opening words were approximately these: 'I have been thinking the matter over again and agree with your plan to make First Panzer Army fight its way through to the west. I have also decided – with great reluctance – to provide an SS Panzer Corps of 9 and 10 SS Panzer Divisions which we have just set up in the west, plus 100 Light and 367 Infantry Division, for Fourth Panzer Army's proposed assault group.'

I reported that I had meanwhile turned down a fresh request from General Hube to break out to the south and had insisted that his army must drive west. I said I thought the thrust would succeed because the two enemy tank armies appeared to be scattering their forces in the direction of the Dniester crossings. After this my operations officer, Lieutenant-Colonel Schulze-Büttger, read out the text of my operation order to First Panzer Army.

In view of the unexpected change in Hitler's attitude, I followed up with one or two ideas of my own on the future conduct of operations. Southern Army Group's task, I said, must be to erect a stable front between the Carpathians and the Pripet Marshes, and in this connexion we had ordered First Hungarian Army to assemble in the area of Stryj to guard the hilly country between the mountain range and the Upper Dniester.

Eighth Army, I went on, must henceforth be under command of Army Group A, to whose lot it would fall to protect Rumania. As for the gap between the two army groups, this was something we must provisionally accept. It could be sealed off at the Carpathian passes by the forces still in Hungary.

I then made the suggestion that a unified command should be constituted to cover all forces on the southern wing, including the allied armies. Having regard to the defence of Rumania, I felt it might be advisable to bring in Marshal Antonescu in conjunction with a German Chief-of-Staff. Hitler, however, did not take this up, merely expressing the opinion that the Marshal would refuse for political reasons.

Following this talk, which, in contrast to that held at midday, had proceeded most harmoniously, Hitler came out with us into the anteroom to inquire whether there was a meal laid on for us. With every sign of satisfaction he read me a Turkish Press comment that Germany had not acted a moment too soon in Hungary, where, it said, things had gone much further than most people supposed.

Early on 26th March I flew back to the Army Group. Eighth Army had meanwhile passed under command of Army Group A.

The next day I visited Fourth Panzer Army to discuss the thrust it would be delivering towards First Panzer Army with the new forces promised by Hitler. General Rauss was confident that he would make contact with the other army, although he was not entirely happy about things on his own front. Tarnopol, having previously been declared a 'stronghold' by Hitler, was surrounded. On the left wing of the army a similar fate threatened 13 Corps at Brody, but this it managed to elude.

Now that Hitler had given in to our demands, however, we could

confidently expect to get First Panzer Army out and concentrate it
with Fourth Panzer Army north of the Carpathians. But although my
success at the Obersalzberg talks on 25th March guaranteed the survival of First Panzer Army, it soon emerged that the pressure I had
exerted on Hitler on that occasion had tired him of working with me
any longer. The same applied in the case of Field-Marshal v. Kleist,
who arrived at the Obersalzberg two days after me to get some definite
action taken about withdrawing his Army Group to the Lower
Dniester.

On the morning of 30th March I was awakened with the startling
news that Hitler's Condor aircraft, which had already picked up v.
Kleist from his headquarters, would shortly land in Lwów to take the
pair of us to the Obersalzberg. While I, Schulz-Büttger and my
A.D.C., Stahlberg, were awaiting its arrival on Lwów airfield, my
Chief-of-Staff talked to Zeitzler on the telephone. The latter revealed
that Hitler – as we had already guessed – was going to relieve both
Kleist and myself of our commands.

On reaching Berchtesgaden, we first had a talk with General
Zeitzler, as Hitler did not wish to see us until just before the evening
conference. Zeitzler told us that after the last Obersalzberg talks, Göring and Himmler, and probably also Keitel, had again started agitating
against me in particular. This, he thought, had probably contributed
towards Hitler's decision to part company with Kleist and myself.
When Hitler had informed him of his intention, he (Zeitzler) had instantly tendered his resignation on the grounds that he had always
fully agreed with me and could not remain in office if I went. His request, though repeated in writing, had met with a curt refusal. This
upright attitude of Zeitzler's did him great credit.

In describing my last meeting with Hitler, I propose to quote an
entry I made in my diary the following day, while my memory was
still fresh.

'Saw the Führer in the evening. After handing me the Swords to
my Knight's Cross, he announced that he had decided to place the
Army Group in other hands (Model's), as the time for grand-style
operations in the east, for which I had been particularly qualified,
was now past. All that counted now, he said, was to cling stubbornly
to what we held. This new type of leadership must be inaugurated

under a new name and a new symbol. Hence the change in the command of the Army Group, whose name he also intended to alter.

'He expressly wished to state that there was not the least question of a crisis of confidence between us, as had previously been the case with other field-marshals (whose names he mentioned). He still had the utmost faith in me: indeed, far from ever having had any criticism of the way the Army Group was led, he had always been in complete agreement with it. At the same time, however, he realized that the Army Group had had an excessive burden of responsibility to bear for a period of one and a half years and that it now appeared in need of a rest. He knew me to be one of his most capable commanders and for this reason intended to give me another appointment before long. At the moment, however, there was no further scope for me in the east. For the tasks now pending there he considered Model, who had stopped a difficult retreat in Northern Army Group, to be especially suitable. After once again assuring me that there was no crisis of confidence between us, the Führer added that he would never forget that prior to the western campaign I had been the only man to advise him of the possibility of deciding the whole issue in the west by a breakthrough at Sedan.

'In reply, I told the Führer that I naturally could not object if he thought he would be able to work better with another army group commander in the present situation. Furthermore, I did not think any great harm would be done by my handing over to Model now, as the decisions regarding the release of First Panzer Army had already been taken – partly by Hitler's decision to bring over the SS Panzer Corps from the west and partly by my order to the army to fight its way out north of the Dniester. By and large, I said, this largely concluded what the Army Group had to do at the moment. Its only remaining commitment was to assist the fighting troops and give them moral support. That Model would certainly be able to do.

'The Führer emphatically agreed that Model was a particularly suitable choice in this respect, as he would "dash round the divisions" and get the very utmost out of the troops. To this I retorted that the Army Group's divisions had long been giving of their best under my command and that no one else could get them to give anything more.'

Whatever one may think of Hitler's various remarks to me at what was destined to be our last meeting, he had at any rate chosen to conduct it on decent lines. This was due at least in part to Zeitzler's insistence that Hitler owed it to Kleist and myself to inform us in person of his motives for relieving us of our commands. That Göring and Himmler had long been working for my removal I was well aware. Yet the main reason for Hitler's decision was probably the fact that he had had to give in to me on 25th March when he had already rejected my proposals in front of a large audience. As he shook hands with me before I left, I said: 'I trust, *mein Führer*, that the step you have taken today will not have any untoward effects.'

After me, Field-Marshal v. Kleist was dismissed in similar fashion. As we left the Berghof, our successors were already waiting at the door – Colonel-General Model, who was to take over Southern Army Group (now re-designated North Ukrainian Army Group), and General Schörner, who was to replace v. Kleist.

The next morning I flew back to Lwów in my Ju 52. My successor was grounded in Cracow by a snowstorm, as a result of which I was able to issue a last Army Group order ensuring the co-operation of our two panzer armies in the breakthrough operation which had now started. On the afternoon of that day I visited Fourth Panzer Army to discuss the employment of the SS Panzer Corps with the army commander and also to say goodbye. My farewells to the other army commanders had to be said in writing.

On the afternoon of 2nd April I handed over to my successor, who had meanwhile arrived in Lwów. As far as anyone could judge, the measures to extricate First Panzer Army and to bring about the concentration of both armies – so decisive for the overall situation – between the Carpathians and the Pripet Marshes were guaranteed, even if they were still to involve some bitter fighting.

On 5th April Fourth Panzer Army duly began its thrust to the east, and by 9th April First Panzer Army was freed.

I still had to take leave of my staff, and was not alone in finding the parting a hard one. These comrades-in-arms had accompanied me through the victorious Crimean battles; they had lived to see the eventual success of that arduous winter campaign of 1942–3; and they had stood beside me throughout the critical months of 1943 and 1944. It was deeply gratifying to know how close our mutual trust had grown in those years and what genuine sorrow they felt now that our work together was finished. I feel entitled to say the same of the army commanders who had served under me.

My staff were thunderstruck by my dismissal. My closest collaborators, the Chief-of-Staff, the Chief of Operations, the Assistant Quartermaster-General and the Assistant Adjutant-General, all put in for postings. Their requests were duly granted, though General Busse had to stay on for some time to preserve the continuity.

As far as I personally was concerned, my removal was a release from responsibility which it had become increasingly difficult to bear under the conditions which I have described.

What had weighed most heavily of all on my staff and myself – to say nothing of the commanders and staffs of our subordinate armies – was the perpetual struggle we had had to wage with the Supreme Command to get operational necessities recognized.

Our repeated demands for the establishment of a *clear focal point of effort at the decisive spot* in this campaign (i.e. on the northern wing of the Army Group) and for *operational freedom of movement* in general (more particularly for our southern wing) were merely outward manifestations of the struggle. The basic issue was between two incompatible conceptions of strategy and grand tactics:

(i) *Hitler*'s, which arose from the personal characteristics and opinions which have already been fully discussed in the chapter dealing with him as a Supreme Commander, and

(ii) that of *Southern Army Group Headquarters*, which was based on the traditional principles and outlook of the German General Staff.

On one side we had the conceptions of a dictator who believed in the power of his will not only to nail down his armies wherever they might be but even to hold the enemy at bay. The same dictator, however, who fought shy of risks because of their inherent threat to his prestige and who, for all his talent, lacked the groundwork of real military ability.

On the other side stood the views of military leaders who by virtue of their education and training still firmly believed that warfare was an *art* in which clarity of appreciation and boldness of decision constituted the essential elements. An art which could find success only in mobile operations, because it was only in these that the superiority of German leadership and German fighting troops could attain full effect.

It is only fair to add, however, that recourse to the kind of operations which the Army Group had in mind would have compelled Hitler to accept considerable risks in other theatres of war and other sectors of the Eastern Front, as well as serious drawbacks in the political and economic spheres. Nonetheless, it would probably have been the only way to exhaust the Soviet Union's offensive power in 1943, and thus to pave the way to a political stalemate in the east.

Even if the Army Group was largely unsuccessful in its struggle for a different operational policy, and therefore deceived in its belief that it could master the enemy, it still had one achievement to its credit. The enemy had not succeeded in encircling the whole southern wing, which the operational situation and his tremendous superiority offered him every prospect of doing. Southern Army Group, though bleeding from a thousand wounds, had *maintained itself in the field*!

The greatest satisfaction of all for my staff and myself was that in this unequal struggle with a far superior opponent, as indeed with a Supreme Command which would not recognize what was clearly forseeable, we had still been able to prevent any forces under our command from suffering the fate of Stalingrad. At Cherkassy, and now with First Panzer Army, it was still possible to deprive the enemy of the prey which he believed to have safely in his grasp.

What made it hard for me to hand over my command was solely the fact that I could no longer be of assistance to the troops who had always trusted in the Army Group's leadership.

I left our headquarters in Lwów on 3rd April 1944. All my faithful comrades had come to the station to see me off. The train had already begun moving when someone called out to me. It was my personal pilot, Lieutenant Langer – the man who had flown me safely through every imaginable kind of weather. Now he had volunteered for the fighter arm, in whose ranks he was soon to give his life. For me his words were a last salute from my comrades.

'*Herr Feldmarschall*,' he cried, 'today we took the Crimean Shield – our victory sign – off the aircraft!'

TRANSLATOR'S NOTE

IN ORDER to shorten these memoirs to a size suitable for publication in Britain and the U.S.A., it has been necessary to excise a number of passages from the original version. As most of them were devoted to personal reminiscences, often in lighter vein, their exclusion was thought unlikely to detract from the book's value in a strictly historical sense. A number of detailed appendices, however, have also been omitted, leaving only those which were considered to be of more than specialist interest.

It may be mentioned here that Chapter 14 (Operation 'Citadel') is a new translation of material originally contributed by the Author to the U.S. *Marine Corps Gazette*, instead of being taken from the equivalent chapter in the German edition of the book, which is considerably longer. We should like to take the opportunity to thank the *Marine Corps Gazette* for allowing us to use this material.

The formation symbols employed in the sketch-maps of this edition are those now current in the NATO countries. They were adopted for the sake of greater clarity and uniformity.

Finally I should like to add a personal note of thanks to Capt. B. H. Liddell Hart for his kind assistance in checking the technical details of this translation and for his many helpful comments.

APPENDIX I

From Commander, Sixth Army.

Gumrak Station
26th Nov. 42
(*written by hand of officer*)

Field-Marshal v. Manstein,
Commander, Don Army Group.

Dear Field-Marshal,

I beg to acknowledge your signal of 24th November and to thank you for the help you propose giving.

To assist you in forming an appreciation of my position, I am taking the liberty to report the following:

(1) When the large-scale Russian attacks on the army's right- and left-hand neighbours started on 19th November, both my flanks were exposed within two days and quickly penetrated by Soviet mobile forces. When our own mobile formations (14 Pz. Corps) were pulled westwards across the Don, their spearheads ran into superior enemy forces west of the river. This put them in an extremely difficult situation, particularly as their movement was restricted by fuel shortage. Simultaneously the enemy moved into the rear of 11 Corps, which in accordance with orders had fully maintained its positions towards the north. Since it was no longer possible to take any forces out of the front to ward off this danger, I was left with no alternative but to fold 11 Corps' left wing back to the south and subsequently to have the Corps fall back initially into a bridgehead west of the Don in order that the elements on that side of the river were not split off from the main body.

While these measures were being carried out, an order was received from the Führer calling for an attack on Dobrinskaya with 14 Pz. Corps' left wing. This order was overtaken by events and could not be complied with.

(2) Early on 22nd November 4 Corps, which had hitherto belonged

to Fourth Pz. Army, came under my command. Its right wing was falling back from south to north through Buzinovka, which meant that the entire south and south-west flank was laid open. To prevent the Russians from marching unchecked through the army's rear towards Stalingrad, I had no choice but to pull forces out of the city and the front in the north. There was a possibility that these would arrive in time, whereas they would not do so if drawn from the area west of the Don.

With the forces supplied by us from the Stalingrad front 4 Corps succeeded in establishing a weak southern front with its western wing at Marinovka. This, however, was penetrated several times on 23rd November, and the outcome is still uncertain. On the afternoon of 23rd November strong enemy armour, including 100 tanks alone, was identified in the area west of Marinovka. In the whole of the area between Marinovka and the Don there were nothing but flimsy German protective screens. The way to Stalingrad lay open to the Russian tanks and motorized forces, as did that to the Don bridge in the direction of Pestkovatka.

For the past thirty-six hours I had received no orders or information from a higher level. In a few hours I was liable to be confronted with the following situation:

(a) Either I must remain in position on my western and northern fronts and very soon see the army front rolled up from behind (in which case I should formally be complying with the orders issued to me), or else

(b) I must make the only possible decision and turn with all my might on the enemy who was about to stab the army from behind. In the latter event, clearly, the eastern and northern fronts can no longer be held and it can only be a matter of breaking through to the south-west.

In case of (b) I should admittedly be doing justice to the situation but should also – for the second time – be guilty of disobeying an order.

(3) In this difficult situation I sent the Führer a signal asking for freedom to take such a final decision if it should become necessary. I wanted to have this authority in order to guard against issuing the only possible order in that situation too late.

I have no means of proving that I should only issue such an order in an extreme emergency and can only ask you to accept my word for this.

I have received no direct reply to this signal. On the other hand, we have today received the two attached O.K.H. signals (enclosures 1 and 2) [1] which restrict me further still. In this connexion I might note that both I and all my formation commanders are firmly resolved to hold out to the last. However, in view of my responsibility to the Führer for the odd 300,000 men entrusted to my charge, it will be appreciated why I have asked for permission to take appropriate action in the last extreme. The situation I have indicated can, incidentally, arise again any day or hour.

Today's situation is being communicated to you by map. Even though it has been possible to move more forces up to the south-western front, the position there is still strained. The southern front (4 Corps) has consolidated somewhat and beaten off heavy enemy infantry and armoured assaults throughout the last few days, though not without considerable losses to ourselves and a heavy expenditure of ammunition.

The Stalingrad front is from day to day resisting strong enemy pressure. On the northern front there is trouble in the north-east quarter (94 Inf. Div.) and on the western wing (76 Inf. Div.). As I see it, the main assaults on the northern front have still to come, as up here the enemy has roads and railways with which to bring up reinforcements. My problem in the next few days will be to get reinforcements to the northern front from the west.

The airlift of the last three days has brought only a fraction of the calculated minimum requirement (600 tons = 300 Ju daily). In the very next few days supplies can lead to a crisis of the utmost gravity.

I still believe, however, that the army can hold out for a time. On the other hand – even if anything like a corridor is cut through to me – it is still not possible to tell whether the daily increasing weakness of the army, combined with the lack of accommodation and wood for constructional and heating purposes, will allow the area around Stalingrad to be held for any length of time.

As I am being daily bombarded with numerous understandable inquiries about the future, I should be grateful if I could be provided

---

[1] No longer available. *Author.*

with more information than hitherto in order to increase the confidence of my men.

Allow me to say, *Herr Feldmarschall,* that I regard your leadership as a guarantee that everything possible is being done to assist Sixth Army. For their own part, my commanders and gallant troops will join me in doing everything to justify your trust.

Yours etc.

PAULUS

P.S. In the circumstances I hope you will overlook the inadequacy of the paper and the fact that this letter is in longhand.

APPENDIX II

TOP SECRET

By Hand of Officer Only   9th Dec. 42

To: Chief-of-Staff O.K.H.
     Operations Branch O.K.H.

APPRECIATION OF SITUATION

1. *Information about the Enemy.* Enemy has committed further strong forces against this Army Group in last ten days. These consist primarily of the reserves expected in our appreciation of 28th Nov. but also include additional forces. Total formations identified by Army Group are:

    86 rifle divisions
    17 rifle brigades
    54 tank brigades
    14 motorized brigades
    11 cavalry divisions,

i.e. 182 formations. In addition to these, we have identified thirteen independent tank regiments, tank battalions and anti-tank brigades.

Following is detailed break-down of enemy forces:

(*a*) Surrounding Stalingrad fortress area:

Volga front. – Sixty-Second Army (eight rifle divisions, three rifle brigades and one tank brigade up; two rifle, two tank and two motorized brigades in reserve).

Northern front. – Sixty-Sixth and Twenty-Fourth Armies (seventeen rifle divisions and one motorized brigade up; four rifle and four tank brigades in reserve).

Western front. – Sixty-Fifth and Twenty-First Armies (ten rifle divisions, seven tank and two motorized brigades, five tank regiments and one anti-tank brigade up; four tank brigades in reserve).

Southern front. – Fifty-Seventh and Sixty-Fourth Armies (seven rifle divisions, six rifle, six tank and six motorized brigades and two tank regiments up; apparently two rifle divisions, two rifle, five tank and one motorized brigade and five motorized regiments in reserve).

In the last ten days the enemy had attacked the northern, western and southern fronts in turn. His main pressure is undoubtedly directed against the western front, whereas he is relatively weak on the southern one.

(*b*) Soviet assault on Stalingrad is being covered to the south-west [1] – on the Chir front – by Fifth Tank Army (twelve rifle divisions, five cavalry divisions, two motorized cavalry divisions, four tank brigades, one tank regiment and two motorized brigades up; two rifle divisions, four tank brigades and one motorized brigade in reserve). Immediately to the north, facing the centre and left wing of the Hollidt Group, are three more rifle divisions.

Covering the assault in a southerly direction, east of the Don, is Fifty-First Army (four rifle and four cavalry divisions, one tank and one motorized brigade up; one tank and one rifle brigade in reserve). Reason for concentration of further motorized forces behind this front is still not clear.

(*c*) Reconnaissance during last few days has revealed unloading operations east of Stalingrad and troop movements across the Don to the south, past the eastern front of the Hollidt Group. While the Soviet covering front east of the Don has remained largely passive, probably because the concentration of motorized forces to the rear is not yet complete, the enemy has attacked across the Chir in strength on the Chir bridgehead and west of the Chir railway station. On account of the north-to-south movements in front of the Hollidt Group we must expect this attack to be extended further westwards.

(*d*) In the fighting to date the enemy has undoubtedly lost a considerable amount of his armour, but hitherto he has been able to fill the gaps by bringing up new tank regiments etc. The offensive capacity of his infantry remains low; the effect of his artillery has considerably increased, notably on the western front of Stalingrad.

2. *Information About Own Troops.*

(*a*) *Sixth Army.* So far the army has beaten off all enemy assaults,

---

[1] i.e. West of the Don. *Author.*

though at the cost of considerable losses. Special report is being submitted on its present fighting capacity. The following were the holdings of the main types of ammunition on 5th December 42, given in percentages of primary issues:[1]

5-cm. vehicle-drawn gun	59%	15-cm. mortar .	.	25%
7·5-cm. ,, ,,	39·4%	Light howitzer	.	34%
8-cm. mortar	30·8%	10-cm. cannon 19	.	21·6%
Light infantry gun.	28%	Heavy howitzer	.	36%
Heavy infantry gun	25%			

Present ration stocks, with bread cut to 200 gr., will last till about 14 Dec. for bread, 20 Dec. for midday meal and 19 Dec. for evening meal.

Despite exemplary efforts of the Luftwaffe, biggest airlift attained to date was 300 tons on 7th Dec. owing to bad weather. Of 188 aircraft used that day, two were shot down and nine failed to return. On all other days tonnage lifted varied between 25 tons (27th Nov.) and 150 tons (8th Dec.), at a daily minimum requirement of 400 tons.

(b) *Fourth Pz. Army*. Assembly of 57 Pz. Corps not materially completed until 10th Dec., instead of 3rd Dec. as hoped, owing to bogging-down of wheeled elements of 23 Pz. Div. 48 Pz. Corps (336 Inf. Div., 11 Pz. Div. and 3 Luftwaffe Fd. Div.) had initially to be thrown in on the Chir front to restore situation there. Battle still in progress.

(c) *Rumanian Formations*. Fourth Rumanian Army, lying north of 16 Mot. Inf. Div., at present standing fast. It cannot, however, be expected to withstand an attack of any strength from the north, particularly as it has been directed by Marshal Antonescu to avoid being cut off. In the case of Third Rumanian Army, apart from reasonably intact 1 Rum. Corps forming part of the Hollidt Group, the fighting power of the remnants of the Rumanian divisions committed forward amounts to no more than one or two battalions. No artillery worth mentioning any longer exists. Because of weapon shortage, reconstitution of formations in rear areas has produced no tangible results. It must also be faced that Rumanian formation staffs are not acting with necessary energy. They attribute their defeat to '*force majeure*', in which they include the German Command. For the rest, entire front of Third Rum. Army is held by various types of emergency unit. In view of the absence of artillery and anti-tank guns there must be no illusions about

---

[1] A 'primary issue' amounted to approximately the amount required for three days' continuous fighting. *Author*.

ability of this front to hold out for any length of time should enemy attack it in strength, particularly with armoured forces. This motley collection of forces, which have nothing to hold them together from within, must shortly be relieved by proper combat units, since neither their composition nor their combat efficiency qualify them for a protracted spell at the front. Apart from this, those of them formed from specialist units from communications zones cannot be withheld from their proper functions without prejudicing the overall supply position.

3. *Own Intentions*. Army Group intends, as already reported, to attack as early as possible with Fourth Pz. Army in order to make contact with Sixth Army. For the time being, however, soft state of ground precludes any advance by 57 Pz. Corps. Whether divisions of 48 Pz. Corps can be fully released on the Chir front by 11 Dec. is still uncertain. It will be necessary to bring 17 Pz. Div. into the attack, and orders have been given to this effect. As enemy must thus be expected shortly to extend his attacks on Chir front in general direction of Morosovskaya, Hollidt Group must co-operate to relieve pressure on this front, either by attacking in general direction of Perelasovsky or by handing over one German division.

4. *General Conclusions*. The weight of forces brought in by enemy against Don Army Group makes it clear that he sees his main point of effort here. He will carry on the struggle in this sector as long as possible by bringing over forces from other fronts.

Regardless of how Sixth Army's own position may develop in the immediate future, therefore, it will still be necessary to maintain a steady flow of reinforcements to Don Army Group. Of decisive importance in this connexion is that everything be done to increase their rate of arrival. At the present rate we shall always lag behind the Russians. I further consider it essential that everything be done to restore the usefulness of the Rumanian Army, particularly as regards its will to fight and its confidence in the German Command.

As to whether Sixth Army should be taken out of the pocket once contact is re-established, I consider that the following factors must be carefully weighed:

(a) Should the army be left in the fortress area, it is entirely possible that the Russians will tie themselves down here and gradually fritter away their manpower in useless assaults. At the same time it must be faced that Sixth Army is having to live and fight under particularly unfavourable conditions in the fortress and that if the present ratio of strengths remains in force much longer, contact may well be lost again. At best it must be assumed that there will be no decisive change in the next few weeks.

(*b*) On the other hand, one must also allow for the possibility that the Russians will take the proper action and, while maintaining their encirclement of Stalingrad, launch strong attacks against Third and Fourth Rumanian Armies with Rostov as their target. If this happens our most vital forces will be operationally immobilised in the fortress area or tied down to keeping the link with it open, whereas the Russians will have freedom of action along the whole of the Army Group's remaining front. To maintain this situation throughout the winter strikes me as inexpedient.

(*c*) The corollary of any decision to keep Sixth Army at Stalingrad must therefore be the decision to fight this battle through to a completely decisive ending. This will necessitate:

(i) providing Sixth Army with extra forces to maintain its defensive capacity, in the form of Luftwaffe field divisions which would be incorporated in its existing formations.

(ii) Initial reinforcement of the adjoining fronts of Third and Fourth Rumanian Armies by German forces, as these fronts cannot be guaranteed to hold with Rumanian remnants and ad hoc units.

(iii) launching a decisive offensive as soon as our own forces permit.

Whether the forces required can be made available and brought into action at short notice is not for me to judge.

v. MANSTEIN
Field-Marshal
Commanding Don Army Group

APPENDIX III

By Hand of Officer Only   3 Copies Issued
                 Copy Nr. 3

TOP SECRET   19th Dec., 1435 hrs.

To: Chief-of-Staff of the Army
 for immediate submission to the Führer

In conjunction with developments in Army Group B, and in consequence of the fact that these have stopped the arrival of any further forces, the situation of Don Army Group is now such that Sixth Army cannot be expected to be relieved in the foreseeable future.

Since an airlift is not possible for reasons of weather and the inadequate forces available (which means, as four weeks' encirclement have shown, that the Army cannot be maintained in the fortress area), and as 57 Pz. Corps by itself obviously cannot make contact with Sixth Army on the ground, let alone keep a corridor open, I now consider a break-out to the south-west to be the last possible means of preserving at least the bulk of the troops and the still mobile elements of Sixth Army.

The breakthrough, the first aim of which must be to make contact with 57 Pz. Corps on about the Yerik Myshkova, can only take place by forcing a gradual shift of Sixth Army towards the south-west and giving up ground sector by sector in the north of the fortress area as this movement progresses.

As long as this operation is in progress it will be essential to safeguard the airlift by adequate fighter and bomber cover.

As there are signs even now of enemy pressure on the northern wing of Fourth Rumanian Army, it is also vital that forces be quickly brought up from the Caucasus front to safeguard the execution of 57 Pz. Corps' task by protection of its deep right flank.

In the event of delay, 57 Pz. Corps is likely to become stuck on or north of the Myshkova or else tied down by attacks in its right flank.

At the same time Sixth Army needs a few days to regroup and stock up with fuel before moving off.

Rations in the pocket will last till 22 Dec. Troops already badly weakened (only 200 gr. a day for last fortnight). According to Sixth Army, most of the horses have already been put out of action by exhaustion or slaughtered for food.

v. MANSTEIN
Field-Marshal
Commanding Don Army Group

APPENDIX IV

TOP SECRET   5 Copies Issued
By Hand of Officer Only   Copy No. 4
To: Sixth Army   19th Dec., 1800 hrs.
     Fourth Pz. Army

1. Fourth Pz. Army (57 Pz. Corps) has beaten enemy in area Verkhnye Kimsky and reached Myshkova at Nizh Kimsky. Attack launched against strong enemy grouping in area Kamenka and north of here. Hard fighting still expected.

Situation on Chir front does not permit forces west of Don to advance on Kalach. Chirskaya in enemy hands.

2. Sixth Army will begin 'Winter Tempest' attack earliest possible. Aim will be to link up with 57 Pz. Corps, if necessary by advancing beyond Donskaya Tsaritsa, for purpose of getting convoy through.

3. Development of situation may make it necessary to extend task in para 2 up to Myshkova. Code-word 'Thunderclap'. In this case the aim must likewise be to establish contact with 57 Pz. Corps in order to get convoy through, and then, by covering flanks on the lower Karpovka, to bring army forward towards the Myshkova simultaneously with sector-by-sector evacuation of fortress area.

It is essential that Operation 'Thunderclap' should immediately follow 'Winter Tempest' attack. Supply by air must be carried out in the main without advance stockpiling. Important to hold Pitomnik airstrip as long as possible.

All weapons and artillery which can be moved, primarily guns needed for the fighting and also any weapons and equipment which are difficult to replace, will be taken along. To this end they will be moved in good time to the south-west of the pocket.

4. All necessary preparations to be made for action laid down in para. 3. Only to be implemented on express issue of 'Thunderclap'.

5. Report day and time on which you can attack in accordance with para. 2.

v. MANSTEIN

Field-Marshal

Copy No. 1: Signal Office File

„ „ 2: Air Fleet 4

„ „ 3: Q Branch

„ „ 4: War Diary

„ „ 5: Draft

MILITARY CAREER

ERICH v. MANSTEIN was born in Berlin on 24th November 1887. His original surname (which he is still entitled to use with the one under which he is better known) was v. Lewinski, his father being Eduard v. Lewinski, an artillery officer who ultimately rose to command an army corps. The name v. Manstein was acquired after Erich v. Lewinski's adoption by General v. Manstein, his mother's brother-in-law.

Erich v. Manstein went to school in Strasbourg and then spent six years in the Cadet Corps. After his passing-out in 1906 he entered the 3rd Regiment of Footguards. In 1913–14 he was at the War Academy.

On the outbreak of war he first served as adjutant of the 2nd Reserve Regiment of Guards in Belgium, East Prussia and South Poland. From May 1915, after being badly wounded in November 1914, he successively served on the staffs of armies commanded by Generals v. Gallwitz and v. Below. In the summer of 1915 he took part in the offensive in North Poland, and from the autumn of the same year until the following spring he saw fighting in Serbia. In the spring of 1917 he was at Verdun, in the Battle of the Somme and in the fighting on the Aisne. That autumn he was made G.S.O. I of 4 Cavalry Division in Courland, and in May 1918 he held the same appointment with 213 Infantry Division in the west. He took part in the Rheims offensives in May and July 1918 and continued to serve in France until the Armistice.

During the post-war years v. Manstein held various staff and regimental appointments. In 1934 he became Chief-of-Staff of III Military Region in Berlin, and in 1935 Chief of the Operations Branch of the General Staff of the Army. By October 1936 he had risen to major-general and become *Oberquartiermeister I*, which made him deputy to General Beck, the Chief of the General Staff.

In connexion with the dismissal of Baron v. Fritsch in February 1938 he was relieved of his staff appointment and transferred to Liegnitz to command 18 Division. The same year he took part in the occupation of the Sudetenland as Chief-of-Staff of an army.

On general mobilization in 1939 v. Manstein became Chief-of-Staff of v. Rundstedt's Southern Army Group, with which he went through the campaign in Poland. In October 1939, in the same capacity, he went with v. Rundstedt to Army Group A on the Western Front. It was here that he became involved in the struggle for an offensive plan which was only adopted by Hitler after v. Manstein had been posted away from the Army Group to command a corps. He led this corps throughout the campaign in the west and was awarded the Knight's Cross.

After the end of the fighting in France, v. Manstein was kept busy for a time training his corps for the invasion of Britain.

In March 1941 he was made commander of 56 Panzer Corps and as such led an armoured dash from East Prussia to Lake Ilmen when Germany attacked the Soviet Union. In September of the same year he was given command of Eleventh Army, at the head of which he conquered the Crimea and smashed the Russian counterlandings at Kerch. On the fall of Sevastopol he was promoted Field-Marshal.

In August 1942 v. Manstein was entrusted with the task of taking Leningrad, but this was never carried out. He was, nonetheless, responsible for the destruction of a Soviet Army on Lake Ladoga.

In 1942, after the Russians had broken through on both sides of Stalingrad and completely surrounded the Sixth Army there, v. Manstein assumed command of Don (later Southern) Army Group. After a vain attempt to free Sixth Army, he directed the heavy fighting to save the German southern wing and finally won a big victory at Kharkov in March 1943. For this he was awarded the Oak Leaves to his Knight's Cross.

In summer 1943 v. Manstein took part in the last German offensive in the east: Operation 'Citadel'. After this had been called off, he took Southern Army Group through a number of difficult defensive battles, including the withdrawal behind the Dnieper. At the end of March 1944, when the German armies were already back on the Polish frontier, v. Manstein was relieved of his command as the result of his differences with Hitler over the conduct of operations in the east. Though awarded the Swords to the Knight's Cross in recognition of his services, he was not employed again.

GLOSSARY OF MILITARY TERMS

GERMAN

ASSAULT GUN Self-propelled (SP) gun with built-in armour mounted on Mark III tank chassis. Intended for close-support role with infantry. (See 'regiment'.)

BRIGADE Roughly equivalent to British independent brigade group or U.S. regimental combat team. (The German equivalent of the British 'brigade' was a 'regiment'—see below.)

MOTORIZED DIVISION Composed of motorized infantry—later redesignated Panzer Grenadier Division.

O.K.W. *Oberkommando der Wehrmacht*—Supreme Command of the Armed Forces.

O.K.H. *Oberkommando des Heeres*—Army High Command.

O.K.L. *Oberkommando der Luftwaffe*—High Command of the Air Force.

O.K.M. *Oberkommando der Kriegsmarine*—High Command of the Navy.

PANZER CORPS Army corps consisting of panzer (armoured) divisions.

PANZER GRENADIER DIVISION See 'motorized division' above.

REGIMENT An infantry regiment consisted of 14 companies—usually nine rifle, three machine-gun, one assault-gun, and one anti-tank.

RUSSIAN

'FRONT' Approximately equivalent to an army group.

MECHANIZED CORPS Composed of three mechanized brigades and one tank brigade, plus artillery and special weapons. Establishment of a mechanized corps was 231 tanks and/or SP guns.

TANK CORPS Composed of three tank brigades and one motorized rifle brigade, plus artillery and special weapons. Establishment of tank corps was 231 tanks and SPs.

RIFLE DIVISION Roughly equivalent to a German infantry division.

INDEX

Notes: (1) Military formations and general information on national armies are under *Army*;

(2) Names of officers are given the highest rank ascribed to them *in the text.*